Commercial Law

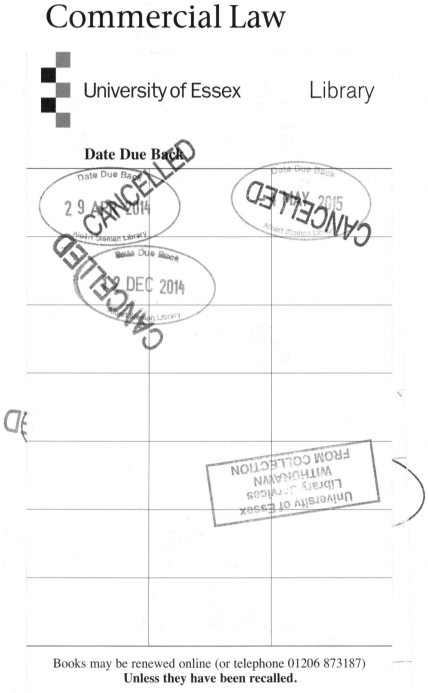

University of Essex   Library

Date Due Back

Books may be renewed online (or telephone 01206 873187)
Unless they have been recalled.

Form No. L.43 April 2004

Commercial Law

Robert Bradgate MA (Cantab), Solicitor

Professor of Commercial Law, Institute for Commercial Law Studies,
University of Sheffield

and

Fidelma White BCL, LLB, LLM (NUI), LLM (Lond)

Senior Lecturer in Law,
University College, Cork

OXFORD
UNIVERSITY PRESS

OXFORD
UNIVERSITY PRESS

Great Clarendon Street, Oxford OX2 6DP

Oxford University Press is a department of the University of Oxford.
It furthers the University's objective of excellence in research, scholarship,
and education by publishing worldwide in

Oxford New York

Auckland Cape Town Dar es Salaam Hong Kong Karachi
Kuala Lumpur Madrid Melbourne Mexico City Nairobi
New Delhi Shanghai Taipei Toronto

With offices in

Argentina Austria Brazil Chile Czech Republic France Greece
Guatemala Hungary Italy Japan South Korea Poland Portugal
Singapore Switzerland Thailand Turkey Ukraine Vietnam

Oxford is a registered trade mark of Oxford University Press
in the UK and in certain other countries

Published in the United States
by Oxford University Press Inc., New York

British Library Cataloguing in Publication Data

Data available

Library of Congress Cataloging in Publication Data

Data available

ISBN 0-19-927729-X

1 3 5 7 9 10 8 6 4 2

Typeset by Newgen Imaging Systems (P) Ltd., Chennai, India
Printed in Great Britain
on acid-free paper by
Antony Rowe Ltd, Chippenham, Wiltshire

OUTLINE CONTENTS

DETAILED CONTENTS

PREFACE

This *Guide* is intended for students taking optional courses in commercial law on the Legal Practice Course. In preparing it we immediately faced a difficulty in deciding what to include: we have seen a number of LPC commercial law syllabuses, all different. The likelihood is that no one course will cover all the material included in this *Guide*, but we have sought to cover as much as possible of the material likely to be covered on a range of courses.

We have taken as our 'core' the material included in the draft syllabus circulated as a model by a number of City firms, but we have not stuck rigidly to it: for instance, we have included a short section on Commercial Dispute Resolution because it seems to us that, whilst commercial litigation may be a specialist topic, and in some institutions will be the subject of a separate course, all students and practitioners of commercial law must have some knowledge of the means by which commercial disputes will be resolved, even if for no other reason than to ensure that they include in contracts appropriate provisions to enable them to make use of appropriate procedures, such as arbitration.

The coverage of the material in this *Guide* is necessarily superficial: we would not claim in 30 pages, for instance, to have provided a comprehensive coverage of intellectual property or competition law. Our objective has been to provide a basic grounding in these subjects for the general commercial practitioner so that on the first day of practice he or she will, for instance, know the difference between agency and distributorship, copyrights and patents or c.i.f. and f.o.b. contracts. Many of the topics we have included may be taught in some institutions in different courses, either, as in the case of, say, intellectual property, commercial litigation and commercial credit and security, developed as options in their own right or, as in the case of agency and distributorship, or the Sale of Goods Act 1979 implied terms, as part of the business law compulsory course. Nevertheless they form an integral part of the core knowledge of the commercial practitioner and we have therefore included them here.

Because of the breadth of the syllabus, possibly more than any other course on the LPC, commercial law involves the study of substantive law rather than of 'practice' or 'procedure'. We make no apologies for this: it seems to us that it is not merely a result of the breadth of the syllabus but an accurate reflection of the work of the general commercial practitioner, much of whose work involves advising clients on points of law. We have tried, where possible, to give the material a practical slant, for instance, by suggesting typical clauses which might be found in commercial contracts, and the reasons for their inclusion. We have also included a number of specimen documents and contracts concerned with international trade to give students a feel for a typical commercial contract and some experience of the more common standard forms. The book includes a section on 'Drafting an Agency Agreement' and a complete chapter on 'Standard Terms of Trading' including specimen sets of terms of sale and purchase with explanatory commentaries.

There are a number of significant omissions. We have not covered insurance law, although it is important in commercial practice, because most institutions indicated that they were not including it in their syllabus. Similarly, we have not covered consumer credit which seems to us to be part of a consumer, rather than commercial, law course.

This is the twelfth edition of the *Guide*. As usual we have undertaken a general updating exercise, taking account of material available to us up to 30 November 2004. The most significant changes this year relate to European Competition law and include changes to the enforcement regime under articles 81 and 82 of the EC Treaty. There are also a number of new developments in the section on Intellectual Property law. We have also included brief introductory and summary sections at the beginning and end of each chapter to facilitate use of the manual by students, and have added some other new material. The selection of forms in the International Trade section has been updated. As usual, wherever possible, we have sought to illustrate the practical implications of legal developments. As a result the *Guide* has once again grown in size, although some of the legal developments have enabled us to cut some material.

Once again we must express our thanks to the staff at OUP for their continued patience, help and support in production of the *Guide*.

Robert Bradgate
Fidelma White
December 2004

ACKNOWLEDGEMENTS

The authors and the publishers would like to express their thanks to the following for permission to reproduce their standard forms and supplying copies:
The Grain and Feed Trade Association
SITPRO

TABLE OF CASES

TABLE OF PRIMARY LEGISLATION

European Primary Legislation

International legislation

TABLE OF SECONDARY LEGISLATION

Contract law and commercial contracts

Part I

Contract law and commercial contracts

The role of the commercial lawyer

1.1 Introduction

The work of a commercial practitioner may cover a wide area, including company and partnership law and all aspects of the law relating to the domestic or international supply of goods and services, including sale, agency, distribution and franchising, carriage, credit, finance and security, intellectual property, competition and tax law. A practitioner may specialise in one, or even in a particular aspect of one, of these areas. Essentially, however, commercial work may encompass any aspect of the law relating to the affairs of the firm's business clients. The role of the commercial practitioner is therefore to provide advice to the firm's business clients on matters relating to their business activities, in a contentious and/or non-contentious context. In either case the commercial practitioner's role is to facilitate the client's commercial activities. He must therefore understand the client's business and the client's needs.

It is, of course, impossible to generalise about the needs of commercial clients but as a rule they will require speedy, practical and accurate advice. Where important transactions, possibly involving large sums of money, are at stake, delay, or inaccurate advice, may be costly for the client and, as a result, for the legal adviser. The commercial lawyer therefore needs to have:

(a) a knowledge of substantive law covering a wide area;

(b) an understanding of business practices and of the practical implications of the substantive law for those practices;

(c) the business needs of the client, including both an understanding of the typical needs of a commercial client and the particular needs of the individual client.

This book concentrates mainly on the law relating to commercial transactions. Its aim is to provide a broad overview, rather than a specialist knowledge, of some of the main areas of substantive law relevant to the work of the commercial practitioner, placing that law, so far as possible, in its practical commercial context. The commercial lawyer must at all times remember that it is his or her job to apply that law in a practical and commercially realistic way.

1.2 Commercial law and contracts

Commercial transactions are generally effected through the medium of contracts and many of the rules of commercial law are applications and, sometimes, modifications, of the general principles of contract law. The commercial lawyer must therefore have an understanding of those basic principles and the way they relate to common business and commercial practices, and in particular the rules governing formation and variation of contracts, incorporation of terms, exclusion clauses, breach of contract and remedies, for those rules underpin the rules applicable to particular types of commercial contract.

Many business practices are difficult to reconcile with theoretical contract law. The courts have sometimes recognised this. The commercial lawyer must therefore also understand those commercial practices and the way the law applies to them.

Chapters 2 and **3** of this book aim to provide an overview of the main principles of general contract law as they apply to commercial and business contracts.

1.2.1 Contentious and non-contentious commercial work

Broadly, a commercial practitioner may be called upon to advise on either (a) the drafting and formation of a contract or (b) its termination and the consequences of its termination. It would be tempting to see these stages as the province respectively of the non-contentious practitioner and the commercial litigator. However, such a division is unrealistic. Practitioners dealing with both kinds of work need to have a knowledge of all the relevant principles: for instance, whilst advice on the quantum of damages may be a matter for the litigator in a given case, the drafter preparing a contract must understand the principles which may govern an award of damages in order to advise the client and draft an appropriate provision, such as a liquidated damages or exclusion clause, to cover that contingency.

The commercial litigator will, of course, need a specialist knowledge of litigation procedures and, in particular, of the procedures special to commercial disputes. However, the non-contentious practitioner will also need an understanding even of those matters, for instance so that contracts can be drafted in such a way as to take advantage of fast and convenient methods of enforcement or to draft arbitration or similar clauses. Some aspects of this material are examined in **Part 9** of this book.

Practitioners dealing with both contentious and non-contentious work therefore need a common knowledge of a wide range of substantive law. The difference between their two areas of work lies in their specialist skills as litigators or drafters.

1.2.2 Commercial and consumer law

The precise relationship between commercial and consumer law is a matter of some academic debate. Some see the two as separate subjects; others see consumer law as a special sub-category within commercial law. In many areas the same rules apply to consumer and commercial transactions. In others the rules applicable to commercial transactions are modified in their application to consumer transactions. Even, however, where this is the case the commercial practitioner cannot afford to be ignorant of consumer law. Many of the practitioner's commercial, or business, clients will be engaged for some or all of the time in dealing with consumers, and a transaction which might be classified as a consumer transaction from the perspective of one party is almost always a business transaction from the point of view of the other. Consider for example the case of a car dealer. The transactions by which the dealer acquires new vehicles for resale will be 'commercial' in the sense that they will involve two businesses. However, the essence of the dealer's business will be the sale of vehicles, many of which will be to private individuals who when buying will be dealing as consumers. The practitioner advising on the dealer's contracts will therefore have to take account of the law applicable to consumer as well as business transactions.

The focus of this guide is on commercial law. There is not scope within this volume to examine all aspects of the law of consumer protection. Rules applicable to consumer transactions are, however, dealt with where especially relevant—notably in relation to the rules governing unfair terms and the special rules applicable to consumer sales. It must be borne in mind, however, that many other aspects of 'consumer protection' law, such as those concerned with consumer credit, trade descriptions, distance selling and electronic commerce, may impinge on the business of clients dealing with consumers.

1.2.3   Drafting commercial contracts

When drafting a commercial contract it is crucial to have in mind at all times what the contract, and what each term within it, is intended to do.

1.2.3.1   The need for certainty

The main purpose of a commercial contract is to provide a clear, certain framework to govern a particular commercial transaction or relationship for the client. An agreement which is vague or uncertain may not be a contract at all. Even if the agreement is legally binding, any uncertainty may lead to disputes between the parties and even to litigation.

Disputes may arise if the law on a particular subject is unclear. A contract is made against the background of legal 'default' rules applicable (a) to contracts generally and (b) to contracts of that particular type. Some of these rules are mandatory—for instance, those concerned with matters of public policy such as illegality—but many apply only insofar as they are not varied or excluded by the express terms of the contract. Many of the legal 'default' rules applicable to commercial contracts may be stated simply but are difficult to apply; for instance:

    (a) 'breach of contract by one party justifies the other terminating the contract if the consequences of the breach are sufficiently serious';

    (b) 'terms may be implied into a contract if they are necessary to give business efficacy to the contract';

    (c) 'goods supplied under a contract of sale must be reasonably fit for the buyer's purpose'.

A well drafted contract will seek to avoid this legal uncertainty by including express provisions to minimise the scope for application of uncertain legal 'default' rules such as those concerned with termination of the contract for breach, the implication of terms at common law, the quality of performance required by the contract and frustration.

Other legal 'default' rules may be inappropriate. The drafter may wish to exclude them.

Disputes may also arise if the language of the contract is unclear. The contract should therefore be drafted in clear language to avoid disputes. A contract term which is unclear may be construed against the party relying on it or may be held unreasonable or unfair.

1.2.3.2   Typical provisions

The contract should therefore take account of the relevant law and the needs of the client. It must be tailored to the needs of the particular client and its business.

    (a) It should define the obligations of the parties and the consequences of and remedies for non-performance.

    (b) It should include provisions facilitating the use of 'self-help' remedies and provide mechanisms such as arbitration clauses for resolving any disputes which arise from the contract, so as to enable clients to avoid, so far as possible, costly and time consuming litigation.

(c) It may include provisions to encourage performance of the contract, such as providing for payment of deposits and/or for payment of liquidated damages on breach.

(d) If it is to govern an international transaction it may include provisions to avoid difficult problems of conflict of laws, including choice of law and choice of forum clauses to make clear what law is to govern the contract and where any dispute arising from it is to be litigated.

1.2.3.3 Allocation of risks

So far as possible the contract should seek to allocate the risks arising out of the trading relationship of the parties to the contract. A party to whom a particular risk is allocated by the contract may seek protection against it by insurance and a contracting party should always be advised to consider insuring against such risks as (for instance) the risk of the other party's failure to perform or his incurring liability for breach. The drafter may seek to minimise the risks falling on the client and throw as many of them as possible onto the other party to the contract, for instance by excluding, so far as possible, obligations imposed by the general law; by limiting liability for breach of contract; and by imposing obligations on the other contracting party. However, the drafter must bear in mind that there are legal and commercial constraints on this process. Thus the contract must be drafted with an awareness of the rules which limit the effectiveness of certain provisions, in particular the Unfair Contract Terms Act 1977 and, where applicable, the Unfair Terms in Consumer Contracts Regulations 1999, whilst bearing in mind that a contract which is excessively one-sided may be commercially damaging. It may provide a basis for negotiation, but may damage the client's trading relationships and reputation.

1.2.3.4 Classification of transactions

Contractual arrangements with similar commercial purposes and effects can have different legal incidents. Classification of an arrangement as (say) a sale (or distributorship) as opposed to an agency can therefore make important differences to the rights and obligations of the parties. Moreover some types of commercial arrangement are subject to special legal requirements relating to (e.g.) their form. Thus, for instance, a contract of guarantee must be evidenced by a written memorandum signed by the guarantor; certain types of charge created by a company must be registered. On the other hand a contract of indemnity may achieve much the same effect as a guarantee but avoids the need for a written memorandum, and a creditor may be able to obtain security for a debt almost as effective as that provided by a charge without actually taking a charge. In order to determine the legal effect and incidents of any particular transaction it may therefore be necessary first to determine its proper classification.

The classification of transactions is a matter of law. Transactions are classified according to their substance rather than their form. Thus the label attached to a transaction by the parties will not be decisive as to its effect. On the other hand 'substance' means 'legal substance' rather than 'commercial purpose'. This means that a court seeking to classify a transaction will look to its terms. If, say, a contract contains terms appropriate to an agency agreement it will be, in law, an agency agreement, even if its commercial purpose and effect is to provide one of the parties with a form of security for payment of a debt.

The process of classification and its relationship to the process of interpretation was considered by the Privy Council in *Agnew v Comrs of Inland Revenue* [2001] 2 AC 710. The first task of the court is to determine the terms of the agreement. The court must then construe the terms to determine their meaning. These first two steps require the court to determine the intentions of the parties. Having done so the court must then determine the legal effect of an agreement containing those terms in order to classify the agreement. That process is a matter of law and not dependent on the intention of the parties. In short it does not matter that the parties intended to create (say) an agency if the terms of their agreement give them rights and obligations appropriate to a charge.

This approach to classification means that the drafter of a commercial agreement enjoys a considerable degree of freedom to control its classification by careful drafting and ensuring that the agreement contains appropriate terms, and it seems that it will make no difference to the classification of an agreement that it was drafted in a particular way so as to avoid legal requirements such as those requiring registration of company charges or that guarantees be evidenced in writing.

1.2.4 European law and commercial practice

In recent years the European Community has begun to exert an ever stronger influence on commercial law and the work of the commercial practitioner. That influence has been strongest in areas such as intellectual property and competition law and in areas outside the scope of this book, such as financial services regulation and company law. Some of these—such as the EC provisions on competition law—exert a wide influence across commercial law and practice, influencing the drafting of a wide range of commercial agreements. To date, however, EC law has had relatively little direct impact on the law applicable to commercial transactions. On the other hand there is now a considerable body of EC law, mainly in the form of Directives, applicable to consumer transactions, some of which are considered in this book. Moreover there are now Directives (such as Directive 86/653 on self-employed commercial agents: see Chapter 7) which directly affect common, mainstream commercial activities. It seems likely that the influence of EC law will continue to grow in the coming years. In 2001 the European Commission issued a communication on European contract law in which it canvassed the possibility of further harmonising European contract and commercial law. That communication initiated a period of consultation which is continuing.

Most EC measures in the field of commercial law are in the form of Directives. They are therefore binding on Member States as to the result to be achieved but require implementation by Member States to give them domestic legal effect. As a general rule a Directive cannot be relied upon in litigation in a domestic court, except against a party who may be regarded as under the control or subject to the authority of the state (see C-91/92 *Faccini Dori* v *Recreb Srl* [1994] ECR I-3325; C-192/94 *El Corte Ingles SA* v *Rivero* [1996] I-1281). On the other hand it is well established that (in accordance with what has become known as the doctrine of 'indirect effect', first established in *Marshall and von Colson* v *Land Nordrhein-Westfalen* (case 14/83 [1984] ECR 1891) domestic law must, wherever possible, be interpreted in accordance with the requirements of EC Law so to achieve, so far as possible, the objective of the relevant directive (*Marleasing SA* v *La Comercial International de Alimentacion SA* (C-106/89 [1990] ECR I-4135). This principle applies not only to domestic laws implementing Directives but also to pre-existing law.

The commercial practitioner therefore cannot afford to ignore EC law and its impact. Where domestic law is inconsistent with relevant EC law it will be necessary to take account of the latter.

Formation of contracts

2.1 Introduction

Commercial transactions are effected through the medium of contracts. This chapter and the next seek to provide a summary overview of the main principles of contract law, with an emphasis on practical considerations. The emphasis in this chapter is on contract formation and the way in which contractual obligations arise. In it we examine:

- the requirements for a binding contract to come into being;
- the factors which may arise during negotiations and invalidate what would otherwise be a valid contract;
- the ways in which a binding contract can be varied;
- how the terms of the contract are identified and interpreted;
- the rules of privity of contract which determine who can enforce and who is bound by contractual obligations.

2.1.1 Formation issues

Commercial contracts are formed in a variety of ways. At one extreme there may be a formal document drawn up for a particular transaction to embody the terms of the contract and then executed by the parties; at the other the contract may be concluded wholly informally—for instance, orally, during a telephone conversation. In between is a range of other possibilities. Often the contract will be based on, or include terms in, a standard printed form which may be the standard terms of one of the parties, an industry standard form contract for the particular type of transaction or a standard form negotiated by the parties to regulate all their mutual dealings. In some cases (e.g. bills of exchange, see **Chapter 22** or guarantees, see **Chapter 26**) a particular form is prescribed by law.

Similarly the lawyer may play a variety of roles in the formation process. Every contract must contain some individually negotiated (or agreed) terms: what is to be supplied, where, when, in what quantity and at what price? These are essentially matters for commercial agreement and in a simple contract lawyers will often play no part in these aspects; indeed, their involvement may be positively obstructive. At the other end of the spectrum, where a detailed formal contract is prepared for a particular transaction or set of transactions it may be necessary to negotiate individual terms covering such matters as warranties, exclusions, arbitration clauses and so on. The detailed negotiation and drafting of such terms will often be a matter for the lawyer, although they also involve matters of commercial judgment on which the business client may have to take the final decision, on the basis of legal advice as to the consequences of accepting a particular form of words. In between these two extremes are a number of intermediate positions: for instance, where a contract is 'negotiated' starting from one party's standard terms. Where both parties have different standard terms, the contract may be concluded after an exchange of terms or 'battle of forms' in which there may be an exchange of documentation with no real negotiation. The lawyer may be called on to draft a set of standard terms but play no part in the formation of individual contracts, or to advise on standard terms put forward by the other side.

In many cases, however, the lawyer is not concerned with formation questions until a dispute arises, when questions such as 'When/where was the contract made?', 'What were its terms?' or even 'Was there a contract at all?' may have to be answered. Often the question is whether one party is bound by a particular undertaking—was it effectively incorporated into the contract? Have the terms been effectively varied? In order to answer such questions the lawyer must have an understanding of the rules governing formation of contracts and their practical implications.

The general rule of contract law is that an undertaking is not legally binding unless:

(a) it was intended to be binding;

(b) it was accepted; and

(c) consideration was provided for it by the person seeking to enforce it or it is contained in a deed.

2.2 Consideration

Commercial contracts usually involve some form of exchange—generally of goods or services for payment, either in money or other goods or services. The requirement that a person can only enforce an undertaking as a contract if either he provided consideration for it or it is contained in a deed therefore rarely causes difficulties in relation to the *formation* of commercial contracts. However, consideration is important, especially in the contexts of the variation of contracts and incorporation of terms.

The most important aspects of the consideration doctrine in the commercial context are the following.

2.2.1 Consideration must not be past

A person wishing to enforce an undertaking must provide consideration at the same time as or after the undertaking is given. A practical consequence of this rule is that new terms cannot be introduced after a contract has been concluded.

EXAMPLE

'Natty Nigel's' telephones Phil's Fashions and orders 40 suits. A price and delivery date are agreed. Two days later Phil's Fashions send out an 'acknowledgement of order' which includes their standard terms of trading, including a term which purports to exclude Phil's Fashions' liability for late delivery. Delivery is late. If Phil's Fashions seek to rely on the terms, Natty Nigel's will argue that the contract was already concluded by telephone and that they are therefore not bound by the exclusion. Even if Nigel's can be said to have agreed the terms, Phil's have provided no consideration for their agreement: the agreement to supply the goods is past consideration.

2.2.2 Performance of existing duties

Generally performance by A of a duty under a contract with B is no consideration for a fresh promise from B. Thus, in the example above, Phil's cannot argue that actual delivery of the goods to Nigel's is consideration for their acceptance of Phil's terms because Phil's were already bound to deliver the goods under the terms of the contract. Phil's must provide fresh consideration for Nigel's' agreement to the terms, for instance by agreeing to a reduction in the price or undertaking some additional duty not imposed by the original contract. This is especially important in the context of variations of contracts.

Recent case law suggests that any slight variation of A's existing duty may be regarded as providing consideration for B's promise and that performance of an existing duty *may* provide consideration if it confers a practical commercial benefit on the promisor (see, e.g., *Williams* v *Roffey Bros and Nicholls (Contractors) Ltd* [1991] 1 QB 1; see **2.5**).

Performance by A of a duty owed under a contract with B *is* consideration for a fresh promise from C who is not party to the existing contract.

2.3   Agreement

It may often be necessary to decide when a contract is concluded. This may affect such matters as:

(a) the terms which govern the contract;

(b) the price (for instance if the contract provides that 'the price shall be the market price current at the date of conclusion of this contract'); and even

(c) the place where the contract is concluded, which may have a bearing on such questions as which law governs the contract.

A contract is only concluded when an offer is unequivocally and unconditionally accepted. The rules of offer and acceptance may be familiar but their application to standard business transactions is often difficult.

2.3.1   Offer

Any statement may be an offer if, objectively interpreted, it contains an unequivocal indication of a willingness to be legally bound if its terms are accepted.

A statement is only likely to be construed as an offer if it contains the essential terms of the contract, expressed in reasonably certain terms. However, this requirement may be relatively easily satisfied: for instance, under a contract for the sale of goods the only requirements are probably identification of the (type and quantity of) the goods, the price and the delivery date, and even silence on these matters may not be fatal if other terms have been agreed.

Whether any particular statement amounts to an offer therefore depends on the facts of the particular case but the normal effect of some common business practices has been considered in case law. Generally estimates, price lists, circulars and advertisements are assumed not to be intended to be contractually binding. Invitations for submission of tenders generally are regarded as invitations to treat, so that a business which invites potential suppliers to submit tenders does not bind itself to accept any tender.

None of these presumptions is an absolute rule, so that in an appropriate case a price list (for instance) may be construed as an offer. Moreover, even when a document is properly construed as an invitation to treat rather than an offer, it may still be contractually significant. For instance, a business may include its standard terms of supply in price lists which it sends out to customers; when a customer orders goods it may be argued that it makes an offer to buy on the terms set out in the price list. Further, the relatively limited requirements for a valid offer mean that even a relatively informal statement—such as a telephone request for delivery of goods—may be construed as an offer.

2.3.2 Acceptance

An acceptance of an offer must unconditionally assent to all the terms of the offer. A response which introduces new terms or qualifies any of the terms of the offer is not an acceptance but a counter-offer which rejects the original offer. Such a counter-offer will only produce a contract if it is accepted.

The general rule is that acceptance is ineffective until communicated to the offeror. The only exceptions are that (a) the offeror may waive the need for communication and (b) where acceptance is sent by post, it is effective on posting. Communications sent by telephone, fax, telex or computer are not effective until received. However, it may be difficult to decide when exactly a fax, telex or computer message, or a message left on a telephone answering machine is 'received'. Case law on the subject suggests that the time when such a message becomes effective depends on a number of factors including normal business practices, the expectations of the parties and the court's assessment of which of them should bear the risk (see e.g. *Brinkibon Ltd* v *Stahag Stahl GmbH* [1983] 2 AC 34). In other words there is no fixed rule to cover all situations. The time at which an acceptance sent by e-mail becomes effective has not yet been considered by the courts. It has been suggested that since an intermediary is involved, as with ordinary ('snail') mail, the postal rule could be applied. Conversely it has also been argued that since the transmission is almost instantaneous and there are ways for the sender to find out whether or not an e-mail message is delivered, the general rule should apply. These arguments seem stronger, but it is likely that if and when the question arises for consideration a court will resolve it by taking into account the sort of factors which have been considered in cases concerned with fax and telex, so that there may be no absolute hard and fast rule.

Where a contract governs a continuing relationship it may contain provisions to deal with the time at which notices become effective, for instance, by providing that, messages sent by fax are to be effective when printed out on the recipient's machine. However, such provisions are unlikely to be helpful in relation to the initial formation of the contract.

An offer may be accepted by conduct. Thus, for instance, if B places an order for goods, S may accept it by conduct by sending the goods.

2.3.3 The terms must be complete and certain

An agreement will not constitute a legally binding contract unless it is sufficiently certain to be enforced. If its terms are incomplete or uncertain it may be decided that the parties have not yet reached a concluded agreement or that they do not intend the agreement to be legally binding. Clearly a lawyer should not normally prepare a contract on vague or incomplete terms; however, many business agreements use vague language (sometimes deliberately) and the lawyer may be called on to advise clients on the effects of such agreements entered into, perhaps, by telephone or at trade fairs or over lunch.

2.3.3.1 Minimum terms

Courts will generally seek to enforce commercial and business agreements, especially where one or both parties have commenced performance, and all that is generally required is agreement in clear terms on the core provisions of the contract, such as the price and date for performance. Even silence on these matters may not be fatal since in contracts for the supply of goods or services it will be an implied term that if no price is agreed the buyer should pay a reasonable price and that if the contract does not fix a date for performance, the contract should be performed within a reasonable time (see **16.3** and **11.2.4**).

2.3.3.2 Uncertain agreements

Any uncertainty in the terms agreed may mean that the particular term is ineffective or even that the parties have not concluded a binding agreement. For instance, agreement that a contact was to be subject to 'usual force majeure conditions' was ineffective as uncertain, since there are no 'usual force majeure conditions' (*British Electrical and Associated Industries (Cardiff) Ltd* v *Patley Processing Ltd* [1953] 1 WLR 280). An agreement to supply goods 'on hire purchase terms' was similarly uncertain and in this case it was held that there was no concluded contract (*G. Scammell and Nephew Ltd* v *Ouston* [1941] AC 251). On the other hand an agreement by which one party undertakes to use 'reasonable' or 'best endeavours' to achieve a result is not uncertain and is enforceable as a contract (*Lambert* v *HTV Cymru* [1998] FSR 874). This type of formula is frequently used in some types of commercial contract. Its effect is that the party has not given an absolute undertaking to achieve a result, but merely to use his reasonable, or best, endeavours to bring it about.

2.3.3.3 Agreements to agree

Certain expressions may indicate that the parties have not yet concluded a binding contract. As a general rule the courts will not enforce 'agreements to agree' or agreements to negotiate. Thus if A and B agree that A should supply B with machinery 'at a price to be agreed' they will probably be held not to have concluded a binding agreement. Since they have agreed that the price is to be agreed they have excluded the implied term that a reasonable price should be paid.

2.3.3.4 Lock out agreements

Although an agreement to negotiate is generally not enforceable, a 'lock-out agreement' under which A agrees with B that he will, for a fixed period, not enter into negotiations with anyone other than B, may be enforceable by B (see *Walford* v *Miles* [1992] 2 AC 128; *Pitt* v *PMH Assett Management Ltd* [1993] 4 All ER 961). A 'lock-out agreement' of this type may be particularly valuable to parties negotiating the sale and purchase of a business, where a potential buyer may have to incur considerable legal and other expenses in investigating the condition of the business to be purchased and wish to be assured of a 'free run' at the purchase.

2.3.4 Formation and standard forms

Problems of formation frequently arise in the context of disputes as to whether particular terms are incorporated into the contract, especially where the parties use standard terms and there is a so-called 'battle of forms'. This aspect of the problem is considered below (**2.6.2.5**).

2.3.5 Intention to create legal relations

A court will not enforce an agreement as a contract unless it is intended to be legally binding. The parties' intention to create legal relations is assessed objectively and it will generally be assumed that commercial and business agreements are intended to be legally binding. Nevertheless, this is not an absolute rule and the parties to a commercial agreement may expressly agree that the agreement is not to be legally binding.

Certain common commercial arrangements, such as letters of comfort and letters of intent, will generally be presumed *not* to be intended to be binding. Letters of comfort are examined at **26.11**.

Where parties are negotiating a contract a letter of intent may be used in order to require one to commence performance while negotiations continue. It will generally be assumed that a letter of intent is not intended to create legal relations. If the parties fail to reach final agreement there may therefore be no contract; however, when the parties do reach agreement its terms may impliedly or expressly apply to work already carried out under the letter of intent (see *G. Percy Trentham Ltd* v *Archital Luxfer Ltd* [1993] 1 Lloyd's Rep 25).

2.3.6 Formalities for contract formation

In general there are no formal requirements for the creation of a valid, binding contract in English law. However, the general rule is qualified by a number of statutory exceptions which require particular types of contract to be either made or evidenced in writing. Thus contracts for the sale or disposition of interests in land, contracts of guarantee, consumer credit and hire contracts, certain contracts of insurance, and certain contracts for the sale or supply of goods or services to consumers are all now subject to some formal requirements. In some cases non-compliance means that the contract is void, in others that it is unenforceable by one or other of the parties, or that one of the parties is subject to some other sanction. Many of these formal requirements are for the protection of consumers. The requirements applicable to commercial transactions, and the consequences of non-compliance with them, are discussed where appropriate in subsequent chapters. It remains true, however, that it is possible to create a valid contract not covered by any of the specific statutory provisions without complying with any particular formalities.

2.3.7 Electronic commerce

Electronic commerce is already growing in importance and is likely to become even more important in future years. It offers businesses the opportunity to reach a wider customer base without the need to maintain an expensive infrastructure of physical outlets, while enabling consumers and businesses to purchase goods and services from a wider range of suppliers than would be accessible to them by traditional means. However, the full potential of electronic commerce is unlikely to be realised unless its legal status is secure and certain: parties need to be assured that electronic contracts are as effective as contracts made by traditional means. A number of legislative instruments have now been adopted to address such concerns. In 1996 the United Nations Commission on International Trade Law (UNCITRAL) published a Model Law on Electronic Commerce which has been used as the basis for national legislation in a number of jurisdictions. More recently the EU has produced Directives on Electronic Commerce and Digital Signatures and, partly to implement the Directives, the Electronic Communications Act 2000 has been passed, and subsidiary regulations have been made, in the UK.

The Electronic Commerce Directive (2000/31/EC) seeks to establish a framework for the supply of 'information society services' (defined in Directives 98/34/EC and 98/84/EC) throughout the EU. It prohibits Member States from making the provision of information society services subject to prior approval and provides that a person who provides a service consisting of transmitting information, providing access to a communication network or storing information, shall not, without more, be liable for the information transmitted or stored. Member States cannot require service providers to monitor the information transmitted by or stored on their systems. It also requires Member States to ensure that their laws allow contracts to be concluded electronically, and the Electronic Signatures Directive (99/93/EC) requires Member States to recognise the effectiveness of electronic signatures. In order to implement these last two requirements the Electronic Communications Act 2000 contains power for the appropriate Secretary of State by statutory instrument to modify 'in such manner as he may think fit for the purpose of authorising or facilitating the use of electronic communications or electronic storage' the provisions of any existing primary or secondary legislation or scheme, licence or approval issued under any legislation which require anything to be done or evidenced in writing or by use of a document or by post or other specified means of delivery, or to be signed or sealed, or that records to be kept, and so on. The Act also provides for electronic signatures 'incorporated into or logically associated with' electronic communications to be admissible in evidence as to the authenticity and/or integrity of the communication (s. 7).

It is anticipated that in the foreseeable future electronic documents will be digitally signed by means of public/private key encryption, in which messages are encoded using a secret 'key'—a piece of digital code unique to the user. Such a message would be decoded by using a corresponding unique key. Since the encoding 'key' is secret and unique to the user, a message encoded using a particular key can be said to have been authenticated, and thus 'signed' by the key holder. In order for such encryption to be evidence of authentication by the key holder, however, it must be possible to connect the particular key with the key holder. In order to satisfy this requirement the Act provides for 'third party certification': details of keyholders and their keys will be kept by certification authorities. If the authenticity of a signature should be questioned in any proceedings, a certificate from the relevant authority may be produced as evidence of the identity of the key holder and the Act makes such a certificate admissible in proceedings (s. 7(1)(b)). The Electronic Signatures Regulations 2002 (SI 2002, No. 318) provide for the Secretary of State to keep under review the activities of certification service providers established in the UK, and to keep a register of such providers. They further provide for certification service providers to be liable to the public if certificates are inaccurate or incomplete. Where a certification service provider issues a certificate to the public and a person who reasonably relies on the certificate for certain prescribed matters suffers loss as a result, the service provider is liable to that person unless the service provider can prove that they were not negligent. In effect, therefore, the Regulations impose a statutory duty of care on service providers, with a rebuttable presumption of negligence.

The Electronic Commerce (EC Directive) Regulations 2002 (SI 2002, No. 213) partly implement the Electronic Commerce Directive by making provision for certain aspects of electronic contract formation. (Contracts for the supply of financial services are covered by separate regulations.) They apply to information service providers established in the UK who supply information services in the UK or any other EU Member State. Amongst other things they require a service provider to provide certain prescribed information to the service recipient before an order is placed (reg. 9), and provide that where a customer places an order by 'technological means' the service provider must (a) acknowledge receipt of the order by electronic means and without undue delay and (b) provide means for the customer to identify and correct input errors prior to placing the order (reg. 11). No derogation from these requirements is permitted where the customer is a consumer; in other cases derogation is permitted with the customer's consent. The requirements for provision of information are additional to any other requirements for the provision of information under other legislation. These duties are enforceable by an action for damages for breach of statutory duty. In addition if the provider fails to provide the customer with a means to identify and correct any input errors before placing of the order, any resulting contract is voidable at the instance of the customer. Significantly, however, neither the information requirements nor the error correction requirements apply to contracts concluded exclusively by e-mail.

These instruments therefore regulate to some degree the formation of contracts in an e-commerce environment. However, the answers to many of the core questions concerning the effectiveness of electronic contracts are likely to depend on application of the traditional rules governing contract formation and, in particular, the rules governing offer and acceptance to questions such as 'is a web-site an offer?' and 'if an acceptance is sent by e-mail, when and where does the acceptance take effect?'. It seems likely that no hard and fast answer can be given to these questions. Instead the answers are likely, in line with the modern approach to such issues (see **2.3.1**, **2.3.2**), to depend on all the circumstances of any particular case.

2.4 Defects in formation

Even where parties appear to have reached a concluded agreement, that agreement may be defective because of the conduct of one or both parties, or because of other events, during formation. As a result the contract may be *void* or *voidable*.

If the contract is wholly void, for instance because of mistake, it has no legal effect. No action is needed to set it aside, although where there is a dispute a court order may be needed to declare the contract void or to recover money paid or property transferred under the contract.

If the contract is merely voidable it is legally effective unless and until the innocent party takes steps to have it set aside. The contract may be rescinded without a court order, for instance by the innocent party giving clear and unequivocal notice to the other that he wishes to rescind the contract, but the assistance of the court may be required to recover property transferred or money paid. Even if the contract is voidable the right to rescind may be lost if the innocent party affirms the contract or unreasonably delays before seeking to rescind. The innocent party should therefore act promptly to protect his position.

The distinction between void and voidable contracts is important where property has been transferred under the contract. If the original contract was void, the original owner can recover the property, even if it has come into the hands of a bona fide purchaser; however, if the original contract was merely voidable the original owner may be unable to recover the property from a bona fide purchaser (see **15.3.4.1**).

2.4.1 Mistake

It is rarely argued that a contract is void for mistake. Moreover, the argument that the contract is void for mistake will only rarely succeed. If the argument succeeds, the contract is void; the parties are therefore excused from performance of the contract and property transferred under it can be recovered, but there is no right to damages.

2.4.1.1 Both parties mistaken

If the parties enter into a contract sharing the same mistaken belief the contract may be void for mistake. The mistake must be fundamental: for instance, a mistake as to the existence of the subject matter of the contract (see *Associated Japanese Bank (International) Ltd* v *Crédit du Nord SA* [1988] 3 All ER 902), or as to the possibility of performing the contract. Thus for instance if S contracts to sell to B goods to be imported, the contract may be void for mistake if, unknown to either of them, import of the goods has been prohibited before they make the contract.

A mistake as to the qualities of the subject matter of the contract will only make the contract void if it is fundamental so that it makes the subject matter essentially different from the subject matter the parties believed to exist (see *The Great Peace* [2002] EWCA Civ 1407; [2002] 2 All ER (Comm) 999). This test is likely to be satisfied only in exceptional cases and a mistake as to the value of the contractual subject matter will rarely make the contract void.

Special rules apply to contracts for sale of goods where without the knowledge of the parties the goods have perished before the contract is made (see **14.3.2**).

2.4.1.2 One party mistaken

A mistake by one party alone will generally not affect the contract. The only exceptions seem to be where the mistake is induced by the conduct of the other party or where one party is mistaken as to the terms of the contract and the other is aware of that mistake.

Often where one party is mistaken, the mistake may have been induced by the other party. In that case the innocent party may be able to claim that the other has been guilty of misrepresentation or even of breach of contract.

2.4.1.3 Parties at cross purposes

If the parties are at cross purposes so that it is impossible objectively to decide what they have agreed, or what their agreement means, the agreement will be void.

2.4.2 Misrepresentation

A misrepresentation is a false statement of fact made by A to B prior to formation of a contract.

If B enters into the contract as a result of A's misrepresentation, the contract is voidable and B may rescind it. It is irrelevant for this purpose that the misrepresentation was not fraudulent, or even non-negligent. Damages may also be recovered for misrepresentation (see **3.3.2.2**).

Failure to disclose relevant information does not generally amount to misrepresentation. There are some exceptions to this general principle, the most important of which is that there is a duty of disclosure if the contract is one of utmost good faith (*uberrimae fidei*). The most important examples of such contracts in the commercial context are insurance contracts and contracts between partners. Where circumstances change between the making of a statement and the conclusion of the contract so that the statement, although true when made, becomes false in light of the changed circumstances, the representor will be under a duty to inform the representee of the change of circumstances (see, e.g., *Spice Girls Ltd* v *Aprilia World Service* [2002] EWCA Civ 15).

A statement made during negotiations may also be a term of the contract so that if it is false the innocent party may claim remedies for breach of contract (see **2.6.1**).

In practice the victim of a misrepresentation will often bring claims for misrepresentation and breach of contract in the alternative.

2.4.3 Duress

If a person is induced to enter into a contract as a result of duress by the other party, the contract is voidable. Threats to a person's life or person and threats to damage property may all amount to duress. 'Economic duress' may also make a contract voidable: a threat to break an existing contract may amount to economic duress which will vitiate any agreement made as a result of the threat. This is important in the context of variations of contracts: if one party to a contract threatens to break the contract unless the other party agrees to vary its terms, the threat may amount to economic duress so that the agreement to vary is voidable (see **2.5.1.2**).

2.4.4 Undue influence

A contract is voidable on the grounds of undue influence if:

(a) one party exercised a dominating influence over the other; and

(b) its terms are manifestly unfair.

Certain relationships give rise to a presumption of undue influence. There will not normally be such a presumption between the parties to a commercial contract, although the relationship between principal and agent may sometimes give rise to a presumption of undue influence. However, even where there is no presumption of undue influence, a contract may be voidable on the grounds of undue influence if it is shown that on the facts of the particular case, one party exercised a dominating influence over the other. (See e.g. *Lloyds Bank Ltd* v *Bundy* [1975] QB 326.)

2.5 Variation of contract

After a contract has been concluded either or both parties may wish to vary its terms or their obligations under it. This may be especially important under long term contracts such as construction, distributorship, loan and requirements contracts where changed circumstances may necessitate variation. For instance, one party may wish to increase the contract price as a result of inflation.

EXAMPLE

Evil Genius Transport Ltd (EGT) contracts with Phil's Fashions of Fulchester Ltd (Phil's) for a period of one year to transport Phil's' goods to retail outlets at a price of £10 per item. After five months the price of diesel is increased as a result of an international oil crisis and EGT wishes to increase the price payable under the contract.

2.5.1 Agreed variation

The general rule is that a contract can only be varied if both parties agree to the variation and each party's agreement to the variation is supported by consideration from the other.

2.5.1.1 Consideration

Where the variation benefits both parties, or may benefit either, each party's consent to it will be consideration for the other's and the variation will therefore be binding. This will not be the case in the example above.

Where the variation benefits only one party, as in the example, the party who benefits from the variation must provide consideration for the other's acceptance of it, for instance by undertaking some extra obligation. Performance of existing obligations will generally not be consideration for the new promise from the other party (see **2.2.2**).

EXAMPLE

If, in the situation described in 2.5 above, Phil's agrees to an increase to £12 per item, the agreement will not be binding. EGT is already bound to carry the goods for the remainder of the year. However, the agreement will be binding on Phil's if EGT provides new consideration for it, for instance by agreeing to insure the goods whilst in transit.

The need for consideration can be avoided by making the variation in a deed.

2.5.1.2 Duress

Even if a variation is agreed and supported by consideration it may not be binding if consent to it was obtained by duress. A threat to break the exisiting contract unless the variation is accepted may amount to economic duress (**2.4.3**). Thus in the above example, if EGT does agree to insure the goods in transit, the agreement will still not be binding on Phil's if their agreement is obtained by EGT threatening to break the contract unless Phil's agrees to the new terms.

2.5.1.3   Informal variation

In many cases parties may respond to changed circumstances by simply varying their performance without any formal agreement to that effect. If a contracting party, A, accepts without objection a varied performance from the other party, B, it may be possible to argue that there is an implied agreement to vary the contract, which will become binding on B if it can be shown that A provided consideration for B's implied agreement to vary. Alternatively, if the variation is wholly unilateral it may be argued that B is estopped from denying that the contract has been effectively varied with the result that B is bound without receiving consideration. However, although these arguments may be deployed after the event in order to argue that the informal variation has become binding, if parties are contemplating a variation of their contract they should be advised to do so formally, either by agreement supported by consideration or by deed.

2.5.1.4   Novation

Where it is intended to vary the contract by introducing a new party there must be a novation of the contract—an agreement between the existing parties and the new party by which it is agreed either to add the new party as a party to the existing agreement, or to substitute the new party for one of the parties to the existing agreement. In either case the agreement will only be binding if supported by consideration. For instance, if A owes money to B and B agrees, at C's request, to release A in return for C's promise to pay the debt, A provides consideration for C's promise by releasing B. In order to avoid problems of consideration a novation agreement may be contained in and executed as a deed.

2.5.2   New contract after discharge

The parties are free to enter into a new agreement if their original contract is discharged. Where circumstances are so fundamentally changed that the contract is frustrated, the parties are discharged from the original contract and may therefore replace it with a new contract. This will rarely be the case since the contract will only be frustrated by a fundamental and unforeseeable change in circumstances. In particular, it will be rare that a contract is frustrated by inflation so as to justify price increases.

Where both parties have outstanding unperformed obligations under a contract they may discharge the contract by agreement. In that case each party agrees to release the other from their unperformed obligations, and each party's agreement to the discharge provides consideration for the other party's agreement. Having discharged the original agreement they are then free to make a new contract on any terms: see *Compagnie Noga D'Importation et D'Exportation v Abacha* [2003] EWCA Civ 1100; 2 All ER (Comm) 915.

EXAMPLE

Thus, in the example given in **2.5**, above, a simple agreement to increase the price payable to £12 per item will not be binding unless EGT provide additional consideration for the increased price. But if after 5 months the parties agree to discharge the original agreement, it will be open to them to make a new contract under which EGT agrees to carry Phil's goods for the remaining 7 months at a price of £12 per item. There is no need for EGT to provide extra consideration because it no longer has any duties under the original contract.

Where it is wished to vary an existing contract before completion of performance it will therefore be preferable to do so by discharging the original contract and replacing it with a new one. Whether a variation agreement operates as a simple variation or as an agreement to discharge the original agreement and replace it with a new one will be largely a matter of form, depending on the way the agreement is expressed. A solicitor advising on the variation of an existing contract should therefore seek to draft the variation as an agreement to discharge and make a new contract. It should be emphasised, though, that this approach is only possible if both parties have unperformed obligations under the original contract. Where one party has completely performed its obligations an agreement to vary the contract will only be binding on that party if it receives some additional consideration for its agreement to the variation or the agreement is contained in a deed.

2.5.3 Variation sanctioned by the original contract

A variation which is sanctioned by the terms of the original contract is binding without fresh consideration. Thus, if in the example above the original contract between EGT and Phil's permitted EGT to increase the price payable by Phil's, the increase to £12 per item is binding even if EGT undertakes no extra obligations.

A term allowing one party unilaterally to vary the terms of a contract is valid at common law. However, such a term may be subject to a test of reasonableness under Unfair Contract Terms Act 1977, s. 3 (see **3.4.3.5**). Such a term in a contract with a consumer may not be binding on the consumer as a result of the Unfair Terms in Consumer Contracts Regulations 1999 (see **3.4.4**). In addition, a contract term granting a discretion to one party to vary the terms of the contract may be subject to an implied restriction that the discretion will be exercised 'honestly and in good faith' and not arbitrarily, capriciously or for an improper purpose: see *Paragon Finance Ltd* v *Nash* [2001] EWCA 1466; [2001] 2 All ER (Comm) 1025.

2.5.4 Variation of performance without variation of contract

A contract may include a term which makes the content of one party's obligation variable without the need for any action by either party. For instance, the contract between EGT and Phil's could contain a clause linking the price payable by Phil's to the price of diesel fuel and providing for the price automatically to increase in the event of fuel price rises.

2.5.5 Practical implications

Because of the difficulties in fulfilling the legal requirements for a binding variation to a contract, a long term contract should generally contain provisions allowing at least some of its terms to be varied where it can be foreseen that changes in circumstances, such as increases in materials or labour costs, may occur.

2.6 Negotiations, statements and terms

There may be extensive negotiations between the parties leading to conclusion of the contract. This may encompass oral and written communications, including letters, price lists, advertising and sales literature as well as formal contract documents.

If a dispute arises it may be necessary to decide what exactly was said and written and what effect, if any, these communications had. Did they form part of the contract?

Were they terms or representations, or mere sales talk with no legal effect? Even where the event-ual contract is set out in a formal document, statements outside that document may have to be considered as representations, supplemental terms or collateral contracts.

Proof of what was said and written is a matter of evidence. The effect of a particular statement is a matter of law.

2.6.1   Terms and representations

The classification of statements made during negotiations is important because it will affect the remedies available if the statement proves false. Breach of a term gives the claimant the right to damages; liability is strict; misrepresentation gives a right to damages only if the misrepresentation was fraudulent or negligent. However, in some cases the measure of damages for misrepresentation may be more favourable than that for breach of contract (see **3.3.2.2**). Conversely misrepresentation always gives the claimant a right to rescind the contract but breach of a term gives a right to terminate the contract only if the term broken is a major term (i.e. a condition) or the breach has important consequences.

In some cases a statement may be both a representation and a term of the contract, in which case the claimant may be able to pursue remedies for either misrepresentation or breach of contract (Misrepresentation Act 1967, s. 1(a)).

2.6.1.1   Representations

A representation is a statement of past or present fact made during negotiations which induces the representee to enter into the contract. Statements of law, opinion and future intention cannot generally constitute representations.

2.6.1.2   Terms

A statement made during negotiations will become a term of the contract if, viewed objectively, it was intended to be binding as a promise. The following factors may be relevant to the question of classification:

(a) the relative knowledge of the parties: a statement made by the party with greater knowledge is more likely to be regarded as a term;

(b) the importance of the statement to the parties;

(c) the time when the statement was made: statements made close to the time of conclusion of the contract are more likely to be regarded as terms;

(d) where the parties record their agreement in a formal written document, statements not included in the document are less likely to be regarded as terms; however, it may be possible in an appropriate case to show that such statements were intended to have contractual effect, either as terms of the written contract, or as a separate, collateral, contract.

In order to avoid the difficulty of classifying statements and the consequent uncertainty in defining the terms of the contract, a written contract (including one on standard terms) may include an 'entire agreement' clause. Such clauses are designed to reinforce the presumption referred to above that where the parties have entered into a written contract they intend the written document to contain all the terms of their agreement, by making clear that no statements outside the written contract are intended to have contractual effect, either as terms of the contract or as collateral contracts. A simple example might thus provide:

The terms of this contract shall constitute the entire agreement between the parties.
The following points should, however, be noted.

(a) Such a provision in a contract with a consumer will be subject to a test of fairness under the Unfair Terms in Consumer Contracts Regulations 1999 unless the term is individually negotiated, and it appears that the Office of Fair Trading generally regards entire agreement clauses as unfair for the purposes of the Regulations (see **3.4.4**).

(b) It seems, too, that an entire agreement clause which denies contractual effect to pre-contractual statements which would otherwise take effect as collateral contracts is subject to a test of reasonableness under s. 3 of the Unfair Contract Terms Act 1977 if it appears in either (i) the written standard terms of the party seeking to rely on it or (ii) a contract with a consumer (*SAM Business Systems Ltd* v *Hedley & Co.* [2002] EWHC 2733 (TCC); [2003] 1 All ER (Comm) 465; see **3.4.3.4**).

(c) An entire agreement clause does not of itself prevent statements outside the written agreement operating as representations inducing the contract. An entire agreement clause will therefore commonly be combined with terms excluding or limiting liability for misrepresentation and restricting the authority of employees and others to make statements binding on the party relying on the clause, such as the following.

The terms of this contract shall constitute the entire agreement between the parties. No variation of these terms shall be binding on the seller unless agreed to in writing signed on the seller's behalf by the seller's marketing director; no other employee or agent has authority to agree to any variation of these terms. The buyer acknowledges that in entering into this contract it has not relied on any statements or representations made by or on behalf of the seller.

This clause contains (i) an entire agreement clause; (ii) a provision limiting the authority of employees to vary the terms of the contract, and (iii) an acknowledgement that the buyer has not relied on any statements or representations made by the seller. This last provision creates an estoppel against the buyer, preventing it asserting (contrary to the term) that it did rely on any such statements. Its effect is therefore to prevent any false statement made by the seller giving rise to liability for misrepresentation. A simple exclusion of liability for misrepresentation would be subject to a test of reasonableness under the Misrepresentation Act 1967, s. 3; it is not clear whether a clause such as this is subject to the 1967 Act. Note, however, that the seller will not be able to rely on the clause if it is aware that the buyer *has* relied on any such statements. (See *Lowe* v *Lombank Ltd* [1960] 1 All ER 611; *Watford Electronics Ltd* v *Sanderson CFL Ltd* [2001] 1 All ER (Comm) 696.)

2.6.2 Incorporation of terms

A key issue in disputes arising out of commercial contracts is whether a particular statement formed part of the contract. Where there is a formal written contract it will be rebuttably presumed to contain the terms of the parties' agreement. In relation to other statements and documents it will be necessary to consider the time when the statement was made and the nature of the document in which it was contained. Particular problems arise when a party wishes to rely on clauses contained in standard terms and argues that those terms were incorporated into the contract. A remarkably large number of commercial disputes are decided on the question whether an alleged term, such as an exclusion clause, was effectively incorporated into the contract.

2.6.2.1 Timing

A statement cannot be part of a contract unless it was made before the contract was concluded. Statements or new terms introduced after conclusion of the contract can only become terms of the contract if there is a contractually binding variation of the contract. Thus terms printed on a document sent out after conclusion of the contract, cannot become part of the contract.

EXAMPLE 1

Phil's Fashions receives an order from Del Sauvage for 10 suits and agrees over the telephone to fulfil his order. Two days later it sends out an 'acknowledgement of order' form which sets out its standard terms of business.

EXAMPLE 2

As above, but Phil's' terms are printed on the back of an invoice sent out with the suits delivered to Del.

In neither case would Phil's' terms be incorporated into the contract, which was made over the telephone. Terms on an invoice delivered after performance of the contract will never form part of the contract. The only exception would be if Phil's could establish a course of dealing with Sauvage (see **2.6.2.4**).

2.6.2.2 Written documents

Incorporation of terms in a written document depends on two factors:

(a) was the document signed; and, if not,

(b) had reasonable steps been taken to draw the terms to the notice of the
     other party?

Signed documents   As a general rule, in the absence of fraud or misrepresentation, a person who signs a document containing or referring to contract terms is bound by those terms even if he has not read them (*L'Estrange* v *Graucob* [1934] 2 KB 394). However, a business may not be able to rely on this rule if it misrepresents the existence or effect of the terms (see *Curtis* v *Chemical Cleaning and Dyeing Co. Ltd* [1951] 1 KB 805; *Harvey* v *Ventilatoren Fabrik Oelde GmbH* [1988] BTLR 138).

A person who has signed a document will also not be bound by it if he can establish a plea of 'non est factum' but it is clear that such a plea will rarely succeed, especially in the context of commercial agreements.

Unsigned documents   A person will not be bound by terms in an unsigned document unless he was aware that the document contained writing or printing. Subject to this, he will be bound if:

(a) he was aware that the document contained contract terms; or

(b) if the person seeking to rely on the terms had taken reasonable steps to give
     him notice of the terms.

The requirement of reasonable notice requires that the document in which they appear should be the sort of document which might reasonably be expected to contain contract terms. Typical business documents, such as orders, acknowledgements and so on, generally contain or refer to contract terms and so should satisfy this requirement, although difficulties can arise if (for example) terms are printed on documents such as tickets or receipts.

It is probably sufficient for terms to be printed on the back of a business document; this is common practice. However, incorporation is more likely if the terms are at least referred to on the face of the document by some formula such as 'We acknowledge receipt of your order and agree to supply you subject to the terms set out overleaf'.

Terms contained in a separate document may be incorporated by reference, e.g.: 'We acknowledge receipt of your order and agree to supply you, subject to our standard terms of trading, a copy of which is available on request'. However, although such a reference might be sufficient to incorporate the terms into the contract, lack of notice of the *content* of the terms might lead to any exclusion clauses being considered unreasonable (see **3.4.3.5**).

2.6.2.3 Special notice for individual terms

If a document contains terms which are unusual or unreasonable, a greater degree of notice may be required to incorporate those terms into the contract. Lord Denning spoke graphically of the need to highlight such terms by printing them in red ink with a red hand pointing to them. This requirement does not apply only to exclusion clauses, but to any clause which may be judged unreasonable or unusual (see *Interfoto Picture Library Ltd* v *Stiletto Visual Programmes Ltd* [1989] QB 433; *AEG (UK) Ltd* v *Logic Resource Ltd* [1996] CLC 265).

2.6.2.4 Course of dealing

Where parties do business together on the same terms on a regular basis over a period of time there may be a course of dealing as a result of which the terms normally used between them will be impliedly incorporated into their contracts. Consider the first example in **2.6.2.1**: if Phil's had regularly done business with Del Sauvage and had always sent out an acknowledgement containing its standard terms, those terms might be included in the contract on this occasion when the contract is made over the telephone.

Terms will only be incorporated by a course of dealing if there has been regular trading between the parties over a period of time on the same terms. It is not clear when a course of dealing will be recognised in this way. Course of dealing is therefore an argument of last resort; a business should be advised to take proper steps to incorporate its terms into its contracts. It may nevertheless be necessary to rely on a course of dealing in litigation.

2.6.2.5 Standard terms and the battle of forms

Businesses often use standard terms to govern their contracts. The incorporation of such terms into individual contracts depends on the factors discussed above. Problems may arise when two businesses wish to contract and each seeks to rely on its standard terms.

EXAMPLE

Phil's Fashions Ltd orders fabric from Broadweave Fabrics Ltd on its own standard order form which incorporates Phil's' standard terms of purchase. Broadweave acknowledges the order with a form which purports to accept the order, but contains Broadweave's own standard terms of sale, which differ from Phil's' terms.

Such dealings tend to be analysed in terms of offer and acceptance. Thus in the example Broadweave has made a counter-offer to Phil's' offer and there is no contract at this stage (see *Butler Machine Tool Co. Ltd* v *Ex-Cell-O Corp.* [1979] 1 WLR 401). The effect of this interpretation is that the 'battle' is won by the party who fires the last shot. For instance, if in the example Broadweave sends out the fabric and Phil's keeps it without objecting to

Broadweave's terms, Phil's may be taken to have accepted Broadweave's counter-offer by conduct. If, on the other hand, Phil's replies to Broadweave's acknowledgement by referring again to its own terms of purchase, Broadweave could be taken to accept Phil's' terms by manufacturing and supplying the fabric without objecting to the terms.

In order to avoid losing the 'battle of forms', standard business terms often contain a provision such as the following:

The terms of this order are to govern any contract between the Buyer and the Seller and shall prevail over any terms put forward by the Seller.

The effect of such terms is unclear. The term above could be read as preventing any conduct of the buyer being interpreted as acceptance of the seller's terms. However, if the seller's terms include a similar provision it is not clear how the situation would be resolved. It might be argued that neither party has accepted the other's terms, so that there is no contract at all, or that there is a contract but neither set of terms applies. Alternatively it could be argued that one party has impliedly waived all of its terms, including the term excluding the other party's terms.

It is generally acccepted that whilst a business can, by objecting to any terms presented by the other side, ensure that it does not lose the battle of forms, it cannot ensure that it wins. In theory if both parties were equally determined there could be a 'stalemate' resulting in there being no contract at all, or a contract on neither party's terms. In practice the battle tends to be won or lost by default and problems are dealt with not when the contract is formed but if a dispute arises and either party seeks to rely on its terms.

A business faced by a battle of forms with a customer might be advised to negotiate a compromise with the customer in order to try and avoid disputes.

2.6.3 Implied terms

The express terms in a contract may be supplemented by terms which may be implied into the contract by statute or at common law.

2.6.3.1 Statutory implied terms

Statutory implied terms are particularly important in commercial contracts: the Sale of Goods Act 1979 and the Supply of Goods and Services Act 1982 respectively imply terms into contracts for the sale of goods and contracts involving the supply of services. These terms are considered in **Chapters 12** and **17**.

2.6.3.2 Common law implied terms

At common law terms may be implied:

(a) to reflect customs of a particular trade;

(b) as a matter of law into all contracts of a particular type: for instance there is a body of terms which may be implied into contracts of agency or contracts of guarantee;

(c) into a particular contract in order to give it 'business efficacy'.

In (b) the implied terms become incidents of the particular type of contract, which are always implied into contracts of that type unless excluded by the express terms. In (c) implication depends on all the facts of the case.

It should only be necessary to rely on an implied term when an event for which no express provision is made occurs. A term cannot be implied if it would contradict an express term of the contract; a well drafted, comprehensive contract therefore minimises the scope for implication of terms, although it will generally be impossible to provide for all eventualities.

2.6.4 Interpretation of contracts

In many cases the most contentious issue between contracting parties is the correct interpretation of the contract. A commercial lawyer needs to be aware, both when drafting a contract and advising on its effect, of the approach a court is likely to take to interpretation. There have been important developments in this area in recent years. The correct approach to contract interpretation has been the subject of judicial analysis in several cases. The leading authority now is the House of Lords' decision in *Investors Compensation Scheme Ltd* v *West Bromwich Building Society* [1998] 1 All ER 98. The following principles can be extracted from the cases.

1. The court's objective when interpreting a contract is to ascertain the intention of the contracting parties, in order to give effect to it.

2. The parties' intention is to be determined objectively, by reference to the words used in the contract.

3. A court will, however, strive to give effect to what it perceives to be the commercial objective of the parties, and to interpret the contract in a 'common sense' manner.

4. This means, in particular, that the words used are interpreted against the background of the commercial and factual context in which they were used. Words in a particular clause are therefore interpreted in the light of the contract as a whole; contracts are interpreted against their commercial and factual background, including any previous dealings of the parties and any relevant trade practices or customs.

5. The court will seek to ascertain the commercial objective of the contract as a whole and then interpret particular clauses or terms so as to give effect to that objective.

6. On the other hand, evidence of the parties' negotiations is normally excluded from consideration as not necessarily reflecting the parties' final intention. Similarly evidence of the parties' conduct *subsequent* to the making of the contract is normally excluded from consideration when determining the meaning of the original contract. However, the fact that the parties performed the contract other than in accord-ance with its original terms may indicate an implied agreement to vary the contract as originally drawn, or operate so as to raise an estoppel against one of the parties (see **2.5.1.3**).

7. Finally, a court will generally be reluctant to give a contract term a meaning which produces a result which the court considers to be unreasonable. Thus if a clause is capable of two or more interpretations, the court is likely to favour that which it considers more reasonable. If an 'unreasonable' result is intended, the parties must make that unambiguously clear by using explicit language.

2.6.5 Classification of terms

Where a term is breached it may be necessary to classify it in order to decide what remedies are available for its breach. Terms may be classified as conditions, warranties or innominate terms.

Breach of any term permits the injured party to claim damages for any loss caused by the breach. Classification becomes important, however, where the innocent party wishes to use the breach as a reason for withholding performance of his own obligations or terminating the contract. Careful advice must be given because if a person purports to withhold performance or terminate in circumstances where such action is not justified, he himself will be in breach of contract.

2.6.5.1 Breach of warranty

Termination is never allowed for a breach of a term classified as a warranty.

2.6.5.2 Breach of condition

Conversely, if the term is classified as a condition, the injured party has the option to withhold performance until the condition is fulfilled and to terminate, in addition to claiming damages, for any breach, no matter how serious. He is not obliged to terminate but may elect to affirm the contract, and will lose the right to terminate if he does affirm; for instance if, knowing of the breach, he does any act which indicates an intention to keep the contract alive and continue with performance.

2.6.5.3 Breach of innominate term

Whether there is a right to withhold performance or to terminate for breach of an innominate term depends on the seriousness of the breach and of its consequences. Unfortunately it is difficult to predict when this test will permit termination of a contract.

2.6.5.4 Express classification

It seems likely that most express terms will be classified as innominate terms. However, certain terms, especially in commercial contracts, will normally be regarded as conditions in the interests of certainty; for instance, provisions as to time in commercial contracts are normally regarded as conditions (*Bunge Corp.* v *Tradax Export SA* [1981] 2 All ER 513).

In order to avoid the problems and unpredictability of classification of express terms a well drafted contract will expressly classify the terms, or the consequences of their breach. If it is intended to give a right to terminate the contract for any breach of a particular term, that term may be expressly defined as a condition. A statement that a term is a 'condition' may not be conclusive if a court takes the view that the parties could not have intended that any breach would give rise to a right to terminate (*Schuler AG* v *Wickman Machine Tools Sales* [1974] AC 235). Parties may seek to avoid any uncertainty as to the classification of a term of the contract by expressly defining the consequences of its breach, for instance as follows:

If the seller commits any breach of this term the buyer may terminate the contract forthwith.

Such a provision makes it more likely that the buyer will be able to terminate the contract in the event of breach by the seller. However, the effect of such a provision will depend on its proper construction, and a court may be reluctant to permit termination for trivial breaches. It is therefore open to a court to conclude that the intention of the parties is to permit termination only in the event of serious breach (see *Rice* v *Great Yarmouth BC, The Times*, 26 July 2000). To avoid such a construction the clause must therefore make it clear beyond doubt that termination is to be permitted for any breach, regardless of its seriousness.

2.7 Privity of contract and contracts for the benefit of third parties

It is a fundamental rule of the common law that a contract can only be enforced by and against a person who is a party to it. The rule applied even where the parties made a contract expressly to confer a benefit on a third party.

Coupled with a second rule, that a person claiming damages for breach of contract can only recover compensation in respect of losses he himself suffered, this rule, has, in the past, often been inconvenient in a commercial context because a large number of commercial transactions involve complex, multi-partite arrangements. So, for instance, if A and B made a contract requiring A to pay money to C, C could not enforce the contract if A defaulted. Similarly, if A contracted to perform services for B but sub-contracted his performance to C, the doctrine of privity could cause difficulties. If C was negligent in his performance and thus caused loss to B, B might be able to sue C in negligence. Both the contracts between A and B and between A and C might contain exclusion and other protective clauses. However, C would not be able to rely against B on such clauses in either contract because of the lack of privity between himself and B, for C was not party to the contract between A and B and B was not party to the contract between A and C.

The inconvenience of the privity rule is somewhat mitigated, especially in commercial contexts, by the existence of a number of exceptions developed by statute and common law. For instance, a person may enforce and be held liable on contracts made on his behalf by his agent, and a court may be prepared to find an implied agency even where there is no formal agency agreement, in order to circumvent the privity of contract doctrine (see generally **Part 2**). The benefit (but not the burden) of a contract may be assigned to a third party. Thus, a creditor may assign to a third party the right to recover payment under a contract in return for a cash payment, as where a creditor sells debts under a factoring arrangement. However, in order to be fully effective an assignment must be in writing and notice must be given to the party against whom the assigned rights are to be enforced. These restrictions reduce the effectiveness of assignment in a commercial contract. Similarly, a contract may be novated so as to add a new party, or substitute a new party for an existing one, but an effective novation requires the consent of all the parties to the arrangement (see **2.5.1.3**). In addition, a number of special exceptions have been created to circumvent the rule in specific situations, such as carriage of goods by sea (see **20.4**) and in relation to negotiable instruments (see **22.2.5**).

The common law rule of privity of contract has, moreover, been significantly modified by the Contracts (Rights of Third Parties) Act 1999 which creates a new general exception to the rule of privity of contract which applies where a contract is made for the benefit of a third party not privy to it. The existing common law and statutory exceptions to the doctrine are untouched by the new Act.

Under the Act, a person who is not party to a contract may nevertheless enforce a term of the contract, including by taking the benefit of an exclusion or similar clause, (a) if the contract expressly provides that he may do so, or (b) if the term purports to confer a benefit on him *and* it appears that, on a proper construction of the contract, the parties to the contract intended him to be able to enforce the contract. So, for instance, if A and B make a contract requiring A to make payment to C, C may be able to enforce the contract and demand payment from A if either the contract so provides or it appears that the parties intended him to be entitled to enforce the contract. The third party's right to enforce is without prejudice to the rights of the parties to enforce the contract, although there are provisions to protect the promisor from double liability. Moreover, where a third party is entitled to enforce a contract in accordance with the provisions of the Act, the contracting parties may in certain circumstances not be able to rescind or vary the contract so as to alter or extinguish his entitlement under the contract, without his consent. In order to avoid any uncertainty a well drafted contract will contain a clear statement that it either is, or is not, intended to confer an enforceable benefit on a third party. (In practice many contracts contain statements expressly excluding any third party right of enforcement under the Act.)

2.8 Summary

Having completed this chapter you should:

- be familiar with the rules governing
    - contract formation;
    - the formation defects which may make a contract void or voidable;
    - variation of contracts;
    - the identification and interpretation of contract terms;
    - who may enforce and who is bound by contractual obligations;
- understand the practical implications of those rules; and
- apply them in a practical context.

Performance and breach of contracts

3.1 Introduction

Disputes frequently arise where a party fails to perform his obligations under the contract. In that case the commercial lawyer may be called upon to advise on whether failure to perform is justified, or may be excused, and on the consequences of such failure.

In this chapter we consider the ways in which contractual obligations are discharged and the remedies available for their non-performance. The topics covered include:

- discharge of contractual obligations, by agreement, performance, breach and frustration;
- remedies for breach of contract and for misrepresentation, including damages and rights to withhold performance of, avoid or terminate contractual obligations; and
- terms which exclude or limit liability for breach of contract and/or misrepresentation; legal controls on the enforceability of such terms; and considerations relevant to their drafting.

These topics are inextricably bound up. One of the most effective remedies available to a contractor who alleges that the other contract party is in breach of contract is to withhold performance of their own obligations. They may be entitled to do so if the other party is in serious breach of contract or if they are entitled to rescind the contract. However, a party who wrongfully withholds performance when not entitled to do so will themself commit a breach of contract for which they will be liable in damages. Thus a claim may arise where A sues B for non-performance; B defends on the grounds that they were entitled to withhold performance on grounds of a prior breach or misrepresentation by A. An effective exclusion or limitation clause in a contract may provide a complete or partial defence to a party who would otherwise by liable for a breach or misrepresentation.

3.2 Discharge

A party who fails to perform his obligations under the contract may seek to justify his failure on the grounds that he is discharged from his obligations under the contract. Alternatively he may argue that his performance is not due because it is dependent on performance by the other party and the other party has not discharged his obligations under the contract. Contractual obligations can be discharged by agreement, performance, breach or frustration.

3.2.1   Discharge by agreement

Contractual obligations are created by agreement; they can be discharged by agreement. An agreement will only discharge a party's contractual obligations if it constitutes an enforceable contract: both parties must agree to the discharge, and the party being discharged must provide consideration for the other's agreement to his discharge.

3.2.1.1   Discharge of both parties

Where both parties have unperformed obligations they can agree to discharge the contract and each provides consideration for his own release by agreeing to release the other.

3.2.1.2   Discharge of one party

Where one party has already performed his obligations his agreement to release the other will only be binding if he receives some other consideration or the discharge is by deed.

3.2.1.3   Discharge in accordance with terms of the contract

The parties may agree in advance that their contract will be discharged in specified circumstances, by including an express term to that effect: for instance, a contract for the export of goods might provide that the parties should be discharged if it proves impossible to obtain a required export licence.

3.2.2   Performance

Generally contractual obligations are discharged when they are fully performed in accordance with the terms of the contract. The question whether a party has discharged his obligations by performing them generally arises where one party demands performance from the other; typically, when a person who has supplied goods or services demands payment from the other (see **3.3.2.1**).

3.2.3   Breach

Generally a term cannot be said to have been broken until the time for its performance has expired.

Breach of contract does not discharge a contract, but a breach by one party may give the other the option to treat himself as discharged and thus refuse further performance of the contract.

Breach will entitle the innocent party to treat himself as discharged if either:

(a) the term broken is properly classified as a condition; or

(b) the term broken is an innominate term and the breach is serious or has serious consequences (see **2.6.5.3**);

(c) the contract so provides.

Termination for breach may be a commercially attractive option where the innocent party has not yet performed his obligations. Termination will be especially attractive where changes in circumstances mean that the innocent party no longer needs the contract goods or services, or can obtain them elsewhere more cheaply. However, where he has performed, termination will be less effective: he will need the assistance of the court to recover money paid or damages for the other party's failure to perform.

3.2.4 Frustration

A contract is frustrated if performance becomes impossible or illegal or if circumstances so change that the commercial purpose of the parties is frustrated. This will only happen where circumstances are so changed that performance in the changed circumstances would be radically different from what the parties anticipated.

It is clear that this test will only rarely be satisfied. A contract will not be frustrated merely because a change in circumstances makes performance more difficult or more expensive than was anticipated.

A contract will only be frustrated by events which were unforeseeable at the time the contract was made. A contract therefore cannot be frustrated by an event for which the contract makes express or implied provision.

A party may not rely on his own act as frustrating a contract.

Where a contract is frustrated both parties are automatically discharged from future performance. The other rights of the parties depend on the Law Reform (Frustrated Contracts) Act 1943 which enables the court to allocate financial losses caused by the frustration by allowing a party who has received payment before frustration to retain some or all of it, or allowing a party to recover payment for work done before frustration.

Special rules apply to contracts for the sale of goods (see **14.3.2**).

3.3 Remedies

The primary judicial remedy for breach of contract is an award of damages. Other remedies are available through the courts, including orders for specific performance or rescission of a contract, but they are generally discretionary and are relatively rare in commercial contracts.

Businesses will prefer, if at all possible, to avoid litigation which consumes time and money and may damage both a trading relationship and a business's public image. Where a dispute arises out of a contract, therefore, a business will generally seek to resolve it by negotiation. If that fails, the business may prefer to obtain redress by means of self-help remedies, rather than through the courts, for instance by withholding performance or forfeiting money or property of the party in default.

If litigation is necessary, it is preferable that judgment can be obtained speedily and easily, preferably on an application for summary judgment without need for a full trial. Actions for liquidated sums are generally preferable to actions for unliquidated damages which raise difficult issues of proof of loss and mitigation and may require a full trial to assess quantum.

These points should all be borne in mind when drafting a contract and the contract should be drawn in such a way as to enable the client to invoke self-help remedies and bring liquidated rather than unliquidated claims.

3.3.1 Self-help remedies

Self-help remedies may enable a party to obtain redress for a breach of contract without resort to litigation; alternatively the withholding of performance or the threat of seizure of property by one party may act as a powerful incentive to the other party to reach a settlement of the dispute.

A number of self-help remedies are available under the general law: for instance, where one party breaks a condition of the contract, the other may simply withhold performance. An unpaid seller has a lien over the goods which entitles him to withhold delivery until he is paid (see **16.4.2.1**). The law recognises a limited right of set-off which will permit a party to a contract to defend an action for breach of that contract on the grounds that he has a claim for payment of money against the claimant. However, the express terms of the contract may extend or supplement the self-help remedies available under the general law.

3.3.1.1   Withholding performance

A party is entitled to withhold performance of his obligations under the contract where the other is in breach of a condition of the contract, or where the contract gives him an express right so to do. A party who withholds performance when he is not entitled so to do, either under the general law or the terms of the contract, will himself be in breach of contract (see **3.2.4**).

3.3.1.2   Set-off

Rights of set-off are available under the general law, under statute and in equity, and set-off is compulsory in insolvency (Insolvency Act 1986, s. 323 (individual insolvency); Insolvency Rules 1986, r. 4.90 (corporate insolvency)).

There is a detailed and technical body of law governing rights of set-off, but the law on set-off outside insolvency can be summarised as follows. If A makes a claim for payment of money against B, B can set-off against his liability to A any claim for payment of money (including damages) he has against A, provided that either both claims are for liquidated amounts (common law, or 'statutory' set-off) or B's claim is closely connected with A's claim and 'impeaches' it so that it would be inequitable for A to obtain judgment for the full amount of his claim without giving credit for B's claim (equitable set-off). Where both claims arise under the same contract B will generally be able to set-off his claim against A's claim. In each case B's right of set-off therefore operates as a partial, or total, defence to A's claim. If B's claim exceeds the value of A's claim, B may claim the excess by way of counterclaim.

Under contracts for the supply of goods the buyer has a right of abatement which allows him to withhold some or all of the price if the goods or work are defective. This is confirmed by the Sale of Goods Act 1979, s. 53(1)(a) which gives the buyer of goods a right to set up against the seller's claim for the price a claim for damages in respect of defects in the goods (see **12.6**).

These rights under the general law may be supplemented by express or implied terms in the contract making set-off available where it would not be permitted under the general law. Clear wording is required to exclude a right of set off which would otherwise be available. A contract term restricting the right of set-off will be subject to a test of reasonableness under the Unfair Contract Terms Act 1977 (see **3.4.3.5**) and may also be subject to challenge under the Unfair Terms in Consumer Contracts Regulations 1999 (see **3.4.4**).

If either party becomes insolvent the relationship between the parties depends on the statutory rules governing set-off in insolvency and contractual provisions extending or restricting those rights are ineffective (see *British Eagle Airlines Ltd* v *Compagnie Nationale Air France* [1975] 2 All ER 390).

3.3.1.3   Deposits and pre-payments

A contract may require one party to pay a sum of money to the other before performance, as part payment or as a deposit to ensure performance. Such a term provides a powerful incentive for the payer to perform his contract, especially if the contract allows the payee to forfeit and retain the payment if the payer is in breach. The payee may be able to retain the payment if the contract is terminated and, in any case, the payer may need to resort to litigation to recover the payment.

Under the general law the payee may retain an advance payment if the contract is terminated and the payment is properly construed as a deposit, i.e. a payment to guarantee the payer's performance. However, if the payment is not a deposit in this sense, but simply a part-payment, the payee must return it if there is a total failure of the consideration for which it is paid, even if the contract is terminated because of the payer's breach.

The contract may therefore provide for payment of a deposit which is to be forfeit on termination of the contract. Such a provision may, however, be subject to the court's power to give relief against forfeiture or to the rule against penalties and the amount of the deposit must therefore not be excessive or unreasonable.

3.3.1.4 Interest

Interest may be payable on sums due under a commercial contract on one of several bases. They are:

(a) in accordance with the express or implied terms of the contract,

(b) under the Supreme Court Act 1981, s. 35A or the County Courts Act 1984, s. 69,

(c) under the Late Payment of Commercial Debts (Interest) Act 1998.

In addition the court may, exceptionally, award damages to compensate for losses caused by late payment of a debt (but not of damages) where the creditor can prove that he has suffered quantifiable loss as a result of late payment and that such loss was in the reasonable contemplation of the debtor at the time the contract was made (*President of India* v *La Pintada Compañia Navigacion* SA [1985] AC 104).

A commercial contract will often provide for interest to be payable if sums due under the contract are not paid on time. Such a provision makes interest payable as a contract debt. It thus serves a dual function, providing an incentive for the debtor to make prompt payment and compensating the creditor for the loss of use of the value of the payment during the period of delay. Alternatively the contract may provide for the buyer to receive a discount for prompt payment, which may have much the same effect.

In the absence of such a provision the court has no general power at common law to award interest on sums due under a contract but paid late. There is power, however, for the court to award simple (not compound) interest on both debts and damages paid after the commencement of court proceedings (Supreme Court Act 1981, s. 35A, or County Courts Act 1984, s. 69). Once proceedings for recovery of a debt or payment of damages are initiated, a claim for such interest may therefore be made and interest becomes payable, but the interest recoverable under these provisions does not run for the period prior to the commencement of proceedings.

Prior to 1998, the position thus was that, provided the relevant contract contained no express provision for payment of interest, a debtor could, in effect, obtain an extended period of interest free credit simply by withholding payment until the last possible moment before the issue of proceedings. The Late Payment of Commercial Debts (Interest) Act 1998 was passed to rectify this situation. In addition, on June 29, 2000, the European Commission adopted a directive on combating late payment in commercial transactions (Dir 2000/35/EC) to address the same issues.

The Directive applies to all 'commercial transactions', that is, transactions between 'undertakings' (effectively all businesses), and between undertakings and public authorities, which lead to the delivery of goods or provision of services. Member States are required to provide for interest on sums due under the contract to become payable at the latest 30 days after the date of the creditor's invoice or request for payment, or of the delivery of the goods or services, whichever is later, and for interest to be payable at a rate of at least seven per cent per annum over the interest rate set by the European Central Bank (or, for states such as the UK not participating in economic and monetary union, seven per cent above the rate set by the national central bank). In addition, Member States are required to ensure that creditors with 'unchallenged claims' for payment can obtain a court judgment or order for payment within 90 days of lodging a claim with the court. In the UK the rules of court already provide for default and summary judgment to be available in unchallenged cases, but these provisions should prove beneficial to businesses seeking to recover debts in the courts of some other EU countries where similar procedures are not currently available. Finally, and significantly, the Directive requires Member States to ensure that 'adequate and effective means exist to prevent the continued use of terms' which seek to exclude or depart from the statutory interest regime and are grossly unfair to creditors. Such means must include permitting organisations 'having a legitimate interest in representing small and medium sized enterprises' to take representative action before national courts to prevent the continued use of such terms.

In the UK the position is therefore covered by the 1998 Act as amended by the Late Payment of Commercial Debts Regulations 2002 (SI 2002, No. 1674) to bring it into conformity with the Directive. The Act provides that it is an implied term of a contract for the supply of goods or services where both parties act in the course of business that debts created by the contract carry simple interest (s. 1). Certain classes of contract are excluded, including consumer credit agreements (s. 2). Interest under the Act runs from the date specified in the contract for payment, or, if none is specified, from the day after the last day of the period of thirty days commencing with either the date of the supplier's performance or the date on which the debtor has notice of the amount due or claimed to be due (s. 4). In the case of advance payments the period runs from the day after the date on which the obligation to which the advance payment relates is performed (s. 11). The rate of interest payable under the Act is to be fixed by order by the Secretary of State (s. 6). The rate currently fixed is eight per cent per annum over the official dealing rate announced from time to time by the Monetary Policy Committee of the Bank of England (Late Payment of Commercial Debts (Rate of Interest) (No. 3) Order, 2002, SI 2002, No. 1675). Once a supplier becomes entitled to statutory interest on a qualifying debt they also become entitled to demand from the debtor payment of a fixed sum by way of compensation for the inconvenience of pursuing the debt (s. 5A). The amount payable depends on the size of the debt. For debts less than £1,000 it is £40; for debts of more than £1,000 but less than £10,000 it is £70; and for debts of £10,000 or more, £100.

The court has power to remit, wholly or in part, interest due under the Act (s. 5) but any term of a contract which purports to exclude or vary the right to interest under the Act is automatically void unless the contract provides a 'substantial remedy' for late payment (s. 8). A remedy is not 'substantial' if either (a) it is insufficient either for deterring late payment or for compensating the supplier for late payment or (b) it would not be fair or reasonable to allow the remedy to oust or vary the statutory right (s. 9). In assessing whether it would be fair or reasonable to allow a contract provision to oust or vary the statutory right the court is directed to consider factors similar to those relevant to the assessment of reasonableness under Schedule 2 of the Unfair Contract Terms Act 1977. A term which purports to postpone the date at which a debt becomes payable under the Act is subject to the test of reasonableness under s. 3(2) of the 1977 Act, whether it appears in the debtor's written standard terms or otherwise (s. 14).

A small business may be reluctant to challenge a term ousting the right to interest, either because of the cost of proceedings or for fear that such a challenge might damage the business' trading relationship with an important customer. To protect such businesses, as required by the EC Directive, the late Payment of Commercial Debts Regulations 2002 therefore provide that where a person acting in the course of a business contracts, or intends to contract, on written standard terms of purchase which seek to oust or vary the statutory right to interest, organisations established to represent the collective interests of small and medium sized enterprises, either in general or in a particular trade sector or geographical area, may bring proceedings in the High Court for an injunction restraining the continued use of the relevant term or terms (reg. 3).

The 1998 Act was brought into force in stages by statutory instrument, but as from 7 August, 2002 it applies to all business-to-business contracts for the supply of goods or services (Late Payment of Commercial Debts (Interest) Act 1998, Commencement No. 5 Order, SI 2002, No. 1673).

The effect of these provisions is that interest is always payable on debts due under business (as opposed to consumer) contracts, and that that right cannot be excluded or restricted by any contract term unless the contract provides an alternative, substantial remedy for late payment. Moreover such interest, together with speedy judgments for unchallenged debts, should be available in all member states of the EU. A business supplier will therefore not be denied interest merely because it lacked the commercial bargaining power to insist on the inclusion of such a right in a contract with a customer. However, neither the 1998 Act nor the Directive do anything to overcome the commercial difficulties which a business, especially a small business, may face in enforcing the right to interest, where a claim may damage a trading relationship with an important customer, and doubts have therefore been expressed as to whether the Act will greatly assist small businesses. This problem may be partly ameliorated by the new provisions for representative action to be taken against unfair terms, preventing larger businesses seeking to exclude the statutory provisions by terms in contracts with smaller suppliers.

It should be noted, however, that both the Act and the Directive provide only for simple, not compound, interest to be payable. An express contract term may provide for payment of compound interest, and/or fix a rate of interest higher than the statutory rate, provided only that the rate is not so high as to infringe the rule against penalties. Where possible, therefore, businesses may prefer to incorporate in their contracts express rights to interest, rather than rely on the statutory right.

3.3.1.5 Other devices

A term requiring one party to pay by bill of exchange (see **Chapter 22**), or to deposit property with the other and grant a lien over it (**25.3**), may also provide simple enforcement mechanisms and an incentive to perform the contract.

3.3.2 Financial remedies

Claims for payment of money may be liquidated—e.g. a claim for a fixed sum of money such as a claim for payment of the price due under a contract—or unliquidated, where the amount payable is to be assessed by the court, such as a claim for damages. If litigation is necessary, there may be procedural advantages to a liquidated claim. In particular, if summary judgment is obtained it will be final and can be executed. Where summary judgment is obtained on an unliquidated claim, it may be necessary to have a further hearing to assess damages.

3.3.2.1   Action for liquidated sum/the price

A claim for payment of money due under the contract may be made if the money is due in accordance with the terms of the contract.

Where payment is due on performance by the payee (for instance, if under a building contract payment is due on completion of the work) it will be necessary to decide if the supplier has performed so as to be entitled to payment. This will depend on whether the payee's obligation to perform is severable or entire. If the obligation is entire, the supplier must perform the whole of his obligation, in accordance with the terms of the contract before claiming payment.

A supplier who has performed only part of an entire obligation may be able to claim payment less an allowance for defects if he has substantially performed his obligation; alternatively if his partial performance is voluntarily accepted by the other party, the supplier is entitled to be paid a reasonable fee (a *quantum meruit*) for the performance rendered.

To avoid such difficulties a contract may provide for payment of the price in stages. For instance, a building or engineering contract may provide for the price to be paid in instalments as stages of the work are completed. The effect is that the obligations to pay and perform are severable and the supplier can claim payment for each stage as it is completed. Where the price is payable in instalments in this way the contract may also contain an *acceleration clause* which provides that if the contract is terminated because of the customer's breach, all further payments immediately become due, allowing the supplier to bring a liquidated claim for payment.

3.3.2.2   Damages

Damages may be awarded for breach of contract or for misrepresentation. In either case the claim is an unliquidated one for damages to be assessed by the court. The objective of the award of damages is to compensate the injured party rather than to punish the defendant, and the claimant must prove that the losses in respect of which he claims were caused by the breach, or misrepresentation, complained of. However, damages for breach and misrepresentation are assessed differently.

Damages for breach   The basic objective of damages for breach of contract is to put the injured party in the position he would have been in had the contract been performed. Damages thus protect the claimant's *expectations* and will generally include the profit the claimant would have made had the contract been performed. However, where a person has spent money in reliance on a contract, for instance in performing his obligations, he may claim, as an alternative, to be compensated for the sum spent in reliance on the contract (wasted expenditure). Such a claim will be advantageous where it is impossible to quantify the profit the claimant would have made had the contract been performed. The claimant may combine claims for wasted expenditure and loss of expected profits, provided that this does not result in him being compensated twice.

EXAMPLE

Phil's Fashions contracts to buy 100 rolls of fabric from Peak Mills at a price of £50 per roll. Phil's Fashions employs a carrier at a cost of £100 to collect the fabric from Peak Mills but no fabric is available. Phil's can buy replacement fabric locally for £60 per roll. Phil's Fashions may claim from Peak Mills £1000, i.e. the difference between the cost of fabric from Peak Mills and the cost of buying it from another supplier. However, it cannot also claim the wasted cost of employing the carrier because that cost would have had to be incurred to collect the fabric and make the anticipated profit.

If the replacement fabric is not available locally and Phil's Fashions has to pay the carrier a further £50 to collect it from another supplier, the wasted carriage costs may be recovered. Phil's' damages

> would then be £1,050, i.e. the difference between the total amount to buy and collect the fabric and the amount which Phil's would have spent had Peak Mills fulfilled the original contract.

Damages may be awarded to compensate for damage to property, personal injuries and economic losses, including lost profits. In the case of a consumer contract, damages may also be awarded for vexation, loss of amenity and/or enjoyment (see, e.g. *Ruxley Electronics and Construction Ltd* v *Forsyth* [1996] AC 344, [1995] 3 All ER 268) even if the provision of peace of mind or enjoyment is not the sole or even the main object of the contract (*Farley* v *Skinner* [2001] UKHL 49, [2001] 4 All ER 801). Damages for such non-pecuniary losses will however not normally be awarded for breach of a commercial contract.

In all cases the claimant is required to take reasonable steps to mitigate his loss, for instance, as in the example above, by buying replacement goods. He will recover no damages in respect of losses which he could have avoided by taking reasonable steps.

The damages recoverable by the claimant are further limited by the rules of remoteness. Essentially this means that the defendant is only liable for losses of a type which he foresaw, or could have foreseen, as not unlikely to result from his breach of contract when the contract was made. Losses are foreseeable according to the rule in *Hadley* v *Baxendale* (1854) 9 Ex 341 if either:

(a) they arise naturally from the breach, in the ordinary course of events; or

(b) they could reasonably be supposed to have been in the contemplation of the parties when they made the contract as the probable result of a breach.

Thus where a party to a contract incurs special losses due to his special circumstances, he may only recover damages in respect of those losses if the special circumstances were known, or ought to have been known, to the other party when the contract was made.

EXAMPLE

Phil's Fashions enters into a contract for Peak Mills to supply it with fabric, to be used in the manufacture of men's suits. The suits are to be supplied to the renowned Wallies Ltd retail chain and Phil's has been told that Wallies may enter into further contracts with Phil's if the suits are satisfactory. Peak Mills fails to deliver on time. Phil's is unable to fulfil its contract with Wallies; it may recover damages from Peak Mills in respect of the profits it would have made on that contract and for the loss of possible future contracts only if (a) it takes reasonable steps to mitigate its loss, for instance by trying to find an alternative fabric supplier and (b) Peak Mills was, or should have been, aware of the contract with Wallies, and the possibility of further contracts, when it entered into the contract with Phil's.

Damages for misrepresentation   A person who enters a contract as a result of a false statement made by the other party during negotiations may claim damages. The basis of assessment depends on:

(a) whether the statement became a term of the contract (see **2.6.1**); and

(b) the state of mind of the person who made the statement.

If the false statement was a term of the contract, the claimant may claim damages for breach of contract, assessed as described above.

The claimant may always rescind the contract for misrepresentation. Rescission will restore both parties to their pre-contract positions; however, the court has a discretion to refuse rescission and may award damages in lieu of allowing rescission, even if the misrepresentation was made wholly innocently (Misrepresentation Act 1967, s. 2(2)).

Such damages will produce the same effect as if the contract had been rescinded; however, they are discretionary and consequential losses cannot be compensated on this basis.

The claimant may however claim damages for misrepresentation on three different grounds:

(a) in the tort of deceit if he can prove that the defendant made the false statement fraudulently;

(b) in the tort of negligence in accordance with the principle in *Hedley Byrne & Co.* v *Heller & Partners Ltd* [1964] AC 465 if he can prove that the defendant acted negligently;

(c) under the Misrepresentation Act 1967, s. 2(1) unless the defendant can show that in making the statement he was not negligent.

In each case damages are awarded to put the claimant in the same position as if the misrepresentation, and therefore the contract, had not been made. However, different rules of remoteness apply to the different claims. A claimant who proves fraud is entitled to be compensated for all losses caused by the fraudulent statement, no matter how remote, and it has been held that damages under the Misrepresentation Act are to be assessed in the same way as damages for fraud (*Royscott Trust Ltd* v *Rogerson* [1991] 2 QB 297). In contrast damages for common law negligent misstatement are subject to the general rules governing remoteness of damage in negligence.

Damages for fraud may be more generous than damages under the 1967 Act in one respect. Damages awarded under s. 2(1) and for negligent misstatement at common law may be reduced to take account of any contributory negligence of the claimant which contributed to his loss (*Gran Gelato Ltd* v *Richcliff Group Ltd* [1992] 1 All ER 865) whereas damages for fraud in the tort of deceit are not subject to reduction on the grounds of contributory negligence (*Standard Chartered Bank plc* v *Pakistan National Shipping Corp* [2002] UKHL 43; [2002] 2 All ER (Comm) 933). Generally, however, damages available under the Act will be as generous as those for fraud and the claimant will therefore bring his claim under the Act. Fraud is difficult to prove and a claimant who alleges fraud may face procedural difficulties; in particular summary judgment may not be available if the claimant alleges fraud. These difficulties do not apply to a claim under the Act. The measure of damages is the same as for fraud and more generous than the common law measure and, by claiming under the Act, the claimant avoids the burden of proving negligence: it is for the defendant to prove that he was not negligent. However, if the defendant discharges that burden the claimant can only recover damages by showing that the misrepresentation had become a term of the contract.

Damages need not necessarily be assessed at the date of the contract but can sometimes be assessed as at the date the misrepresentation is discovered. Thus, e.g., if the claimant buys goods as a result of a misrepresentation and by the time the misrepresentation is discovered the goods have declined in value, the claimant may be able to recover damages to compensate for the decline in their value (*Naughton* v *O'Callaghan* [1990] 3 All ER 191 contrast *Smith New Court Securities Ltd* v *Scrimgeour Vickers (Asset Management) Ltd* [1994] 4 All ER 2251).

In an action for damages for misrepresentation the claimant cannot recover compensation for profits he would have made if the representation had been true. However, he may claim damages for profits he would have earned had he not entered into the contract. For instance, a claimant who bought a loss making business as a result of a misrepresentation recovered damages to compensate for profits she would have earned had the misrepresentation not been made and she had bought a different (probably profitable) business (*East* v *Maurer* [1991] 2 All ER 733).

Comparison of the remedies for misrepresentation and breach of contract   The different bases for assessment of damages in cases of breach of contract and misrepresentation mean that the way a case is framed or pleaded can affect the amount recovered. It is therefore important for the commercial lawyer to understand the two measures and their relative advantages. The following examples illustrate the two different measures.

EXAMPLE 1

Phil's Fashions Ltd contracts to buy a second-hand computerised knitting machine from Notts Knitts Ltd for a price of £10,000. During negotiations a representative of Notts Knitts asserts that the machine is a 1992 model. Other 1992 machines are available for around £12,000, and on the basis of this statement Phil's Fashions agrees to buy the machine. In fact the machine is only a 1991 model, which has a lower capacity than a 1992 model and would normally cost around £8,000.

   Phil's Fashions may claim damages either for breach of contract or for misrepresentation.

   (a) *Damages for breach* seek to put Phil's in the same position as if the statement about the machine had been true: damages will therefore be the difference between £8,000 (the actual value of the machine) and £12,000 (the amount the machine would have been worth had the statement been true).

   (b) *Damages for misrepresentation* seek to put Phil's into the position it would have been in had the statement not been made. Damages will therefore be the difference between £8,000, i.e. the value of the machine Phil's now has, and £10,000, i.e. the amount of money Phil's had before buying the machine.

EXAMPLE 2

If instead the value of a 1992 machine would have been only £9,000 (so that Phil's has made a bad bargain), misrepresentation damages will be more generous to Phil's.

   (a) *Damages for breach* will now be the difference between £8,000 (the actual value of the machine) and £9,000 (the value of a 1992 machine).

   (b) *Damages for misrepresentation* are still £2000.

EXAMPLE 3

Phil's bought the machine to fulfil a contract to manufacture and supply knitwear to the S&M retail chain. The 1991 machine is unable to perform the necessary operations so that Phil's is unable to fulfil the contract and loses the profits it would have made under the contract.

   (a) *Damages for breach of contract* may include damages for the lost profits provided they are not too remote. Damages may therefore not be recoverable if Nott's Knitts were not aware of the contract with S&M.

   (b) *Damages for misrepresentation* may include damages for the lost profits if Phil's can show that had the statement not been made it would have bought a different machine and would have fulfilled the S&M contract. Damages are not limited by remoteness so it is irrelevant that Nott's Knitts were unaware of the S&M contract.

3.3.2.3   Liquidated damages

Commercial contracts often contain provisions fixing the amount of compensation payable on breach. The effect of such a clause is that, in the event of a breach, the specified sum is payable and can be claimed as a debt. The claimant thus has the procedural advantages of a liquidated claim; the (potential) defendant knows the amount of his potential liability at the time the contract is made and it may therefore be easier for him to obtain insurance against liability.

Such provisions are valid and enforceable provided the amount payable under the clause is a 'genuine pre-estimate of the loss' likely to be caused by the breach and not a penalty. It may be a penalty if the amount payable is disproportionately greater than any loss likely to be caused by the breach, or if one fixed amount is payable in respect of several different breaches or breaches of differing degrees of seriousness. A clause fixing damages for late performance should therefore provide for the amount payable to be on a sliding scale increasing in line with the length of the delay.

3.3.3   Other remedies

A court may order rescission of a contract entered into as a result of misrepresentation or duress.

The court has a discretion to order specific performance of a contract, or to award an injunction ordering a party to perform, or not to perform, a contract. However, these remedies are all discretionary. Specific performance will only be awarded where damages would not provide an adequate remedy for the claimant.

3.4   Exclusion clauses

Most commercial contracts include terms intended to prevent one or other party being in breach, or to exclude or restrict liability for any breach which does occur. Typical provisions include terms which:

(a) allow a supplier to alter the mode of performance, for instance, by supplying alternative goods or varying the date for performance;

(b) prevent one party terminating in the event of breach by the other;

(c) limit the amount of damages payable on breach;

(d) provide that one party shall not be liable for certain types of loss caused by breach;

(e) impose procedural restrictions on claims for breach of contract, for instance, by requiring all claims to be made within a stated period;

(f) exclude obligations which would otherwise be imposed by law, such as the terms implied into sale contracts by the Sale of Goods Act 1979 (see **Chapter 12**).

We will refer to all such provisions as 'exclusion clauses'. Their effectiveness is restricted by both common law and statutory rules.

3.4.1   Common law controls on exclusions

An exclusion clause will only be effective to exclude or modify liability under a contract if it is incorporated into the contract so as to be binding on the claimant, and if on its proper construction it covers the claimant's claim. Although exclusion clauses are now regulated by statute the common law restrictions on their effectiveness remain important. Incorporation of terms in the contract has been considered above (see **2.6.2**).

3.4.1.1   Construction of exclusion clauses

The first step in determining the effectiveness of an exclusion clause is to construe it so as to determine its effect and scope. The application of the statutory test of reasonableness under the Unfair Contract Terms Act 1977 will depend on the proper interpretation of the clause. The general rules governing the interpretation of contract terms (see **2.6.4**) apply to exclusion clauses just as to other terms. However, additional rules apply specifically to exclusion and similar clauses. In particular, the courts have tended to construe exclusion clauses strictly, i.e. *contra proferentem*, so that any ambiguity in the wording of the clause will be resolved against the interests of the party seeking to rely on it. Exclusion clauses must therefore be clearly worded.

(a) Clear words must be used to exclude or limit liability for negligence; for instance, by specifically referring to 'negligence' or some synonym for it (see e.g. *Canada Steamship Lines* v *R* [1952] AC 192; *Smith* v *South Wales Switchgear Ltd* [1978] 1 WLR 165). In particular, where a party may be strictly liable and liable for negligence, a general exclusion may be interpreted as covering only the strict liability. A clause which excludes liability for all loss 'howsoever caused' may be interpreted as excluding negligence liability; a claim which excludes 'any loss whatsoever' will not be so interpreted.

(b) Similarly clauses which exclude liability for breach of 'warranty' may be interpreted as not excluding liability for breach of conditions; clauses excluding liability for breach of implied terms may be interpreted as not excluding liability for breach of express terms.

(c) There is no rule of law that an exclusion cannot cover liability for a 'fundamental' breach of contract, but the court will generally assume that an exclusion is not intended to cover a case of fundamental breach or total failure to perform unless very clear words are used.

In general, clauses which limit liability may be less strictly construed than those which seek wholly to exclude liability. However, they are still susceptible to *contra proferentem* construction. Thus, for instance, a clause which excludes liability for 'consequential loss' will be interpreted as excluding liability for losses which do *not* arise naturally, in the ordinary course of events, from the breach of contract, and which would therefore be not recoverable under the 'first limb' of the rule in *Hadley* v *Baxendale* (see **3.3.2.2**): *Croudace Construction Ltd* v *Cawoods Concrete Products Ltd* [1978] 2 Lloyd's Rep 55; *British Sugar plc* v *NEI Power Products Ltd* [1997] BLR 42.

3.4.2 Statutory control

Many statutes impose restrictions on exclusion clauses in particular types of contract. The main statutory controls on exclusion clauses are UCTA 1977 and the Unfair Terms in Consumer Contracts Regulations 1999.

3.4.3 The Unfair Contract Terms Act 1977

UCTA 1977 distinguishes between consumers and non-consumers; it imposes more stringent restrictions on exclusions in contracts with consumers. Exclusions of liability for certain types of loss are rendered wholly ineffective; exclusions of other types of liability are permitted only so far as the exclusion satisfies a test of reasonableness.

3.4.3.1 The scope of UCTA

UCTA 1977 applies to contract terms and notices which seek to restrict 'business liability', that is for breach of contractual and tortious obligations which arise from things done in the course of a business or from occupation of premises for business purposes of the occupier (UCTA 1977, s. 1(2)).

UCTA 1977 does not apply to certain classes of contract including international supply contracts as defined (s. 26; see *Amiri Flight Authority* v *BAE Systems plc* [2003] EWCA 1447; [2004] 1 All ER (Comm) 385), contracts of insurance (sch. 1, para. 1(a)) or any contract insofar as it relates to:

(a) the creation, transfer or termination of interests in land or of intellectual property rights;

(b) the formation, dissolution or constitution of companies;

(c) the creation and transfer of securities (sch. 1 para. 2).

3.4.3.2 Clauses regulated by UCTA 1977

The main restrictions on exclusions are imposed by UCTA 1977, ss. 2, 3, 6 and 7, as extended by s. 13.

Liability for negligence   UCTA 1977, s. 2 restricts attempts to exclude liability for negligence. A person cannot by any contract term or notice restrict or exclude liability for death or personal injury caused by his negligence. Liability for property damage or other loss caused by negligence can be excluded/restricted in so far as the exclusion satisfies the test of reasonableness.

Implied terms relating to goods   UCTA 1977, ss. 6 and 7 restrict attempts to exclude liability for the statutory implied terms relating to goods in contracts for the sale and supply of goods. Such exclusion is wholly ineffective where the buyer is a consumer; where the buyer is not a consumer the exclusion is effective in so far as it satisfies the test of reasonableness.

Other breaches of contract   UCTA 1977, s. 3 restricts clauses which exclude or restrict liability for breach of contract where the party against whom liability is to be excluded deals as a consumer, or on the other party's written standard terms of business. In either case the exclusion is effective only in so far as it satisfies a test of reasonableness.

Extending the scope of UCTA 1977 Insofar as UCTA 1977 restricts the effectiveness of clauses which exclude or restrict liability for breach of duty it also restricts clauses which:

(a) make liability or its enforcement subject to restrictive or onerous conditions (e.g. 'all claims to be notified within 30 days of delivery');

(b) exclude or restrict any right or remedy in respect of the liability (e.g. 'the seller's liability in damages for breach of this contract shall be limited to £100'; 'no refunds'; 'the buyer may not withhold payment on any grounds');

(c) subject a person to any prejudice as a consequence of pursuing any such right or remedy;

(d) exclude or restrict rules of evidence or procedure ('the certificate of quality shall be conclusive that the goods comply with the contract'; 'no refunds without receipt').

In addition the restrictions imposed by ss. 2, 6 and 7 also apply to clauses which exclude or restrict the relevant duty, for instance, clauses which seek to exclude a duty of care in tort or which exclude the implied terms in contracts for the sale or supply of goods.

UCTA 1977 does not apply to arbitration clauses but their effectiveness against consumers is restricted by the 1999 Regulations and by other legislation (Consumer Arbitration (Agreements) Act 1988).

Clauses excluding or limiting liability for misrepresentation are subject to a test of reasonableness (Misrepresentation Act 1967, s. 3).

3.4.3.3　Consumers and non-consumers

A person deals as a consumer for the purposes of UCTA 1977 if:

(a) he neither makes the contract in the course of a business, nor holds himself out as so doing; and

(b) the other party (who wishes to rely on the exclusion) does make the contract in the course of a business; and

(c) where the contract involves the transfer of ownership or possession of goods, the goods are of a type ordinarily supplied for private use or consumption (UCTA 1977, s. 12). (This requirement is likely to be abolished when the European Commission's Directive on the Sale of Consumer Goods and Associated Guarantees is implemented.)

A person makes a contract 'in the course of a business' for this purpose if either:

(a) the contract is integral to the business, for instance, where goods are bought for resale; or

(b) there is sufficient regularity of similar transactions (*R&B Customs Brokers Ltd* v *United Dominions Trust Ltd* [1988] 1 All ER 847).

This test may be difficult to apply; however, it means that a business, including a limited company, may be 'dealing as a consumer' for the purposes of the Act: for instance, a small freight forwarding company which bought a car for the use of its directors and had bought three such cars in the previous five years was dealing as a consumer when it bought the car (*R&B Customs Brokers Ltd* v *UDT Ltd*). Moreover, the phrase 'in the course of a business' also appears in the Sale of Goods Act and in that context has been given a different, wider meaning (see *Stevenson* v *Rogers* [1999] 1 All ER 613, below **12.4.1.1**). Since both the relevant statutory provisions originated in the same Act, the Supply of Goods (Implied Terms) Act 1973, it must be open to question whether the two approaches can both be correct.

3.4.3.4　Section 3: restrictions on liability for breach of contract

UCTA 1977, s. 3 may have a particularly significant impact on commercial contracts. It applies where one party deals as a consumer or on the other's written standard terms of business and provides that the other may not by reference to any contract term:

(a) when himself in breach of contract exclude or restrict any liability of his in respect of that breach; or

(b) claim to be entitled

　(i) to render a contractual performance substantially different from that which was reasonably expected of him; or

　(ii) in respect of the whole or any part of his contractual obligation, to render no performance at all

unless the term satisfies the test of reasonableness.

There is no statutory definition of 'written standard terms of business', but it seems likely that the expression will be given a wide interpretation to include both terms prepared by or for an individual business and those prepared for a particular trade by or under the auspices of a trade association or similar body. A contract may still be on 'written standard terms' if standard terms are incorporated by reference or by a course of dealing (see *McCrone* v *Boots Farm Sales Ltd* 1981 SLT 103, considering the equivalent Scottish provision). Where standard terms are varied for an individual contract the question whether the contract is on 'written standard terms' will be one of fact and degree. Minor variations, or the inclusion of express provisions to deal with such matters as delivery dates, price and so on, will not prevent the application of s. 3. However, where parties use a set of standard terms as a basis for negotiation and make alterations to suit the particular case, the resulting contract may fall outside the ambit of s. 3 depending on the extent of negotiations and the nature and degree of the alterations made: see *Salvage Association* v *CAP Financial Services Ltd* (1993), unreported.

Where the section applies it clearly imposes a test of reasonableness on a clause which restricts or excludes liability for breach, such as 'in the event of late delivery the seller's liability is limited to £100'. The ambit of paragraph (b) is not clear. It seems that it applies to clauses which purport to allow a contractor to vary its own contractual obligations but not to clauses which purport to allow a contractor to demand a varied performance from the other contracting party (although such clauses may be subject to common law control: see *Paragon Finance Ltd* v *Nash* [2001] EWCA 1466; [2001] 2 All ER (Comm) 1025, above **2.5.3**). It has been held that for the purposes of paragraph (b)(i) the nature of the performance 'reasonably expected' should first be determined without reference to the clause in dispute (see *Zockoll Group* v *Mercury Communications Ltd* (1998) ITCLR 104). Thus, for instance, where a contract for the sale of goods quotes a delivery date, a provision in the standard terms purporting to permit the seller to vary the delivery date or deliver substitute goods would be one by which the seller purports to be entitled to render a performance different from that 'reasonably expected' of him and would thus be subject to a test of reasonableness. It has been held that s. 3 applies to an entire agreement clause which has the effect of enabling a contractor to render a contractual performance substantially different from that reasonably expected as a result of the pre-contract negotiations between the parties (*SAM Business Systems Ltd* v *Hedley & Co.* [2002] EWHC 2733 (TCC); [2003] 1 All ER (Comm) 465). On this approach s. 3 will apply, subject to a test of reasonableness, to many of the terms commonly found in standard form commercial supply contracts.

3.4.3.5 Reasonableness

The test whether a contract term is reasonable depends on whether the clause was a fair and reasonable one to be included in the contract in light of the circumstances known to the parties when the contract was made; in relation to a notice not having contractual effect the test is whether it would be reasonable to allow reliance on it having regard to the circumstances obtaining when liability arose, or, but for the notice, would have arisen (UCTA 1977, s. 11). It is for the person who wishes to rely on an exclusion to show that it is reasonable (s. 11(5)). A party who wishes to challenge a clause as unreasonable may do so even though he did not plead the point (see *Sheffield* v *Pickfords Ltd* (1997) NLJ 457). A party who wishes to rely on an exclusion clause in litigation must therefore always be prepared to justify it and have evidence available at trial to establish, if necessary, that it is reasonable.

Assessment of reasonableness involves consideration of all the circumstances of the case, but UCTA 1977 indicates some factors which may be taken into account. Where liability is subjected to a financial limit, account should be taken of the resources available to the party in breach to meet the liability, and the extent to which he could have protected himself by insurance (s. 11(4)). Thus, for instance, a clause imposing a financial limit on a contractor's liability may be regarded as unreasonable if the limit is significantly lower than the insurance cover against liability available to the contractor. Clauses limiting liability must therefore be drafted with care, taking account of the amount of insurance cover against liability available to the contractor. The amount of the limit may have to be reviewed from time to time to take account of any increase in insurance cover (see, e.g.: *Salvage Association* v *CAP Financial Services Ltd* (1993), unreported).

UCTA 1977, sch. 2 lists a number of factors which must be taken into account when assessing the reasonableness of exclusions under ss. 6 and 7 of the Act; in practice these or similar factors will be considered in all cases. They include:

(a) the relative bargaining strengths of the parties;

(b) whether the party against whom the exclusion is set up received any inducement to agree to its inclusion in the contract: for instance, where a contract contains an exclusion of liability but the person relying on it offers to accept greater liability for an increased price, the exclusion is more likely to be reasonable;

(c) whether the party against whom the exclusion is set up knew, or ought reasonably to have known, of the existence and extent of the term; a term may therefore be unreasonable if it is printed in small print or drafted in obscure language (see *The Zinnia* [1984] 2 Lloyd's Rep 211);

(d) where the term excludes or restricts liability unless some condition is complied with, whether it was reasonable to expect compliance with the condition when the contract was made: for instance, a clause in a contract for sale of seed potatoes requiring notification of claims within seven days of delivery was unreasonable (*R. Green Ltd* v *Cade Bros Farms* [1978] 1 Lloyd's Rep 602);

(e) whether goods supplied under the contract were manufactured, adapted etc. to the special order of the customer.

Before seeking to apply the reasonableness test the court must first construe the clause in order to determine its true effect and scope (see *Watford Electronics Ltd* v *Sanderson CFL Ltd* [2001] 1 All ER (Comm) 696). A restrictive interpretation may be to the benefit of the party seeking to rely on the clause, by making it more likely that it will be considered reasonable. When it comes to apply the reasonableness test the court is required to assess the reasonableness of the clause as a whole; it cannot 'sever' an unreasonable part of the clause so that, if part of a clause is unreasonable the whole clause is ineffective, even if it would be reasonable to allow reliance on the clause in relation to the particular claim. For instance, a clause restricting a buyer's right of set-off by providing that: 'the buyer may not withhold payment on grounds of any alleged defects in the goods or on any other grounds whatsoever' would be unreasonable because it would mean, for instance, that the buyer could not withhold payment even on grounds that the seller had totally failed to perform the contract (see *Stewart Gill Ltd* v *Horatio Myer & Co. Ltd* [1992] QB 600). Blanket exclusions which provide that a party has no liability in any circumstances are therefore likely to be regarded as unreasonable.

Account must also be taken of the effect of other terms of the contract as properly construed. For example, in *Britvic Soft Drinks* v *Messer UK Ltd* [2002] EWCA Civ 548; [2002] 2 All ER (Comm) 335, a company supplied carbon dioxide to be used in the manufacture of carbonated drinks. The contract warranted the purity of the gas to a prescribed British Standard (BS 4105) and provided that 'all other implied warranties and conditions as to quality or description are excluded.' Unknown to either party the gas supplied was contaminated with benzene, causing extensive losses to the claimants. It was held that on its proper construction the warranty of compliance with BS 4015 did not include a warranty of freedom from benzene contamination, which could therefore arise only under the statutory implied terms as to quality. It was therefore unreasonable to exclude those terms without which the claimants would have no warranty of freedom from contamination. (See also *Bacardi Martini Beverages Ltd* v *Thomas Hardy Packaging Ltd* [2002] EWCA 549; [2002] 2 All ER (Comm) 335.)

3.4.4   The Unfair Terms in Consumer Contracts Regulations 1999

The Unfair Terms in Consumer Contracts Regulations 1999 (SI 1999/2083) came into force on 1 October 1999 and apply to contracts made between businesses and consumers after that date. They provide that a term in a contract between a business and a consumer which has not been individually negotiated may, in certain circumstances, be judged unfair in which case the term in question shall not be binding on the consumer, although the remainder of the contract remains binding if it can continue in existence without the unfair term.

In many respects the Regulations overlap the Unfair Contract Terms Act 1977. However, there are significant differences between the two pieces of legislation and in some ways the ambit of the 1977 Act is wider than that of the Regulations. In particular, the Regulations only apply to standard, pre-drafted terms in consumer contracts and therefore provide no protection to businesses, or to consumers dealing on negotiated, as opposed to standard terms. Moreover, whereas the 1977 Act renders some exclusions wholly ineffective, the Regulations subject all terms to a test of fairness.

The Regulations were introduced to implement the 1993 EC Directive on 'Unfair Terms in Consumer Contracts' (Directive 93/13/EEC; OJ L95 21/4/93). The Directive prescribes a minimum level of protection for consumers but permits Member States to provide higher levels of consumer protection. Thus in those areas in which the 1977 Act, or the common law, provides wider, or more stringent, control of contract terms, that higher level of control is maintained. Anyone advising on the effectiveness of contract terms or drafting a standard term contract must therefore now be fully aware of both sets of regulations and the relationship between them. One must also bear in mind that the Regulations are intended to implement the EC Directive. This means:

(a) that there will be similar regulation of standard terms in consumer contracts in other Member States of the EC;

(b) that decisions on the Directive in other member states, or in the European Court of Justice, may offer guidance as to the meaning and effect of the Directive; and

(c) that the Regulations must be interpreted, so far as possible, so as to give effect to the Directive.

The 1999 Regulations replace the Unfair Terms in Consumer Contracts Regulations 1994 which applied to contracts made between 1 July 1995 and 30 September 1999. There were a number of significant differences between the wording of the 1994 Regulations and the wording of the EC Directive and it was felt that in a number of respects the 1994 Regulations did not properly implement the Directive. The 1999 Regulations follow the wording of the Directive much more closely but there are still a number of differences between the two. If it proves impossible to interpret the Regulations consistently with the Directive, a litigant cannot rely on the Directive in litigation before a UK court except against those contractors who may be regarded as subject to the authority or control of the State. However, in such a case the litigant might be able to recover compensation from the UK Government for breach of its obligations under the Treaty establishing the European Community as amended, under the principle of *Francovich and Bonifaci* v *Italy* [1992] IRLR 84.

3.4.4.1   Scope of the Regulations

The Regulations apply in relation to terms in contracts concluded between a seller or supplier and a consumer. However, certain types of contract are excluded from the scope of the Regulations.

'*Consumer*' is defined for the purposes of the Regulations as:

a natural person who, in making a contract to which these Regulations apply, is acting for purposes which are outside his business (reg. 2(1)).

This is a narrower definition than that in the UCTA 1977, since it clearly excludes corporations: thus the buyer in *R&B Customs Brokers* v *UDT Ltd* [1988] 1 All ER 847 would not be a 'consumer' for the purposes of the Regulations. (See *Cape SNC* v *Ideal Service SRL*, C541/99 [2002] 2 All ER (EC) 657, ECJ.) Sole traders and, possibly, partnerships, may be protected by the Regulations as 'consumers' but only when contracting for 'purposes which are outside his business'. This is wider than the equivalent requirement in the UCTA 1977 that a purchase not be 'in the course of a business' and means that most business partnership contracts will fall outside the Regulations. It is not clear if the Regulations apply where a contract is made partly for private and partly for business purposes, or where a natural person purports to be acting for business purposes, as, for instance, where (say) a business proprietor buys goods for private use using a cheque drawn on a business account.

'*Seller or supplier*' is defined as 'any natural or legal person who, in contracts covered by these Regulations, is acting for purposes relating to his trade, business or profession, whether publicly owned or privately owned' (reg. 2(1)). This is wider than the corresponding provision in the 1977 Act which only applies where the supplier makes the contract in question '*in the course of* a business'. Thus, for instance, a business which occasionally sells off its old vehicles or equipment would be a seller for the purposes of the Regulations even though the sale would not be 'in the course of a business' for the purposes of the 1977 Act. (The corresponding provision in the original 1994 Regulations defined 'seller' as 'a person who sells goods' and 'supplier' as 'a person who supplies goods or services'. This created the impression that the Regulations only applied to contracts for the supply of goods or services *to* consumers. It is now clear that this is not the case, and that the Regulations apply equally to contracts where the consumer is the supplier of goods or services, as, for instance, where a consumer sells a car to a dealer.)

Excluded Contracts   The Regulations are stated not to apply to any contractual term which reflects:

(a) mandatory statutory or regulatory provisions (including such provisions under the law of any Member State or in Community legislation having effect in the United Kingdom without further enactment);

(b) the provisions or principles of international conventions to which the Member States of the Community are party (reg. 4(2)).

The 1994 Regulations also excluded contracts relating to employment, succession rights, family law rights and the incorporation and organisation of companies or partnerships. The recitals to the underlying Directive state that such contracts are to be excluded from its scope. However, there is no such exclusion in the text of the Directive itself and there is no longer any reference to such contracts in the UK Regulations.

There was some doubt about the application of the 1994 Regulations to contracts for the creation or transfer of interests in land. However, it now seems clear that such contracts will be subject to the 1999 Regulations if they fall within the definition of a contract between a seller or supplier and a consumer.

Unlike the 1977 Act the Regulations do apply to contracts of insurance, although their impact on such contracts may be limited.

Standard Terms   The test of fairness under the Regulations applies only to a term which has not been 'individually negotiated'. For this purpose a term is 'always regarded as not

having been individually negotiated where it has been drafted in advance and the consumer has therefore not been able to influence' its substance (reg. 5(1)).

3.4.4.2   The nature of the control

The Regulations impose a general duty on the seller or supplier to ensure that any written
term is expressed in plain and intelligible language (reg. 6). Although the point is not
entirely clear it seems that this requirement applies to all terms and not merely those
which have not been 'individually negotiated'. Where a non-negotiated term is unclear or
unintelligible, that factor may go to make it unfair. Moreover, the Regulations confirm the
contra proferentem rule of construction by providing that where there is any doubt about
the meaning of a term, it shall be given the meaning most favourable to the consumer.

More importantly, the Regulations provide that an unfair term shall not be binding on
the consumer. A term is unfair if 'contrary to the requirement of good faith' it 'causes a significant imbalance in the parties' rights and obligations under the contract to the detriment of the consumer' (reg. 4(1)). The Regulations provide that the assessment of whether
a term is unfair should take account of the nature of the goods or services in question, all
the circumstances attending the conclusion of the contract, and all the other terms of the
contract or any other contract on which it is dependent (reg. 4(2)). In order for a term to be
considered unfair three requirements must therefore be satisfied: the term must create a
significant imbalance in the rights and obligations of the parties; that imbalance must be
'to the detriment of the consumer': and the creation of the imbalance must be contrary to
the requirement of 'good faith' (see *Director General of Fair Trading* v *First National Bank*
[2001] UKHL 52; [2001] 2 All ER (Comm) 1000).

The balance of rights and obligations   A term is only considered unfair if it creates a
'significant imbalance in the rights and obligations of the parties under the contract to
the detriment of the consumer'. The imbalance must favour the supplier. Thus a term
which gives rights to the supplier without giving corresponding rights to the consumer
may be considered unfair.

Good faith   Some commentators have argued that a term which creates a significant
imbalance of rights and obligations to the detriment of the consumer is necessarily 'contrary to good faith'. The better view, however, is that 'good faith' is a separate requirement,
and this view was accepted by the House of Lords in *Director General of Fair Trading* v *First
National Bank*. Thus a term will not be unfair merely because it creates a significant imbalance in the rights and obligations of the parties. The creation of that imbalance must be
'contrary to good faith'.

The 1999 Regulations offer no guidance as to how 'good faith' is to be assessed. Some
guidance may, however, be drawn from the recitals of the 1993 Directive which provide,
inter alia, that in assessing good faith regard should be had in particular to 'the strength of
the bargaining position of the parties; whether the consumer had an inducement to agree
to the term and whether the goods or services were sold or supplied to the special order of
the consumer' and conclude that 'the requirement of good faith may be satisfied by the
seller or supplier where he deals fairly and equitably with the [consumer] whose legitimate
interests he has to take into account'. These are similar to the factors which a court is
directed to consider when making an assessment of reasonableness in accordance with
UCTA 1977, sch. 2, and the 1994 Regulations expressly incorporated a similar list.
According to Lord Bingham in the *First National Bank* case 'the requirement of good faith
in this context is one of fair and open dealing'. This requires that the terms are presented
clearly and legibly to the consumer, and that the supplier should not take advantage of the
consumer's lack of experience, weak bargaining position and so on. On this view it follows
that a term which creates an imbalance in rights and obligations will not necessarily be

unfair if it is presented to the consumer clearly and openly and he genuinely consents to it. On the other hand it seems clear that 'good faith' is not concerned solely with procedural factors. Some terms, such as terms purporting to exclude liability for death or injury caused by negligence, are so substantively unfair that their inclusion could never be considered to be in good faith, even if clearly drawn to the consumer's attention. It therefore seems that the assessment of 'good faith' will require consideration of both substantive and procedural factors.

The Regulations provide that:

'in so far as it is in plain intelligible language, the assessment of fairness of a term shall not relate—

(a) to the definition of the main subject matter of the contract; or

(b) to the adequacy of the price or remuneration, as against the goods or services supplied in exchange.'

The House of Lords has indicated that this provision should be given a narrow interpretation to avoid undermining the purpose of the Regulations. Thus in the *First National Bank* case the House of Lords held that a provision in a consumer credit agreement relating to the payment of default interest was not covered by the provision and was subject to the test of fairness. Similarly the Office of Fair Trading has taken the view that price escalation or variation clauses are subject to the test of fairness and the House of Lords accepted that that was correct. It is clear that the fairness even of a term defining the main subject matter of the contract may be challenged if the term is not expressed in plain, intelligible language, and it seems that the price and other 'core' terms can be taken into account when assessing the fairness of other terms covered by the Regulations (see reg. 4(2)).

The indicative list of unfair terms   Schedule 3 of the Regulations contains an 'indicative and non-exhaustive list' of terms which 'may' be considered unfair. A similar list appears in the Directive. Although the terms included in the list are not necessarily unfair, terms of the types included in the list may be difficult to justify, and although other types of term may be considered unfair, the list provides guidance as to the sorts of terms which may be covered by the Regulations.

Arbitration clauses   By virtue of ss. 89–91 of the Arbitration Act 1996, an arbitration agreement between a consumer and a supplier of goods or services is made subject to the Regulations and is automatically presumed to be unfair where the amount in dispute does not exceed £3,000. It should be noted that 'arbitration agreement' appears to include both an arbitration clause in a contract *and* an agreement to refer a dispute to arbitration made after the dispute has arisen. For the purpose of this provision the definition of 'consumer' is widened to include not only natural, but also legal, persons who are acting for purposes which are outside their business.

3.4.4.3 Enforcement

Individual consumers may rely on the Regulations to challenge unfair terms in contracts to which they are a party. If a term is found to be unfair, the term is not binding on the consumer (reg. 5(1)), but the remainder of the contract remains in force if it is capable of continuing in existence without the term (reg. 5(2)).

In addition, the Regulations provide for the Director General of Fair Trading (DGFT), or any qualifying body, to take action against unfair terms, including by seeking an injunction, against anyone using or recommending the use of an unfair term. The qualifying bodies entitled to enforce the Regulations are listed in sch. 1. They include Regulatory

Officers responsible for particular sectors such as the Data Protection Registrar and the Director General of Telecommunications and also the Consumers' Association.

The DGFT may only take action under the Regulations on the basis of a complaint, but complaints may be made by anyone including individual consumers, local trading standards or other officers, consumer organisations or even by one business against another. Where a complaint is made the DGFT has a duty to consider it, unless he considers it frivolous or vexatious, or a qualifying body notifies him that it agrees to consider it. He must give reasons for his decision to apply or not to apply for an injunction, but may, if he considers it appropriate, accept an undertaking in lieu of an injunction. A special Unfair Contract Terms Unit has been established within the Office of Fair Trading to enforce the Regulations. Where it receives a complaint about a term which it considers to be unfair, it will normally seek first to negotiate a change to the term before seeking an injunction or undertaking and to date it has had little need to resort to formal court proceedings.

Qualifying Bodies now have similar powers to the DGFT to take action against unfair terms. Where a Qualifying Body agrees with the DGFT to consider a complaint about the fairness of a particular term, it is under a duty to do so and must then give reasons for its decision whether or not to apply for an injunction. However, before seeking an injunction, a qualifying body must first give to the DGFT at least 14 days notice of its intention to do so, unless the DGFT agrees to accept shorter notice. Qualifying Bodies may, like the DGFT, accept undertakings in lieu of seeking injunctions. They must notify the DGFT of any undertakings thus accepted.

The 1999 Regulations contain significant new powers for the DGFT and Qualifying Bodies other than the Consumers' Association by notice in writing to require any person to supply copies of standard form contracts used in dealings with consumers and information about their use. In the event of non-compliance with such a notice, the DGFT or Qualifying Body may seek a court order compelling compliance, and if such order is made, it may provide for the costs of the application to be borne personally by the person in default or, in the case of a company or other association, by any officers of the company or association who are responsible for its default.

It seems that one way in which the Regulations aim to discourage the use of unfair terms is by 'naming and shaming' those who use them or encourage their use. The DGFT is under a duty to publish details of undertakings or injunctions obtained by him or notified to him by a qualifying body and of any application to the court to enforce a previous order. In addition, he is given power to disseminate 'in such form and manner as he thinks appropriate' such information and advice concerning the operation of the Regulations 'as may appear to him to be expedient to give to the public and all persons likely to be affected' by the Regulations. The OFT's Unfair Terms Unit has published a series of Bulletins giving details of its activities and guidance as to its approach to the Regulations and the types of terms it considers unfair, including details of the terms against which it has taken action and the businesses using them.

An additional 'fast track' method of enforcement is available under the Stop Now Orders (EC Directive) Regulations 2001 (SI 2001, No. 1422). These regulations, which were made to implement an EC Directive (98/27/EC—'The Injunctions Directive'—OJ L 166, 11.6.98), enable the DGFT and any other 'qualified entity' to take proceedings under Part III of the Fair Trading Act 1973 against any trader who has engaged in conduct which constitutes an infringement of certain specified Community consumer protection legislation, as transposed into domestic law, and which harms the collective interests of consumers. The Unfair Terms Directive and 1999 Regulations are included in the list of specified Community legislation. Thus where the DGFT believes that a trader or other undertaking has engaged in conduct which constitutes a breach of the 1999 Regulations—i.e.: by using unfair standard terms—he may apply to the court for an order under the regulations requiring the trader to desist from that conduct. Such an order, known as a 'stop now order' will, if made, require the trader immediately to desist from the specified conduct, and breach of such an order is punishable as a contempt of court. Unless satisfied that the circumstances require proceedings to be brought without delay, the DGFT is required to seek to obtain the cessation of the infringement by negotiation with the trader concerned. However, the intention clearly is that it should be possible to bring proceedings and obtain a court order speedily. The Secretary of State has power under the regulations to designate other bodies 'whose purpose is to protect the collective interests of consumers' as 'qualified entities' for the purposes of the regulations, and such entities are also given power to bring proceedings for a stop now order. Where a qualified entity proposes to seek an order it must first consult with the DGFT and with the trader concerned in order to attempt to obtain a cessation of the infringement by consultation, but if no cessation is achieved within two weeks, it may bring proceedings without further delay. A trader threatened with proceedings for an order has therefore only a very short time to seek a negotiated settlement and little opportunity to 'play for time'. The Regulations identify various regulatory bodies as 'qualified entities', but it is clear that other organisations will in due course be so designated. Moreover, the intention of the underlying Directive is to harmonise enforcement procedures, and 'qualified entities' from other EU Member States therefore have similar powers to seek 'stop now orders' in the UK courts, whilst the DGFT and UK qualified entities are empowered to seek similar orders, where necessary, under corresponding legislation in the courts of other Member States.

3.4.4.4   Impact on contracts

In many respects the control on contract terms imposed by the 1999 Regulations is similar to that imposed by the Unfair Contract Terms Act. In particular, many terms likely to be considered 'unfair' under the Regulations would probably be regarded as 'unreasonable' under the Act. However, there are important differences between the two sets of controls and standard term contracts should therefore be drafted with both in mind. The different definitions of 'consumer' and similar phrases in the two sets of provisions may make the contract drafter's job more difficult. The possiblity of the Director General of Fair Trading seeking an injunction against unfair terms under the Regulations is particularly important. An injunction could prohibit a business from continuing to use its standard term contracts and require them to be re-drafted, causing bad publicity and serious administrative difficulties. The OFT's Unfair Terms Unit has been vigorous in its enforcement of the Regulations to date. The main difficulty it has faced has been the sheer volume of potentially unfair terms referred to it for consideration. The extension of enforcement powers to other qualifying bodies, including the Consumers' Association, will obviously lessen the burden on the OFT and will almost certainly mean that many more terms will be subject to scrutiny in the future. Businesses dealing on standard terms with consumers should therefore be advised to keep their terms under review and, in particular, to keep abreast of publicity relating to decisions on the fairness of terms, and advice and action from the Office of Fair Trading.

In its Bulletins published so far the OFT has emphasised that it regards certain types of term as *prima facie* unfair. These include:

(a) 'entire agreement' clauses and clauses restricting a contractor's obligation to respect, perform or be bound by statements or undertakings made by his agents and employees;

(b) 'hidden clauses'—i.e., clauses incorporated in circumstances which make it impossible or difficult for the consumer to become acquainted with the content and meaning of a clause before a contract is made (for instance, where a consumer is required to sign a document purporting to incorporate by reference terms not available for inspection by the consumer prior to signature);

(c) penalties—e.g.: clauses allowing retention of deposits;

(d) clauses purporting to permit the supplier unilaterally to vary the terms of the contract;

(e) 'inappropriate' exclusion clauses, such as clauses:

    (i)   which effectively remove any obligation on the part of the supplier to perform the contract;

    (ii)   stating that delivery/performance dates are not contractual obligations;

    (iii)   excluding liability for death, injury or loss caused by negligence;

    (iv)   excluding liability for the quality of goods supplied.

3.4.5   Force majeure clauses

Most commercial contracts contain provisions to deal with the effects of outside events or changed circumstances which hinder or prevent performance or make performance more difficult or expensive than anticipated. Such provisions are especially important in a long term contract. They include such provisions as price variation, force majeure and hardship clauses.

3.4.5.1   Force majeure clauses

A force majeure clause is intended to cover the situation where one party is prevented or hindered from performing the contract by circumstances outside their control, such as war, trade embargoes, adverse weather conditions, strikes etc. The effect of such a clause is, to some extent, similar to that of an exclusion clause, in that it may protect the contracting party from liability in the circumstances in which it applies. However, it may have wider effects, for instance by suspending or extending the time for performance. Such clauses tend to be construed less strictly than outright exclusion clauses; however, many force majeure clauses in standard form contracts may be subject to a test of reasonableness under UCTA 1977, s. 3.

Many of the circumstances which lead to the application of a force majeure clause might otherwise frustrate the contract. However, where an event is covered by a force majeure clause it cannot frustrate the contract. A major advantage of a force majeure clause is therefore that it avoids the uncertainties of the doctrine of frustration and may allow for a more flexible and commercially sensible set of responses to force majeure circumstances. A force majeure clause might provide that if force majeure prevents one party from performing:

(a) he is not to be liable; or

(b) the time or method of performance is to be varied; or

(c) the contract is to be discharged with specified consequences.

For instance, a contract to export goods might contain a clause providing that if the seller is unable to load the goods on time due to adverse weather conditions, the loading period should be extended by a period equal to the period of the delay, whereas if the contract were frustrated it would be automatically discharged.

A well drafted force majeure clause may stipulate a procedure which must be followed before it can be invoked—for instance by requiring the party relying on the clause to give notice of that fact to the other. It should then define what may be regarded as 'force majeure' so as to allow its invocation and then stipulate the consequences of the force majeure event. For instance:

If performance of the Seller's obligations is prevented, delayed or hindered by circumstances amounting to force majeure (as defined) the following provisions shall apply.

(a) The Seller shall, as soon as reasonably practicable, give the Buyer notice of the reasons for the delay, hindrance or failure to perform. However, provision of such a notice shall not be a contractual obligation and failure to provide such notice shall not prevent the Seller relying on the remaining provisions of this clause.

(b) The Seller's duty to perform shall be suspended for so long as the circumstances continue and the time for performance of the Seller's obligations shall be extended by a period equal to the duration of the force majeure circumstances.

(c) If the force majeure circumstances continue for [30 days] both parties shall be released from their obligations under this contract. The Seller shall return to the Buyer all sums paid prior to such discharge, provided that the Seller may retain [a sum not exceeding £n] to cover its expenses incurred in performing this contract.

This clause is intended to protect a seller of goods. 'Force majeure circumstances' would be defined elsewhere in the contract. The clause requires the seller to serve notice on the buyer before invoking the clause, in order to ensure that the buyer is informed of the situation. However, without more, such a requirement might mean that the seller would be in breach of contract if he failed to serve notice, or that service of such a notice was a condition precedent to the seller's right to rely on the clause. Sub-clause (a) therefore excludes these possibilities. The clause then provides for the consequences of force majeure—the seller's duty to perform is suspended and the time for performance is extended; the seller therefore cannot be liable for breach of contract in such a case. However, such suspension must be limited in time, and the clause therefore continues by providing that if the force majeure circumstances continue (in this case for a relatively short period) the contract is to be discharged. Finally, the clause defines the consequences of discharge (sub-clause (c)).

3.4.5.2 Hardship clauses

Another provision sometimes found in a commercial contract, especially one intended to govern a long-term relationship such as a long-term supply contract, is a so-called 'hardship clause'. Such a clause provides that in the event of a change in circumstances which makes performance more difficult or onerous for one of the parties, the parties should seek to negotiate an adjustment of the contract to alleviate the effect of the changed circumstances. Such a clause should define the circumstances in which it applies, the procedure by which it can be invoked and the procedure to be followed thereafter. However, a bare agreement to negotiate, or to negotiate in good faith, is not binding in English law (*Walford* v *Miles* [1992] 2 AC 128, above **2.3.3.4**). In order to be effective, such a clause must therefore contain some procedure to deal with the changed circumstances in the event that the parties fail to reach agreement within a specified time, for instance by providing for the matter to be referred to arbitration or for a nominated third party to determine the issue for them.

3.5 Summary

Having completed this chapter you should:

- be familiar with the rules governing
  - discharge of contractual obligations by agreement, performance, breach and frustration;
  - the consequences of discharge of a contract, especially by breach or frustration;
  - the assessment of damages for breach of contract and misrepresentation;
  - rescission of contracts for misrepresentation;
  - the incorporation, interpretation and validity of exclusion clauses;
- understand the practical implications of those rules;
- be able to advise a client on
  - whether it can lawfully withhold performance of its own obligations under a contract;
  - the remedial consequences of a breach of contract including the choice of the most appropriate remedy in any particular case;
  - the likely calculation of damages for a particular breach of contract or misrepresentation;
  - the effectiveness of an exclusion or similar clause;
- be able to draft an effective exclusion or similar clause.

Part II

Agency

Agents in commerce

4.1 Introduction

Most businesses use intermediaries in their dealings with the outside world. Such intermediaries may be employed for a variety of reasons: because they possess special skill or expertise; have special knowledge of a particular market, area or commodity; because the business needs someone 'on the spot' to negotiate the contract; or simply because the proprietor of the business cannot be personally responsible for all its dealings. They may be used to market and sell goods or services in order to maximise the exploitation of a product, to find customers and introduce them to the business, to negotiate contracts, or to purchase goods or services for the business. Many such intermediaries are referred to as 'agents'; the need for them is particularly acute where the business wishes to trade on an international basis.

In a partnership, each partner is by law treated as an agent of the firm and of each of the other partners for the purposes of the business of the firm (Partnership Act 1890, s. 5). Where the business is conducted through the medium of a limited liability company, which is in law a separate person from its shareholders, the company must act through human agents.

4.1.1 Agency distinguished from other marketing arrangements

The words 'agent' and 'agency' must be used with care. The law attaches special legal incidents to an agency relationship. Not all those referred to as 'agents' in commercial parlance are agents in *law*. Conversely, a person who is an agent in law may not be called an agent: for instance, 'factors' and 'brokers' are agents, whilst confirming houses and freight forwarders may act as agents in particular transactions; such persons therefore have the legal powers, rights and obligations of agents. Moreover, the concept of agency may be invoked by the courts from time to time in order to produce results which are (or are thought to be) commercially convenient or socially desirable, and parties may find that they have entered into an agency relationship without being aware of it.

It is therefore important for the commercial lawyer to have an understanding of the concept of agency and of its legal uses and incidents: where one person has acted, or purported to act, on behalf of another it will be necessary to consider whether their relationship is that of principal and agent, generating the legal consequences of agency, or some other relationship. When preparing an agreement under which one person is to represent another it will be necessary to consider whether a true, legal agency, or some other relationship, will best fulfil the requirements of the parties.

In this chapter we will examine the different relationships which may exist between a business and the intermediaries through whom it acts and the various types of 'agency' relationship which may be found in commerce. In **Chapters 5–7** we examine the legal incidents of the agency relationship and finally, in **Chapter 8**, consider alternative marketing arrangements which may be used by a business.

4.2   The nature and consequences of agency

In law, 'agency' is the relationship which exists between two persons, principal and agent, who have both consented to the creation of that relationship. A number of consequences flow in law from the creation of the agency relationship.

4.2.1   The agent has power to bind the principal

The law recognises an agent as having power to affect the principal's legal position, creating, by his actions, rights and obligations enforceable by and against the principal. Thus the agent's actions, whilst acting in his capacity as agent, are attributed to the principal. The most significant aspect of the agent's power in the commercial context is that, as an exception to the doctrine of privity, contracts made by the agent on behalf of the principal are treated in law as the principal's contracts and are directly enforceable by and against him. However, the agent's actions may affect the principal's position in other ways. He may make binding dispositions of the principal's property or acquire property on the principal's behalf; his statements may bind the principal, both in a contractual context and otherwise; for instance in the law of evidence, if he exerts duress or undue influence on the other contracting party during negotiations, or in obtaining that party's signature to a document, his actions will be attributed to the principal who may therefore be unable to enforce the contract; and his actions may even make the principal criminally liable, especially for offences concerned with the 'sale' or 'supply' of goods (see, e.g. *Gardner* v *Akeroyd* [1952] 2 QB 743).

4.2.2   Agent's rights and duties

The law gives the parties certain rights, and imposes on them certain duties, against each other. Most importantly, the agent generally occupies a fiduciary position *vis-à-vis* the principal and owes him duties similar to those owed by a trustee to trust beneficiaries. In return the agent is given certain rights at common law, most notably a right to be indemnified against expenses incurred whilst acting on the principal's behalf; in certain circumstances he may also be entitled to be paid for his work, either at common law. A commercial agent, as defined, may have additional duties and more extensive rights, including the right to be paid for his work and a right to a statutory payment (termed either 'compensation' or 'indemnity') under the Commercial Agents Regulations 1993 (SI 1993, No. 3053).

4.2.3   Basis of agency

The relationship of principal and agent can only arise by consent of the parties; however, agency is a legal concept and two persons may be found to have consented to the creation of an agency relationship without there being any express agreement to that effect or even without their realising it. Moreover, a person may have power in law to affect another position even though that other has not agreed to his having such power.

4.3   Common commercial agency arrangements

A number of agency relationships are common in commerce, each with their own special legal incidents as a result of legal recognition of commercial usage.

4.3.1   General and special agents

A general agent has general authority to act for the principal in a particular trade or class of transactions; a special agent is authorised only to act in one particular transaction. The distinction is no longer so significant in practice as it once was but is sometimes found in cases.

4.3.2   Factors and brokers

A factor (or 'mercantile agent') is an agent whose business is to sell or otherwise deal with goods on behalf of his principal; the principal gives the factor possession of the goods for that purpose.

A broker negotiates contracts for the sale and purchase of goods and other property on behalf of his principal but does not have possession of the goods.

The terms 'factor' and 'broker' are not always used in modern practice, but the distinction between the two types of agent remains important, as the law (Factors Act 1889) gives factors extensive powers to make binding dispositions of their principals' property in order to protect third parties who deal with them (see **Chapter 15**).

4.3.3   Del credere agents

A del credere agent negotiates contracts for a principal and guarantees to the principal that the third party will pay any sums due under the contract; this may be important where the third party is not known to the principal. The del credere agent charges the principal an extra commission for providing the guarantee.

4.3.4   Commission agents

A commission agent buys or sells property on behalf of a principal, but is not authorised to create privity of contract between the principal and the third party with whom he deals. Thus *vis-à-vis* the third party, the agent contracts as principal and is therefore liable to the third party on the contract; for instance, if he buys goods, he alone is liable for the price; but *vis-à-vis* his principal, the agent owes the duties owed by an agent to his principal. Thus if employed to buy goods he must take reasonable care in performance of his duties but is not strictly liable for their quality as a seller would be (see **Chapter 12**). Commission agency effectively falls halfway between a true agency and the situation where a person acting as an independent contractor buys and resells goods on his own behalf. It is common in civil law systems and there is some authority to suggest that it may be recognised by the common law (e.g. *Aluminium Industrie Vaasen BV v Romalpa Aluminium Ltd* [1976] 2 All ER 552).

4.3.5   Commercial agents

A commercial agent is a self-employed agent with continuing authority to negotiate or to negotiate and conclude contracts for the sale or purchase of goods on behalf of and in the name of a principal. Commercial agents have special rights against and duties to their principals in accordance with the Commercial Agents (Council Directive) Regulations 1993 (SI 1993, No. 3053), implementing an EC Directive (86/653). Commercial Agency is discussed more fully below in **Chapter 7**).

4.3.6 Confirming houses

Confirming houses play an important role in international trade. They normally act on behalf of overseas clients who wish to import goods, and act in different ways according to their client's instructions.

(a) They may simply buy goods in the domestic market and resell them to a client overseas: they then enter into two contracts of sale.

(b) They may act simply as agents, negotiating a purchase on behalf of a client and revealing their capacity as agents; there is then one contract of sale, between domestic supplier and overseas buyer.

(c) Because domestic sellers may be unhappy about dealing solely with overseas customers whose reputation and credit standing may be unknown, a confirming house may make the contract to purchase the goods as agent on behalf of its overseas principal but enter into a separate contract with the supplier to 'confirm', or guarantee, that the buyer will perform its obligations under the sale contract.

The confirming house's obligation to pay is independent of that of the overseas customer, so that the domestic seller has the security of being able to claim the price direct from the confirming house which is both within the jurisdiction of domestic courts and known to be creditworthy.

4.4 Other agents

The following are also agents, at least for some purposes, although their power to bind their principals may be limited.

4.4.1 Company directors and other officers

A company is an artificial, legal person; it acts through human agents. Authority to act on behalf of the company is generally vested in the board of directors as a whole; however, most companies' articles of association contain power for the board to delegate power to individual directors and executive, or managing, directors are often appointed and given wide powers of management, either generally or in relation to a particular aspect of the company's business. Other company officers, such as the company secretary, are also treated as agents of the company in law, although they generally have only limited authority.

4.4.2 Partners

Every partner in a firm is an agent of the firm and all the other partners for the purpose of the business of the firm, and every partner who does any act for carrying on in the usual way business of the kind carried on by the firm binds the firm and the other partners (Partnership Act 1890, s. 5). Agency principles are generally applied by statute to partnerships in their dealings with outsiders.

4.4.3 Employees

Employees may be agents of their employers for certain purposes connected with their-employment: for instance, a shop assistant will be an agent of the shop's proprietor when contracting with customers. The scope of the employee's authority to bind the employer as an agent may be limited: generally, the more senior the employee, the greater the authority which he is likely to possess. Employers are also vicariously liable for torts committed by their employees when acting in the course of their employment.

4.4.4 Professionals

Solicitors, accountants and other professionals may be agents for their clients when dealing with third parties on their clients' behalf in accordance with their instructions, for instance in negotiations. Note, however, that the authority of some professional agents is limited unless specifically extended, either expressly or by implication: for instance, estate agents generally have only very limited authority to bind their clients and generally have no authority to sign a contract of sale. The rules of agency are modified somewhat when applied to certain categories of agents, such as insurance agents.

4.5 Alternatives to agency

As we noted earlier, there is a range of arrangements using representative intermediaries open to a business which wishes to market its goods or services, but not all of them amount to agency even though the representative may be referred to as an 'agent'.

4.5.1 Distributorship

A business may use a network of distributors to market its products. The relationship between the business and an individual distributor will generally be governed by a master agreement which may impose restrictions on both parties: for instance, the business may agree not to sell products in competition with the distributor, or not to appoint other distributors in the same area; the distributor may agree to promote the business's products and not to sell products of a rival manufacturer. Although the relationship between the parties is close, it does not amount to one of agency. When the business supplies goods to the distributor they enter into a relationship of seller and buyer, and when the distributor resells to the public, it does so on its own behalf, so that it, rather than the business, will be liable to customers for performance of the contract of sale. Distributorship is examined in more detail in **Chapter 8**.

4.5.2 Franchising

The relationship between franchisor and franchisee may be even closer than that between a business and its distributors. Again there will be a master agreement which will impose restrictions on the parties. In return for payment of a fee and acceptance of those restrictions, the franchisee will be given the right to use the franchisor's product or business idea and also its general style, including intellectual property rights such as copyrights and trade marks; indeed, it will generally be obliged to adopt the franchisor's style. The individual franchisee thus gets the benefit of appearing to be part of a large organisation and of the goodwill generated by the franchisor and other franchisees. The franchisee will be obliged to purchase some or all of the products to be used in its business from the franchisor. However, once again, when goods are supplied from franchisor to franchisee the relationship is that of seller and buyer; and when the franchisee resells to the public it does so as seller on its own behalf and not as agent for the franchisor.

4.5.3   Subsidiaries

A company may choose to market its goods or services through a network of subsidiary companies. Parent and subsidiary are separate persons in law. The relationship between parent and subsidiary will depend on the facts of the particular case: the subsidiary may be appointed to act as the parent's agent; alternatively it may buy goods from the parent for resale on its own behalf.

4.5.4   Classification of the agreement

The distinction between a true agency and other representative arrangements such as distributorship may often be difficult to draw. The proper approach to classification of an agreement is to determine whether its provisions are consistent with its being an agency or some other relationship. It will therefore be necessary to consider whether the rights and duties of the parties under the agreement are consistent with the normal duties of principal and agent. An agreement which contains provisions inconsistent with an agency relationship will not be an agency in law. As a general rule an agent is not entitled to make any profit from his agency other than his agreed commission without the knowledge and consent of his principal. An agreement under which A is allowed to resell P's products at prices determined by A and keep the profit will therefore not normally be an agency. However, there is no hard and fast rule that an agent must be remunerated by commission and it is not impossible for an agency agreement to provide for the agent to be remunerated by retaining any 'mark up', so that an arrangement allowing the agent to retain all or part of the profit obtained on selling the principal's products may nevertheless be an agency if its other provisions are consistent with its so being (see *Mercantile International Group plc* v *Chuan Soon Huat Industrial Group* [2002] EWCA Civ 288; [2002] 1 All ER (Comm) 788).

4.6   Practical consequences of the distinctions

It may be important to distinguish these various marketing arrangements for a number of reasons, including the following.

4.6.1   Responsibility for defective performance

The marketing arrangements must be capable of being distinguished in order to decide who is answerable to the ultimate customer who complains of defective performance of the supply contract—for instance, because goods supplied are not of satisfactory quality. If the representative is an agent in law, the business is potentially liable, as principal, on the supply contract and the representative has no liability to the ultimate customer. Otherwise primary contractual liability falls on the representative (although in the case of defective products the business may incur tortious or statutory product liability direct to the ultimate customer; see **Chapter 13**).

4.6.2   Determination of the parties' rights and duties

The marketing arrangements need to be capable of being distinguished in order to determine the rights and duties of the parties *inter se*. Generally these will be defined by the agreement between the parties, but where a point is not covered by express provision it may be necessary to consider the general law applicable to such agreements, for instance in order to decide whether the business can compete with its representative. In addition, some agents have extensive rights under the Commercial Agents' Regulations 1993—see **7.1.1**.

4.6.3   Insolvency

Where the representative becomes insolvent, the marketing arrangements may have to be classified in order to determine whether the business is entitled to claim payment direct from customers, or to claim moneys received from customers. Where goods are sold by an agent, the principal's goods in the agent's hands remain the principal's property until sale. Contracts with customers are directly enforceable by the principal who can therefore claim sums due direct from the customers. Sums received from customers by the agent may be held in a fiduciary capacity in which case they too are the principal's property. The principal may thus be able to recover goods held by the agent and claim proceeds of the agent's sales by way of a proprietary claim rather than being limited to a claim as a creditor in the agent's insolvency.

4.6.4   Contravention of competition law

The types of representative arrangement under discussion may contravene domestic or European competition law; in particular, any agreement whose object or effect is the prevention, restriction or distortion of competition within the Common Market is contrary to Art. 81 of the E.C. Treaty and void unless exempted under Art. 81(3) (see **Chapter 29**). However, vertical agreements, between organisations at different levels in the supply chain, are generally considered not to be anti-competitive and in 1999 the European Commission issued a block exemption covering certain categories of vertical agreements (2790/99, 1999 OJ L 336/21). Distributorship agreements (other than those for motor vehicle distributorship, which are covered by a separate exemption, Reg. 1475/95) are protected by the block exemption provided that they do not contain certain prohibited terms. Distributorship agreements should therefore be drafted so as to conform to the terms of the block exemption. (At present if an agreement falls outside the terms of the Block Exemption the parties must seek individual exemption for it from the Commission, which requires them to give prior notice of it to the Commission. However, from May 2004 this system will be discontinued. National courts will have an obligation to rule on the application of Art. 81 to agreements in litigation. More importantly it will no longer be necessary or possible to give the Commission prior notification of an agreement for individual exemption. As a result where an agreement falls outside the terms of the Block Exemption the parties will proceed with it at their own risk, subject to the possibility that in the event of litigation a court may rule that it infringes Art. 81.) Agency agreements, on the other hand, fall outside the exemption because they are regarded as not being anti-competitive: the agent is effectively regarded as being part of the principal's organisation. A Commission Notice accompanying the block exemption indicates that true agency agreements will be regarded as exempt provided that the agent undertakes no 'financial risk'. An agency agreement may thus fall outside the terms of the notice if, for instance, the agent maintains stocks of goods at his own risk or cost, or takes responsibility for customers' performance of their contracts (see Commission Notice, Guidelines on Vertical Restraints (2000 OJ C291/01) Chapter 2, Section II).

Agent's power and authority

5.1 Introduction

In this chapter we are concerned with the agent's power to legally bind the principal. For instance, the agent may make binding dispositions of the principal's property or acquire property on the principal's behalf; he may sign documentation on behalf of the principal; and his statements may bind the principal, both in a contractual context and otherwise. But arguably, the most significant aspect of the agent's power in the commercial context is that, as an exception to the doctrine of privity, contracts made by the agent on behalf of the principal are treated in law as the principal's contracts and are directly enforceable by and against him.

In this chapter we:

- identify the different bases on which an agent may have power to bind their principal;
- examine the ways in which these different types of of power arise; and
- note the overlapping nature of some types of authority and the consequences of this overlap.

5.1.1 The agency relationships

Agency involves three relationships:

(a) the principal/agent relationship;

(b) the agent/third party relationship; and

(c) the principal/third party relationship.

These relationships can be represented diagramatically as where, for example, an agent negotiates a contract on behalf of his principal.

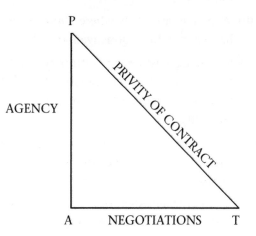

The principal/agent relationship is usually consensual and in a commercial context is commonly based on a contract. The relative rights and duties of the principal and agent are considered further in **Chapter 7**. Although the agent is not privy to the contract he negotiates on behalf of the principal, he may, in certain circumstances, incur liability to the third party. Such liability is considered further in **Chapter 6**. In this chapter we are concerned with the principal/third party relationship and, in particular, the agent's power to affect his principal's legal position. Where the agent negotiates a contract on behalf of his principal the effect is to create privity of contract between the principal and the third party (see further **Chapter 6**).

While it is useful, for the purpose of analysis, to separate these three relationships, it should be borne in mind that these three relationships are connected and in any practical situation it may be necessary to consider all three.

We will use the abbreviations P, A and T to refer respectively to the principal, the agent and the third parties with whom the agent contracts on the principal's behalf.

5.2   The agent's power

The basis of the principal/agent relationship is consent: P consents to A having power to bind him. P is therefore said to *authorise* A. However, as against T, A may have power to bind P even without P's consent so that, strictly speaking, his actions are *unauthorised*.

The tendency is to define A's power to bind P, even where P has not consented to A's actions, in terms of different types of 'authority' and for consistency we will follow this tendency. It is probably more accurate however to think in terms of A being recognised by the law as having *power* in a number of situations to bind P. In some cases this power may derive from P's consent to, or authorisation of, A's actions, but generally it is recognised on public policy grounds: commerce would grind to a halt without the facility of agency.

5.2.1   Types of authority

A's authority will be categorised under the following five headings.

(a) 'Actual' authority where P consents in advance to A's actions, giving A actual authority to act in a certain manner and bind P. Actual authority may be express or implied.

(b) 'Apparent' authority where A appears to T to have authority, whether he actually has it or not; his actions again bind P.

(c) 'Usual' or 'customary' authority where A has authority which a person in his position usually, or customarily, has; this type of authority can either expand the scope of A's actual or apparent authority, or be seen as an independent head of authority.

(d) Authority by 'ratification' where, although A does not have authority at the time when he acts on P's behalf, P later ratifies or adopts A's actions and is thus bound by them.

(e) Agency of 'necessity', where due to an emergency situation, A is vested, by operation of the law, with authority to act in a way not actually authorised by P.

EXAMPLE

P appoints A to buy a particular personal computer, and to pay no more than £1,200 for it. A buys a machine as described but for £1,500. A has exceeded his actual authority, and is in breach of his duties to P. P is not bound unless T can rely on A's apparent authority. Alternatively if P ratifies A's purchase the contract can be enforced by T and A's breach of duty is excused.

Unfortunately, judges and academics have not been consistent in their use of terminology to describe agency. Different writers use the same word to mean different things and different words to mean the same thing: actual authority is sometimes referred to as 'real' authority, apparent authority as 'ostensible' or 'held-out' authority, and the boundaries between implied, usual and customary authority are malleable. Commercial lawyers must therefore be familiar with the full range of terminology.

5.3 Actual authority

Actual authority is the authority which A *actually* has as a result of the consensual arrangement between P and A.

Actual authority is crucial as between P and A. If A acts outside his actual authority he is not entitled to remuneration, for example, and he may be sued for breach of his duties as agent (see **Chapter 7**).

As we have noted, P's consent need not be contractual, but most commercial agency relationships are likely to be based on contract. There are no formal requirements for the appointment of an agent, though if A is appointed to execute a deed, he must be appointed by a special type of deed, known as a power of attorney.

Furthermore:

...actual authority can be express or implied. It is express when it is given by words such as when a board of directors pass a resolution which authorises two of their number to sign cheques. It is implied when it is inferred from the conduct of the parties and the circumstances of the case, such as when a board of directors appoint one of their number to be managing director. They thereby impliedly authorise him to do all such things as fall within the usual scope of that office (*Hely-Hutchinson* v *Brayhead Ltd* [1968] 1 QB 549 at 583).

5.3.1 Express actual authority

A's express actual authority depends on the express words used by P, whether oral or written. Proof of the scope of A's express actual authority is therefore a matter of evidence of the words used and construction of those words as a matter of law.

5.3.2 Implied actual authority

The scope of A's express actual authority may be broadened by implication. In the case of a written agency agreement the normal principles of construction of written documents allow the implication of additional authority from the express words used, the usage of the trade or the course of business between the parties.

EXAMPLE

A is 'instructed to run a car sales business for four weeks'. He would impliedly have authority to do all acts necessary in order to run the business for that period. In order to determine the extent of his implied authority a court would seek to give effect to the intentions of the parties and ask (i) if this person had acted in this capacity previously and, if so, what powers he had then and (ii) what is normal in the car trade. A might thus be impliedly authorised to sell cars, buy cars, pay wages, and incur expenses in the day to day running of the business (note the four week period only), but not, for example to incur major capital expenditure, to raise finance by using the business as security, or to sell the business. None of these powers was expressly granted to A by P.

5.3.2.1   Implied incidental authority

A court will imply authority in order to give effect to the agency agreement, so that every agent has implied authority to do everything necessary for, and ordinarily incidental to, carrying out his express authority. The scope of A's implied actual authority will therefore depend on what he is expressly authorised to do.

EXAMPLE 1

An agent authorised to find a purchaser for property has implied authority to describe the property to prospective purchasers (*Mullens* v *Miller* (1882) 22 Ch D 194).

EXAMPLE 2

An agent authorised to find a purchaser and conclude a contract does not have implied authority to receive the purchase money (*Mynn* v *Joliffe* (1834) 1 Mood & R 326).

EXAMPLE 3

An agent authorised to receive payment of money has no authority to accept payment in any other form or under any other arrangement (*Pearson* v *Scott* (1878) 9 Ch D 198).

EXAMPLE 4

An agent instructed to *sell* a house and to be paid commission on the purchase price, has implied authority to make a binding contract and to sign an agreement of sale (*Rosenbaum* v *Belson* [1900] 2 Ch 267).

EXAMPLE 5

An agent instructed to *find a purchaser* but not to sell does not have any implied authority to conclude a contract of sale (*Hamer* v *Sharp* (1874) LR 19 Eq 108).

5.3.2.2   Implied usual/customary authority

In other cases an agent may have implied authority to do what is usual or customary for an agent in his particular trade or profession. Thus, for instance, cases have considered the 'usual' authority of solicitors, estate agents, company directors and secretaries and ship's captains, amongst others. 'Usual' and 'customary' authority are considered further below (see **5.5**).

5.4 Apparent authority

Whereas actual authority is based on an agreement between P and A, to which T is an outsider, apparent authority is based on a representation from P to T which does not directly concern A. Apparent authority is thus said to be based on estoppel: if P makes a representation to T that A has authority and T relies on it, P is estopped from later denying that statement. Otherwise, T would be burdened with constantly having to confirm A's authority before dealing with him.

A may therefore have 'apparent authority' to do things which he is not actually authorised to do; however, his actual and apparent authority may often coincide when A *appears* to have the authority he *actually* does have.

5.4.1 Requirements for apparent authority

The leading case of *Freeman & Lockyer* v *Buckhurst Park Properties (Mangal) Ltd* [1964] 1 All ER 630 set out three requirements which must be fulfilled before P can be bound by A's apparent authority:

(a) there must be a representation that A has authority;

(b) that representation must come from someone with authority to make that representation, usually, though not always, P; and,

(c) that representation must be relied upon by T.

If these requirements are fulfilled P will be bound by A's actions even though he did not actually authorise them. The law favours T by allowing him to rely on appearances: this facilitates commerce in general and, specifically, the ease with which transactions can be completed. However, T can only rely on appearances where they have been, in some way, created or corroborated by P.

5.4.1.1 Representation

The representation that A has authority can be express or implied.

Express representation   In *Summers* v *Saloman* (1857) 7 El & Bl 879 the defendant employed his nephew to run his jewellery shop. As part of his functions the nephew often placed orders for jewellery for which the defendant then paid. The nephew left the defendant's employ, thus terminating the agency, but no notice of this was given to the plaintiffs. The nephew obtained more jewellery from the plaintiffs in the defendant's name and fled. The plaintiffs' claim against the defendant for the price succeeded. While the nephew had *actual* authority only when in his uncle's employ, the *representation* that he had general authority continued even after termination of the agency until third parties were given notice to the contrary. According to Crompton J:

As soon as you have given the agent authority to pledge your credit, you render yourself liable to parties who have acted upon notice of such authority until you find the means of giving them notice that the authority is determined.

On termination of an agency P should therefore notify persons who have done business with A that A no longer has authority to act on his behalf.

Implied representation   The representation can also be implied from previous dealings or from conduct. For instance, by placing A in a position, and allowing him to act in a manner consistent with that position, P represents to the world that A has the authority which an agent in that position usually has. For instance, if A is allowed to act as a managing director of a company even though he is never *actually* appointed he may have apparent authority to do what a managing director usually does (*Freeman & Lockyer* v *Buckhurst Park Properties*). Similarly, if A is actually appointed managing director he may have apparent authority to do all things which a managing director is usually authorised to do, even if his actual authority is limited by the principal. So also by honouring orders placed with a supplier by an employee a business may impliedly represent that the employee has authority to place such orders and be estopped from denying such authority in relation to future orders (see *Pharmed Medicare Private Ltd* v *Univar Ltd* [2002] EWCA Civ 1569; [2003] 1 All ER (Comm) 321).

5.4.1.2 By whom?

The representation must be made by someone with authority to make it, usually P. In *Freeman and Lockyer* v *Buckhurst Park Properties* it was the board of directors, which had actual authority to act on behalf of the company, which made the representation, by allowing the director to act as *de facto* managing director.

An agent usually cannot make representations about his own authority except, possibly, where he has actual or apparent authority to make such representations (see *The Rafaella* [1985] 2 Lloyd's Rep 36). Such cases will be rare. When A acts in a way which is usual for an agent in his position recent cases suggest that T can assume that A does have the authority that he appears to have (*First Energy Ltd* v *Hungarian International Bank Ltd* [1993] 2 Lloyd's Rep 194). Where T deals with A in a transaction which is not usual for an agent in A's position, T will not normally be able to rely on A's own assertion that he has received actual authority to enter into the particular transaction since T cannot claim that A has apparent authority to claim authority (see *Armagas Ltd* v *Mundogas Ltd* [1985] 1 Lloyd's Rep 1; [1986] 2 All ER 385). In such a situation the third party should seek confirmation of the agent's authority from the principal or someone who is authorised to manage the principal's business.

A senior manager might have authority (actual or apparent) to make statements about the running of a business, including statements about the authority of agents including himself (*First Energy Hungarian International Bank Ltd* [1993] 2 Lloyd's Rep 194).

5.4.1.3 Reliance

T must rely on the representation that A has authority and change his position as a result. Entering into a contract with A will be sufficient change of position; it seems that there is no further requirement of 'detriment'. T must therefore know of the representation: constructive notice is insufficient (*Rama Corpn* v *Proved Tin and General Investment Ltd* [1955] 2 QB 147).

T cannot claim to have relied on the representation if he knows the representation to be false. In certain circumstances the court may find that T ought to be aware of A's lack of authority. In *Overbrooke Estates Ltd* v *Glencombe Properties Ltd* [1974] 3 All ER 511, T purchased property at an auction having relied on the auctioneer's statement which proved false. T alleged that P was liable for the statement on the basis of apparent authority, but failed. The auction particulars stated that the auctioneer had no authority to make such statements and T therefore could not claim to rely on any representation that he had authority.

There may be a duty on T to enquire as to the extent of A's authority if A is acting in a manner which would be unusual for an agent in A's position (*British Bank of the Middle East* v *Sun Life Assurance* [1983] 2 Lloyd's Rep 9).

5.5   Usual/customary authority

Usual and customary authority are similar concepts. In most cases they are really types of actual or apparent authority. However, there is some support for the existence of a separate category of usual authority, distinct from both actual and apparent authority.

5.5.1   Usual authority

If A is appointed to a position he may impliedly have the authority which any agent in that position usually has; if his authority is expressly limited, so that it is less than an agent in that position would usually have, he may nevertheless have apparent authority to do what such agents may usually do, and third parties who are unaware of the limitation may rely on the appearance of authority.

EXAMPLE

A is appointed to act as company secretary to company P but is expressly told that he may not enter into any contract without the approval of the company's chief executive. A enters into a contract with T, who is unaware of the limitation on A's authority, for the supply to the business of a photo-copier. P is bound by the contract, notwithstanding the limitation on A's authority, if it is within the usual authority of a company secretary, because A appears to have that authority.

Deciding what is usual for an agent in a particular position is a matter for evidence. For instance, in *Panorama Developments (Guildford) Ltd* v *Fidelis Furnishing Fabrics Ltd* [1971] 2 QB 711, it was stated that a company secretary would have usual authority to sign contracts 'dealing with the administrative side of [the] company's affairs', and on the facts it was held that a company secretary had actual implied usual authority to hire cars on behalf of the company.

5.5.2   Customary authority

A may also, impliedly or apparently, be authorised to do what is customary for agents in his particular trade. Such customary authority is a variety of usual authority and may be particularly important in the context of commercial transactions where particular markets, for instance certain commodity markets, may have settled customs and practices.

A custom will only be recognised if it is certain, notorious and reasonable.

5.5.3   Relationship between implied, apparent and usual authority

Where A is appointed to a position the scope of his actual authority depends on what he is expressly instructed to do and what is usual for an agent in that position. If no limitations are imposed by P on his authority he may be held impliedly to have actual authority to do everything which an agent in his position is usually authorised to do. He may be said to have the *usual* authority of an agent in his position but his authority is *actual*. Thus if he acts in a way which is usual for an agent in his position he binds P and acts in accordance with his duty as P's agent.

Even if express limitations are placed on A's *actual* authority, he may nevertheless appear to outsiders to have the authority which an agent in his position usually has. He may be said to have the *usual* authority of an agent in his position, but his authority is now only *apparent*. Thus if he acts in a way which is usual for an agent in his position he will bind his principal but be liable to him for exceeding his actual authority.

Thus both *actual* and *apparent* authority can be described as *usual*. Moreover, in the first situation A will *appear* to have the authority which he *actually* has. This can cause confusion, as is illustrated by the decision in *Hely-Hutchinson* v *Brayhead Ltd* [1968] 1 QB 549. A was appointed chairman of Brayhead Ltd. He also, with the acquiescence of the board of directors, acted as *de facto* managing director of the company. As part of a corporate financing deal A gave an indemnity, on behalf of Brayhead, to the plaintiff, T. T sought to enforce the indemnity against Brayhead. The crucial issue was whether A had authority to give the indemnity so as to bind Brayhead. It was argued that A had both implied and apparent authority. Roskill J at first instance refused to hold that A had implied authority to give an indemnity merely by virtue of being appointed chairman of Brayhead; however, he had apparent authority because he was allowed to act as and appear to be managing director. The Court of Appeal, however, held that he had actual authority, not by virtue of his appointment as chairman, because a company chairman would not usually have authority to enter into such a contract, but because by allowing him to act as if he were managing director the board of directors (acting on behalf of the company) had impliedly authorised A to do such things as a managing director would usually do.

Since T generally has no knowledge of the arrangements between P and A he will generally rely on A's apparent authority.

5.5.4 A separate head of usual authority?

There is some authority that there may be a separate category of 'usual' authority which is neither actual nor apparent, so that where A is appointed to a position any acts he does which would be usual for a person in that position are binding on P.

In *Watteau* v *Fenwick* [1893] 1 QB 346, A was appointed to manage a public house, which he had previously owned. His name was still over the door as licensee. P expressly limited his actual authority by forbidding him to purchase anything other than bottled beer and mineral water. In defiance of that prohibition he bought cigars. P was held liable for their price.

Clearly, A did not have actual authority. Nor could this be a case of apparent authority as T believed A to be owner of the business and was not aware of P, and so could not rely on a representation made by P. The correct basis of this decision is therefore unclear and various explanations have been offered; one is that an agent appointed to a position has power to bind his principal by doing acts which would be usual for an agent in his position. The case is old and has been doubted but has not been overruled in England (but see criticism of Bingham J in *The Rhodian River* [1984] 1 Lloyd's Rep 373) and could be significant. It suggests that where a proprietor appoints a manager to run a business on his behalf he may be bound by any acts of the manager which would be normal for a manager, or even a proprietor, of such a business, even though they have been expressly prohibited. In order to avoid this outcome the proprietor should ensure that third parties who deal with the business, such as suppliers and customers, are aware that he is the proprietor of the business, and of the scope of the manager's authority.

5.6 Ratification

Where A, purporting to act on P's behalf, enters into a transaction without P's actual prior authority, P can retrospectively approve A's actions and adopt the transaction. P is then said to ratify A's actions and the result is as if A had, at all relevant times, acted with authority. This process of ratification can occur when A acts without authority because he is not P's agent at all or when A merely exceeds his authority.

5.6.1 Requirements for ratification

P can only ratify A's actions if the following conditions are met.

(a) A must have purported to be acting for a principal. An undisclosed principal can therefore never ratify a contract: *Keighley, Maxstead & Co.* v *Durant* [1901] AC 240.

(b) P must have been in existence, competent and capable of being ascertained at the time when A purported to act on his behalf.

Thus if the promoters of a company make a contract on behalf of the company prior to its incorporation, the company cannot later ratify (*Kelner* v *Baxter* (1866) LR 2 CP 174). The promoters are personally liable on, and entitled to enforce, the contract, subject to any agreement to the contrary (Companies Act 1983, s. 36C; see *Braymist Ltd* v *Wise Finance Co. Ltd* [2002] EWCA Civ 127; [2002] 2 All ER 333). Where such a 'pre-incorporation contract' is made the parties should, after incorporation, enter into a novation arrangement by which the promoters are released from liability and the company takes over the contract (see **2.5.1.3**).

P is 'ascertainable' even if not expressly named provided that T is given sufficient information to enable him to identify P.

One consequence of this rule is that if a contractor enters into a contract, such as a building or engineering contract, intending to sub-contract some of the work, sub-contractors appointed after conclusion of the main contract cannot ratify the contract so as to take advantage of exclusion clauses in the main contract, even if they were intended to have the benefit of them. In *Southern Water Authority* v *Carey* [1985] 2 All ER 1077, a contractor entered into a contract which contained exclusion clauses which also purported to protect sub-contractors. When the employer sued one of the sub-contractors in tort the sub-contractor was unable to claim the benefit of the exclusion clauses because:

(i)   they were not party to the main contract;

(ii) they had not authorised the main contractors to act on their behalf; and

(iii) being unascertainable to the employer at the time the contract was made, they could not later ratify the contract.

The outcome of this case might now be different as a result of the Contracts (Rights of Third Parties) Act 1999, which would allow the sub-contractors to take the benefit of the exclusion clauses provided that the main contract either (a) expressly provided that they may enforce the contract or (b) on its proper construction showed that the parties intended the sub-contractors to be able to enforce the exclusion clauses (see **2.7**). However, in the absence of an express provision as to enforceability the application of the 1999 Act is uncertain. Moreover the 1999 Act only allows a third party beneficiary to take the benefit of the contract. He is not bound by it. In contrast a person who ratifies a contract made in his name becomes fully a party to it. In cases of doubt it may therefore be preferable to arrange for a novation of the contract to make the intended third party beneficiaries (such as the sub-contractors in *Carey*) full parties to the contract.

Again the problem can be overcome by a novation of the contract by all the parties.

(c) P can ratify acts which are both lawful and unlawful but cannot ratify a nullity. Thus it has been said that P cannot ratify a forged signature on a cheque (*Brook* v *Hook*

(1871) LR 6 Ex 89), but can ratify the unauthorised issue of a writ (*Presentaciones Musicales SA* v *Secunda* [1994] 2 All ER 737).

(d) P must ratify within a reasonable time. Generally P cannot ratify a contract after the time for its performance or the commencement of performance has arrived (*Metropolitan Asylums Board (Managers)* v *Kingham* (1890) 6 TLR 217) except, perhaps, where such ratification benefits T (*Bedford Insurance Co. Ltd* v *Instituto de Resseguros do Brasil* [1985] QB 966).

(e) P cannot ratify unless he has full knowledge of all relevant circumstances.

5.6.2 The effect of ratification

The effect of ratification is that A is retrospectively deemed to have had authority, so that:

(a) P can sue, or be sued by, T on the contract made by A;

(b) any liability A may have had to T for breach of warranty of authority is extinguished (see **6.5.2.2**);

(c) A cannot be held liable to P for exceeding his authority; and

(d) A is entitled to remuneration on the contract and to be indemnified against any expenses incurred by him (see **7.3.1.1** and **7.3.1.2**).

The anomalous effect of ratification is illustrated by the case of *Bolton Partners* v *Lambert* (1889) 41 Ch D 295, where it was held that if T makes an offer to A which A, without authority, accepts on P's behalf but P later ratifies the contract, T is bound by the contract even if he has purported to withdraw his offer *before* ratification.

5.6.3 Methods of ratification

Ratification can be express or implied. P may be taken to have ratified if he does any act which indicates an intention to adopt the contract. Indeed, he may also be bound (on the basis of estoppel) if he passively agrees to acts done on his behalf (*Spiro* v *Lintern* [1973] 3 All ER 319).

5.6.4 Limitations on ratification

If T contracts with an agent whom he knows to be acting without authority there are a number of steps which T may take to protect himself against the harshness of ratification and its retrospective effect.

(a) T may agree with A that the contract is conditional on ratification, so that P is required to ratify within a reasonable time.

(b) T may stipulate a time within which P must ratify.

(c) If T agrees with A to terminate the contract before it is ratified, this should be done on the basis that any later ratification will be ineffective.

5.7 Agency of necessity

According to *Bowstead on Agency*, 16th edn, Art. 35:

A person may have authority to act on behalf of another in certain cases where he is faced with an emergency in which the property or interests of that other person are in imminent jeopardy and it becomes necessary, in order to preserve the property or interests, so to act.

Agency of necessity can operate to extend an agent's authority or to give authority to someone not already an agent. Its application is particularly important in the context of the carriage of goods by sea (*Prager* v *Blatspiel, Stamp and Heacock Ltd* [1924] 1 KB 566; *Jebara* v *Ottoman Bank* [1927] 2 KB 254) where it has been held to give a ship's master further authority to deal with the vessel or its cargo in emergencies. For instance, a master may jettison some cargo to preserve a ship and its remaining cargo (*The Gratitudine* (1801) 3 C Rob 240); he may sell part or whole of the vessel to pay for repairs to the vessel (*Gunn* v *Roberts* (1874) LR 9 CP 331); and he may incur expenses in order to preserve the cargo (*Notora* v *Henderson* (1872) LR 7 QB 225).

5.7.1   Requirements for agency of necessity

There are four preconditions for agency of necessity to arise:

(a) it must be shown that A could not get instructions from P;

(b) A must have acted in P's interests and *bona fide*;

(c) A's actions must be reasonable; and

(d) there must have been some necessity or emergency which caused A to act as he did.

Developments in modern communications mean that the first requirement will rarely be satisfied (see *The Choko Star* [1989] 2 Lloyd's Rep 42; and *Surrey Breakdown Ltd* v *Knight* [1999] RTR 84).

5.7.2   Effects of agency of necessity

Where the requirements for creation of agency of necessity are fulfilled, two consequences follow.

(a) A has power to bind P to transactions entered into with third parties: for instance, A might contract with T on P's behalf for T to warehouse P's goods; P will be bound by (and entitled to enforce) the contract with T.

(b) The relationship of principal and agent is constituted between P and A even if it did not already exist, so that A is entitled to the rights of an agent (see **7.3**). Thus, for instance, if in an emergency A pays T to warehouse P's goods, A can claim an indemnity from P to cover that payment.

5.8 Summary

At the end of this chapter you should:

- be aware of the different bases on which an agent may have power to bind their principal;

- be familiar with the pre-requisites for these different types of power; and

- be able to identify, in a particular factual situation, what, if any, types of power(s) may exist and accordingly whether P is bound by A's actions.

Effects of agency

6.1 Introduction

In this chapter we concentrate on the effects of agency, for P, A and T. The effects depend largely on the nature and extent of A's authority and power to act on P's behalf. In particular:

- we identify and distinguish disclosed and undisclosed agencies;
- we outline the effects of a disclosed agency;
- we examine the consequences of an undisclosed agency;
- we consider the effects of settlements with agents; and
- lastly, we examine the issue of agent liability, both contractual and personal.

As already stated, the basic rule is that where A concludes a contract with T within the scope of his authority, privity of contract is established between P and T.

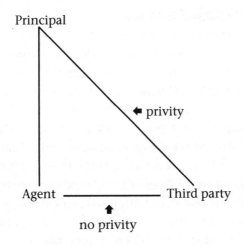

There are however refinements to this rule depending on whether the agency is *disclosed* or *undisclosed*.

6.1.1 Disclosed and undisclosed agency

(a) If T is aware that A is an agent, and hence acting on behalf of someone else, there is a *disclosed agency*.

(b) If T believes that A is acting on his own behalf, and not for any other person, there is an *undisclosed agency*.

If the agency is disclosed it is of no legal significance that P is not *named*.

The disclosed/undisclosed distinction is important as it affects:

(a) P's ability to ratify A's actions (see **5.6.1**); and

(b) A's liability to T.

6.2 Disclosed agency

Where A, with P's actual authority, concludes a contract on P's behalf with T and the agency is disclosed, a direct contractual relationship is created between P and T, and each party can sue the other on the contract.

If A acts without P's actual authority P can ratify his actions provided that A purported to act on his behalf; therefore only a disclosed principal can ratify an unauthorised contract.

If A concludes a contract outside his actual but within his apparent authority P will be bound by but cannot enforce the contract: as apparent authority is based on a form of estoppel it can be used only as 'a shield and not a sword'. Since it depends on a representation by P that A has authority, apparent authority can only arise where the (purported) agency is disclosed; P could, of course, therefore ratify A's unauthorised actions if he wished to enforce the contract made by A.

If A concludes a contract without, but claiming to have, P's authority, T can enforce the contract against P if the conditions for A having apparent authority are fulfilled. T may also hold A personally liable in tort or for breach of warranty of authority (see **6.5.2.1** and **6.5.2.2**).

6.3 Undisclosed agency

It is not uncommon for a person to make a contract and then, when faced with legal action on the contract, to claim that he acted as agent for another. In such a case the other contracting party will have to investigate the facts in order to try and discover if the claim to have acted as agent is true. If A contracts with T without disclosing that he is acting as agent for P, so that the agency is undisclosed, the contract is initially between A and T and each may enforce the contract against the other. However, if T discovers P's existence, he may enforce the contract against either A or P; moreover, provided that A acted with his actual authority, P can intervene and enforce the contract against T.

The rule that the undisclosed principal may intervene and enforce the contract has often been described as anomalous but is best explained in terms of commercial convenience. In addition, the doctrine prevents circuity of action; otherwise P could require A to lend his name to enforce the contract against T, and P would have to indemnify A for any liabilities he incurs towards T.

6.3.1 T's right of election

Even where P's existence is discovered, A remains liable on the contract and T may choose to enforce it against *either* P or A, but not both. Once T elects to sue one party, his option to sue the other is extinguished. It seems that T will not be bound by an election unless he has unequivocally indicated his intention to hold one liable and release the other. In *Clarkson, Booker Ltd* v *Andjel* [1964] 3 All ER 260, A had failed to pay for airline tickets which he had purchased from T on behalf of an undisclosed P. Having discovered the existence of P, T wrote to both P and A requesting payment, and then served a writ on P. However, P was insolvent and T therefore sought payment from A. The Court of Appeal, while stating that this was a borderline case, found that serving a writ did not amount to an unequivocal election: T had never withdrawn the threat to sue A and was therefore free to pursue the action against A.

If P denies that A was acting on his behalf, T faces a dilemma. He cannot know if P's claim is true since that depends on A's actual authority and thus on arrangements between P and A to which T was not privy. He should therefore threaten and, if necessary, commence proceedings against both as co-defendants, for if he does any act which may be construed as electing to sue one and not the other he may be bound by that election.

6.3.2 Limitations on P's right to intervene

The undisclosed principal's right to intervene on and enforce the contract made on his behalf, is limited in several situations.

6.3.2.1 Capacity

An undisclosed P can only intervene if he was in existence and had the legal capacity to make the contract at the time it was made. This rule mainly affects pre-incorporation contracts made on behalf of companies.

6.3.2.2 A had actual authority

P can only intervene if A had actual authority to conclude the contract. An undisclosed principal can never ratify a contract made without his prior consent.

6.3.2.3 The contract does not exclude P's intervention

P cannot intervene if such intervention is prohibited by the contract, either expressly or impliedly.

P will be impliedly prohibited from intervening if the language of the contract implies that no-one other than A is interested in it. However, it is not clear what language has this effect. Case law suggests that where the contract relates to property and describes A as having a proprietary interest in the property, A may be taken impliedly to have undertaken that no-one else is interested in the contract so that P will be excluded; but language describing A as contracting party will not exclude P's intervention (see per Viscount Haldane in *F Drughorn Ltd* v *Rederiaktiebolaget Trans-Atlantic* [1919] AC 203). Thus P was excluded where A signed a contract to charter a ship as '*owner* of the good ship or vessel called *Anne*' (*Humble* v *Hunter* (1848) 12 QB 310) and where A described himself as 'owner' or 'proprietor' of property (*Formby Bros* v *Formby* (1910) 102 LT 116) but not where T executed a lease as 'tenant' (*Danziger* v *Thompson* [1944] KB 654 at 657 *per* Lawrence J) or 'landlord' (*Epps* v *Rothnie* [1945] KB 562) or a contract of insurance as 'proposer' (*Siu Yin Kwan* v *Eastern Insurance Co. Ltd* [1994] 1 All ER 213).

6.3.2.4 Personal selection of A

P cannot intervene if T contracted with A for personal reasons, for example, where it is clear that T intended to contract only with A, for instance due to some personal skill or solvency of A. Thus if T employs A to paint a picture this contract cannot be performed other than by A. In *Greer* v *Downs Supply Co.* [1927] 2 KB 28, T contracted with A so that he could set-off a debt owed to him by A and the Court of Appeal refused to allow P to intervene (although if P had intervened he would have done so subject to the right of set-off available against A (see **6.3.3**)). It has been held that a contract of insurance is not such a personal contract as to prevent the intervention of an undisclosed proposer (*Sin Yiu Kwan* v *Eastern Insurance Co. Ltd* [1994] 1 All ER 213).

6.3.2.5   Personal opposition to P

In some cases it has been said that P cannot intervene where T has personal reasons for not contracting with him (see e.g. *Said* v *Butt* [1920] 3 KB 497 where a theatre critic denied a ticket for a first night could not buy a ticket through an undisclosed agent). However, it is clear that this rule can only apply where there is a 'striking personal element' to the contract; it is unlikely to apply in the context of ordinary commercial transactions. In *Dyster* v *Randall & Sons* [1926] Ch 932, the plaintiff, knowing that the defendant would not sell certain property to him, engaged A to conclude a contract, without disclosing his interest in the matter. The defendant unsuccessfully resisted the plaintiff's attempt to enforce the contract. The court held that this was not a personal contract and so the identity of P was not material. A could, in any case, have enforced the contract in his own name and re-sold the property to P.

6.3.2.6   Misrepresentation by A

If A positively misrepresents the identity of P, for instance by expressly denying P's interest in the contract, the contract is voidable for misrepresentation and neither P nor A may be able to enforce it.

6.3.3   P enforces on the same terms as a would have done

If an undisclosed principal does intervene he generally does so on the same terms on which the agent could have enforced the contract, so that a third party can raise any defences against P which he would have had against A. These may include purely personal defences, such as rights of set-off available against A (*Cooke & Sons* v *Eshelby* (1887) 12 App Cas 271).

6.4   Settlement

Where an agent is employed to negotiate a contract the question of the effect of either party paying the agent may arise. This is likely to be important where the agent has received payment from P or T but has failed to hand it over to the intended recipient. Although privity of contract is between P and T, there are instances where settlement by either party with A can discharge his liability to the other party. If it does not do so, the payer must pay a second time.

6.4.1   Settlement by T with A

Payment by T to A will discharge T's liability to P if the agency is undisclosed.

If at the time of payment T is aware of P's existence (whether the agency was initially disclosed or undisclosed) such a payment will only discharge him of liability if A is authorised to receive payment.

6.4.2   Payments by P to A

Where money is payable by P to T it may be paid through A but P's liability will only be discharged if T's conduct induced him to settle with A, for instance, because T gave P a receipt showing that he had already been paid by A (*Heald* v *Kenworthy* (1855) 10 Ex 739).

6.5 The agent's liability

Despite the general rule that where A concludes a contract on behalf of P, the contract is between P and T, A may be liable:

(a) on the contract; or

(b) personally; either

    (i)   in tort; or

    (ii) under a collateral 'warranty of authority'.

6.5.1 Agent is liable on the contract

A is liable on the contract in the following circumstances.

6.5.1.1 A is party to the contract

Where on its proper construction A is a party to the contract, for instance, where A contracts on behalf of himself and P. Where A executes a contract in his own name he should use clear words to make clear that he is acting in a representative capacity and not undertaking personal liability. Merely signing 'A, agent' may not be enough.

6.5.1.2 Deeds

If A executes a deed in his own name other than under a power of attorney he is personally liable on the deed. A deed executed under a power of attorney should recite that fact.

6.5.1.3 Bills of exchange

If A signs a bill of exchange or cheque in his own name he will become liable on the contract in the bill unless his signature makes clear that he is acting in a representative capacity (**22.2.7.2**).

6.5.1.4 Custom

In some markets there may be a custom that an agent is personally liable on the contracts he makes, especially if he does not name his principal.

6.5.1.5 Agent acting on own behalf

There is some authority that a person who has purported to enter into a contract as an agent but who in fact is acting on his own behalf may be held liable on and enforce the contract.

6.5.1.6 Collateral contract

Where the agent enters into a collateral contract he may be liable on that. An example is the obligation undertaken by a confirming house which confirms an order placed on behalf of its overseas principal (see **4.3.5**).

6.5.1.7 Undisclosed agency

In cases of undisclosed agency T may elect whether to enforce the contract against A or P. A may enforce the contract if P does not do so (see **6.3**).

6.5.2 A's personal liability

Where A purports to have authority to act on P's behalf but in fact is unauthorised we have seen (**5.4**) that A's claim will not normally give him apparent authority. However, it may make him liable to T either in tort or for breach of warranty of authority.

6.5.2.1 Tortious liability

If A can be shown to have acted fraudulently, knowing that he had no authority, he is liable to T in the tort of deceit. Alternatively he may be liable in negligence, under the ruling in *Hedley Byrne & Co. Ltd* v *Heller & Partners Ltd* [1964] AC 465, if it can be shown that he was negligent in claiming to have P's authority. In either case T may claim damages from A on a *tortious* basis; they will seek to restore T to the position he was in before he entered the supposed contract with P.

6.5.2.2 Warranty of authority

A will also be liable if he falsely claims P's authority even though his claim is wholly innocent. In contracting on behalf of P, A is taken impliedly to warrant that he does have P's authority; if he has no such authority A can then be sued for breach of warranty of authority. A's warranty of authority is viewed as being collateral to the main contract; T provides consideration for it by entering into the (supposed) main contract with P. Since A's liability is contractual it is strict; thus in *Yonge* v *Toynbee* [1910] 1 KB 215 solicitors were instructed by their client to defend an action. Unknown to them the agency was terminated due to their client's insanity; nevertheless they continued to act on his behalf and were held liable for breach of warranty of authority.

Damages for breach of warranty of authority are awarded to put T in the same position as if the warranty had been true and are assessed under the normal common law rules as set out in *Hadley* v *Baxendale* (1854) 9 Ex 341. They will therefore seek to put T in the same position as if he had had a contract with P and will thus be limited to the amount which could be obtained from P. So, if P is bankrupt, T's damages against A are limited to the amount which could be recovered from P by way of dividend in the bankruptcy.

In order to sue A for breach of warranty of authority T must establish:

(a) that A was purporting to act as an agent (if A was acting on his own behalf, or for an undisclosed P, A is personally liable to T anyway);

(b) that A lacked authority;

(c) that A expressed no doubts about his authority which would put T on notice to enquire further; and,

(d) that T did rely on A's representation of authority.

Since liability for breach of warranty of authority is strict, T will generally prefer to hold A liable on this basis, rather than in tort, unless the damages recoverable in tort are more favourable to him.

Where there is any doubt about A's authority T will probably seek to pursue P (on the supposed contract, on the grounds that A had actual or apparent authority) and T (for breach of warranty of authority) in the alternative.

6.6 Summary

Having concluded the chapter, you should now:

- be able to distinguish a disclosed agency from an undisclosed agency;
- understand the consequences of a disclosed agency;
- with regard to an undisclosed agency, be aware of the circumstances when—
  - an undisclosed principal can be held liable on a contract concluded by their agent, and
  - an undisclosed principal can enforce a contract concluded by their agent;
- be able to identify the circumstances in which T can discharge liability by settling with A;
- be aware of the circumstances in which A may be liable, either on the contract or personally.

The relationship between principal and agent

7.1 Introduction

In the previous chapter we examined the external effects of agency. In this chapter we consider the internal relationship between principal and agent, and in particular the duties imposed on the parties as a matter of law.

As we noted earlier, an agency relationship is consensual but need not be contractual. However, even where A agrees to act gratuitously the relationship of principal and agent, giving rise to mutual rights and duties, will still arise.

In particular the agency relationship is regarded at common law as a fiduciary one under which the agent is subject to strict fiduciary duties. However, a special category of commercial agent is now recognised by statute. *Commercial agents* enjoy special rights against their principals. In this chapter we therefore examine:

- the rights and duties of agents and principals at common law;
- the meaning of 'commercial agent';
- the special rights and duties of commercial agents and their principals;
- the drafting of agency and commercial agency agreements in the light of the above.

7.1.1 Regulation of the agency relationship

The primary source of the parties' rights and obligations is their agreement. However, the common law gives an agent certain rights and imposes on him extensive duties because of the fiduciary nature of the agency relationship. In addition, many agency agreements will now be subject to the Commercial Agents (Council Directive) Regulations 1993 (SI 1993, No. 3053 as amended by SI 1993, No. 3173 and SI 1998, No. 2868) which partly codify and partly modify the common law. The Regulations were passed to implement a European Directive (86/653) and similar provisions apply in other Member States of the EC. They came into force on 1 January 1994 and apply both to agreements entered into after their commencement and to existing agreements which must be amended to correspond with them. Their main impact is to give agents more extensive rights than they enjoy at common law. However, although the Regulations apply to many important commercial agency arrangements, they do not apply to all agencies and it is therefore necessary to consider the common law rules applicable to agency alongside the Regulations.

The 1993 Regulations apply (a) to the agent's activities in Great Britain where the contract is governed by the law of any part of the United Kingdom, and (b) where the agent acts in another Member State if (i) the parties have chosen to subject their contract to the law of England and Wales or Scotland and (ii) the law of that Member State permits such a choice.

Thus when the agent's activities take place outside Great Britain the Regulations only apply if the agreement expressly incorporates them. It is not clear that the Regulations as drafted properly implement the underlying Directive. In *Ingmar GB Ltd* v *Eaton Leonard Technologies Inc* [2001] 1 All ER (Comm) 329 the ECJ held that the provisions of the Directive relating to the agent's rights on termination of the agency (Arts. 17 and 18: see **7.4.3.2**) are mandatory in nature and cannot be derogated from to the detriment of the agent (see Art. 19) and are therefore applicable wherever a commercial agent carries on activities as an agent within the territory of a Member State, even if (a) one of the parties to the contract is a national of a non-EU state and (b) the contract expressly provides for it to be governed by the law of a non-EU state. It therefore seems that the restriction of the UK Regulations' application to cases where the agency contract is governed by the law of any part of the UK is inappropriate and the mandatory provisions of the Directive, at least, should apply to all cases where the agent undertakes activities in the UK unless the contract is subjected to the law of another EU Member State. However, some of the Directive's provisions are non-mandatory in nature and may be derogated from by the parties. The result would therefore seem to be that where an agent undertakes activities within the EU under an agency contract expressed to be subject to the law of a non-EU state the agency is nevertheless subject to the mandatory provisions of the Directive, but in relation to other matters, including those covered by non-mandatory provisions of the Directive, is governed by the chosen law of the contract.

A 'commercial agent' is a self-employed agent with continuing authority to negotiate the sale or purchase of goods on behalf of the principal, or to negotiate and conclude such transactions on behalf of the principal and in his name. There must be a direct agency relationship between principal and agent. Thus where P employs an agent who recruits sub-agents to negotiate sales of P's goods to customers, the sub-agents will not be commercial agents of P (*Light* v *Ty Europe Ltd* [2003] EWCA 1238; [2003] Eu L 858). To be protected by the Regulations the 'agent' must be acting as an agent in law, negotiating and/or concluding contracts on behalf of his principal. The Regulations thus do not apply where a person negotiates contracts for the supply of a manufacturer's products and then purchases goods and resells them on his own behalf in order to fulfil the contracts (*AMB Imballaggi Plastici SRL* v *Pacflex* [1999] 2 All ER (Comm) 249, CA). They therefore do not apply to other distribution arrangements, such as distributorship or franchising, nor to agents acting in one-off transactions, nor to agents dealing in services. They also include a list of exceptions, which includes:

(a) company directors, partners and insolvency practitioners;

(b) agents operating on commodity exchanges or markets; and

(c) persons whose activities as commercial agents are secondary.

7.2 Agent's duties

An agent generally stands in a fiduciary position to his principal; all agents are therefore subject to duties imposed by the general law. These may be modified where the 1993 Regulations apply.

Agents in the financial services industry are also subject to the rules of various self-regulatory bodies which police that industry, including rules designed, for instance, to avoid conflicts of interest. The relationship of such rules with the general common law rules applicable to agents and, in particular, the question whether an agent who has complied with regulatory rules may nevertheless be held to have breached his common-law duties, is unclear.

7.2.1 At common law

Agents are subject to the following duties at common law. The duties apply whether the agency is contractual or gratuitous but if the agency is contractual, the terms of the contract may modify or define the scope of the duties, although they probably cannot exclude them altogether.

7.2.1.1 To obey instructions

A must obey P's lawful instructions. Where the agency is contractual A is liable for breach of contract if he fails to perform. It is not clear if a gratuitous agent can be held liable for simple non-feasance. There can clearly be no contractual obligation to perform if the agency is non-contractual. If failure to perform were to cause loss to P, it might be that A could be held liable in tort but there is generally no duty of care in negligence to avoid causing loss by omissions as opposed to positive acts.

Whether the agency is contractual or not A will be liable for misfeasance if he acts otherwise than in accordance with his instructions, for instance, by exceeding his authority.

7.2.1.2 To exercise reasonable skill and care

All agents are required to act with reasonable skill and care, although the standard of reasonable care may be lower where the agency is gratuitous (*Chaudhry* v *Prabhakar* [1988] 3 All ER 718). This may require A to offer advice to P, including on the wisdom of any instructions given by P. When the agency is contractual, there will be concurrent duties of care in contract and tort (*Henderson* v *Merett Syndicates Ltd* [1995] 2 AC 145) but it may be possible to limit liability for breach of the duties, subject to the UCTA 1977.

7.2.1.3 To perform personally

Since A is often chosen for his personal qualities the general rule is that he must perform his duties personally and cannot delegate performance ('*delegatus non potest delegare*') unless delegation is authorised by P. Authority to delegate may be given expressly or impliedly, for instance where the parties must know because of the circumstances that A must employ a sub-agent, or where delegation is customary: for instance, provincial solicitors conducting litigation in London have customary authority to employ London agents.

Where delegation is permitted and A employs a sub-agent (S), the agency agreement must be construed in order to determine whether the relationship of principal and agent is created between P and S. Generally where delegation is authorised S will be the agent of A so that there will be no legal relationship between P and S; A will remain liable to P for performance of his duties.

7.2.1.4 To avoid conflicts of interest

A must not allow his personal interests to conflict with those of P. This duty, which applies to all fiduciaries, is strictly applied. There is a breach if, for instance, A, employed to buy property, sells his own property to P, or if A, employed to sell property, buys it for himself, unless all the circumstances are disclosed to P and P consents to the transaction.

If A commits a breach of this duty P may rescind the resulting contract. If P affirms the contract he may require A to account for any profit he makes or claim damages.

7.2.1.5 Not to make a secret profit from his position

A must account to P for all profits made from his position; he may only keep a profit if it is disclosed to P who with full knowledge consents to his retaining it. There will be a breach of this duty if, for instance:

(a) A receives a secret commission from a third party for negotiating a contract between P and T; or

(b) A receives discounts on contracts entered into for P's benefit; or

(c) A profits from the use of P's property (for instance by investing money), or information which he receives in his capacity as agent, or otherwise from his position as agent.

7.2.1.6   Not to accept a bribe

A bribe is any payment made to an agent by a third party with whom A contracts on behalf of P as an inducement to enter into the contract. It is therefore a particular species of secret profit. If A receives a bribe P may:

(a) dismiss A forthwith;

(b) withhold any commission due to A on that transaction and recover any commission already paid;

(c) rescind the contract with T;

(d) require either A or T to account for the amount of the bribe as money had and received (A holds any bribe on constructive trust for P);

(e) claim damages (in the tort of deceit) for any loss he suffers as a result of payment of the bribe and entry into te consequent contract. A and T are jointly and severally liable for such damages.

Although the position is not clear it seems that P cannot claim both damages and an account of the bribe; however, the other remedies are cumulative. In addition if it can be shown that the bribe was paid or received with a corrupt motive, T and/or A may be guilty of an offence under the Prevention of Corruption Act 1916.

7.2.1.7   To account

A must account to P for all property of P he receives in the course of the agency. He must therefore keep his own moneys and property separate from those of P unless mixing is expressly or impliedly authorised. If A wrongfully mixes his property with that of P, P may claim the whole of the mixed fund. Since the relationship between P and A is fiduciary, P may trace his property in equity and thus claim any replacement asset if A wrongfully disposes of it.

A must keep complete books of account and on termination of the agency must deliver up to P any property of P in his possession unless he is entitled to exercise a lien over it. P's right to inspect A's accounts in relation to transactions effected on P's behalf during the agency may continue after termination of the agency (see *Yasuda Fire & Marine Insurance Co. of Europe Ltd* v *Orion Marine Insurance Underwriting Agency Ltd* [1995] 3 All ER 211).

7.2.2   Duties under the 1993 Regulations

In general the 1993 Regulations merely restate A's common law duties in broad terms. They provide (reg. 3) that A must:

(a) look after the interests of his principal and act dutifully and in good faith;

(b) make proper efforts to negotiate and, where appropriate, conclude transactions P instructs him to carry out;

(c) communicate to P all necessary and available information; and

(d) comply with all reasonable instructions given by P.

The parties cannot derogate from these duties.

7.3 Rights of the agent

At common law an agent enjoys only limited rights. These are greatly enhanced where the 1993 Regulations apply. We will therefore examine the general common law before considering the impact of the Regulations.

7.3.1 At common law

The agent has three basic rights at common law: the right to remuneration; the right to an indemnity; and the right to a lien.

7.3.1.1 Remuneration

The agent is entitled to be paid in accordance with the terms of the agreement if remuneration has been agreed, either expressly or impliedly. Remuneration may be by retainer and/or commission. Where an agent is employed in circumstances in which an agent would normally be paid it may be implied that he is entitled to remuneration. Where it is agreed that A should be paid but the amount of remuneration is not agreed, A is entitled to a reasonable sum as a quantum meruit.

The agency agreement will normally set out the terms of payment; it will therefore be necessary to construe the agreement to decide when commission is earned; for instance, it may be payable on conclusion, or performance, of the contract A is instructed to negotiate.

Where a commission is payable on A bringing about a result he will only be entitled to payment if he is the effective cause of that result.

Where A is to be remunerated by commission it may be necessary to decide whether P may prevent him earning his commission, for instance by refusing to perform a contract negotiated by A. In the absence of any express provision in the agency agreement this depends on whether an appropriate term may be implied into the agency contract. Generally the courts have been reluctant to imply terms which would restrict P's right to deal with his own property. Thus in *Luxor (Eastbourne) Ltd* v *Cooper* [1941] AC 108 the House of Lords refused to imply into a contract of estate agency a term that Ps should not refuse to sell to a buyer introduced by the agents. In *French & Co.* v *Leston Shipping Co. Ltd* [1922] 1 AC 451, the House of Lords refused to imply a term which would prevent P ship-owners selling the ship during the course of a charter-party negotiated by the agent, where the effect of the sale was to deprive the agent of commission. However, in *Alpha Trading* v *Dunshaw-Patten* [1981] QB 290 where agents were employed to negotiate a contract for the sale of cement and were entitled to commission on performance of the contract, the principals broke the contract negotiated with the third party (paying damages to the third party) in order to take advantage of a rising market. It was held that this was a breach of an implied term in the agency contract so that the agents were entitled to damages equal to the amount of commission of which they had been deprived by the breach. In general it will probably be easier for such a term to be implied in a continuing contract rather than in a one-off contract. A well-drafted agency contract will seek to avoid such problems.

Where A is appointed 'sole agent' to effect a contract, P commits a breach if a second agent is appointed. If the second agent then concludes a contract, the first is entitled to damages, equal to the amount of commission of which he is deprived, for breach of that term. There is no breach in such a case if P effects the contract himself; however, if A is given 'sole right to sell' property, there is a breach if P negotiates a sale himself.

7.3.1.2 Indemnity

A is entitled to be indemnified against any expenses incurred on behalf of P in performance of his duties when acting within the scope of his authority or if his actions are later ratified. Where the agency is contractual the right to indemnity will be an implied term of the contract; where the agency is gratuitous the right will be restitutionary.

7.3.1.3 Lien

A is entitled to a lien over property, including papers, of P in his possession to secure payment of any remuneration or indemnity due to him. Most agents are entitled only to a particular lien, i.e. a right to retain property until sums related to that property or any related transaction are paid. Some agents, however, are entitled to a general lien, a right to retain any property of P to secure payment of any sums due from P, whether connected to that property or not. Factors, bankers, solicitors and stockbrokers are entitled to general liens (see **25.3.3**).

A commission agent employed to purchase goods, who therefore stands in the same position *vis-à-vis* his principal as a seller of goods, is entitled to a lien over the goods until paid by his principal (Sale of Goods Act 1979, s. 38(2); see **16.4.2.1**).

7.3.2 Rights under the 1993 Regulations

Where the Regulations apply they modify the agent's right to remuneration and give him certain additional rights. The common law rights to indemnity and lien remain.

7.3.2.1 The right to remuneration

In the absence of express agreement on the amount of remuneration payable to A, A is entitled to receive such remuneration as is customarily paid to a commercial agent dealing in the type of goods to which the agreement relates in the area in which A operates.

When A is to be remunerated wholly or partly by commission he is entitled to receive commission:

(a) on contracts concluded during the agency which result from his actions;

(b) on contracts concluded during the agency which result from repeat orders from customers introduced by A; and

(c) where A has the exclusive right to represent P in a particular area or in relation to a particular class of goods, on all contracts for such goods or from customers in that particular area.

Further provisions govern A's right to commission on contracts entered into after termination of the agency (see **7.4.3.2**).

7.3.2.2 When payable

Broadly speaking under the Regulations commission becomes payable when either P or T performs his obligations under the contract. Where P fails to perform, commission is payable when he should have performed, or when T should have performed had P not breached the contract. The result is that P cannot deprive A of commission by failing to perform the contract with T. The parties cannot vary these provisions to the prejudice of A. However, A is not entitled to commission on orders where the contract is not performed for some reason other than P's breach.

7.3.2.3 Provision of information

The Regulations require P to provide A with a detailed statement indicating the amount of commission due to him and how it is calculated. Either party may require the other to provide a written statement of the terms of the agency, including any variation.

7.4 Termination of the agreement

Since it depends on consent, the relationship between P and A can be terminated at any time by either party withdrawing consent; it may also terminate automatically in certain circumstances by operation of law. However, in certain circumstances an agency may be irrevocable; moreover, even where an agency is revocable, termination of the relationship and of A's actual authority to act for P may leave A with apparent authority and may therefore not deprive him of power to bind P by his actions (see **5.4.1.1**). In addition, as between P and A, termination of the agency may give rise to consequent rights, especially where the agency is contractual and termination amounts to a breach of contract.

Once again the general rules of the common law are modified by the 1993 Regulations. We will therefore consider the ways in which agencies may be terminated before considering the consequences of termination, taking account, where appropriate, of the impact of the Regulations.

7.4.1 Termination of agency at common law

At common law an agency, unless irrevocable, may be terminated automatically by operation of law or by the act of either or both parties.

7.4.1.1 Irrevocable agencies

In the following cases A's authority cannot be revoked either by action of P or by operation of law.

(a) Where authority is given to A in order to give him security to protect his own interest (referred to as 'a power coupled with an interest'): in such cases A really acts to protect his own position. The interest must exist at the time authority is given; A's interest in earning commission is not sufficient.

(b) Where authority is given by power of attorney, expressed to be irrevocable, and given to secure a proprietary interest of the donee or performance of an obligation owed to the donee then, so long as the interest exists or the obligation remains unfulfilled, the authority cannot be revoked without the consent of the donee (Powers of Attorney Act 1971, s. 4).

7.4.1.2 Termination by operation of law

An agency may be terminated automatically by effluxion of time, performance, frustration, or by bankruptcy or insanity of either party.

(a) *Effluxion of time*
Where an agency is expressed to be for a fixed period the relationship, and A's actual authority, are automatically determined on expiry of the agreed period.

(b) *Performance*
Where A is appointed to perform a particular task—for instance, to sell a particular piece of property—the agency is terminated on performance of the task.

(c) *Frustration*
A contractual agency may be terminated by any event which frustrates the contract (see **3.2.4**). Thus it will be terminated if performance becomes illegal or impossible, for instance, because of the death of either party, or if a change in circumstances destroys the commercial purpose of the contract.

Since the relationship is personal, death of either party will terminate the agency. Where P dies, A is deprived of both actual and apparent authority. Where one of the parties is a company the agency is similarly terminated by winding up of the company.

(d) *Bankruptcy*

P's bankruptcy terminates the agency and deprives A of authority (although there are a number of rules designed to protect A and T in respect of acts done before they have notice of the bankruptcy). A's bankruptcy will terminate the agency if it makes him unfit to continue to act.

(e) *Insanity*

The agency is automatically terminated by the insanity of either party. However, if A is appointed under an enduring power of attorney, P's insanity will not automatically terminate the agency.

Where A's authority is terminated by P's insanity, he may nevertheless continue to have apparent authority as against third parties who deal with him without knowledge of the termination (*Drew* v *Nunn* (1879) 4 QBD 661); however, there is also authority that if A continues to act he may incur personal liability for breach of warranty of authority (*Yonge* v *Toynbee* [1910] 1 KB 215).

7.4.1.3 Termination by act of the parties

Since agency is a consensual relationship it can be terminated if either party withdraws consent.

(a) *Mutual consent*

Contractual and non-contractual agencies can be determined by the agreement of both parties.

(b) *Unilateral action*

The agency relationship is terminated if either party withdraws consent to its continuance. Where A withdraws consent he is said to 'renounce' the agency; where P withdraws he is said to 'revoke' A's authority. No formality is required for a renunciation or revocation.

Revocation or renunciation is effective even if it is in breach of contract. Thus, for instance, the authority of an agent appointed for a fixed term may be revoked before expiry of the term and the revocation will be effective to terminate A's actual authority. However, A may continue to have apparent authority and revocation may give rise to liability for breach of contract. Where possible P should therefore publicise the termination of A's authority in order to draw it to the attention of those who have dealt with A in the past.

Where A is appointed for an indeterminate period the agency can be terminated in accordance with any provision in the agreement for termination by notice. In the absence of any express term it will normally be implied that the agency can be terminated by either party on reasonable notice. What is reasonable will depend on the facts of the particular case. In *Martin Baker Aircraft Co. Ltd* v *Canadian Flight Equipment Ltd* [1955] 2 QB 556 where A agreed, in return for a commission, to promote P's products and not to sell competing products, it was held that twelve months' notice was required to terminate the agency.

7.4.2 The 1993 Regulations

A commercial agency agreement governed by the 1993 Regulations can be terminated in any of the ways described above. However, in the case of termination by notice the notice required by the contract cannot be less than one month in the first year of the relationship, two months in the second and three months thereafter. The parties can agree to longer notice; in that case the notice to be given *to* A cannot be shorter than that to be given *by* A. Where A is initially appointed for a fixed term but continues to act after expiry of the term, the agency is treated as continuing for an indeterminate period.

7.4.3 Consequences of termination

Where an agency relationship is terminated in any of the ways described above it will be necessary to consider:

(a) what, if any, effect that termination has on the relationships of P and A with third parties with whom A deals; and

(b) what, if any, rights P and A have against each other as a result of the termination.

7.4.3.1 Relations with third parties

A may continue to act even after his authority has been terminated. In such a case A may incur liability to any third party with whom he deals for breach of his warranty of authority. Since liability for breach of the warranty is strict, it is irrelevant that A is unaware of the termination of his authority, for instance, where it is brought about automatically by P's insanity (*Yonge* v *Toynbee* [1910] 1 KB 215).

However, where A continues to act after termination of his authority P may also be held liable for his actions since A may continue to have apparent authority (*Drew* v *Nunn* (1879) 4 QBD 661) until T has notice that the agency has been terminated (see **5.4.1.1**).

7.4.3.2 Relations between principal and agent

Although either party may terminate the agency unilaterally by withdrawing consent to its continuance, where the agency is contractual unilateral action will not automatically terminate the contract and may give rise to liability for breach of contract.

Existing liabilities   Termination of agency, whether by operation of law or by action of one or both parties, does not affect existing liabilities. Thus, for instance, A is entitled to commission earned and to an indemnity in respect of liabilities incurred before termination of the agreement.

Rights to commission   A may be entitled to commission on contracts performed after termination of the agency where they were entered into prior to termination. In certain circumstances A may also be entitled to commission on contracts entered into after termination. This may be the case where the agreement entitles A to commission on 'repeat orders'. The issue will depend on the proper construction of the contract and a provision entitling A to commission on 'repeat orders' may be interpreted as applying to repeat orders from customers introduced by A and placed during the agency. Care must therefore be taken in drafting agency contracts in order to make clear whether A is entitled to commission in such cases.

In cases of commercial agency covered by the 1993 Regulations A is entitled to commission on contracts which result from orders placed before termination of the agency and on contracts entered into after termination which result mainly from A's efforts and which are entered into within a reasonable time of termination of the contract (reg. 8, see, e.g., *Tigana Ltd* v *Decoro Ltd* [2003] EWHC 23) L; approved, *Light* v *Ty Europe Ltd* [2003] EWCA 1238; [2003] EuLR 858.

Liability for breach of contract   Termination by either party without notice will be justified where the other party has been guilty of a serious breach of contract. In other cases termination without notice, or with less than the full notice required by the agreement will terminate A's authority but may give rise to liability for breach of contract where the agency is contractual.

Some agencies are correctly analysed as unilateral contracts; the best example is estate agency. Under such an agreement P agrees to pay A commission if he brings about a particular result, but A does not undertake to do anything. Other agreements where A is to be remunerated by commission if he brings about the sale of property may be subject to a similar analysis. Since A is not committed to any action, he may renounce his authority without liability; similarly P can without liability revoke A's authority at any time before the result is achieved; strictly such revocation by P amounts to no more than the revocation of an offer. However, in some cases it may be possible to imply a collateral agreement which restricts P's freedom to revoke, for instance, after A has begun to act and has incurred expenses or liabilities.

It seems that the general rule applies that a breach of contract by one party will not terminate the contract unless accepted by the other; thus if P revokes A's authority in breach of contract, P's action, although repudiatory, will not terminate the contract unless accepted by A. However, since agency is a personal and confidential relationship, the court will not normally order specific performance of an agency contract; nor will it grant an injunction whose effect would be specifically to enforce the contract. A will therefore normally have to pursue a remedy in damages.

Where termination of an agency contract involves a breach of contract, the innocent party may have a claim against the other for breach of contract. Normally this will be a claim against P by a dismissed agent. Where A is employed under a bilateral contract and is dismissed in breach of contract, he may claim damages in respect of the loss of the opportunity to earn commission had the contract been performed. Thus in the case of a fixed term contract damages will be calculated by reference to the commission A would have earned in the unexpired term of the contract. Where the agency is terminable by notice damages will be based on the commission A would have earned had the contractually required notice been given. The normal rules governing a claim for damages for breach of contract will apply (see **3.3.2.2**). In particular the agent will be required to take reasonable steps to mitigate his loss, e.g. by seeking an alternative agency.

Where A is an employee he may have an additional claim for a redundancy payment or for compensation for unfair dismissal in accordance with the general rules applicable to contracts of employment.

In cases of commercial agency covered by the 1993 Regulations, A is entitled on termination of the agency to receive either compensation or an indemnity (reg. 17). An indemnity is only payable when the agency contract expressly so provides. The parties are therefore free to choose between indemnity and compensation; compensation will, however, be the norm.

Both 'indemnity' and 'compensation' differ significantly from common law damages, and may be payable where damages would not be. Both are payable where the agency is terminated by the agent's death (reg. 17(8)) and both may be payable where the contract is frustrated, where the agent resigns in response to a breach of contract by the principal, where the agent retires on grounds of old age, illness or infirmity, or where, with the principal's consent, the agent assigns his rights and obligations under the contract (reg. 18). It has been held that the agent is entitled to an indemnity or compensation payment (as appropriate) where the agency is terminated by the expiry of a fixed term contract (*Barrett McKenzie & Co. Ltd* v *Escada (U.K.) Ltd* [2001] ECC 50; *Tigana Ltd* v *Decoro Ltd* [2003] EWHC 23). On the other hand, neither indemnity nor compensation is payable where the contract is terminated by the principal because of default by the agent which would justify immediate termination. It is not clear if payment is due where the contract is for a fixed term which expires. The Directive states that the parties may not derogate from the indemnity and commission provisions to the detriment of the agent before the contract expires (Art. 19). This would seem to leave open the possibilities that (a) an agreement to grant the agent rights greater than those provided for by the Directive, and (b) an agreement to derogate from the Directive's provisions made after termination of the agency contract would be valid. In *Ingmar GB Ltd v Eaton Leonard Technologies Inc* [2001] 1 All ER (Comm) 329, however, the Advocate General seems to have considered that an agreement to derogate from the Directive's provisions would be invalid even if made after termination of the agency. If correct this would make it impossible to compromise a claim for compensation or indemnity, and given the uncertainty about the correct method of calculating the payment under either basis, this seems an unattractive interpretation of the Directive. The ECJ itself made no pronouncement on the point. The concepts of 'compensation' and 'indemnity' in the Directive are derived from French and German law respectively. It has therefore been held that in the interests of furthering the harmonising objective of the Directive, a UK court applying the compensation and indemnity provisions of the Regulations may take account of the law and practice of the courts of the country in which the relevant provision originated ((*Moore v Piretta PTA Ltd* [1999] 1 All ER 174— indemnity; *Roy v M.R. Pearlman* [1999] 2 CMLR 1155, Ct of Session— compensation).

(a) *Compensation*

A is entitled to compensation for damage he suffers as a result of termination of his relationship with P. He is deemed to suffer such damage where termination occurs in circumstances which either:

(i) deprive him of commission he would have received had the contract been properly performed, while providing P with substantial benefits linked to A's activities; or

(ii) prevent A recouping his costs and expenses incurred in performing the contract.

It seems that the contract may not be performed 'properly' for the purposes of paragraph (i) even though it is performed strictly in accordance with its terms. In *Page v Combined Shipping & Trading Ltd* [1997] 3 All ER 656, the terms of the agency contract allowed the principal to control the amount of business handled by the agent, and thus the amount of commission he earned, so that the agent might earn no commission if the contract were performed strictly in accordance with its terms. The Court of Appeal, hearing an appeal on an interim matter, held that it is at least arguable that the reference to 'proper performance of the contract' in the Regulations requires compensation to be assessed by reference to the amount of commission the agent would have earned had the agency contract been performed *normally*, in accordance with the expectations of the parties. On the facts of the case, therefore, it was arguable that performance strictly in accordance with the terms of the contract, with the principal passing no business through the agent, would not be 'proper' and that the principal was therefore liable to pay substantial compensation following termination of the agency.

Neither the 1993 Regulations nor the Directive offers any guidance as to how compensation is to be calculated. French law treats the agency as being a 'quasi partnership' for the common interest of principal and agent and on termination awards the commercial agent a sum to compensate for his loss of a chance to participate in the business. The practice of the French courts is, apparently, to award a sum equal to two years' average commission, and in the Scottish case of *King v Tunnock Ltd*

[2000] EuLR 531 the Court of Session held that the French practice should be followed and awarded the agent two years' commission although the principal was closing down the business in which the agent had been involved. The agent may thus be entitled to substantial compensation without proof of loss or any duty to mitigate his loss. However, the award of two years' commission is not an absolute rule in France and can be varied at the discretion of the judge, and in a series of first instance decisions the English High Court has declined to follow the French approach, preferring instead to assess compensation by reference to the facts of the particular case taking account of such factors as the duration of the agency, the value of the benefit derived by the principal from the agency, any expenditure by the agent, the contractual notice provisions, any commission payable under reg. 8, and so on (see, eg: *Ingmar GB Ltd v Eaton Leonard Inc* (2001) unreported; *Barrett McKenzie & Co. Ltd v Escada (U.K.) Ltd* [2001] ECC 50; *Tigana Ltd v Decoro Ltd* [2003] EWHC 23). The court may in any case require the practice of the French courts to be proved by expert evidence.

(b) *Indemnity*

An indemnity is payable if the agreement so provides and A has brought P new customers or significantly increased the volume of business from existing customers and payment of an indemnity is 'equitable having regard to all the circumstances'. In assessing the amount of the indemnity the court must take account of the value of the agent's activities over the whole period of the agency, including any period before the 1993 Regulations came into force (*Moore v Piretta PTA Ltd* [1999] 1 All ER 174). So where an agent is employed under a series of fixed-term contracts, he is entitled on termination to an indemnity based on his efforts over the whole period of the agency relationship, and not merely the period covered by the last contract. The maximum amount of any indemnity is one year's commission based on the average of the last five years.

In order to claim compensation or an indemnity under the Regulations, A must deliver a written claim to P within one year of termination of the agency. The notice need not be in any particular form. It is sufficient if there is some communication in writing which communicates to the reasonable reader that the agent intends to pursue a claim for compensation or indemnity, without necessarily specifying which, under the Regulations. (*Hackett* v *Advanced Medical Computer Systems Ltd* [1999] CLC 160.)

The Regulations expressly state that the grant of an indemnity shall not prevent the agent seeking damages at common law for breach of contract. Where, as will be more common, the agent is entitled under the Regulations to compensation rather than indemnity, the Regulations are silent as to the availability of common law damages. However, it has been held that an agent may seek both common law damages and statutory compensation, but may not aggregate the two. It seems therefore that compensation and damages may both be payable provided that the agent does not thereby receive double compensation for the same loss. Where a clause in an agency agreement providing for payment of liquidated damages on termination was held to be penal and unenforceable at common law, it was held that the agent was nevertheless entitled to claim compensation under the Regulations (*Duffen v FRA BO SpA* (1998) 17 Tr Law 460).

Restraint of trade Because of the confidential nature of the relationship and the special relationship A is likely to develop with P's customers, P may wish to restrict A's activities after termination of the agency and to that effect may include a restrictive covenant in the agency agreement. Such a covenant is subject to the general rules of the common law and will only be valid provided it is not an unreasonable restraint of trade. It must therefore protect a legitimate interest of P; normally P will have a legitimate interest in protecting his trade connection. In addition the covenant must be reasonable both in duration and geographical extent. What is reasonable will be a question of fact in each case.

In cases of commercial agency covered by the 1993 Regulations similar restrictions on the effectiveness of covenants are imposed. However, under the Regulations a covenant must not apply for more than two years after termination of the agency (reg. 20).

7.5   Drafting an agency agreement

As has already been explained, an agency relationship may arise without any formal agreement between principal and agent; indeed, although agency depends on the consent of principal and agent, they may be found to have consented to the creation of such a relationship without realising it. Moreover, even where they have not agreed to such a relationship, one person may have apparent authority to act on behalf of another. However, where a business wishes to appoint a person to act as its agent, it will often want a formal agreement to be prepared to regulate their relationship. The agency agreement will govern the relationship between principal and agent although it should be borne in mind that it will not be decisive as against third parties who deal with the agent. Where the agent is employed to negotiate or conclude contracts for the sale or purchase of goods, the drafter should bear in mind the requirements of the 1993 Commercial Agents Regulations and the similar provisions which apply in other EC countries. The drafter should also bear in mind the possible impact of competition law and the need to comply with the Commission's 2000 Notice Guidelines on Vertical Restraints (2000/C291/01) (see **4.6.4** and **29.2.1.4**).

An agency agreement should contain provisions to cover the points set out below. For examples of agency agreements see *Schmitthoff's Agency and Distribution Agreements*; Christou, *Drafting Commercial Agreements*, Chapter 7, p. 229; and *Encyclopaedia of Forms and Precedents*, vol. 1, paras 1210–1320.

7.5.1   Parties

The agreement should identify the parties.

7.5.2   Duration

The agency may be for a fixed or indeterminate period; in the latter case it will be terminable by notice although there is no reason why a fixed term agreement should not contain provision for early termination by notice.

7.5.3   Scope of agency

The agreement should define the scope of the agent's activities. An agent employed to buy or sell goods will often be given responsibility for a defined area or group of customers. The agreement should define the area and the goods in which he is to deal and state whether the agent is to have sole or exclusive rights for the area of his operations.

The agreement should define the agent's authority and state whether he has authority to conclude or merely to negotiate sales. It should be borne in mind that although the agreement may impose limitations on the agent's authority, the agent may have apparent authority to bind the principal to transactions with third parties outside the scope of his actual authority; however, limitations in the agreement will be decisive as between principal and agent. In order to reinforce the principal's rights against the agent, it may expressly require the agent to indemnify the principal against any liabilities caused by the agent's exceeding his authority or failing to comply with any relevant laws.

Where the agent is employed to negotiate contracts or merely to introduce customers the agreement may impose a duty on the principal to accept orders from or to perform contracts with customers introduced by the agent.

7.5.4   Principal's duties

The agreement may provide for the principal to provide the agent with information, advertising material and other documentation, samples etc. required for the performance of the agent's duties. The 1993 Regulations impose a duty on the principal to supply such information and require the principal generally to act in good faith towards the agent.

7.5.5   Agent's duties

A general duty of good faith is imposed at common law and under the Regulations. The agreement should expressly impose such a duty and require the agent to comply with the prin-cipal's lawful instructions. It will normally require him to keep accounts, to keep the principal's property separate from his own and to account to the principal for moneys and property received in his capacity as agent; it may require him to pay all sums due to the principal promptly, without deduction, so as to exclude any right of lien or set-off to which he would otherwise be entitled. If the agent is employed to sell goods the agreement may require him to hold stock; however, in that case the agreement may fall outside the EC Commission Guidelines on Vertical Restraints of 2000 for the purposes of Art. 81 of the Treaty of Rome (see **4.6.4**). The agent may agree to provide guarantees of performance as del credere agent.

The agreement should require the agent to provide the principal with information relating to the agency and the principal's business and to keep confidential all information relating to the principal's business received by him in the course of the agency.

7.5.6   Remuneration

The agreement should define the amount of remuneration payable to the agent, including how any commission is to be calculated, and state when (and how) moneys due to the agent are payable. The principal may agree to idemnify the agent against liabilities incurred in performance of his duties. It should state whether the agent is entitled to remuneration on repeat orders from customers introduced by him, including on orders received after termination of the agency; the 1993 Regulations require remuneration to be paid on such orders.

7.5.7   Termination of the agency

The agreement should stipulate the period of notice required to terminate the agency, bearing in mind the minimum periods prescribed by the 1993 Regulations. It may provide for the agency to be terminated automatically—for instance in the event of the agent's bankruptcy.

Where the 1993 Regulations apply the agreement should state whether the agent is to be entitled to an indemnity or to compensation on termination of the agency. In view of the comments made earlier it seems that compensation may be more generous to the agent.

The agreement should expressly require the agent, on termination, to deliver up all documents and property of the principal in his possession and exclude the agent's lien.

The agreement may impose restrictions on the activities after termination of the agency; any such restrictions will be in restraint of trade and will therefore be void unless it can be shown that they are reasonably required to protect a legitimate interest of the principal (see *Marshall* v *N.M. Financial Management Ltd* [1995] 4 All ER 785). They must be reasonable in duration and geographical extent and should not be for more than two years where the 1993 Regulations apply.

7.5.8 Other provisions

The agreement may contain other provisions commonly included in commercial contracts including force majeure clauses, provision for service of notices, a choice of law and forum clause (if relevant). Where the agent is to perform duties outside Great Britain the agreement should state whether the 1993 Regulations are to apply to it.

7.6 Summary

Having completed this chapter you should:

- be familiar with the rights and duties of principal and agent vis à vis each other;
- in particular be familiar with
  - the agent's fiduciary duties at common law and the extent to which they may be modified;
  - the rights of a commercial agent under the 1993 Regulations;
  - the ways in which an agency may be terminated (a) at common law and (b) under the regulations and the legal consequences of termination;
- be aware of the main considerations to be taken into account when drafting an agency agreement.

Distributorship contracts

8.1 Introduction

Agency is only one of a range of possible commercial marketing arrangements. Another arrangement commonly used is distributorship. We have already mentioned the distinction between a distributorship agreement and a true agency (see **4.5.1**). We will now consider distributorship in a little more detail.

In this chapter we examine:

- legal and commercial factors affecting the choice of agency or distributorship agreements;
- the different types of distributorship arrangement;
- the legal incidents of distributorship contracts;
- legal controls on the drafting of distributorship contracts, especially under competition law.

8.1.1 Relative advantages of agency and distributorship

Both distributorship and (true) agency may offer both parties advantages and a business wishing to market its goods will therefore need to be advised on and consider the relative merits of the two types of arrangement.

8.1.2 Control

A business is likely to be able to exert greater control over agents than over independent distributors. An agent sells goods on behalf of its principal; the contracts it makes are, in law, the principal's contracts. The principal is therefore entitled to control the terms of those contracts. A distributor is an independent business, trading on its own behalf, and although the supplier may exert control over its distributors through the terms of its agreements with them, there are limitations on the effectiveness of such terms imposed by domestic and European competition law.

8.1.3 Product liability

Since the distributor sells on its own behalf, it alone incurs contractual liability to its customers for the goods it supplies. The supplier is, in turn, liable to the distributor, but may be able to limit its liability for those goods by the terms of its contract with the distributor. Where an agent sells on behalf of a principal, privity is established between principal and customer; the principal is therefore answerable to the customer for the goods and, if the customer is a consumer, the principal may be unable to limit its liability for the goods.

However, even where sales are effected through a distributor the supplier may incur liability directly to the end customer, or to any person damaged by defects in the goods, in the law of negligence, under the Consumer Protection Act 1987, or if it offers a guarantee, under the terms of that guarantee (see **Chapter 13**).

8.1.4 Credit risk

A business which markets goods through an agent must look for payment to the ultimate customers, not the agent. The business must therefore consider the credit-worthiness of all the end customers introduced by its agent.

A distributor buys and resells on its own behalf and is therefore responsible for recovering the price from the end customers; the supplier need look only to the distributor for payment.

Conversely, a principal may authorise its agent to receive payments from customers. If the agent becomes insolvent, the principal can recover payment direct from any customer who has not already paid the agent. In addition he may claim in priority to the agent's other creditors any moneys held by the agent which represent payments made to the agent by his customers.

The failure of ultimate customers to pay for goods supplied may affect the viability of a distributor, but if the distributor becomes insolvent the supplier can neither claim payment direct from the ultimate customer nor establish a priority claim to moneys due to the distributor from its customers (except, possibly, under a reservation of title clause: see **16.4.3**).

8.1.5 Impact on prices

Since a distributor takes the primary risk of the failure of customers to pay for goods supplied, it will wish to increase its profit margin in order to reflect that increased risk. As a result the supplier must either:

(a) reduce its price to the distributor, reducing its own profit margin; or

(b) accept that the ultimate market price of its goods will increase (to cover the distributor's profit), thus possibly reducing its competitiveness.

8.1.6 Termination and dismissal

In light of the 1993 Commercial Agency Regulations it may be easier for a supplier to dismiss an unsatisfactory distributor than an agent.

8.1.7 Competition law

Distribution agreements must be carefully drafted in order to avoid contravention of competition law. Agency agreements are less likely to contravene competition law, in particular being wholly exempt from the provisions of Art. 81 of the Treaty of Rome.

8.2 Types of distributorship arrangement

If a business decides to use distributors rather than agents there are several different types of arrangement which may be used. In particular, there is an important distinction between 'sole' and 'exclusive' distributorship arrangements. In each case there will be a master agreement defining the continuing relationship of the parties; the parties will then enter into further, individual contracts for the sale of goods each time goods are supplied to the distributor. Although the terms on which goods will be sold may be set out in the master agreement, that agreement is not itself a sale of goods contract.

8.2.1 Selective distributorship

The supplier may simply establish a network of distributors without giving any of them any exclusive rights. Effectively the supplier allows distributors, often retailers, to stock and supply its products provided that they meet certain criteria, for instance in relation to staff training, after-sales service, facilities and so on. The arrangement allows the supplier to decide who may sell its products and thus establish and maintain its product reputation. Such arrangements may be used, for instance, for computers, hi-fi equipment and for some cars. Individual distributors are then free to compete against each other.

8.2.2 Sole distributorship

Under a sole distributorship agreement the supplier appoints another to act as its distributor for some or all of its products in a specified area and undertakes in return that it will not appoint another distributor to deal in those goods in that area. However, the supplier is free to sell products direct to customers in competition with the distributor.

8.2.3 Exclusive distributorship

Under an exclusive distributorship agreement the supplier undertakes not to appoint another distributor in the area covered by the agreement, nor to sell goods itself in direct competition with the appointed distributor. Such an agreement therefore offers the distributor more protection than a sole distributorship. An agreement expressed to give the distributor the 'sole right to sell' the supplier's products has the same effect: *WT Lamb and Sons* v *Goring Brick Company Ltd* [1932] 1 KB 710.

8.2.4 Exclusive purchasing

A looser arrangement is possible where the distributor agrees merely that it will purchase its requirements of particular products from a named supplier. The purchaser may agree to purchase a specified quantity of the goods in question or merely to purchase all its requirements of the specified goods from the supplier; in the latter case the purchaser is not committed to take any particular quantity of goods.

8.3 Legal incidents of distributorship contracts

The obligations of the parties to a distributorship agreement will be derived primarily from the express and implied terms of the agreement itself. Unlike agency agreements there are relatively few standard incidents of distributorship agreements, although terms may be implied into an individual agreement where justified by the circumstances of the particular case. A well drafted agreement will set out the rights and obligations of the parties in some detail. However, if the agreement is silent the following terms may be implied.

8.3.1   Exclusivity

The meaning of 'sole' and 'exclusive' distribution rights has been considered above (see **8.2.2** and **8.2.3**).

8.3.2   Agent's obligation to promote supplier's goods

It will generally be an implied term of a sole or exclusive distributorship agreement that the distributor should use his best endeavours to promote the supplier's goods.

8.3.3   Duration

If the agreement is not expressed to be for a fixed term it will be for an indefinite term, terminable by notice from either party. If no notice period is specified in the agreement, it will be terminable by reasonable notice. What is reasonable will depend on the facts of the particular case. In view of the continuing relationship contemplated by a distributorship agreement and the fact that the distributor will be expected to have invested time, effort and money in developing the market for the supplier's products, long notice will often be required. For instance in *Decro-Wall SA* v *Marketing Ltd* [1971] 1 WLR 361 it was held that twelve months' notice was required to terminate a distributorship agreement which had run for over two years.

In any case the agreement may be terminated by either party without notice where the other has been guilty of a repudiatory breach of contract. Case law suggests that in view of the continuing relationship between the parties the courts may be reluctant to find that a solitary breach justifies termination (see e.g. *Decro-Wall SA* v *Marketing Ltd* [1971] 1 WLR 361; *Wickman Tools Ltd* v *Schuler AG* [1974] AC 235).

8.4   The impact of competition law

Prima facie distributorship and similar agreements are likely, by virtue of the restrictions undertaken by the parties to them, to offend domestic and/or EC competition law. Competition law is discussed more fully below (**Part 7**). However, there are special provisions in both European and domestic law designed to deal with such agreements.

8.4.1   EC competition law

Sole and exclusive distributorship agreements *prima facie* contravene Art. 81 of the EC Treaty. On 22 December 1999, however, the European Commission published a new block exemption (Regulation 2790/99; see 1999 OJ L 336/21) which applies generally to 'vertical agreements'—that is, agreements between organisations operating at different levels in the supply chain—and which is therefore capable of applying to both sole and exclusive distributorships. The new block exemption came into force on 1 January 2000 and applies with effect from 1 June 2000. It replaces an earlier block exemption (Regulation 1983/83) which applied prior to 2000 to exclusive, but not to sole, distributorship agreements.

In order to take the protection of the block exemption, an agreement must be drafted in accordance with its terms. First, the exemption will never apply where the supplier's share of the market on which it sells the relevant goods or services exceeds 30 per cent. Second, the exemption will never apply to agreements which have one of a number of listed objects, including the restriction of the buyer's right to determine his sale price (Art. 4(a)), the restriction of active or passive sales to end-users by members of a selective distribution system operating at the retail level (Art. 4(c)), or the restriction of 'cross-supplies' by one distributor to another within a selective distribution system (see Art. 4 of the Regulation for a complete list). Third, the exemption does not apply to provisions in a vertical agreement which:

(a) directly or indirectly impose a non-competition obligation of more than five years' duration;

(b) directly or indirectly prevent the buyer from manufacturing, purchasing, selling or reselling any goods or services after termination of the agreement unless the obligation

- relates to goods or services which compete with the contract goods or services,
- is limited to the premises from which the buyer sold the contract goods or services,
- is indispensable to protect know how transferred by the supplier to the buyer, and
- is for a period not extending more than one year beyond the termination of the contract;

(c) directly or indirectly prevents members of a selective distribution system from selling 'the brands of particular competing suppliers' (Art. 5).

Those drafting distributorship agreements thus now have considerably more freedom as to the terms which may be included than was the position prior to the introduction of the new exemption. In general, however, a distributorship agreement should be drafted so as to comply with and take the benefit of the Block Exemption. In the past there was a procedure whereby an agreement which fell outside the terms of the Block Exemption could be notified to the Commission to obtain an individual exemption for it. Since May 2004, however, it is no longer possible to seek individual exemption from the Commission by prior notification in this way. Domestic courts now have an obligation to rule on the application of Art. 81 to agreements in litigation before them. Where an agreement falls outside the terms of the Block Exemption the parties therefore proceed with it at their peril, subject to the risk that it may subsequently be declared to infringe Art. 81, and with no possibility of obtaining prior clearance from the Commission.

8.4.2 Domestic law

UK competition law is now governed by the Competition Act 1998. The 1998 Act is closely modelled on EU competition law and replaces earlier legislation, notably the Restrictive Trade Practices Act (RTPA) 1976 and Resale Prices Act (RPA) 1976 (see **Chapter 30**). The 1998 Act came into force with effect from 1 March 2000. Prior to the coming into force of the 1998 Act distributorship agreements were subject to the RTPA 1976 and RPA 1976. All distributorship agreements are now subject to the 1998 Act, although agreements made prior to 1 March 2000 may take the benefit of transitional arrangements (see **30.2.6**).

Section 2 of the 1998 Act prohibits all agreements which affect trade in the UK and which have as their object or effect the prevention, restriction or distortion of competition in the UK ('the Chapter I prohibition'). This precisely mirrors the control contained in Art. 81 of the EC Treaty. The Act expressly provides that it is to be interpreted and applied so far as is possible in a manner which is consistent with Community competition law (s. 60). Moreover, an agreement which is exempt from Art. 81 of the EC Treaty, either under a block or individual exemption, is automatically exempt from the Chapter I prohibition (s. 10). As noted above, 'vertical agreements' are now covered by a block exemption from the provisions of Art. 81. The result is that a distributorship agreement which conforms to the EC block exemption will not infringe either Art. 81 or the domestic Chapter I prohibition. Agreements with an effect on trade between Member States of the EU should therefore be drafted in accordance with the terms of the block exemption. They will then be valid under both domestic and EU law.

Agreements with a purely domestic effect are governed solely by domestic law, which is even more favourable than EC law to vertical agreements. Vertical agreements, including distributorship agreements, are exempt from the Chapter I prohibition (Competition Act 1998 (Land and Vertical Agreements Exclusions) Order 2000, SI 2000, No. 310), provided only that the agreement does not directly or indirectly have the object or effect of restricting the buyer's ability to determine its sale price (Art. 4). The only exception is that it is permissible for a supplier to fix a maximum resale price or to stipulate a recommended resale price. The result is that, provided that they do not contain impermissible restrictions on the distributor's power to fix resale prices, distributorship agreements with a purely domestic impact are now exempt from the Chapter I prohibition.

8.4.2.1   Restraint of trade

Restraints contained in a distributorship agreement are also potentially open to challenge under the common law doctrine of restraint of trade. A party seeking to enforce an agreement must therefore be prepared to meet such a challenge by showing that its restrictions are justified and are not unreasonable in duration or extent.

8.5   Drafting distributorship agreements

The first thing to be considered when preparing a distributorship agreement is the form of agreement best suited to the needs of the parties, taking account of the factors indicated above (see **8.1**). Assuming that distributorship rather than true agency is preferred, the following paragraphs set out (in outline) the main points which the agreement should cover. Care should be taken when drafting the agreement to ensure, so far as possible, that it does not fall foul of the competition rules described above (see **8.4**) and that it can, where appropriate, take advantage of the various exemptions available under those rules.

8.5.1   Nature of the agreement: exclusivity

The agreement should state whether it is for an exclusive, sole or selective distributorship. In a sole distributorship agreement there will generally be express obligations on the supplier not to appoint another competing distributor in the area covered by the agreement and, in an exclusive distributorship, not to compete by selling direct to customers in the territory. The supplier may also agree to pass on to the distributor queries from customers in the territory.

8.5.2   Scope of the agreement

The scope of the agreement should be defined by reference to both the area and the type of goods covered.

8.5.3   Duration

The agreement may be specified to be for a fixed period. However, even in a fixed term agreement it may be prudent to provide a break clause allowing the supplier to terminate the agreement at some earlier date by notice, for instance, if the number of orders falls below a specified level. If no fixed period is stated the agreement should state the notice required from each party to terminate it; as noted, in the absence of an express provision it will be implied that reasonable notice must be given, and 'reasonable notice' in this context may be quite long. However, if an express notice period is agreed there is no provision in English law requiring any minimum period of notice to be given (unlike the provisions which apply to employment and, under the 1993 Regulations, agency contracts).

8.5.4   Distributor's obligations

The agreement should impose an express obligation on the distributor to promote the goods covered by the agreement. It may, for instance, specify a minimum number of advertisements to place, or require a minimum number of visits to be made to (named) potential customers. The distributor may be required to use (only) promotional material supplied by the supplier. The distributor may be required to keep detailed records of orders and transactions, and to make them available to the supplier. The agreement may require the distributor to place a minimum number of orders, or to hold a minimum level of stock.

8.5.5   Supplier's obligations

The supplier may undertake to provide the distributor with advertising and promotional material and other information relating to the products. The supplier should undertake promptly to fulfil orders placed by the distributor; a fixed time limit may be stated. However, the supplier will probably want to ensure that any such time limit is not a binding contractual commitment, or provide for non-compliance to be excused in cases of force majeure, in order to avoid liability for breach of contract if orders are not satis-fied in time.

8.5.6   Intellectual property rights

The distributor will normally be required to make use of the supplier's promotional material. The agreement should therefore contain provisions to protect the supplier's intellectual property rights in both the goods themselves and in the promotional material. The distributor should be required to keep confidential any manufacturing know-how or information relating to the supplier's business received during the course of the agreement.

8.5.7   Distributor's authority

The agreement should make clear that the distributor is not an agent for the supplier and has no authority to bind the supplier in its dealings with third parties. However, such provision, although binding on the parties, will not be binding on third parties so that the supplier may still be bound by the distributor's actions if it allows it to appear that the distributor is its agent and the other requirements for apparent authority are fulfilled (see **5.4**).

8.5.8   Termination and post-termination matters

The agreement should require the distributor to deliver up to the supplier all promotional material and information relating to the goods and the supplier's business on termination of the agreement. In addition the agreement may impose restrictions on the distributor to prevent it competing with the supplier after termination of the agreement. Such provisions will only be valid if they can be shown to be reasonable and not to be in restraint of trade. A provision restricting the distributor for a fixed period from soliciting orders for goods similar to those covered by the agreement, from customers with whom it has dealt may be justifiable provided it is restricted to the contract territory and not unreasonable in duration.

8.5.9 Conditions of sale

Although it is not itself a sale contract, the agreement may include the terms on which goods will be supplied by the supplier to the distributor; those terms will then be incorporated, expressly or impliedly, into the individual sale contracts. Drafting conditions of sale is considered below (see **18.2**). However, care should be taken when drafting the terms to ensure that they are suitable for application over the whole period of the distributorship agreement, for instance, by including provision allowing them to be varied. In particular, provision should be made for the price to be varied; the agreement may therefore provide that the price should be the price stated in the supplier's price list from time to time.

8.5.10 Consequences of breach

Since the agreement anticipates a long term relationship, care should be taken to define the consequences of a breach of its provisions and, in particular, the rights of the party not in breach. The supplier may wish to reserve a right to terminate the agreement in the event of a breach by the distributor. If so the agreement should make clear that breach may permit the supplier to terminate; it may not be enough simply to state that the distributor's obligations are 'conditions', unless the agreement defines 'condition' as a term breach of which gives the other party a right to terminate the agreement (see *Wickman Tools Ltd* v *Schuler AG* [1974] AC 235).

8.5.11 Other provisions

The agreement should contain the other provisions commonly found in commercial agreements. It should be borne in mind that the agreement anticipates a continuing relationship; provisions such as those allowing for the service of notices and force majeure clauses may therefore be particularly important.

8.6 Summary

Having completed this chapter you should:

- be aware of the legal and commercial factors affecting the choice of agency or distributorship and be able to advise on the suitability of either as an appropriate marketing arrangement in a particular case;
- be aware of the different types of distributorship contract and their different legal incidents;
- be aware of the legal controls on the drafting of distributorship contracts, especially those arising under competition law;
- be able to advise on the main terms to be included in a distributorship agreement.

The sale and supply of goods and services

Commercial supply contracts

9.1 Introduction

Goods and services may be supplied under a range of different contracts (see **1.2.3.4** and **9.4**). Different types of contract may be subject to different legislation which may result in the rights and obligations of the parties varying according to the classification of the contract. In this chapter:

- we identify, in broad terms, the legislative framework for the supply of goods and services;
- we concentrate on contracts for the sale of goods and examine, in detail, the statutory definition thereof; and
- we identify and distinguish other types of supply contracts from sale of goods contracts.

9.1.1 The legislative framework

Contracts for the sale of goods are governed by the Sale of Goods Act 1979 (SoGA 1979), a consolidating Act which closely resembles its predecessor, the Sale of Goods Act 1893. Contracts for the supply of services are regulated by the Supply of Goods and Services Act 1982 (SGSA 1982). These two principal Acts set out the rights and duties of the parties to the contract, and contain rules as to delivery, passing of risk and property, measure of damages etc. However, neither statute is a detailed code in the sense that they do not contain all the rules applicable to these types of contracts. Much of the law can be found outside these statutes in the common law or other statutes. Moreover, both statutes have been amended a number of times.

- The Sale and Supply of Goods Act 1994 made important changes to both Acts in relation to the quality of goods supplied and buyer's remedies (see **12.4, 11.2.5** and **11.3**). This Act came into force on 3 January 1994.

- The Sale of Goods (Amendment) Act 1994 amended SoGA 1979 by abolishing the market overt exception to the *nemo dat* rule (see **15.3.6**). This Act came into effect on 3 January 1994 also.

- The Sale of Goods (Amendment) Act 1995 amended the rules on the passing of property in unascertained goods from an identified bulk in SoGA 1979 (see **14.2.4.5**). The 1995 Act came into force on 17 September 1995.

- The Sale and Supply of Goods to Consumers Regulations 2002 (SI 2002 No. 3045) made important changes to both SoGA 1979 and SGSA 1982 where the buyer/recipient of goods is a consumer. This legislation seeks to give effect to the EC Directive on certain aspects of the sale of consumer goods and associated guarantees

([1999] OJ L 171/12). New provisions deal with the quality of goods supplied and a new remedy regime is introduced for consumers (see **12.4** and **11.3**). The Regulations also contain provisions dealing with manufacturers' guarantees (see **13.5.1**). The Regulations came into effect on 31 March 2003.

Many of the default rules in SoGA 1979 applicable to contracts for the supply of goods will often be unsuitable for the needs of a particular buyer or seller and it will be desirable to modify them by express terms. However, a lot of business supply contracts involve relatively small amounts: to negotiate individual sets of terms for all such contracts would be impracticable and (prohibitively) expensive. Many businesses therefore have sets of standard terms which they apply to all their supply contracts; many purchasers use sets of standard terms of purchase. The drafting of such standard terms is a common task for the commercial practitioner and **Chapter 18** therefore includes some guidance on the drafting of standard terms, together with specimen terms which might be used by a typical business. The following chapters examine the default rules applicable under the general law, together with the ways in which they might be modified. Where appropriate, cross-references are provided to the specimen terms in **Chapter 18**.

9.1.2   Consumer transactions

When dealing with supply contracts the commercial lawyer should be aware of the distinction between consumer and non-consumer transactions. A considerable body of legislation has been enacted to protect the weaker position of consumers. This includes the Hire Purchase Act 1964, the Trade Descriptions Act 1968, the Supply of Goods (Implied Terms) Act 1973, the Consumer Credit Act 1974, the Unfair Contract Terms Act 1977, the Consumer Protection Act 1987 and the Sale and Supply of Goods to Consumers Regulations 2002 (SI 2002 No. 3045). The provisions of both SoGA and SGSA apply equally to sales to consumers and non-consumers; however:

(a)   some provisions of both Acts apply only when the *seller/supplier* acts in the course of a business;

(b)   the Unfair Contract Terms Act 1977 (UCTA 1977) restricts the ability of the seller/supplier to modify the liabilities imposed on him by SoGA and SGSA where the *buyer* deals <u>as a consumer</u> and further protection may be offered to consumers under the Unfair Terms in Consumer Contracts Regulations 1999 (see **3.4.2** and **12.1.1**); and

(c)   there are differences between the rights of consumer and non-consumer buyers to reject goods as a result of s. 15A, SoGA 1979.

(d)   new provisions as to quality, a new remedy regime and new rules dealing with manufacturers' guarantees apply to protect consumer buyers/recipients of goods under SoGA and SGSA as amended by the Sale and Supply of Goods to Consumers Regulations 2002 (see **12.4**, **11.3** and **Chapter 13**).

9.2   Different types of supply contracts

There are many ways of transferring ownership and possession of goods other than by selling them, such as by gift, bailment, hire, or barter. The popularity of these and other arrangements tends to rise and fall with changes in the social and economic environment. For example, hire-purchase was very popular in the 1950s and 1960s, but has today been overtaken in popularity by the conditional sale arrangement. While many of these arrangements resemble a sale there are fundamental differences, often technical and obscure, with which a commercial lawyer must be familiar.

In this chapter we will first define 'a contract for the sale of goods'; SoGA only applies to contracts which come within the statutory definition. Other similar transactions will then be defined and distinguished from sale, identifying the applicable legislation.

9.3   Contract for the sale of goods defined

Section 2(1) of SoGA 1979 defines a contract of sale of goods as:

a contract by which the seller *transfers* or *agrees to transfer* the property in goods to the buyer for a money consideration, called the price.

The property in the goods, or their ownership, can therefore pass either:

(a) at the time of the contract, if the seller *transfers* the property immediately; or,

(b) at some time after the contract is concluded, if the seller *agrees to transfer* the property at some future date.

These two options are further elucidated in s. 2(4) and (5) which provide that:

Where under a contract of sale the property in the goods is transferred from the seller to the buyer the contract is called a *sale*.

Where under a contract of sale the transfer of the property in the goods is to take place at a future time or subject to some condition later to be fulfilled the contract is called an *agreement to sell*.

The elements of this definition will now be examined.

9.3.1   A contract

First, there must be 'a contract'. Therefore, there must be an offer, acceptance, sufficient consideration and an intention to create legal relations. There are no formal requirements for the contract. SoGA 1979, s. 4 provides:

Subject to this or any other Act a contract of sale may be made in writing ... or by word of mouth, or partly in writing and partly by word of mouth, or may be implied from the conduct of the parties.

Exceptions to s. 4 include contracts of hire-purchase and credit-sales which come under the provisions of the Consumer Credit Act 1974, ss. 60–65, and contracts for the purchase of a British ship or a share therein which are subject to the Merchant Shipping Act 1894.

9.3.2   The parties

Secondly, the requirement that the property be transferred from one party to another means that there must be two distinct parties with capacity to enter into contracts. However, there may be a sale by one part owner to another (s. 2(2)).

9.3.3   The price

Thirdly, the goods must be sold for 'a price'. This must be 'money consideration'. Money has been defined as 'chattels issued by the authority of the law and denominations with reference to a unit of account and meant to serve as a universal means of exchange in the State of issue' (Mann, *The Legal Aspect of Money*, 5th edn, OUP, 1991). If the consideration is in any form other than money, the contract will, technically, not be one of sale (for example, see **9.4.3**).

According to s. 8, the price can be:

(a) fixed by the contract;

(b) left to be fixed by an agreed manner; or,

(c) determined by the course of dealings between the parties (s. 8(1));

otherwise, a reasonable price is payable (s. 8(2)). What is a reasonable price is a question of fact dependent on the circumstances of each case (s. 8(3)).

It is not uncommon for the parties to fail to fix a price before commencing performance, perhaps because performance has to begin while the parties are still negotiating or because of a wish to leave things vague. A failure to agree a price may be taken to indicate that the parties have not yet concluded a valid contract but the courts will lean against this construction, especially where the parties have commenced performance or have otherwise acted on the assumption that they have a binding agreement (see e.g. *Foley* v *Classique Coaches Ltd* [1934] 2 KB 1) and will find a contract subject to a requirement that the buyer pay a reasonable price (see **2.3.3**).

If the contract provides that the price is 'to be agreed', s. 2 cannot apply because the parties' agreement indicates that the price is to be agreed between them. In that case, if the parties fail to agree, the only conclusion may be that there is no concluded contract (*May & Butcher* v *R* [1934] 2 KB 17n) since an agreement to negotiate is not legally enforceable. However, if goods have been delivered under such an arrangement the 'buyer' may have to pay a reasonable sum for them under restitutionary principles (*British Steel Corporation* v *Cleveland Bridge and Engineering Ltd* [1984] 1 All ER 504).

If a price is agreed after performance has begun, that agreement may apply to deliveries which have already taken place, either on the basis that the parties' agreement fixes the amount of the reasonable price payable under the contract, or that the agreement expressly or impliedly has retrospective effect.

9.3.4   Goods

Finally, the contract of sale must be a sale of 'goods'. Goods are defined in s. 61 of the 1979 Act as including:

... all personal chattels other than things in action and money ...; and in particular 'goods' includes emblements, industrial growing crops, and things attached to or forming part of the land which are agreed to be severed before sale or under the contract of sale.

Choses in action, such as debts, shares, and intangible property, are not goods, and money is also excluded except where coins are sold as curios or artefacts.

The status of computer software and contracts for computer software is unclear. In *St Albans City and District Council* v *International Computers Ltd* [1996] 4 All ER 481, Sir Ian Gildewell stated *obiter*, in the Court of Appeal, that while a floppy disk was clearly goods, a computer program or software, 'being instructions or commands telling the computer hardware what to do', of itself was not. But, where a disk carrying a program is supplied, or where hardware and software are supplied together and the software program is defective, the defect in the program would make the disk or hardware on which the program is loaded defective, and the supplier would be in breach of the statutory implied terms as to quality. In the *St Albans* case, as is common, the defective program was not sold or hired, it was simply copied from a disk onto the plaintiff's computer without delivery of the disk. The property in the disk remained with the supplier, while the plaintiffs were licensed to use it. In these circumstances, the program was not 'goods' so there were no statutory implied terms as to quality. But in the absence of any express terms, his Lordship held that there would be a term implied at common law that the program should be reasonably fit for its intended purpose.

Where a software engineer is retained to write a program for a client a further possibility is that, even if the program is capable of being goods, the contract could be categorised as one for work and materials, or professional services, in which the engineer undertakes to perform his work with reasonable skill and care.

The classification of such contracts is likely to be most important where the customer complains of defects in the software and seeks to hold the supplier liable on the basis of the quality and fitness terms implied into contracts of sale under the Sale of Goods Act 1979 (see **Chapter 12**). The classification of the contract may therefore not be decisive as to the parties' rights and obligations. It is clear that terms equivalent to those implied by the Act could (as Sir Iain Glidewell recognised in the *St Albans* case) be implied into other contracts at common law. Conversely many of the other rules applicable to contracts for the sale of goods—such as those concerned with delivery and passing of property—are unlikely to be appropriate to contracts for the supply of software as such.

9.3.4.1 Classifications of goods

SoGA distinguishes between (a) existing and future goods and (b) specific and unascertained goods. These distinctions have important consequences, especially in relation to the passing of property and risk (see **Chapter 14**).

9.3.4.2 Existing and future goods

Section 5 states:

The goods which form the subject of a contract of sale may be either existing goods, owned or possessed by the seller, or goods to be manufactured or acquired by him after the making of the contract of sale, in this Act called future goods.

Where by a contract of sale the seller purports to effect a present sale of future goods, the contract operates as an agreement to sell the goods.

9.3.4.3 Specific and unascertained goods

A contract is for the sale of *specific* goods if the *particular* goods to be sold are identified and agreed upon at the time when the contract is made (s. 61); a contract is therefore for the sale of *unascertained* goods if the actual goods to be used in performance of it are not specifically identified at the time of the contract. The following examples may clarify this distinction.

EXAMPLE 1

B agrees to buy a second hand Volkswagen Golf, registration ROB 07 from S. The contract is for the sale of specific goods.

EXAMPLE 2

B agrees to buy a new Volkswagen Golf from S. The contract is for unascertained goods. Note that the contract may include a detailed specification of the car to be delivered, for instance, it may specify that the car should be a black, 1.8l GL model with 5 speed gear box, sun roof and CD player. The contract is nevertheless for unascertained goods because the particular car to be delivered by S has not been agreed: any new Golf will do so long as it matches the contract specification.

EXAMPLE 3

B agrees to buy 50,000 tonnes of grade A soya meal. The contract is for unascertained goods.

It will be noted that in examples 2 and 3 the contract is for the sale of generic goods by description. In such a case S may use any goods in performance of the contract, so long as they correspond to the contract description. However, the contract may still be for unascertained goods even though the parties have agreed on the source from which the goods are to come, as in the following examples.

EXAMPLE 4

B agrees to buy 500 tonnes of wheat forming part of a cargo of 1,000 tonnes on board the ship *Challenger*. S must supply wheat from the cargo of the *Challenger* but is free to supply any 500 tonnes from that cargo. The contract is for unascertained goods.

EXAMPLE 5

B agrees to buy 10 cases of vintage burgundy from S's cellar. S must supply wine from his cellar (he cannot buy in other goods to fulfil the contract) but subject to that he can supply any cases from the cellar which correspond to the contract. The contract is therefore for unascertained goods.

Such contracts, where the buyer agrees to buy goods forming part of a larger, specified bulk source, are common. They are sometimes referred to as contracts for 'quasi-specific goods', and this may be a useful label to distinguish them from contracts for wholly unascertained goods. Technically, such contracts are for unascertained goods, but there are several important differences between the rules applicable to them and those applicable to contracts for wholly unascertained goods (see **14.2.4.5**).

Many commercial contracts are therefore for the sale of unascertained goods. It is important to bear in mind however that goods are specific if identified and agreed upon *at the time when the contract is made*. Thus if a consumer buys goods in a supermarket the contract is for specific goods, because when the contract is made the contract is for the sale of the actual items presented at the check-out.

9.3.4.4   Relationship between the classifications

Existing goods may be specific or unascertained. In most cases future goods will be unascertained. However, although the position is not clear, it would seem that future goods may be specific.

EXAMPLE

S agrees to acquire and sell to B a particular antique desk owned by X. The desk is 'future goods' since it is not yet owned or possessed by S. However, it is clearly identified and agreed upon at the time the contract is made and S cannot tender any other desk in performance of the contract. The contract between B and S would therefore appear to be for the sale of specific future goods.

This may be important in the context of the rules on passing of risk and frustration of the contract if the goods are lost or damaged before risk passes to B (see **14.3.2**); however the normal rules on passing of property in specific goods cannot apply in such a case.

9.4   Sale of goods distinguished from other transactions

In many cases the classification of the contract will not affect the obligations of the parties as SoGA 1979 and the legislation governing other supply arrangements are similar on certain points, such as implied terms as to quality. The House of Lords has expressed strong views on the undesirability of drawing unnecessary distinctions between different types of contract (*Young & Marten Ltd* v *McManus Childs Ltd* [1969] AC 454).

9.4.1   Gift

A gift of goods involves a voluntary transfer of property in or ownership of goods by one person to another. What distinguishes a gift from a sale is the lack of consideration for the transfer. An executory gift, i.e. a promise to make a gift at a future date, is not binding unless made by deed.

Gifts may be commercially significant. In *Esso Petroleum Co. Ltd* v *Commissioners of Customs & Excise* [1976] 1 All ER 117, customers who bought petrol at a garage received a 'coin' as a 'free gift' with every purchase of four gallons. The issue was whether this amounted to sale or a gift, for tax purposes. The House of Lords held that it was not a gift because the garage was contractually obliged to supply the coin, but nor was it a sale. Instead it was a contract for the supply of a coin in consideration of the customer buying petrol, a type of collateral contract to the sale of petrol (this would now make it subject to the SGSA 1982).

9.4.2   Bailment

A bailment is a transaction whereby one party (the bailor) delivers, and so transfers possession of, goods to another party (the bailee) on terms which normally require the bailee to hold the goods and eventually to redeliver them to the bailor or in accordance with his directions. Unlike a sale, bailment involves the transfer only of possession, not property or ownership.

Everyday examples of a bailment include:

(a) leaving your bag or coat in a cloakroom;

(b) hiring a TV; or,

(c) putting goods into storage.

Where the bailee holds the goods to the bailor's order, for instance, under a storage contract, it is said that the bailor remains in 'constructive possession' of the goods while the bailee has 'actual possession'. But where the bailee holds for his own interest, as under a hire contract, it seems that the bailee has 'exclusive possession'.

Bailments can be 'voluntary' or 'involuntary'. An example of the latter occurs where goods are left in a person's possession without their consent. An involuntary bailee may have a statutory right to sell unclaimed goods under the Torts (Interference with Goods) Act 1977, ss. 12, 13.

Bailments can also be 'gratuitous' or 'for reward'. Commercial bailments are usually of the latter type.

A voluntary bailee, whether gratuitous or not, is required by law to exercise due care while the goods are in his possession. Where the goods are lost or damaged while in his possession, due to his negligence, he is liable to the bailor for that loss or damage. It appears that an involuntary bailee is only liable for gross negligence or deliberate damage to the goods. In either case the burden of proof is on the bailee to prove he has not been negligent.

A bailee, like the owner, has sufficient interest, known as an 'insurable interest', in the goods in his possession to insure them, and to pursue claims against any third party who interferes with or damages the goods.

9.4.3   Barter

Whereas under a contract of sale the consideration must be money, under barter arrangements goods are transferred in return for goods or services, so the consideration for the transfer is not money. Contracts of barter or exchange are governed by the SGSA 1982.

Before money was coined, barter was the only means of trading. It is still commercially significant today.

9.4.3.1   Countertrade

Countertrade, a system whereby countries, usually developing countries, require that persons wanting to supply goods to them can only do so if they in turn purchase goods from the developing country, is probably a type of barter.

9.4.3.2   Part exchange

When goods are transferred in return for goods plus money, as where goods are part exchanged, the contract may be analysed as a barter but other analyses are possible.

The leading authority in this area is the case of *Aldridge* v *Johnson* (1857) 7 El & Bl 885 where the transaction involved an exchange of 52 bullocks valued at £192, for 100 quarters of barley valued at £215, with the difference in value to be made up in money (£23). It was assumed by the court that this was a sale. This can be explained on the basis that each item was attributed a money value.

In determining whether a transaction is a sale or a barter the following questions should be addressed:

(a) What was the intention of the parties?

(b) What was the 'substantial' consideration, the money or the goods?

(c) Can a notional price be given to the goods?

In an Irish case, *Flynn* v *Mackin* [1974] IR 101, car X was traded for car Y and £250. This was held to be a barter or exchange because no value was or could be placed on the goods, and the barter dominated the transaction. In *Dawson (Clapham)* v *Dutfield* [1936] 2 All ER 232, the exchange was of two lorries for £475; this £475 was made up of £250 in cash and two other lorries in part exchange. This was held to be a sale because the vehicles had been valued, and could be closely attributed an exact value. In *Bull* v *Parker* (1842) 2 Dowl NS 345, an exchange of new riding equipment for old riding equipment plus £2 was also held to be a sale. Although the parties had not valued the goods, the court deduced a value of £4 for the new equipment. This case suggests that where the value of the goods is apparent, a contract may be construed as a sale, despite the fact that no value has been attributed to the goods.

In the more recent case of *Connell Estate Agents* v *Begej* [1993] 39 EG 125, the Court of Appeal stated obiter that in the 1990s a part-exchange consumer transaction would probably be regarded as a sale. It seems that such a transaction could be treated as two sales with a set-off of one price against the other.

9.4.4   Hire

As already noted, a contract of hire is a form of bailment, so that while goods are supplied under this arrangement, only possession and not ownership of the goods is transferred to the hirer. Hire is the legal basis for many everyday transactions, including the domestic and commercial rental of equipment. The hiring may be for a short or long term. It has the advantage of avoiding large capital outlay by spreading the cost over a period of time and is especially useful at a time of rapid technological development when products can quickly become outdated.

9.4.5 Hire purchase

The ultimate result of hire purchase and sale are the same, i.e. the transfer of ownership of the goods, but legally, the transactions are very different.

Hire purchase involves <u>a hiring (a bailment) of the goods from</u> the owner to the hirer. Payment is made by instalments and the hirer is granted an <u>option to purchase</u> the goods at the end of the hire period in return for <u>a final optional payment</u>. The hirer is not legally obliged to purchase the goods at this point. In practice, this option is always exercised because the total sum of the instalments far exceeds the normal cost of hiring, and the final payment is often a nominal figure. Effectively, it is a way to purchase goods over a period of years.

Hire purchase offers the buyer the advantage that he does not have to pay a lump sum, but acquires the goods on credit, while the supplier is secured since he remains owner of the goods until the final optional payment is made. If the hirer defaults in his payments the owner can repossess his goods according to the agreement, subject to restrictions imposed by the Consumer Credit Act 1974 where it applies.

In practice, the buyer does not purchase direct from the supplier. Instead, a finance company buys the goods from a supplier and enters into the hire purchase arrangement with the ultimate buyer. The supplier of the goods and the ultimate consumer therefore normally have no direct contractual relationship with each other, unless a collateral contract can be implied.

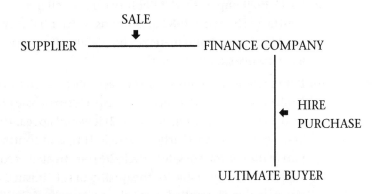

Hire purchase is governed by the Supply of Goods (Implied Terms) Act 1973, which implies terms as to title and quality of the goods supplied under hire purchase agreements similar to those implied by SOGA 1979 (see **Chapter 12**).

Hire purchase arrangements must be distinguished from two types of sale contracts: conditional sales and credit sales.

9.4.5.1 Conditional sale

Being a sale, this transaction is governed by SoGA 1979. It is similar to hire purchase in that the buyer is given credit, the price often is paid by instalments and <u>no property passes until the condition is met</u>, usually when the full price is paid. However, here the parties are committed to the sale from the outset unlike hire purchase where there is only an option to buy. A contract under which the 'buyer' will become owner of goods by paying instalments unless he exercises an option NOT to acquire the goods is a conditional sale, not hire purchase (*Forthright Finance plc* v *Carlyle Finance Ltd* [1997] 4 All ER 90). Conditional sales are now more popular than hire purchase arrangements.

9.4.5.2   Credit sale

Again, as a sale, this arrangement is governed by SoGA 1979. The buyer is given credit, and payment may be by instalments, so in this respect credit sales resemble hire purchase agreements and conditional sales. However, unlike hire purchase agreements and conditional sales, property in the goods passes to the buyer at the time of the contract of sale, or, at least, at the time of delivery of the goods, so that it does not offer the seller the security of a hire purchase or conditional sale. Only an imprudent seller would offer a purchaser substantial unsecured credit without first being assured of his creditworthiness.

Where parties are in a continuous trading relationship, credit sale arrangements are often utilised, with accounts being settled at predetermined times, monthly or quarterly, thereby reducing paper work.

These last three arrangements, i.e. hire purchase, conditional sale and credit sale, share many similarities and, from a consumer perspective, can be difficult to distinguish. For this reason, legislation has to a large extent assimilated these arrangements and the Consumer Credit Act 1974 may apply to them all.

9.4.6   Work and materials

In many cases it will make no difference to the rights of the parties whether a contract is one of sale or for work and materials. Contracts for the supply of services are governed by the SGSA 1982 (see **Chapter 17**). The distinction between the two types of contract remains important, however, for the following reasons.

(a) SoGA 1979 imposes strict liability on the seller for the goods supplied under the contract. The SGSA 1982 also imposes strict liability for goods supplied under a contract for work and materials but liability for the provision of services is based on a negligence standard (see **17.4**).

(b) But in relation to consumer transactions a different liability standard may apply. Under the EC Directive on certain aspects of the sale of consumer goods and associated guarantees ([1999] OJ L 171/12) it would appear that contracts to manufacture and supply a finished article (Article 1(4)) and contracts where installation forms part of the contract of sale (Article 2(5)) are treated as contracts of sale and hence the supplier is strictly liable for the quality of the finished article and for work/services if installation is supplied. The Sale and Supply of Goods to Consumers Regulations 2002 which seek to implement this Directive do not address these points. The thinking seems to have been that existing law was in compliance with the Directive. However, as it clear from above, it is arguable that the Directive is not properly implemented in this regard.

(c) Where the purchaser is a consumer, UCTA 1977 prevents the exclusion of the implied terms under the 1979 Act but the duty of care under the 1982 Act can be excluded if the exclusion satisfies the test of 'reasonableness'.

(d) The classification can affect a buyer's right to reject the goods (see **11.3.1.3**) and terminate the contract and the passage of property (see **14.2**).

(e) The distinction is also important where the contract requires the buyer to pay some or all of the price before performance by the seller/supplier and the contract is terminated before performance. In such a case the payment will be refundable if there is a total failure of the consideration for which it was paid. Under a contract of sale such payments will therefore normally be refundable, unless paid by way of deposit.

Under a contract for work and materials the supplier will often be entitled to retain or sue for the advance payment notwithstanding termination, provided that he has performed some of the work required by the contract.

9.4.6.1 Drawing the distinction

In classifying a contract the commercial lawyer should ask:

(a) What is the intention of the parties?

(b) What is the substance of the contract, the sale element or the services element or a combination of both (*Robinson* v *Graves* [1935] 1 KB 579)?

Case law sheds some light on the matter, but some cases cannot easily be reconciled as the following examples show.

EXAMPLE 1

A contract to supply a meal in a restaurant was held to be a sale (*Lockett* v *Charles* [1938] 4 All ER 170).

EXAMPLE 2

A contract to build a ship's propeller to a design provided by the customer was held to be a sale of the finished product (*Cammell Laird & Co. Ltd* v *Manganese Bronze & Brass Co. Ltd* [1934] AC 402).

EXAMPLE 3

Contracts for the repair of a car (*Myers* v *Brent Cross* [1934] 1 KB 46), the application of hair dye (*Watson* v *Buckley, Osborne & Garrett* [1940] 1 All ER 174) and the administration of medicine by a vet (*Dodd & Dodd* v *Wilson & McWilliam* [1946] 2 All ER 691) were all held to be contracts for performance of services.

EXAMPLE 4

A contract for a printer to print a book, where the printer was to supply the paper was held to be a contract for work and materials (*Clay* v *Yates* (1856) 1 Hurl & N 73).

EXAMPLE 5

A contract requiring a painter to paint a picture was held to be for work and materials (*Robinson* v *Graves* [1935] 1 KB 579) (although the court also said in that case that a contract for a sculptor to produce a statue might be a sale of a finished product!).

In all these cases the court applied the 'substance of the contract test' and seemed to regard the question of classification as a simple one of 'sale or service'. However, more recent authority recognises the possibility of a hybrid contract (*Hyundai Heavy Industries Co.* v *Papadopoulos* [1980] 2 All ER 29: a contract to build and supply a ship was a sale of the ship, but not a pure sale, as it had elements of a building contract).

In general it seems that a contract for the performance of a service which also involves the supply of goods, such as a contract to service a car, will normally be classified simply as one for work and materials, governed by SGSA 1982. A contract for professional services will usually be one for services even though documents may be passed to the client and become his property (*Lee* v *Griffin* (1861) 1 B & S 272). Classification may be more difficult and more important where the contract involves the manufacture and supply of a finished product. Such contracts are treated as contracts for the sale of the finished product under the EC Directive on the Sale of Consumer Goods and Associated Guarantees (Art. 1(4)), with the result that the Directive's provisions apply to the finished product (see **Chapter 17**).

9.5 Summary

You should now be able, both in theory and in practice:

- to identify a contract for the sale of goods, in light of the statutory definition;
- to distinguish between contracts of sale and other forms of supply of goods;
- to identify the legislation applicable to different forms of supply contract.

Duties of the parties

10.1 Introduction

In this short chapter we:

- outline the essential duties of buyer and seller under a typical sale of goods contract;
- consider the terms of the sales contract, and specifically their classification—
  - as express or implied terms, and
  - as conditions, warranties or innominate terms and the remedies available for breach thereof.

10.2 Duties of the parties

The basic duties of the parties to a contract for sale of goods are set out in SoGA 1979, s. 27:

It is the duty of the seller to deliver the goods, and of the buyer to accept and pay for them, in accordance with the terms of the contract.

These duties are fundamental and failure by either party to perform his duties allows the innocent party to repudiate the contract and sue for damages. Section 28 states that unless otherwise agreed, these duties are concurrent conditions:

... that is to say, the seller must be ready and willing to give possession of the goods to the buyer in exchange for the price and the buyer must be ready and willing to pay the price in exchange for the goods.

It is not unusual in commercial sales for the goods to be bought on credit terms—'payment 30 days after delivery' for example—so this general rule of 'payment on delivery' is often displaced.

10.3 The terms of the contract

The duties of the parties are further defined by the terms of the contract. SoGA 1979 requires the parties to deliver/accept and pay for the goods 'in accordance with the terms of the contract'. Those terms may be expressed in the contract or implied by law. In an oral contract the type of basic terms which are usually expressed include a description of the goods to be sold, their price, mechanisms for payment, mode and time for delivery. Under a written contract, including one on a standard form, more detail is generally provided.

A court may imply terms to give effect to the contract under the normal rules of construction (see **2.6.3**), but many terms are implied into contracts for the sale of goods by SoGA 1979. Some of the Act's provisions are mandatory and cannot be contracted out of (for example s. 16, see **14.2.1**) but others are default rules which apply subject to the contrary intention of the parties. Many of the default rules will be inappropriate in a commercial contract and a well drafted contract may modify and replace them by provisions which better meet the needs of the parties, or the party who prescribes the terms of the contract. For instance, SoGA 1979, s. 29 states that the place of delivery of the goods is the seller's place of business or residence. This provision clearly favours the seller by placing the burden on the buyer to collect the goods. If the buyer is in a stronger bargaining position than the seller, he could require the seller to deliver the goods to his place of business or elsewhere by express provision in the sales contract.

Even where the default rules are considered appropriate, it may be better to restate them in the contract, so that the contract can give a complete picture of the rights and duties of the parties. However, in order to draft and understand a contract, it is necessary to have a clear understanding of the default rules. Our main concern is therefore with the statutory implied terms rather than any specific express terms.

10.4 Remedies for non-performance

If either party to a sale contract is in breach of contract, a range of remedies is available to the other. These include:

(a) damages;

(b) refusal to perform his own obligations under the contract;

(c) termination of the contract;

(d) an order that the other party perform his obligations.

We examine these remedies in more detail in **Chapters 11, 12** and **16**. However, the availability of the rights to withhold performance and terminate the contract depends on the classification of the term broken. We must therefore briefly examine the classification of terms in sale contracts.

10.5 Conditions and warranties

SoGA 1979 classifies contract terms as either conditions or warranties. Only 'warranty' is defined:

'warranty' means an agreement with reference to goods which are the subject of a contract of sale, but collateral to the main purpose of such contract, the breach of which gives rise to a claim for damages, but not to a right to reject the goods and treat the contract as repudiated. (SoGA s. 61.)

By implication a condition is a primary, more important term of the contract, breach of which gives rise to a right to reject the goods, treat the contract as repudiated and therefore terminate it (although in certain circumstances the right of a non-consumer buyer to reject goods for breach of condition is limited (SoGA 1979, s. 15A: see **11.3**). Whether a term is a condition or a warranty depends in each case on the construction of the contract

(s. 11(3)); and a stipulation may be a condition though it is referred to as a warranty in the contract and vice versa.

No reference is made in the Act to innominate terms, but in *The Hansa Nord* [1976] QB 44, the Court of Appeal held that an *express* term in a sale contract could be classified as innominate. The result is that terms implied into sale contracts by SoGA 1979 are all either conditions or warranties but express terms may be classified as conditions, warranties or innominate terms, in line with the general rules of contract law (see **2.6.4**).

Where a contract is subject to a condition to be fulfilled by the seller, the buyer may waive the condition or elect to treat the breach of the condition as a breach of warranty and not as a ground to repudiate the contract (s. 11(2)). A buyer might do so if, for instance, faced with a minor breach or in order to maintain good trading relations.

10.6 Summary

In this chapter we:

- outlined the duties of the seller and the buyer of goods, as set out in the SoGA and under the terms of the contract—subsequent chapters expand on this chapter;

- in the next chapter, **Chapter 11**, we explore, in more detail, the seller's duty to deliver the goods and the remedies available to the buyer for breach of this obligation;

- in the subsequent chapter, **Chapter 12**, we concentrate on the statutory implied terms in relation to the goods supplied and the remedies available to a buyer for breach of these obligations.

Seller's duties and buyer's remedies

11.1 Introduction

The seller's basic duty is to deliver the goods in accordance with the terms of the contract. Therefore if the seller fails to deliver in the manner required by the contract, or delivers goods which do not comply with the terms of the contract, he is in breach.

In this chapter we are concerned with:

- the meaning of delivery;
- the terms relating to the way in which delivery is to be effected, including—
  - the time of delivery;
  - the place of delivery;
  - the quantity to be delivered;
- the consequences of the seller's failure to deliver in accordance with the terms of the contract; and
- the main remedies for non-performance of the contract.

In the next chapter, we examine the terms concerned with the nature and quality of the goods to be delivered under the contract.

11.2 Meaning of delivery

Delivery is defined simply as the 'voluntary transfer of possession from one person to another' (SoGA 1979, s. 61). The Act contains detailed rules as to where, when and how delivery is to take place. Generally, however, these default rules will be modified by the express terms of the contract.

11.2.1 Modes of delivery

The voluntary transfer of possession from one party to another can be effected by actual delivery or constructive delivery. 'Actual delivery' involves the physical handing over of the goods by the seller to the buyer. 'Constructive delivery' is concerned with the transfer of *control* over the goods without the physical transfer of possession.

11.2.1.1 Physical delivery

The obvious means of delivery is by the seller physically delivering the goods to the buyer; equally the seller, by allowing the buyer to collect the goods himself from the premises or a warehouse, performs his duty to deliver. Section 29(1) provides:

Whether it is for the buyer to take possession of the goods or for the seller to send them to the buyer is a question depending in each case on the contract, express or implied, between the parties.

The contract should therefore contain an express provision (see **18.5.1**, Clause 2).

However, actual physical delivery may not always be necessary. There are at least four types of constructive delivery.

11.2.1.2 Continuance in possession in his own right

Where the buyer already has the goods in his possession, as a bailee for instance, physical delivery is not necessary. Here the buyer's continuing in possession in his own right notionally represents constructive delivery.

11.2.1.3 Transfer of documents of title

Where goods are represented by a document of title, such as a bill of lading covering goods at sea (see **20.2**), the transfer of the document of title from seller to buyer, with the intention to transfer possession, gives the buyer legal control over the goods, and so represents constructive delivery of the goods. The goods may be in the actual possession of some third party, such as the sea carrier in the case of sea carriage, but in the constructive possession of the buyer.

11.2.1.4 Attornment

The goods may be in the physical possession of the seller or a third party. If the person in possession acknowledges that he holds the goods for the buyer rather than for himself or the seller, he is said to *attorn* to the buyer. The effect of such an attornment is to put the buyer in constructive possession of the goods with the person in physical possession of the goods acting as bailee on the buyer's behalf.

11.2.1.5 Delivery to a carrier

When the buyer does not deal as a consumer, delivery to a carrier can constitute constructive delivery to the buyer (s. 32(1)).

11.2.2 The place of delivery

Unless the parties have otherwise agreed (see **18.5.2**, Clause 6.2) the place of delivery is the seller's place of business, or if he has no place of business, his residence. If however the sale is for specific goods which the parties know at the time of the sale to be in some other place, that is the place of delivery (s. 29(2)). If at the time of the sale the goods are in the possession of a third party, there is no delivery of the goods until that third party acknowledges that he is holding the goods on the buyer's behalf or attorns to the buyer (s. 29(4)).

11.2.3 The cost of delivery

All expenses for putting the goods in a deliverable state are borne by the seller, unless otherwise agreed (s. 29(6) and see **18.5.2**, Clause 6.4). As a general rule all expenses of and incidental to delivery are for the seller's account and all expenses of and incidental to taking delivery are for the buyer's account.

11.2.4   The time of delivery

Although s. 27 states that delivery and payment should happen simultaneously this does not always occur. Often the time of delivery is expressed in the contract. This may be a specific time ('8 a.m. Monday 3 January 2004), or, more usually, a time period within which delivery should be made ('between 1 May and 7 May 2004).

If the seller is obliged under the contract to send the goods to the buyer and no time is fixed, the seller is required to send them within a reasonable time (s. 29(3)). What is reasonable will depend on a variety of factors, for instance, the type of goods (e.g. perishable or not) and on the market.

Demand for and tender of delivery must be made at a reasonable hour (s. 29(5)).

11.2.4.1   Effect of late delivery

If goods are delivered late, the seller is in breach of contract and the buyer can sue for damages. However, if the duty to deliver at a specific time is classified as a condition, time is said to be 'of the essence' and late delivery entitles the buyer to reject the goods, terminate the contract and sue the seller for damages, even if the delay is slight. Whether the time for delivery is 'of the essence', or merely a warranty, depends on the terms of the contract (SoGA 1979, s. 10(2)). However,

in ordinary commercial contracts for the sale of goods the rule is clearly that time is prima facie of the essence with respect to delivery (McCardie J in *Hartley* v *Hymans* [1920] KB 475).

Thus late delivery will generally allow the buyer to terminate the contract. The buyer may of course be willing to accept late delivery in order to preserve a good trading relationship, because of a scarcity of the goods in the market, or because he got a good price on the goods, but he has the right to terminate the contract if he so wishes, and he may expressly reserve this right in the contract (see **18.5.2**, Clause 6.1).

This strict rule is justified as providing certainty and facilitating trade, especially in 'string transactions' where there is a series of sales of the same goods, each dependent on the one before it. Such 'string' contracts are particularly common in large scale commodity dealing. Conversely the time for payment is not generally of the essence (s. 19(1)).

Where time is of the essence the buyer may lose or waive his right to terminate the contract for late delivery by acting in such a manner as to lead the seller to believe that he intends to continue to perform that contract. This is exactly what happened in the case of *Hartley* v *Hymans* where the contract was for the sale of yarn to be delivered between September and 15 November. In fact deliveries did not commence until late October and did not cease until 13 March. The buyer pressed the seller for delivery until 13 March when the buyer wrote to the seller terminating the contract on the grounds of late delivery. The court found that the buyer was in breach by terminating the contract. In pressing for delivery he had waived his right to insist on prompt delivery.

A buyer who has waived the right to prompt delivery may set a new delivery date and make time of the essence afresh by giving reasonable notice. In *Charles Rickards Ltd* v *Oppenhaim* [1950] 1 KB 616, a car chassis was to be built and delivered by 20 March. It was not delivered in time but the buyer continued to press for delivery until 29 June at which point he gave notice to the seller that he would not accept delivery unless it was made within four weeks. Delivery was not made until October at which time the buyer refused to accept it. The Court of Appeal found that in giving the notice he had made time of the essence and was therefore entitled to reject the goods.

11.2.4.2   Excluding liability for late delivery

Although the buyer may want the right to terminate the contract in the event of late delivery, the seller will be anxious to avoid this possibility. There are a number of ways in which the seller may seek to restrict the buyer's right to terminate the contract and/or claim damages for late delivery (see **18.5.1**, Clause 2.4). For instance the contract may:

(a) provide that delivery will take place 'on or about' a certain date so that there is no absolute commitment to deliver on the stated date and late delivery is not necessarily a breach of contract at all; in addition time is unlikely to be of the essence in such a case; the clause is likely to be interpreted as requiring delivery within a reasonable time of the stated date;

(b) expressly provide that the buyer is not to terminate for late delivery, or that the time of delivery is not of the essence;

(c) give the seller to right to vary the delivery date;

(d) simply provide that the seller is not to be liable for late delivery;

(e) state that the quoted delivery date is an estimate only and not a contractual commitment; probably the effect of such a provision is to require delivery within a reasonable time.

In any case the clause must be carefully construed in order to determine whether it excludes the buyer's right to terminate (see **18.5.1**, Clause 2.4), the seller's liability for damages (see **18.5.1**, Clause 2.4.1) or both. Most such clauses are probably subject to a test of reasonableness under UCTA 1977, s. 3 (see **3.4.3.4**) and, in a consumer contract, to a test of fairness under the Unfair Terms in Consumer Contracts Regulations 1999 (see **3.4.4**).

11.2.5   The quantity to be delivered

The contract will normally contain an express term fixing the quantity of goods to be delivered. SoGA 1979, s. 30 defines the rights of the buyer where the seller delivers less or more than the right quantity. The basic rule is one of 'strict compliance' so that unless the seller delivers exactly the correct quantity, the buyer can reject the goods. However, he is not obliged to do so, and his right to reject is subject to two restrictions.

(a) If the seller delivers a quantity less than that contracted for the buyer can:
    (i)   reject the goods; or
    (ii)   accept them, paying at the contract rate (s. 30(1)).

(b) If the seller delivers a quantity greater than that contracted for the buyer can:
    (i)   reject the whole delivery; or
    (ii)   accept and pay for the whole delivery at the contract price; or
    (iii) accept the contract quantity and reject the remainder (s. 30(2)).

These rules are subject to two restrictions. First, a deviation from the contract quantity will be disregarded if it is *de minimis*. However, this exception has been very narrowly construed so that only a very slight deviation from the contract quantity will be sanctioned on this basis. In *Shipton Anderson & Co.* v *Weil Bros.* [1912] 1 KB 574, an excess of 0.0005 per cent was found to be so slight that the buyer could not reject. More importantly, as a result of amendments made by the Sale and Supply of Goods Act 1994, a buyer who does not deal as a consumer may not reject the whole delivery where the excess or shortfall is so slight that it would be unreasonable for him to reject (SoGA 1979, s. 30(2A)). It seems that this restriction is intended to be more favourable to the seller than the *de minimis* exception.

However it is for the seller to prove that the excess or shortfall is so slight that rejection would be unreasonable. Note that the buyer's right in the event of delivery of more than the contract quantity to reject the excess is unaffected.

These rules are supplemented by the rule that the buyer is not obliged to accept delivery by instalments unless the contract so provides (s. 31(1)) so that if the seller delivers less than the contract quantity he cannot claim to be entitled to make up the shortfall in a second delivery unless the contract gives him that right.

Once again these rules will often be modified by express terms in the contract, including provisions allowing the seller to deliver in instalments and allowing for tolerances in the amount to be delivered (e.g. 'plus or minus 5 per cent') (see **18.5.1**, Clause 3; **18.5.2**, Clause 4). Again, such provisions may be subject to a test of reasonableness under UCTA 1977, s. 3 (see **3.4.3.4**) and, in a consumer contract, will be subject to a test of fairness under the Unfair Terms in Consumer Contracts Regulations 1999 (see **3.4.4**).

11.3 Buyer's remedies

Any breach of contract by the seller entitles the buyer to damages for losses caused by the breach (see **11.3.2**). In addition, where the seller commits a breach of a condition or a serious breach of an innominate term, the buyer may reject the goods and terminate the contract (see **11.3.1**). Moreover, where the buyer is a consumer and the goods do not conform to the contract at the time of delivery the buyer may have additional rights to require the seller to repair or replace the goods, or to require the seller to reduce the price or to rescind the contract, under ss. 48A–F SoGA (inserted by the Sale and Supply of Goods to Consumers Regulations 2002, see **11.3.3**). Other remedies may be available under the general law of contract, including specific performance and damages and/or rescission of the contract for misrepresentation (see **Chapter 3**).

11.3.1 Rejection

As noted above (see **10.4**) breach by the seller of a condition of the contract allows the buyer to reject the goods and terminate the contract. Although the position is not clear, there seems no reason why the buyer should not reject the goods without terminating the contract, in which case the contract will remain alive and the seller may be able to re-tender goods to replace those rejected.

The right to reject goods for breach of condition may be restricted or modified by the express terms of the contract (see, e.g., **18.5.2**, Clause 9.2); In addition, SoGA 1979 (as amended) restricts the right of a non-consumer buyer to reject in certain circumstances and provides that the right to reject goods for breach of condition may be lost if the buyer 'accepts' the goods.

11.3.1.1 Effect of rejection

'Rejection' involves the buyer refusing to perform his duty to accept the goods. Effective rejection requires an unequivocal indication by the buyer that he intends to reject the goods. It is not necessary that he physically return the goods to the seller, but he must make the goods available for the seller to repossess them. It is important that a buyer who wishes to reject goods for breach of contract does indicate his intention to reject in unequivocal terms since otherwise he may be taken to have accepted the goods and thus have lost the right to reject (see **11.3.1.3**).

Rejection by the buyer has the following consequences.

(a) If property in the goods has passed to the buyer, it revests in the seller.

(b) Risk of loss of or damage to the goods revests in the seller.

(c) The position is as if the seller had not delivered: if the buyer has paid the price, he is entitled to recover it by means of a restitutionary claim; alternatively he may claim damages for non-delivery (see **11.3.2.1**).

(d) If the buyer remains in possession of the goods after rejection he is in the position of an involuntary bailee.

Rejection is therefore particularly attractive where the buyer has not already paid for the goods; in that case it is a 'self-help' remedy which involves the buyer refusing to perform his obligations to accept and pay for the goods. It must nevertheless be exercised with care, since if the buyer rejects in circumstances where he is not entitled to do so, he himself will be in breach of contract.

Where the buyer has already paid for goods rejection is less attractive, especially in a commercial context since, if the seller refuses to accept the buyer's rejection the buyer may be forced to take legal proceedings in order to recover the price.

11.3.1.2   A right to cure?

Where the seller delivers goods which do not comply with the contract, there is authority for the proposition that he has a right to tender another delivery provided he can do so within the contract delivery period and that a buyer who refuses to accept this second valid tender is in breach of contract for non-acceptance. However, most of the leading cases in this area concern international sale contracts where delivery is effected by the tender of documents rather than actual physical delivery of the goods (see e.g. *Borrowman Phillips & Co.* v *Free and Hollis* (1878) 4 QBD 500); whether a right to re-tender exists in domestic sales where documents do not represent the goods remains uncertain. If the seller wishes to have the right to 'cure' any defective delivery he should therefore reserve that right expressly in the contract (see **18.5.1**, Clause 4.3). Alternatively, the buyer may wish to include an express right to demand cure—for instance by requiring the seller to repair or replace defective goods (see **18.5.2**, Clause 9.3). Interestingly, rights to cure exist in relation to international and consumer sale of goods contracts. Under the Vienna Convention on the International Sale of Goods (1980) there is provision both for the seller to cure a defective performance (Articles 34, 37 and 48) and the buyer to demand repair or replacement of the goods (Article 46). While the Vienna Convention has not been incorporated into domestic law parties to a sales contract can expressly adopt the Convention, or conflict of laws rules may result in the application of the Convention. Further, under ss. 48A–F SoGA (inserted by the Sale and Supply of Goods to Consumers Regulations 2002), a consumer buyer has a limited right to demand cure in the form of a right to demand repair or replacement (see **11.3.3**).

11.3.1.3   Loss of the right to reject

The seller may want to prevent the buyer rejecting the goods, especially in the case of international transactions where rejection by the buyer may leave the seller with the goods on his hands in a foreign country. The contract may therefore contain express terms restricting or excluding altogether the right to reject. Such terms will generally be subject to the Unfair Contract Terms Act 1977: terms restricting the right to reject for breach of the statutory implied conditions in SoGA 1979, ss. 12–15 will be regulated by UCTA 1977, s. 6;

terms restricting the right to reject for breach of other conditions will be regulated by UCTA 1977, s. 3 (see **3.4.3.4**).

In consumer contracts, such terms will also be subject to a test of fairness under the Unfair Terms in Consumer Contracts Regulations 1999.

In addition, SoGA 1979 imposes restrictions on the right to reject. First, it provides that a buyer who does not deal as a consumer may not reject goods for breach of one of the implied terms in ss. 13–15 of the Act (s. 15A; see **Chapter 12**) where the breach is so slight that rejection would be unreasonable. 'Deals as consumer' has the same meaning here as it does under the Unfair Contract Terms Act 1977 (see **3.4.3.3**). Secondly, it provides that where the contract is not severable, the buyer loses the right to reject if he accepts the goods or part of them (s. 11(4)). It then goes on to provide that the buyer may accept the goods, and thus lose the right to reject, in three ways:

    (a) by expressly intimating that he accepts the goods:

    (b) by doing an act inconsistent with the seller's ownership of the goods; or

    (c) by lapse of time if the buyer retains the goods without rejecting them (ss. 34–5).

Acceptance operates in some ways like affirmation of a contract following a breach. However, whereas an innocent party is not taken to have affirmed the contract unless he has full knowledge of the breach, it is clear that a buyer can accept the goods, and so lose the right to reject them, even before he is aware of the breach of contract.

Express intimation of acceptance   The buyer loses the right to reject the goods if he expressly indicates that he accepts them. In order to take advantage of this provision the seller may attempt to get the buyer to sign an 'acceptance note'. The effect of such notes is not entirely clear: if the note clearly states that the buyer accepts the goods as delivered as being in conformity with the contract, it may be held to prevent the buyer rejecting the goods. However, a court may be reluctant to interpret an acceptance note as having this effect unless it is clearly worded: such a note may be construed as simply acknowledging receipt of the goods and such an interpretation is likely especially where the buyer is a consumer.

Where the note is signed by an agent of the buyer, rather than by the buyer in person, it will only bind the buyer if it is signed by someone who has authority to bind the buyer by accepting the goods (see **Chapter 5**).

An act inconsistent with the seller's ownership of the goods   It has been suggested that this means merely 'an act inconsistent with rejecting the goods'. It is not entirely clear what acts will be regarded as having this effect. In the past the following have been regarded as acts inconsistent with the seller's ownership of the goods:

    (a) any dealing with the goods, such as reselling or making a gift of them;

    (b) using the goods more than is necessary in order to ascertain whether they conform to the contract;

    (c) consuming the goods so that they cannot be returned;

    (d) attempting to repair the goods and even, possibly, asking the seller to repair the goods, at least if the buyer does not make clear that he reserves the right to reject.

As a result of changes made by the Sale and Supply of Goods Act 1994 such actions may not always bar rejection (see SoGA 1979, s. 35(6) discussed below). However, such acts are still capable of being 'acts inconsistent with the seller's ownership' which may bar rejection.

Lapse of time   The buyer loses the right to reject if he retains the goods beyond the lapse of a reasonable time without intimating that he is rejecting them. What is a 'reasonable time' will be a question of fact in each case. The following factors may be relevant in deciding what is a reasonable time for rejecting the goods:

(a) the nature of the goods: for instance, if the goods are perishable, the time for rejection may be relatively short: if the goods are complex machinery, a longer time may be allowed to enable the buyer to try them out;

(b) the conduct of the parties: for instance, where a buyer seeks from the seller information to enable the buyer to decide whether to accept, reject or seek cure, a court may be willing to disregard the time taken to receive this information (*Clegg and another* v *Olle Andersson* [2003] EWCA Civ 320; [2003] 1 All ER (Comm) 721);

(c) the nature of the market: where prices are volatile, the time for rejection will probably be shorter;

(d) any custom of the trade;

(e) what the parties expected the buyer to do with the goods; thus if goods are bought for resale and it is not expected that they will be inspected prior to resale, a reasonable time for rejection will be such time as it might reasonably take to resell the goods and for the buyer's customer to examine them (see *Truk (UK) Ltd* v *Tokmakidis GmbH* [2000] 1 Lloyd's Rep 543);

(f) the need for the seller to close his account.

SoGA 1979, s. 35(5) provides that in assessing what is a reasonable time the court is to consider (*inter alia*) whether the buyer has had a reasonable time to examine the goods to ascertain whether they are in conformity with the contract. It is clear, however, that the time for rejection runs from the date of delivery, not the date of discovery of the defect, and the nature of the defect is not relevant when considering what is a reasonable time. The issue is whether the buyer has had a reasonable time to examine the goods generally, not a reasonable time to discover the particular defect (*Truk (UK) Ltd* v *Tokmakidis GmbH*). In some cases the time may be rel-atively short.

In order to avoid uncertainty the contract may impose an express time limit on rejection (see **18.5.1**, Clause 4 and **18.5.2**, Clause 9.2). The effectiveness of such a provision will be subject to UCTA 1977.

11.3.1.4   The buyer's right to examine the goods

SoGA 1979, s. 35(2) provides that the buyer is not to be taken to have accepted the goods by express acceptance or by doing an act inconsistent with the seller's ownership unless he has first had an opportunity of examining them in order to ascertain whether they are in conformity with the contract and, if the goods are sold by sample, that the bulk corresponds with the sample. The contract may seek to exclude this right to examine; however, where the buyer deals as a consumer (as defined in the UCTA 1977: see **3.4.3.3**) he cannot lose his right to examine the goods by agreement, waiver or otherwise (SoGA 1979, s. 35(3)) so that a contract term excluding the right to examine will be ineffective against a consumer. A contractual restriction on the right of a non-consumer buyer to examine the goods may be effective if it satisfies the test of reasonableness in UCTA 1977, s. 6. The buyer may want to include an express right to examine the goods, in order to clarify the position (see **18.5.2**, Clause 9.1).

11.3.1.5   Resolving disputes

SoGA 1979, s. 35(6) provides that the buyer is not to be taken as having accepted goods 'merely because (a) he asks for, or agrees to, their repair by or under an arrangement with the seller or (b) the goods are delivered to another under a sub-sale or other disposition'. Clearly, therefore, such acts will not automatically be construed as 'acts inconsistent with the seller's ownership' so as to bar rejection. However, the lapse of time involved in attempting repair or in reselling and recovering the goods may prevent rejection. A buyer who agrees to the seller's attempting to repair the goods should therefore make clear that he does so without prejudice to his right to reject if the repair proves ineffective and that the time involved in attempting the repair should not be taken into account in assessing what is a reasonable time.

Further, it has been held that where buyer seeks information from the seller to enable the buyer to decide whether to accept, reject or seek repair, a court may be willing to disregard the time taken to receive this information is assessing what is a reasonable time under s. 35(4). In *Clegg and another* v *Olle Andersson* [2003] EWCA Civ 320; [2003] 1 All ER (Comm) 721 a yacht was delivery August 2000 and at the time of delivery the sellers informed the buyers that the keel of the yacht was substantially heavier than the manufacturer's specification. Between August and September the buyers sought information about the overweight keel, its consequences and possible remedies from the sellers. This information was not received until 15 February 2001. Three weeks later the buyers sought to reject the yacht. The court held that time did not start to run for the purpose of s. 35(4) until the relevant information was supplied and further that three weeks was not an unreasonable time. Therefore the buyers had not lost their right to reject the goods.

Where the buyer claims to be entitled to reject but the seller disputes that right, perhaps on the basis that there has been no breach of contract, the parties may agree that the buyer should dispose of the goods without prejudice to the claim to reject. Such an arrangement avoids storage costs for the goods whilst the dispute is settled and may be especially important where the goods are perishable. The seller's agreement to such an arrangement is important since if the buyer resells the goods without the seller's agreement but with knowledge of the defect he may be taken to have accepted them.

11.3.1.6 Rejection of part

The SoGA 1979, s. 35A gives the buyer a right of partial rejection and provides that where the buyer has a right to reject the goods because of a defect affecting some of them but accepts some of the goods, including all of those unaffected by the breach, he does not lose the right to reject some or all of the goods affected. However, this is subject to the rule in s. 35(6) that if the buyer accepts some of the goods comprising a 'commercial unit' he is taken to have accepted the whole of that commercial unit. A 'commercial unit' is defined as 'a unit division of which would materially impair the value of the goods or the character of the unit'. Thus, for instance, the buyer could not reject one of a pair of shoes or one chair from a dining suite.

The overall position where some of the goods delivered are affected by a breach is therefore as follows:

(a) the buyer may reject all of the goods, provided that if the buyer is a non-consumer, he may not reject where the breach is so slight that rejection would be unreasonable;

(b) the buyer may retain all of the goods unaffected by the breach and reject some or all of the goods affected; however, if he retains any of the unaffected goods he must retain all of them;

(c) where only part of a 'commercial unit' is affected by the breach the buyer must accept or reject the unit as a whole.

There is no reason why the contract should not contain express provisions modifying these rules (see **18.5.1**, Clause 4.3 and **18.5.2**, Clause 9.2), subject only to the UCTA 1977 and the Unfair Terms in Consumer Contracts Regulations 1999 (where applicable).

11.3.1.7 Severable contracts

The buyer's rights to reject and terminate are modified where the contract is severable.

A contract is severable where the goods are to be delivered in separate instalments, separately paid for (s. 31(2)). The courts have also interpreted contracts as severable in other circumstances. For instance contracts were severable where goods were to be paid for by monthly account (*Longbottom* v *Bass Walker* (1922) WN 245) or where the contract provided for the goods to be delivered in instalments to be determined by the seller or buyer (*Jackson* v *Rotax* [1910] 2 KB 937; *Regent OHG* v *Francesco of Jermyn St* [1981] 3 All ER 327).

Where the contract is severable and the seller makes one or more defective deliveries it may be necessary to decide whether (a) the buyer can reject the defective delivery and/or (b) terminate the contract and refuse future deliveries.

Rejection of the defective delivery   Where a contract is severable, acceptance of one instalment does not prevent the buyer rejecting another instalment. In addition, s. 35A, giving the buyer a right of partial rejection, applies to an instalment under a severable contract in the same way as it applies to a contract as a whole so that where part of an instalment is defective the buyer may reject some or all of the defective goods and retain the rest.

Termination of the contract   Where the seller makes one or more defective deliveries under a severable contract, whether or not those breaches allow the buyer to terminate the whole contract depends on the terms of the contract and all the circumstances of the case. Factors which may be taken into account include:

(a) the ratio of the breach to the contract as a whole; and

(b) the likelihood of the breach being repeated.

The question whether the buyer is entitled to terminate the contract as a result of a breach by the seller may be crucial: if the buyer terminates in circumstances in which he is not entitled to do so he will be in breach. However, the application of the test is difficult to predict, as the following cases illustrate, so that the commercial practitioner may not be able to advise the buyer with certainty as to his right to terminate the contract.

(a) *Maple Flock Co. Ltd* v *Universal Furniture Products (Wembley) Ltd* [1934] 1 KB 148
    S contracted to sell 100 tons of rag flock in weekly instalments of 1.5 tons each. The first 15 deliveries were satisfactory and were accepted; the sixteenth was contaminated and the buyer purported to terminate the contract; a further four satisfactory deliveries were tendered. It was held that the breach was not so serious as to justify termination.

(b) *Robert A Munro & Co. Ltd* v *Meyer* [1930] 2 KB 312
    S contracted to sell 1,500 tons of bonemeal to be delivered in weekly instalments of 125 tons. After half the goods had been delivered it was discovered that all the deliveries were contaminated with cocoa husks. In this case it was held that the buyer was entitled to terminate the contract.

11.3.2 Damages

Any breach of contract by the seller entitles the buyer to claim damages in respect of any losses caused by the breach. Generally damages are assessed in accordance with the general rules governing damages for breach of contract; the buyer must therefore show that his losses were caused by the breach in question, that they are not too remote to be compensatable and that he has taken reasonable steps to mitigate his loss. However, these rules are modified by SoGA 1979 and different rules apply to claims for (a) non-delivery, (b) late delivery and (c) breach of warranty. The rules on damages for breach of warranty are examined at **12.6.1**.

11.3.2.1 Non-delivery

(a) *The basic measure*

The basic measure of damages for non-delivery is 'the estimated loss directly and naturally resulting, in the ordinary course of events, from the seller's breach' (s. 51(2)). However, where there is an available market for goods of the contract description, this basic rule is modified so that the buyer's damages for non-delivery are the difference between the contract price and the market price for similar goods on the date when goods should have been delivered (s. 51(3)). The rationale of this rule is that the buyer is expected to take reasonable steps to mitigate his loss and, where there is an available market, can mitigate by buying replacement goods in the market.

There is an 'available market' for this purpose if there is an available source of supply from which the buyer could buy replacement goods. There is no available market if the contract goods are unique or if demand for goods of the contract description exceeds supply. In such a case, damages will be assessed in accordance with the basic measure above.

(b) *Special damages*

Where the buyer has contracted to resell the goods but the seller fails to deliver, generally no account is taken of the price at which the buyer contracted to resell: a replacement purchase in the market will enable him to satisfy his resale contract. However, the market price rule does not prevent the buyer recovering special damages where they would be recoverable in accordance with general principles (s. 54). Thus where the buyer loses a resale because he cannot satisfy his resale by buying in the market, special damages may be recoverable to compensate the lost resale provided they are not too remote. Such damages are therefore recoverable where:

(i)   the buyer contracts to resell the goods as *specific* goods (so that he cannot tender other goods to his buyer);

(ii) he does so before the seller's breach;

(iii) such resale was foreseeable by the seller as a reasonable probability; and

(iv) the resale price is not extravagant (*Re R & H Hall & Co. Ltd and W H Pim (Jnr) & Co. Ltd's Arbitration* (1927) 30 Ll L Rep 159).

11.3.2.2 Late delivery

The basic measure of damages for late delivery is similarly modified where there is an available market for goods of the contract description. The basic measure of damages is then the difference between the value of the goods at the date when they should have been delivered and their value at the date when they are delivered. Where there is an available market the value of the goods will be assessed by reference to the market price for such goods at the relevant dates.

11.3.3 Additional remedies in consumer cases

The EC Directive on the sale of consumer goods and associated guarantees has introduced an additional scheme of remedies for consumers. The Directive applies where a seller (meaning a natural or legal person who sells good in the course of his trade business or profession) sells consumer goods (defined as any tangible moveable item) to a consumer (that is, any natural person who is acting for purposes which are not related to his trade, business or profession) (Art. 1). Under Article 2 of the Directive the seller must deliver goods which conform with the contract. Where there is a lack of conformity the Directive provides that a consumer's primary rights are to require the seller to repair or replace the goods, unless this is impossible or disproportionate. Under the Directive a remedy is disproportionate in comparison to another remedy if it imposes on the seller, in comparison to the alternate remedy, costs which are unreasonable taking into account (i) the value of the goods, (ii) the significance of the goods failure to conform to the contract, (iii) the inconvenience of the alternative remedy to the consumer. In more limited circumstances, a consumer may be entitled to a reduction in the price or to have the contract rescinded (that is, reject the goods and get a refund of the price) (Art. 3). Under Article 5 a seller remains liable for any lack of conformity for two years following delivery. Further, any lack of conformity which becomes apparent within six months of delivery will be presumed to have existed at the time of delivery (Art. 5).

This Directive has been transposed in the UK by the Sale and Supply of Goods to Consumers Regulations 2002 (SI 2002 No. 3045). Under the Regulations 'consumer' is defined as any natural person who is acting for purposes which are outside his trade, business or profession; and 'goods' has the same meaning as under s. 61 of SoGA 1979 (Reg. 2). The intention in transposing this Directive was not to reduce existing levels of consumer protection. Therefore, the Directive's remedial scheme co-exists with remedies under SoGA 1979. The result is a complex remedial scheme for consumers. First, consumers continue to enjoy an absolute right to reject goods for breach of condition, albeit for a relatively short time after delivery, under ss. 34 and 35, SoGA 1979. Secondly, any existing right to damages for breach of warranty remains, and such a claim to damages is available for up to six years after the time of sale. Thirdly and additionally, a new Part 5A (ss. 48A–F) is inserted in SoGA 1979 setting out additional rights where the buyer deals as a consumer and the goods do not conform to the contract at the time of delivery (Reg. 5). Goods do not conform to a contract of sale where there is a breach of an express term of the contract or a term implied by ss. 13–15 of SoGA 1979 (s. 48F). As noted above, under the Directive the remedial scheme for buyers is only available where a lack of conformity manifests itself within two years of the date of delivery. To avoid confusion between the normal six year limitation period and this two year manifestation period this aspects of the Directive was not implemented in the Regulations. Hence the only procedural restriction for consumers is the normal limitation period of six years. Moreover, section 48A(3) provides that a lack of conformity which manifests itself within the period of six months from delivery is rebuttably presumed to have existed at the time of delivery. Beyond this six month period, the burden of proving lack of conformity shifts back to the buyer.

Section 48A(2) provides that a buyer has the right:

(a) to require the seller to repair or replace the goods (see further s. 48B), or

(b) (i) to require the seller to reduce the purchase price by an appropriate
        amount; or

    (ii) to rescind the contract (see further s. 48C).

Under s. 48B a buyer may require a seller to repair or replace the goods (s. 48B(1)). If so requested, the seller must repair or replace the goods within a reasonable time but without causing significant inconvenience to the buyer, and the seller must bear any necessary cost (s. 48B(2)). Any question as to what is a reasonable time or significant inconvenience is to be determined by reference to (a) the nature of the goods, and (b) the purpose for which the goods are required (s. 48B(5)). The buyer cannot require repair or replacement if it would be

(a) impossible;

(b) disproportionate in comparison to other remedies; or

(c) disproportionate in comparison to price reduction or rescission under the Regulations (s. 48B(3)).

A remedy is disproportionate in comparison to another if the one imposes costs in the seller which are unreasonable, taking into account:

(a) the value which the goods would have if they conformed to the contract;

(b) the significance of the lack of conformity; and

(c) whether the other remedy could be effected without significance inconvenience to the buyer.

Under s. 48C a buyer may require price reduction by an appropriate amount or rescission of the contract provided that

(a) the buyer may require neither repair or replacement under s. 48B(3), or

(b) the buyer has required repair or replacement but the seller has failed to do so within a reasonable time or without significant inconvenience to the buyer.

Lastly, where a buyer rescinds a contract, any reimbursement to the buyer may be reduced to take account of any use he has had of the goods since delivery (ss. (3)).

A consumer who receives goods which do not conform to the contract therefore has an initial choice between the remedies of rejection and/or damages derived from the SoGA and the new remedies under Part 5A of the Act derived from the Directive. Where the lack of conformity amounts to a breach of condition the consumer is therefore entitled to reject the goods and is not required to act reasonably in deciding whether or not to exercise the right to reject (*Clegg and another* v *Olle Andersson* [2003] EWCA Civ 320; [2003] 1 All ER (Comm) 721). However, if the consumer elects to seek repair or replacement of the goods under s. 48B, he may not then reject the goods unless and until the seller has had a reasonable time to effect repair or replacement, as the case may be (s. 48D).

11.3.4 Specific performance

Generally the court may order specific performance of a contract to sell goods but will only do so where the contract is for the sale of specific or ascertained goods. Since the remedy is discretionary it will only be awarded where the goods are unique. Consumer buyers now have rights to have goods repaired or replaced if they do not conform with the contract (SoGA, Part 5A; see **11.3.3**). The rights of repair and replacement are effectively forms of specific performance. The court is therefore given power to order specific performance of the obligations to repair and replace goods in consumer cases (s. 48E(2)).

11.3.5 Re-drafting the delivery obligations

As noted above many of the obligations as set out in the 1979 Act apply 'unless agreed otherwise'. Where the above rules do not suit one party's or both parties' needs, they should be expressly amended, preferably in written form for evidential reasons.

The seller cannot wholly exclude the delivery obligation as this would render the contract useless; however, most of the other rules as to delivery, such as those as to the place of delivery (**11.2.2**) can be altered. The contract will often contain express provisions dealing with the following.

(a) Responsibility for the cost of delivery: to avoid uncertainties this should be expressly provided for (see **18.5.1**, Clause 2.1 and **18.5.2**, Clause 6.4).

(b) Storage costs: who is to bear the cost of storing the goods if delivery is delayed (see **18.5.1**, Clause 2.2)?

(c) The time of delivery (see **11.2.4**): the seller may want the right to vary the time of delivery; the buyer might want to make such a variation conditional upon his consent (see **18.5.2**, Clause 6.1).

(d) The giving of notice that the goods are ready for collection (see **18.5.1**, Clause 2.2).

(e) Risk in transit: normally the buyer bears this cost but if he is in a stronger bargaining position, this burden could be shifted back to the seller (see **14.3** and **18.5.2**, Clause 8.2).

(f) Quantity: as the statutory rules as to the quantity to be delivered are strict, the seller will want the contract to allow for variation; for instance, 'the seller shall be entitled to deliver a quantity of goods up to 5 per cent greater or less than the contract quantity and the buyer shall accept the actual quantity' (see **18.5.1**, Clause 3 and **18.5.2**, Clause 4).

(g) A force majeure clause excusing the seller where delivery is hindered or prevented by circumstances outside his control (see **2.8.3**, **18.5.1**, Clause 2.4.2 and **18.5.2**, Clause 12).

11.4 Summary

Having completed this chapter you should:

- understand the concept of delivery and how delivery is effected in law;
- be aware of the legal rules governing the time and place of delivery and the quantity of goods to be delivered;
- be aware of the remedies available to the buyer in the event of breach by the seller and in particular—
  - the availability of the right to reject for breach of condition;
  - the remedies available for delivery of the wrong quantity;
  - the rights of the buyer in the event of late delivery;
  - the calculation of damages for non-delivery, late delivery and defective delivery;
- be aware of the legal controls on terms defining the delivery obligation and/or exclusion of the seller's liability for breach of his delivery obligation;
- be aware of the main considerations to be taken into account when drafting terms relating to delivery in a sale contract.

Terms relating to the goods

12.1 Introduction

In this chapter we examine the statuory implied terms in relation to the goods under a sales contract. These terms impose legal obligations on the sellers of goods as regards their right to sell the goods and the quality of the goods. In practice, where a buyer wishes to escape from the contract, it may be argued that the seller has breached one or more of these statutory implied terms. In particular:

- we examine, in detail, the obligations placed on sellers by the implied terms in relation to the goods in ss. 12–15 of SoGA 1979;
- we note the overlapping nature of these terms;
- we consider the extent to which these terms can be altered using exclusion clauses and other express terms; and
- we outline the buyer's remedies for breach of these terms.

12.1.1 The implied terms

Sections 12–15 of SoGA 1979 imply into contracts of sale a series of terms concerned with the condition of the goods sold and the seller's right to sell them. The terms can be broadly categorised into five groups:

(a) an implied *condition* that the seller has the right to sell the goods, and implied warranties that the goods are free from any encumbrances or charges and that the buyer will enjoy quiet possession of the goods (s. 12);

(b) an implied *condition* that the goods will correspond with their description (s. 13);

(c) an implied *condition* that the goods will be of satisfactory quality (s. 14(2));

(d) an implied *condition* that, where the buyer makes known to the seller his purpose for buying the goods, the goods will be fit for that purpose (s. 14(3)); and

(e) an implied *condition* that where goods are sold by sample, they will comply with that sample (s. 15).

The contract may contain other terms relating to these and similar matters, but the statutory implied terms are significant because:

(a) they are easy to prove: some apply automatically to every contract of sale, so that there is no need to prove the term by evidence of the words used;

(b) they are expressly classified by the Act as either conditions or warranties; however, the right of a non-consumer buyer to reject the goods for breach of the implied conditions in ss. 13–15 is limited in certain circumstances (see **11.3.1**);

(c) liability for breach is strict;

(d) exclusion or limitation of the terms or of liability for their breach is restricted by UCTA 1977 (see **12.1.1**).

The seller will generally want to minimise the effects of these provisions in order to minimise his liability; the buyer will want to maximise their effect and, perhaps, to supplement them by express terms.

12.1.2 Excluding the implied terms

The seller's power to exclude the statutory implied terms is restricted by the common law and by UCTA 1977. Any attempt to exclude the terms may be construed strictly, *contra proferentem*. Since the protection offered by the implied terms may overlap, so that the same event may amount to a breach of two or more terms, any attempt to exclude the implied terms must therefore be drafted with care (see **18.5.1**, Clause 4.5).

The limitations imposed by UCTA 1977 tend now to be more significant. UCTA 1977, s. 6 provides that:

(a) the implied terms relating to title and the seller's right to sell the goods (SoGA 1979, s. 12) can never be excluded;

(b) the implied terms relating to correspondence with description, quality, fitness for purpose and correspondence with sample (SoGA 1979, ss. 13–15) can never be excluded where the buyer deals as a consumer (see **3.4.3.3**) and in other cases can be excluded only insofar as the exclusion satisfies the test of reasonableness.

UCTA 1977, s. 7 imposes similar restrictions on attempts to exclude the corresponding implied terms in other contracts involving the supply of goods.

In addition, it is a criminal offence to include in a contract a term, or to display a notice, which purports to exclude the statutory implied terms, or restrict liability for their breach, etc., as against a person who deals as a consumer (Consumer Transactions (Restrictions on Statements Order) 1976 (SI 1976, No. 1813)). Sellers will often wish to restrict liability for breach of the statutory implied terms, or exclude them altogether; care must therefore be taken when drafting any such exclusion to avoid committing a criminal offence. This causes particular difficulty when preparing standard contract terms which may be used for both consumer and non-consumer buyers; in such a case the relevant exclusion might be prefaced with words such as:

Where the buyer deals as a consumer within the meaning of s. 12 of the Unfair Contract Terms Act 1977, sub-clause (a) of this clause shall have no effect.

Such a provision contradicts the spirit of the restrictions on exclusion clauses but may be effective (see *R & B Customs Brokers Ltd* v *United Dominions Trust Co. Ltd* [1988] 1 All ER 847 where such a clause received no adverse comment).

An attempt to exclude or limit the implied terms in a consumer contract may also be subject to a test of fairness under the Unfair Terms in Consumer Contract Regulations (see **3.4.4**), but since such exclusion is wholly prohibited by UCTA 1977, s. 6, the Regulations have little significance in this context.

12.2 Title—Sale of Goods Act 1979, section 12

We have noted that the essence of a sales contract is the transfer of property from the seller to the buyer. We have also noted that the seller's duty to deliver is defined in terms of the transfer of possession not title, ownership or property. However, s. 12 goes some way to fill this lacuna. Section 12 implies three terms:

(a) an implied condition that the seller has the right to sell the goods;

(b) an implied warranty that the goods are free from any encumbrances or charges; and

(c) an implied warranty that the buyer will enjoy quiet possession of the goods.

These terms cannot be excluded or restricted in any domestic contract of sale (UCTA 1977, s. 6; since UCTA 1977 does not apply to international supply contracts (UCTA 1977, s. 26) the terms can be excluded in an international contract). However, liability under SoGA 1979, s. 12(2) can be avoided by disclosure of charges or encumbrances before the contract is concluded (see **12.2.2** and **12.2.3**). In addition, where the seller contracts to sell only a limited title, these implied terms are replaced by more restricted implied undertakings (s. 12(3): see **12.2.4**).

12.2.1 The right to sell

Section 12(1) provides:

In a contract of sale … there is an implied condition on the part of the seller that in the case of a sale he has a right to sell the goods, and in the case of an agreement to sell he will have such a right at the time when the property is to pass.

This section does not require that the seller be the owner of the goods sold, but only that he has *the right to sell*. So for instance an agent is empowered to sell goods which belong to his principal, on his principal's behalf.

Conversely there may be a breach of s. 12 where a person sells goods which he does own if they infringe someone's intellectual property rights. This is what happened in *Niblett* v *Confectioners' Materials Co. Ltd* [1921] 3 KB 387, where the defendants, an American company, sold 3,000 tins of condensed milk to the plaintiffs, but when the goods arrived in England, customs officials seized the goods on the grounds that the labels infringed a well known company's trademark (see **Chapter 35**). It was held that as the trade mark owner could have obtained an injunction to restrain the sale of the goods, the sellers had no right to sell them.

12.2.1.1 At what time?

The implied term imposes different requirements on a sale and an agreement to sell. In the case of an outright sale, the seller must have the right to sell at the time the contract is made; in contrast, in the case of an agreement to sell, the requirement is that the seller must have the right to sell at the time the property is to pass. However, the terms of the contract may expressly or impliedly contain an undertaking that the seller owns, or has the right to sell the goods at the time the contract is made. For instance, a contract provision in a conditional sale agreement that the 'property in the goods shall remain with the seller until payment' may be held to imply an undertaking that the seller has property in the goods at the time the contract is made (see *Barber* v *NWS Bank plc* [1996] 1 WLR 641) and it has been held that such a term may be implied at common law as a legal incident of a conditional sale agreement. Such express or implied provision may be held to be a condition. It would be broken if, for example, the seller had purchased the goods under a conditional sale agreement (for instance, under a sale subject to a reservation of title) under which property had not yet passed to him at the time of the sale. Care must be taken when drafting conditional sale agreements and reservation of title clauses to try to ensure that such additional undertakings are not given inadvertently.

EXAMPLE

On Monday A agrees to sell C's car to B on Friday. Section 12 is not breached although at the time of the agreement C still owns his car. However, A will be in breach of s. 12 if he fails to obtain the right to sell the car by Friday.

Even where the seller has no right to sell when the property is to pass, it is possible for the seller to acquire that right later, and that right will feed into the sale so that any breach of s. 12 is retrospectively cured. This occurred in *Butterworth* v *Kingsway Motors Ltd* [1954] 2 All ER 694. A took a car on hire-purchase and, mistakenly believing that she had the right to sell it subject to her continuing to pay the instalments, purported to sell the car to B. B resold it to C, who sold it to the defendant, who sold it to the plaintiff. Despite these transactions the hire purchase company remained owners of the car and after the plaintiff had had the car for over eleven months, the hire purchase company repossessed the car. The plaintiff then claimed repayment of the complete purchase price from the defendant, on the basis of a breach of the implied term in s. 12. Eight days later A made the final payment under the hire purchase contract. It was held that when A made the final payment, she acquired title to the goods and this 'fed' through to the defendants. The court did not address the issue of whether the plaintiff would have succeeded if the claim had been made after the title had fed through.

12.2.1.2 Effect of breach

Since the implied term in s. 12(1) is a condition, breach allows the buyer to reject the goods and terminate the contract. However, it has been held that the rule that the buyer loses the right to reject goods for breach of condition if he has accepted them (s. 11(4): see **11.3.1.3**) does not apply where there is a breach of s. 12, on the grounds that breach of s. 12 gives rise to a total failure of consideration entitling the buyer to a refund of any money paid for the goods. This anomalous rule is a result of the case of *Rowland* v *Divall* [1923] 2 KB 500. There the plaintiff bought a car from the defendant for £334 and re-sold it for £400 to a sub-buyer, who used it for four months. It turned out that the car had never belonged to the defendant because he bought it in good faith from someone without title. The car was reclaimed by its original owner and the plaintiff refunded the sub-buyer £400 and then claimed from the defendant £334 on the basis that there had been a total failure of consideration due to the breach of the condition. The defendant admitted liability for breach, but argued that there was not a total failure of consideration as the plaintiff and the sub-buyer had had four months' use of the car. The Court of Appeal found that there was a total failure of consideration and allowed him a total refund; the breach was so fundamental that the plaintiff could not have accepted the goods.

12.2.2 Freedom from encumbrances

Section 12(2) provides:
In a contract of sale . . . there is an implied warranty that—

(a) the goods are free and will remain free until the time when the property is to pass, from any charge or encumbrance not disclosed or known to the buyer before the contract of sale.

This appears to add little to s. 12(1), as the law does not recognise real encumbrances over chattels by someone not in possession of them, and even equitable rights must give way to a bona fide purchaser without notice. The measure of damages for a breach of this warranty would usually be the amount it takes to discharge the charge or encumbrance.

12.2.3 Peaceful enjoyment

Section 12(2) also provides:

In a contract of sale . . . there is also an implied warranty that—

(b) the buyer will enjoy quiet possession of the goods except so far as it may be disturbed by the owner or other person entitled to the benefit of any charge or encumbrance so disclosed or known.

It appears that this warranty will be breached if the buyer is disturbed by the wrongful act of the seller or by any person claiming through him, or by a lawful act of any other person, including the true but dispossessed owner: *Mason* v *Burningham* [1949] 2 KB 545. For example, in *Rubicon Computer Systems Ltd* v *United Paints Ltd* (2000) 2 TCLR 453, there was a contract to supply a computer system. Following installation and part-payment a dispute arose. The supplier had installed a 'time-lock', which when activated rendered the system unusable. It was held, *inter alia*, that the supplier's installation of the 'time-lock' constituted wrongful interference with the goods and accordingly there was a breach of s. 12(2)(b). The section imposes a continuing warranty, so that it was breached in *Microbeads AG* v *Vinhurst Road Markings Ltd* [1975] 1 All ER 529, where the Court of Appeal awarded damages under s. 12(2) to a buyer whose quiet possession was disturbed by a patentee who had been granted a patent after the sale, so there was no breach of s. 12(1).

12.2.4 Sale of a limited title

Where it appears from the contract or the surrounding circumstances that it is intended that the seller should transfer only such title as he or a third party has, the implied terms in s. 12(1)–(2) are replaced by more limited implied warranties that:

(a) all charges or incumbrances known to the seller and not to the buyer have been disclosed to the buyer before the contract is made; and

(b) the buyer's possession will not be disturbed by the seller, by the third party whose title is transferred, or by any person claiming through the seller or that third party, except where they claim under an encumbrance disclosed to the buyer (s. 12(3)–(5)).

These provisions govern the situation where, e.g., goods seized in execution are sold by a bailiff or sheriff who is unsure of the execution debtor's title to the goods. There seems to be no reason why other sellers should not take advantage of these provisions by contracting to sell only such title as they have so that, for instance, if the goods breach the intellectual property rights of a third party there would be no breach of the implied terms.

12.3 Sale by Description—Sale of Goods Act 1979, section 13

Sections 13 and 14 imply three conditions relating to the goods supplied under the contract, each offering the buyer greater protection than the one before. These provisions tend to overlap and the same circumstances may amount to a breach of two or even all three implied conditions; in practice a case is often pleaded as a breach of all three. The overlap between the provisions must also be borne in mind when drafting contract terms seeking to exclude or restrict the implied terms since any exclusion clause may be interpreted strictly, *contra proferentem*.

Section 13(1) provides:

Where there is a contract for the sale of goods by description, there is an implied condition that the goods will correspond with the description.

12.3.1 Application

Unless excluded, section 13 applies to all sales whether the seller acts in the course of a business or privately; where the buyer acts as a consumer the implied term cannot be excluded.

In considering s. 13, three questions must be addressed.

(a) When is a sale a sale by description?

(b) What is the contractual description?

(c) Do the goods correspond with the description?

12.3.2 When is a sale a sale by description?

Clearly where future or unascertained goods are sold there must be a description by which the goods can be identified, so the sale would be a sale by description. However, SoGA 1979 and cases decided under it make clear that a sale may be by description in other circumstances. Section 13(3) states that:

A sale of goods is not prevented from being a sale by description by reason only that, being exposed for sale or hire, they are selected by the buyer.

Thus sales from retail outlets where goods are packaged and/or labelled in some way and set out for display, such as in supermarkets, may be sales by description.

However, in order for goods to be sold *by* description, the descriptive words must be influential in the sale. The circumstances must be such that the parties might reasonably expect the description to influence the buyer in his decision to buy the goods. In *Harlingdon & Leinster Ltd* v *Christopher Hull Fine Art Ltd* [1990] 1 All ER 737, a painting sold by the defendant for £600 was described as being by Munter, a German expressionist. However, the seller emphasised that he had no expertise in this area of fine art and the buyer obtained the opinion of its own expert. It was later discovered that the painting was a fake, worth about £50–£100. The buyer sought to reject the goods on the basis that they did not comply with the description. The Court of Appeal held that in view of the disclaimer by the seller the buyer could not reasonably be expected to rely on the description of the painting as a Munter so that the sale was not a sale by description. This case suggests that a seller could avoid liability under s. 13 by simply disclaiming any knowledge or expertise as to the goods; however, it should be noted that the contract was for the sale of a painting, an essentially speculative venture and a similar disclaimer might not be effective in other circumstances.

It should therefore be assumed that as a general rule most sales where descriptive words are used to refer to the goods may be sales by description.

12.3.3 What words form the description?

In order to minimise the overlap between the implied terms in ss. 13 and 14 the courts have sought to restrict the ambit of s. 13, and case law makes clear that not every statement about quality or fitness of the goods can be treated as a part of the description. However, it is not easy to predict when words will be construed as forming part of the contract description. Modern cases have tended to adopt a more restrictive approach, under which words 'which were intended by the parties to identify the kind of goods to be supplied' (Lord Diplock in *Ashington Piggeries Ltd v Christopher Hill Ltd* [1972] AC 441 at 503), or which identify an essential commercial characteristic of the goods to be supplied are taken as part of the contract description. However, older cases interpreted s. 13 more widely.

The following have been held to form part of the description by which goods are sold:

(a) a statement in a contract for sale of wooden staves that the staves should be half an inch thick (*Arcos Ltd v E A Ronaasen & Son* [1933] AC 470);

(b) a statement in a contract for the sale of 3,000 tins of fruit that the tins should be packed in cases of 30 tins (*Re Moore & Co. Ltd and Landauer & Co. Ltd* [1921] 2 KB 519); there was therefore a breach when the seller delivered the full quantity of tins but some were packed in cases of 24 tins, so that the buyer could reject the goods for breach of s. 13.

(c) the date of shipment of goods (*Bowes v Shand* (1877) 2 App Cas 455);

(d) markings on the goods (*Smith Bros (Hull) Ltd v Gosta Jacobsson & Co.* [1961] 2 Lloyd's Rep 522).

Conversely in *Reardon Smith Line Ltd v Yngvar Hansen-Tangen* [1976] 3 All ER 570, shipbuilders contracted to build a ship to a detailed specification at Yard No. 354 at Osaka Zosen. The ship was in fact built elsewhere, but the House of Lords held that the words as to the location of construction were of no legal significance, they did not form part of the description of the goods; the description of the ship was to be found in the specifications. Lord Wilberforce stated that the implied term as to description was concerned with words which identify 'an essential part of the description of the goods'.

Case law must therefore be treated with care; each case must be looked at in the light of the surrounding circumstances, the language used and its commercial setting; older cases especially should be treated with caution. However, from the seller's perspective, although not all words of description form part of the contractual description and come within s. 13, care should be taken in describing goods for sale in light of the case law.

12.3.4 Breach

Once it is decided that a word or phrase forms part of the description by which the goods are sold, the goods must exactly correspond to that description or there will be a breach of the condition implied by s. 13 enabling the buyer to reject the goods, terminate the contract and sue for damages.

Where the goods delivered are totally different from those contracted for there is clearly a breach. However, in other cases it may be more difficult to decide whether goods do correspond to their description. The *Ashington Piggeries* case concerned a sale of herring meal for feeding to mink. The meal turned out to be contaminated by a substance which made it unsuitable for feeding to mink. It was held that there was no breach of s. 13 because the goods could still be properly be described as 'herring meal', i.e. contaminated herring meal is still herring meal. (This case is notable for the very narrow interpretation it gives to s. 13 but in fact the buyers were successful in their claim under s. 14: see **12.4**.)

The courts have found a breach of s. 13 where:

(a) Western Madras cotton was tendered for Long Staple Salem cotton (*Azemar* v *Casella* (1867) LR 2 CP 677);

(b) a mixture of hemp and rape oil was tendered under a contract for foreign refined rape oil (*Nichol* v *Godts* (1854) 10 Exch 191);

(c) copra cake was contaminated with so large an admixture of castor bean as to render it poisonous (*Pinnock Bros* v *Lewis & Peat Ltd* [1923] 1 KB 690);

(d) meat and bone meal was contaminated with 5 per cent cocoa husks (*Robert A Munro & Co.* v *Meyer* [1930] 2 KB 312);

(e) under a contract for sale of wooden staves half an inch thick, around 95 per cent of the staves delivered were about $\frac{9}{16}$ inches thick, even though they were found to be merchantable (now satisfactory) and perfectly suitable for the buyer's intended purpose (*Arcos Ltd* v *E A Ronaasen & Son* [1933] AC 470); specifications in commercial contracts are usually interpreted strictly.

Liability for breach of the implied condition is strict; it is therefore no defence for the seller to argue that the failure of the goods to correspond with the contract description was not his fault.

12.3.5   Practice

Commercial contracts will often contain provisions which affect the application of s. 13. For instance, the contract may expressly provide that certain statements, such as those relating to packaging or dates of arrival, are not to form part of the contractual description; or, in a case such as *Arcos* v *Ronaasen*, provide for a tolerance or margin, e.g. 'lengths of between 98 and 102 cm' or 'lengths of 1 metre, plus or minus 2 per cent'. Where the term amounts to an exclusion of liability its effectiveness will be regulated by the common law and by UCTA 1977.

12.3.5.1   Exclusion of liability

A clause which seeks to exclude liablity for breach of the implied condition in s. 13 may be construed strictly. It is unlikely that a court would construe a clause as permitting the seller to deliver goods wholly different from those contracted for, and a clause excluding or limiting liability for 'defects' may be construed as referring to liability under s. 14 but not that under s. 13.

Exclusion of the term implied by s. 13, or of liability etc. for its breach, is also controlled by UCTA 1977, s. 6 (see **12.1.1**).

12.4   Quality and fitness—Sale of Goods Act 1979, section 14

Having stated the basic common law principle of *caveat emptor* (let the buyer beware) in subsection (1), SoGA 1979, s. 14 implies two conditions to protect the position of the buyer, which require that the goods supplied must be:

(a) of satisfactory quality; and

(b) reasonably fit for the buyer's purpose.

12.4.1   Application

12.4.1.1   Sale in the course of business

Unlike s. 13, s. 14 only applies to sales 'in the course of a business' and hence not to purely private sales. The meaning of this term, in the context of s. 14, was considered for the first time in *Stevenson* v *Rogers* [1999] 1 All ER 613 where a person, who carried on the business of fisherman, sold his trawler to another fisherman. The Court of Appeal held that the sale was 'in the course of a business'. This finding was based on an examination of the legislative history of the term (see *Pepper* v *Hart* [1993] AC 593). Accordingly, a business seller of goods, whether or not habitually dealing in goods of the type sold, will be considered to be acting 'in the course of a business'. In reaching this finding, the court distinguished cases that had interpreted the term more restrictively, such as *Davies* v *Sumner* [1984] 3 All ER 831 where the House of Lords held that a courier who sold his car had not acted 'in the course of a business' for the purposes of the Trade Descriptions Act 1968; and *R&B Customs Broker Ltd* v *United Dominions Trust Ltd* [1988] 1 All ER 847, where the Court of Appeal held that a freight forwarding company who had bought three cars over a period of five years was not acting 'in the course of a business' when buying the cars for the purposes of the Unfair Contract Terms Act 1977 (see **3.4.3.3**).

12.4.1.2   Scope

The conditions in s. 14 apply to *goods supplied under the contract*, not merely the goods sold, so that a defect in the packaging of the goods might render the goods of unsatisfactory quality, even if the packaging is returnable (*Geddling* v *Marsh* [1920] 1 KB 668).

12.4.2   Satisfactory quality: s. 14(2)

SoGA 1979, like the Sale of Goods Act 1893, required that goods supplied under a sale contract be of 'merchantable quality'. This has now been replaced by a requirement of 'satisfactory quality' (Sale and Supply of Goods Act 1994). The 1994 Act defines 'satisfactory quality' and contains a non-exhaustive list of factors to be taken into account in assessing quality. These changes are based on a Law Commission Report (No. 160) and they seek to clarify the law rather than change it. In the absence of a significant body of case law on the meaning of satisfactory quality, cases on the meaning of merchantable quality may still be relevant. In one case on the meaning of 'satisfactory quality', the court was referred to a number of cases decided before 1994, although the court found them not to be 'of much assistance' (see *Thain* v *Anniesland Trade Centre* 1997 SLT (Sh Ct) 102).

Section 14(2) now provides:

Where the seller sells goods in the course of a business, there is an implied term that the goods supplied under the contract are of satisfactory quality.

Section 14(6) provides that the term implied by subsection (2) is a condition. However, where the buyer is not a consumer, his right to reject the goods for breach is limited (see **11.3.1**).

12.4.2.1   The meaning of satisfactory

Section 14(2A) provides:

. . . goods are of satisfactory quality if they meet the standard that a reasonable person would regard as satisfactory, taking account of any description of the goods, the price (if relevant) and all the other relevant circumstances.

The description applied to goods will affect the standard reasonably expected of them; for instance a higher standard would be expected from goods described as 'brand new' than those described as 'second-hand'. In *Rogers* v *Parish (Scarborough) Ltd* [1987] QB 933, a buyer bought a 'new Range Rover' for £16,000. The car suffered from a number of minor defects and was held to be unmerchantable. The Court of Appeal emphasised the importance of the descriptions 'new' and 'Range Rover':

> In the present case the car was sold as new. Deficiencies which might be acceptable in a second-hand vehicle were not to be expected in one purchased as new. Next, the description 'Range Rover' would conjure up a particular set of expectations, not the same as those relating to an ordinary saloon car, as to the balance between performance, handling, comfort and resilience (*per* Mustill LJ at 944).

A lower standard would be expected of a second-hand vehicle (see *Bartlett* v *Sidney Marcus Ltd* [1965] 2 All ER 753; *Thain* v *Anniesland Trade Centre* 1997 SLT (Sh Ct) 102) or goods described as 'seconds' or 'shop-soiled'.

Price is also expressly referred to. In *Rogers* the car was bought for £16,000 whereas in *Bartlett* the car was bought at a 'reduced price'. This is clearly relevant to the standard of quality which would be expected from goods.

Section 14(2B) states:

> . . . the quality of the goods includes their state and condition and the following (among others) are in appropriate cases aspects of the quality of the goods—
>
> (a) fitness for all purposes for which goods of the kind in question are commonly supplied,
>
> (b) appearance and finish,
>
> (c) freedom from minor defects,
>
> (d) safety, and
>
> (e) durability.

Similar factors were taken into account when assessing merchantability. We will examine each of these factors in turn, seeking guidance from the case law on merchantability.

(a) *Fitness for all common purposes*

It is now clearly established that to be of satisfactory quality goods must be fit for all their common purposes. The test of merchantability had required that goods must be fit for the *purpose or purposes* for which they are commonly bought. However, in *Aswan Engineering Establishment Co.* v *Lupdine Ltd* [1987] 1 All ER 135 it was held that, where goods had more than one common purpose they would be merchantable provided they are reasonably fit for any one of their common purposes. This clearly favoured the seller by placing the onus on the buyer to make known to the seller his purpose for buying the goods, and hence forcing him to rely on s. 14(3) (see **12.4.3**). The new test of satisfactory quality restores the balance in favour of the buyer of goods.

(b) *Appearance and finish*

Issues of appearance and finish of the goods will probably be more relevant to the sale of new, as opposed to second-hand, goods and to consumer, rather than commercial sales.

In *Rogers* v *Parish*, Mustill LJ at p. 944 in referring to the test of merchantability stated:

> . . . one would include in respect of any passenger vehicle not merely the buyer's purpose of driving the car from one place to another but of doing so with the appropriate degree of comfort, ease of handling and reliability and, one might add, of pride in the vehicle's outward and interior appearance. What is the appropriate degree and what relative weight is to be attached to one characteristic of the car rather than another will depend on the market at which the car is aimed.

(c) *Freedom from minor defects*

'Minor defect' is not defined in the new legislation because it was felt that any definition would have to be too vague or else too detailed to cover the variety of circumstances. Hence what amounts to a minor defect will remain uncertain and develop on a case by case basis. What is clear is that it is not intended that goods which have minor defects will necessarily be of unsatisfactory quality.

'Minor defects' can include defects relating both to the appearance and to the purpose of the goods, for example, the operation of a machine. As with appearance and finish, freedom from minor defects will probably be more relevant to the sale of new, as opposed to second-hand, goods and to consumer, rather than commercial sales.

Again in *Rogers* v *Parish*, the defects in a new Range Rover included misfiring, oil leaks, paint scratches and engine noise. These were categorised as minor but the car was nevertheless found to be unmerchantable. Both Mustill LJ and Sir Edward Eveleigh were of the opinion that the fact that the car was sold with a manufacturer's warranty did not make it merchantable at the time of delivery. In contrast, in the earlier case of *Millars of Falkirk Ltd* v *Turpie* 1976 SLT 66, where a car was delivered with a slight oil leak in the power steering system, it was held, on appeal, that the car was merchantable. One of the factors which led to this decision was that the defect was minor and could readily and easily be repaired. It is not clear whether a court would reach the same conclusion applying the test of satisfactory quality.

In the past, the courts were reluctant to find that goods were of unmerchantable quality, so as to allow the buyer to reject them, where the defect was minor. For instance, in *Cehave NV* v *Bremer Handelsgesellschaft mbH* [1976] QB 44 it was found that a cargo of citrus cattle food pellets which was overheated was 'far from perfect' but the court found that the goods were merchantable as they could still be used for the buyer's purpose. Similar cases will now be decided using s. 15A (see **11.3.1.3**).

(d) *Safety*

Defects which render goods unsafe may make them unsatisfactory. In *Clegg and another* v *Olle Andersson* [2003] EWCA Civ 320; [2003] 1 All ER (Comm) 721 a yacht was bought but the keel of the yacht was substantially heavier than the manufacturer's specification. The Court of Appeal found that a reasonable person would consider that the yacht was not of satisfactory quality because of the overweight keel, the adverse effect it had on rig safety and the need for more than minimal remedial work and hence there was a breach of s. 14(2). However, safety is not an absolute requirement so that, for instance, goods are not necessarily unsatisfactory merely because they could have been made safer (see e.g. *Medivance Instruments* v *Gaslane Pipework Services* [2002] EWCA Civ 500).

Safety has also been emphasised in a number of cases concerning motor cars, notably *Lee* v *York Coach & Marine* [1977] RTR 35 and *Bernstein* v *Pamsons Motors (Golders Green) Ltd* [1987] 2 All ER 220. In the latter case, a new Nissan Laurel car, bought for just under £8,000, seized up after three weeks and about 140 miles driving due to a blob of sealant which blocked the oil supply. It was held that the car was unmerchantable. Although the defect was repairable, it had major consequences. The court emphasised the potentially disastrous consequences of the car seizing up while being driven at speed.

Clearly safety will be a particularly important factor in cases concerned with consumer goods.

(e) *Durability*

In order to be of satisfactory quality the goods must be reasonably durable, i.e., in such a condition when delivered that they will remain usable for a reasonable time. In *Mash and Murrell* v *Joseph I Emmanuel* [1961] 1 All ER 485 (reversed on facts [1962] 1 All ER 77, but followed in *The Rio Sun* [1985] 1 Lloyd's Rep 350), sellers in Cyprus sold potatoes, c. & f. Liverpool. The potatoes, although sound when loaded, had deteriorated by the time the ship reached Liverpool. It was held that the seller had breached the merchantability requirement because the goods should have been loaded in 'such a state that they could endure the normal journey and be in a merchantable condition on arrival'.

It should be noted, however, that the requirement that goods be supplied in a reasonably durable condition applies to their condition at the time of supply. If the goods break down or deteriorate earlier than would reasonably be expected, that may be evidence of a lack of durability or of a defect in the goods at the time of supply. If, however, it is shown that a breakdown is due to some other factor, such as misuse by the buyer, rather than a defect present at the time of supply, the goods will not be of unsatisfactory quality on grounds of lack of durability.

In any case the standard of durability to be expected will be affected by other factors, such as the price and description of the goods. In *Thain* v *Anniesland Trade Centre* (1997) SLT (Sh Ct) 102, the plaintiff bought a five year old, second-hand Renault car, which had done some 80,000 miles, for a price of £2,995. About two weeks after the sale the gear box began to show signs of wear, and within a few weeks it wore out completely so that the car was unusable. It was found as fact, however, that the car was fit for its purpose at the time of sale and that the defect was one which could occur at any time in a car of this age and mileage, and that the car was therefore not unsatisfactory on the grounds of lack of durability.

(f) *Public statements about the goods*

The Sale and Supply of Goods to Consumers Regulations 2002 (SI 2002 No. 3045, introduced to transpose the EC Directive 1999/44/EC on the sale of consumer goods and associated guarantees) expressly identify a further factor as being relevant in assessing satisfactory quality. Section 14(2D) SoGA 1979 now provides that where the buyer deals as a consumer any public statement on the specific characteristics of the goods made about them by the seller, the producer or his representative, particularly in advertising or on labelling is relevant in assessing satisfactory quality. However, such public statements may not be relevant if the seller shows that

(a) at the time the contract was made, he was not, and could not reasonably have been aware of the statement;

(b) before the contract was made, the statement had been withdrawn in public or, to the extent that it contained anything that was incorrect or was misleading, it had been corrected in public, or

(c) the decision to buy the goods could not have been influenced by the statement (s. 14(2E)).

(g) *Other relevant factors*

The various aspects of quality listed in s. 14(2B) and the newer s. 14(2D) are not intended to be exclusive and in appropriate cases other factors and circumstances may be relevant. For instance, s. 14(2F) SoGA 1979 (inserted by the Sale and Supply of Goods to Consumers Regulations 2002) makes clear that any public statement about the goods may be relevant and not just those made under the terms of

s. 14(2D) and (2E). In *Clegg and another v Olle Andersson* [2003] EWCA Civ 320; [2003] 1 All ER (Comm) 721 where a yacht with an overweight keel was bought, the Court of Appeal considered, *inter alia*, the extend of remedial work which was needed in determining whether the yacht was satisfactory or not. Moreover, it was stated that the cost of remedial works was not a reliable indication of whether the yacht was satisfactory or not. Under the old law it was established that packaging and instructions could be relevant when assessing merchantable quality (*Niblett* v *Confectioners' Materials Co. Ltd* [1921] 3 KB 387). More recently, in *Albright & Wilkinson* v *Biachem Ltd & ors* [2000] All ER(D) 530 (successfully appealed to House of Lords on other grounds [2002] UKHL 37; [2002] 2 All ER (Comm) 753), it was held at first instance, following the old law and without reference to s. 14(2B), that inaccurate documentation was capable of making goods unsatisfactory.

12.4.2.2 When must goods be of satisfactory quality?

It seems most likely that the goods must be of satisfactory quality when the risk passes from the seller to the buyer: usually at delivery. Latent defects present at this time which manifest themselves after delivery also render goods unsatisfactory.

12.4.2.3 Exceptions

Section 14(2) SoGA 1979 does not extend to any matter making the quality of goods unsatisfactory:

(a) which is specifically drawn to the buyer's attention before the contract is made; or

(b) where the buyer examines the goods before the contract is made, which that examination ought to reveal, or

(c) in the case of a sale by sample, which would have been apparent on a reasonable examination of the sample (s. 14(2C)).

Thus if the seller discloses a defect to the buyer, the buyer cannot complain that *that* defect means that the goods are of unsatisfactory quality.

In relation to item (b) there is no duty on the buyer to examine the goods, but if he does he may not complain about any defects which his examination should have revealed. However, his right to complain about other defects which his examination could not discover remains unaffected. There is authority for the proposition that if the buyer is given the opportunity to examine the goods and leads the seller to believe that he has done so, then the seller is not liable for any defects which would have been revealed by the examination the buyer claims to have carried out. In *Thornett & Fehr* v *Beers & Son* [1919] 1 KB 486, the buyer, who was pressed for time, examined some barrels of glue from the outside only, though it was made clear to him by the seller that a fuller examination was possible. It was held that the above exception applied and the seller avoided liability.

12.4.2.4 Exclusion of the implied term

Liability for breach of the implied term in s. 14(2) is strict. Any attempt to exclude liability should use clear wording such as 'no liability for any faults' or 'goods sold with all defects' (see **18.5.1**, Clause 4.5). All attempts to exclude the term or liability for its breach are restricted by UCTA 1977, s. 6.

12.4.2.5 The relevance of merchantable quality

In assessing satisfactory quality, it seems likely that the judiciary will have recourse to the case law on merchantability. In particular, many of the factors referred to in s. 14(2B) were considered by the courts in applying the test of merchantable quality.

Merchantable quality was first defined in the Supply of Goods (Implied Terms) Act 1973 as follows:

Goods of any kind are of merchantable quality . . . if they are as fit for the purpose or purposes for which goods of that kind are commonly bought as is reasonable to expect having regard to any description applied to them, the price (if relevant) and all the other relevant circumstances.

The merchantable quality test, as applied by the courts, was an amalgam of two tests: the 'acceptability test', whereby goods supplied would be merchantable if they would be acceptable to a reasonable buyer without any reduction of price; and the 'usability test', whereby goods would be regarded as merchantable as long as they could be used for any purpose for which goods of that contract description would commonly be used. One reason for changing the implied term from a requirement of merchantable quality to one of satisfactory quality was the perception that the courts were using the 'usability test' in consumer cases to the disadvantage of consumers. However, more recent case law (see e.g. *Rogers* v *Parish* [1987] QB 933), suggests that the courts were applying the 'acceptability test', which can favour the buyer because it takes account of non-functional aspects of the goods, in 'consumer' cases, and the 'usability test' in 'commercial cases'.

12.4.3 Fitness for the buyer's particular purpose: s. 14(3)

The function of s. 14(2) is to establish a general standard of quality which goods are required to reach. In contrast, s. 14(3) is designed to ensure that goods are fit for a particular purpose made known to the seller (*Jewson Ltd* v *Kelly* [2003] EWCA Civ 1030; [2003] All ER(D) 470). Therefore, section 14(3) places a greater burden on the seller. It states:

Where the seller sells goods in the course of a business and the buyer, expressly or by implication, makes known—

(a) to the seller . . .
    any particular purpose for which the goods are being bought, there is an implied condition that the goods supplied under the contract are reasonably fit for that purpose, whether or not that is the purpose for which such goods are commonly supplied, except where the circumstances show that the buyer does not rely, or that it is unreasonable for him to rely, on the skill or judgment of the seller . . .

12.4.3.1 Particular purpose

For s. 14(3) to apply the buyer must make known, either expressly or impliedly, the particular purpose(s) for which the goods are bought. 'Particular' here means the purpose indicated by the buyer, rather than any special, abnormal purpose. Thus where the buyer buys goods for their normal purpose he impliedly makes known that he requires the goods for their normal purpose and can rely on s. 14(3). In such a case if the goods are unfit for their normal purpose there will be a breach of both the implied terms in s. 14(2) and s. 14(3).

Where there has been a course of dealings between the same parties the buyer may be held to have impliedly made his purpose known to the seller.

The implied term requires that the goods be *reasonably fit* for the purpose indicated by the buyer; thus the more precisely the buyer expresses his purpose the more closely the goods must fit that purpose, so a buyer should try to be as explicit as possible about the purpose for which the goods are being bought. In *Ashington Piggeries Ltd* v *Christopher Hill Ltd*, herring meal which was compounded into mink food proved to be toxic to mink. Herring meal was commonly used as animal food and fertiliser. The sellers knew that the herring meal was to be used for animal feed but not that it was to be used to feed mink. It was held that the buyer had sufficiently made known the particular purpose for which the meal was bought. The making of mink food fell within the broader category of animal feed and was not an unforeseeable use. There was therefore a breach of s. 14(3).

However, there is no breach of s. 14(3) where the failure of the goods to meet the intended purpose arises from an abnormal feature or idiosyncrasy, not made known to the seller, either of the buyer or in the circumstances of the use of the goods by the buyer. In *Slater* v *Finning Ltd* [1997] AC 473 the plaintiff owners of a 'fishing vessel *Aquarius II*' wanted to upgrade the power of the engine, and accordingly the defendants installed a new camshaft into the engine. This proved unsatisfactory, causing excessive noise and wear and tear to parts of the camshaft. Two further replacement camshafts caused similar difficulties and the plaintiffs had to replace the whole engine with a different model. The plaintiffs sued for breach of s. 14(3). It was accepted by both sides that the damage caused to the camshaft was caused by some unascertained force external to the engine and the camshafts themselves: an idiosyncratic feature of the vessel. Nevertheless, the plaintiffs argued that they had made known the particular purpose for the camshafts, i.e., to be installed in *Aquarius II*, idiosyncrasies included. The House of Lords rejected this notion that the defendants took the risk that *Aquarius II* might have unknown or unusual features: there was no breach of s. 14(3).

12.4.3.2 Reliance

Section 14(3) requires that (a) the buyer rely on the seller's skill and judgment and (b) such reliance be reasonable. In many cases these requirements will easily be satisfied: for instance, consumer buyers will generally be taken to rely on retailers; a person buying from a manufacturer will generally be taken to rely on him.

However, where the buyer's purpose is insufficiently communicated, the buyer may not be able reasonably to rely on the seller's skill and judgment. In *Jewson Ltd* v *Kelly* [2003] EWCA Civ 1030; [2003] All ER(D) 470 the defendant bought 12 electrical boilers and materials from the claimants for installation in a building to be converted into individual flats. The defendant did not pay for all the goods and the claimant took proceedings to recover the shortfall. The defendant counter-claimed, *inter alia*, that the boilers were not fit for their purpose, in breach of s. 14(3), because the boilers reduced the 'SAP' ratings (home energy ratings) of the flats. The Court of Appeal found that whilst the defendant had told the claimant that he wanted the boilers for installation in flats for sale, he had given the claimant no information about the nature of the building being converted. Therefore, it could not be held that the defendant had relied on the skill and judgment of the claimants. The court found that this was a matter for the defendants and his advisors. This was a case of partial reliance where the defendant relied on the claimants as to the intrinsic quality of the boilers but not as to whether the boilers were suitable for those particular flats having regard to the SAP ratings.

Similar issues of partial reliance may arise where goods are manufactured to a specification provided wholly or partly by the buyer. However, even in such a case the buyer will rely on the seller to follow the specification, provide materials and actually manufacture the goods; there may be a breach of the implied term if the finished article proves unfit for the buyer's purpose due to any defect within the area of the seller's responsibility. In *Ashington Piggeries*, B gave S specifications as to how the mink food was to be compounded, but it was held that B was entitled to rely on S that the ingredients used would be fit for animal feed, which they were not. In *Cammell Laird & Co. Ltd* v *Manganese Bronze & Brass Co. Ltd* [1934] AC 402, the defendants agreed to build two propellers for the plaintiffs according to the plaintiffs' specification. However, these specifications were silent on certain points, such as the thickness of the blades, and these matters were left to the defendants. One propeller was unsatisfactory due to defects in matters not covered by the specifications. The House of Lords held that there was a breach of the equivalent of s. 14(3) because 'there was a substantial area outside the specification which was not covered by its directions and was therefore necessarily left to the skill and judgment of the seller' (p. 414).

In the interests of clarity in such a case the contract should define the scope of each party's responsibility and perhaps include an express provision such as:

the seller is not liable for any loss or damage caused by any errors in the formula or specification provided to him.

12.4.3.3   Time of fitness

As with merchantability it appears that the goods must be fit when risk passes, usually on delivery (see, e.g. *Viskase Ltd* v *Paul Kiefel GmbH* [1999] 3 All ER 362, where the Court of Appeal decided that, for the purposes of the Brussels Convention on Jurisdiction and the Enforcement of Judgments in Civil and Commercial Matters 1968, the seller's obligations under the contract were completely performed at the time of delivery). Where goods display defects within a shorter period of time than normal this may evidence lack of fitness at delivery.

12.4.3.4   Exceptions

Again liability is strict.

Exclusion of the term in s. 14(3) or liability for its breach is regulated by UCTA 1977, s. 6. Any attempt to exclude liability should use clear wording: for instance, an exclusion of liab-ility for 'defects' may not cover the case where the goods are unfit for the buyer's purpose.

12.5   Sale by sample—Sale of Goods Act 1979, section 15

Where goods are sold by sample, s. 15 now implies two conditions:

(a) that the bulk will correspond with the sample; and

(b) that the goods will be free from any defect, making their quality unsatisfactory, which would not be apparent on reasonable examination of the sample.

Section 15(1) provides that a sale is by sample where there is an express or implied term to that effect in the contract. In general it seems that in order for a contract to be regarded as one for sale by sample a sample must be used to *define* the goods to be supplied. There is no reason why a sale cannot be by sample *and* description, in which case both ss. 13 and 15 will apply. Where a sample is provided to the buyer the contract may therefore include a term making clear whether the sale is or is not a sale by sample within the meaning of the Act: for instance a provision that any sample provided is merely for the purposes of demonstration might prevent the sale being by sample.

12.5.1   Exclusion of liability

Exclusion of liability for breach of the terms in s. 15 is restricted by UCTA 1977, s. 6 in the same way as the implied terms in SoGA 1979, ss. 13 and 14.

12.6 Buyer's remedies

If the seller delivers goods which do not comply with the terms of the contract the buyer may claim damages. In addition, where the term broken is a condition the buyer may reject the goods and terminate the contract. However, the right to reject may be lost if the buyer has accepted the goods (see **11.3.1.3**); alternatively the buyer may elect to keep the goods despite the breach of contract. In either case the buyer is entitled to claim damages for breach of warranty. Where the buyer does keep the goods he may set up his claim for damages for breach of warranty against the seller's claim for the price and thus withhold some, or all of the price (SoGA 1979, s. 53(1)(a)).

Even where the buyer does reject he may be able to claim damages for any losses caused by the breach of contract.

Furthermore, where the buyer deals as a consumer and there is a breach of an express term of the contract or any of the implied terms in ss. 13–15 of SoGA 1979, the consumer buyer may have the right to require the seller to repair or replace the goods, or to require the seller to reduce the price or to rescind the contract under ss. 48A–F SoGA 1979 (as inserted by the Sale and Supply of Goods to Consumers Regulations 2002, see **11.3.3**).

12.6.1 Damages for breach of warranty

The basic measure of damages for breach of warranty is 'the estimated loss directly and naturally resulting, in the ordinary course of events, from the breach of warranty' (s. 53(2)). This measure also applies where the seller commits a breach of condition but the buyer elects, or is compelled (e.g. because he has accepted the goods) to treat the breach as a breach of warranty.

In the case of a breach of warranty of quality, e.g. where the seller delivers goods which are defective and thus unsatisfactory, the basic measure is the difference between the value of the goods at the date of delivery and the value they would have had had they complied with the warranty (s. 53(3)). This will often be the cost of repairing the goods. Special damages may also be recovered provided they are not too remote. Additional damages may therefore be awarded for:

(a) the buyer's lost profits as a result of being unable to use the goods;

(b) loss of future orders or damage to goodwill;

(c) damage to any property of the buyer;

(d) personal injury suffered by the buyer;

(e) an indemnity against any damages payable by the buyer to his customer;

(f) in a consumer case, disappointment.

12.6.2 Damages following rejection

Where the buyer rejects the goods for breach of condition the effect is as if the seller has not delivered; the buyer may either (a) claim damages for non-delivery (see **11.3.2.1**) or (b) where he has already paid the price, reclaim the price in a restitutionary claim.

Where the goods cause other losses to the buyer prior to rejection, e.g. where the goods are defective and damage the buyer's other property—the buyer may claim damages for those losses in addition to rejecting the goods.

12.7   Express terms

A commercial supply contract will often contain express terms giving undertakings about the goods, either in substitution for or as a supplement to the statutory implied terms. Such express undertakings are often called 'warranties' and we will use that term here; however, it should be understood that in this section we are using the term 'warranty' to mean 'product guarantee', rather than in its strict legal sense of a contract term of minor importance. Such express warranties offer advantages to both parties.

12.7.1   Advantages for the buyer

Express product warranties may offer the buyer protection which the statutory implied terms do not provide. In particular, whereas the implied requirement that goods be of satisfactory quality applies only at the time of delivery, an express product warranty can require the seller to maintain and support the goods for a lengthy period after delivery. An express warranty can also provide the buyer with remedies not available under the general law: in particular, with a right to demand repair or replacement and, perhaps, an obligation for the seller to maintain a stock of spare parts etc. Such provisions may be commercially more attractive to the buyer than the bare right to reject the goods, which may be lost relatively quickly, and the right to claim damages. The contract may also expressly state that the seller warrants the goods fit for a particular purpose, thus freeing the buyer from the problems of proving that he made his purpose known to the seller and relied on him, or that the seller warrants that the goods comply with a specified standard or with legal requirements. In an appropriate case, for instance, when the goods are to be resold, the buyer may also require the seller expressly to indemnify him against liability which he may incur to third parties.

12.7.2   Advantages for the seller

From the seller's point of view express warranties offer a number of practical, commercial and legal advantages. First, the presence of an express warranty under which the seller undertakes to repair or replace defective goods *may* affect the standard of satisfactory quality, so that goods may be held to be of satisfactory quality despite defects (although this is less likely in the case of consumer goods than complex items such as, say, computer software).

Secondly, an express warranty may offer the buyer more limited remedies than are available under the general law: for instance, if defined as a warranty in the strict legal sense, the term may limit the buyer to a claim for damages while preventing him rejecting the goods. Alternatively the warranty may restrict the buyer still further, by obliging him to accept repair or replacement of defective goods. Often, therefore, an express product support warranty or warranty of quality will be coupled with a blanket exclusion of the statutory implied terms and all other undertakings relating to the goods, such as:

This warranty defines the seller's liability in respect of the goods. Except as expressly stated in this contract, all other conditions, warranties or other undertakings concerned with the goods, whether express or implied by statute, common law, custom, usage or otherwise are excluded from this contract.

Such an exclusion would, of course, be ineffective to exclude the statutory implied terms as against a consumer and should not be used in a consumer contract (see **12.1**); but as against a non-consumer buyer it would be effective if it satisfied the test of reasonableness.

The dangers of such 'blanket' exclusions have been described elsewhere (see **3.4.3.5**) but the presence in the contract of an express warranty *might* increase the likelihood of the exclusion being held reasonable. The scope of the express warranty offered will be a relevant factor when assessing the reasonableness of the exclusion. The more limited the warranty offered, the less likely it is that exclusion of the implied terms will be reasonable. (See, e.g., *Britvic Soft Drinks* v *Messer UK Ltd* [2002] EWCA Civ 548, [2002] 2 All ER (Comm) 335; [2002] 2 Lloyd's Rep 368 and *Bacardi Martini Beverages Ltd* v *Thomas Hardy Packaging Ltd* [2002] EWCA 549; [2002] 2 All ER (Comm) 335, above **3.4.3.5**.)

Finally, the fact that the seller is prepared to offer an express warranty, especially one which provides long term cover, is generally taken as an indication of the seller's faith in his product and may be a good selling point and generate commercial goodwill.

12.8 Summary

At the end of this chapter you should be able:

- to advise sellers of their legal obligations in relation to the goods;
- to draft exclusion clauses and other express terms to the advantage of the seller;
- to advise buyers how the implied terms can be used as a means of escaping contractual liability and what remedies may be available.

Manufacturer's and product liability

13.1 Introduction: the effect of privity

Liability for defective goods falls primarily on the contractual supplier who is strictly liable under the contract of supply, especially by virtue of the statutory implied terms (see **Chapter 12**).

A person who has purchased a defective product will generally pursue his contractual claim against his supplier because (a) liability is strict; (b) exclusion and limitation of liability is restricted (UCTA 1977, s. 6); and (c) compensation can be awarded for all kinds of loss, including injury, damage to property and even economic losses, including the diminished value of the defective product itself.

Since liability under the implied terms is contractual, it is limited by privity, so that the injured claimant may only enforce them against his immediate supplier. Thus unless the manufacturer supplied the product direct to the claimant he will not be liable under SoGA for defects in the goods. However, liability for defective goods may still fall on the manufacturer in four ways:

(a) by liability being passed back up the contractual supply chain;

(b) under the rule in *Donoghue* v *Stevenson* [1932] AC 562;

(c) as a result of Part I of the Consumer Protection Act 1987;

(d) as a result of a direct (collateral) contract between manufacturer and end user of the product.

Manufacturers and their advisers must be aware of these potential liabilities, the ways in which they may be avoided or minimised, and the need to insure against all possible heads of liability.

In this chapter we examine the ways in which the manufacturer or producer may incur liability as a result of any defects in its products.

13.2 Contractual liability

Goods reach the ultimate consumer via a chain of supply contracts, as follows:

Manufacturer (M)

↓

Wholesaler (W)

↓

Retailer (R)

↓

Consumer (C)

Each of the parties in the distribution chain is in privity with the next. Thus if the goods prove defective and C brings an action against R, R can, in turn, bring an action on his purchase contract against W; his damages may include an indemnity against any liability he has incurred to C. W, in his turn, can claim against M. However, the ability of R and W to pass liability back in this way is limited by two factors.

(a) Since neither R nor W is a consumer for the purposes of UCTA 1977, M can limit or exclude his liability to W, and W his to R, by an appropriate term in their contracts, provided the term satisfies the statutory test of reasonableness (UCTA 1977, s. 6).

(b) W or M may become insolvent, or cease trading. If W is insolvent, R cannot pursue his contractual claim and M will avoid liability.

If defective goods harm someone other than C, who purchased them, that person has no contractual right of action.

13.3 Tortious liability

According to the rule in *Donoghue* v *Stevenson* a manufacturer of products owes a duty to the ultimate consumer to take reasonable care in their manufacture. The only exception is where, at the time the goods leave his control, there is a reasonable probability of the goods being subject to an examination which will reveal any defect. If in breach of this duty the manufacturer is guilty of negligence in manufacture he is liable in damages to the consumer for any loss or damage caused by the product.

In order to bring a claim on this basis the claimant must show that the manufacturer was negligent and that a causal link exists between that negligence and his injury. In practice the claimant will often be able to rely on the maxim *res ipsa loquitur* and thus avoid the need to prove negligence.

13.3.1 Types of damage

The claimant may claim damages in respect of:

(a) any personal injury; or

(b) damage to property caused by the defective product,

subject to the limitations imposed by the rules of remoteness of damage. However, generally no claim lies on this basis for pure economic loss, including the diminished value of the defective product itself, unless there is an especially close relationship between the claimant and the manufacturer.

13.2.2 Exclusion of liability

The manufacturer's freedom to exclude or restrict his liability for losses caused by negligent manufacture is restricted by UCTA 1977, and by the general absence of privity between manufacturer and ultimate consumer.

(a) Any attempt to exclude or restrict liability for death or personal injury caused by negligence is ineffective (UCTA 1977, s. 2(1)).

(b) Exclusion of liability for other types of damage may be valid provided the exclusion is reasonable (UCTA 1977, s. 2(2)). However, where as a result of negligence in manufacture a product proves defective in consumer use, any exclusion of liability for any type of loss is ineffective if contained in a guarantee (UCTA 1977, s. 5).

The combined effect of these provisions is that the manufacturer will generally be unable to exclude liability for loss caused by defective products in consumer use since terms outside a guarantee will generally not be binding on the product user due to the absence of privity.

In the case of products which prove defective outside consumer use, liability for property damage and economic loss can be excluded provided the exclusion satisfies the requirement of reasonableness.

13.4 Consumer Protection Act 1987

Part II of the Consumer Protection Act 1987 imposes strict liability for defective products on their manufacturers and certain others. The Act was passed to implement a European Directive (85/374/EEC). It is not clear that the Act does fully implement the Directive; however, the Act expressly states that it is to be construed in accordance with the Directive (s. 1) and therefore when advising on questions under the Act one should refer to both the Act and the Directive. In July 1999 the European Commission initiated a review of the operation of the 1985 Directive with a view to its possible amendment in 2000.

13.4.1 Who can sue?

Any person injured by a defective product can sue under the Act.

13.4.2 Defective products

'Product' includes goods and electricity (s. 1(2)). Where a component or raw material used in manufacture of a finished item is defective, both component and finished item are products for the purposes of the Act. As originally drafted the 1987 Act did not apply to a person who supplied agricultural produce unless, at the time of supply, it had undergone 'industrial processing' so that, for instance, a farmer could not be held liable for illness caused by beef produced on his farm being affected by BSE. However, in 1999 the Directive was amended to remove the exclusion for primary agricultural produce and the 1987 Act has now been amended accordingly (Consumer Protection Act 1987 (Product Liability) (Modification) Order 2000, SI 2000, No. 2771). (The amendment may however prove difficult to apply as there has been no corresponding amendment to the definition of 'producer'.)

A product is defective if its safety is 'not such as persons generally are entitled to expect' (s. 3). Safety takes into account the risk of both injury and damage to property. The Act includes a list of factors to be taken into account by the court in assessing product safety under this test (s. 3(2)). In cases decided to date the courts appear to be adopting a common sense test of what the public are entitled to expect. In *A* v *National Blood Authority* [2001] 3 All ER 289 it was held that blood products contaminated with the Hepatitis C virus and supplied to patients were not as safe as 'persons generally [were] entitled to expect' and that the National Blood Authority, which had supplied the products, was therefore liable to patients who had received contaminated blood products and contracted hepatitis as a result. It made no difference that at the time of supply there was no effective way of screening blood products for the virus. The public had a legitimate expectation that such products would be free from viral contamination. (See also *Abouzaid* v *Mothercare (UK) Ltd* [2000] All ER (D) 2436.)

13.4.3   Who is liable?

Primary liability is imposed on the 'producer' of the defective product. 'Producer' is defined as:

(a) the manufacturer;

(b) in the case of a product which was won or abstracted (e.g. minerals such as oil), the person who won or abstracted it;

(c) in relation to goods which are neither manufactured nor won nor abstracted, but where an essential characteristic of the product is attributable to an industrial process, the person responsible for that process (s. 1(2)(a)).

In addition the following may also be liable:

(d) own branders;

(e) the person who imported the product into the EC;

(f) any person who supplied the product unless, on request by a person injured by the product, he can identify either his supplier *or* its 'producer' (s. 2(2)).

13.4.4   What losses are compensatable?

Damages may be awarded under the Act for death or personal injury or for damage to private property (s. 5), but

(a) the claimant must prove the losses were caused by the defect in the product; and

(b) no claim may be brought in respect of property damage where the total amount of compensation would be £275 or less.

Damages cannot be recovered for damage to business property or economic losses, including the diminished value of the defective product itself.

13.4.5   Defences

A number of defences are available under the Act (s. 4), including:

(a) that the defendant did not supply the product;

(b) that the defendant did not manufacture or supply the product in the course of a business;

(c) that the defect did not exist at the time the product was put into circulation;

(d) in the case of components, that the defect constitutes a defect in the finished product and was due either to the design of the finished product or compliance with instructions given by the manufacturer of the finished product;

(e) the development risks defence: that the state of scientific and technological knowledge at the time the product was put into circulation was not such that a producer of such products might be expected to have discovered it if it had existed in his products while they were under his control. It seems that the defence will be narrowly construed. It will only be available if the state of scientific and technical knowledge makes the defect undiscoverable, in the sense of being unknown. In *Abouzaid* v *Mothercare (UK) Ltd* [2000] All ER (D) 2436 the Court of Appeal held that the risk of injury caused by an elastic strap snapping back violently was not covered by the defence even though there was no record of such an incident at the relevant time: the absence of accident records was not 'scientific and technical knowledge'. In *A* v *National Blood Authority* [2001] 3 All ER 289 it was held that the defence was not available where there was no satisfactory test for discovering whether a particular batch of blood was contaminated, because the risk of blood being contaminated was known.

Liability under the Act cannot be excluded or restricted by any contract term or notice (s. 7). However, a clause requiring a third party to indemnify the manufacturer against liability may be effective.

13.5 Collateral contract

A manufacturer may incur contractual liability to the end user of his products even where he does not supply the goods direct to the end-user.

13.5.1 Guarantees

Where a manufacturer offers a guarantee with a product the guarantee may be contractually binding either at common law or under the Sale and Supply of Goods to Consumers Regulations 2002 (SI 2002, No. 3045).

The SSGCR 2002 implement an EC Directive (1999/44 on the sale of consumer goods and associated guarantees). They provide that where goods sold or otherwise supplied to a consumer (defined as a 'natural person who . . . is acting for purposes which are outside his trade, business or profession') are offered with a consumer guarantee, the guarantee takes effect at the time the goods are delivered as a contractual obligation owed by the guarantor under the conditions set out in the guarantee and any associated advertising (SSGCR reg. 15). 'Consumer guarantee' is defined as 'any undertaking by a person acting in the course of his business to a consumer, given without extra charge, to reimburse the price paid or to replace, repair or handle consumer goods in any way if they do not meet the specifications set out in the guarantee statement or in the relevant advertising' (SSGCR 2002 reg. 2). The Regulations therefore apply to typical guarantees, whether given by the manufacturer or any other party to the supply chain, which offer repair or replacement of goods which prove defective in use. They do not apply to so-called 'extended warranties' of the type often sold with electrical goods, which are not provided without extra charge, and it is not clear if they apply to so-called 'satisfaction guarantees' whereby a guarantor offers to refund the price paid if the consumer is not satisfied with the goods, since such guarantees do not depend on the goods meeting any specification.

Guarantees which fall outside the scope of the SSGCR, such as 'satisfaction guarantees' or guarantees given to non-consumer buyers, may nevertheless be contractually binding on the guarantor at common law. In order for a guarantee to be binding on this basis it is necessary to find all the elements for creation of a valid contract at common law. Thus it will be necessary to find that the end user of the goods has accepted an offer of a guarantee made by the guarantor, and provided consideration for the guarantor's promise. Typically the end-user will provide consideration and accept the guarantor's offer if he buys the goods knowing of and on the strength of the offer of the guarantee, or does some act such as completing and returning a guarantee registration card. Where however the end user is not aware of the guarantee at the time of purchase and does no additional act after purchase it may be difficult to find the necessary consideration to make the guarantee binding.

13.5.2   Advertising and similar claims

Where a manufacturer makes claims for his product addressed directly to a particular purchaser who buys the product on the strength of those claims, they may be held to give rise to a collateral contract between manufacturer and purchaser and thus become binding on the manufacturer. General advertising claims are not normally contractually binding at common law, often because such claims lack the required degree of certainty to be contractual or are not intended to be legally binding. However, a manufacturer's product claims may now have some legal effect as a result of the Sale and Supply of Goods to Consumers Regulations 2002. Where a manufacturer's advertising contains an undertaking to reimburse the price paid or to replace, repair or handle consumer goods in any way if they do not meet specifications set out in the advertising, it will constitute a consumer guarantee and be binding under SSGCR reg. 15 (see **13.5.1** above). In addition public statements made about goods by the seller or by producer of the goods or his representative are directly relevant as between a consumer buyer and the seller of the goods in determining whether the goods are of satisfactory quality (see **12.4.2.1**(f)).

13.6   Summary

After reading this chapter you should:

- understand the different ways liability for defective or substandard products may be imposed on their manufacturer or producer;
- understand the differences in the nature and extent of the manufacturer's liability under the different bases of liability;
- be able to advise on the most appropriate route by which to pursue an action against a manufacturer or producer in a particular case;
- be able to advise a manufacturer or producer on its potential liability and the extent to which and how it may be excluded or limited.

The passing of property and risk

14.1 Introduction

We have seen that the legal objective of a contract for the sale of goods is the transfer of property in the goods from seller to buyer and that this is recognised by the statutory definition of a contract of sale (SoGA 1979, s. 2: see **9.3**) and is one of the features which distinguishes sale from other, apparently similar, transactions involving the transfer of possession and use of goods.

In this chapter we examine:

- the meaning of the legal concepts of 'property' and 'risk';
- the legal and commercial consequences of the transfer of property in goods and risk of their loss or damage from seller to buyer;
- the legal rules governing the transfer of property and risk from seller to buyer;
- the special rules which may excuse the seller from liability for non-performance of the contract where performance is rendered impossible.

14.1.1 The meaning of property

'Property' is defined by SoGA as 'the general property in goods and not merely a special property' (s. 61). It seems that, legally, this means the *absolute interest* in the goods sold; for practical purposes it can be regarded as meaning 'ownership'.

The transfer of property has important practical and legal consequences which the commercial practitioner may have to consider when advising a client whether to acquire or dispose of goods by means of outright sale or some other transaction, or on a question relating to the rights of either buyer or seller, the answer to which depends on whether or not property in the goods had passed.

14.1.2 Practical consequences of the passing of property

The owner of goods has the absolute legal right to use them in any way he thinks fit (subject to such legal restrictions as those imposed, for instance, by the law of criminal damage, nuisance and environmental law) including the right to sell or otherwise dispose of them, permanently or temporarily, to consume them and to use them as security. There may also be tax reliefs available to the owner of goods and when considering whether to buy goods outright or to acquire them in some other way, for instance, under a contract of hire, a business should consider what it intends to do with the goods and the availability of such tax advantages.

Generally speaking, if a person wishes to acquire goods in order to dispose of them, by way of resale or gift, or to consume them, it will be necessary to acquire the property in those goods and therefore to buy them.

14.1.3   Legal consequences of passing of property

The passing of property is important in the following circumstances.

(a) The goods are lost or damaged. Risk of loss or damage normally passes from seller to buyer at the same time as property, so that if property has passed the buyer bears the risk.

(b) A third party interferes with or damages the goods. Only the owner, or a person with a right to immediate possession, of goods has the right to sue a third party who interferes with or damages them.

(c) The buyer fails to pay for goods delivered. If the seller has tendered delivery of goods and property has passed to the buyer, the seller is entitled to claim the contract price if the buyer fails to pay; if property has not passed the seller may be limited to a claim for damages (see **16.4.1** and **16.2.3**).

(d) The seller fails to deliver the goods. If property has passed to the buyer, he may be able to demand specific delivery of the goods as his property, or claim damages for wrongful interference with goods; if no property has passed he is restricted to a claim for damages for non-delivery.

(e) The buyer (B1) purports to resell the goods to a sub-buyer (B2). If property has passed to B1, then property will be transferred to B2; if property has not passed to B1, B2 will only acquire a title to the goods by virtue of the provisions of SoGA concerned with title and priority conflicts and B1 will be liable to B2 for breach of his implied undertaking that he has the right to sell the goods (see **15.3.4**, **15.3.5** and **12.2**).

(f) The seller purports to resell the goods to another customer (B2) after selling them to the buyer (B1). If property has passed to B1, he can claim the goods from B2 (unless the latter can rely on the statutory provisions concerned with title and priority conflicts: see **15.3.3**); if no property has passed, B2 will acquire property, although B1 may have a claim against the seller for non-delivery of the goods.

(g) The seller becomes insolvent after the buyer has paid for the goods. If property has not passed to the buyer, the goods fall into the insolvent seller's estate leaving the buyer with, at best, a claim as an unsecured creditor for damages for non-delivery; if property has passed, the buyer is entitled to demand delivery of and retain them.

(h) After the goods are delivered the buyer becomes insolvent without paying for them. If property has passed to the buyer, the goods fall into his estate, leaving the seller to claim as an unsecured creditor, but if property remains in the seller, he can recover the goods relying on his proprietary right and, effectively, gain priority over all other creditors (see **16.4.3**).

Because of the legal and commercial importance of property and ownership, SoGA contains detailed rules governing various aspects of its transfer including the time when property is transferred from seller to buyer (ss. 16–19; see **14.2**), the seller's undertaking that he has the right to sell them and that they are unencumbered (s. 12; see **12.2**) and the effect of a purported transfer by someone who is not the owner of the goods (ss. 21–26; see **Chapter 15**).

14.2   The passing of property

Sections 16–20A of SoGA 1979 contain a set of detailed rules governing the transfer of property and risk from seller to buyer. Different rules apply according to whether the goods are (1) specific or unascertained and (2) existing or future goods (see **9.3.4**).

14.2.1   Rules of presumed intention

The basic rule of English law is that under any contract for the transfer of property in goods, property in the goods passes from transferor to transferee when the parties intend it to pass. This rule is reflected in SoGA 1979, s. 17 which provides that the parties may indicate their intention expressly or impliedly. Section 18 then sets out a series of rules of presumed intention which determine when property is to pass when there is no express or implied indication in the contract. However, both sections 17 and 18 are subject to the overriding rule in s. 16 which provides that:

> where there is a contract for the sale of unascertained goods no property in the goods is transferred to the buyer unless and until the goods are ascertained.

This rule cannot be excluded or varied by the parties. Where the goods to be used in performance of the contract are not identified at the time the contract is made, no property in any goods can pass to the buyer until the goods to be used are identified in some way, when they are said to be 'ascertained'. This rule is subject to one important exception, in SoGA, s. 20A, when the contract is for the sale of unascertained goods from a designated bulk source (see **14.2.4.5**).

14.2.2   Discovering the intention of the parties

Subject to the provisions of s. 16, the basic rule in s. 17 is that property passes when the parties intend it to pass. Section 17 provides that in ascertaining their intention regard should be had to:

(a) the terms of the contract;

(b) their conduct; and

(c) all the surrounding circumstances.

Express provision for the passing of property is now common (see **18.5.1**, Clause 6 and **18.5.2**, Clause 8); sellers regularly include in their contract terms a reservation of title clause which stipulates that property should not pass until the buyer has paid in full for the goods (or, possibly, paid other sums due to the seller). This is expressly permitted by s. 19 of the Act which permits the seller to reserve a right of disposal of the goods until certain conditions are fulfilled (see **16.4.3**).

If the contract contains no express provision, the parties may be held to have impliedly indicated their intention as to the passing of property and reference may be had to the other terms of the contract and to the circumstances surrounding the contract. For instance, if payment is deferred, that may implicitly indicate that property is not to pass until payment. Similarly, since risk normally passes with property, an express provision as to the time when risk is to pass may be held impliedly to indicate that property will pass at the same time. However, an express provision as to the passing of risk may also be construed as indicating that risk and property are intended to be separated. There are conflicting authorities on this point and each case will depend on its own facts. In order to avoid difficulties a well drafted contract will therefore contain an express provision indicating when property is to pass.

Even where the contract is for unascertained goods, the parties are free to agree when property is to pass, although they cannot agree that property should pass before the contract goods have been ascertained. Thus a contract for the sale of unascertained goods may provide that no property is to pass until the price of the goods is paid.

If there is no express or implied indication of the parties' intention as to the passing of property, it will pass in accordance with the rules in s. 18.

14.2.3 Passing of property in specific goods

The first three rules in s. 18 apply to contracts for the sale of specific goods. The basic rule applicable to such contracts is set out in rule 1:

Where there is an unconditional contract for the sale of specific goods in a deliverable state the property in the goods passes to the buyer when the contract is made, and it is immaterial whether the time of payment or the time of delivery, or both, be postponed.

It is generally thought that the reference to an 'unconditional contract' means that the contract does not make the passing of property conditional on the happening of any event: in other words, rule 1 applies provided that there is no reservation of title clause in the contract. Any attempt to introduce a reservation of title into a contract for the sale of specific goods after the contract is made will be ineffective because property will have passed in accordance with rule 1 (*Dennant v Skinner & Collom* [1948] 2 KB 164).

Rule 1 only applies if, when the contract is made, the goods are in a 'deliverable state'. This means 'such a state that the buyer would, under the contract, be bound to take delivery of them' (s. 61(5)), but it seems that goods may be in a deliverable state in this sense even though they are so defective that the buyer would be entitled to reject them for breach of the implied conditions in the contract. Goods are in a deliverable state so long as nothing remains to be done to them by the seller before the buyer can be required to take delivery (*Underwood Ltd v Burgh Castle Brick and Cement Syndicate* [1922] 1 KB 343).

EXAMPLE

B agrees to buy S's car. Since the car is specific, property passes to B when the contract is made, even though B does not pay and S retains possession of the car while B obtains the price and arranges insurance.

Conversely if the parties in the above example agree that before B takes delivery S should replace one of the tyres, the car is not in a deliverable state and rule 1 will not apply to the contract; property will pass in accordance with r. 2 in s. 18 (see 14.2.3.1).

Note that where rule 1 applies property in the goods passes immediately the contract is made, and this may be so even though the seller retains possession of the goods and/or payment is deferred; this may be counter to the expectations of both parties. If payment or delivery is deferred it may be possible to infer a contrary intention (see, e.g. *R V Ward Ltd v Bignall* [1967] 1 QB 534; *Dobson v General Accident Fire and Life Assurance Co. Ltd* [1990] 1 QB 274). However, it would be unwise to rely on such unpredictable rules and parties dealing in specific goods should consider including in their contracts specific provisions as to the passing of property if rule 1 is thought inappropriate.

14.2.3.1 Goods not in a deliverable state

Where the goods are not in a deliverable state at the time of the contract, rule 2 in s. 18 applies.

Where there is a contract for the sale of specific goods and the seller is bound to do something to the goods for the purpose of putting them into a deliverable state, property does not pass until the thing is done *and the buyer has notice that it has been done* (emphasis supplied).

Thus, in our example above, property in the car will not pass until S has fitted the new tyre *and* B has notice of that fact. Again the parties may wish to exclude the application of the rule by an express contract provision.

Rule 3 applies

where there is a contract for the sale of specific goods in a deliverable state but the seller is bound to weigh, measure, test, or do some other act or thing with reference to the goods for the purpose of ascertaining the price.

Property does not pass until the necessary act has been done *and* the buyer has notice of that fact.

14.2.4   Passing of property in unascertained goods

Where the parties contract for the sale of unascertained goods, s. 16 provides that no property in any goods is transferred to the buyer unless and until the goods to be used in performance of the contract are ascertained. Goods are ascertained when they are 'identified in accordance with the agreement after [the] contract . . . is made' (per Atkin LJ in *Re Wait* [1927] 1 Ch 606). Thus, until the goods to be used in performance of the contract are identified, no property can pass to the buyer. However, the effect of s. 16 is purely negative and even if the contract goods are identified so as to be ascertained, no property in them will pass to the buyer unless either (a) the parties intend it to pass; or (b) if there is no express or implied indication of the parties' intention, goods of the contract description are unconditionally appropriated to the contract by one party with the consent of the other, in accordance with s. 18, r. 5.

These rules apply both to contracts for the sale of wholly unascertained, or generic, goods by description—such as a contract to purchase '1,000 tonnes of Western wheat'— and to contracts to purchase unascertained goods from an identified bulk source—such as a contract to purchase '1,000 tonnes of Western wheat forming part of the cargo of the ship *Challenger*'. In the latter case, so long as the goods remain part of the bulk they are unascertained even though the source is identified and the buyer therefore may not claim property in any particular goods. Many commercial and consumer contracts are therefore for unascertained goods, and these rules may prejudice a buyer who pays for goods prior to delivery if the seller becomes insolvent without delivering the goods. However, the rules are modified in one important respect when the source from which the contract goods are to be supplied is identified. In that case a buyer who pays part or all of the price of the goods may become a tenant in common of the bulk with the seller and/or any other buyers—thus obtaining proprietary rights over the bulk which may afford him some protection if the seller becomes insolvent.

14.2.4.1   Appropriation

As noted above, under a contract for the sale of unascertained goods, subject to s. 16 and in the absence of any contrary intention, property passes to the buyer when goods of the contract description in a deliverable state are unconditionally appropriated to the contract by one party with the consent of the other (s. 18, r. 5). It seems that 'deliverable state' here has the same meaning as it has under rule 1 and 'description' has the same meaning as it has under SoGA s. 13, so that the goods appropriated to the contract must be of the right commercial *type*. The key to the passing of property in unascertained goods is therefore 'unconditional appropriation'.

Goods are 'unconditionally appropriated' to the contract if they have been 'irrevocably earmarked' for use in its performance (*Carlos Federspiel SA v Charles Twigg & Co. Ltd* [1957] 1 Lloyd's Rep 240); generally this requires the seller to do some act which puts the goods out of his control, so that he cannot use them in performance of another contract.

EXAMPLE 1

S agreed to manufacture and sell a quantity of bicycles to B who paid for them in advance. The bicycles were placed in crates marked with B's name. They were not 'unconditionally appropriated' to B's contract and when S became insolvent the liquidator was entitled to remove the bicycles from the crates and sell them to another customer, leaving B an unsecured creditor (*Carlos Federspiel SA* v *Charles Twigg & Co. Ltd*).

EXAMPLE 2

Where S sent B an invoice showing the serial number of engines to be delivered to B, it was held that the engines had been 'unconditionally appropriated' to B's contract. Having sent the invoice identifying the particular items to be delivered to B, S could no longer substitute them for other goods without B's consent (*Hendy Lennox Ltd* v *Graham Puttick Engines Ltd* [1984] 1 WLR 485).

Generally 'appropriation' will be the last act the seller has to do in order to perform the contract.

It seems that the requirement that the appropriation be 'unconditional' means that S must not reserve a right of disposal of the goods.

14.2.4.2 Delivery to a carrier

Where the seller delivers goods to an independent carrier or bailee for transmission to the buyer, he is to be taken as having unconditionally appropriated the goods to the contract unless he reserves a right of disposal of the goods (s. 18 rule 5(2)). Thus if S puts goods in the post for delivery to B he will be taken to have unconditionally appropriated them to the contract. Conversely, if S gives goods to an independent carrier but makes them deliverable to himself or his agent, he has retained control over them and they are not unconditionally appropriated to the contract.

EXAMPLE

S puts goods, intended for B, onto a train to be delivered, but provides for them to be collected at their destination by his own agent and then allocated to B. The goods are not unconditionally appropriated to B's contract when they are put on the train and thus remain S's property during the journey.

Delivery of the goods to a carrier will only be treated as an appropriation of them to the contract with B if the carrier is independent of S. If the carrier is S's employee or agent, the goods remain in S's control; conversely, if the carrier is B's employee or agent, the goods are delivered to B and must be unconditionally appropriated to the contract.

14.2.4.3 Consent

In order to pass property the appropriation must be made by one party with the consent of the other. Consent may be express or implied, and may be given before or after the appropriation. In most cases goods will be appropriated to the contract by the seller and it will be clear that the buyer has (impliedly) consented to such appropriation in advance.

14.2.4.4 Ascertainment and appropriation

In many cases the same act will both ascertain the goods to be used in performance of the contract and appropriate those goods to the contract. Thus, for example, where the contract is for the sale of goods from a designated bulk source, the contract goods will become ascertained 'by exhaustion' if the bulk is reduced to a quantity equal to or less than the contract quantity (see SoGA, s. 18, r. 5(3)). No further act of appropriation will be required since the seller cannot fulfil the contract by delivering any other goods. However, there is no hard and fast rule. In some cases the goods may be ascertained but no property will pass because they are not unconditionally appropriated to the contract. In other cases (especially under international sale contracts for unascertained goods on c.i.f terms) there may be a 'notice of appropriation' before the contract goods are ascertained (see **21.3.3.2**).

14.2.4.5   Contracts for the sale of goods from a designated bulk source

As noted above, a contract for the sale of unascertained goods from a designated bulk source—such as a contract for '1,000 tonnes of Western wheat forming part of the cargo of the ship *Challenger*'—is a contract for the sale of unascertained goods, and, as a result of the rule in s. 16 of SoGA 1979, no property in any particular goods can pass to the buyer until the goods to be supplied under his contract are ascertained. However, s. 20A of SoGA 1979 (inserted by the Sale of Goods (Amendment) Act 1995 to implement recommendations made by the Law Commission) creates an important exception to the rule in s. 16 with the result that in certain circumstances the buyer may acquire a property interest in the whole bulk as a tenant in common with the seller and/or any other buyers, and thus obtain a measure of protection if the seller becomes insolvent after the buyer has paid for the goods but before they have been delivered from the bulk.

For s. 20A to apply, three conditions must be fulfilled: (a) the contract must be for the sale of a specified quantity of goods; (b) from an identified bulk source; and (c) the buyer must have paid for some or all of the goods forming part of the bulk. These requirements need a little more explanation.

(a)   *A specified quantity*

Section 20A only appllies where the contract is for the sale of a specified *quantity* — such as '100 tonnes' or '1000 litres'—of goods. It does not apply to contracts to sell a share or proportion of the goods forming a specified bulk, such as a contract to sell 'half of the grain in my warehouse', under which the buyer becomes a tenant in common of the bulk at common law without the need for the application of s. 20A.

(b)   *An identified bulk source*

Section 20A only applies when the parties indentify a bulk source from which the contract goods are to be supplied. 'Bulk' is defined as 'a mass or collection of goods of the same kind which—

(a) is contained in a defined space or area; and

(b) is such that any goods in the bulk are interchangeable with any other goods therein of the same number or quantity' (SoGA 1979 s. 61(1)).

The parties may indentify the bulk source to be used to satisfy the contract either in the contract, or by subsequent agreement. Thus although a contract to sell '1000 tonnes of grain' is a contract for wholly unascertained goods to which s. 20A would not apply, the section will apply if, after the contract is made the parties agree that the buyer's goods should be supplied form the cargo of a named ship or from a particular warehouse. This is particularly important in the context of international sales where, under contracts for sales of unascertained goods on c.i.f terms, the seller will serve on the buyer a 'notice of appropriation' indicating his intention to fulfil the contract by delivering goods from a particular ship (see **21.3.3.2**).

(c)   *The buyer must have paid for some or all of the goods*

Section 20A only applies if the buyer has paid for some or all of the goods to be supplied and which form part of the bulk. The size of the buyer's share of the bulk depends, in part, on the quantity of goods he has paid for.

Unless otherwise agreed, once these three conditions are fulfilled the buyer becomes owner of an undivided share of the bulk, as a tenant in common with the seller and/or any other buyers of goods from the bulk. The parties are free to exclude the operation of s. 20A, for instance by expressly agreeing that the buyer should not own any part of the bulk until he has paid the whole of the contract price.

Although the buyer has agreed to buy a specified quantity of goods, the effect of s. 20A is to make him owner of a *share* of the bulk. The size of his share is determined by s. 20A(3) which provides that 'the undivided share of a buyer in a bulk at any time shall be such share as the quantity of goods paid for and due to the buyer out of the bulk bears to the quantity of goods in the bulk at that time'. The size of the buyer's *share* of the bulk will therefore vary according to the quantity in the bulk at any time.

EXAMPLE 1

S agrees to sell B 5,000 tonnes of grain from a silo thought to contain 20,000 tonnes. In fact the silo contains 15,000 tonnes. B therefore becomes a tenant in common of the grain, owning a one third share of the bulk. If S now removes 5,000 tonnes for his own purposes B owns 5,000 out of the remaining 10,000 tonnes and therefore owns half of the bulk.

The Act contains special, detailed provisions to deal with the position where the bulk contains more or less than it is thought to contain and to allow the owners of the bulk to deal with their shares. As a result of s. 20A(3) described above, if the bulk contains less than it is thought to contain, the loss falls first on the seller. Where however the aggregate of the shares of buyers in a bulk would exceed the whole of the bulk each buyer's share is reduced proportionately (s. 20A(4)).

EXAMPLE 2

S agrees to sell to each of A, B, C and D 5,000 tonnes of grain from a silo thought to contain 20,000 tonnes. In fact it contains only 16,000 tonnes. Prima facie each buyer is entitled to five sixteenths of the whole. However, the effect of s. 20A(4) is to reduce the size of each buyer's share of the bulk so that each owns four sixteenths (one quarter) of the whole.

EXAMPLE 3

S agrees to sell 10,000 tonnes of grain to A and 5,000 tonnes each to B and C from a silo thought to contain 20,000 tonnes. In fact it contains only 16,000 tonnes. The effect of s. 20A(4) is to reduce A's share to eight sixteenths and B's and C's shares to four sixteenths.

In order to facilitate dealings in the goods by the co-owners, the Act provides that each co-owner is deemed to consent to any delivery to another co-owner of goods due to him under his contract and to any removal, dealing with, delivery or disposal of goods in the bulk by any other co-owner insofar as the goods fall within his undivided share (s. 20B(1)). The effects of these provisions may be complex but their main effect is that if any buyer takes delivery of the quantity of goods due to him under his contract with the seller, the other co-owners cannot recover any of the goods even if, in fact, the buyer has taken more than his share of the bulk. Thus in Example 2 above, if A takes delivery of 5,000 tonnes of grain he has actually taken more than his share but B, C and D are deemed to have consented to the delivery. Their shares of the remaining bulk will therefore be reduced and they cannot recover any part of the goods from A; nor (in the absence of an agreement to the contrary) can they recover compensation from A for any shortfall in the goods delivered to them (see SoGA s. 20B(3)(a)). The Act expressly provides that its provisions do not affect 'the rights of any buyer under his contract' (s. 20B(3)(c)). B, C and D therefore remain entitled, as against S, to delivery of the quantities due to them under their contracts with him—ie: to 5,000 tonnes each—and may therefore be able to sue S for (partial) non-delivery, but that right may be practically worthless if S is insolvent. The effect therefore is that co-owning buyers take delivery out of the bulk on a 'first come, first served' basis. The buyers are free, however, to modify the statutory rules so as to vary their rights against each other.

Difficult problems may arise where the seller sells more shares than the bulk can actually support. Later buyers may then acquire a share in the bulk, at the time the requirements of s. 20A are fulfilled, or title to any goods delivered to them out of the bulk, if they can rely on s. 24, SoGA (see **15.3.3**).

As already noted, the effect of s. 20A is to make the buyer co-owner of the bulk, rather than owner of any particular goods. When goods are delivered to a buyer out of the bulk, those goods will then be ascertained and property in them will pass to the buyer. In addition, s. 18, r. 5(3) (confirming a rule established in *The Elafi* [1982] 1 All ER 208) provides that where there is only one buyer entitled to goods from the bulk and the bulk is reduced to (or less than) the quantity due to the buyer under his contract, then the goods are treated as having been appropriated to his contract and property in them passes to the buyer.

14.2.4.6   Reservation of ownership

The rules in s. 18, r. 5 and s. 20A are rules of presumed intention. They may therefore be excluded by the parties, and may often be modified by express contractual provision, for instance providing that no property shall pass to the buyer until he has paid for his goods, or until he has paid other debts due to the seller. It should be noted, too, that in order to pass property under s. 18, r. 5 an appropriation must be *unconditional*. Thus if the seller appropriates goods to the contract conditionally, by reserving a right of disposal until the price is paid, the appropriation will not pass property even if there was no reservation of ownership in the *contract*.

14.2.4.7   Subsequent mixing

Once the goods to be used in performance of the contract have been ascertained and unconditionally appropriated to the contract, property passes to the buyer. If the buyer's goods are subsequently remixed with other similar goods the buyer becomes a joint owner of the resulting mixture as a tenant in common with the owners of the other goods in the mixture (*Indian Oil Corp. Ltd* v *Greenstone Shipping Corp.* [1988] QB 345).

14.2.5   Future goods

It is not clear if future goods can be specific (see **9.3.4**); however, it is clear that s. 18, r. 1 cannot apply to future goods. Property in future goods will therefore pass when the parties intend it to pass.

Where the contract is for future goods sold by description, in the absence of any indication of the parties' intention s. 18, r. 5 applies. Thus where a manufacturer contracts to sell goods to be manufactured by him, property will pass when goods of the contract description are unconditionally appropriated to the contract by one party with the consent of the other.

EXAMPLE

M, a manufacturer, receives an order for goods from a customer, C1. He manufactures goods for the contract but, before they are delivered, receives another order for similar goods from another customer, C2. Provided that the goods already manufactured have not been unconditionally appropriated to C1's contract, M is free to appropriate them to the contract with, and deliver them to, C2, although, as a result, M may incur liability to C1 for late delivery.

14.2.6   Sale or return

Goods may be delivered to a potential buyer in order for him to evaluate their suitability for his purposes, or to try and resell them, under terms which allow him to return them if they prove unsuitable or unsaleable. In such cases the goods are said to be delivered on approval, or on sale or return terms. Such arrangements have obvious advantages for the potential buyer, who avoids the risk of buying goods which he cannot use or resell. However, they may also be advantageous for the seller, by offering some protection against the buyer's failure to pay and insolvency.

14.2.6.1   Sale or return and other arrangements compared

Such arrangements may outwardly resemble an agency contract, or a conditional sale or an outright sale subject to an express right for the buyer to return the goods if they prove unsuitable or unsaleable; however, the rights of the parties may be different under each of these arrangements. In addition, the rights of third parties who acquire an interest in the goods may be affected by the classification of the transaction. Where goods are delivered to a person on terms which allow their return it may therefore be necessary to examine the terms of the agreement and all the circumstances in order to identify the legal relationship between the parties. Similarly, where a client wishes to enter into an arrangement which allows him to take or supply goods on approval, it will be necessary to consider which of these arrangements best suits his needs.

Strictly, where goods are delivered on sale or return terms, or on approval, there may at the time of delivery be no contract of sale; there will instead be a standing offer by the 'seller' to sell the goods, which the buyer may accept by retaining, reselling or approving the goods. In effect, therefore, the 'buyer' has an option to buy the goods. This may offer tax advantages making such arrangements attractive to potential buyers; where goods are supplied on such terms there is no chargeable supply for VAT purposes until either:

(a) the buyer adopts the transaction; or

(b) the time for return of the goods expires; or

(c) (at the latest) 12 months after the delivery of the goods to the 'buyer' (Value Added Tax Act 1983, s. 4(2)(c)).

'Sale or return' and similar arrangements may therefore be used as part of common commercial arrangements, including stock financing agreements, for instance in the motor trade, consignment stocking arrangements, and as part of distribution arrangements.

It is important to emphasise that although under a sale or return there is initially no contract of sale, the goods must be delivered at the request of the potential buyer and there will often be a detailed contract between the parties. If the delivery is not requested by the buyer the goods are unsolicited and the buyer may be entitled to treat them as a gift under the Unsolicited Goods and Services Act 1982.

14.2.6.2   Passing of property under sale or return transactions

The sale or return agreement may contain detailed provisions dealing with the buyer's right to return the goods and the passing of property in them. In the absence of any express or implied agreement as to the passing of property, rule 4 in s. 18 of the SoGA 1979 applies. It provides that property passes to the buyer:

(a) when he signifies his approval or acceptance of them; or

(b) when he does any act adopting the transaction; or

(c) if without giving notice of rejection of the goods the buyer retains them

　　(i)   if a time is fixed by the contract for the return, beyond that time; or

　　(ii)   if no time is fixed, beyond a reasonable time.

The buyer may adopt the transaction under (b) by dealing with the goods, normally by reselling them, or by using them for longer than is necessary to assess their suitability. However, the buyer does not adopt the transaction where he is prevented by circumstances outside his control from returning the goods, for instance because they are accidentally damaged or destroyed (*Elphick* v *Barnes* (1880) 5 CPD 321).

Even if the buyer does not expressly adopt the transaction he will, in effect, impliedly do so under (c) if he retains the goods beyond the time for their rejection without giving notice of rejection. The terms of an effective notice may be prescribed by the agreement under which the goods are delivered to the buyer. It may provide for the goods to be returned, to be made available for return, or simply for notice of rejection to be given by a prescribed date. The notice must specify the goods to which it relates, but it is sufficient for this purpose if it refers to them by generic description. If such notice is given by the buyer it effectively rejects the seller's offer to sell and brings an end to the buyer's right to possess the goods. The buyer does not have to return the goods physically to the seller unless the agreement so prescribes, but he must make the goods available for collection by the seller in accordance with the express or implied terms of the original supply agreement. If the buyer does not make the goods available for collection after serving notice of rejection he may be liable to the seller for wrongful interference with goods. (See generally *Atari Corp (UK) Ltd* v *Electronics Boutique Stores (UK) Ltd* [1998] 1 All ER 1010.)

The buyer will be a bailee of the goods for the seller from the time when they are delivered to him until he either returns them or adopts the transaction.

In order to guard against the uncertainty inherent in rule 4 and to provide extra protection for the supplier, the contract under which the goods are delivered should contain express provision as to the time when property is to pass. The supplier can, for instance, expressly reserve property beyond the time when it would pass in accordance with rule 4 (*Weiner* v *Gill* [1906] 2 KB 574). The agreement should also deal with the risk of loss while the goods are in the possession of the potential buyer and, perhaps, require him to insure them against accidental loss or damage.

14.2.7   Express terms as to the passing of property

In many cases the rules in s. 18 will be inappropriate; in addition their application may often be unpredictable. A well drafted contract should therefore contain an express provision as to when property is to pass. Any express provision offers the advantage that it allows the parties to know where they stand.

(a) Where the seller is allowing the buyer credit he will generally want to retain property until the price, and possibly other sums, are paid (see **18.5.1**, Clause 6).

(b) A buyer who pays for goods before delivery may want to include some provision to protect him against non-delivery (see **18.5.2**, Clause 8).

Where the contract is for specific goods an express provision reflecting s. 18 rule 1, or providing for property to pass on payment, will give the buyer some protection against the seller's insolvency by giving him property in the goods. Where the goods are to be supplied from a designated bulk source, the buyer may receive some protection as a result of the provisions of s. 20A. However, his rights may still be defeated if the seller contracts to sell more goods than the bulk contains. Moreover, s. 20A will not apply at all if the contract is for wholly unascertained goods. In such cases it may therefore be necessary to consider the use of some other device, for instance requiring the seller to provide a guarantee of performance or security for repayment of the price.

14.3 Risk

The basic rule of English law is that the owner of property bears the risk of its damage, deterioration or destruction (*'res perit domino'*). This is reflected in SoGA 1979, s. 20:

Unless otherwise agreed, the goods remain at the seller's risk until the property in them is transferred to the buyer, but when the property in them is transferred to the buyer the goods are at the buyer's risk whether delivery has been made or not.

(It will be noted that English law thus links the passing of risk to the passing of property, rather than possession.)

It is important to understand the consequences of this rule. If goods are damaged whilst at the seller's risk, the seller may not be able to require the buyer to accept them in performance of the contract of sale and may therefore have to repair them or find replacement goods in order to perform his contract; such repair or replacement will be at his expense. If he is unable to do so within the time for performance of the contract he may incur liability for late or non-delivery, unless he is excused by the contract or on the grounds of impossibility.

If the goods are damaged whilst at the buyer's risk, the buyer must accept and pay for them under the contract of sale. The party who bears the risk of loss of or damage to goods therefore bears the risk that they may have to be replaced or repaired and may wish to insure against that risk.

EXAMPLE

Phil agrees to buy a second hand car from Nigel, but agrees that Nigel should keep the car until the next day to allow Phil to arrange insurance and finance. The car is specific goods so that, prima facie, property passes to Phil when the contract is made; the car is therefore prima facie at Phil's risk from that time. If the car is stolen before Phil returns to take possession of it, Phil bears the risk of loss and must nevertheless pay for it.

It is not entirely clear how the rule that risk passes with ownership applies where there is a contract to sell unascertained goods from a specified bulk. As explained earlier, s. 20A of the SoGA now provides that in such a case a buyer who pays for some or all of the goods contracted for becomes owner of an undivided share in the bulk. The effect of the rules outlined earlier is that the seller bears the risk of partial destruction of the bulk, and it seems that it is intended that the seller should bear the risk of any loss of or deterioration in the goods prior to delivery to the buyer, since the Act provides that the rights of the buyer 'under his contract' are not affected by the new provisions. However, it could also be argued that the buyer should bear the risk of deterioration as a co-owner of the bulk from the time his co-ownership arises, and when a contract is drafted to govern dealings from bulk it will be advisable to include express provisions to deal with the passing of risk.

14.3.1 Exceptions to the general rule

The rule in s. 20 may be displaced by express or implied agreement; in addition it is subject to a number of exceptions or modifications.

14.3.1.1 Contract provisions

(a) *Express provision*

The contract may contain an express provision as to the passing of risk (see **18.5.2**, Clause 8.2). Where the seller retains title to the goods until they are paid for, the contract should expressly provide that, notwithstanding the retention of title, the goods are to be at the buyer's risk from the time of delivery (if not earlier) (see **18.5.1**, Clause 6.1). Similarly where goods are delivered on sale or return or approval, the contract may contain a provision placing them at the 'buyer's' risk. In both cases the contract might expressly require the buyer to insure the goods and to ensure that the insurance covers the seller's interest in them. A person who bears the risk of loss of or damage to property has sufficient interest in that property to insure it (*Inglis* v *Stock* (1885) 10 App Cas 263).

(b) *Implied provision*

Even if the contract contains no express provision as to the passing of risk it may be possible to find an implied term governing the subject. For instance, in the example of the car given above, it might be possible to find an implied term that the car should remain at the seller's risk until delivery, especially in view of the fact that the buyer was to arrange insurance. The same result could be reached by finding an implied agreement that property should not pass until the buyer paid for the car.

Conversely, risk may impliedly pass before property. A person who buys goods forming part of bulk has an insurable interest in them (*Inglis* v *Stock*).

Under many common commercial arrangements the passing of risk will generally be covered by a conventional implied term. For instance, under international contracts where goods are sold on f.o.b or c.i.f terms the goods are normally understood to be at the buyer's risk from the time they are shipped, even if the seller retains property (see **21.2.5** and **21.3.7**).

When preparing a contract of sale, it is preferable to include an express provision to deal with the passing of risk rather than rely on the unpredictability of an implied term.

14.3.1.2 Bailment

The Sale of Goods Act 1979, s. 20 is expressed to have no impact on any duty owed by either party to the other as a bailee (s. 20(3)). Where the buyer takes possession of the goods before the passing of property he will be a bailee for the seller and thus owe the seller a duty to take reasonable care of the goods (see **9.4.2**); similarly where the seller remains in possession after the passing of property, he will be a bailee for the buyer. Thus in the example of the car in **14.3**, S is a bailee of the car pending its collection by B, and will be liable to B if the loss of the car is caused by S's negligence.

14.3.1.3 Delay in delivery

Where delivery is delayed through the fault of seller or buyer, the party at fault must bear the risk of any loss which might not have occurred but for that fault (s. 20(2)); for instance, in *Demby Hamilton & Co. Ltd* v *Barden* [1949] WN 73, B agreed to buy 30 tons of apple juice in accordance with a sample. The juice was placed in casks to await collection but was not appropriated to the contract so that no property passed to B. B delayed collecting the juice and when he did collect it it was discovered that the juice had deteriorated. It was held that B must bear the risk of deterioration on the grounds that delivery was delayed by his default and that delay had caused the deterioration.

14.3.1.4 Goods damaged in transit

The allocation of risk of damage in transit is covered by SoGA 1979, s. 32. Where the seller is authorised to send the goods to the buyer, delivery of the goods to a carrier for transmission to the buyer is treated as delivery to the buyer (see **11.2.1.5**). The buyer is therefore treated as being in possession of the goods (and thus a bailee of them) through the agency of the carrier whilst they are in transit. This rule does not apply, however, where the buyer deals as consumer, in which case delivery of goods to the carrier is not deemed to be delivery to the buyer (s. 32(4) inserted by the SSGCR 2002) and risk of loss or damage to the goods does not pass to the consumer buyer until they are delivered to him (SoGA, s. 20(4)).

This rule only applies where the seller is authorised or required to send the goods to the buyer. In order to apply the rule it is necessary to determine the contractual point of delivery of the goods. If a carrier is employed by the seller to carry the goods to the contractual delivery point, that carrier is the agent of the seller and the seller therefore remains in constructive possession of the goods up to that time. Conversely, once the goods have reached the contractual delivery point they are treated as having been delivered to the buyer so that thereafter any carrier is treated as the agent of the buyer.

EXAMPLE 1

S contracts to sell goods to B, to be delivered at B's premises. The goods are given to an independent carrier, C, to deliver them to B's premises. C is treated as the agent of S, and S is therefore in constructive possession of the goods until they reach B's premises.

EXAMPLE 2

S contracts to sell goods *ex works* to B, so that the delivery point is at S's own premises. S agrees to arrange for the goods to be *physically* delivered to B's premises and entrusts them to a carrier, C. Delivery to C is treated as delivery to B, who is therefore in constructive possession of the goods whilst they are in transit.

EXAMPLE 3

S, in England, contracts to sell goods to B, in Hamburg, to be delivered free on board (f.o.b) at Hull. S gives the goods to C, a road haulier, to carry them to Hull for loading on board ship. The contractual delivery point is Hull; C is therefore S's agent and S is in possession until the goods are loaded on board ship; the sea carrier, however, is B's agent, even if the contract of sea carriage is made by S on B's behalf.

The rule in s. 32 is further modified by other provisions.

(a) *Seller to make reasonable contract*

Where the seller makes a contract of carriage on behalf of the buyer, he must make a reasonable contract. If he fails to do so and the goods are damaged or lost in transit, the buyer may decline to treat delivery of the goods to the carrier as delivery to himself, or claim damages from the seller in respect of the damage, thus throwing the risk of loss during transit back onto the seller (s. 32(2)). What is a reasonable contract will depend on all the circumstances of the case. This rule becomes especially important in the context of international sales (see **21.2.3.4**).

(b) *Buyer to bear risks necessarily incidental to transit*

Where the goods are to be delivered at some place other than their location when the contract is made and the carriage is to be at the seller's risk, the buyer must bear the risk of any deterioration of the goods *necessarily* incident on the carriage (s. 33).

(c) *Express provision*

In order to avoid the uncertainty of the statutory rules on loss in transit, the contract should generally contain express provisions allocating the risk of loss or damage during transit.

The practical effect of the rules on passing of property and risk is thus that in many cases the buyer will bear the risk of loss of or damage to the goods in transit. In consumer cases, however, the risk of such loss will normally be borne by the seller.

14.3.1.5   Goods damaged by third parties

If property and risk are separated, difficulties may arise if the goods are damaged by the act or default of a third party. The only persons entitled to sue the third party in negligence for damaging the goods are their owner and the person with an immediate right to possession of them. A person who bears the risk of damage but does not have property may therefore be unable to recover damages from any third party by whom they are damaged; the owner, although entitled to sue, will have no interest in doing so since the goods are not at his risk. However, the person at risk has sufficient interest in the goods to insure them and therefore should do so.

14.3.2   Impossibility

If goods to be sold are lost, or are damaged or deteriorate so as to become no longer of satisfactory quality whilst at the seller's risk, he will be unable to insist on the buyer accepting them under the contract and may have to repair or replace them. Where the contract is for specific goods, replacement is not possible without the buyer's consent, so that the seller may be unable to perform the contract, and in any case the delay involved in arranging repair or replacement may put the seller in breach of contract. However, SoGA 1979, ss. 6 and 7 contain rules broadly analogous to the general common law rules of frustration and mistake which may excuse the seller from liability if performance becomes impossible. Where they apply the general common law rules on mistake and frustration are displaced.

Section 6 provides that:

Where there is a contract for the sale of specific goods and the goods without the knowledge of the seller have perished at the time the contract is made, the contract is void.

Section 7 provides that:

Where there is an agreement to sell specific goods and subsequently the goods, without any fault on the part of the seller or buyer, perish before the risk passes to the buyer, the agreement is avoided.

Section 6 is the equivalent of the common law rules on mistake; s. 7 is the equivalent of the rules on frustration.

14.3.2.1   Perishing

An item is generally regarded as having perished if it has 'so changed as to become an unmerchantable thing which no buyer would buy and no honest seller would sell'

(Lord Esher in *Asfar & Co.* v *Blundell* [1896] 1 QB 123). However, cases on the meaning of 'perishing' are not easy to reconcile.

EXAMPLE 1

Dates which were impregnated with river water and sewage when the barge on which they were carried sank, had perished, even though they still existed and were recovered from the river (*Asfar* v *Blundell*).

EXAMPLE 2

Rotten potatoes were still potatoes and had not perished (*Horn* v *Minister of Food* 65 TLR 1906).

EXAMPLE 3

Goods may be treated as having 'perished' when they are stolen, or even when part of the goods is stolen, since the buyer cannot be required to accept less than the agreed contract quantity (*Barrow, Lane and Ballard Ltd* v *Phillip Phillips & Co.* [1929] 1 KB 574).

The effect of partial loss of the contract goods is not clear. Theft of part may result in the whole of the goods being treated as having perished, but cases decided under analogous rules at common law (not strictly cases concerned with specific goods) suggest that where part of the contract goods are lost:

(a) the buyer cannot be required to take the reduced quantity;

(b) the seller cannot be held liable for non-delivery in respect of the lost goods; but

(c) the seller must offer the remaining goods to the buyer.

It is not clear if similar results could be reached under the statutory rules.

The statutory rules apply only to contracts for the sale of specific goods and only where the goods have perished. In other cases where performance becomes impossible due to circumstances outside the seller's control, the outcome will depend on the application of the common law rules of frustration, mistake and implication of terms.

14.3.2.2 Express provision

To avoid the uncertainty of these rules the contract may contain express provisions to cover cases where performance is rendered impossible. A suitably worded force majeure clause may cover cases where performance is hindered or made impossible, including by total or partial failure of the anticipated source of supply. It may apply even where the statutory rules would not apply, and may produce results which are more commercially attractive than those provided for by ss. 6 and 7.

EXAMPLE

S contracts to sell 500 tons of raspberries to each of B1 and B2, intending to grow the fruit on his own farm. Due to a wet summer the farm produces only 600 tons in total, leaving S with insufficient raspberries to satisfy both B1 and B2. If S delivers less than 500 tons to either customer, he may be liable for short delivery. Since the contracts are not for specific goods he cannot argue that either is affected by s. 7 of the Sale of Goods Act 1979, or that either is frustrated at common law. It may be possible to imply a term allowing him to apportion the available crop between the customers, depending on the circumstances of the two contracts.

The difficulty in this example might be avoided if the contracts between S and B1 and B2 contained an appropriate term allowing S to appropriate the available crop between his customers in the event of his farm producing less than the anticipated quantity of fruit.

14.4 Summary

After reading this chapter you should understand:

- the legal concepts of property and risk;
- the legal and commercial consequences of the transfer of property from seller to buyer;
- the difference between *specific* and *unascertained* goods;
- the legal rules governing the transfer of property in (a) specific goods, (b) unascertained goods and (c) goods *ex bulk*;
- the rules governing the transfer of risk of loss of or damage to goods;
- the rules governing perishing of goods and impossibility of performance.

Title and priority conflicts

15.1 Introduction

It is a fundamental rule of English law that no-one can transfer a better title to property than he himself has ('*nemo dat quod non habet*'). This basic rule is restated in SoGA 1979, s. 21. However, exceptions to the basic rule were developed to protect bona fide purchasers and thus encourage commercial activity by reinforcing the security of sale transactions, and several exceptions are now set out in SoGA 1979, ss. 21–26. Thus if a person [S] purports to sell goods which he does not own, his buyer [B] will get no title to them unless he can rely on one of the statutory exceptions to the *nemo dat* rule. Such a situation can arise in a number of ways.

(a) S may be a thief who stole the goods from their rightful owner, or may have purchased the goods from a thief.

(b) S may have agreed to buy the goods but under a contract containing a reservation of title clause, so that title has not passed to him at the time he resells to B.

(c) S may have already sold the goods to X, but remained in possession of them after the transfer of property to X.

(d) S may have held the goods under a hire purchase agreement.

(e) S may have obtained the goods from their owner by deception, under a contract which as a result is voidable.

In each case B may find that, having bought goods, they are claimed by another person [O] who asserts that he is the true owner of the goods, or has a prior right to possession of them, and was dispossessed of them by the wrongful act of S or of a third party. B may be entirely innocent; however O will generally seek to recover the goods from B by suing in conversion.
In this chapter we examine:

- the *nemo dat* rule;

- the means by which a dispossessed owner can recover his property; and

- the statutory exceptions to the *nemo dat* rule which in some circumstances allow a person who buys goods from someone other than their owner nevertheless to obtain good title to them.

15.2 Conversion

The practitioner is most likely to encounter the *nemo dat* rule and its exceptions in litigation between a dispossessed owner and a subsequent buyer, although the rules are also significant where goods are sold subject to reservation of title (see **16.4.3**). A person in possession of goods who is wrongfully deprived of possession, or a person with an immediate right to possession of goods, may sue in the tort of conversion any person who deprives him of possession or who, without his authority, deals with the goods intending to assert a right to them inconsistent with his right. Provided the defendant has this intention, liability in conversion is strict, in that the defendant may be liable even though he was unaware of the claimant's right to them or honestly believed that he himself was their true owner. An owner of goods deprived of them by the wrongful act of a third party may therefore sue in conversion the wrongdoer or any person who subsequently deals with them.

In practice the dispossessed owner (O) will generally seek to recover the goods from B, the person in possession. If he can, O is entitled to recover the goods without court action; however, if B resists O's claim, O will need to bring an action in conversion. If his claim succeeds the court has a discretion (Torts (Interference with Goods) Act 1977, s. 3) either to:

(a) order specific delivery of the goods; or

(b) allow the claimant to choose between:

    (i) an award of damages; and

    (ii) an order for specific delivery of the goods but giving the defendant the option to pay damages in lieu.

Damages under (b)(i) and (ii) are the value of the goods at the date of the conversion. If the defendant has improved the goods the court may award him an allowance for the value of the improvement (Torts (Interference with Goods) Act 1977, s. 6).

However, if B can rely on any of the exceptions to the *nemo dat* rule, B will acquire a title to the goods superior to that of O and therefore be able to resist O's claim. The goods may have changed hands several times via a chain of transactions before coming into B's hands. In order to dispute O's entitlement to the goods B must therefore examine each of the transactions in the chain in order to see if any fell within any of the *nemo dat* exceptions. Note that if *any* of the transactions in the chain fell within any of the *nemo dat* exceptions all subsequent parties in the chain will have a good defence to O's claim.

EXAMPLE

O supplies a car to X under a conditional sale agreement. O therefore remains owner of the car. X then resells the car to Y in circumstances which allow Y to rely on one of the *nemo dat* exceptions so that Y acquires a title to the car superior to that of O. Y then sells the car to Z who resells it to S. Finally S sells the car to B. The chain of transactions may be represented thus:

$$O \rightarrow X \rightarrow Y \rightarrow Z \rightarrow S \rightarrow B$$

The title acquired by Y will be transferred, via the sales to Z, S and B, to B allowing him to resist O's claim. Note that B is protected even though the sale by S to him did not fall within any of the *nemo dat* exceptions.

Even if O's claim against B fails because B can rely on one of the *nemo dat* exceptions, O may still succeed against other, earlier, parties in the transaction chain who are unable to rely on a *nemo dat* exception. Thus in the example above, where the sale from X to Y fell within a *nemo dat* exception, the title acquired by Y in that transaction will give him, Z, S and B a defence to O's conversion claim. However, X has no such defence and will thus be liable to O.

If B cannot rely on any of the *nemo dat* exceptions he will be forced to surrender the goods, or pay their value, to O. B then has a claim against S, his vendor, for breach of the implied terms in the contract of sale that S should have had the right to sell the goods and that B should enjoy quiet possession of them (SoGA 1977, s. 12; see **12.2**). B will therefore join S into the proceedings as a third party. S will have a similar claim against his vendor, Z, and so on. Each party involved in the transaction chain can thus be joined into the action, and liability be passed back up the chain. In theory, liability could be passed back in this way all the way to X, the original wrongdoer. However, in practice X will often be untraceable or unable to satisfy any judgment.

15.3 Exceptions to the *nemo dat* rule

Before examining the exceptions to the general *nemo dat quod non habet* principle we should note that, although we are primarily concerned with disputes between a person who has bought goods and a person who claims to be their owner, the exceptions may also be used to decide disputes between a buyer and a person who claims to be entitled to a prior limited interest, or between a dispossessed owner and a person who claims to be entitled to a subsequent limited interest in the goods.

Most of the exceptions apply only in favour of a buyer who receives the goods in good faith and without notice of the seller's lack of title or the rights of the original owner. In all cases but one (s. 23) the burden of proving good faith lies on the buyer who asserts it and relies on the exception. He will only be deprived of protection on this basis if he has actual, rather than constructive, notice of any defect in the seller's title and he is generally under no duty to investigate the seller's right to sell or to scrutinise documents with great care. However, in deciding if the buyer has actual notice of any facts, the court applies an objective test, so that he will be deemed to have actual notice of any facts to which he deliberately shuts his eyes, and if the circumstances of the disposition are suspicious the court may infer that he must have had notice, that he deliberately shut his eyes to the facts, or that he acted in bad faith.

15.3.1 Agency

O will be bound by any disposition of his goods by his agent acting with his actual or apparent authority (SoGA 1979, s. 21(1); see **Chapter 5**).

15.3.1.1 Mercantile agency

A mercantile agent, or factor, is a special type of agent entrusted with the possession of goods in order to sell or otherwise deal with them. Since the mercantile agent is given possession of his principal's goods, he may appear to be their owner. Special rules were therefore devised to protect persons who dealt with factors relying on this appearance of ownership. The current legislation is the Factors Act 1889 which provides (at s. 2):

> Where a mercantile agent is, with the consent of the owner, in possession of goods or of the documents of title to goods, any sale, pledge or other disposition of the goods, made by him when acting in the ordinary course of business of a mercantile agent, shall, subject to the provisions of this Act, be as valid as if he were expressly authorised by the owner of the goods to make the same; provided that the person taking under the disposition acts in good faith and has not, at the time of the disposition, notice that the person making the disposition has not authority to make the same.

The third party who deals with a mercantile agent will only be protected by this provision if a number of requirements are fulfilled.

(a) The agent must be a mercantile agent, defined as

> a mercantile agent having, in the customary course of his business as such agent authority either to sell goods or to consign goods for the purposes of sale, or to buy goods, or to raise money on the security of goods (Factors Act 1889, s. 1).

Thus the agent must be in business to deal in goods on behalf of others, rather than on his own behalf (*Belvoir Finance Ltd* v *Harold G. Cole Ltd* [1969] 1 WLR 1877). Where it is alleged that a person in possession of another's goods is a mercantile agent it is therefore necessary to examine the basis on, and purpose for, which he was in possession of the goods. It is enough that the agent acts as a mercantile agent only for one principal or in one transaction, so that the agent's first transaction as such can be protected (*Lowther* v *Harris* [1927] 1 KB 393).

(b) The agent must be in possession of the goods, or of a document of title to the goods, at the time of the sale, or other dealing with them. For this purpose 'document of title' has a wider meaning than it does at common law (see **20.2.3**) and includes:

> any bill of lading, dock warrant, warehouse keeper's certificate, and warrant or order for the delivery of goods, and any other document used in the ordinary course of business as proof of possession or control of goods, or authorising or purporting to authorise, either by endorsement or by delivery, the possessor of the document to transfer or receive the goods thereby represented (Factors Act 1889, s. 1(4)).

A car's log book, and presumably therefore a car registration document, is not a document of title for this purpose (*Folkes* v *King* [1923] 1 KB 282).

The agent may be in possession through a third party, such as an employee or agent (s. 1(2)).

(c) The agent must be in possession of the goods with the consent of the owner. The burden of proof is on the owner to prove that he did not consent to the agent's possession. It is irrelevant that his consent was obtained by deception (*Pearson* v *Rose & Young* [1950] 1 KB 275) and provided that the owner consented to the agent's initial possession of the goods, it is irrelevant that he has withdrawn consent at the time of the agent's disposition (Factors Act 1889, s. 2(2)).

(d) The owner must consent to the agent possessing the goods *as* a mercantile agent, for sale or one of the other purposes listed in the Factors Act 1889, s. 1. Thus if he gives the goods to the agent for repair, he will not be bound by the agent's disposition.

(e) The agent must deal with the goods 'in the ordinary course of business as a mercantile agent'. It has been held that this means that the agent must act 'in such a way as a mercantile agent in the ordinary course of business as a mercantile agent would act, that is to say within ordinary business hours, at a proper place of business, and in other respects in the ordinary way in which a mercantile agent would act, so that there is nothing to lead the disponee to believe that anything is done wrong' (*Oppenheimer* v *Attenborough* [1908] 1 KB 221). This does not require that the particular transaction be one which is usual for an agent in the agent's particular trade or business. What is 'in the ordinary course of business' will be a question of fact in each case.

(f) The disponee must take the goods in good faith and without notice of any lack of authority on the agent's part. The burden of proof is on the disponee.

15.3.2 Estoppel

The SoGA 1979, s. 21 provides that:

> where goods are sold by a person who is not their owner, and who does not sell them under the authority or with the consent of the owner, the buyer acquires no better title to the goods than the seller had, *unless the owner of the goods is by his conduct precluded from denying the seller's authority to sell* (emphasis supplied).

The words in italics reproduce a common law exception to the general *nemo dat* rule which may apply in two different types of case:

(a) where the owner's conduct makes it appear that the seller is the owner's agent (cases of apparent authority); and

(b) where the owner's conduct makes it appear that the seller is the owner of the goods (apparent ownership).

In either case the owner will be prevented from recovering his goods, and the buyer will acquire title to them, provided the seller's dealing in the goods is consistent with the appearance created by the owner's conduct.

The owner's representation may be by words or by conduct; however, the estoppel exception has generally been narrowly interpreted. For instance:

(a) the owner's representation will only estop him if it was voluntarily made, so that where O surrendered his car to a robber, and, at gunpoint, completed a document stating that he had sold the car to the robber, O was not estopped from denying the robber's right to sell the car (*Debs* v *Sibec Developments Ltd* [1990] RTR 91);

(b) merely parting with possession of goods, even if voluntarily, is generally insufficient to give rise to an estoppel (*Farqharson Bros & Co.* v *King & Co.* [1902] AC 325); normally a positive representation that the seller has the right to sell is required;

(c) the owner's negligence in dealing with his property will not estop him from recovering it from an innocent buyer unless he owes the buyer a duty of care: a duty of care to avoid causing economic loss will only be recognised in exceptional cases, and it therefore seems that it will very rarely be possible for a buyer to establish a title to goods on the basis of estoppel by negligence (see *Moorgate Mercantile Co. Ltd* v *Twitchings* [1977] AC 890).

15.3.3 Sellers in possession

A person [S] who has contracted to sell goods may retain possession of them after the contract and thus appear still to own the goods, even if property in them has in fact already passed to the buyer [B1]. Other people may therefore deal with S as if he were still owner of the goods, for instance by agreeing to buy the same goods, or to take security over them. A series of provisions may protect such a person who deals with the seller who thus remains in possession of goods after selling them.

15.3.3.1 Where property has not passed

Provided that property has not passed to B1 under the first contract of sale, S may continue to deal with the goods as owner. If he resells them, the second buyer (B2) will acquire property in the goods and a title superior to that of B1, although S may incur liability to B1 for failure to deliver if the contract with B1 was for specific goods.

Similarly, if S creates an encumbrance over the goods, the encumbrance will bind B1, but S may be liable to B1 for breach of the implied terms in the Sale of Goods Act 1979, s. 12.

15.3.3.2 Where S has a lien

Even if property has passed to B1, if S has not been paid for the goods he will have a lien over them for the purchase price so long as he remains unpaid and in possession (SoGA 1979, ss. 41–43: see **16.4.2.1**). If S then resells the goods to B2, B2 acquires a good title as against B1 (SoGA 1979, s. 48(2)).

15.3.3.3 Sale of Goods Act 1979, s. 24

Even where property has passed to B1 under the original contract of sale, if S remains in possession of the goods, or the documents of title to them, and resells, pledges or otherwise disposes of them to B2, B2 may take priority over B1 by virtue of the SoGA 1979, s. 24.

It provides that the transfer to B2 has the same effect as if S were authorised by the owner of the goods to make it, provided that B2:

(a) acts in good faith and without notice of the first sale; and

(b) takes delivery of the goods or documents of title.

S is thus treated as if he were B1's agent and B1 is therefore bound by S's dealings with the goods. (A similar, wider provision in the Factors Act 1889, s. 8 protects B2 even though he receives possession of the goods under an *agreement* for sale, pledge or other disposition.)

These provisions apply regardless of the capacity in which S remains in possession of the goods (*Pacific Motor Auctions Property Ltd* v *Motor Credits (Hire Finance) Ltd* [1965] AC 867; *Worcester Works Finance Ltd* v *Cooden Engineering Ltd* [1972] 1 QB 210) and even though S remains in possession unlawfully or without B1's consent (*Worcester Works Finance Ltd* v *Cooden*); however, once S has released possession of the goods, the provisions do not apply even though S subsequently regains possession in some capacity other than as seller, for instance to repair the goods.

In order to be protected by s. 24 B2 must take delivery of the goods. However, physical delivery is not required: it is sufficient if B2 takes constructive delivery. Constructive delivery will occur if a seller who has sold goods remains in possession of them but recognises that his buyer is entitled to possession of them and that he retains possession as bailee. Thus if A sells goods to B but remains in possession of the goods, and then enters into a sale and lease back arrangement relating to the same goods with C, C will get a title to the goods superior to that of B, even though the goods remain throughout in A's possession: see *Michael Gerson Leasing Ltd* v *Wilkinson* [2000] 2 All ER (Comm) 890. Of course, since A remains in possession of the goods after the sale to C, C's title is also vulnerable to a further resale by A.

B2 takes priority over B1 provided he takes possession of the goods (or documents of title), in good faith and without notice of the sale to B1, under a sale, pledge or 'other disposition'. 'Other disposition' has been given a wide meaning but the disposition to B2 must involve a voluntary act by S (*Forsythe Inc. (UK) Ltd* v *Silver Shipping Co. Ltd* [1994] 1 All ER 851) and the creation of a *proprietary*, rather than of a mere *possessory*, interest (*Worcester Works Finance Ltd* v *Cooden*).

15.3.3.4 Sales from bulk

Section 24 may be important where goods are sold from bulk. A seller who contracts to sell goods from bulk may, deliberately or unwittingly, contract to sell more goods than the bulk can actually satisfy, thus, effectively, selling the same goods twice. Consider the following example.

EXAMPLE

S agrees to sell 5,000 tonnes of grain to each of A, B and C, from a silo thought to contain 20,000 tonnes. In fact it contains 15,000 tonnes. S then sells a further 5,000 tonnes to D.

D acquires no interest in the bulk under s. 20A because S has no interest in it to transfer. However, D may acquire an interest in the bulk under s. 24 if S is in possession of a document of title and transfers it to him. More importantly, if S is in possession of the bulk and D takes delivery of the goods out of the bulk, he may be able to rely on s. 24 and thus obtain title to the goods delivered in priority to A, B and C.

15.3.4   Sale under a voidable title

Where a person (B) buys goods from a seller (S) who has only a voidable title to them, B may nevertheless acquire a good title to the goods provided he buys them in good faith, without notice of the defect in B's title before S's title has been avoided (SoGA 1979, s. 23).

This section applies (a) where S acquired the goods under a transaction which was voidable as a result of his misrepresentation, duress or undue influence and (b) where S's title is defective because one of his predecessors in title acquired the goods under a voidable contract.

EXAMPLE 1

Nigel exerts duress on Phil in order to persuade Phil to sell him a valuable antique desk; Nigel thus acquires title to the desk but his title is voidable at Phil's instance. Nigel immediately gives the furniture to Peter; Peter acquires no better title than Nigel had and his title is therefore voidable. However, if Peter now sells the furniture to Alistair, Alistair may acquire a good title to the furniture provided the requirements of s. 23 are fulfilled.

EXAMPLE 2

Oliver contracts to sell his car to Sheila, the price to be paid by a cheque drawn by Sheila. On presentation Oliver discovers that the cheque was stolen and it is dishonoured. The contract between Oliver and Sheila is voidable on the grounds of misrepresentation (where a person buys goods and contracts to pay for them by cheque he impliedly represents that the cheque will be honoured on presentation; thus if the cheque is dishonoured there is a misrepresentation) and Sheila's title to the car is therefore voidable. However, if Sheila resells the car to Brenda before her title is avoided by Oliver, Brenda will acquire a title to the car which is good against Oliver provided the requirements of s. 23 are fulfilled.

Section 23 only applies where S has a voidable title to the goods; it does not apply where S has no title at all. Thus it cannot apply where the contract under which S acquired the goods purported to transfer only possession of the goods, or was an agreement to sell under which property is to pass at a later date or was wholly void, as opposed to voidable, since a void contract has no legal effect at all.

15.3.4.1   Void and voidable contracts

Where B claims to have acquired a good title under s. 23, the original owner (O) may therefore argue that the contract under which he transferred the goods to S was not merely voidable but was wholly void, typically on the grounds of mistake. Where S contracts to buy goods, and by falsely claiming to be someone else persuades O to give him credit, or to accept a cheque there is clearly a misrepresentation by S, which makes the contract voidable; however, O may seek to argue that the contract is void on the grounds of mistake of identity. The authorities show that the distinction between a contract which is void (on the grounds of an operative mistake of identity) and one which is merely voidable for misrepresentation is a fine one, and difficult to draw but it seems that O will only succeed in arguing that the contract was void if he can establish that he intended to contract with someone other than the actual buyer and that the identity of the other contracting party was a vital feature of the contract. Where contracting parties deal face to face there will be a strong presumption that each intends to contract with the person physically present before him (see *Lewis* v *Averay* [1972] 1 QB 198). Where, however, the contract is made in writing the identity of the contracting parties is a matter of construction of the relevant contract in light of the surrounding circumstances and it may then be possible for O to establish that his intention was to contract with the person named in the contract rather than with S, so that there is no contract between O and S. (See *Cundy* v *Lindsay* (1878) 3 App Cas 459; *Shogun Finance Ltd* v *Hudson* [2003] UKHL 62.)

15.3.4.2   Requirements for s. 23 to apply

B can only rely on s. 23 if he acquires the goods:

(a) in good faith; and

(b) without notice of the defect in S's title;

(c) before S's title is avoided.

It seems that under this exception, unlike others, the burden is on O, who challenges B's title, to establish that B bought the goods in bad faith or with notice of the defect.

Where O has parted with property under a voidable contract he should take immediate steps to rescind the contract, in order to recover the property and prevent its sale to a bona fide purchaser who may be protected by s. 23. He may do so without court proceedings merely by notifying S of his intention to avoid the contract between them. However, where S is untraceable, O may be able to rescind the contract by taking other steps to recover his property, such as notifying the police (see *Car and Universal Finance Co. Ltd* v *Caldwell* [1965] 1 QB 525). Note however, that in such a case B may be able to rely on s. 25: see **15.3.5**.

Section 23 only protects a person who *buys* goods from a seller who has a voidable title. However, it reflects a more general common law rule which would also protect a person who, in good faith, took a limited interest in goods, for instance by taking a pledge of them.

15.3.5   Sale by a buyer in possession

A person who has agreed to buy goods (B1) may take possession of them before title passes to him and, by being in possession of the goods, appear to be the owner of the goods. If he resells or otherwise disposes of them before property passes to him a title or priority dispute may then arise between S, the person who sold the goods to B1, and B2, the person to whom B1 transferred them.

SoGA 1979, s. 25 may protect B2 in such a case. Provided the requirements of s. 25 are fulfilled the disposition by B1 has the same effect as if he were a mercantile agent in possession of the goods with the consent of their owner, allowing B2 to take priority over S. Section 25 repeats an almost identical provision in the Factors Act 1889 (s. 9).

15.3.5.1   Requirements for s. 25 to apply

In order for s. 25 to apply, the following conditions must be satisfied.

(a) *B1 must have bought or agreed to buy the goods*
Section 25 only applies where B1 acquired possession of the goods under a sale or agreement for a sale; it thus applies in the common commercial situation where S sells goods to B1 subject to a reservation of title pending payment (see **16.4.3**). It does not apply where B1 acquired the goods under:

(i)   a hire purchase contract (*Helby* v *Matthews* [1895] AC 471);

(ii)   a conditional sale agreement where the price is payable by instalments (SoGA 1979, s. 25; Factors Act 1889, s. 9);

   (iii) an agency agreement (*Shaw* v *MPC* [1987] 1 WLR 1332);

   (iv) a sale or return agreement (*Weiner* v *Harris* [1910] 1 KB 285); or

   (v) a contract for work and materials (*Dawber Williamson Roofing* v *Humberside CC* (1979) 14 BLR 70),

although a person who acquires goods from B1 in any of these circumstances may acquire a good title to them by virtue of other rules.

Section 25 also applies where B1 has bought goods under a contract which is voidable at the instance of S, and may protect B2 even though he acquires the goods *after* S has avoided B1's title so that SoGA 1979, s. 23 does not apply *(Newtons of Wembley Ltd* v *Williams* [1965] 1 QB 560; see **15.3.4**). Rescinding a voidable contract therefore does not guarantee that the dispossessed owner will be able to recover his property.

(b) *B1 must be in possession of the goods with the consent of S*

At the time of the disposition to B2, B1 must be in actual or constructive possession of the goods, or of documents of title to them. He must have acquired possession with the consent of S; however, provided S has given actual consent to B1's possession it is irrelevant that B1 obtained his consent by deceiving him. Provided that B1 *acquired* possession of the goods with S's consent, it is also irrelevant that S withdraws consent prior to B1's disposition of them.

(c) *B1, or a mercantile agent acting for him, must deliver or transfer the goods, or documents of title to them, to B2 under a sale, pledge or other disposition*

This requirement is identical to that under s. 24. As under s. 24, constructive delivery will suffice.

(d) *B2 must act in good faith and without notice of any right of S*

The burden of proof under s. 25 is on B2 to prove that he acted in good faith and without notice of S's rights.

Where S relies on a reservation of title clause in his contract with B1, B2 will be able to rely on s. 25 unless he has notice both of the clause and that S was unpaid (and therefore owned the goods) at the time of the sale to him *(Forsythe Inc. (UK) Ltd* v *Silver Shipping Co. Ltd)*.

15.3.5.2 Effect of s. 25

Where the requirements of s. 25 are satisfied, the disposition by B1 to B2 has the same effect as if B1 'were a mercantile agent in possession of the goods with the consent of the owner'. These words have been interpreted as requiring that B1 must act in the way in which a mercantile agent acting in the ordinary course of business would act in disposing of the goods *(Newtons of Wembley Ltd* v *Williams)*. Since a disposition by a mercantile agent is only binding on the owner of goods if the agent is in possession of them with the consent of the owner, s. 25 only applies where B1 is in possession with the consent of the owner *(National Employers Mutual General Insurance Association Ltd* v *Jones* [1990] 1 AC 24). Thus if S steals goods from O and sells them to B1, a resale by B1 to B2 is not within the section since B1, although in possession with the consent of his *seller* is not in possession with the consent of the *owner*.

15.3.5.3 Sale of vehicles let under hire purchase

Goods let on hire purchase remain the property of the owner/bailor. The hirer/bailee does not become owner of the goods until he has paid all instalments and any option fee due under the agreement. If he purports to resell the goods before that time his buyer, prima facie, acquires no title to them, and is not protected by SoGA 1979, s. 25 because the hirer is not a person who has 'bought or agreed to buy goods' (see **15.3.5.1**). However, Part III of the Hire Purchase Act 1964 applies a special rule to sales of *motor vehicles* let on hire purchase so that, in certain circumstances, a private, as opposed to a trade, purchaser of a motor vehicle let on hire purchase may take a good title, in priority to the owner/bailor (HPA 1964, s. 27). The same rule applies to vehicles sold under conditional sale agreements where the price is payable by instalments. However, the relevant provisions of the HPA can only apply where the vehicle has been bailed under a valid hire purchase agreement or agreed to be sold under a valid conditional sale agreement. They therefore do not apply where the initial hire purchase or conditional sale agreement is void for mistake of identity (*Shogun Finance Ltd* v *Hudson* [2003] UKHL 62. See **15.3.4.1**).

15.3.6   Sales in a market overt

There was formerly an exception to the *nemo dat* rule, where goods were sold in *market overt*, which allowed the buyer to take a good title to them. This exception was abolished by the Sale of Goods (Amendment) Act 1994.

15.3.7   Sales under special powers of sale or orders of the court

Nothing in SoGA affects 'the validity of any contract of sale under any special common law or statutory power of sale or under the order of a court of competent jurisdiction' (s. 21(2)(b)). This includes sales by sheriffs, bailiffs, bailees and pledgees and allows the buyer to acquire a good title to goods sold in such transactions.

15.4   Summary

After reading this chapter you should understand and be able to apply:

- the general rule *nemo dat quod non habet*;
- the statutory exceptions to the *nemo dat* rule;
- the conditions for application of the various exceptions.

Buyer's duties and seller's remedies

16.1 Introduction

In this chapter we examine:

- the buyer's duties to accept and pay for the goods;
- the seller's remedies in the event of the buyer's failure to perform including
    - the right to claim the price;
    - the right to claim interest on unpaid sums;
    - the right to claim damages for non-acceptance;
    - the right to withhold delivery and/or recover possession of goods after delivery;
    - the effectiveness of contractual terms reserving title to goods after delivery and the drafting of such terms.

SoGA 1979 provides that it is the buyer's duty to accept and pay for the goods in accordance with the terms of the contract (s. 27). In addition, where the seller is ready and willing to deliver the goods and requests the buyer to take delivery, the buyer must compensate the seller for any losses caused by his failure to take delivery within a reasonable time (s. 37): an obligation to accept delivery of the goods is therefore indirectly imposed. Where performance of the seller's obligations requires the buyer's co-operation, as for instance where the seller requires to have access to the buyer's premises to deliver or install goods, a term requiring the buyer to co-operate in performance of the contract will generally be implied at common law.

SoGA 1979 provides the seller with a range of real and personal remedies for non-performance of the buyer's obligations. However, a well drafted contract will generally contain express terms covering these matters. Where the terms of the contract are dictated by the seller, the contract will expand and supplement the obligations imposed on the buyer by the general law and provide the seller with a range of enhanced remedies, including:

(a) provision for the payment of interest on late payment;

(b) liquidated damages for failure to accept or take delivery of the goods; and

(c) reservation of title clauses to secure payment of the price.

16.2 The duties to accept and take delivery of the goods

These duties are not necessarily the same. The buyer commits a breach of the duty to accept the goods if he rejects them in circumstances where he has no right to do so, either because there are no grounds for rejection, or because he has lost the right to reject, including by accepting the goods under SoGA 1979, ss. 34–5 (see **11.3.1.3**). A buyer may therefore take delivery of the goods but then reject them; conversely, a buyer who is prepared to accept the goods may be in breach of contract by failing to take delivery of them at the correct time. However, where the buyer refuses to take delivery of the goods and indicates that he will not accept them in the future he commits a breach of both duties and repudiates the contract.

16.2.1   Time for performance

Unless the contract otherwise provides, the buyer is required to accept the goods when the seller is ready and willing to deliver them. Where the seller is ready and willing to deliver the goods and requests the buyer to take delivery of them, the buyer must take delivery within a reasonable time. In order to avoid doubt and disputes the contract will generally contain provisions fixing the time for performance of the buyer's obligations (see **18.5.1**, Clause 2.2).

16.2.2   Damages

If the buyer fails to accept or take delivery of the goods at the proper time, the seller is entitled to damages. In either case damages are assessed in accordance with the general rules governing damages for breach of contract including those concerned with causation, remoteness and mitigation (see **3.3.2.2**). However, these general rules are modified in some respects by SoGA 1979, s. 50.

16.2.3   Damages for non-acceptance

Damages for non-acceptance are assessed similarly to damages for non-delivery.

(a) Where there is an available market for goods of the contract description, the prima facie measure of damages is the difference between the contract price and the market price of the goods at the date when they should have been accepted (SoGA 1979, s. 50). There will only be an available market for the purposes of a claim for damages for non-acceptance where there are sufficient [potential] buyers to buy the contract goods, so that there will be no market where supply exceeds demand.

(b) If there is no available market, the seller will be entitled to damages to compensate for the profit he would have made had the contract been performed.

(c) In any case, he may also recover damages in respect of other losses caused by the buyer's breach, including the costs of storing the goods and the costs of advertising or modifying them for sale, provided such losses are not too remote.

16.2.4   Damages for failure to take delivery

Where the buyer fails to take delivery of the goods within a reasonable time of being required by the seller so to do, he is liable to the seller for any loss caused by his failure to take delivery and must pay the seller a reasonable charge for the care and custody of the goods (SoGA 1979, s. 37).

16.2.5   Express terms

The contract is likely to contain express terms covering the duties to accept and take delivery of the goods and the consequences of the buyer's failure so to do. It will often fix the time for performance. For instance, where the buyer is to take delivery of the goods it may provide for the seller to serve notice that the goods are ready for delivery and require the buyer to collect them within a stated time.

16.2.5.1 Classification of the terms

Generally stipulations in commercial contracts requiring one of the parties to perform some act within a stated time are construed as conditions, but a well drafted contract should expressly classify the obligations or define the consequences of non-performance. The buyer will want them to be warranties, whereas the seller may prefer to make them conditions so that he may terminate the contract if the buyer fails to perform on time. (See generally **18.5.1** and **18.5.2**.)

16.2.5.2 Consequences of breach

A typical term might provide for the seller to serve notice when the goods are ready for delivery and require the buyer to collect them within a fixed time (see **18.5.1**, Clause 2.2). It might further provide that if the buyer fails to take delivery at that time:

(a) the goods should be at the buyer's risk;

(b) the seller may make arrangements for the storage of the goods and the buyer should reimburse the seller any costs so incurred;

(c) the seller may terminate the contract on the grounds of the buyer's non-performance (see **18.5.1**, Clause 2.3).

The contract may require the buyer to pay liquidated damages if he fails to accept or take delivery in accordance with the terms of the contract. Such provision will be valid provided the clause is a genuine pre-estimate of the loss likely to be incurred by the seller and not a penalty (see **3.3.2.3**). In a consumer contract such a provision may also be subject to the test of fairness under the Unfair Terms in Consumer Contracts Regulations 1999 (see **3.4.3**).

16.2.5.3 Other provisions

Where performance of the seller's duties requires the buyer's co-operation, the contract will generally contain express provisions, for instance allocating responsibility for providing facilities or services, obtaining licences or consents and arranging testing.

16.3 The duty to pay the price

The seller's main interest is to obtain payment of the price. SoGA 1979 requires the buyer to pay the contract price for the goods 'in accordance with the terms of the contract'. The contract will generally fix the amount of the price and contain detailed provisions governing how, when and where it is to be paid. However, if the contract is silent, the following default rules apply.

(a) If the contract does not expressly fix the price or a method for determining it (for instance, by providing that the price shall be fixed by an independent assessor), the buyer must pay a reasonable sum.

(b) The normal rule is that payment is due in cash at the seller's premises, but it will generally be implied that the buyer may pay by any commonly used method; payment by cheque will generally be permitted. A cheque is only a conditional payment, so that the buyer's obligation to pay the price revives if the cheque is not honoured. However, payment by credit card operates to discharge the buyer's obligations absolutely (*Re Charge Card Services Ltd* [1989] Ch 497).

(c) If the contract is silent, payment is due on delivery. Most commercial contracts will allow the buyer credit. The time for payment is generally not of the essence (SoGA 1979, s. 10(1)). Thus if the buyer fails to pay at the correct time, the seller may not terminate the contract. This is especially important where the contract requires payment by instalments, since if the buyer fails to pay any instalment at the due date the seller cannot terminate the contract.

16.3.1   Express provisions

The default rules will often be inappropriate and the contract will therefore generally contain express provisions to cover these matters. The contract will therefore contain provisions covering the following matters.

16.3.1.1   The amount of the price

A seller may want to reserve the right to vary the price, especially in the case of a long term contract. The price may be indexed, for instance to raw material prices. Alternatively the seller may reserve the right unilaterally to vary the price. Such provisions are perfectly valid at common law, but may be subject to challenge under the Unfair Contract Terms Act 1977, s. 3 or the Unfair Terms Consumer Contracts Regulations (when applicable). In the absence of such a provision the price can only be varied by a contractually binding agreement, supported by consideration.

16.3.1.2   The method of payment

Where payment by cheque is permitted, the contract may provide that the price is not paid until the cheque is cleared.

16.3.1.3   Rights of set-off

The contract may require the buyer to pay the price in full, without deduction in respect of any claim or set-off the buyer may have against the seller, for instance on the grounds of alleged defects in the goods (see **18.5.1**, Clause 5.2). Such a provision will be subject to statutory control under the Unfair Contract Terms Act 1977, s. 6 (*Stewart Gill Ltd* v *Horatio Myer and Co. Ltd* [1992] QB 600) and thus be wholly ineffective against a consumer and, in a non-consumer contract, subject to a test of reasonableness.

16.3.1.4   The time for payment

Most commercial contracts, and many consumer contracts, allow the buyer credit, although where there are doubts about the buyer's ability to pay, the seller may require payment before delivery. The contract may make prompt payment of the price 'of the essence', especially where payment by instalments is permitted. Where payment is by instalments the contract will generally also contain an acceleration clause under which, on breach of contract by the buyer, all outstanding instalments immediately become due. The effect of such a clause is that if the buyer does commit a breach the seller can immediately sue for the whole balance due under the agreement. In order to encourage prompt payment the contract may require the buyer to pay interest if payment is late, or offer the buyer a discount for early payment. In the absence of such a provision interest may be payable under the Late Payment of Commercial Debts (Interest) Act 1998 (see **3.3.1.4**).

16.3.1.5   Deposits and pre-payments

Where a contract for the sale of goods requires the buyer to make part payment of the price before delivery, the character of the payment must be determined in order to decide if it can be retained by the seller in the event of the contract being terminated on any basis. If the payment is properly characterised as a deposit, to guarantee the buyer's performance, the seller may retain it if paid, or sue for it notwithstanding termination. However, if the payment is properly characterised as a part payment it must be refunded in the event of termination (*Dies* v *British and International Mining and Finance Corp Ltd* [1939] 1 KB 724). The position may be different under contracts for work and materials where advance payments may be for preparatory work, design etc. In such cases the seller may retain pre-payments unless there is a total failure of the consideration for which they were paid. Thus where under a contract to design, build and supply a ship the contract provided for 20 per cent of the price to be payable on completion of the vessel's keel but the buyer failed to pay, the shipbuilder was entitled to terminate the contract and sue for the amount of the part payment, as money payable in respect of the design and construction work. If the payment had been made the builder would have been entitled to retain it. (See *Hyundai Heavy Industries Co. Ltd* v *Papadopoulos* [1980] 1 WLR 1129; *Stocznia Gdanska SA* v *Latvian Shipping Co.* [1998] 1 All ER 883.)

16.4 Remedies for non-payment

Where the buyer fails to pay the price in accordance with the terms of the contract, SoGA offers the seller a number of real and personal remedies. Again the statutory rights will often be supplemented by additional rights granted by the contract.

16.4.1 Claim for the price

The seller may sue for the price if either:

(a) property has passed to the buyer; this provision will not apply even if it is the buyer's breach of contract which prevents property passing (for instance, because the buyer fails to take delivery of the goods); or

(b) the contract makes the price payable 'on a day certain irrespective of delivery' (SoGA 1979, s. 49).

Where neither of these conditions is fulfilled the seller will only be able to claim damages for non-acceptance.

From the seller's point of view a claim for the price has advantages over a claim for damages for non-delivery. It is a liquidated claim so that the seller may be able to obtain summary judgment for the amount of the price which can be executed immediately; there is no duty to mitigate and no problems of remoteness or proving causation or loss. The contract may contain express provisions extending the seller's right to claim the price, for instance allowing him to claim the price even though property has not passed to the buyer (see **18.5.1**, Clause 5.3).

16.4.2 Real rights

As a personal claim, the right to sue for the price will be of little use where the buyer is insolvent and unable to pay. SoGA 1979, s. 39 gives the seller three real remedies which offer him some measure of protection against the buyer's failure to pay. They are:

(a) a lien over the goods;

(b) a right to stop the goods in transit; and

(c) a right in certain circumstances to resell the goods and terminate the contract.

The rights of lien and stoppage are available even if property in the goods has passed to the buyer, so long as the seller is unpaid. For these purposes the seller is 'unpaid' until he has received payment in full for the goods. Where he has received conditional payment, such as a cheque, the seller is unpaid until the condition is fulfilled (s. 38).

16.4.2.1 Lien

A right of lien is a right to retain possession of the goods as security for payment of the price (see **25.3**). It is available only where:

(a) the goods are supplied 'without any stipulation as to credit', or any credit period allowed has expired, or the buyer is insolvent (s. 41); and

(b) the seller retains possession of the goods; it is lost if the seller delivers the goods to the buyer, his agent, or to an independent carrier or bailee for transmission to the buyer (s. 43).

The statutory lien is of little practical value in modern commercial circumstances when goods are normally supplied on credit and the seller rarely remains in possession of the goods after expiry of the credit period.

16.4.2.2 Stoppage in transit

As a lien depends on continued possession, the seller loses his lien over the goods when he delivers them to an independent carrier for transmission to the buyer. However, if the buyer becomes insolvent while the goods are in transit, the seller is allowed to stop them, retake possession of them and retain them until paid for (ss. 44–5).

16.4.2.3 Resale

A seller who has exercised his right of lien or stoppage in transit may in certain circumstances resell the goods (s. 48). The consequences of such a resale are:

(a) the original contract of sale is terminated and the seller may claim damages from the buyer for any losses he suffers as a result of the buyer's breach of contract: for instance, the difference between the original contract price and the amount realised on the resale; and

(b) the resale passes a good title to the goods to the second buyer to whom the goods are resold, even if property in the goods had already passed to the first buyer.

The right of resale is available where:

(a) the goods are perishable;

(b) the seller gives the buyer notice that he intends to resell the goods and the buyer fails within a reasonable time to tender the price; or

(c) resale is authorised by the contract.

16.4.3 Reservation of title

The seller's rights to sue for the price and for damages for non-acceptance are personal rights; they will be worthless if the buyer is insolvent, for as an ordinary unsecured creditor the seller's rights will rank behind those of the buyer's preferential and secured creditors. In most cases the seller will only receive a small percentage of the sum due to him as a dividend; in many he will receive nothing. In modern commercial circumstances the statutory rights of lien, stoppage in transit and resale offer the seller only very limited protection against the buyer's failure to pay the price. The seller may therefore require additional protection against the buyer's inability to pay. For instance, he may require the buyer to provide a guarantee from some third party, such as a bank (see **Chapter 26**); in international transactions payment by documentary credit is often required (see **Chapter 23**). Alternatively he may require the buyer to provide security in some other form.

The simplest option will often be to use the goods supplied to the buyer as security by retaining title to them until paid for. In appropriate cases the seller may lease the goods to the buyer; alternatively, they may be supplied on hire purchase terms. However, leasing and hire purchase are inappropriate where the goods are supplied to the buyer for resale or for use in manufacturing. A further alternative is for the seller to supply the goods under a conditional sale agreement, retaining title to them until they are paid for, and it is now common for commercial sale contracts to contain 'reservation of title' clauses retaining title to the goods supplied until they are paid for in order to provide the seller with security against the buyer's failure to pay the price. Such clauses are often complex and must be drafted with care.

Reservation of title is sanctioned by SoGA 1979, ss. 17 and 19 and at its simplest a sale subject to reservation of title is essentially a conditional sale agreement. However, whereas traditionally goods were only supplied on conditional sale terms where it was expected that they would be retained by the buyer in the form in which they were supplied, reservation of title clauses are used in contracts even where it is expected from the outset that the goods may be resold, consumed or used in a manufacturing process before they are paid for. (See **18.5.1**, Clause 6.)

16.4.3.1   Challenges to reservation of title

A seller will not normally seek to enforce a reservation of title clause unless the buyer is insolvent. A successful claim under a reservation of title clause will remove the assets claimed by the seller from the pool of assets available for distribution to other creditors, and insolvency practitioners will therefore seek to resist a seller's claim under a reservation of title clause if at all possible.

There is now a substantial body of case law and an extensive academic and practical literature surrounding reservation of title clauses. Nevertheless many aspects of the law relating to reservation of title clauses are unclear and insolvency practitioners may use that uncertainty in order to resist claims, or at least negotiate a settlement of a seller's claim. Possession of the goods or other assets gives the insolvency practitioner a strong bargaining position *vis-à-vis* an unpaid seller. However, most insolvency practitioners will be reluctant to become involved in litigation and they may therefore prefer to negotiate a settlement of a reservation of title claim if pressed by a determined seller.

The arguments advanced by insolvency practitioners in order to resist reservation of title claims can be grouped under four main headings.

(a) *Effective imposition of the clause*

Receivers and liquidators will generally reject a reservation of title clause unless the clause was effectively incorporated in the relevant sale contract. The wording of SoGA 1979, ss. 18 and 19 suggests that in the case of a contract for the sale of unascertained goods a right of disposal of the goods may be reserved by the terms of the appropriation of the goods to the contract. However, since there is no modern case law on the point, insolvency practitioners can be expected strongly to resist a claim where the clause was imposed after the contract was made.

(b) *The clause must relate to the assets claimed*

An insolvency practitioner may resist a reservation of title claim on the simple grounds that there are no assets of the class or classes to which the clause in question relates. For instance, where the clause reserves title merely to the goods supplied by the seller, he may assert that the goods have been consumed or resold leaving nothing for the seller to claim. For this reason the seller may seek to extend his claim to cover manufactured goods or proceeds of resales. Alternatively it may be argued that, although there are in stock goods supplied by the claimant seller, they have been paid for and have become the buyer's property, or cannot be identified as the seller's property, leaving nothing for the seller to claim.

(c) *The seller's claim amounts to a charge over the assets claimed*

This is the most contentious of the arguments advanced against reservation of title claims. Its essence is that, although the contract purports to make the seller owner of the assets to which it relates, those assets are in law the buyer's property and the effect of the contract is to grant the seller a security interest over them. Where (as in most cases) the insolvent buyer is a company it will be argued that the clause amounts to a charge over the relevant assets. Certain classes of charge created by a company are void against a liquidator or creditor unless registered (Companies Act 1985, ss. 395–6); the rights created by a reservation of title clause may amount to:

(i) a floating charge on the company's property; or

(ii) a charge over book debts or a charge created by an instrument which, if executed by an individual would require registration under the Bills of Sale Acts 1878 and 1882.

In practice the rights created by reservation of title clauses are never registered because first, registration would generally be impracticable, since each individual contract would require a fresh registration, and secondly, any charge so registered would rank in priority behind any charge over the relevant assets already registered. Since in practice most companies will have given floating charges over their whole undertaking to their banks, registration by the seller of a charge over goods supplied would achieve nothing unless the bank agreed to waive priority in favour of the seller.

Although the Companies Act 1985 does not expressly make an unregistered charge void against a receiver, receivers regularly reject reservation of title claims on the grounds that the clause in question creates an unregistered charge, and it seems to have been accepted by the courts that they are entitled so to do.

Where the buyer is not a company it may be claimed that a contract containing a reservation of title clause amounts to a bill of sale which must be registered in accordance with the Bills of Sale Act 1878 (see **25.6.1**). An unregistered bill of sale is void against a trustee in bankruptcy. Moreover, if the bill is held to be a 'security bill' it is wholly void, even against the buyer, unless in the statutory form prescribed by the Bills of Sale Act 1882. Where a clause lays claim to the proceeds of sale of goods supplied by the seller it may be construed as a general assignment of future book debts which requires registration under the 1878 Act in the same way as a bill of sale.

The Insolvency Act 1986, s. 11 imposes a further restriction on the enforcement of reservation of title clauses. Where an application is made to the court for an administration order in respect of a company, no steps may be taken to repossess goods supplied subject to a reservation of title until the hearing of the application and, if the order is made, so long as the order remains in force.

16.4.3.2   Types of reservation of title clause

Reservation of title clauses can be classified into various 'types'.

(a) Simple clause: retains title to the goods supplied under the contract in which it is included until the price for those goods is paid.

(b) Current account clause: retains title to goods supplied until their price and other debts are paid. A common form provides that property in the goods shall not pass until the buyer has paid all sums due to the seller on any account (see **18.5.1**, Clause 6.2).

(c) Products clause: claims that products manufactured using the goods supplied by the seller are to be the seller's property until the buyer has paid for goods supplied to him and used in the manufacture of the new products.

(d) Proceeds of sale clause: claims that if the goods supplied by the seller are resold, the proceeds of sale belong to the seller until the buyer pays the price of the goods (see **18.5.1**, Clause 6.4).

We will use these 'types' in order to explain the relevant law. In practice a clause will often be a hybrid of the various 'types'. For instance the seller may use a current account clause which also lays claim to proceeds of sale of the goods supplied, products manufactured from the goods supplied and proceeds of sale of those new products.

16.4.3.3   Simple clause

It is now settled that a simple clause which retains title to the goods supplied until they are paid for is effective and does not create a charge (*Clough Mill Ltd* v *Martin* [1985] 1 WLR 111). However, it is essential that the clause retain *legal* title: it has been held that a clause which retained 'equitable and beneficial ownership' of goods supplied allowed the legal title to pass to the buyer subject to the grant back to the seller of an equitable charge, which was void unless registered (*Re Bond Worth Ltd* [1980] Ch 228).

Under a simple clause the seller retains title to goods supplied under the particular contract in which the clause appears until sums due under that contract are paid. Where the seller relies on such a clause an insolvency practitioner may therefore often require him to prove that any goods in stock were not only supplied by him but also were supplied under the particular contract under which he claims, so that they remain the seller's property. In many cases this may prove difficult. Suppliers of goods should therefore be advised that, wherever possible, the goods they supply should be capable of being identified and linked with the particular contract under which they are supplied—for instance by including serial numbers in contracts or invoices, or marking goods with batch or contract numbers.

It is, however, not clear that it is necessary for a supplier to identify goods in this way. It was accepted in *Ian Chishohm Textiles Ltd* v *Griffith* [1994] BCC 96, that in order to make a successful claim under a reservation of title clause the supplier must positively identify particular items as his property. However, in *Glencore International AG* v *Metro Trading Inc* [2001] 1 All ER (Comm) 103 it was held that where goods (in this case, oil) of several owners were stored together and commingled so that it became impossible to identify each owner's goods, it was not necessary for any particular owner to identify particular goods as his own. Provided that a claimant could show that (a) he had supplied goods to the defendant and (b) that he had not withdrawn his goods from the mixture, each supplied was entitled to recover an equivalent quantity of goods to that supplied, unless the defendant could positively show that the goods in stock were *not* the claimant's property. In effect the judge applied the rules applicable to tracing claims (following *dicta* of Lord Millett in *Foskett* v *McKeown* [2000] 3 All ER 97) and held that in a case of wrongful mixing the risk of any loss of goods from the mixture should fall, first, on the party responsible for the mixing.

Glencore was not a reservation of title case but the reasoning would appear to be applicable in the retention of title context. It is also consistent with the earlier decision in *Indian Oil Corpn Ltd* v *Greenstone Shipping Corp* [1988] QB 345, where it was held that where A wrongfully mixed his goods with those of B so that the two became indistinguishable, A and B would own the resulting mixture as tenants in common and that B would be entitled to recover from the mixture a quantity of goods equivalent to his 'contribution' to it.

16.4.3.4   Current account clause

Where the seller relies on a simple clause the seller is only entitled to claim a batch of goods so long as sums remain due under the contract under which they were supplied. If the goods have been resold or consumed, the seller is left with no security even if other goods supplied by him remain in stock.

EXAMPLE

Phil's Fashions Ltd supplies designer suits to Wallies Ltd under contracts which include a simple reservation of title clause and which require payment at the end of the month following delivery. It supplies 10 suits in January, and a further 10 in February. At the end of February Wallies pays for the suits delivered in January but, in March, Wallies becomes insolvent without paying for the suits delivered in February. It is then discovered that all of the suits delivered in February have been sold, but eight of the suits supplied in January are still held in stock. Phil's has no claim to the suits: they became the property of Wallies at the end of February when Wallies paid for them.

In order to avoid such problems a seller may use a 'current account clause'. Thus Phil's might avoid the difficulties outlined above if its clause provided that:

Suits supplied by us remain our property until you have paid all sums due to us on any account.

Taking the facts of the example given above, when Wallies pays for the January consignment at the end of February, it owes Phil's for the February consignment. The current account clause therefore prevents title in the January consignment passing to Wallies and, when it becomes insolvent, Phil's can claim those suits.

In *Armour* v *Thyssen Edelstahlwerke GmbH* [1990] 3 All ER 481 it was held that a current account clause was effective to prevent title passing to the buyer until its conditions were fulfilled and it therefore seems that such a clause does not create a charge. However, since *Armour* was decided on a point of Scots law, insolvency practitioners still tend to resist claims under current account clauses, arguing that such clauses allow property to pass to the buyer subject to a charge back in favour of the seller. Current account clauses should therefore be used with care. Moreover, a current account clause does not avoid the need for goods to be identifiable. If the buyer's account with the seller is clear at any time, property in all goods supplied prior to that time will pass to the buyer so that it will be necessary to differentiate between goods supplied before and after that date.

As the example given above shows, where a seller enforces a claim under a current account clause he may repossess goods for which the buyer has already paid. It is not clear whether, in such a case, he may retain the money paid for those goods.

16.4.3.5   Manufactured products

Where the seller's goods are used in the manufacture of a new product the seller's rights depend primarily on the nature and effect of the manufacturing process.

(a) If the goods supplied by the seller can be removed from the manufactured product without doing damage to them or other components, the seller may retain title to them by means of a simple clause, and, if necessary, recover them from the manufactured product.

EXAMPLE

In *Hendy Lennox Ltd* v *Graham Puttick Engines Ltd* [1984] 1 WLR 485 diesel engines supplied by the seller were incorporated into generator sets. The seller was able to recover them under a simple reservation of title clause.

(b) Where the manufacturing process results in the seller's goods being irreversibly incorporated into a new product, or losing their identity, the seller's title to the original goods will be extinguished as they will cease to exist as an independent item. For instance, where a seller supplied resin his title was extinguished when the resin was used to manufacture chipboard (*Borden v Scottish Timber Products Ltd* [1981] Ch 25). It will be assumed that property in the goods is intended to pass to the buyer as soon as they enter a manufacturing process which will result in the loss of their identity (see *Re Peachdart Ltd* [1984] 1 Ch 131).

In order to overcome this problem the seller may seek to claim title to products manufactured using his goods. However, it will generally be assumed that new products manufactured by the buyer will be the buyer's property, since to recognise them as belonging to the seller would allow him to take the benefit of the buyer's labour and of any other goods or materials used in their manufacture including, perhaps, some supplied by other traders also subject to reservation of title clauses. If the seller's reservation of title clause lays claim to such manufactured products it will normally give him no more than a charge over the manufactured product to secure the sums owed to him (see *Clough Mill v Martin; Re Peachdart Ltd; Borden v Scottish Timber Products Ltd*).

(c) Where the goods supplied by the seller are incorporated into realty they will become part of the realty, and therefore the property of its owner, if the annexation is such as to make them a fixture.

16.4.3.6   Claims to proceeds of sale

If the buyer resells the goods before paying for them, the seller's rights will normally be extinguished because the sub-buyer will take a good title to the goods by virtue of SoGA 1979, s. 25 (see **15.3.5**). In order to overcome this problem the seller may seek to claim an interest in the proceeds of the resale. In *Aluminium Industrie Vaasen BV v Romalpa Aluminium* [1976] 2 All ER 552 the Court of Appeal held that, in such a situation, the seller was entitled to trace his goods into the proceeds of their resale. However, although in a number of subsequent cases reliance has been placed on the *Romalpa* precedent, there is no other reported case in which a seller has been able to establish a claim to proceeds of sale.

(a) *Fiduciary relationship*

A seller's claim to proceeds will only succeed if he can show that the relationship between him and his buyer is fiduciary and thus establish a right to trace in equity. The establishment of a fiduciary relationship will depend on the wording and construction of the particular reservation of title clause and the other provisions of the contract in which it appears. In *Romalpa* the sellers sold aluminium foil to the buyers subject to a reservation of title clause which provided that:

(i)   the foil should be stored in such a way as to identify it as the seller's property;

(ii)   products made from the seller's foil were to belong to the seller and be stored so as to make them identifiable as such;

(iii)   that until resale, the buyer was to hold manufactured products in the capacity of 'fiduciary owner' for the seller; and

(iv)   on demand the buyer should 'hand over' to the seller claims against its customers who bought manufactured products.

The buyer went into receivership without paying for a quantity of foil; however, prior to the receivership the buyer sold a quantity of foil and that was paid for after the appointment of a receiver. The seller claimed the proceeds of sale from the receiver. The contract contained no express provision to cover such a situation. Counsel for the receiver conceded that the buyer held the foil as bailee for the seller, and the Court of Appeal held, in light of that concession and the provisions of the contract, that (1) a right for the buyer to sell foil must be implied and (2) that the relationship between seller and buyer was fiduciary so that on a resale of the foil the seller could trace into the proceeds of sale.

Subsequent cases have refused to find the requisite fiduciary relationship, for instance on the ground that:

(i)   the contract did not require separate storage of the seller's goods; or

(ii)   there was no requirement for the buyer to keep proceeds of resales separate from his own money; or

(iii) implication of a fiduciary relationship would be inconsistent with the express terms of the contract, and especially with the grant of credit to the buyer.

Generally it seems that the courts regard imposition of a fiduciary relationship as unreal, in that such a relationship would entitle the unpaid seller to the whole of the proceeds of the buyer's resale, including any profit element.

(b) *A claim to proceeds creates a registrable charge*

A clause which makes an express claim to proceeds of resale is likely to be regarded as an assignment of future book-debts, or a charge on the proceeds of resale, which will require registration as a charge or bill of sale (see **25.6.1**). Even where the seller manages to establish a fiduciary relationship and an equitable right to trace into proceeds of resale, his interest in the proceeds of sale may be regarded as a charge on the proceeds which, arising from the terms of the contract, will be a registrable charge created by the buyer since, if the seller's interest only subsists until payment of the price due to the seller, being both limited to the amount of the outstanding debt and defeasible on payment of that debt, that interest possesses the characteristics of a charge.

The courts therefore seem unlikely to uphold a seller's claim to an interest in proceeds of the buyer's resale, and a receiver can be expected strongly to contest any such claim. In many cases there will, in any event, be nothing for the seller to claim. A claim to proceeds will only be worthwhile where, as in the *Romalpa* case itself, the proceeds of resale are received after commencement of the insolvency. If they are received before the insolvency they are likely to be lost in the buyer's bank account which, by definition, will be overdrawn (thus defeating any attempt to trace).

(c) *The impact of factoring*

In many cases the buyer will have factored his book debts. In such a case the seller who attempts to claim proceeds of the buyer's resale will find himself competing for those proceeds with the factor. Priority as between the two will go to the first of them to give notice to the debtor (i.e. sub-buyer) of the assignment to him (in accordance with the so called 'rule in *Dearle* v *Hall* ' (1828) 3 Russ 1) (see *Compaq Computer Ltd* v *Abercorn Group Ltd* [1991] BCC 484). In practice this means that the factor will normally have a prior claim to the proceeds since the seller will rarely give such notice.

16.4.3.7   Drafting a reservation of title clause

In light of the case law, a reservation of title clause must be drafted with care. Consideration should be given to the nature of the goods, the likely uses to which they will be put and the identity and corporate status of the seller's customers in order to decide what form the clause should take.

Even though claims to proceeds of resale and manufactured products are unlikely to be upheld by a court, many clauses will include such claims, and it may be felt appropriate to include such claims where resale or use in manufacturing are foreseen as a basis for bargaining with an insolvency practitioner. It seems that even if a clause contains a claim to proceeds or products which is construed as a charge, that will not colour the construction of the claim to the original goods sold. However, in order to avoid any doubt the clause should be drafted in separate sub-clauses to facilitate severance of the different parts.

A simple clause should contain at least the following provisions:

(a) a reservation of legal title to the goods until full payment is received (see **18.5.1**, Clause 6.2); care must be taken in drafting the clause: a clause which states that 'the goods shall remain the property of the seller until paid for' may be construed as an express undertaking that the goods are the seller's property at the time of the contract, exposing the seller to wider liability than under the implied condition in SoGA 1979, s. 12;

(b) since risk normally passes with property, an express provision that risk of loss or damage is to pass to the buyer on delivery; this may be coupled with a requirement for the buyer to insure the goods for the seller's benefit (see **18.5.1**, Clause 6.1);

(c) a requirement that the goods be stored separately from the buyer's property so that they are identifiable as the seller's property (see **18.5.1**, Clause 6.3);

(d) a right for the seller to enter onto the buyer's premises in order to recover the goods in the event of non-payment or the buyer's earlier insolvency (see **18.5.1**, Clause 6.6).

Where a current account clause is required the reservation of property will be until the buyer has paid all sums due to the seller on any account (see **18.5.1**, Clause 6.2).

If a claim to manufactured products is included, the clause should provide that new products manufactured using the seller's goods shall belong to the seller and be held by the buyer on the same basis as the original goods; in particular, separate storage and insurance of manufactured products should be required.

If a claim to proceeds of resale is made, the clause must be drafted so as to create a fiduciary relationship between buyer and seller. In order to achieve this the clause should:

(a) require the buyer to hold the seller's goods (including manufactured products) as bailee for the seller, and keep them separate from the buyer's other property;

(b) permit the buyer to resell the goods, but as (undisclosed) agent for seller; however, the clause should make clear that the buyer has no authority to create privity of contract between the seller and the sub-buyer;

(c) require the buyer to hold proceeds of any resale on trust for the seller and keep them separate from the buyer's own moneys by paying them into a separate bank account (see **18.5.1**, Clause 6.4).

Since a reservation of title clause will prevent property passing to the buyer, it will restrict the seller's right to claim the price under SoGA 1979, s. 49. The seller will therefore want to include in the contract a provision allowing him to claim the price for the goods even where property has not passed to the buyer.

16.4.3.8   Enforcing a reservation of title clause

It can be expected that insolvency practitioners will resist all but the most clear-cut reservation of title claims. A seller seeking to rely on a clause must therefore be prepared to argue his case and justify his claim. In addition the following points should be noted.

(a) If the seller proves in the insolvency, or claims VAT bad debt relief, in respect of the unpaid price, he may be taken as acknowledging that property has passed to the buyer and that his reservation is ineffective.

(b) Where an administration order is made, the seller may not enforce his reservation of title without a court order (Insolvency Act 1986, s. 11)

16.5 Summary

After reading this chapter you should:

- understand the buyer's duties to accept and pay for the goods and the remedies available to the seller for their non-performance;
- understand the circumstances in which the seller may sue for the price in the event of non-payment;
- understand the circumstances in which the seller may be entitled to withhold delivery or recover possession of goods on grounds of non-payment;
- understand the different types of claim which may be included in a reservation of title clause;
- understand the factors affecting the effectiveness of the different forms of reservation of title clause and the likelihood of such claims being upheld;
- be able to advise a creditor or insolvency practitioner on the likely effectiveness of a claim under a reservation of title clause;
- understand the main considerations to be taken into account when drafting a reservation of title clause.

Contracts for the supply of services

17.1 Introduction

The supply of services is an increasingly important part of commercial activity. A wide range of transactions involves the supply of services including: the servicing and repair of vehicles and machinery; professional services such as legal, financial and accountancy services; commercial activities such as agency and storage and carriage of goods; and domestic or 'consumer' services such as travel agency.

In this chapter we examine the legal rules applicable to contracts involving the supply of a service and in particular:

- the rules governing the quality of the service to be performed;
- the time for performance;
- the price payable.

17.2 Supply of Goods and Services Act 1982

Contracts involving the supply of services are subject to the Supply of Goods and Services Act 1982 (SGSA) which implies into such contracts terms relating to

(a) the standard of performance of the service (s. 13);

(b) the time for performance (s. 14); and

(c) the price (s. 15).

The Act applies to all contracts for the supply of services either alone or together with goods. It thus applies to both (e.g.) contracts for professional services, such as accountancy or for private health care, and also to contracts for the supply of goods and services, such as contracts for the repair or servicing of vehicles or for installation of double glazing (although there is power in s. 12 for the Secretary of State by order to exempt certain classes of contract from the provisions of the Act and some classes of contract have been exempted by orders made under this section).

A contract to manufacture and supply a product may be classified either as a contract for the supply of work and materials, covered by the 1982 Act, or as a contract for sale of the finished item, covered by the Sale of Goods Act 1979 (see **9.4.6**). The significance of this is examined below.

17.3   Common law implied terms

Additional terms may be implied into contracts for services at common law and this possibility is expressly recognised by the Act (SGSA 1982, s. 16(3)). Where performance of one party's obligations requires the co-operation of the other party, a term requiring such co-operation will generally be implied. In the case of common types of contracts for services, such as banking and agency, case law has recognised a body of terms which are generally implied into such contracts.

It will generally be preferable for the terms of a contract for services to be spelt out expressly, to avoid reliance on the implied terms, and to modify and supplement them.

17.4   The quality of the service

It is an implied term in a contract involving the supply of a service that the supplier will perform the service with reasonable skill and care (SGSA 1982, s. 13). A similar term was implied at common law (*Bolam* v *Friern Hospital Management Committee* [1957] 2 All ER 118).

The implied term is not classified as either a condition or warranty. It is therefore an innominate term and the customer's remedy in the event of breach depends on the seriousness of the breach and its consequences and the other circumstances of the case.

Exclusion or limitation of the implied term or remedies for its breach is regulated by UCTA 1977, s. 2 and/or by the Unfair Terms in Consumer Contracts Regulations 1999: see **3.4.3, 3.4.4**. In addition, any attempt to exclude liability for breach of the implied term will be subject to the common law *contra proferentem* rule of construction. Since the basis of liability is negligence, the clause must make clear that negligence liability is to be excluded. To be effective the clause must refer to negligence, or use some synonym (see **3.4.1.1**). The implied term may also be supplemented by a tortious duty of care.

17.4.1   Undertaking to achieve a result

The supplier of a service is liable under statute only for failure to take reasonable care in the supply of the service. Generally there is no implied undertaking by a supplier of services to achieve any given result and if the buyer wants such an undertaking he should make it an express term of the contract. There is thus an important distinction between contracts for services and contracts for the sale of goods, under which the seller does undertake strict liability for the quality of the goods supplied.

Where a contract involves the supply of goods **and** services the supplier impliedly undertakes:

(a) to perform the service with reasonable skill and care; and

(b) that the goods supplied are of satisfactory quality and reasonably fit for the buyer's purpose, correspond with the contract description etc.

However, where the contract requires the supplier to use his skill to produce and supply a finished object, the distinction between a contract for the sale of goods and one for work and materials becomes crucial.

EXAMPLE

An engineer contracts to design, build and supply a piece of machinery.

If construed as a sale of the finished machine, the supplier impliedly undertakes that the finished item will be of satisfactory quality, fit for the buyer's purpose etc., and the supplier's liability is strict.

However, if construed as a contract for work and materials the supplier undertakes that he will exercise reasonable skill and care in the work of design and assembly (negligence liability) and that the parts (strict liability) used in the manufacture of the machine will be of satisfactory quality etc. There is no statutory undertaking as to the quality or fitness of the finished machine. However, where the supplier knows the purpose for which the machine is to be used there may be a common law implied term requiring the finished product to be reasonably fit for the buyer's purpose (*IBA* v *EMI Electronics and BICC Construction Ltd* 14 BLR 9).

In a contract to manufacture and supply a finished article there may therefore be implied terms as to the quality of the parts used, requiring the work to be performed with reasonable care and as to the quality and/or fitness of the finished product. The supplier may want to exclude some or all of these; conversely the customer will probably want to replace them with express undertakings, especially as to the fitness for his purpose of the finished item.

17.4.1.1 Consumer contracts

The position described above is modified where the customer is a consumer as a result of the EC Directive 44/1999 and amendments made to the SGSA to implement it. The Directive applies to two types of contract involving the supply of a service.

First, under the Directive a contract between a business supplier and a consumer 'for the supply of consumer goods to be manufactured or produced' is deemed to be a contract for the supply of the finished product so that the manufacturer is strictly liable for any failure of the finished product to conform with the contract (art. 1(4); see generally Chapter 12), whether the lack of conformity originates in the materials or from defective workmanship. The only exception is that the Directive provides that the supplier is not liable for any lack of conformity which 'has its origin in materials supplied by the consumer' (art. 2(3)).

EXAMPLE

A joiner contracts to build and supply a book case to a consumer. The joiner is liable under the Directive for any lack of conformity in the finished book case, whether due to the quality of the materials or the quality of his workmanship. But if the consumer supplies the wood to be used by the joiner, the joiner is not liable for any lack of conformity in the finished bookcase which is due to (say) the wood being warped.

In effect therefore under the Directive the supplier under a contract to manufacture and supply goods is strictly liable for both the materials and the service element of the contract. There is no provision in the Sale and Supply of Goods to Consumers Regulations 2002 to implement arts 1(4) or 2(3), so that there is no corresponding provision in domestic law. This may amount to a failure properly to implement the Directive. However, an English court would be required to interpret domestic law so far as possible so as to conform to the Directive. A contract to manufacture and supply a finished product would therefore have to be classified as a contract for supply of the finished item, or be found to contain common law implied terms relating to the quality, fitness for purpose and compliance with description of the finished item.

Second, the Directive contains special provision for contracts to supply and install goods. It provides that where installation of goods supplied to a consumer 'forms part of the contract of sale' and the goods are installed 'by the seller or under his responsibility', any lack of conformity resulting from 'incorrect installation' shall be deemed to be equivalent to a lack of conformity in the goods themselves (art. 2(5)). In effect therefore the Directive provides that under a contract with a consumer for the supply and installation of goods the supplier is strictly liable for the installation. Under domestic law such a contract—for instance a contract to supply and fit a shower—would probably be classified as one for work and materials under which the supplier would be strictly liable for the materials but liable only for failure to take reasonable care in the installation. The Sale and Supply of Goods to Consumers Regulations 2002 seek to implement this provision by amending the SGSA to provide that where under a contract for the supply of goods installation of the goods forms part of the contract and the goods are installed by or under the responsibility of the supplier there is a lack of conformity in the goods if the goods are installed in breach of the term implied by s. 13, SGSA. However, since s. 13 only requires that a service be performed with reasonable skill and care this again seems insufficient to implement the Directive, which seems to require that the supplier should be strictly liable for any lack of conformity in the goods as installed, whether that results from the goods themselves of the manner of their installation.

EXAMPLE

A plumber contracts to supply and install a shower. When the work is completed the shower fails to work properly. The shower as installed therefore does not conform to the contract. Under the Directive the plumber is strictly liable for the failure, whether it originates in the shower itself or the installation work. Under the SGSA the plumber is strictly liable for the quality, fitness and compliance with description of the shower but only liable for the installation work if he failed to perform it with reasonable skill and care. This is not sufficient to satisfy the Directive.

Under the Directive a supplier of goods may not exclude or limit liability for the goods' conformity with the contract. An attempt by the supplier to exclude liability for the installation work should therefore be ineffective.

17.5 Time for performance

The contract will normally fix a time for performance of the service; alternatively it may provide a means by which the time for performance may be determined or it may be possible to determine the time for performance by reference to previous dealings between the parties. However, if the time for performance is not expressly or impliedly fixed by the contract, it is an implied term that the service will be performed within a reasonable time (SGSA 1982, s. 14).

17.6 Price

If the price payable for the service is not fixed expressly or impliedly in the contract, it is an implied term that the customer will pay a reasonable price (SGSA 1982, s. 15). This is more significant than may at first appear, since many contracts for services are entered into without the parties first agreeing a price, for instance because it is not known at the time the contract is made how much work will be involved. The parties may, of course, agree an hourly or other rate in such a case but if no rate is agreed the implied term applies so that the customer may challenge an account which is unreasonably high. If the price is not paid at the due date, interest may be payable, in accordance either with the terms of the contract or with statute (see **3.3.1.4**).

17.6.1 Part payments and deposits

Where a contract for the supply of services requires the customer to make part payment of the price before completion of the service and the contract is terminated before completion, the supplier may be entitled to retain the payment, if made, or sue for it. Such repayment will be refundable to the customer only where there is a total failure of the consideration for which it was paid. It will therefore not be refundable where it can be characterised as a deposit, or where it can be regarded as referable to work to be done by the supplier before termination. (See *Hyundai Heavy Industries Co. Ltd* v *Papadopoulos* [1980] 1 WLR 1129; *Stocznia Gdanska SA* v *Latvian Shipping Co.* [1998] 1 All ER 883.)

17.7 Summary

After reading this chapter you should understand and be able to advise on:

- the legal rules applicable to contracts involving the supply of a service, including those relating to
  - the quality of the service;
  - the time for performance;
  - payment;
- the suitability of those rules for any particular case; and
- the need to modify the general rules in any particular case (whether for supplier or customer); the legal restrictions on terms modifying or excluding the general rules; and the extent to which such terms may be upheld in any particular case.

Standard terms of trading

18.1 Introduction

Many businesses use standard terms to govern their supply or purchase of goods and services. We have already mentioned standard terms at several places in the preceding chapters. In this chapter we examine:

- the advantages and disadvantages of using standard terms;
- the legal controls on the use and drafting of standard terms;
- issues to be considered when preparing a set of standard terms.

Finally we set out a set of standard terms of sale and standard terms of purchase for a hypothetical business, together with a commentary on the terms and their likely effectiveness (see **18.5**).

18.1.1 Advantages of standard terms

Standard terms allow businesses to obtain many of the advantages of individually drafted contracts for all their transactions, at very little unit cost. They offer a number of advantages.

(a) They may provide a detailed code of rules, varying the default rules applicable under the general law and replacing them with provisions more appropriate to the individual business.

(b) Contracts on detailed and sophisticated terms can be arranged at a relatively low level within the organisation.

(c) By using one set of terms for most or all of its contracts the business can become familiar with the terms and thus use them to resolve speedily any disputes which may arise.

18.2 Dangers of standard terms

The benefits of standard terms are only obtained if they are both prepared and used with care.

18.2.1 Incorporation of terms

A set of standard terms will only be effective to govern an individual contract if the terms are properly incorporated into that contract. The rules governing incorporation of terms have been considered elsewhere (see **2.6.2**). Terms printed in catalogues and price lists, on order forms, order acknowledgements, or even delivery orders may be incorporated into a contract provided that reasonable steps are taken to bring them to the attention of the other contract party before the contract is concluded. Terms on an invoice sent out after the contract has been performed will never be effective, unless it is possible to establish their incorporation by a course of dealing.

Problems may occur where contracts are made by telephone, fax or similar media, or face to face. If the terms are to be incorporated into such contracts they must at least be referred to when the contract is made.

18.2.2   Battle of forms

Since many businesses now use standard terms of purchase, there is a real danger that a battle of forms may result (see **2.6.2.5**). A business's set of standard terms may contain provisions which seek to prevent any action by the business being regarded as acceptance of terms put forward by its trading partners. However, as explained elsewhere, the effect of such provisions is not clear and their effectiveness cannot be guaranteed. In order to avoid losing the battle of forms a business must be advised:

(a) never to return any documentation originating from its trading partners; and

(b) always to respond to any terms put forward by its partners with a document which contains or refers to its own terms.

18.2.3   The Unfair Contract Terms Act 1977

Where a business trades on its own standard terms, UCTA 1977, s. 3 will apply and will apply a test of reasonableness to any exclusion clause or clause which purports to allow the business to render a contract performance substantially different from that which was expected of it or, in respect of all or part of its obligation, to render no performance at all (see **3.4** and **3.4.3.4**). Many of the terms included in a set of standard terms will therefore be subject to a test of reasonableness.

18.2.4   The Unfair Terms in Consumer Contracts Regulations 1999

Where a business uses standard terms to contract with consumers the 1999 Regulations will apply and all of the terms will be subject to the test of fairness. A term is considered 'unfair' if it creates a 'significant imbalance in the rights and obligations of the parties under the contract to the detriment of the consumer' (see **3.4.4**).

18.3   Drafting standard terms

A set of standard terms will have to govern a number of contracts with different parties and, possibly, for a range of goods and services. It may therefore be necessary to prepare more than one set of terms.

(a) A business may want separate sets of terms of supply and purchase.

(b) Where the business supplies different types of goods or services it may need two or more different sets of terms; for instance, a computer manufacturer and supplier may want different sets of terms to govern contracts for the supply of hardware, of software and of hard- and software together; a business whose business involves both sale and hire of plant and equipment will want separate sets of terms for sale and hire contracts.

(c) Where a business deals with consumers and non-consumers it may want to use separate sets of terms for each, in order to accommodate the different restrictions on exclusion clauses imposed by UCTA 1977 and by the Unfair Terms in Consumer Contracts Regulations 1999. However, it should be borne in mind that the UCTA and the Regulations have differing definitions of 'consumer'.

Each set of terms will govern a large number of individual transactions so that it may have to be more flexible than would a one-off contract prepared for a specific transaction. Nevertheless, the objectives of a set of terms are broadly the same as those of any other commercial contract:

(a) to minimise the scope for dispute;

(b) to define the obligations of the parties and the consequences of non-performance of those obligations;

(c) to exclude and/or modify those default rules applied by the general law which are inappropriate to the needs of the particular business and its contracts;

(d) to allocate risks between the parties;

(e) to provide machinery for speedy resolution of any disputes which do arise.

Since a set of standard terms will not be negotiated, they may be more favourable to the business for whom they are prepared than would be the case with a one-off negotiated contract. However, they should not be too one-sided for both commercial and legal reasons. A business which uses excessively one-sided terms may find that its trading partners are reluctant to agree to those terms, or simply that it acquires a bad reputation for unfair treatment of customers or suppliers. The fact that the terms as a whole are one-sided may also influence a court considering the reasonableness or fairness of any particular term. Unnecessary provisions should be omitted.

18.3.1   Use of precedents

There is a range of materials which may be used in the preparation of standard terms. Encyclopaedias and other precedent books may provide guidance; many solicitors' firms have their own 'office' precedent which may be adapted; and the terms used by other businesses in the same area of business may provide guidance as to what is common or accepted in the particular trade.

18.4   Contents of the terms

The contents of the terms will depend on a number of factors including the nature of the business and its goods or services; its customers; the value of its transactions; the problems the business has encountered and is likely to encounter. However, the following are commonly included in standard terms and in many cases provisions to cover the following points should be considered. Other provisions may be required in a particular case.

18.4.1   Delivery/performance

A contract for the supply of goods should define what is to be delivered, and where, when and how delivery is to be effected (see **18.5.1**, Clause 2 and **18.5.2**, Clause 6). It should contain appropriate (force majeure) provisions to deal with delay in delivery caused by circumstances outside the supplier's control and liability for loss caused by late or non-performance (see **18.5.1**, Clause 2.4.2 and **18.5.2**, Clause 12). It may contain provision for performance by instalments and allow some variation from the contract quantity (see **18.5.1**, Clause 3 and **18.5.2**, Clause 4).

18.4.2 Quality of the goods/services

Express provisions to cover these matters will almost always be necessary. A seller of goods may want to exclude the statutory implied terms, so far as permitted by UCTA 1977, or perhaps replace them by more limited, express, warranties (see **18.5.1**, Clause 4). A buyer may want to replace or supplement the statutory terms by express warranties giving more extensive or more appropriate rights in the event of breach, such as a right to demand repair or replacement (see **18.5.2**, Clause 3).

18.4.3 Payment

The parties will generally fix the amount of payment; alternatively the price may be fixed by reference to some external document, such as the seller's current price list.

The terms may cover such matters as the manner and place of payment and provide for remedies for late payment, such as a requirement to pay interest (see **18.5.1**, Clause 5.1), or allowance of discounts (see **18.5.2**, Clause 7.2) for early payment.

In a long term contract a price variation clause may be needed.

The contract may exclude the buyer's right of set-off and contain express provision to allow the seller to sue for the price (see **18.5.1**, Clauses 5.2 and 5.3).

18.4.4 Security

The contract may provide the supplier with security, for instance by allowing him a lien over goods or other property of the customer. Where goods are sold on credit a reservation of title clause will normally be included (see **18.5.1**, Clause 6).

18.4.5 Exclusion and limitation of liability

Many of the provisions included in a set of standard terms will be intended to exclude or limit liability for breach of contract. It may also be appropriate to include a general limitation on liability, especially where individual contracts are likely to be of relatively low value. For instance, the contract might include a clause such as:

Without prejudice to other provisions of this contract the supplier's liability for breach of this contract shall in any case be limited to £x.

18.4.6 Formation and construction

The contract may contain provisions to define its scope and interpretation including:

  (a) a definition clause defining terms used in the contract;
  (b) a term indicating whether other documents (e.g. plans, specifications, quotations) are to be regarded as forming part of the contract;
  (c) a term defining the authority of agents and employees to make statements binding on the business and to agree to variations of the contract;

(d) a term stating that the business will only contract on its own terms and that no conduct is to be regarded as acceptance of any terms put forward by the other party (see **18.5.1**, Clause 9 and **18.5.2**, Clause 1);

(e) an entire agreement clause indicating that the contract document contains the entire agreement of the parties and that therefore no other statements outside that document have contractual effect; such a clause may be combined with a clause excluding liability for misrepresentation or confirming that no statements made by or on behalf of the business have been relied on by the other party. (For the effectiveness of such provisions see **2.6.1.2**.)

18.4.7   Dispute resolution

A term may require disputes arising from the contract to be referred to arbitration or some other dispute resolution scheme, in order to avoid the expense and trouble of litigation (see **18.5.2**, Clause 13.2).

Provision can also be made requiring claims to be notified, and/or litigation commenced within a specified period and limiting the evidence which may be used in any dispute, for instance by providing that one party's record of correspondence or transactions is to be final.

18.4.8   International contracts

International contracts should include express choice of law and choice of forum clauses to avoid problems of conflict of laws.

18.5   Specimen terms

Set out below are two sets of standard terms, the first a set of terms of sale, the second a set of terms of purchase, which might be used by a typical small business. The terms have been drafted for Phil's Fashions of Fulchester Ltd, a relatively small business manufacturing and supplying designer menswear. Although Phil's sells direct to the public through its own retail outlets, it also supplies clothing to other retailers for resale. The standard terms of sale have been drafted to govern such sales to other retailers; they would not be used for direct sales to consumers where many of them would be inappropriate and the use of some might be considered unfair under the Unfair Terms in Consumer Contracts Regulations 1999 or be prohibited by the UCTA 1977 and the Consumer Transactions (Restrictions on Statements) Order, 1976. The standard terms of purchase are to be applied to purchases of fabric and other materials for use in Phil's' business.

Students should note that these terms are specimens, not precedents. They are intended to illustrate the sort of terms which might be used by a business such as Phil's Fashions, rather than to provide precedents either of standard terms or of individual terms.

18.5.1   Specimen terms of sale

These terms would be applied to domestic sales to other businesses. They would be printed on the back of Phil's Fashions' acknowledgement of order form. They would apply to single contracts, rather than to long term 'requirements' contracts where other terms might be required. They should be clearly referred to on the face of acknowledgment, for instance, as follows:

We acknowledge receipt of your order and agree to supply you with the goods set out below, at the price indicated, subject to our standard terms of sale, printed overleaf.

Phil's Fashions Ltd
Terms of Sale

Clauses	Comment
1. Scope of Contract	
1.1 The terms set out overleaf and below, together with any specification referred to overleaf, comprise all the terms of the contract between the Seller and the Buyer. No other statement, written or oral, including statements in any brochure or promotional literature of the Seller, shall be incorporated into the contractor have any legal effect.	1.1 This term seeks to define the contract and ensure that other statements do not have legal effect. Such statements might otherwise be terms of the contract (subject to the parol evidence rule) or take effect as misrepresentations or collateral contracts. Insofar as this term prevents statements having effect as representations it may be subject to a test of reasonableness under Misrepresentation Act 1967, s. 3 (see **3.4.3.2**). The contract will contain a specification which will define the goods to be supplied. (A provision such as this would almost certainly be considered unfair in a contract with a consumer.)
1.2 The terms set out below shall prevail over any terms put forward by the Buyer and [except as provided for in 1.3 below] no conduct of the Seller shall constitute acceptance of any terms put forward by the Buyer unless the Seller expressly agrees to them in writing signed by its duly authorised agent.	1.2 This term is included in an attempt to prevent Phil's Fashions losing the battle of forms: see **2.6.2.5**.
1.3 No employee or agent of the Seller has any authority to vary these terms orally or to make any representation on behalf of the Seller as to their effect. No addition to or variation of these terms shall be binding on the Seller unless in writing signed by the Seller's Marketing Manager.	1.3 This term limits the authority of employees to make statements binding on Phil's Fashions, and supplements the preceding terms. Insofar as, by limiting the authority employees would otherwise have, the term prevents statements having effect as terms or representations it may be subject to a test of reasonableness under UCTA 1977 or Misrepresentation Act 1967. The term also seeks to ensure that Phil's is not bound by employees' statements as to the meaning of the contract: such statements might otherwise give rise to an estoppel. If such a term is included it is important that it also indicate which employees do have authority to bind the business. Such a clause would almost certainly be open to challenge as unfair if included in a contract with a consumer.
2. Delivery	
2.1 Unless otherwise agreed and stated overleaf the price agreed for the goods is for delivery ex works and it shall be the Buyer's duty to take delivery of the goods at the Seller's premises.	2.1 This clause places the burden of taking delivery on the buyer. This may be onerous: a seller may often be willing to undertake to deliver the goods at the buyer's premises (see **11.2.2**).
2.2 When the goods are ready for delivery the Seller will give the Buyer notice of readiness for collection. It is a condition of this	2.2 A clause such as this must be included if the contract requires the buyer to collect the goods, to ensure that the consequences of the buyer's failure to collect the goods are defined. 'Condition' is defined in Clause 9.

Clauses	Comment
contract that the Buyer shall then within seven days of service of that notice either: (a) collect the goods or (b) give the Seller instructions for their delivery at the Buyer's expense. 2.3 If the Buyer fails either to collect the goods or give the Seller instructions for their delivery in accordance with Clause 2.2, the Seller may exercise either of the following rights: 2.3.1 treat the Buyer's failure as a repudiation of the contract and terminate the contract with immediate effect; in that case the Seller may do any of the following, either alone or in any combination: (a) dispose of the goods as it thinks fit; (b) retain any payments made by the Buyer before termination of the contract; (c) recover from the Buyer any costs incurred in respect of the costs of storage of the goods or of their disposal, together with damages for any other losses caused by the Buyer's breach; or 2.3.2 arrange for storage of the goods, in which case: (a) the goods shall be stored at the Buyer's risk; (b) the cost of storage shall be for the Buyer's account and the Buyer will indemnify the Seller against all costs incurred by the Seller in arranging such storage; (c) the Buyer will pay the Seller a reasonable fee for its services in arranging for storage of the goods; (d) the Seller may at any time give the Buyer notice to collect the goods and, if the Buyer fails to comply with such notice, treat the Buyer's breach as repudiatory, in accordance with clause 2.3.1 above, or continue to store them in accordance with this clause. 2.4 The Seller will endeavour to have the goods ready for delivery by the date agreed for delivery but it is agreed that the Buyer shall not be entitled to terminate this contract by reason of the Seller's failure to deliver by the agreed date. 2.4.1 The Seller shall not be liable to the Buyer for any losses caused to the Buyer by late delivery of the goods. 2.4.2 If delivery is delayed by force majeure circumstances, the following provisions shall apply: 2.4.2.1 the Seller shall as soon as is reasonably practicable give the Buyer notice of the reasons for the delay, provided that the Seller shall incur no liability by reason of any failure to give notice; 2.4.2.2 the Seller's duty to deliver shall be suspended for so long as the force majeure	2.3 This clause sets out the seller's rights if the buyer fails to take delivery. Many of these rights would be available under the general law (see **16.4.2.3**) but their inclusion clarifies the parties' rights. Under the general law the seller probably would not be entitled to terminate the contract and retain payments made by the buyer. Arguably a provision allowing the seller to terminate the contract in this way is subject to a test of reasonableness under UCTA 1977, s. 3. In a consumer contract it would almost certainly be unfair. 2.3.2 Clause (c) of 2.3.2 might fix a rate by way of liquidated damages; such a provision will be effective provided it is not penal (see **3.3.2.3**). Clause (d) is necessary to ensure that the seller is not irrevocably bound by an election to store the goods. 2.4 The provisions of this clause seek to protect the seller against liability for failure to deliver on time. 2.4, 2.4.1 and 2.4.2 would all be subject to a test of reasonableness under UCTA 1977, s. 3; they are drafted as separate sub-clauses to ensure that if one is held unreasonable it will not necessarily prevent Phil's relying on the others (see **3.4.3.5**). See generally **11.2.3**, and **3.4.3**.

Clauses	Comment
circumstances continue and the time for delivery shall be extended by an equivalent period;	
2.4.2.3 the Seller may at any time, and at its sole discretion, give notice to the Buyer to terminate the contract. In that case the Seller shall incur no liability to the Buyer for any losses caused as a result of the termination.	
3. Quantities	3. See **11.2.5.**
3.1 The Seller shall be entitled to deliver the contract goods by instalments of any size and in any order.	3.1 The buyer is not obliged to accept delivery by instalments unless he agrees to do so.
3.2 If the Seller delivers more or less than the agreed quantity of goods the following provisions shall apply.	
3.3 The Seller shall have no liability to the Buyer in respect of the excess or shortfall unless the Buyer gives the Seller notice of the excess or shortfall within ten days of delivery. If the Buyer does give such notice:	3.3 Is considerably more flexible, and more favourable to the seller, than the rules in s. 30 SoGA 1979. Note that the clause gives the seller the option of either making good the shortfall or allowing a reduction of the price.
3.3.1 in the case of excess delivery the Seller will make arrangements for the excess to be returned to the Seller at the Seller's expense;	3.3, 3.4 and 3.5 would probably be subject to a test of reasonableness under UCTA 1977, s. 3.
3.3.2 in the case of short delivery the Seller may at its own discretion either:	
(a) make good the shortfall by one or more further deliveries; or	
(b) reduce the contract price by the same proportion as the shortage bears to the contract quantity.	
3.4 The Buyer shall not be entitled to reject any delivery on the grounds of any excess or short delivery but shall pay the contract price or, where the Seller exercises the option referred to in 3.3.2(b) above, the reduced price in accordance with that provision.	
3.5 Save as provided in Clauses 3.1–3.4 above, the Seller shall not be liable for any losses caused by excess or short delivery.	
4. Seller's Warranty	4. This clause provides the buyer with a very limited warranty and then excludes the other terms which would otherwise be implied under the general law. It then limits the seller's liability and the buyer's rights for breach of that limited warranty. See generally **Chapter 12** and **3.4**. Again it contains several sub-clauses which would all be construed as exclusion clauses and be subject to UCTA 1977. They provide the seller with several layers of protection, so that even if one is held unreasonable the seller may be able to rely on one or more of the others.
4.1 The Seller warrants that the goods conform to the contract specification and with any sample referred to in the specification.	
4.2 The Seller shall have no liability for any alleged failure of the goods to conform to the contract specification unless such failure is notified within 21 days of their being delivered.	
4.3 If any of the goods are found not to be in accordance with the contract specification the Buyer shall notify the Seller within 21 days of their being delivered. The Seller's representative will then visit the Buyer's premises and examine the relevant goods and if any are	

Clauses	Comment
found not to conform to the contract specification the Seller may, at its sole option, either: (a) at its own expense replace the goods found not to be in accordance with the specification; or (b) reduce the contract price by an amount equivalent to that proportion of the price payable in respect of the goods found not to conform to the contract specification.	
4.3.1 The Buyer shall in any case accept and pay at the contract rate for all goods which conform to the contract specification. 4.3.2 The Seller shall not be liable for any economic loss suffered by the Buyer as a result of the failure of any goods to conform to the contract specification, including loss of profits, business, goodwill or other consequential losses. 4.4 The Seller does not warrant that the goods are fit for any particular purpose of the Buyer. 4.5 Save as provided for in this clause the Seller shall have no liability for any defect in the quality of the goods or their failure to correspond to any description or sample or to be fit for any purpose and all other conditions, warranties, stipulations and undertakings, whether express or implied by statute or common law are excluded.	Exclusion of liability for 'consequential loss' is a commonly used formula. Note, however, that as interpreted by the courts this does not exclude liability for all economic loss flowing from a breach of contract: see **3.4.1.1**.
5. Payment	
5.1 Payment for goods delivered is due not later than the last day of the month following the month in which the goods are delivered. The Buyer will pay interest on sums paid late at the rate of 1% above the base lending rate of Midlays Bank plc in force from time to time.	5.1 A right to interest on late payment is expressly reserved: this will effectively exclude the statutory right to interest under the Late Payment of Commercial Debts (Interest) Act 1998, provided that it is regarded as providing a 'substantial remedy' for late payment (see **3.3.1.4**).
5.2 Except where the Seller reduces the contract price in accordance with Clauses 3.3.2(b) or 4.3(b) the Buyer will pay the full invoice price of goods delivered with-out any deduction, set-off or abatement on the grounds of any alleged shortfall in delivery, defect in quality or failure to conform to specification, or other breach of contract by the Seller.	5.2 Excludes the buyer's rights of set-off and abatement which would otherwise exist under the general law. It is therefore subject to a test of reasonableness under UCTA 1977 (see **3.4.3.5**).
5.3 If the Buyer fails to pay in full for goods delivered by the date for payment under Clause 5.1 above the Seller shall be entitled to bring an action for the price notwithstanding that property in the goods has not passed to the Buyer.	5.3 Extends the seller's right to sue for the price (see SoGA 1979, s. 49; **16.4.1**): such a provision is necessary where the contract contains a reservation of title.
6. Title and Risk	6. This is a fairly straightforward reservation of title (see **16.4.3**).
6.1 Goods delivered shall be at the Buyer's risk from the time they are delivered.	6.1 Is necessary to exclude the general rule in SoGA 1979, s. 20.
6.2 Property in goods delivered shall not pass to the Buyer until the Buyer has paid all sums	6.2 This is a 'current account clause'. Such clauses have been upheld by the courts but

Clauses	Comment
due to the Seller (a) in respect of the goods and (b) on any other account.	their effectiveness is often challenged by insolvency practitioners; however, the seller may be able to argue that the current account provision (sub-clause (b)) is severable from the simple reservation.
6.3 Until property in the goods passes to the Buyer in accordance with Clause 6.2, the Buyer shall hold them as bailee for the Seller and shall store them separately from any similar goods of the Buyer or any other person in such a way that they remain identifiable as the Seller's property.	6.3 Serves two functions: (a) it requires separate storage so that the goods are identifiable as the seller's property and (b) by so doing may enable the seller to argue that the contract creates a fiduciary relationship allowing the seller to trace into proceeds of resale of the goods.
6.4 The Buyer may resell the goods before the conditions in Clause 6.2 are satisfied on the following conditions: (a) any sale shall be effected by the Buyer as agent for the Seller, provided that the Buyer shall have no authority to create privity of contract between the Seller and any customer to whom the goods are sold; (b) the Buyer will hold the proceeds of any such resale as trustee for the Seller, separate from its own monies in a separate, identifiable bank account.	6.4 The goods are sold to retailers and will be resold. This provision is designed to enable the seller to claim that there is a fiduciary relationship between seller and buyer, so that he can trace into the proceeds of the goods if they are sold. However, it is unlikely to be accepted by an insolvency practitioner and probably will not be upheld by a court. Nevertheless, such provisions are often included in contracts. The clause does not lay claim to new products manufactured from the goods: such a provision is unlikely to succeed and is unnecessary here since the contract is for the sale of finished garments.
6.5 The Buyer's right to possession of goods supplied by the Seller shall terminate if the Buyer is declared bankrupt or makes any proposal to his creditors for any composition or voluntary arrangement or, if the Buyer is a company, an administrator, administrative receiver or liquidator is appointed in respect of its business.	
6.6 The Buyer hereby grants the Seller, its agents and employees an irrevocable licence at any time to enter any premises where the goods are stored in order to inspect them or, where the Buyer's right to possession has terminated, recover them.	
7. Intellectual Property	7. This clause deals with two separate points.
7.1 The Seller will transfer to the Buyer such title as it has to the goods.	7.1 Limits the seller's liability for breach of contract if the goods infringe the rights of any third party (contrary to SoGA 1979, s. 12 see **12.2**).
7.1.1 The Seller believes that the goods do not infringe any intellectual property rights of any third party and warrants that it is not aware of any adverse third party intellectual property rights affecting the goods, other than those expressly disclosed to the Buyer.	
7.1.2 If it is alleged that the goods infringe any intellectual property right of any third party the Buyer shall: (a) promptly notify the Seller of the alleged infringement; (b) allow the Seller to defend such third party claim as it thinks fit and have sole control,	

Clauses	Comment
at the Seller's expense, of any litigation and/or negotiations relating there-to; (c) not without the Seller's consent make any admission of liability. 7.2 The Buyer will not without the Seller's permission resell any goods supplied under this contract from which any label or logo has been removed or altered. **8. Applicable Law and Jurisdiction** 8.1 The formation, construction and performance of this contract shall be governed in all respects by English Law. 8.2 It is agreed that the English courts shall have the sole jurisdiction to decide any dispute arising out of or in connection with the formation, construction or performance of this contract. **9. Interpretation** In this contract: 'the Seller' means Phil's Fashions Ltd 'the Buyer' means the person or organisation named as the Buyer overleaf 'the goods' means the goods forming the subject matter of this contract indicated overleaf 'condition' means a term of this contract, any breach of which shall entitle the party not in breach to terminate the contract forthwith and without notice to the party in breach 'force majeure circumstances' means circumstances beyond the Seller's control, including fire, flood, storm, Act of God, war, riot, civil commotion, strikes, lock-outs and other industrial action 'Seller's premises' means the Seller's premises at 40 Flash Lane, Fulchester 'intellectual property rights' means patents, copyrights, registered and unregistered design rights, registered and unregistered trade and service marks, confidential information and such rights as are protected by the law of passing off.	7.2 Is intended to protect Phil's' intellectual property rights and, especially, its trade marks to ensure that its reputation is not diluted by resale of goods not identified as manufactured by Phil's (see **Chapter 35**). 8. Since these terms are intended for domestic contracts this provision might be excluded, but a choice of law clause might be needed if goods were sold to a Scottish buyer and the inclusion of these provisions guards against problems if the terms are used for international contracts.

18.5.2 Specimen terms of purchase

The terms of purchase set out below are printed on the back of Phil's Fashions Order Form. Details on the front of the Order Form would include the goods to be purchased, their price and name of the supplier. These terms are drafted for a once-off, domestic purchase of goods.

Phil's Fashions Ltd
Terms of purchase

Clauses	Comment
1. Definitions	
1.1 'Seller' means the person who supplies or agrees to supply goods to the buyer, as specified overleaf.	1.1 The seller should be identified overleaf.
1.2 'Buyer' means Phil's Fashions of Fulchester Ltd, of 40 Flash Lane, Fulchester.	
1.3 'Buyer's place of business' means 40 Flash Lane, Fulchester.	
1.4 'Goods' means the goods indicated overleaf as the subject-matter of the contract.	
1.5 'Price' means the price as indicated overleaf.	
1.6 'Condition' means an important term of the contract, any breach of which, regardless of seriousness, allows the party not in breach to terminate the contract, and/or reject the goods supplied under the contract, and/or sue for damages for any loss caused.	1.6 This mirrors the SoGA 1979 definition.
1.7 Headings are not to be taken into account in interpreting this contract.	1.7 and 1.8 are common provisions in written agreements.
1.8 Any clause, or part thereof, which is or may be void or unenforceable shall be treated as severable from the remainder of this contract and shall not affect any other provisions of this contract.	
1.9 'Writing' shall include fax, telex, and e-mail messages and 'written notice' shall be construed accordingly.	
2. Application of Terms	
2.1 These terms of purchase shall apply to the contract between the Seller [..............] and the Buyer, to the exclusion of all other terms including those which the Seller may purport to apply to any such transactions.	2.1 This clause seeks to avoid problems of 'battle of the forms' and ensure the primacy of the purchaser's terms.
2.2 Unless acceptance occurs at an earlier date in time, despatch of goods from the Seller to the Buyer shall be deemed to be conclusive evidence of acceptance of these terms.	2.2 This clause reinforces Clause 2.1.
2.3 Any variation of these terms must be agreed in writing by the Buyer.	2.3 A clause such as this could specify a particular person with authority to amend the contract, for instance, the General Manager, and emphasise that no other persons have the necessary authority. In doing so the clause prevents any statements, actions or inaction of the company being construed as representations as to an employee's authority. Such a clause may be subject to a test of reasonableness under s. 3 of UCTA 1977.

Clauses	Comment
3. Nature and Quality of Goods	The provisions of this clause largely reflect those in SoGA 1979 but are included here in order to present a complete picture of the parties' rights and duties.
3.1 Specifications	
It is a condition of this contract that the goods supplied shall conform in all respects with all specifications and any other requirements communicated by the Buyer to the Seller, including any sample supplied by the Buyer to the Seller.	3.1 This clause includes SoGA 1979, s. 15.
3.2 Description	
It is a condition of this contract that all goods supplied will conform with the description given by the Buyer. 'Description' shall be deemed to include all references to markings, labels, warnings, patterns and specifications.	3.2 The clause mirrors SoGA 1979, s. 13 and goes further to expand on the meaning of description.
3.3 Quality	
It is a condition of this contract that all goods supplied will be of satisfactory quality (as defined in the Sale and Supply of Goods Act 1994) and fit for all their common purposes.	3.3 This clause mirrors SoGA 1979, s. 14(2) as amended but extends the statutory requirement by making it an absolute requirement that goods should be fit for all their common purposes.
3.4 Fit for Buyer's Particular Purpose	
It is a condition of this contract that all goods supplied will be fit for any particular purpose made known to the Seller by the Buyer.	This clause mirrors SoGA 1979, s. 14(3).
4. Quantity	
4.1 Subject to Clause 4.4 below, it is a condition of this contract that the Seller will deliver the exact quantity of goods specified overleaf.	4.1 This establishes that the basic rule is one of strict compliance.
4.2 Subject to Clause 4.4 below, if the Seller delivers a quantity less than the quantity specified overleaf, the Buyer may elect: (i) to terminate the contract, or (ii) to accept the lesser quantity and pay for it at the contract rate, subject to a deduction of 5% of the contract price to compensate the Buyer for any inconvenience caused.	4.2 This clause is similar to SoGA 1979, s. 30, but includes provision for compensation for inconvenience caused. This would probably be subject to UCTA 1977, s. 3 and/or the rule against penalties.
4.3 Subject to Clause 4.4 below, if the Seller delivers more than the quantity specified overleaf, the Buyer may elect: (i) to accept and pay for all the goods delivered at the contract rate, (ii) to accept and pay for the contract quantity and reject the excess, or (iii) to reject the whole quantity.	4.3 This mirrors SoGA 1979, s. 30.
4.4 Any discrepancies in quantity of less than 1% shall be regarded as *de minimis*, and shall not entitle the Buyer to terminate the contract or reject the goods or sue for damages.	4.4 This represents a proviso to Clause 4.1 and hence overrides the strict compliance rule in relation to *de minimis* quantity discrepancies. SoGA 1979, s. 30(2A) restricts the right of

Clauses	Comment
	rejection where any shortfall or excess is so slight that it would be unreasonable to reject: this clause seeks to define the circumstances where rejection is prohibited.
5. Title to Goods	
5.1 Right to Sell	
It is a condition of this contract that: (i) the Seller has the right to sell the goods to the Buyer at the time of delivery, and (ii) the goods sold will be free of all encumbrances, and (iii) the Buyer will enjoy quiet possession of the goods supplied.	5.1 This mirrors SoGA 1979, s. 12 but raises all the undertakings to the level of condition.
5.2 Right to Indemnity on Infringement of Intellectual Property Rights.	
Where the Buyer's ownership, possession, or use of the goods infringes any other person's intellectual property rights, then the Seller will indemnify the Buyer for all resulting losses, expenses and liabilities.	5.2 This clause provides for an express right of indemnity. Such a right would probably be available under the general law but is expressly included in the interests of clarity.
6. Delivery	
6.1 Time	
It is a condition of this contract that goods shall be delivered promptly on the date specified overleaf, or as varied by the Buyer. If the Seller fails to deliver the goods on the specified delivery date the Buyer may terminate the contract.	6.1 This clause makes time of the essence and specifies the consequences of breach.
6.2 Place of Delivery	
Unless otherwise specified, the place of delivery shall be the Buyer's place of business.	6.2 This clause overrides SoGA 1979, s. 29(2) by making the place of delivery the buyer's premises. This is clearly more convenient for the buyer, although the price of the goods may reflect this extra cost on the seller's account.
6.3 Variation	
The Buyer reserves the right, by written notice, to vary the time and/or place of delivery, provided the Buyer has given the Seller reasonable notice. It shall be a condition of this contract that the Seller will deliver in accordance with the Buyer's instructions.	6.3 Provision could also be made for the seller to give notification of readiness.
6.4 Expenses	
All expenses associated with delivery shall be for the Seller's account.	
6.5 Instalments	
The Buyer is not obliged to accept delivery by instalments.	6.5 This mirrors SoGA 1979, s. 31(1).
6.6 Liquidated Damages	
Where the Seller fails to deliver the goods in accordance with Clause 6.1 above, damages shall be payable at the rate of £x per week, or part thereof.	6.6 Obviously a figure should be inserted in place of x. The appropriate amount might vary from contract to contract.

Clauses	Comment
7. Payment of Price	
7.1 The Price	
The price payable shall be the price specified overleaf. This price is inclusive of VAT, taxes and all other duties.	
7.2 Mode of Payment	
The price is payable in full 30 days after delivery of the goods. The Buyer shall be entitled to a discount of 10% of the price if payment is made within 7 days of delivery.	7.2 This overrides the general rule of cash on delivery specified in SoGA 1979, s. 28. If the price is not paid when due, interest will be payable under the Late Payment of Commercial Debts (Interest) Act 1998. Any attempt to exclude the statutory right to interest will be ineffective (see **3.3.1.4**).
7.3 Right of Set-off	
The Buyer may set-off against the price any sums due from the Seller to the Buyer whether under this contract or others.	7.3 This clause makes express provision for a right of set-off, and extends the right available at common law.
8. Passing of Property and Risk	
8.1 Property	
Property in the goods supplied under this contract shall pass to the Buyer at the time the contract is made, or at the very latest when the goods are despatched to the Buyer. Passing of property will not prejudice the Buyer's right to reject the goods under Clause 9 below.	8.1 This clause specifies that property will pass to the buyer at the earliest reasonable date in order to allow the buyer to deal with the goods as soon as possible. It also makes clear that property passes provisionally so that if the goods are defective, the buyer can reject them.
8.2 Risk	
The goods shall be at the seller's risk until the goods are delivered in accordance with the terms of the contract.	8.2 The passage of risk however, is delayed as late as possible. The effect of this along with Clause 6.2 is that goods are at the seller's risk during transit.
9. Right to Reject and Replace	
9.1 Right of Inspection	
The Buyer shall not be deemed to have accepted the goods until he has inspected them to determine whether they comply with the contract.	9.1 This mirrors ss. 34 and 35 of SoGA 1979, as amended. This clause makes it clear that the right to inspect applies to all forms of acceptance.
9.2 Right to Reject	
The Buyer shall have the right to reject any or all of the goods within 6 months of their delivery, for any breach of condition.	9.2 This would probably be subject to UCTA 1977, s. 3, because allowing the buyer a long-term right to reject may be interpreted as allowing him to refuse performance.
9.3 Right to Demand Replacement	
Where the Seller has supplied goods in breach of Clause 3 which are not in conformity with the contract, the Buyer may elect: (i) to reject the goods and terminate the contract, or	This clause goes beyond the remedies offered by SoGA 1979 and expressly gives the buyer a right to demand replacement.

Clauses	Comment
(ii) to demand that the Seller supply replacement goods within a time specified by the Buyer, and in either case claim damages for all losses, expenses and liabilities incurred as a result of the Seller's breach.	
10. Right to Indemnity The Seller shall indemnify the Buyer against all claims by or liabilities to customers of the Buyer arising out of any breaches by the Seller of this contract.	10. This clause provides for an express right of indemnity to cover claims by the buyer's customers. Such a right would probably be available under the general law but is expressly included in the interests of clarity.
12. Force Majeure The Buyer shall not be liable for any failure of performance due to act of God, war, strike, lock-out, industrial action, fire, flood, storm or any other event beyond the control of the Buyer.	12. This is a standard short form, force majeure clause.
13. Waiver The Buyer may waive any of its rights under this contract without prejudice to any other rights under this or other contracts.	
14. Cancellation The Buyer may, by written notice and at any time, cancel any order before delivery, without any liability to the Seller.	14. This clause would probably be subject to UCTA 1977, s. 3.
15. Proper Law and Forum 15.1 This contract is governed by the law of England and Wales.	
15.2 All disputes arising out of or connected with this contract shall be resolved by arbitration. The arbitrator shall be appointed by agreement of the parties or in default within 30 days by the President of the Law Society.	15.2 The preference is for arbitration rather than litigation.

18.6 Summary

After completing this chapter you should:

- understand the advantages and disadvantages of using standard terms;
- be able to advise on the use of standard terms;
- be aware of the legal controls on the use of standard terms and understand their effect on drafting;
- be aware of the matters to be covered in a set of standard terms of sale or purchase;
- be able to draft a set of standard terms of sale or purchase.

Part IV

International sales

International sales transactions

19.1 Introduction

When we examined sale of goods contracts (Part 3), we were predominantly concerned with domestic sales. In this Part, we look at the special problems which international sale of goods transactions pose and examine how commercial law has adapted to resolve these problems and meet the needs of the international trading community. In particular, in this chapter we:

- identify the different sources of international sales law;
- consider the factors that determine whether a sale is 'international' or not;
- highlight the special problems associated with international sales.

Moreover, special payment mechanisms have been devised for international contracts: they are examined in **Chapter 23**. Insurance is particularly important in international transactions. Marine insurance law is beyond the scope of this book: for detailed coverage see *Schmitthoff's Export Trade*, 2000, chapter 19; *Chalmer's Marine Insurance Act 1906*, 1993; Hardy Ivamy, *Marine Insurance*, 1985; Templeman, *Marine Insurance*, 1986.

At the end of this Part various standard form documents are reproduced in order that students can see and examine them, at first hand. The following documents are included:

- a standard form f.o.b. contract—GAFTA No. 82;
- a standard form c.i.f. sales contract—GAFTA No. 100;
- a standard shipping note;
- a dangerous goods note;
- a short form bill of lading;
- a bill of lading for combined transport;
- a sea waybill;
- a collection/delivery order;
- an invoice.

19.2 Sources of international sales law

International sales law is a mixture of common law and statute, international conventions, rules, terms and customs.

The first point to be considered when dealing with problems arising out of an international contract is what law governs the contract. A well drafted contract will normally contain an express choice of law clause. If not, the question will be decided in accordance with rules of private international law designed to identify the proper law of the contract.

Where English law is the proper law of the contract, the parties' obligations are defined mainly by trade custom, the common law and the SoGA 1979; this Act is not limited to domestic sales. However, the UCTA 1977 generally does not apply to international sales (s. 26).

In practice, English law is often the proper law of international sales contracts, even when neither of the parties to the contract is English, and the High Court in London is frequently the chosen forum for resolution of disputes arising out of the contract.

19.2.1 The Vienna Convention

The International Convention on the Sale of Goods (the Vienna Convention) came into effect on 1 January 1988. However, the UK has not ratified the Convention, so it is not part of UK law (it should be noted that the DTI is undertaking a fresh consultation on the possibility of the UK ratifying the Convention). Nevertheless, parties to a sales contract can expressly adopt the Convention, or conflict of laws rules may result in the application of the Convention, so it is advisable, for a commercial lawyer to have a working knowledge of the Convention.

The Convention covers issues such as its application, contract formation (but not validity), rights and duties of the parties, risk and remedies, but not the passing of property. The obligations of the parties under the Convention are largely similar to those under domestic law but there are differences in relation to contract formation and remedies. Some notable features of the Convention are set out below.

19.2.1.1 Formation of the contract

(a) An offer can be irrevocable if:

    (i) it indicates, whether by stating a fixed time for acceptance or otherwise, that it is irrevocable; or

    (ii) it was reasonable for the offeree to rely on the offer as being irrevocable and the offeree has acted in reliance on the offer (Art. 16(2)).

(b) Acceptance does not become effective until it reaches the offeror, and may be withdrawn if the withdrawal reaches the offeror before or at the same time as the acceptance would have. So, mere despatch of acceptance does not bind the offeree, but it suffices to prevent the offeror from revoking the offer (Arts 16(1), 18(2) and 22).

(c) An acceptance containing additional or different terms, which does not materially alter the terms of the offer, may constitute an acceptance, unless the offeror objects (Art. 19).

19.2.1.2 Breach of contract and remedies

(a) There is no mention of conditions or warranties; instead the Convention uses a test similar to that in *Hong Kong Fir Shipping Co.* v *Kawasaki Kisen Kaisha* [1962] 2 QB 226 to determine whether the innocent party may terminate the contract (Art. 25).

(b) The seller may have a right to 'cure' defective performance (Arts 34, 37 and 48).

(c) The buyer may have a right to demand specific performance, replacement or repair of the goods (Art. 46).

(d) There is a two years' time limit from physical delivery for rejection (Art. 39(2)).

(e) Where defective goods are delivered, the buyer can claim a reduction in price proportionate to the defect (Art. 50).

(f) Where the contract has been avoided and the innocent party makes a substitute transaction, then the innocent party can recover the difference between the contract price and the substitute transaction, provided the substitute transaction was made in a reasonable manner and within a reasonable time after avoidance (Art. 75).

19.2.1.3   Risk

The passage of risk is not linked to property but to control (Arts 67–69).

19.2.2   Standard contracts and terms

International sales contracts are often concluded using standard form contracts, such as GAFTA (The Grain and Feed Trade Association) 100 (see Specimen 2 at the end of this Part), or else they incorporate established trade terms into the contract. The most authoritative document defining these terms is the ICC's (International Chamber of Commerce) INCOTERMS. The adoption of these terms helps avoid disputes as to their exact meaning and they also have the advantage of being neutral as between the parties. Therefore when drafting a contract for the international sale of goods, express reference to INCOTERMS may be used to define the duties of the parties.

19.2.2.1   INCOTERMS

INCOTERMS are designed to define the method of delivery of the goods sold, the different duties of the parties, passing of property, risk, the calculation of purchase price and incidental charges. They are not limited to sea carriage. The definitions in INCOTERMS reflect commercial practice and hence they are revised periodically: the latest revision dates from 2000. They allow many of the parties' obligations to be defined by use of short-hand terms.

The following are examples of some of the terms defined in INCOTERMS.

(a) *Ex works*

Here the seller must make the goods available for collection outside his own premises. This involves minimum duties on the seller's part and this is reflected in the price.

(b) *Free alongside ship (f.a.s.)*

The seller fulfils his delivery obligations when he places the goods alongside the ship, e.g. on the quay.

(c) *Free on board (f.o.b.)*

The seller must put the goods on board the ship. He bears the cost of the stevedore company for loading, for example, but recovers it in the price.

(d) *Cost and freight (c & f)*

Here the seller must pay the costs and freight necessary to bring the goods to the named port of destination.

(e) *Cost, insurance and freight (c.i.f.)*

As above but the seller also has to procure marine insurance.

(f) *Delivered ex ship*

The seller must make goods available on board ship, uncleared for import, at the port of destination.

(g) *Delivered ex quay*

The seller must make goods available on the quay or wharf, at the port of destination, cleared for importation.

19.3 When is a sale international?

In determining whether a sale is international, the law concentrates on the place of business of the parties to the contract and not whether the goods are dispatched and delivered in different countries. This is the approach of UK sales law (see UCTA 1977, s. 26) and international sales law (see Vienna Convention, Art. 1). So, although the goods may never leave a jurisdiction, where the parties to the sale contract have their places of business in different jurisdictions, a commercial lawyer must be able to assess what effect this international character has on the parties' rights and obligations.

19.4 Special problems of international sales

Set out below are some of the problems inherent in international sales, which do not arise in the domestic context.

(a) An international sale will usually involve a sea transit. Often, the time between dispatch of the goods by the seller and actual delivery to the buyer can be substantial, thus increasing the risk of loss of or damage to the goods while in transit. As well as the sale contract, which must be negotiated, further contracts for the carriage of the goods by sea and the insurance of the goods while at sea need to be arranged. Customs need to be cleared. Import and export licences may need to be obtained.

(b) International sales raise conflict of laws problems: what is the proper law of the contract, where is the proper forum for dispute resolution and under what procedures can a judgement be enforced abroad?

(c) Where the sale is on credit terms, how can the buyer's creditworthiness be assessed and how best can the seller ensure payment of the price?

(d) Fluctuations in currency due to exchange rates can render unprofitable what was once considered a good deal.

(e) Political instability can lead to changes in government policy on imports or exports for example.

Some of these problems may be dealt with by appropriate contract terms such as choice of law and forum clauses and price variation clauses. Contracts can provide for payment in a strong currency. A documentary letter of credit can be used to provide a reliable paymaster (see **Chapter 23**).

The commercial lawyer needs to be aware of these special problems and the means of addressing them.

19.5 Summary

Having read this chapter you should be:

- familiar with the different sources of international sales law;
- able to determine when a sale is 'international'; and
- aware of the special problems inherent in international sales.

Carriage of goods by sea

20.1 Introduction

International sales contracts often require the goods to be shipped, so it is important for the commercial lawyer to have an understanding of contracts for the carriage of goods by sea.

In this chapter we:

- set out a typical shipping transaction;
- examine one of the main shipping documents, the bill of lading, and how it operates as—
  1. evidence of the contract of carriage;
  2. a receipt for the goods;
  3. a document of title;
- identify and distinguish alternatives to the bill of lading, namely, the sea waybill and delivery order; and
- outline the rights of action by a shipper of goods against the carrier under the Carriage of Goods by Sea Act 1992.

Depending on the terms of the sale contract, it may be the seller's or the buyer's duty to arrange shipment of the goods. For the purposes of this chapter, the person who arranges the carriage will be referred to as the shipper.

20.1.1 A typical shipping transaction

In *Heskell* v *Continental Express* [1950] 1 All ER 1033, Devlin J outlined the practice when shipping goods.

(a) First, the shipper or his agent (a freight forwarder) needs to determine when a suitable ship is sailing to the particular port and then book space on the ship for the goods with the carrier or his agent (a loading broker) and deliver the goods to the port.

(b) On delivering the goods to the carrier, the shipper receives a mate's receipt for the goods and, using this, fills in the details on the bill of lading.

(c) Next, the bill of lading is presented to the carrier or his representative, perhaps the master of the ship, who checks the details on the bill (dates, ports of shipment and destination, description, quantity of goods and apparent condition, etc.) against the goods and, if there are no discrepancies, signs the bill, making any necessary amendments, and issues it to the shipper, in return for the mate's receipt.

(d) The shipper forwards the bill, by post, to the person responsible for collecting the goods, the consignee. The consignee may be a buyer or someone acting for the shipper. If the former, the shipper usually only transfers the bill in return for payment of the price.

(e) Finally, the consignee presents the bill of lading to the carrier at the destination: the master usually will not release the goods without presentation of the bill (see e.g. *The Sormouskiy 3068* [1994] 2 Lloyd's Rep 266). One way, in practice, around this is through the use of an indemnity, whereby the consignee agrees to indemnify the carrier against any claims that may arise due to the carrier handing over the goods, without presentation of the bill of lading.

20.1.1.1   Modern practice

Important changes have occurred in practice since *Heskell*. For instance, mates' receipts are not often used today; instead goods are usually forwarded to the port with a Standard Shipping Note or, if necessary, a Dangerous Goods Note containing details of the goods which, when signed, is issued to the shipper as a receipt (see Specimens 3 and 4). Also, it is more common now for the carrier to prepare the bill of lading by computer from the details given by the shipper when booking space on the ship. Indeed, the use of bills of lading has declined, especially when the voyage is short, where they have been replaced by the sea waybill (see **20.3.1**).

Nevertheless, the bill of lading still plays a vital role in many shipping transactions and therefore warrants further examination.

20.2   Bill of lading

A bill of lading (see Specimens 5 and 6) is a transport document with unique characteristics. It has three functions:

(a) it evidences the contract of carriage;

(b) it is a receipt for the goods; and

(c) it is a document of title.

We will examine each of these in more detail.

20.2.1   As evidence of the contract of carriage

The contract of carriage is concluded between the shipper and the carrier, or through their agents, usually before the goods are shipped, often when the shipper books space on the ship for his goods, or perhaps on loading of the goods or acceptance for loading by the carrier (*Heskell* v *Continental Express* [1950] 1 All ER 1033). Hence, the bill cannot be the contract: but it can evidence the contract.

On the back of modern standard form bills are detailed the terms and conditions of carriage, so when the bill is issued or signed by the master it merely evidences a contract that was previously concluded.

In order to regulate the shipment of goods, rules were developed by the international shipping community which set out the duties and liabilities of the parties to the carriage contract. Today, three different sets of rules (each an amendment to its predecessor) are in force:

(a) the Hague Rules 1924;

(b) the Hague-Visby Rules 1968/1979; and

(c) the Hamburg Rules 1978 (which came into force on 1 November 1992).

20.2.1.1   Application

The Hague-Visby Rules have been incorporated into UK law by the Carriage of Goods by Sea Act 1971. Basically these Rules apply when:

(a) a bill is issued in a Contracting State;

(b) the carriage is from a port of a Contracting State; or,

(c) the Rules are expressly adopted.

Therefore, all bills for goods shipped from the UK are subject to the Hague-Visby Rules.

20.2.1.2   Duties of the parties

The Rules set out the rights and duties of the parties. For example, the rules require the carrier:

(a) to exercise due diligence before, and at the beginning of, the voyage, to provide a seaworthy ship, properly man, equip and supply the ship and generally make the ship fit and safe for the reception, carriage and preservation of the goods (Art. III r. 1);

(b) properly and carefully to load, handle, stow, carry, keep, care for and discharge the goods carried (Art. III r. 2);

(c) on demand from the shipper, to issue a bill of lading showing (i) leading marks of identification, (ii) either the number of packages or pieces, or the quantity, or weight, and (iii) the apparent order and condition of the goods (Art. III r. 3); and

(d) only to make a reasonable deviation or a deviation to save or attempt to save life or property, otherwise the carrier will be liable for any resulting loss or damage (Art. IV r. 4).

The shipper, on the other hand, is required not to ship dangerous goods without informing the carrier (Art. IV r. 6).

20.2.1.3   Exclusion of liability

Article IV r. 2 states that the carrier has no liability for loss or damage arising or resulting from, *inter alia*: act, neglect or default of the master in the navigation or in the management of the ship; fire, unless caused by the actual fault or privity of the carrier; act of God; act of war; seizure under legal process; quarantine restrictions; strikes; riots; insufficient packing; latent defects and any other fault arising without the actual fault or privity of the carrier.

20.2.1.4   Limitation of liability

Unless the nature and value of the goods has been declared before shipment and entered on the bill of lading, the carrier's liability is limited under Art. IV r. 5 on the basis of package or weight.

Article III r. 8 provides that any clause relieving or lessening the liability of the carrier, as set out in the Rules, shall be null and void.

20.2.1.5   Limitation period

The limitation period for claims is one year from delivery of the goods or when they should have been delivered (Art. III r. 6).

20.2.2   **As a receipt**

It has been stated that a ship must 'deliver what she receives, as she receives it' (*FC Bradley & Son Ltd* v *Federal Steam Navigation Co. Ltd* (1927) 27 Ll L Rep 395 at 396, *per* Lord Sumner). This means that if the goods are lost or damaged while in transit, the carrier may be liable. In order for a shipper to pursue such a claim it is necessary to know the quantity and condition of the goods on receipt by the carrier or on shipment. Also, if a shipper is planning to deal with goods while they are at sea, by selling or pledging them for instance, he will require some form of evidence that proves that the goods exist and provides details as to the quantity and condition of the goods. Written records are relied on as evidence for these purposes, the most important being the bill of lading. A bill of lading can be either:

(a) a *'received for shipment'* bill, that is, a bill of lading evidencing the quantity and condition of the goods when they are received for shipment; or,

(b) a *'shipped'* bill, that is, a bill of lading which evidences the quantity and condition of the goods on shipment.

The evidential status of the bill of lading is dealt with:

(a) at common law, as amended by the Carriage of Goods by Sea Act 1992; and,

(b) in the Hague-Visby Rules.

20.2.2.1   As between shipper and carrier

Both regimes, in effect, provide that as between the shipper and the carrier, the bill is prima facie evidence of the quantity and condition of the goods at the time of loading. As this raises only a presumption, the carrier can produce evidence to dispute any statements in the bill.

20.2.2.2   As between the carrier and a third party

(a) Where the Hague-Visby Rules apply, evidence which contradicts the bill is not admissible provided the third party buyer acts in good faith, so that the bill is conclusive evidence (Art. III r. 4).

(b) When the Hague-Visby Rules do not apply, the position is governed by the common law as amended by the 1992 Act, which states that a bill of lading representing goods that are received or shipped in the hands of the lawful holder shall be conclusive evidence of quantity and condition against the carrier (Carriage of Goods by Sea Act 1992, s. 4).

With regard to non-transferable bills of lading which are outside the statutory definition of a bill of lading in the 1992 Act, the common law still applies and draws a distinction between statements as to condition and quantity.

(a) *Condition*

If the bill states that the goods are loaded in 'good order and condition' the carrier is estopped from denying the truth of this statement. This estoppel operates only in favour of a transferee who takes the bill for value in good faith and relies on it. However, if the bill is claused, that is, there is an annotation on the bill to the effect that the goods are in some way defective, the carrier can raise evidence to prove the condition of the goods when loaded.

(b) *Quantity*

At common law a ship's master has no authority to sign a bill where goods are not loaded (*Grant* v *Norway* (1861) 10 CB 665) so, where the bill overstates the quantity loaded or no goods are loaded at all, the carrier may dispute the statement in the bill as to the amount shipped.

As noted above, when the Hague-Visby Rules apply the shipper is entitled to demand from the carrier a bill showing:

(a) the leading marks necessary to identify the goods;

(b) the quantity of the goods by reference to number of packages, pieces, weight; and

(c) the apparent order and condition of the goods (Art. III r. 3).

A shipper should therefore always demand a bill with these details.

20.2.3 As a document of title

In *Lickbarrow* v *Mason* (1794) 5 TR 683, the bill of lading was recognised as a document of title because, in practice, it was treated as such. The bill of lading thus symbolises the goods and proper transfer of the bill effects a transfer of property in or ownership of the goods.

In order to be recognised as a document of title at common law a document must possess two characteristics:

(a) it must be regarded as proof of possession or control of the goods; and,

(b) it must give the possessor the right to deal with the goods.

20.2.3.1 Transfer of property

The time when property passes by transfer of a bill depends on:

(a) the intention of the parties (SoGA 1979, s. 17);

(b) the wording of the bill; and

(c) the surrounding circumstances.

(a) *Intention*

When a bill is assigned to a bank as security for a loan, the transfer does not cause property in the goods to pass to the bank because the necessary intention is lacking. Instead the bank has a security interest in the goods represented by the bill.

(b) *Wording*

Bills can be classified into three classes:

(i)   bearer bills;

(ii)   straight bills; and

(iii) order bills.

Bearer bills   Where no consignee is named in the bill, the bill is a *'bearer bill'* which may be transferred by simple delivery, so that any person can present the bill at the port of destination and seek delivery of the goods. This type of bill is rarely used due to the danger of theft and the potential for fraud.

Straight consigned bills   If the bill is made out to a named consignee it is known as a *'straight consigned bill'*. Such a bill cannot be transferred and only the named consignee can seek delivery of the goods at the port of destination. This type of bill is useful when the shipper is shipping goods to himself or where the shipper has no intention of selling the goods while at sea.

Order bills   The most common type of bill in use is known as an *'order bill'*, where a bill is made out to a named party and the words 'or order' are included: for instance, 'to Fidelma White or order'. The inclusion of the two words 'or order' makes the bill transferable so, where it is contemplated that the goods may be sold or pledged while afloat, these words should be included. The bill is transferred by indorsement and delivery of the bill, and often the goods are sold numerous times over with the bill being indorsed and delivered each time.

On transfer of an order bill, the carrier attorns that he holds the goods as bailee for the benefit of the transferee and subject to his directions. Where the buyer may want to deal with the goods, by re-sale or pledge, while they are at sea, he should contract for the seller to provide an order bill.

Where goods are shipped and the bill of lading provides that the goods are deliverable to the seller or his agent, the seller is prima facie to be taken to have reserved the right of disposal (SoGA 1979, s. 19(2)). Usually, the seller retains the right of disposal, or title, until the goods are paid for. This presumption can however be rebutted.

20.3 Other transport documents

Despite the unique legal status of the bill of lading, it may not always be necessary or practical to use a bill and other transport documents will suffice. The contract of sale may therefore provide for the seller to tender some other document.

20.3.1 Sea waybill (see Specimen 7)

With short voyages, the ship may arrive at the port of destination before the bill of lading. There is no implied term in the contract of carriage that the bill must arrive before the ship: this must be expressly contracted for. Where the ship is expected to arrive before the bill of lading (for instance, due to a short voyage, or because the bill is being delayed in the banking system where a letter of credit is being used to finance the transaction) the seller should expressly provide for the substitution of a letter of indemnity. However, the carrier may not be happy to accept an indemnity against liability, especially from a stranger. The use of sea waybills avoids these problems. The waybill performs some of the functions of a bill of lading, in that it both:

(a) evidences the carriage contract; and,

(b) acts as a receipt.

However, unlike a bill of lading, a waybill is not a document of title. Therefore, there are no means of selling the goods while at sea. As the possibility of sale is unlikely during a short voyage, this is not a great disadvantage. Indeed, the waybill has several advantages over a bill of lading. With a waybill:

(a) there is no need for the consignee to produce the waybill to obtain delivery of the goods, so delays in collection due to the late arrival of the documents can be avoided, along with consequent storage charges;

(b) a lot of the detailed checking at either end of the voyage, which is associated with a bill of lading, is avoided; and,

(c) the waybill can be given to the shipper as soon as the carrier has taken charge of the goods, so that it can be used immediately to obtain payment under a letter of credit (see **Chapter 23**) or as security for a bank loan.

Waybills are widely used in container transport.

20.3.2 Delivery order

The delivery order (see Specimen 8) is most often used in the transportation of bulk cargoes (oil or grain for instance) in order to break up the bulk into smaller consignments. A delivery order is an undertaking by the shipper (merchant's delivery order) or by the carrier (ship's delivery order) that the goods will be delivered to the person named therein, or to the holder of the order.

20.3.3 Mate's receipt

This is a temporary form of receipt, given by the mate of a ship, for goods which have been received on board. As seen above, this receipt is usually handed to the carrier or his loading broker in exchange for the bill of lading.

20.4 Actions against the carrier

If the shipper retains ownership of the goods during the transit and, on discharge, it materialises that some or all of the goods have been lost or damaged, the shipper has a contractual right of action against the carrier on the terms of the contract of carriage. Where the goods are sold while in transit the new owner is not privy to the contract of carriage and so would appear to have no contractual recourse against the carrier. In fact, the buyer has a statutory right of action under the Carriage of Goods by Sea Act 1992. A buyer who has statutory rights under the 1992 Act is not entitled to rely on the Contracts (Rights of Third Parties) Act 1999 (*ibid* s. 6(5); see **2.7**).

20.4.1 The Carriage of Goods by Sea Act 1992

The Act provides that where certain transport documents are used, on transfer of the document contractual rights of action are transferred to the transferee, the rights of action of previous holders of the document are extinguished and, in some cases, liability on the contract is transferred to the transferee.

20.4.1.1 Definitions

Section 1 defines the terms bill of lading, sea waybill and delivery order, for the purposes of the Act. The lawful holder of a bill of lading is defined as a person who holds the bill in good faith (s. 5(2)).

20.4.1.2 Transfer of contractual right of action

The Act provides that the lawful holder of a bill of lading, or person entitled to delivery under a sea waybill or ship's delivery order shall have transferred to and vested in him all rights of suit as if he had been a party to the contract of carriage (s. 2(1)).

Rights of suit are still transferred by s. 2 notwithstanding that the goods have ceased to exist after the issue of the relevant document (for instance, where the ship is lost) or where the goods cannot be identified—for instance, where they form part of a bulk (s. 5(4)).

20.4.1.3 Extinction of contractual rights of action

Where rights are transferred under s. 2, the Act extinguishes any rights to enforce the contract previously vested in any other person (s. 2(5)). The defect which the 1992 Act sought to remedy was that contractual rights evidenced by the bill of lading could remain vested in persons other than those having property in the goods or at risk in relation to the goods. This might occur because general property in the goods did not pass at all or because property did not pass 'upon or by reason of endorsement' of the bill, as was required by the Bill of Lading Act 1855. The solution provided in the 1992 Act is to transfer contractual rights to any holder of the bill, as defined. However, it is now clear that this results in a new class of cases where the contractual rights under the bill of lading vest in persons not at risk. In *East West Corporation* v *DKBS 1912 A/S and another; Utaniko Ltd* v *P&O Nedlloyd BV* [2003] EWCA Civ 83; [2003] 2 All ER 700, the claims related to alleged losses of goods in containers delivered to a Chilean company, GC, without presentation of the bills of lading. The defendants were the carriers and it was through their agents that the goods were delivered to GC. The bills of lading issued by the carrier identified the claimant as shippers; GC was named as the notify party; and the bills were endorsed by the claimants and sent to their banks, as their agents, to collect the price due from GC. Importantly, the goods remained at all times the property of the claimants. The goods were delivered to GC without presentation of the bills and GC did not pay in full for the goods. As a result the claimants commenced proceedings against the defendants for release of the goods without presentation of the bills. The Court of Appeal held that the claimants' rights of action under the contract of carriage were transferred to the banks when they became the holders of the bills under the authority of the claimants, as their agents, under the 1992 Act. As a result the claimants contractual rights of action were extinguished. However, Mance LJ stated *obiter* that the sole effect of the 1992 Act is on contractual rights and where there is no intention to pass any possessory right, possessory rights in bailment remain unaffected.

20.4.1.4   Transfer of liabilities

Where rights are transferred to any person under s. 2, that person becomes liable under the contract as if he was an original contracting party if:

(a) he takes or demands delivery of the goods;

(b) he makes a claim under the contract of carriage; or

(c) he took or demanded delivery before the rights under the contract were vested in him (s. 3).

It seems that the vesting of liabilities that occurs as a result of taking or demanding delivery of the goods may not be final. In *The Berge Sisar* [1999] QB 863, the buyers of a cargo of propane received a sample of the cargo from the carriers for testing. On discovering that the sample did not meet their requirements they resold the cargo and transferred the bill of lading to the new buyers. It was held that the first buyers had taken delivery of the cargo for the purposes of the Act and therefore became subject to liabilities under the bill. They ceased to be liable when they transferred the bill to the new buyers (at which time they also ceased to be entitled to rights under the contract of carriage). Presumably the result would be the same where a buyer rejects a cargo after taking delivery of it and returns the bill of lading to the seller.

The Act came into effect on 16 September 1992 and applies to bills or orders issued after that date (s. 6(3)).

20.5 Summary

After reading this chapter you should:

- be aware of standard shipping practices;
- be familiar with the main types of shipping documentation in use, and their differing legal consequences;
- be able to advise both a shipper and a carrier of their respective rights and liabilities under the Carriage of Goods by Sea Act 1992.

International sales contracts

21.1 Introduction

Although governed by the general law of sale, international sales contracts contain trade terms which are not customary in domestic trade and which define many of the obligations of the parties. Each of the common types of contract is recognised by custom as having different legal incidents and classification of the contract may therefore affect the rights and duties of the parties and the effects of the contract on such matters as the passing of property and risk. The most common are 'free on board'—'f.o.b.'—and 'cost, insurance and freight'—'c.i.f.', although there are several variants to these basic terms, all of which place different rights and duties on the parties to the sales contract.

In this chapter, we concentrate on the f.o.b. and c.i.f. contracts which together dominate international sales. With regard to each type of contract we:

- consider its nature and its relative popularity in the market;
- examine the obligations of the seller and buyer; and
- analyse the rules on the passing of property and risk.

A commercial lawyer must be able to identify these terms, and hence the type of sale contract, in order to advise on the rights and duties of the parties, although in some cases the distinction between different types of contract may not be clear cut.

21.2 F.o.b. contracts

F.o.b. stands for 'free on board'. The abbreviation is usually followed by the name of a port, for instance 'f.o.b. London', which is the port of shipment. At its most basic, the f.o.b. contract requires the seller to supply the goods and place them on board a ship at the named port at his own expense, hence, from the buyer's perspective, 'free on board'. The price naturally includes an element to cover this cost but the advantage for the buyer is that he does not have to concern himself with loading the goods as this, and sometimes more, is the seller's responsibility.

The buyer must pay the cost of carriage and insurance of the goods during transit and thus will have to bear the risk of any changes in those costs.

21.2.1 Types of f.o.b. contracts

The f.o.b. contract is flexible: the parties may vary many of its incidents without changing its nature as an f.o.b. contract. Three basic types have been recognised (*per* Devlin J in *Pyrene and Co. Ltd* v *Scindia Navigation Co. Ltd* [1954] 2 QB 402 at 424):

(a) the strict, or 'classic' f.o.b. contract;

(b) an f.o.b. contract with additional duties; and

(c) the modern f.o.b. contract.

In view of this, an f.o.b. contract should make clear the duties of the parties, and hence the type of contract intended.

21.2.1.1   The strict or classic f.o.b. contract

Here, the buyer is obliged to nominate the ship. When it arrives, it is the seller's duty to place the goods on board under a contract of carriage which the seller makes with the carrier for the account of the buyer. The seller receives the bill of lading which names him as consignor or is made out to his order and he transfers it to the buyer, usually on payment of the price. The carriage contract is therefore originally between the seller and the carrier.

21.2.1.2   F.o.b. with additional services

This is similar to the classic f.o.b., in that the seller enters into a contract of carriage with the carrier, places the goods on board and transfers the bill to the buyer, but here the seller will have accepted additional duties, such as nominating the ship and/or arranging the insurance of the cargo. As a result this type of contract may closely resemble a c.i.f. contract.

21.2.1.3   Modern f.o.b. contract

Here, the buyer himself makes the carriage contract, either directly or through his agent. So it is the buyer who nominates the ship and, when it arrives at the port, the seller must place the goods on board, but the bill of lading goes directly to the buyer, usually through his agent, and does not pass through the seller's hands. Today, this type of contract has replaced the classic f.o.b. as the norm.

21.2.2   Relations with the carrier

Under a classic f.o.b. contract or f.o.b. with additional services contract, the contract of carriage is initially made by the seller but is transferred to the buyer when the bill of lading is transferred (Carriage of Goods by Sea Act 1992: see **20.4.1**). Under the modern f.o.b. contract the contract of carriage is between the buyer and the carrier. However, the seller needs the assistance of the carrier to load the goods and fulfil his obligations under the sale contract and a court may find an implied contract between the seller and the carrier on the terms of the bill of lading (see *Pyrene and Co. Ltd* v *Scindia Navigation Co. Ltd* [1954] 2 QB 402). This means that relations between the seller and the carrier are governed by the terms of the contract of carriage and may be significant if the goods are damaged by the carrier during loading whilst at the seller's risk (see **21.2.5** and **21.3.7**). In that case therefore the seller may have an action against the carrier but the carrier will be protected by the terms of the bill of lading.

21.2.3   Obligations of the parties

The duties of the seller and the buyer depend on the terms of the contract and classification of the contract as a classic, additional duties or modern f.o.b. contract.

Unless there is provision to the contrary, the basic duties of the parties are as set out below.

(a) *Classic f.o.b.*

Generally, under a classic f.o.b. contract, the buyer must:

(i)   nominate a ship;

(ii) notify the seller of the nomination, so that the seller can fulfil his obligations in time;

(iii) pay the price.

The seller must:

(i)   make a reasonable contract in accordance with SoGA 1979 s. 32(2);

(ii) provide the necessary information so that the buyer can insure the goods (SoGA 1979, s. 32(3));

(iii) load conforming goods;

(iv) load the goods at the proper time (time is *prima facie* of the essence in commercial contracts); and

(v)   load the goods at his expense.

(b) *F.o.b. with additional duties*

Here the duties of the parties are the same as under a classic f.o.b. contract except that the seller must perform the extra duties imposed on him by the contract, such as arranging insurance.

(c) *Modern f.o.b.*

Under a modern f.o.b. the the buyer must:

(i)   make the contract; and

(ii) pay the price.

The seller must:

(i)   load conforming goods;

(ii) load the goods at his expense;

(iii) provide the necessary information so that the buyer can insure the goods (s. 32(3)); and

(iv) transfer the relevant shipping documents, usually a mate's receipt, so that the buyer can obtain the bill of lading.

We will examine some of these duties in more detail.

21.2.3.1 Nomination

Where the buyer is obliged to nominate a ship, as under strict f.o.b. and modern f.o.b. contracts, he must nominate an 'effective or suitable ship'.

(a) *Effective ship*

A ship is suitable if it is ready, willing and able to carry the goods from the of shipment to the destination. The ship will not be effective or suitable if, for example:

(i)   it does not arrive in time to enable the seller to perform his obligations, or at all;

(ii) meat is being transported, and the ship is not equipped with cold stores; or,

(iii) oil needing heating is being transported, and the ship does not have heating coils.

Failure to nominate a suitable ship entitles the seller to terminate the contract (*Bunge Corp.* v *Tradax Export SA* [1981] 2 All ER 513) releasing him from his obligation to perform and allowing him to seek damages from the buyer for non-acceptance. However, where the goods have not been loaded, property will generally not have passed from seller to buyer, so the seller will not be able to sue for the price of the goods.

(b) *Time for nomination*

Time for nomination is usually of the essence, i.e., it is a condition of the contract, allowing the seller to treat the contract as repudiated if the buyer fails to nominate a ship within the specified time, or if no time is specified, within a reasonable time (*Bunge Corp.* v *Tradax Export SA* [1981] 2 All ER 513).

Where a contract provides for a 'shipment period', for example, 'shipment in August or September', the buyer must nominate a suitable ship at a time which will allow for shipment during the period. Equally, the seller must load within the specified shipment period.

If the buyer's nomination is ineffective, for instance because the nominated ship is delayed, he may be able to nominate a substitute ship provided he can still give sufficient notice of the replacement nomination to comply with the contract. He must do so as soon as possible and at his own expense. If however there are specified time limits, a substitution can only be made within these limits, unless trade custom to the contrary can be proved.

If the buyer is entitled to make a substitute nomination, failure by the seller to accept it may put the seller in breach of contract (*Agricultores Federatos Argentinos* v *Ampro* [1965] 2 Lloyd's Rep 157).

It is not clear who bears the costs of storage of the goods or risk of their deterioration while awaiting arrival of the substitute vessel; the contract should therefore contain express provisions to determine whether the buyer is entitled to make a substitute nomination, and the consequences of such a substitution.

21.2.3.2 Notify the nomination

The contract will usually require the buyer to give notice, within a stated time, of the probable readiness of the ship to load, so that the seller can have the goods ready for loading. This is customary in the oil trade. The requirement to give notice of the stipulated length will be a condition of the contract. In *Bunge Corp.* v *Tradax Export SA* [1981] 2 All ER 513, an f.o.b. buyer was required to give 'at least fifteen consecutive days' notice' of probable readiness of their ship to load the goods. The notice given was five days short. The House of Lords held that the stipulation as to time was a condition, so that breach allowed the seller to terminate the contract.

21.2.3.3 To provide information to allow the goods to be insured

Section 32(3) of SoGA 1979 provides:

Unless otherwise agreed, where goods are sent by the seller to the buyer by a route involving sea transit, under circumstances in which it is usual to insure, the seller must give such notice to the buyer as may enable him to insure them during their sea transit; and if the seller fails to do so, the goods are at his risk during such sea transit.

This provision would apply to a classic or a modern f.o.b. contract, where the seller is under no duty to insure, for example, but not if the seller is himself responsible for obtaining insurance cover under an additional duties contract.

If the seller fails to provide the necessary information, risk does not pass to the buyer on loading, as is normal (see **21.2.5**), but remains with the seller during transit.

Since the seller may not himself have insurance to cover loss of the goods during transit he will probably have to bear any such loss himself; he should therefore be advised of the importance of providing the buyer with the necessary information. This will normally be at least details of the ports of loading and delivery and of the nature and value of the goods.

21.2.3.4   To make a reasonable contract

The Sale of Goods Act 1979, s. 32(2) provides:

Unless otherwise authorised by the buyer, the seller must make such contract with the carrier on behalf of the buyer as may be reasonable having regard to the nature of the goods and the other circumstances of the case; and if the seller omits to do so, and the goods are lost or damaged in the course of transit, the buyer may decline to treat delivery to the carrier as a delivery to himself or hold the seller responsible in damages.

This provision applies to classic and additional duties f.o.b. contracts where it is the seller who makes the contract. What is reasonable depends on the nature of the goods and other circumstances, so that a reasonable contract would make provision for refrigeration for frozen food, or heating coils for certain types of oil.

A contract which allows for excessive deviation may be unreasonable. In *Thos Young & Sons* v *Hobson & Partners* (1949) 65 TLR 365, where the seller made a contract for carriage at the consignee's risk, although the goods could have been carried at carrier's risk for no extra cost, it was held that the seller was in breach of s. 32(2).

21.2.3.5   To load conforming goods

Goods must conform with both the express and implied terms of the contract, including those implied by SoGA 1979.

(a) *Description*

It has been held that in international contracts statements as to country of origin and the date of loading form part of the contract description for the purposes of SoGA 1979, s. 13 (see **12.3**), so that if (say) goods are loaded outside the contract period they may be rejected. In *Bowes* v *Shand* (1877) 2 App Cas 455, the contract was for '600 tons of Madras rice to be shipped at Madras during March and April'. The cargo tendered was shipped during February. It was held that the buyer could reject the goods for breach of s. 13 because the shipment period formed part of the description.

The seller will generally wish to avoid this and will wish to include in the sale contract terms which restrict the scope of the description, for instance by expressly stating that statements as to date of loading do not form part of the contract description, or limit the right of rejection. Such exclusions are not subject to control under UCTA 1977 in an international contract (s. 26).

(b) *Quality and fitness for purpose*

The quality and fitness for purpose of goods (SoGA 1979, ss. 14(2)–(3)) is assessed when the goods are loaded and risk of loss passes to the buyer, as this is the time of delivery under a f.o.b. contract.

In order to be satisfactory, goods must be fit when loaded to survive the transit under normal conditions (*Mash & Murrel* v *Emmanuel* [1961] 1 All ER 485). Deterioration during transit will therefore be the seller's responsibility if it occurs because the goods were not satisfactory on loading.

21.2.4   **Passing of property**

As with domestic sales, property passes when the parties intend it to pass (SoGA 1979, s. 17), and the seller may reserve a right of disposal (s. 19). Where the goods are specific, property may pass at the time of the contract (s. 18, r. 1). However, no property can pass so long as the goods remain unascertained (s. 16).

Where the goods are ascertained it is presumed in f.o.b. contracts, on the basis of trade practice, that property passes on shipment when the goods pass the ship's rail, unless title is retained until some condition is fulfilled, for example, until the goods are paid for. Every case must be assessed on its own facts and the time when property passes depends on:

(a) the intention of the parties;

(b) the wording of the bill of lading; and,

(c) the surrounding circumstances.

Although the normal rule is that property passes on loading it has been held that an f.o.b. seller may reserve title until payment (*Mitsui & Co. Ltd* v *Flota Mercante Grancolombiana SA* [1989] 1 All ER 951).

If the seller takes the bill of lading in his own name he is *prima facie* taken to have reserved a right of disposal (SoGA 1979, s. 19(2)) and this provision does apply to an f.o.b. contract so that, if the seller takes the bill in his own name and has not received full payment at the time of shipment, he may be taken to have impliedly reserved title under this provision.

However, s. 19(2) raises only a rebuttable presumption and a court may hold, on examination of all the facts of the case that even though the seller takes the bill in his own name, property passes on loading.

EXAMPLE

In *The Parchim* [1918] AC 157, the seller took the bill in his own name but it was held on examination of all the facts of the case that property passed on loading.

Conversely, in *Kronprinsessan Margareta* [1918] AC 517, the seller took a bill in the buyer's name but retained possession of it. It was held that property had not passed because the bill was retained by the seller.

In order to avoid disputes the contract should contain express provisions as to the passing of property and if the seller wants a reservation of title to guard against non-payment he should expressly so provide.

21.2.5   Passing of risk

The general rule is that under an f.o.b. contract risk passes on loading when the goods pass the ship's rail (*Pyrene and Co. Ltd* v *Scindia Navigation Co. Ltd* [1954] 2 QB 402). The seller thus bears the risk of loss or damage prior to loading; the buyer bears the risk of loss during the voyage. If the goods are damaged during the loading process, allocation of the risk of that damage will depend on whether the goods had crossed the ship's rail before it occurred. This general rule applies even if property does not pass on loading, because, for example, the seller reserves ownership.

The buyer may therefore be at risk before owning the goods, but for insurance purposes, once the goods are at the buyer's risk, he has an insurable interest in them and can therefore insure the cargo against loss or damage (*Inglis* v *Stock* (1885) 10 App Cas 263). Once the bill of lading is transferred to the buyer he may enforce the contract of carriage against the carrier and sue for any damage to the goods which occurs during the voyage, including damage which occurred before transfer of the bill of lading (Carriage of Goods by Sea Act 1992, s. 2).

Conversely, the seller must bear the risk of loss or damage prior to loading even if loading is delayed. This is illustrated in *Cunningham* v *Munro* (1922) 28 Com Cas 42 where the contract was for the sale of bran f.o.b. Rotterdam for October shipment. The seller delivered the cargo to the port on 14 October but the buyer could not find shipping space until two weeks later and nominated a ship loading at Rotterdam on 28 October, by which time the bran had deteriorated due to overheating. The buyers refused to accept it on loading. It was held that they were entitled to reject: the bran was at the seller's risk until it passed the ship's rail.

21.2.5.1   **Exceptions to the general rule**

By using the trade term 'free on board' the parties are taken to have intended that risk is to pass on loading. This presumed intention may be excluded by an express provision in the contract.

(a) *Passing of risk delayed*

The buyer may delay the passing of risk by contracting for the goods to be sold 'free on board stowed': risk will then not pass until the goods are properly stowed.

(b) *Risk passes prior to shipment*

There is some authority that if the buyer instructs the seller to deliver the goods to the port prematurely and they deteriorate as a result, for instance, as a result of a subsequent delay in loading, the buyer must bear the risk of that deterioration (*Cunningham* v *Munro*).

EXAMPLE

B contracts to buy 100 tons of tomatoes, f.o.b. Southampton April shipment. B gives 5 April as the loading date. S therefore delivers the goods to the port on 3 April, but B then substitutes 15 April as the loading date. Between 3 and 15 April the goods deteriorate so that on loading they are no longer fit to survive the voyage and are therefore unsatisfactory.

As a result:

(i) B may reject the tomatoes as unsatisfactory; but

(ii) B is liable to S in damages for the deterioration.

To avoid possible disputes it would be better if this situation were expressly provided for in the contract.

(c) *Seller fails to provide buyer with information to insure*

Risk of loss remains with S if he fails to give B the information necessary for B to insure the goods (SoGA 1979, s. 32(3)). However, in order to insure the goods, B needs only to know the ports of loading and destination, and the nature and value of the goods. As a result, the only information an f.o.b. buyer normally needs from his seller in order to arrange insurance is details of the port of loading where that is chosen by the seller (see *Wimble, Sons & Co.* v *Rosenberg & Sons* [1913] 1 KB 279).

(d) *Seller fails to make reasonable contract*

Risk may also remain with the seller under s. 32(2) if he fails to make a reasonable carriage contract on behalf of the buyer, allowing the buyer to refuse to treat delivery to the carrier as delivery to himself (see **21.2.3.4**).

21.3 C.i.f. contracts

Under a c.i.f. contract, the seller is responsible for supplying the goods, insuring them and shipping them: hence 'cost, insurance and freight'. A c.i.f. contract therefore involves the seller entering into not only a sale contract but also, at a later date, insurance and carriage contracts. The seller, therefore, fixes a price to cover all these costs and it is he who carries the risk of fluctuations in insurance and freight costs.

This type of contract is now more common than the f.o.b. contract. Hybrids can occur by intention or default.

21.3.1 C.i.f. defined

Under a c.i.f. contract, the seller undertakes to be responsible for transportation and insurance cover to a named port of destination (the port named in the contract, for example, 'c.i.f. London', is the port of destination), while the buyer agrees to pay, not against delivery of the goods but against the tender of the shipping documents. The seller fulfils his part of the bargain by tendering the correct documents; he does not have to ensure the arrival of the goods, but is under a negative duty not to prevent them being delivered. He can therefore demand payment on tender of the documents.

21.3.2 Business rationale

A c.i.f. contract is a contract for the sale of goods. However, from a business point of view, it can be said that the purpose of a c.i.f. contract is not a sale of the goods themselves, but a sale of the documents relating to the goods.

The effectiveness of the c.i.f. contract depends on the transfer of the documents which give the buyer control, and a right of disposal of the goods, and rights to recover compensation if they are damaged due to the default of the carrier or due to some insured peril. It offers the parties certain advantages. Thus the buyer obtains:

(a) the means to take delivery of the goods;

(b) the means to dispose of the goods in order to resell them or to secure a bank advance using them as security before they actually arrive at their destination; and

(c) the right to enforce the contract of carriage and/or the contract of insurance and recover the value of the goods if they are lost or damaged during transit.

The seller obtains the following advantages:

(a) he accommodates the buyer;

(b) he secures increased profits by providing carriage and insurance;

(c) he retains the right of disposal until payment; and

(d) he is not answerable for loss or damage to the goods during carriage.

21.3.3 The seller's obligations

Unless there is provision to the contrary, the seller's duties under a c.i.f. contract are:

(a) to ship goods of the description contained in the contract;

(b) to procure a contract of carriage, under which the goods will be delivered to the destination contemplated in the contract;

(c) to arrange for an insurance, upon the terms current in the trade, which will be available for the benefit of the buyer;

(d) to make out an invoice;

(e) where necessary, to appropriate goods to the contract; and

(f) to tender the shipping documents to the buyer so that he may know what freight he has to pay in order to obtain delivery of the goods if they arrive, or to recover for their loss if they are lost on the voyage.

21.3.3.1   To ship the goods

The seller need not actually ship the goods himself. He can fulfil his obligations under the sale contract by:

(a) allowing his supplier to ship goods, which correspond with the contract description, within the relevant shipping period, as his agent;

(b) appropriating to the buyer's contract goods which correspond with the contract description, already shipped by him or his agent, provided they were shipped within the relevant shipping period; or

(c) buying goods already afloat which match the contract description and were shipped within the relevant shipping period by a third party, and then appropriating them to the buyer's contract.

If one method becomes impossible, the general rule is that the seller must use another, so if the seller intended to ship the goods himself but cannot, he is expected, for instance, to buy compatible goods afloat.

21.3.3.2   To appropriate the goods to the contract

Unless the contract is for specific goods, the seller must appropriate goods to the contract. Here the word 'appropriation' is used not in its proprietary sense but rather in its contractual sense. In this context appropriation means that the goods are nominated, or earmarked, for the buyer's contract: property only passes when goods are *unconditionally* appropriated (SoGA 1979, s. 18, r. 5).

Some sales contracts expressly require that a notice of appropriation be sent to the buyer so that he can in turn deal with the goods. Once this happens the goods cannot be used for any other contract, and if they are, the buyer can sue the seller for breach of contract. Conversely, the seller cannot, without the buyer's consent, substitute other goods for those appropriated to the contract.

Usually appropriation occurs on service of notice of appropriation or when the shipping documents are tendered.

A buyer should contract for service of notice of appropriation as this enables him to make arrangements to resell or pledge the goods.

21.3.3.3   To tender the shipping documents

The contract normally requires the seller to tender the following:

(a) a bill of lading;

(b) insurance policy; and

(c) an invoice.

The first two ensure that if the goods are lost or damaged during transit, the buyer will generally have a right of action against either the carrier or the insurer. The invoice contains a description of the goods and a statement of the price; it may be needed to clear goods through customs.

These basic requirements may be varied by the express terms of the contract, either by imposing qualifications on the basic documents to be tendered or by requiring the tender of additional documents.

(a) *Buyer's requirements*

Buyers should be advised to be as specific as possible in defining, in the sale contract, the shipping documents to be tendered. In practice, buyers usually demand that the shipping documents include the following.

(i)   A full set of clean, shipped, transferable bills of lading covering the whole transit (bills are usually issued in sets of three).

(ii)   An assignable marine insurance policy on the usual terms covering only the goods being sold, for the whole transit. The buyer could also require that the insurance be taken out with a company which meets its approval; that the policy covers 'all risks'; or that the goods be insured to an agreed valuation.

(iii)   An invoice, identifying the goods in accordance with the sale contract description, inclusive of the c.i.f. price. If freight is not pre-paid by the seller, the invoice should be discounted for the amount of freight due. Where a letter of credit is being used to finance the transaction, the description of the goods in the invoice and the letter of credit should correspond (see **23.4.3**).

The buyer can reject the documents tendered if they do not correspond to the contract requirements. The more specific the buyer's requirements, therefore, the greater the scope for rejection. So in the above example, the buyer could reject the tender if:

(i)   the bill is not clean, i.e. it is claused;

(ii)   the bill is a received for shipment, as opposed to a shipped, bill (a received for shipment bill can be tendered where the words 'since shipped' and a date are attached, thus effectively turning the bill into a shipped bill);

(iii)   the bill tendered is a straight consigned bill, because it is not transferable;

(iv)   anything less than an insurance policy, such as an insurance certificate or a cover note, is tendered;

(v)   the insurance contract fails to cover the whole transit or the usual risks; or

(vi)   the invoice does not identify the goods being sold.

The bill of lading will identify the goods; however, it will generally give the buyer no guarantee that the goods shipped are of the required quality. The buyer will therefore often require additional documents, such as export or import licences, certificates of origin, quality or inspection, to be tendered.

(b)   *Seller's requirements*

Where the seller is consigning the goods to himself, or is in a particularly strong position, or where there is established a good trading relationship between the buyer and the seller, the contract may provide for the tender and acceptance of other, perhaps lesser or more convenient documents, such as delivery orders instead of a bill of lading or an insurance certificate instead of a policy.

21.3.3.4   Time of tender

If a time for tender is specified it must be strictly complied with; if not, the buyer can reject the documents and terminate the contract (*Toepfer* v *Lenersan-Poortman NV* [1980] 1 Lloyd's Rep 143).

Where there is no stipulation as to the time for tender, the documents must be forwarded with reasonable despatch: it is unclear whether failure to do so gives the buyer the right to reject the documents and terminate the contract. However, the buyer may be able to serve notice fixing a time for tender and making time of the essence.

The contract should normally fix a time for tender and expressly deal with the consequences of late tender.

21.3.3.5 A right to re-tender?

There is some authority that a seller who has tendered defective documents may re-tender, if he can do so within the contract period (*Borrowman Phillips & Co.* v *Free and Hollis* (1878) 4 QBD 500; see **11.3.1.2**). However, the position is unclear and the contract should therefore contain an express provision to deal with this possibility.

21.3.4 The buyer's obligations

The general rule that delivery of the goods and payment of the price are concurrent obligations (SoGA 1979, s. 28) is displaced in c.i.f. contracts where, unless otherwise agreed, the buyer must be ready and willing to pay the price against tender of the documents (*Biddel Bros* v *E Clement Horst Co.* [1911] 1 KB 214). Provided that the documents accord with the contract, the buyer must accept them and pay the price: rejection of the documents and non-payment of the price is a breach of contract which allows the seller to terminate the contract and sue for damages. The buyer can therefore only avoid payment at this stage if:

(a) the contract on its true construction is not a c.i.f. contract, but rather some type of arrival contract where the seller is responsible for the arrival of the goods (see *The Julia* [1949] AC 293); or

(b) the shipping documents do not conform with the requirements of the sale contract (see **21.3.3.3**).

21.3.4.1 Where the goods are lost

Even if the goods are lost in transit, the seller is still entitled to tender the documents and claim the purchase price, and this rule applies even if at the time of tender the seller knows that the cargo has been lost (*Manbre Saccharine Co. Ltd* v *Corn Products Co. Ltd* [1919] 1 KB 198; and *State Trading Corporation of India* v *Golodetz* [1988] 2 Lloyd's Rep 182 at 183, *per* Evans J). Generally this causes no hardship to the buyer who has a remedy against the insurers or the carrier. However, the rule applies even where the buyer has no such right, for instance because the goods are lost without fault on the part of the carrier due to an uninsured risk. The buyer must then bear the loss, because he is at risk from shipment.

EXAMPLE

In *Groom* v *Barber* [1915] 1 KB 316, on 20 August, the seller appropriated to the buyer's contract the cargo of a named ship. In fact, unknown to the buyer, the ship was sunk by a submarine on 6 August. On 21 August the sinking became public knowledge and the buyer rejected the tender and refused to pay. It was held that the buyer was obliged to pay, even though the contract of sale provided that war risks were for the buyer's account and so the policy of insurance did not cover loss of the cargo due to enemy action.

21.3.4.2 Where the goods are defective

Provided the documents tendered conform to the contract, the buyer must accept and pay for them even if the goods themselves are defective. The buyer may have a separate right to reject the goods themselves on arrival (see **21.3.5.2**).

21.3.4.3 The seller's remedies (see Chapter 16)

If the buyer fails to perform any of his obligations the seller has the usual remedies of a seller under SoGA 1979 as amended by any express terms of the contract. In particular, if the buyer wrongfully rejects the documents or the goods, the seller can terminate the contract and sue the buyer for non-acceptance.

21.3.5 The buyer's remedies

The buyer's remedies depend on whether the seller has breached a condition of the contract, in which case he can reject the goods and sue for damages, or breached a warranty, in which case he must accept the goods but has a claim in damages.

Breach of a condition under a c.i.f. contract gives the buyer, in effect, two rights to reject:

(a) he can reject the documents when they are tendered;

(b) he can reject the goods when they are landed and when after examination they are found not to be in conformity with the contract (*Kwei Tek Chao* v *British Traders and Shippers Ltd* [1954] 2 QB 459).

21.3.5.1 Right to reject the documents

A buyer can reject documents which do not comply with the contract: for instance, if the bill is claused, showing that the goods were not in good condition when loaded, dated outside the shipment period or discloses deficiencies in quantity; or if an insurance certificate is tendered instead of a policy.

This right to reject the documents is lost if the buyer (or bank where payment is through a letter of credit: see **Chapter 23**) takes up the documents, even though inaccurate, and pays the price without objection.

EXAMPLE

In *Panchaud Frères SA* v *Etablissements General Grain Co.* [1970] 1 Lloyd's Rep 53, the contract of sale was for a quantity of Brazilian maize, c.i.f. Antwerp, shipment June/July 1965. The maize was actually loaded during August but the seller tendered a bill of lading falsely dated 31 July and a certificate of quality from loading supervisors stating that they had drawn samples on 10 and 12 August. This certificate formed part of the shipping documents which were taken up and paid for by the buyer, so the fact of late shipment was apparent. The buyer nevertheless accepted the documents. The buyer was therefore precluded from complaining of the late shipment.

Moreover, if a defect in the goods is apparent on the face of the documents, the buyer who accepts the documents will also be unable to reject the goods themselves on arrival for that defect. It is therefore vital that the buyer, or the bank, checks the documents carefully to ensure they conform to the contract before accepting them.

If the documents do correspond to the contract the buyer cannot reject them on the grounds of defects in the goods, and if the buyer does reject documents in such a case he will be in breach of contract. In *Berger & Co. Inc* v *Gill & Dufus SA* [1984] AC 382 the buyers rejected a tender of documents and tried to justify their rejection on the grounds that the goods, when delivered, did not correspond to the contract description. The House of Lords held that they could not do so and were in breach of contract; however, the fact that the goods would not have conformed to the contract could be taken into account by the court when assessing damages.

21.3.5.2 Right to reject the goods

A buyer who has accepted documents may still reject the goods if, on arrival, they do not comply with the terms of the contract. However, he may only do so for defects not apparent from the documents, so if a buyer accepts documents which show that the goods were damaged on loading he cannot then reject the goods when they arrive on that ground: *Kwei Tek Chao* v *British Traders and Shippers Ltd* [1954] 2 QB 459.

The buyer will accept the documents if he deals with them before the goods arrive, for instance, by using them to resell or pledge the goods. A buyer who deals with the documents in this way therefore loses the right to reject the goods themselves for defects apparent from the documents.

Any rejection must be clear and unequivocal.

21.3.5.3   Damages

Even where the buyer has lost the right to reject the goods, for instance because he accepted documents which indicated that the goods were defective, he may nevertheless claim damages for the seller's breach of contract.

In practice the buyer will generally not reject the goods after acceptance of the documents. He, or his bank, will have paid the price on presentation of the documents and rejection of the goods will therefore leave him in the position of having to pursue the seller to recover the price. It will generally be better for the buyer to accept the goods and then bring a claim for damages for breach of warranty.

Damages will be assessed in accordance with the general rules for buyer's claims for breach of warranty (see **11.3.2**) so that the basic measure will be the difference between the value which goods coresponding with the contract would have had, and the actual value of the goods delivered. Where the market value of the contract goods falls between the date of tender of the documents and the date of delivery of the goods, the buyer may find that a claim in damages leaves him worse off than if he had rejected the documents.

EXAMPLE

On 1 May B contracts to buy 500 tons of grade A soya beans, April shipment, c.i.f. London, at £100 per tonne. On 10 May S tenders documents which appear to comply with the contract and B accepts them. At that time the market price of the soya meal is £100 per tonne. The goods are discharged on 17 May and it is found that the beans are of a lower grade. The market price of grade A soya beans has now fallen to £80 per tonne; the beans delivered are worth only £75 per tonne. B may reject the beans and recover the price paid. If he accepts the beans, he is entitled to damages being the difference between the current market price of grade A beans and the current value of the beans actually delivered, i.e. £5 per tonne. If he had rejected the documents themselves he would have avoided the fall in the market price of soya beans.

21.3.5.4   Claim for additional damages

Where a defect in the documents is concealed by the fraud of the seller (or his predecessors in title), the buyer can claim additional damages to cover any loss he could have avoided if the defect had been apparent on the documents and he had rejected them. Thus in the example just given, if the goods had actually been shipped in March and the bill of lading had been falsely dated, B could recover extra damages to include the amount of the fall in the market value of soya beans (see *Kwei Tek Chao* v *British Traders and Shippers Ltd* [1954] 2 QB 459).

21.3.6   **Passage of property**

Again, the basic rule is that property passes when the parties intend it to pass (SoGA 1979, ss. 17–18), and no property can pass in unascertained goods (s. 16). Under a c.i.f. contract property usually passes when the buyer (or the bank when a letter of credit is being used: see **Chapter 23**) receives the bill and pays the price and the buyer thus acquires the right of disposal. However, this is only a presumption, so that if, for example, the contract is for specific goods, property could pass when the contract is made; or on shipment if the goods are then ascertained; or when the notice of appropriation is given (though this would be rare).

Where the bill of lading is made to the seller's order, he is presumed to have reserved title (SoGA 1979, s. 19(2)).

Express provisions dealing with passing of property will generally avoid disputes and uncertainty.

21.3.7 Passage of risk

Risk of loss of, or damage to, the goods usually passes when the goods pass over the ship's rail, and the goods travel at the buyer's risk, although the seller is responsible for the payment of freight and insurance premium.

If the seller sells goods already afloat, risk passes when the seller tenders documents, but does so retrospectively as from shipment, so that the buyer bears the risk even of loss which had already occurred prior to tender of the documents. He is protected by the availability of actions against either the carrier or the insurers.

SoGA 1979, s. 32(2) applies to c.i.f. contracts so that risk of loss may fall on the seller unless he makes a reasonable contract of carriage (see **21.2.3.4**).

21.4 Summary

Having concluded this chapter you should:

- be able to identify, and distinguish between, an f.o.b. and a c.i.f. contract; and
- be in a position to advise a client which type of contract best suits his needs, in terms of—
  - his rights and obligations under the contract, and
  - the rules on the passing of property and risk.

Specimen 1

Effective 1ˢᵗ January 2003

Gafta No.82

Copyright
THE GRAIN AND FEED TRADE ASSOCIATION

GENERAL CONTRACT
FREE ON BOARD TERMS
(F.O.B.)

Date ....

1   **SELLERS** ....
2
3   **INTERVENING AS BROKERS** ....
4
5   **BUYERS** ....
6   have this day entered into a contract on the following terms and conditions.
7
8   **1.   GOODS-** ....
9
10 **2.   QUANTITY-** ....
11
12 **3.   PRICE-** per tonne of 1000 kilograms, gross weight, delivered free on board Buyers' vessel at ....
13
14 **4.   BROKERAGE**.................................per tonne, to be paid by Sellers on the mean contract quantity, goods lost or not lost,
15 contract fulfilled or not fulfilled unless such non-fulfilment is due to the cancellation of the contract under the terms of the
16 Prohibition or Force Majeure Clause. Brokerage shall be due on the day shipping documents are exchanged, or if the goods are
17 not delivered then the brokerage shall be due on the 30ᵗʰ consecutive day after the last day for delivery.
18
19 **5.   QUALITY-**
20 Specifications ....
21 **Condition-** Delivery shall be made in good condition.
22
23 **6.   PERIOD OF DELIVERY** -Delivery during-.. at Buyers' call.
24
25 **Nomination of Vessel-** Buyers shall serve not less than ....consecutive days notice of the name and
26 probable readiness date of the vessel and the estimated tonnage required.
27 Buyers have the right to substitute the nominated vessel, but in any event the original delivery period and any extension shall not
28 be affected thereby. Provided the vessel is presented at the loading port in readiness to load within the delivery period, Sellers
29 shall if necessary complete loading after the delivery period and carrying charges shall not apply. In case of re-sales a provisional
30 notice shall be passed on without delay, where possible, by telephone and confirmed on the same day in accordance with the
31 Notices Clause.
32
33 **7.   LOADING -** Vessel(s) to load in accordance with the custom of the port of loading unless otherwise stipulated. Bill of lading
34 shall be considered proof of delivery in the absence of evidence to the contrary.
35
36 **8.   EXTENSION OF DELIVERY-** The contract period of delivery shall be extended by an additional period of not more than 21
37 consecutive days, provided that Buyers serve notice claiming extension not later than the next business day following the last day of
38 the delivery period. In this event Sellers shall carry the goods for Buyers' account and all charges for storage, interest, insurance and
39 other such normal carrying expenses shall be for Buyers' account, unless the vessel presents in readiness to load within the contractual
40 delivery period.
41
42 Any differences in export duties, taxes, levies etc, between those applying during the original delivery period and those applying
43 during the period of extension, shall be for the account of Buyers. If required by Buyers, Sellers shall produce evidence of the
44 amounts paid. In such cases the Duties, Taxes, Levies Clause shall not apply.
45
46 Should Buyers fail to present a vessel in readiness to load under the extension period, Sellers shall have the option of declaring Buyers
47 to be in default, or shall be entitled to demand payment at the contract price plus such charges as stated above, less current FOB
48 charges, against warehouse warrants and the tender of such warehouse warrants shall be considered complete delivery of the contract
49 on the part of Sellers.

9. **SHIP'S CLASSIFICATION**- Shipment by first class mechanically self-propelled vessel(s) suitable for the carriage of the contract goods classed in accordance with the Institute Classification Clause of the International Underwriting Association in force at the time of shipment, excluding tankers and vessels which are either classified in Lloyd's Register or described in Lloyd's Shipping Index as "Ore/Oil" vessels.

10. **PAYMENT**-

(a) By cash in ....

against the following documents ....

(b) No obvious clerical error in the documents shall entitle Buyers to reject them or delay payment, but Sellers shall be responsible for all loss or expense caused to Buyers by reason of such error, and Sellers shall on request of Buyers furnish an approved guarantee in respect thereto.

(c) Amounts payable under this contract shall be settled without delay. If not so settled, either party may notify the other that a dispute has arisen and serve a notice stating his intention to refer the dispute to arbitration in accordance with the Arbitration Rules.

(d) **Interest** – If there has been unreasonable delay in any payment, interest appropriate to the currency involved shall be charged. If such charge is not mutually agreed, a dispute shall be deemed to exist which shall be settled by arbitration. Otherwise interest shall be payable only where specifically provided in the terms of the contract or by an award of arbitration. The terms of this clause do not override the parties' contractual obligation under sub-clause (a).

11. **DUTIES, TAXES, LEVIES, ETC.**- All export duties, taxes, levies, etc., present or future, in country of origin or of the territory where the port or ports of shipment named herein is/are situate, shall be for Sellers' account.

12. **EXPORT LICENCE** – if required, to be obtained by Sellers.

13. **WEIGHING**- the terms and conditions of GAFTA Weighing Rules No.123 are deemed to be incorporated into this contract. Final at time and place of loading, as per GAFTA registered superintendent certificate at Sellers' choice and expense. Buyers have the right to attend at loading.

14. **SAMPLING, ANALYSIS AND CERTIFICATES OF ANALYSIS**- the terms and conditions of GAFTA Sampling Rules No.124, are deemed to be incorporated into this contract. Samples shall be taken at time and place of loading. The parties shall appoint superintendents, for the purposes of supervision and sampling of the goods, from the GAFTA Register of Superintendents. Unless otherwise agreed, analysts shall be appointed from the GAFTA Register of Analysts.

15. **INSURANCE**- Marine and war risk insurance including strikes, riots, civil commotions and mine risks to be effected by Buyers with first class underwriters and/or approved companies. Buyers shall supply Sellers with confirmation thereof at least five consecutive days prior to expected readiness of vessel(s). If Buyers fail to provide such confirmation Sellers shall have the right to place such insurance at Buyers' risk and expense.

16. **PROHIBITION**- In case of prohibition of export, blockade or hostilities or in case of any executive or legislative act done by or on behalf of the government of the country of origin or of the territory where the port or ports of shipment named herein is/are situate, restricting export, whether partially or otherwise, any such restriction shall be deemed by both parties to apply to this contract and to the extent of such total or partial restriction to prevent fulfilment whether by shipment or by any other means whatsoever and to that extent this contract or any unfulfilled portion thereof shall be cancelled. Sellers shall advise Buyers without delay with the reasons therefor and, if required, Sellers must produce proof to justify the cancellation.

17. **FORCE MAJEURE, STRIKES ETC.**- Sellers shall not be responsible for delay in delivery of the goods or any part thereof occasioned by any Act of God, strike, lockout, riot or civil commotion, combination of workmen, breakdown of machinery, fire or any cause comprehended in the term "force majeure". If delay in delivery is likely to occur for any of the above reasons, shall serve a notice on Buyers within 7 consecutive days of the occurrence, or not less than 21 consecutive days before the commencement of the contract period, whichever is later.

The notice shall state the reason(s) for the anticipated delay. If after serving such notice an extension to the delivery period is required, then the Sellers shall serve a further notice not later than 2 business days after the last day of the contract period of delivery. If delivery be delayed for more than 30 consecutive days, Buyers shall have the option of cancelling the delayed portion of the contract, such option to be exercised by Buyers serving notice to be received by Sellers not later than the first business day after the additional 30 consecutive days.

If Buyers do not exercise this option, such delayed portion shall be automatically extended for a further period of 30 consecutive days. If delivery under this clause be prevented during the further 30 consecutive days extension, the contract shall be considered void. Buyers shall have no claim against Sellers for delay or non-delivery under this clause, provided that Sellers shall have supplied to Buyers, if required, satisfactory evidence justifying the delay or non-fulfilment.

18. **NOTICES**- All notices required to be served on the parties pursuant to this contract shall be communicated rapidly in legible form. Methods of rapid communication for the purposes of this clause are defined and mutually recognised as: - either telex, or letter if delivered by hand on the date of writing, or telefax, or E-mail, or other electronic means, always subject to the proviso that if receipt of any notice is contested, the burden of proof of transmission shall be on the sender who shall, in the case of a dispute, establish, to the satisfaction of the arbitrator(s) or board of appeal appointed pursuant to the Arbitration Clause, that the notice was actually transmitted to the addressee. In case of resales/repurchases all notices shall be served without delay by sellers on their respective buyers or vice versa, and any notice received after 1600 hours on a business day shall be deemed to have been

120   received on the business day following.   A notice to the Brokers or Agent shall be deemed a notice under this contract.
121

122 **19.** **NON-BUSINESS DAYS**- Saturdays, Sundays and the officially recognised and/or legal holidays of the respective countries and any
123   days, which GAFTA may declare as non-business days for specific purposes, shall be non-business days. Should the time limit for
124   doing any act or serving any notice expire on a non-business day, the time so limited shall be extended until the first business day
125   thereafter. The period of delivery shall not be affected by this clause.
126

127 **20.** **DEFAULT**- In default of fulfilment of contract by either party, the following provisions shall apply: -
128   (a) The party other than the defaulter shall, at their discretion have the right, after serving a notice on the defaulter to sell or purchase,
129   as the case may be, against the defaulter, and such sale or purchase shall establish the default price.
130   (b) If either party be dissatisfied with such default price or if the right at (a) above is not exercised and damages cannot be mutually
131   agreed, then the assessment of damages shall be settled by arbitration.
132   (c) The damages payable shall be based on, but not limited to, the difference between the contract price and either the default price
133   established under (a) above or upon the actual or estimated value of the goods, on the date of default, established under (b) above.
134   (d) In all cases the damages shall, in addition, include any proven additional expenses which would directly and naturally result in the
135   ordinary course of events from the defaulter's breach of contract, but shall in no case include loss of profit on any sub-contracts made
136   by the party defaulted against or others unless the arbitrator(s) or board of appeal, having regard to special circumstances, shall in
137   his/their sole and absolute discretion think fit.
138   (e) Damages, if any, shall be computed on the quantity called for, but if no such quantity has been declared then on the mean contract
139   quantity, and any option available to either party shall be deemed to have been exercised accordingly in favour of the mean contract
140   quantity.
141

142 **21.** **INSOLVENCY**- If before the fulfilment of this contract, either party shall suspend payments, notify any of the creditors that he is
143   unable to meet debts or that he has suspended or that he is about to suspend payments of his debts, convene, call or hold a meeting of
144   creditors, propose a voluntary arrangement, have an administration order made, have a winding up order made, have a receiver or
145   manager appointed, convene, call or hold a meeting to go into liquidation (other than for re-construction or amalgamation) become
146   subject to an Interim Order under Section 252 of the Insolvency Act 1986, or have a Bankruptcy Petition presented against him (any of
147   which acts being hereinafter called an "Act of Insolvency") then the party committing such Act of Insolvency shall forthwith serve a
148   notice of the occurrence of such Act of Insolvency on the other party to the contract and upon proof (by either the other party to the
149   contract or the Receiver, Administrator, Liquidator or other person representing the party committing the Act of Insolvency) that such
150   notice was thus served within 2 business days of the occurrence of the Act of Insolvency, the contract shall be closed out at the market
151   price ruling on the business day following the serving of the notice. If such notice has not been served, then the other party, on
152   learning of the occurrence of the Act of Insolvency, shall have the option of declaring the contract closed out at either the market price
153   on the first business day after the date when such party first learnt of the occurrence of the Act of Insolvency or at the market price
154   ruling on the first business day after the date when the Act of Insolvency occurred. In all cases the other party to the contract shall
155   have the option of ascertaining the settlement price on the closing out of the contract by re-purchase or re-sale, and the difference
156   between the contract price and the re-purchase or re-sale price shall be the amount payable or receivable under this contract.
157

158 **22.** **DOMICILE**- This contract shall be deemed to have been made in England and to be performed in England, notwithstanding any
159   contrary provision, and this contract shall be construed and take effect in accordance with the laws of England. Except for the
160   purpose of enforcing any award made in pursuance of the Arbitration Clause of this contract, the Courts of England shall have
161   exclusive jurisdiction to determine any application for ancillary relief, the exercise of the powers of the Court in relation to the
162   arbitration proceedings and any dispute other than a dispute which shall fall within the jurisdiction of arbitrators or board of appeal
163   of the Association pursuant to the Arbitration Clause of this contract. For the purpose of any legal proceedings each party shall be
164   deemed to be ordinarily resident or carrying on business at the offices of The Grain and Feed Trade Association, (GAFTA),
165   England, and any party residing or carrying on business in Scotland shall be held to have prorogated jurisdiction against himself to
166   the English Courts or if in Northern Ireland to have submitted to the jurisdiction and to be bound by the decision of the English
167   Courts. The service of proceedings upon any such party by leaving the same at the offices of The Grain and Feed Trade
168   Association, together with the posting of a copy of such proceedings to his address outside England, shall be deemed good
169   service, any rule of law or equity to the contrary notwithstanding.
170

171 **23.** **ARBITRATION**-
172   (a) Any dispute arising out of or under this contract shall be settled by arbitration in accordance with the GAFTA Arbitration Rules,
173   No. 125, in the edition current at the date of this contract, such Rules forming part of this contract and of which both parties hereto
174   shall be deemed to be cognisant.
175   (b) Neither party hereto, nor any persons claiming under either of them shall bring any action or other legal proceedings against the
176   other of them in respect of any such dispute until such dispute shall first have been heard and determined by the arbitrator(s) or a
177   board of appeal, as the case may be, in accordance with the Arbitration Rules and it is expressly agreed and declared that the obtaining
178   of an award from the arbitrator(s) or a board of appeal, as the case may be, shall be a condition precedent to the right of either party
179   hereto or of any persons claiming under either of them to bring any action or other legal proceedings against the other of them in
180   respect of any such dispute.
181

182 **24.** **INTERNATIONAL CONVENTIONS**-
183   The following shall not apply to this contract: -
184   (a) The Uniform Law on Sales and the Uniform Law on Formation to which effect is given by the Uniform Laws on International
185   Sales Act 1967;
186   (b) The United Nations Convention on Contracts for the International Sale of Goods of 1980; and
187   (c) The United Nations Convention on Prescription (Limitation) in the International Sale of Goods of 1974 and the amending Protocol

188   of 1980.
189   (d) Incoterms
190   (e) Unless the contract contains any statement expressly to the contrary, a person who is not a party to this contract has no right
191   under the Contract (Rights of Third Parties) Act 1999 to enforce any term of it.

Sellers .... Buyers ....

Printed in England and issued by

GAFTA
(THE GRAIN AND FEED TRADE ASSOCIATION)
GAFTA HOUSE, 6 CHAPEL PLACE, RIVINGTON ST, LONDON EC2A 3SH

82/4

Specimen 2

Effective 1ˢᵗ January 2003

Gafta No.100

Copyright
THE GRAIN AND FEED TRADE ASSOCIATION

**CONTRACT FOR SHIPMENT OF FEEDINGSTUFFS
IN BULK
TALE QUALE - CIF TERMS**

*delete/specify as appropriate   *Date*...

1   **SELLERS** ....

2

3   **INTERVENING AS BROKERS**..

4

5   **BUYERS**...

6   have this day entered into a contract on the following terms and conditions. Wherever the word "cakes" is used, this is agreed to mean

7   goods of the contractual description.

8

9   **1.   GOODS-** ....

10   Broken cakes and/or meal in a proportion, having regard to the characteristics of the goods and methods of handling, to be taken and

11   paid for as cakes. Goods in bulk but Buyers agree to accept up to 15% in stowage bags, such bags to be taken and paid for as cakes

12   and any cutting to be paid for by Buyers. Sellers have the option of shipping the whole or part of the quantity in excess of 15% in

13   bags, in which case the excess over 15% shall be delivered in bulk and Sellers shall be responsible for cutting the excess bags which

14   remain their property.

15

16   **2.   QUANTITY-** .... 2% more or less.

17   Sellers shall have the option of shipping a further 3% more or less than the contract quantity. The excess above 2% or the deficiency

18   below 2% shall be settled on the quantity thereof at shipment at market value on the last day of discharge of the vessel at the port of

19   destination; the value to be fixed by arbitration, unless mutually agreed. Should Sellers exercise the option to ship up to 5% more, the

20   excess over 2% shall be paid for provisionally at contract price. The difference between the contract price and the market price

21   calculated in accordance with the provisions of this clause shall be adjusted in a final invoice. In the event of more than one shipment

22   being made, each shipment shall be considered a separate contract, but the margin of the mean quantity sold shall not be affected

23   thereby.

24

25   **3.   PRICE AND DESTINATION** - At ....

26   * per tonne of 1000 kilograms   }

27   } gross weight, cost, insurance and freight to ....

28   * per ton of 1016 kilograms or 2240 lbs.   }

29

30   **4.   BROKERAGE**....................................per tonne, to be paid by Sellers on the mean contract quantity, goods lost or not lost,

31   contract fulfilled or not fulfilled unless such non-fulfilment is due to the cancellation of the contract under the terms of the

32   Prohibition or Force Majeure Clause. Brokerage shall be due on the day shipping documents are exchanged or, if the goods are

33   not appropriated then brokerage shall be due on the 30th consecutive day after the last day for appropriation.

34

35   **5.   QUALITY-**

36   * **Warranted to contain** .... at time and place of discharge.

37

38   Not less than ....% of oil and protein combined, and not more than 2.50% of sand and/or silica. Should the whole, or

39   any portion, not turn out equal to warranty, the goods must be taken at an allowance to be agreed or settled by arbitration as

40   provided for below, except that for any deficiency of oil and protein there shall be allowances to Buyers at the following rates,

41   viz.: 1% of the contract price for each of the first 3 units of deficiency under the warranted percentage; 2% of the contract price

42   for the 4ᵗʰ and 5ᵗʰ units and 3% of the contract price for each unit in excess of 5 and proportionately for any fraction thereof.

43   When the combined content of oil and protein is warranted within a margin (as for example 40%/42%) no allowance shall be made

44   if the analysis ascertained as herein provided be not below the minimum, but if the analysis results are below the minimum

45   warranted the allowance for deficiency shall be computed from the mean of the warranted content. For any excess of sand and/or

46   silica there shall be an allowance of 1% of the contract price for each unit of excess and proportionately for any fraction thereof.

47   Should the goods contain over 5% of sand and/or silica the Buyers shall be entitled to reject the goods, in which case the contract

48   shall be null and void for such quantity rejected.

49

50   The goods are warranted free from castor seed and/or castor seed husk, but should the analysis show castor seed husk not

51   exceeding 0.005%, the Buyers shall not be entitled to reject the goods, but shall accept them with the following allowances: 0.75%

52   of contract price if not exceeding 0.001%, 1% of contract price if not exceeding 0.002%, and 1.50% of contract price if not

53   exceeding 0.005%. Should the first analysis show the goods free from castor seed and/or castor seed husk such analysis shall be

54   final but in the event of the first analysis showing castor seed husk to be present a second sample may be analysed at the request of

55   either party and the mean of the two analyses shall be taken as final. Should the parcel contain castor seed husk in excess of

56   0.005% Buyers shall be entitled to reject the parcel, in which case the contract shall be null and void for such quantity rejected.

Nevertheless, should Buyers elect to retain the parcel they shall be entitled to a further allowance for any excess over 0.005% of castor seed husk, to be settled by agreement or arbitration. For the purpose of sampling and analysis each mark shall stand as a separate shipment. The right of rejection provided by this clause shall be limited to the parcel or parcels found to be defective.

* **Official** .... certificate of inspection, at time of loading into the ocean carrying vessel, shall be final as to quality.

* **Sample**, at time and place of shipment about as per sealed sample marked.........................in possession of ....
the word "about" when referring to quality shall mean the equivalent of 0.50% on contract price. Analysis as per arrival sample. Difference in quality shall not entitle Buyers to reject except under the award of arbitrator(s) or board of appeal, as the case may be, referred to in the Arbitration Rules specified in the Arbitration Clause.
Condition – Shipment shall be made in good condition.

6.   **PERIOD OF SHIPMENT**- as per bill(s) of lading dated or to be dated ....
The bill(s) of lading to be dated when the goods are actually on board. Date of the bill(s) of lading shall be accepted as proof of date of shipment in the absence of evidence to the contrary. In any month containing an odd number of days, the middle day shall be accepted as being in both halves of the month.

7.   **SALES BY NAMED VESSELS**- For all sales by named vessels, the following shall apply: -
(a) Position of vessel is mutually agreed between Buyers and Sellers;
(b) The word "now" to be inserted before the word "classed" in the Shipment and Classification Clause;
(c) Appropriation Clause cancelled if sold "shipped".

8.   **SHIPMENT AND CLASSIFICATION** - Shipment from ....
direct or indirect, with or without transhipment by first class mechanically self-propelled vessel(s) suitable for the carriage of the contract goods, classed in accordance with the Institute Classification Clause of the International Underwriting Association in force at the time of shipment.

9.   **EXTENSION OF SHIPMENT**- The contract period for shipment, if such be 31 days or less, shall be extended by an additional period of not more than 8 days, provided that Sellers serve notice claiming extension not later than the next business day following the last day of the originally stipulated period. The notice need not state the number of additional days claimed.
Sellers shall make an allowance to Buyers, to be deducted in the invoice from the contract price, based on the number of days by which the originally stipulated period is exceeded, in accordance with the following scale: -
           1 to 4 additional days, 0.50%;
           5 or 6 additional days, 1%;
           7 or 8 additional days 1.50% of the gross contract price.
If, however, after having served notice to Buyers as above, Sellers fail to make shipment within such 8 days, then the contract shall be deemed to have called for shipment during the originally stipulated period plus 8 days, at contract price less 1.50%, and any settlement for default shall be calculated on that basis. If any allowance becomes due under this clause, the contract price shall be deemed to be the original contract price less the allowance and any other contractual differences shall be settled on the basis of such reduced price.

10. **APPROPRIATION**-
(a) Notice of appropriation shall state the vessel's name, the approximate weight shipped, and the date or the presumed date of the bill of lading.
(b) The notice of appropriation shall within (i) 10 consecutive days if shipped from the U.S. Gulf and/or U.S. and/or Canadian Atlantic/Lake Ports, (ii) 14 consecutive days if shipped from any other port, from the date of the bill(s) of lading be served by or on behalf of the Shipper direct on his Buyers or on the Selling Agent or Brokers named in the contract. The Non-Business Days Clause shall not apply.
(c) Notice of appropriation shall, within the period stated in sub-clause (b) be served by or on behalf of subsequent Sellers on their Buyers or on the Selling Agent or Brokers named in the contract, but if notice of appropriation is received by subsequent Sellers on the last day or after the period stated in sub-clause (b) from the date of the bill of lading, their notice of appropriation shall be deemed to be in time if served: -

(1)   On the same calendar day, if received not later than 1600 hours on any business day, or

(2)   Not later than 1600 hours on the next business day, if received after 1600 hours or on a non-business day.

(d) A notice of appropriation served on a Selling Agent or Brokers named in the contract shall be considered an appropriation served on Buyers. A Selling Agent or Brokers receiving a notice of appropriation shall serve like notice of appropriation in accordance with the provisions of this clause. Where the Shipper or subsequent Sellers serves the notice of appropriation on the Selling Agent, such Selling Agent may serve notice of appropriation either direct to the Buyers or to the Brokers.
(e) The bill of lading date stated in the notice of appropriation shall be for information only and shall not be binding, but in fixing the period laid down by this clause for serving notices of appropriation the actual date of the bill of lading shall prevail.
(f) Every notice of appropriation shall be open to correction of any errors occurring in transmission, provided that the sender is not responsible for such errors, and for any previous error in transmission which has been repeated in good faith.
(g) Should the vessel arrive before receipt of the appropriation and any extra expenses be incurred thereby, such expenses shall be borne by Sellers.
(h) When a valid notice of appropriation has been received by Buyers, it shall not be withdrawn except with their consent.

125   (i) In the event of less than 95 tonnes being tendered by any one vessel Buyers shall be entitled to refund of any proved extra expenses
126   for sampling, analysis and lighterage incurred thereby at port of discharge.

127

128 **11.** **PAYMENT**-

129   (a) **Payment** .... % of invoice amount by cash in ....

130   * In exchange for and on presentation of shipping documents;

131   * In exchange for shipping documents on or before arrival of the vessel at destination, at Buyers' option;

132   Sellers, however, have the option of calling upon Buyers to take up and pay for documents on or after.................................

133   consecutive days from the date of the bill(s) of lading.

134

135   (b) **Shipping documents** – shall consist of - 1. Invoice. 2. Full set(s) of on board Bill(s) of Lading and/or Ship's Delivery
136   Order(s) and/or other Delivery Order(s) in negotiable and transferable form. Such other Delivery Order(s) if required by Buyers,
137   to be countersigned by the Shipowners, their Agents or a recognised bank. 3. Policy (ies) and/or Insurance Certificate(s) and/or
138   Letter(s) of Insurance in the currency of the contract. The Letter(s) of Insurance to be certified by a recognised bank if required
139   by Buyers. 4. Other documents as called for under the contract. Buyers agree to accept documents containing the Chamber of
140   Shipping War Deviation Clause and/or other recognised official War Risk Clause.

141   (c) In the event of shipping documents not being available when called for by Buyers, or on arrival of the vessel at destination,
142   Sellers may provide other documents or an indemnity entitling Buyers to obtain delivery of the goods and payment shall be made
143   by Buyers in exchange for same, but such payment shall not prejudice Buyers' rights under the contract when shipping documents
144   are eventually available.

145   (d) Should Sellers fail to present shipping documents or other documents or an indemnity entitling Buyers to take delivery, Buyers
146   may take delivery under an indemnity provided by themselves and shall pay for the other documents when presented. Any
147   recoverable extra expenses, including the costs of such indemnity or extra charges incurred by reason of the failure of Sellers to
148   provide such documents, shall be borne by Sellers, but such payment shall not prejudice Buyers' rights under the contract when
149   shipping documents are eventually available.

150   (e) Should shipping documents be presented with an incomplete set of bill(s) of lading or should other shipping documents be
151   missing, payment shall be made provided that delivery of such missing documents is guaranteed, such guarantee to be
152   countersigned, if required by Buyers, by a recognised bank.

153   (f) Costs of collection shall be for account of Sellers, but if Buyers demand presentation only through a bank of their choice, in
154   that event any additional collection costs shall be borne by Buyers.

155   (g) No obvious clerical error in the documents shall entitle Buyers to reject them or delay payment, but Sellers shall be responsible
156   for all loss or expense caused to Buyers by reason of such error and Sellers shall on request furnish an approved guarantee in
157   respect thereto.

158   (h) Amounts payable under this contract shall be settled without delay. If not so settled, either party may notify the other that a
159   dispute has arisen and serve a notice stating his intention to refer the dispute to arbitration in accordance with the Arbitration
160   Rules.

161   (i) **Interest** – If there has been unreasonable delay in any payment, interest appropriate to the currency involved shall be charged.
162   If such charge is not mutually agreed, a dispute shall be deemed to exist which shall be settled by arbitration. Otherwise interest
163   shall be payable only where specifically provided in the terms of the contract or by an award of arbitration. The terms of this
164   clause do not override the parties' contractual obligation under sub-clause (a).

165

166 **12.** **DUTIES, TAXES, LEVIES, ETC.**- All export duties, taxes, levies, etc., present or future, in country of origin, shall be for Sellers'
167   account. All import duties, taxes, levies, etc., present or future, in country of destination, shall be for Buyers' account.

168

169 **13.** **DISCHARGE**- Discharge shall be as fast as the vessel can deliver in accordance with the custom of the port, but in the event of
170   shipment being made under liner bill(s) of lading, discharge shall be as fast as the vessel can deliver in accordance with the terms of
171   the bill(s) of lading. The cost of discharge from hold to ship's rail shall be for Sellers' account, from ship's rail overboard for Buyers'
172   account. If documents are tendered which do not provide for discharging as above or contain contrary stipulations, Sellers shall be
173   responsible to Buyers for all extra expenses incurred thereby. Discharge by grab(s) shall be permitted unless specifically excluded at
174   time of contract. If shipment is effected by lash barge, then the last day of discharge shall be the day of discharging the last lash barge
175   at the port of destination.

176

177 **14.** **WEIGHING**-the terms and conditions of GAFTA Weighing Rules No. 123 are deemed to be incorporated into this contract.
178   Unless otherwise agreed, final settlement shall be made on the basis of gross delivered weights at time and place of discharge at
179   Buyers' expense. If the place of destination is outside the port limits, Buyers agree to pay the extra expenses incurred by Sellers
180   or their agents for weighing. No payment shall be made for increase in weight occasioned by water and/or oil during the voyage.
181   If final at time and place of loading, as per GAFTA registered superintendents' certificate at Sellers' choice and expense, (in
182   which case the Deficiency Clause will not apply).

183

184 **15.** **DEFICIENCY**- Any deficiency in the bill of lading weight shall be paid for by Sellers and any excess over bill of lading weight
185   shall be paid for by Buyers at contract price, (unless the Pro-rata clause applies).

186

187 **16.** **SAMPLING, ANALYSIS AND CERTIFICATES OF ANALYSIS**- the terms and conditions of GAFTA Sampling Rules No.124,
188   are deemed to be incorporated into this contract. Samples shall be taken at the time of discharge on or before removal from the
189   ship or quay, unless the parties agree that quality final at loading applies, in which event samples shall be taken at time and place
190   of loading. The parties shall appoint superintendents, for the purposes of supervision and sampling of the goods, from the GAFTA
191   Register of Superintendents. Unless otherwise agreed, analysts shall be appointed from the GAFTA Register of Analysts.

192

193 **17.** **INSURANCE**- Sellers shall provide insurance on terms not less favourable than those set out hereunder, and as set out in detail in
194   GAFTA Insurance Terms No.72 viz.:-
195   (a) Risks Covered:-

196		Cargo Clauses (WA), with average payable, with 3% franchise or better terms	- Section 2 of Form 72
197		War Clauses (Cargo)	- Section 4 of Form 72
198		Strikes, Riots and Civil Commotions Clauses (Cargo)	- Section 5 of Form 72

199 (b) Insurers - The insurance to be effected with first class underwriters and/or companies who are domiciled or carrying on business in
200 the United Kingdom or who, for the purpose of any legal proceedings, accept a British domicile and provide an address for service of
201 process in London, but for whose solvency Sellers shall not be responsible.
202 (c) Insurable Value - Insured amount to be for not less than 2% over the invoice amount, including freight when freight is payable on
203 shipment or due in any event, ship and/or cargo lost or not lost, and including the amount of any War Risk premium payable by
204 Buyers.
205 (d) Freight Contingency - When freight is payable on arrival or on right and true delivery of the goods and the insurance does not
206 include the freight, Sellers shall effect insurance upon similar terms, such insurance to attach only as such freight becomes payable, for
207 the amount of the freight plus 2%, until the termination of the risk as provided in the above mentioned clauses, and shall undertake
208 that their policies are so worded that in the case of particular or general average claim the Buyers shall be put in the same position as if
209 the c.i.f. value plus 2% were insured from the time of shipment.
210 (e) Certificates/Policies - Sellers shall serve all policies and/or certificates and/or letters of insurance provided for in this contract,
211 (duly stamped if applicable) for original and increased value (if any) for the value stipulated in (c) above. In the event of a certificate of
212 insurance being supplied, it is agreed that such certificate shall be exchanged by Sellers for a policy if and when required, and such
213 certificate shall state on its face that it is so exchangeable. If required by Buyers, letter(s) of insurance shall be guaranteed by a
214 recognised bank, or by any other guarantor who is acceptable to Buyers.
215 (f) Total Loss - In the event of total or constructive total loss, or where the amount of the insurance becomes payable in full, the
216 insured amount in excess of 2% over the invoice amount shall be for Sellers' account and the party in possession of the policy (ies)
217 shall collect the amount of insurance and shall thereupon settle with the other party on that basis.
218 (g) Currency of Claims - Claims to be paid in the currency of the contract.
219 (h) War and Strike Risks/Premiums - Any premium in excess of 0.50% to be for account of Buyers. The rate of such insurance not to
220 exceed the rate ruling in London at time of shipment or date of vessel's sailing whichever may be adopted by underwriters. Such
221 excess premium shall be claimed from Buyers, wherever possible, with the Provisional Invoice, but in no case later than the date of
222 vessel's arrival, or not later than 7 consecutive days after the rate has been agreed with underwriters, whichever may be the later,
223 otherwise such claim shall be void unless, in the opinion of Arbitrators, the delay is justifiable. Sellers' obligation to provide War Risk
224 Insurance shall be limited to the terms and conditions in force and generally obtainable in London at time of shipment.
225 (i) Where Sellers are responsible for allowances or other payments to Buyers under Rye Terms or other contractual terms, (and which
226 risks are also covered by the insurance provided by Sellers), the Buyers, on receipt of settlement, shall immediately return to Sellers
227 the insurance documents originally received from them and shall, if required, subrogate to Sellers all right of claim against the Insurers
228 in respect of such matters.
229

230 **18. PROHIBITION**- In case of prohibition of export, blockade or hostilities or in case of any executive or legislative act done by or on
231 behalf of the government of the country of origin or of the territory where the port or ports of shipment named herein is/are situate,
232 restricting export, whether partially or otherwise, any such restriction shall be deemed by both parties to apply to this contract and to
233 the extent of such total or partial restriction to prevent fulfilment whether by shipment or by any other means whatsoever and to that
234 extent this contract or any unfulfilled portion thereof shall be cancelled. Sellers shall advise Buyers without delay with the reasons
235 therefor and, if required, Sellers must produce proof to justify the cancellation.
236

237 **19. FORCE MAJEURE, STRIKES, ETC**- Sellers shall not be responsible for delay in shipment of the goods or any part thereof
238 occasioned by any Act of God, strike, lockout, riot or civil commotion, combination of workmen, breakdown of machinery, fire, or
239 any cause comprehended in the term "force majeure". If delay in shipment is likely to occur for any of the above reasons, the Shipper
240 shall serve a notice on Buyers within 7 consecutive days of the occurrence, or not less than 21 consecutive days before the
241 commencement of the contract period, whichever is the later. The notice shall state the reason(s) for the anticipated delay.
242

243 If after serving such notice an extension to the shipping period is required, then the Shipper shall serve a further notice not later than 2
244 business days after the last day of the contract period of shipment stating the port or ports of loading from which the goods were
245 intended to be shipped, and shipments effected after the contract period shall be limited to the port or ports so nominated.
246

247 If shipment be delayed for more than 30 consecutive days, Buyers shall have the option of cancelling the delayed portion of the
248 contract, such option to be exercised by Buyers serving notice to be received by Sellers not later than the first business day after the
249 additional 30 consecutive days. If Buyers do not exercise this option, such delayed portion shall be automatically extended for a further
250 period of 30 consecutive days. If shipment under this clause be prevented during the further 30 consecutive days extension, the
251 contract shall be considered void. Buyers shall have no claim against Sellers for delay or non-shipment under this clause, provided that
252 Sellers shall have supplied to Buyers, if required, satisfactory evidence justifying the delay or non-fulfilment.
253

254 **20. NOTICES**- All notices required to be served on the parties pursuant to this contract shall be communicated rapidly in legible form.
255 Methods of rapid communication for the purposes of this clause are defined and mutually recognised as: - either telex, or letter if
256 delivered by hand on the date of writing, or telefax, or E-mail, or other electronic means, always subject to the proviso that if
257 receipt of any notice is contested, the burden of proof of transmission shall be on the sender who shall, in the case of a dispute,
258 establish, to the satisfaction of the arbitrator(s) or board of appeal appointed pursuant to the Arbitration Clause, that the notice was
259 actually transmitted to the addressee. In case of resales/repurchases all notices shall be served without delay by sellers on their
260 respective buyers or vice versa, and any notice received after 1600 hours on a business day shall be deemed to have been received
261 on the business day following. A notice to the Brokers or Agent shall be deemed a notice under this contract.
262

263 **21. NON-BUSINESS DAYS**- Saturdays, Sundays and the officially recognised and/or legal holidays of the respective countries and any
264 days, which GAFTA may declare as non-business days for specific purposes, shall be non-business days. Should the time limit for
265 doing any act or serving any notice expire on a non-business day, the time so limited shall be extended until the first business day
266 thereafter. The period of shipment shall not be affected by this clause.
267

268 **22. PRO RATA**-

269 (a) Should any of the above mentioned quantity form part of a larger quantity of the same or a different period of shipment of bags of
270 the same mark, or of a similar quality, whether in bags or bulk or whether destined to more than one port, no separation or distinction
271 shall be necessary.
272 (b) All loose collected, damaged goods and sweepings shall be shared by and apportioned pro-rata in kind between the various
273 Receivers thereof at the port of discharge named in the contract, buying under contracts containing this clause. In the event of this not
274 being practicable or any of them receiving more or less than his pro-rata share or apportionment, he shall settle with the other(s) on a
275 pro-rata basis in cash at the market price and each Receiver shall bear his proportion of the depreciation in market value. The pro-rata
276 statement shall be established by the Sellers or their Representatives in conjunction with the Receivers or their Representatives.
277 (c) The above pro-rata apportionment between Receivers shall have no bearing on the establishment of final invoices with Sellers and
278 for the purpose of these invoices, the total quantity of loose collected, damaged goods and sweepings shall be regarded as delivered to
279 those Receivers who did not receive their full invoiced quantity.
280 (d) In the case of excess or deficiency, the difference between the invoiced and the total delivered quantity shall be settled at the market
281 price by final invoices to be rendered by Receivers, who have received more or less than that paid for, to their immediate Sellers
282 without taking into consideration the above pro-rata apportionment between Receivers.
283 (e) If an excess quantity is delivered to one or more Receiver and a deficient quantity is delivered to one or more Receiver, the excess
284 and deficiency shall be settled between them at the market price. Invoices shall be established with immediate Sellers for any balance
285 resulting from this settlement.
286 (f) All Shippers, Sellers and Buyers of any part of such larger quantity as aforesaid under contracts containing this clause shall be
287 deemed to have entered into mutual agreements with one another to the above effect, and to agree to submit to arbitration all questions
288 and claims between them or any of them in regard to the execution of this clause as aforesaid in accordance with the Arbitration
289 Clause of this contract. Sellers and Buyers shall serve all reasonable assistance in execution of this clause. All Sellers shall be
290 responsible for the settlement by the respective Buyers in accordance with this clause within a reasonable time.
291 (g) The market price wherever mentioned in this clause shall be the market price on the last day of discharge of the vessel in the port
292 of destination, such price to be fixed by arbitration unless mutually agreed.
293 (h) In the event of this clause being brought into operation, any allowances payable in respect of condition, or quality, or under any of
294 the other guarantees contained in this contact, shall be based upon the actual weight received by the Buyers and not on the pro-rata
295 weight.
296 (i) In the event of any conflict in terms of apportionment applicable to the port of discharge the method published by GAFTA shall,
297 where applicable, take precedence over sub-clauses (b) to (h) above.
298 (j) In the event that sub-clause (a) applies or that the goods subsequently become co-mingled, and that the goods were shipped by more
299 than one Shipper and destined for one or more ports of discharge then, after the adjustment between Receivers under the terms of this
300 clause, the Shippers shall settle pro-rata between themselves in proportion to their bill of lading quantities. Such settlements shall be
301 made in cash and in the event of two or more discharging ports being involved, then the settlement price shall be the average of the
302 market prices on the last day of discharge in the respective ports.

304 **23. DEFAULT**- In default of fulfilment of contract by either party, the following provisions shall apply: -
305 (a) The party other than the defaulter shall, at their discretion have the right, after serving notice on the defaulter to sell or purchase, as
306 the case may be, against the defaulter, and such sale or purchase shall establish the default price.
307 (b) If either party be dissatisfied with such default price or if the right at (a) above is not exercised and damages cannot be mutually
308 agreed, then the assessment of damages shall be settled by arbitration.
309 (c) The damages payable shall be based on, but not limited to, the difference between the contract price and either the default price
310 established under (a) above or upon the actual or estimated value of the goods, on the date of default, established under (b) above.
311 (d) In no case shall damages include loss of profit on any sub-contracts made by the party defaulted against or others unless the
312 arbitrator(s) or board of appeal, having regard to special circumstances, shall in his/their sole and absolute discretion think fit.
313 (e) Damages, if any, shall be computed on the quantity appropriated if any but, if no such quantity has been appropriated then on the
314 mean contract quantity, and any option available to either party shall be deemed to have been exercised accordingly in favour of the
315 mean contract quantity.
316 (f) Default may be declared by Sellers at any time after expiry of the contract period, and the default date shall then be the first
317 business day after the date of Sellers' advice to their Buyers. If default has not already been declared then (notwithstanding the
318 provisions stated in the Appropriation Clause) if notice of appropriation has not been served by the 10th consecutive day after the last
319 day for appropriation laid down in the contract, the Seller shall be deemed to be in default and the default date shall then be the first
320 business day thereafter.

322 **24. CIRCLE** -Where Sellers re-purchase from their Buyers or from any subsequent buyer the same goods or part thereof, a circle shall be
323 considered to exist as regards the particular goods so re-purchased, and the provisions of the Default Clause shall not apply. (For the
324 purpose of this clause the same goods shall mean goods of the same description, from the same country of origin, of the same quality,
325 and, where applicable, of the same analysis warranty, for shipment to the same port(s) of destination during the same period of
326 shipment). Different currencies shall not invalidate the circle.
327 Subject to the terms of the Prohibition Clause in the contract, if the goods are not appropriated, or, having been appropriated
328 documents are not presented, invoices based on the mean contract quantity shall be settled by all Buyers and their Sellers in the circle
329 by payment by all Buyers to their Sellers of the excess of the Sellers' invoice amount over the lowest invoice amount in the circle.
330 Payment shall be due not later than 15 consecutive days after the last day for appropriation, or, should the circle not be ascertained
331 before the expiry of this time, then payment shall be due not later than 15 consecutive days after the circle is ascertained.
332 Where the circle includes contracts expressed in different currencies the lowest invoice amount shall be replaced by the market price
333 on the first day for contractual shipment and invoices shall be settled between each Buyer and his Seller in the circle by payment of the
334 differences between the market price and the relative contract price in currency of the contract.
335 All Sellers and Buyers shall give every assistance to ascertain the circle and when a circle shall have been ascertained in accordance
336 with this clause same shall be binding on all parties to the circle. As between Buyers and Sellers in the circle, the non-presentation of
337 documents by Sellers to their Buyers shall not be considered a breach of contract. Should any party in the circle prior to the due date
338 of payment commit any act comprehended in the Insolvency Clause of his contract, settlement by all parties in the circle shall be
339 calculated at the closing out price as provided for in the Insolvency Clause, which shall be taken as a basis for settlement, instead of
340 the lowest invoice amount in the circle. In this event respective Buyers shall make payment to their Sellers or respective Sellers shall
341 make payment to their Buyers of the difference between the closing out price and the contract price.

25. **INSOLVENCY**- If before the fulfilment of this contract, either party shall suspend payments, notify any of the creditors that he is unable to meet debts or that he has suspended or that he is about to suspend payments of his debts, convene, call or hold a meeting of creditors, propose a voluntary arrangement, have an administration order made, have a winding up order made, have a receiver or manager appointed, convene, call or hold a meeting to go into liquidation (other than for re-construction or amalgamation) become subject to an Interim Order under Section 252 of the Insolvency Act 1986, or have a Bankruptcy Petition presented against him (any of which acts being hereinafter called an "Act of Insolvency") then the party committing such Act of Insolvency shall forthwith serve a notice of the occurrence of such Act of Insolvency on the other party to the contract and upon proof (by either the other party to the contract or the Receiver, Administrator, Liquidator or other person representing the party committing the Act of Insolvency) that such notice was served within 2 business days of the occurrence of the Act of Insolvency, the contract shall be closed out at the market price ruling on the business day following the serving of the notice.

If such notice has not been served, then the other party, on learning of the occurrence of the Act of Insolvency, shall have the option of declaring the contract closed out at either the market price on the first business day after the date when such party first learnt of the occurrence of the Act of Insolvency or at the market price ruling on the first business day after the date when the Act of Insolvency occurred.

In all cases the other party to the contract shall have the option of ascertaining the settlement price on the closing out of the contract by re-purchase or re-sale, and the difference between the contract price and the re-purchase or re-sale price shall be the amount payable or receivable under this contract.

26. **DOMICILE**- This contract shall be deemed to have been made in England and to be performed in England, notwithstanding any contrary provision, and this contract shall be construed and take effect in accordance with the laws of England. Except for the purpose of enforcing any award made in pursuance of the Arbitration clause of this contract, the Courts of England shall have exclusive jurisdiction to determine any application for ancillary relief, the exercise of the powers of the Court in relation to the arbitration proceedings and any dispute other than a dispute which shall fall within the jurisdiction of arbitrators or board of appeal of the Association pursuant to the Arbitration Clause of this contract. For the purpose of any legal proceedings each party shall be deemed to be ordinarily resident or carrying on business at the offices of The Grain and Feed Trade Association, England, (GAFTA) and any party residing or carrying on business in Scotland shall be held to have prorogated jurisdiction against himself to the English Courts or if in Northern Ireland to have submitted to the jurisdiction and to be bound by the decision of the English Courts. The service of proceedings upon any such party by leaving the same at the offices of The Grain and Feed Trade Association, together with the posting of a copy of such proceedings to his address outside England, shall be deemed good service, any rule of law or equity to the contrary notwithstanding.

27. **ARBITRATION**-

(a) Any dispute arising out of or under this contract shall be settled by arbitration in accordance with the GAFTA Arbitration Rules, No. 125, in the edition current at the date of this contract, such Rules forming part of this contract and of which both parties hereto shall be deemed to be cognisant.

(b) Neither party hereto, nor any persons claiming under either of them shall bring any action or other legal proceedings against the other of them in respect of any such dispute until such dispute shall first have been heard and determined by the arbitrator(s) or a board of appeal, as the case may be, in accordance with the Arbitration Rules and it is expressly agreed and declared that the obtaining of an award from the arbitrator(s) or a board of appeal, as the case may be, shall be a condition precedent to the right of either party hereto or of any persons claiming under either of them to bring any action or other legal proceedings against the other of them in respect of any such dispute.

28. **INTERNATIONAL CONVENTIONS**-

The following shall not apply to this contract: -

(a) The Uniform Law on Sales and the Uniform Law on Formation to which effect is given by the Uniform Laws on International Sales Act 1967;

(b) The United Nations Convention on Contracts for the International Sale of Goods of 1980; and

(c) The United Nations Convention on Prescription (Limitation) in the International Sale of Goods of 1974 and the amending Protocol of 1980.

(d) Incoterms

(e) Unless the contract contains any statement expressly to the contrary, a person who is not a party to this contract has no right under the Contract (Rights of Third Parties) Act 1999 to enforce any term of it.

Sellers .... Buyers ....

Printed in England and issued by

GAFTA
(THE GRAIN AND FEED TRADE ASSOCIATION)
GAFTA HOUSE, 6 CHAPEL PLACE, RIVINGTON ST, LONDON EC2A 3SH

100/6

Specimen 3

© SITPRO 1999

STANDARD SHIPPING NOTE - FOR NON - DANGEROUS GOODS ONLY

IMPORTANT
USE THE
DANGEROUS
GOODS NOTE
IF THE
GOODS ARE
CLASSIFIED AS
DANGEROUS
ACCORDING TO
APPLICABLE
REGULATIONS
SEE BOX 10A

Exporter	1	Customs reference/status	2
		Booking number	3	Exporters reference	4
			Forwarder's reference	5

Consignee	6

Freight forwarder	7	International carrier	8
		For use of receiving authority only	

Other UK transport details (e.g. ICD, terminal, vehicle bkg. ref. receiving dates)	9

10A

The Company preparing this note declares that, to the best of their belief, the goods have been accurately described, their quantities, weights and measurements are correct and at the time of despatch they were in good order and condition; that the goods are not classified as being hazardous by reference to relevant national and international regulations applicable to the intended modes of transport.

Vessel/flight no. and date	Port/airport of loading	10

Port/airport of discharge	Destination	11

TO THE RECEIVING AUTHORITY - Please receive for shipment the goods described below subject to your published regulations and conditions (including those as to liability)

Shipping marks	Number and kind of packages; descripion of goods; non-hazardous special stowage requirements	12	Gross weight (kg) of goods	13A	Cube (m³) of goods	14

For use of Shipping company only

Total gross weight of goods

Total cube of goods

Container identification number/ vehicle registration number	16	Seal number(s)	16A	Container/vehicle size and type	16B	Tare (kg)	16C	Total gross weight (including tare) (kg)	16D

HAULIER DETAILS

DOCK/TERMINAL RECEIPT

RECEIVING AUTHORITY REMARKS

Name and telephone number of company preparing this note

17

Hauliers name

Received the above number of packages/containers/trailers in apparent good order and condition unless stated hereon.

Name/status of declarant

Vehicle reg. no.

Place and date

Drivers signature

Receiving authority signature and date

Signature of declarant

Specimen 4

© SITPRO 1999

DANGEROUS GOODS NOTE

Exporter	1	Customs reference/status	2

		Booking number	3	Exporter's reference	4
				Forwarder's reference	5

Consignee	6	DSHA Notification (in accordance with DSHA Regulations (as amended)) given by:	6A

		Shipper	Cargo agent	Transport operator	Shipping line

Freight forwarder	7	International carrier	8

For use of receiving authority only

Other UK transport details (e.g. ICD, terminal, vehicle bkg. ref., receiving dates)	9

I hereby declare that the contents of this consignment are fully and accurately described below by the proper shipping name, and are classified, packaged, marked and labelled/placarded and are in all respects in proper condition for transport according to the applicable international and national governmental regulations and in accordance with the provisions shown overleaf. The shipper must complete and sign box 17. 10A

Vessel	Port of loading	10

Port of discharge	Destination	11

TO THE RECEIVING AUTHORITY
Please receive for shipment the goods described below subject to your published regulations and conditions (including those as to liability).

Shipping marks	Number and kind of packages; description of goods;	12	Net weight (kg) of goods	13	Gross weight (kg) of goods	13A	Cube (m³) of goods	14
SPECIFY: Proper Shipping Name*, Hazard Class, UN No. Additional information (if applicable) see overleaf For RID/ADR/CDG Road requirements see notes overleaf								

* Proper Shipping Name - Trade names alone are unacceptable

CONTAINER/VEHICLE PACKING CERTIFICATE

I hereby declare that the goods described above have been packed/ loaded into the container/vehicle identified below in accordance with the provisions shown overleaf.

THIS DECLARATION MUST BE COMPLETED AND SIGNED FOR ALL CONTAINER/ VEHICLE LOADS BY THE PERSON RESPONSIBLE FOR PACKING/LOADING

Name of company

Name/Status of declarant

Place and date

Signature of declarant

15	Total gross weight of goods	Total cube of goods

Container identification number/ vehicle registration number	16	Seal number(s)	16A	Container/vehicle size and type	16B	Tare (kg)	16C	Total gross weight (including tare) (kg)	16D

DOCK/TERMINAL RECEIPT

HAULIER DETAILS	RECEIVING AUTHORITY REMARKS	Name and telephone number of shipper preparing this note	17
Haulier's name	Received the above number of packages/containers/trailers in apparent good order and condition unless stated hereon.	Name/status of declarant	
Vehicle reg. no.		Place and date	
Driver's signature	Receiving authority signature and date	Signature of declarant	

630 Non-completion of any boxes is a subject for resolution by the contracting parties

ADDITIONAL INFORMATION (Box 12) – Number and kind of packages; description of goods
•
The following information must also appear with the proper shipping name, hazard class/division and UN Number:
(a)   packaging group – where assigned;
(b)   the words "MARINE POLLUTANT" for substances so designated in the IMDG Code;
(c)   the minimum closed cup (cc) flashpoint in °C – if 61°C or less;
(d)   subsidiary hazards not communicated in the proper shipping name; and
(e)   the words "SALVAGE PACKAGING" for dangerous goods transported in salvage packaging together with the description of the goods.

Additional information is required for:
(f)   substances and articles in Class 1 and 2;
(g)   certain substances in Classes 4.1 and 5.2;
(h)   infectious substances (Class 6.2);
(i)   radioactive materials (Class 7);
(j)   empty packaging/tanks containing residues;
(k)   waste dangerous goods;
(l)   dangerous goods consigned as limited quantities; and
(m)   dangerous goods requiring a weathering certificate.

RID/ADR/CDG Road Information

For hazardous goods moved under RID/ADR or CDG Road Regulations the following information must be given:

(a)   a description (including the substance identification number for RID/ADR);
(b)   the class;
(c)   the item number together with any letter for RID/ADR OR the UN number for CDG Road;
(d)   the initials RID/ADR; and
(e)   any extra information required to determine the transport category and the control temperature and emergency temperature where appropriate (for CDG Road).

Refer to the IMDG Code, RID Regulations, ADR Agreement, CDG Road Regulations and the SITPRO/FTA Completion Guide for further details.

CONTAINER/VEHICLE PACKING CERTIFCATE (box 15)
The signature given overleaf in box 15 must be that of the person controlling the container/vehicle operation.

It is certified that:
1.   the container/vehicle was clean, dry and apparently fit to receive goods;
2.   if the consignment includes goods of class 1, other than division 1.4, the container is structurally serviceable in conformity with section 12 of the introduction to Class 1 of the IMDG Code;
3.   no incomplete goods have been packed into the container/vehicle unless specially authorised by the Competent Authority;
4.   all packages have been externally inspected for damage and only sound packages packed;
5.   drums have been stowed in an upright position, unless otherwise authorised by the Competent Authority;
6.   all packages have been properly packed and secured in the container/vehicle;
7.   when materials are transported in bulk packaging the cargo has been evenly distributed in the container/vehicle;
8.   the packages and the container/vehicle have been properly marked, labelled and placarded. Any irrelevant marks, labels and placards have been removed;
9.   when solid carbon dioxide (CO_2 – dry ice) is used for cooling purposes, the vehicle or freight container is externally marked or labelled in a conspicuous place e.g. at the door end, with the words:
       DANGEROUS CO_2 GAS (DRY ICE) INSIDE,
       VENTILATE THOROUGHLY BEFORE ENTERING
10.   when this Dangerous Goods Note is used as a container/vehicle packing certificate only, not a combined document, a Dangerous Goods Declaration signed by the shipper or supplier has been issued/received to cover each dangerous goods consignment packed in the container.

Note: The container packing certificate is not required for tanks.

THE SHIPPER'S DECLARATION (Box 17) covers the following regulations

The International Maritime Dangerous Goods code (IMDG Code), as revised or re-issued from time to time by the International Maritime Organisation.

Annex 1 (RID) to the Uniform Rules concerning the Contract for international Carriage of Goods by Rail (CIM), as revised or re-issued from time to time.

European Agreement concerning the international carriage of dangerous goods by road (ADR) as revised or re-issued from time to time.

The Carriage of Dangerous Goods by Road Regulations 1996 – S.I. 2095/1996 (the CDG Road Regulations), or any amending or replacement regulations.

If signing the document for the ADR Agreement or CDG Road Regulations the shipper is confirming that in accordance with the applicable Regulations:
i)   the dangerous goods as presented may be carried;
ii)   the dangerous goods and any packaging, intermediate bulk container or tank in which they are contained are in a fit condition for carriage and are properly labelled; and
iii)   where several packages are packed together in an overpack or in a single container, that this mixed packaging is not prohibited.

Specimen 5

*Applicable only when document used as a through bill of lading

Particulars declared by shipper

Shipper	VAT no.

COMMON SHORT FORM BILL OF LADING

B/L no.

Shipper's reference

Forwarder's reference

Consignee	VAT no.'

Name of carrier

Notify party and address

The contract evidenced by this Short Form Bill of Lading is subject to the exceptions, limitations, conditions and liberties (including those relating to pre-carriage and on-carriage) set out in the Carrier's Standard Conditions applicable to the voyage covered by this Short Form Bill of Lading and operative on its date of issue. If the carriage is one where the provisions of the Hague Rules contained in the International Convention for unification of certain rules relating to Bills of Lading, dated Brussels on 25th August, 1924, as amended by the Protocol signed at Brussels on 23rd February, 1968 (the Hague Visby Rules) are compulsorily applicable under Article X, the said Standard Conditions contain or shall be deemed to contain a Clause giving effect to the Hague Visby Rules. Otherwise, except as provided below, the said Standard Conditions contain or shall be deemed to contain a Clause giving effect to the provisions of the Hague Rules.
The Carrier hereby agrees that to the extent of any inconsistency the said clause shall prevail over the exceptions, limitations, conditions and liberties set out in the said Standard Conditions in respect of any period to which the Hague Rules or the Hague Visby Rules by their terms apply. Unless the Standard Conditions expressly provide otherwise, neither the Hague Rules nor the Hague Visby Rules shall apply to this contract where the goods carried hereunder consist of live animals or cargo which by this contract is stated as being carried on deck and is so carried.
Notwithstanding anything contained in the said Standard Conditions, the term Carrier in this Short Form Bill of Lading shall mean the Carrier named on the front thereof.
A copy of the Carrier's said Standard Conditions applicable hereto may be inspected or will be supplied on request at the office of the Carrier or the Carrier's Principal Agents.

Pre-carriage by*	Place of receipt by pre-carrier*
Vessel	Port of loading
Port of discharge	Place of delivery by on-carrier*

Shipping marks; container number	Number and kind of packages; description of goods	Gross weight	Measurement

Freight details; charges etc.

RECEIVED FOR CARRIAGE as above in apparent good order and condition, unless otherwise stated hereon, the goods described in the above particulars.

IN WITNESS whereof the number of original bills of lading stated below have been signed, all of this tenor and date, one of which being accomplished the others to stand void.

C of S
CSF
BL
1987

Ocean freight payable at	Place and date of issue
Number of original Bs/L	Signature for carrier; carrier's principal place of business

Specimen 6

BILL OF LADING FOR COMBINED TRANSPORT SHIPMENT OR PORT TO PORT SHIPMENT   B/L No.:

Shipper	Reference:

P&O Containers

Consigned to the order of	

Notify Party/Address (It is agreed that no responsibility shall attach to the Carrier or his Agents for failure to notify of the arrival of the goods (see clause 20 on reverse))	Place of Receipt (Applicable only when this document is used as a Combined Transport Bill of Lading)

Pre-Carrier	Place of Delivery (Applicable only when this document is used as a Combined Transport Bill of Lading)
Vessel and Voy. No.	

Port of Loading	Port of Discharge	

Undermentioned particulars as declared by Shipper, but not acknowledged by the Carrier (see Clause 11)

Marks and Nos; Container Nos;	Number and kind of Packages; Description of Goods	Gross Weight (kg)	Measurement (cbm)
VOID VOID VOID VOID VOID			

* Total No. of Containers/Packages received by the Carrier	Movement	Freight payable at

Received by the Carrier from the Shipper in apparent good order and condition (unless otherwise noted herein) the total number or quantity of Containers or other packages or units indicated in the box above entitled "*Total No. of Containers/Packages received by the Carrier" for Carriage subject to all the terms and conditions hereof (INCLUDING THE TERMS AND CONDITIONS ON THE REVERSE HEREOF AND THE TERMS AND CONDITIONS OF THE CARRIER'S APPLICABLE TARIFF) from the Place of Receipt or the Port of Loading, whichever is applicable, to the Port of Discharge or the Place of Delivery, whichever is applicable. Before the Carrier arranges delivery of the Goods one original Bill of Lading, duly endorsed, must be surrendered by the Merchant to the Carrier at the Port of Discharge or at some other location acceptable to the Carrier. In accepting this Bill of Lading the Merchant expressly accepts and agrees to all its terms and conditions whether printed, stamped or written, or otherwise incorporated, notwithstanding the non-signing of this Bill of Lading by the Merchant.

Number of Original Bills of Lading	Place and Date of Issue	IN WITNESS of the contract herein contained the number of originals stated opposite has been issued, one of which being accomplished the other(s) to be void.
		For P&O Containers Limited as Carrier:
		As Agent for the Carrier.

DPC B/L 18/94 (C)

Specimen 7

© C of S 1979/1987

*Applicable only when document used as a Through Sea Waybill

Particulars declared by shipper

Shipper	VAT no.

**NON-NEGOTIABLE
SEA WAYBILL**

SWB No

Shipper's reference

Forwarder's reference

Consignee	VAT no.

Name of carrier

Notify Party and Address

The contract evidenced by this Waybill is subject to the exceptions, limitations, conditions and liberties (including those relating to pre-carriage and on-carriage) set out in the Carrier's Standard Conditions of Carriage applicable to the voyage covered by this Waybill and operative on its date of issue: if the carriage is one where had a Bill of Lading been issued the provisions of the Hague Rules contained in the International Convention for unification of certain rules relating to Bills of Lading, dated Brussels, 25th August, 1924, as amended by the Protocol signed at Brussels on the 23rd February, 1968 (the Hague Visby Rules) are compulsorily applicable under Article X, the said Standard Conditions contain or shall be deemed to contain a Clause giving effect to the Hague Visby Rules. Otherwise the said Standard Conditions contain or shall be deemed to contain a Clause giving effect to the provisions of the Hague Rules. In neither case shall the proviso to the first sentence of Article V of the Hague Rules or the Hague Visby Rules apply. The Carrier hereby agrees (i) that to the extent of any inconsistency the said clause shall prevail over the said Standard Conditions in respect of any period to which the Hague Rules or the Hague Visby Rules by their terms apply, and (ii) that for the purpose of the terms of this Contract of Carriage this Waybill falls within the definition of Article 1(b) of the Hague Rules and the Hague Visby Rules.

The shipper accepts the said Standard Conditions on his own behalf and on behalf of the Consignee and the owner of the goods and warrants that he has authority to do so. The consignee by presenting this Waybill and/or requesting delivery of the goods further undertakes all liabilities of the Shipper hereunder, such undertaking being additional and without prejudice to the Shipper's own liability. The benefit of the contract, evidenced by this Waybill shall thereby be transferred to the Consignee or other persons presenting this Waybill.

Notwithstanding anything contained in the said Standard Conditions, the term Carrier in this Waybill shall mean the Carrier named on the front hereof.

A copy of the Carrier's said Standard Conditions applicable hereto may be inspected or will be supplied on request at the office of the Carrier or the Carrier's Principal Agents.

Pre-carriage by*	Place of receipt by pre-carrier*
Vessel	Port of loading
Port of discharge	Place of delivery by on-carrier*

Shipping marks; container number	Number and kind of packages; description of goods	Gross weight	Measurement

Freight details; charges etc.

RECEIVED FOR CARRIAGE as above in apparent good order and condition, unless otherwise stated hereon, the goods described in the above particulars.

: of S
SWB
1987

Ocean freight payable at	Place and date of issue

Signature for carrier; carrier's principal place of business

Authorised and licensed by the Chamber of Shipping ©1979/1987

Specimen 8

(c) SITPRO 1992

COLLECTION/DELIVERY ORDER

Exporter	A

Exporter's reference	U
	N
Forwarder's reference	I
	C

Collection address if different from A	B

Other UK transport details e.g. delivery address	C

Haulier **D**

Vessel/flight no. and date	Port/airport of loading

Port/airport of discharge

DANGEROUS GOODS

Specify proper shipping name: hazard class: UN No.: flashpoint deg C
Shipper must provide the appropriate dangerous goods declaration

Shipping marks: container number	Number and kind of packages description of goods	Gross weight (kg)	Cube (m3)

		Total gross weight of goods	Total cube of goods

IMPORTANT - DOCUMENTS TO BE COLLECTED

Collect documents from **A B**

Deliver documents to **C D** or:-

Prefix and container/trailer number(s)	Seal number(s0	Container/trailer size(s) and type(s)	Tare wt(kg) as marked on CSC plate	Weight of container and goods (kg)

Received the above packages/containers/trailers in apparent good order unless stated hereon	For and on behalf of

Haulier's name

Vehicle reg no.	Date

Driver's signature	Signature and date

SITPRO Licensee No. 000.

Specimen 9

INVOICE RECHNUNG FACTURE FACTURA فاتــــورة

Seller (name, address, VAT reg no.)	Invoice number
	Invoice date (tax point) — Seller's reference
	Buyer's reference — Other reference

(c) SITPRO
1992

Consignee — VAT no.	Buyer (if not consignee) — VAT no.

U
N
I
C

	Country of origin of goods — Country of destination
	Terms of delivery and payment

Vessel/flight no. and date	Port/airport of loading
Port/airport of discharge	Place of delivery

Shipping marks; container number	No. and kind of packages; description of goods	Commodity code	Total gross wt (Kg)	Total cube (m3)
			Total net wt (Kg)	

Item/packages	Gross/net/cube	Description	Quantity	Unit price	Amount
					Invoice total

	Name of signatory
	Place and date of issue
It is hereby certified that this invoice shows the actual price of the goods described, that no other invoice has been or will be issued, and that all particulars are true and correct.	Signature

SITPRO Licensee No. 000.

V6

Part V

Payment mechanisms in commercial transactions

Bills of exchange

22.1 Introduction

A supplier will generally be reluctant to supply goods or services without some assurance of payment which will protect him against the customer's failure to pay both through inability (i.e. insolvency) and unwillingness, including for instance, where liability is disputed on grounds of allegedly defective performance. The customer on the other hand will want to withhold payment at least until the contract is performed, in order to assure himself of satisfactory performance, and will often want credit, so that he is not obliged to pay immediately even on completion of the supplier's performance.

not having money

There are a number of ways in which these competing needs may be satisfied. The seller may take real or personal security (see **Chapters 25** and **26**) or may protect himself by reserving title to goods supplied until the price is paid (see **16.4.3**). In addition, commercial practice has developed a number of payment mechanisms which may be used to satisfy the needs of both parties. These payment mechanisms will often be more convenient than cash, offering a further advantage. Amongst the most important, considered in this and the following chapter, are bills of exchange, cheques, promissory notes, documentary credits and performance bonds; they are especially important in international transactions.

Bills of exchange are probably the most important of the commercial payment mechanisms in widespread use, and there is a body of detailed and technical law relating to their use. Cheques are bills of exchange and are governed by the same rules, albeit with some modifications. Promissory notes are in some ways analogous and are governed by similar rules.

In this chapter we examine some common payment methods used in commercial transactions. In particular we:

- outline the concept of negotiability;
- examine the commercial uses of and the law relating to bills of exchange including their transfer and enforcement and liability on a bill;
- examine the law relating to cheques and their role in the banking system;
- outline the use of and law relating to promissory notes.

22.1.1 Negotiable instruments

Bills, promissory notes and cheques are all negotiable instruments, and it is this status that gives them their special practical value. An instrument is a document which evidences title to 245.a legal right, such as a right to enforce a debt. Such rights are property (choses in action) and can therefore be transferred. Generally, rights under a contract can only be transferred by assignment, either in equity or under the Law of Property Act 1925, s. 136. A legal assignment must be written and notice of it must be given to the debtor against whom the right is to be enforced; even if these requirements are fulfilled, the debtor can set up against the transferee any defence he could have asserted against the transferor. However, a negotiable instrument can be transferred, either simply by delivery to the transferee or by delivery and indorsement with the name of the transferee; the transferee is then able to enforce the legal obligation evidenced by the instrument. Moreover, the transferee of a negotiable instrument may take it free of any defects in the transferor's title and defences which could have been set up against the transferor.

There is a range of instruments in regular commercial use; however, not all are regarded as negotiable: for instance, postal orders and share certificates are instruments but are not negotiable. An instrument is recognised by the law as negotiable if it is regarded as negotiable by mercantile custom. Other instruments which are regarded as negotiable include bearer bonds, share warrants payable to bearer and dividend warrants.

22.1.2 Negotiability and privity

Negotiation of a bill of exchange, promissory note or other negotiable instrument effectively allows the transfer of contractual rights, vesting new rights on the contract in the bill etc in the transferee. Negotiation therefore operates as an exception to the doctrine of privity of contract, which was accepted at common law and confirmed by the Bills of Exchange Act 1882. It is therefore expressly provided that the Contracts (Rights of Third Parties) Act 1999 confers no rights on a third party in the case of a contract on a bill, note or other negotiable instrument (s. 6(1): see **2.7**).

22.2 Bills of exchange

A bill of exchange is an order by one person (the *drawer* of the bill) to another person (the *drawee*) to pay a sum of money to a person (the *payee*). The bill need not name a payee: instead it may be payable simply to 'bearer'. If a payee is named, the payee may be the drawer or a third party. The sum ordered to be paid by the bill may be payable immediately or at a future date. The payee may enforce the bill himself by presenting it for payment in accordance with its terms, or may sell (or 'discount') it to a third party, transferring it to the third party in return for an immediate cash payment. The transferee will then enforce the bill in due course, or may in turn himself transfer it.

A bill contains a contractual undertaking to pay a sum of money to the payee. The drawer and drawee are parties to the bill and are liable to honour the payment undertaking. The drawee is the person primarily liable to honour the bill; however, liability depends on signature. The drawer is therefore immediately liable on the bill but the drawee is only liable on it if it is presented to him for acceptance and he accepts the obligation it contains by signing it. A bill only has to be presented for acceptance if it is drawn payable 'n days after sight' (when presentation for acceptance is needed to fix the date when it is payable) but a bill generally will be presented for acceptance even if not so drawn, since acceptance will make the drawee liable to honour it and thus increase its value. If the drawee fails to accept the bill when presented to him, it is dishonoured by non-acceptance.

22.2.1   Examples of the use of bills of exchange

EXAMPLE 1

S agrees to sell goods to B. B wants credit; S wants immediate payment. S may agree with B that B will accept a bill of exchange drawn on him by S for the price and payable at a fixed, future date. S will therefore draw a bill on B naming himself as payee, and present it to B for acceptance; he will not supply the goods until the bill is accepted. On B's acceptance, S can discount the bill to a bank or discount house in return for an immediate cash payment. A discounter will pay less than the full face value of the bill to take account of both the fact that the bill is not immediately payable and the risk that the bill will be dishonoured on presentation for payment. The value of the bill to a discounter will therefore depend on the credit-worthiness of B; S will take account of this when fixing the price under the contract of sale, which will therefore be higher than if B were to pay cash.

EXAMPLE 2

C agrees to make a loan to D. In order to secure repayment, C requires D to accept a bill for the amount of the loan plus interest; or, where the loan is repayable by instalments, bills payable at future dates for the amounts of the instalments. C can then discount the bill(s) for immediate cash payment.

Because the value of a bill depends on the credit-worthiness of the drawee its value may be increased if drawn on and accepted by a respected and credit-worthy institution, such as a bank. In example 1 above, therefore, B may agree with his bank that it will accept a bill of exchange for the price of goods sold by S; S will therefore reduce the price to reflect the increased marketability and value of a bill accepted by B's bank. B will, of course, have to pay his bank for providing this facility. Arrangements such as this are particularly common in international transactions where goods are paid for by means of a documentary credit under whose terms B's bank agrees to accept a bill of exchange drawn on it for the price (see **Chapter 23**).

22.2.2   Advice on bills of exchange

The legal adviser may be required to advise on a bill of exchange in two situations. A client may seek advice on the consequences and advisability of giving or accepting a bill, perhaps in payment under a commercial contract. Alternatively, when someone seeks to enforce the bill the legal adviser may be asked to advise the person seeking to enforce the bill or the person against whom it is to be enforced. In that case the adviser will need to consider a series of questions.

(a) Is the bill valid?

(b) Is the person seeking to enforce entitled to enforce it?

(c) Is the person against whom it is enforced liable on it and are any defences available?

(d) Can the person against whom the bill is enforced pass on liability by enforcing the bill against someone else?

(e) What steps must be taken to enforce the bill?

These questions are considered in the following paragraphs.

22.2.3   The law relating to bills of exchange

The law relating to bills of exchange is contained in the Bills of Exchange Act (BoEA) 1882.

22.2.4   Definition of a bill of exchange

A bill of exchange is defined as:

an unconditional order in writing addressed by one person to another, signed by the person giving it, requiring the person to whom it is addressed to pay on demand or at a fixed or determinable future time a sum certain in money to or to the order of a specified person, or to bearer (BoEA 1882, s. 3(1)).

An instrument which does not comply with all the elements of this definition is not a bill of exchange (s. 3(2)).

A typical bill of exchange might therefore look like this:-

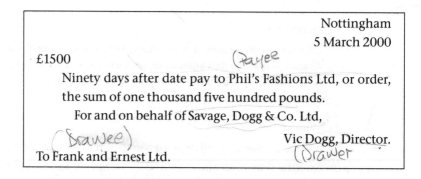

Nottingham
5 March 2000

£1500   (Payee)

Ninety days after date pay to Phil's Fashions Ltd, or order,
the sum of one thousand five hundred pounds.
For and on behalf of Savage, Dogg & Co. Ltd,

(Drawee)   Vic Dogg, Director.
To Frank and Ernest Ltd.   (Drawer)

Here Savage, Dogg & Co. Ltd are drawers of the bill, Frank and Ernest Ltd are the drawees and Phil's Fashions Ltd the payee.

22.2.4.1   Unconditional order

A bill of exchange must contain an order, or demand to pay, as opposed to a mere request. The order must be unconditional, in the sense that there must be no condition on the drawee's liability to pay. An order to pay dependent on a contingency, such as 'provided the goods are satisfactory' or 'if X is made redundant', is not a bill of exchange.

The unconditional nature of the order to pay gives the bill of exchange one of its most important commercial features. The undertaking to pay in a bill is separate from any underlying commercial contract in connection with which the bill is drawn. Thus if B buys goods and accepts a bill drawn on him by S for the price, B cannot avoid liability on the bill on the grounds of an (alleged) breach of the underlying contract of sale. The only exceptions are where a breach of the underlying contract results in a total failure of the consideration for which the bill was given, as where S repudiates the contract and refuses to deliver the goods, or a partial failure of consideration in a quantifiable amount (*Nova Jersey Knit Ltd* v *Kammgarn Spinnerei GmbH* [1977] 2 All ER 463). Thus in Example 1 in **22.2.1**, if S delivers goods which are defective but B keeps the goods, B cannot set up the defects in order to justify refusing to honour the bill. He must honour the bill and then claim damages for S's breach of contract in separate proceedings. If B fails to honour the bill, S can seek summary judgment on it.

In *Esso Petroleum Co. Ltd* v *Milton* [1997] 2 All ER 593 it was held that the same rule applies to direct debits so that a person who has agreed to payment for goods or services by direct debit is liable for breach of contract if the debit is cancelled and cannot justify cancellation on the grounds of a breach of contract by the payee, unless the breach gives rise to a total, or quantifiable partial, failure of consideration.

To avoid abuse, the use of bills of exchange as payment of, or as security for, sums due under a regulated consumer credit agreement is restricted by the Consumer Credit Act 1974.

An order to pay 'provided there are funds available' or out of a specified fund is conditional and is therefore not a bill of exchange. However, an unconditional bill with an indication of a fund out of which the drawee is to reimburse himself is valid (BoEA 1882, s. 3(3)): thus a cheque drawn on a particular account is a valid bill of exchange.

22.2.4.2   In writing

A bill of exchange may be typewritten or printed (BoEA 1882, s. 2) or otherwise represented in visible form (Interpretation Act 1978, s. 5).

22.2.4.3   Addressed by one person to another

Drawer and payee may be the same person (BoEA 1882, s. 5(1)) but drawer and drawee should be different persons. If a person draws a bill on himself, a holder may treat it as a bill or a promissory note, whichever is more favourable (s. 5(2)). The drawee must be named or otherwise indicated in the bill with reasonable certainty (s. 6). A bill addressed to two drawees in succession or in the alternative is not valid (s. 6(2)).

22.2.4.4   Signed by the drawer

Until signed by the drawer a bill is not valid. However, a person may sign through an agent. The effect of forged signatures and signature by agents is examined below (see **22.2.7.2**). The example bill in **22.2.4** is signed by Vic Dogg as agent for Savage, Dogg & Co. Ltd.

22.2.4.5   Payable on demand or at a fixed or determinable future time

A bill payable 'at sight' or 'on presentation' is payable on demand. A bill may be drawn payable at a fixed future date, e.g. on 31 December 2000, or at a determinable future date, e.g. '90 days after date' (in which case it is payable 90 days after the date in the bill) or '90 days after sight' (in which case it is payable 90 days after presentation for acceptance; such a bill must be presented for acceptance in order to fix the date for payment). A bill payable '90 days after acceptance' would not be valid, since it would not contain an *unconditional* order to pay: the payment obligation would be dependent on acceptance by the drawee, but if such a bill is accepted by the drawee it may take effect as a promissory note by the drawee (*Novaknit Hellas SA* v *Kumar Bros International Ltd* [1998] Com LC 971). The example bill in **22.2.4** is payable ninety days after date—i.e. on 3 June 2000.

22.2.4.6   To pay a sum certain in money

A bill may order payment in instalments, with interest at a specified rate or in foreign currency at a stated rate of exchange (s. 9). Where the sum payable is expressed in words and figures and there is a discrepancy between the two, the words prevail over the figures.

22.2.4.7   To or to the order of a specified person or to bearer

A bill may be payable to a named person: e.g. 'pay P Jones'. The addition of the words 'or order' ('pay P Jones or order') confirms that the bill is transferable, although the bill is transferable even without those words unless it is expressed to be payable to 'P Jones only'. Alternatively, the bill may be drawn payable to bearer. A bill payable to a named payee is transferable by delivery plus indorsement; a bearer bill is transferable by simple delivery. The example bill in **22.2.4** is an order bill, payable to Phil's Fashions Ltd or order. An instrument which is payable neither to bearer nor to a named payee (e.g. 'to cash' or 'to wages') is not a valid bill of exchange. A bill payable to a non-existent or fictitious payee is treated as a bearer bill and is thus transferable by delivery without indorsement (s. 7(3)). The case law on this point is complex, but briefly a payee is 'fictitious' for this purpose even though there is a real person with the same name as that given for the payee, provided that the drawer of the bill did not intend that person to receive payment of the bill (see *Bank of England* v *Vagliano Bros* [1891] AC 107; *Clutton* v *Attenborough* [1897] AC 90; contrast *Vinden* v *Hughes* [1905] 1 KB 795).

22.2.4.8   Other information

In addition to the details required by s. 3, a bill of exchange may contain other information.

(a) The bill may be dated with the date when it is drawn. Although this is common, an undated bill is valid unless it is made payable 'n days after date' in which case the date must be included to fix the date of payment. However, if no date is stated, any holder may complete the bill by inserting the date, and if the bill comes into the hands of a holder in due course the date so inserted is deemed to be correct.

(b) The bill may include a statement of the place(s) where it is drawn and/or payable. A bill which is drawn and payable within the British Isles, or drawn in the British Isles on a person resident in the British Isles, is classified as an 'inland bill'. All other bills are 'foreign bills'. The distinction between inland and foreign bills is important if the bill is dishonoured, when a special procedure must be followed before a foreign bill can be enforced against the drawer or indorsers. The example bill in **22.2.4** is an inland bill.

22.2.4.9   Incomplete bills

Although a bill which does not comply with the requirements of s. 3 is not a valid bill of exchange, any person in possession of an incomplete (or 'inchoate') bill has prima facie authority to complete it (s. 20) and if a person signs a paper and delivers it to another person in order that it can be converted into a bill of exchange, the person to whom it is delivered has prima facie authority to complete it as a bill of exchange for any amount, using the signature as the signature either of drawer or drawee. The original signatory is only liable under this provision if the bill is completed within a reasonable time and in accordance with the actual authority given; however, if the bill comes into the hands of a holder in due course it is conclusively presumed that these requirements are fulfilled. Moreover, the bill can be enforced as completed against any person who becomes a party to it after its completion.

22.2.5   Transfer of bills of exchange

The commercial significance of bills of exchange depends on the fact that they are transferable and negotiable. Strictly 'transferability' and 'negotiability' are separate concepts, negotiation of an instrument indicating a transfer which allows the transferee to take the instrument free of any defects in the transferor's title. The Bills of Exchange Act 1882 uses 'negotiate' merely as a synonym for 'transfer'; however, we propose here to use 'negotiate' in its true sense and to talk more generally of the 'transfer' of bills.

Prima facie, all bills are transferable unless their transferability is restricted by the parties. A bill (other than a cheque) payable 'to X only', or crossed 'not transferable' or 'not negotiable' is not transferable (BoEA 1882, s. 8). The effect of crossings on cheques is examined at **22.3.2.1**.

The method by which a bill is transferred depends on whether it is a bearer or order bill.

22.2.5.1   Transfer of bearer bills

A bearer bill can be transferred by simple delivery (BoEA 1882, s. 31(2)), i.e. by transferring physical possession of the bill.

22.2.5.2   Transfer of order bills

An order bill is transferred by indorsement and delivery (BoEA 1882, s. 31 (3)). In order to indorse a bill the payee must sign his name, either on the reverse of the bill or on a slip of paper attached to the bill and known as an 'allonge'. The indorsement may be general, special or restrictive.

(a) *General indorsement*

A general indorsement consists merely of the payee's signature. Its effect is to convert an order bill into a bearer bill, so that after a general indorsement the bill can be transferred by simple delivery. However, any holder can convert a generally indorsed bill back into an order bill by writing the name of a person as transferee/payee above the indorser's signature.

(b) *Special indorsement*

A special indorsement consists of the payee's signature together with the name of a person to whom the bill is to be transferred.

EXAMPLE

Jones draws a bill of exchange payable to 'Savage or order'. Savage can transfer the bill to Daley by a special indorsement, in which case he will write on it 'pay Daley' and sign his name. Alternatively he can indorse it generally, in which case he need only sign his name on the bill and deliver it to Daley.

If the bill is specially indorsed, Daley can transfer it to Trotter by indorsing it. If the bill is generally indorsed, Daley can transfer it to Trotter by simple delivery; alternatively he can re-convert it to an order bill by writing Trotter's name above Savage's signature.

(c) *Restrictive indorsement*

A restrictive indorsement restricts further transfer of the bill, either by prohibiting further transfer or by indicating that it is transferred in order to be dealt with in a particular way. For instance, the bill in the example above might be indorsed by Savage 'pay Daley only' in which case Daley cannot further transfer the bill. Alternatively, he could indorse it 'pay Daley for the account of Savage' in which case it is clear that the bill is transferred to Daley merely in order that he can collect payment on behalf of Savage.

In the absence of a restrictive indorsement there is (in theory) no limit to the number of times a bill may be transferred.

22.2.5.3   Forged and unauthorised signatures

An order bill can only be transferred by indorsement with the signature of the payee or last indorsee. A forged or unauthorised signature has no effect, unless ratified, and the transferee acquires no title to the bill through a forged or unauthorised indorsement (BoEA 1882, s. 24).

The distinction between a forged indorsement and one which is merely unauthorised is unclear and may be difficult to draw but it is clear that an unauthorised indorsement can, while a forged indorsement cannot, be ratified. However, a forged indorsement is not wholly ineffective.

(a) A person who takes a bill as a result of a forged indorsement can enforce the bill against the person who transferred the bill to him (i.e. the forger) but not against persons who became parties to the bill before the forgery.

(b) A person who takes a bill as a result of forged indorsement may be able to retain it as against the true holder if the holder is estopped from setting up the forgery or unauthorised signature.

In addition, where a bill is drawn payable to a non-existent or fictitious payee, it is treated as a bearer bill so that it can be transferred without indorsement (BoEA 1882, s. 7(3): see above **22.2.4.7**). A person to whom such a bill is indorsed can therefore acquire title to it and enforce it, notwithstanding the fact that the signature on the bill is a 'forgery', since his title to the bill does not depend on the signature.

22.2.6 Holders

The person entitled to enforce a bill of exchange, by presenting it for payment or by taking enforcement proceedings if it is dishonoured, is called 'the holder' of the bill. Only payment to the holder of a bill can discharge the payer's liability on the bill.

The holder of a bearer bill is the bearer; the holder of an order bill is the payee or indorsee in possession of it.

The Bills of Exchange Act 1882 recognises three different classes of holder, with different rights:

(a) holders;

(b) holders for value; and

(c) holders in due course.

Since 'holder' status depends, at least in part, on possession of the bill, only one person can be a holder of a bill at any one time. Having decided who is the holder, it will then be necessary to classify the holder into one of these three categories in order to decide what rights he enjoys and what, if any, defences can be raised against him if he seeks to enforce the bill.

22.2.6.1 Holders

A mere holder has fewest rights. He is entitled:

(a) to transfer the bill;

(b) to insert the date in the bill if it has been omitted; and

(c) to present the bill for payment.

In addition every holder is rebuttably presumed to be a holder in due course unless it is shown that the bill was issued, accepted or negotiated 'by fraud or duress or force and fear or illegality', in which case the burden of proof is transferred to the holder to show that the bill has subsequently been transferred for value in good faith (BoEA 1882, s. 30).

22.2.6.2 Holders for value

Since liability on a bill of exchange is contractual, a person against whom a holder seeks to enforce the bill can deny liability if he received no consideration for the bill. However, a holder for value can overcome this objection. A holder will be a holder for value if he or any previous holder provided consideration for the bill and for this purpose the consideration may be any consideration which would be sufficient to support a simple contract, or an antecedent debt, or liability of the person against whom the bill is to be enforced.

EXAMPLE

Smith sells 20 suits to Jones for £1,000. One month after delivery Jones accepts a bill of exchange for £1,000 in favour of Smith. Smith is a holder for value, Jones's existing debt providing consideration for the promise of payment contained in his acceptance of the bill.

Smith subsequently transfers the bill to White as a birthday present. White is also a holder for value, since Smith provided value for it.

22.2.6.3   Holders in due course

A holder for value can enforce the bill even though the person against whom he enforces it received no consideration for his promise to pay. However, other defences may be raised against a holder for value; for instance, that the bill was obtained by fraud or duress. A holder in due course, however, can enforce the bill free from all defences and defects in title of his predecessors in title. A holder in due course is defined in BoEA 1882, s. 29 as:

a holder who has taken a bill complete and regular on the face of it, under the following conditions; namely,

(a)   that he became the holder of it before it was overdue and without notice that it had previously been dishonoured, if such was the fact; and

(b)   that he took the bill in good faith and for value, and that at the time the bill was negotiated to him he had no notice of any defect in the title of the person who negotiated it.

A number of requirements must therefore be fulfilled if a person is to qualify as a holder in due course.

(a)   *He must be a holder*

It has been held that for this purpose the original payee of a bill cannot be a holder in due course in his capacity as payee (*RE Jones Ltd v Waring & Gillow Ltd* [1926] AC 670), but he may be a holder in due course if he transfers the bill and it is later negotiated back to him (*Jade International Steel Stahl und Eisen GmbH & Co. KG v Robert Nicholas (Steels) Ltd* [1978] QB 917).

A person who acquires an order bill by means of a forged indorsement can never qualify as a holder and therefore cannot qualify as a holder in due course.

(b)   *The bill must be complete and regular on its face*

If any of the details which should be included in a bill is missing at the time it is transferred, the transferee cannot qualify as a holder in due course, although he has prima facie authority to complete an inchoate bill (s. 20: see **22.2.4.9**). If he does so a subsequent transferee may qualify as a holder in due course.

It has been held that 'face' includes the rear of the bill so that if an indorsement is missing from the rear of the bill, it is not complete and regular on its face (*Arab Bank Ltd v Ross* [1952] 2 QB 216).

(c)   *The bill must have been transferred to him before it was overdue*

A bill is overdue when the time for payment has passed. A bill payable on demand is overdue if it has been in circulation for 'an unreasonable length of time' (s. 36(3)), which is a question of fact. Banks generally regard cheques as overdue if presented for payment more than six months after they are drawn.

(d)   *He must have taken the bill without notice of its having been dishonoured*

A bill may be dishonoured by non-acceptance or by non-payment.

(e) *He must have taken the bill in good faith and without notice of any defect in the transferor's title*

'Notice' here means actual, not merely constructive notice and, provided that he acts honestly, a person is not regarded as acting in bad faith merely because he is negligent (BoEA 1882, s. 90). However, a person who deliberately disregards suspicious circumstances may be regarded as acting in bad faith and will, in any case, have to discharge an evidential burden in order to convince the court that he was not aware of facts which a reasonable person would have appreciated.

A person's title may be defective for this purpose 'when he obtained the bill, or the acceptance thereof, by fraud, duress or force and fear, or other unlawful means, or an illegal consideration, or when he negotiates it in breach of faith, or under such circumstances as amount to fraud' (s. 29(2)).

(f) *He must have taken the bill 'for value'*

It is sufficient if value is given by the holder himself or has at any previous time been given for the bill: the holder need not himself have given value for it (*Clifford Chance* v *Silver* [1992] 2 BLR 11.

22.2.6.4   Subsequent holders

Once a bill has come into the hands of a holder in due course, all prior defects in title are cured. Subsequent holders can therefore enforce the bill against all persons who became party to it before it came into the hands of the holder in due course, free of all defects in title, even if they are aware of them. The only exception is that a person who acquires a bill through a holder in due course cannot take free of defects if he was party to the conduct which gave rise to the defect.

EXAMPLE

Savage draws a bill of exchange in favour of himself on Jones and obtains Jones's acceptance by duress. Savage then transfers the bill to Smith, for value, in circumstances which allow Smith to qualify as a holder in due course. Smith then transfers the bill to White, who is aware that Savage obtained it by duress; White can nevertheless enforce the bill against Jones who cannot deny liability on the basis that it was obtained by duress. However, if White transfers the bill back to Savage and he tries to enforce it, Jones can raise the defence of duress as Savage was party to the original duress.

22.2.7   Liability on a bill

The general rule is that every person who puts his name to a bill, as drawer, acceptor or indorser, becomes liable on it and the bill can be enforced against him by persons to whom it is subsequently transferred. In addition, a person who transfers a bearer bill may be liable in certain circumstances if it is dishonoured. The person primarily liable is the acceptor or, if the bill is not accepted, the drawer; other parties are only liable if the person primarily liable fails to honour the bill.

22.2.7.1   Capacity

No-one can be held liable on a bill unless he has the capacity to incur contractual liability. A minor cannot be held liable on a bill, even if it is given in payment for a debt he did have capacity to incur.

A company's liability on bills depends on its powers under its constitution. A trading company will generally have implied, if not express, power to draw, accept and indorse bills of exchange.

22.2.7.2 Signature

A person's liability on a bill prima facie depends on him having signed it. Difficulties arise if a person whose signature appears on a bill claims that it was placed there without his authority. The signature may be forged or unauthorised.

(a) *Forged signatures*

A person whose signature on a bill is forged incurs no liability unless he is estopped from asserting the forgery, as, for instance, if having become aware that his signature on the bill had been forged, he stood by while the person seeking to enforce the bill gave value for it.

If the drawer's signature on the bill is forged there is no bill of exchange at all.

(b) *Unauthorised signatures*

A person incurs no liability on a bill through an unauthorised signature unless he is estopped from denying the signor's authority or he subsequently ratifies the signature.

Where a bill is signed by an agent it may indicate that fact by being signed in the name of the principal '*per procurationem*' (or 'per pro' or 'p.p.') the agent, whose name should also be placed on the bill (note that contrary to popular understanding the correct formula is 'principal per pro agent' and not vice versa). The use of such a formula acts as notice that the agent's authority to sign the bill may be limited, and the principal is then only bound by the agent's signature if he had actually authorised it.

(c) *Agent's liability*

An agent who signs a bill on behalf of his principal may incur personal liability on it if he signs his own name, unless his signature clearly indicates that he signs as agent and does not undertake personal liability (s. 26(1)). In deciding whether a signature is that of the agent personally, or that of his principal, the court should adopt the construction most favourable to the validity of the bill (s. 26(2)). Thus a company director who signs a bill on behalf of the company in his own name may be taken to have undertaken personal liability. Even if he adds the word 'director' after his name he may be taken merely to have described his office rather than to have made a clear indication that he does not undertake personal liability, especially if the company would, in any case, be liable on the bill (*see Rolfe Lubell & Co.* v *Keith* [1979] 1 All ER 860).

Every company bill or cheque must contain written or printed details of the company name; if not, any person who signs the bill on behalf of the company is personally liable on it (Companies Act 1985, s. 394). Where the bill does contain details of the company's name, a director who signs his own name may escape personal liability.

22.2.7.3 Delivery

Every contract on a bill is incomplete and revocable until the bill is delivered (s. 21). The only exceptional case, where liability is complete without delivery, is if the drawee of a bill notifies the person entitled to payment that he accepts the bill.

'Delivery' means simply transfer of possession. Delivery may be conditional: for instance, if a person orders goods and gives the seller a bill for the price, he may deliver the bill conditionally on delivery of the goods.

Since delivery is necessary to complete liability on a bill, a person who signs a bill and then loses it, or has it stolen, is *prima facie* not liable on it. However, it is rebuttably presumed that a bill has been delivered by every signatory to it and if the bill comes into the hands of a holder in due course it is irrebuttably presumed that it has been delivered by all prior parties to it. Thus if a person draws a bill payable to bearer and it is then stolen, it can be enforced against him by a holder in due course despite the fact that it was never delivered. If the bill were drawn in favour of a named payee 'or order' no-one claiming through the thief could be a holder in due course since the payee's signature would (necessarily) be missing or forged.

22.2.7.4   The undertakings given by parties to the bill

Each person who becomes a party to a bill by signing and delivering it gives certain undertakings relating to its payment. In addition, each party is bound by certain estoppels relating to existing facts and events prior to his becoming party to the bill.

(a) *Acceptor*

The acceptor is the party primarily liable on the bill. By accepting the bill he undertakes that at maturity he will honour the bill in accordance with the terms of his acceptance. In addition, as against a holder in due course, he is estopped from denying: the drawer's existence, capacity and authority to draw the bill; the genuineness of the drawer's signature and the payee's existence and capacity to indorse the bill (BoEA 1882, s. 54).

(b) *Accommodation parties*

A person may accept a bill in order to increase its marketability by lending the value of his name to the bill to increase its marketability. Such a person is referred to as 'an accommodation party'.

EXAMPLE

If A wishes to borrow money from B, he may draw on C, and get C to accept, a bill in favour of B for the amount of the loan. Effectively C acts as guarantor of the loan; he is then an accommodation party and the bill is an accommodation bill.

Where a person accepts a bill as an accommodation party the drawer, and not the acceptor, is primarily liable on the bill. Thus if C is called on to pay the bill he may seek re-imbursement from A.

(c) *The drawer*

The drawer undertakes that on presentation the bill will be accepted and paid and that if not he will compensate the holder or any indorsee who pays the bill, provided that the necessary dishonour proceedings are taken. As against a holder in due course, he is estopped from denying the existence of the payee and his capacity to indorse the bill.

(d) *Indorsers*

Each person who indorses the bill becomes party to it and gives the same undertakings as the drawer. He is estopped, as against a holder in due course, from denying the genuineness and regularity of the drawer's signature or of any indorsements prior to his own. In addition, as against subsequent indorsees, he is estopped from denying that the bill was valid and that he had a good title to it at the time of his indorsement.

EXAMPLE

A draws a bill of exchange on B, payable to C. It is stolen by D, who forges C's indorsement and transfers it to E, who transfers it to F.

A ➡ B ➡ C D ➡ E ➡ F

Since no title to a bill is conferred by a forged signature, F has no title to the bill as against A, B and C; however, both D and E are bound as indorsers and both are estopped from denying that they had a good title to it at the time of their indorsements. F can therefore enforce the bill against D or E; similarly if E pays F, E can enforce the bill against D.

(e) *Other parties*

Any other person who signs a bill is liable on it as if he were an indorser.

(f) *Signature without recourse*

The drawer and indorsers of the bill can avoid liability on it by drawing/indorsing it 'without recourse', in which case he will add the words 'without recourse' or '*sans recours*' after his signature to indicate to future parties that he accepts no liability for the bill's being honoured.

(g) *Transferor of a bearer bill*

A person who transfers a bearer bill by simple delivery gives the following warranties to the transferee:

(i)   that the bill is genuine as it purports to be;

(ii)   that he has the right to transfer it; and

(iii) that he is not aware of any facts which make the bill worthless.

22.2.8   Enforcement of the bill

Unless a bill is an accommodation bill the person primarily liable to honour it is the drawee. However, if he fails to honour it, either by refusing to accept or pay it, the holder may take steps against any prior party to the bill to enforce their undertakings with regard to the bill, as described above. The BoEA 1882, prescribes certain steps which the holder must take on dishonour if he is to enforce the bill against anyone other than the drawee; generally failure to take the prescribed steps will release some or all previous parties from liability on the bill.

22.2.8.1   Presentation of the bill

The holder must present the bill:

(a) for acceptance; and

(b) for payment.

Although a bill may be presented to the drawee in person, it is common for bills to be presented by the holder's bank to the drawee's bank, the banks acting as agents.

(a) *Presentation for acceptance*

Presentation for acceptance is not necessary if the bill is payable on demand. However, bills other than cheques payable at a future date will generally be presented for acceptance since acceptance will increase their marketability by adding the drawee's undertaking to pay the bill to that of the drawer. A bill payable 'n days after sight' or 'n days after presentation' must be presented for acceptance in order to fix the date of maturity. The holder of such a bill must present it for acceptance or transfer it within a reasonable time, otherwise the drawer and any previous indorser will be released from liability.

When the drawee accepts a bill presented to him he will endorse his acceptance on the bill and sign it as acceptor.

The drawee should accept the bill as drawn; if he imposes conditions or varies the terms of the bill, it is dishonoured. If the holder accepts a qualified acceptance of the bill, the drawer and previous indorsers are released from liability unless they agree to the qualification. However, if the acceptor gives a partial acceptance, for instance by accepting the bill for only part of the amount for which it is drawn, the holder may:

(i)   treat the bill as wholly dishonoured; or

(ii)   treat the bill as dishonoured only as regards the difference.

He may therefore enforce the bill against the acceptor for the amount of the acceptance and take dishonour proceedings for the balance.

(b) *Presentation for payment*

All bills must be presented for payment at the time and place indicated by their terms. Failure to present at the proper time and place will generally release prior parties from liability.

22.2.8.2   Notice of dishonour

If the drawee fails to accept the bill as drawn, or having accepted it, fails to pay it, the bill is dishonoured by non-acceptance or non-payment as appropriate. In that case the holder can enforce the undertakings given by the drawer or indorsers but in order to do so must within a reasonable time give notice of dishonour to every previous party to be held liable. Notice of dishonour is excused in certain circumstances (BoEA 1882, s. 49) but generally failure to notify any party of dishonour will release that party from liability on the bill.

A notice of dishonour given by one party to another protects not only the person giving the notice but also all intermediate parties in the liability chain.

EXAMPLE

A draws a bill on B, payable to C. C indorses it in favour of D who presents it to B. B refuses payment and D gives notice of dishonour to A and C. He can then take enforcement proceedings against either C or A; if he takes proceedings against C, C can in turn take proceedings against A, relying on the notice given by D.

22.2.8.3   Noting and protesting

If a foreign bill (see **22.2.4.8**) is dishonoured the holder must also have it noted and protested by a notary public (s. 51). This procedure provides evidence of dishonour which is acceptable in enforcement proceedings overseas.

22.2.9   Defences to liability on a bill

A person against whom it is sought to enforce a bill of exchange may raise a number of defences in order to seek to avoid liability. The validity of some of these defences depends on whether the relationship between the person seeking to enforce the bill and the person against whom the bill is to be enforced is immediate or remote. The relationships between drawer and drawee, drawer and payee and between indorser and indorsee are all immediate; all other relationships are remote. Thus the relationship between a person to whom a bill is indorsed and the original acceptor of the bill is remote.

(a) As against an immediate party a person may avoid liability on a bill by showing that his undertaking on the bill is voidable on the grounds of duress, misrepresentation or undue influence.

(b) As against an immediate party a person may avoid liability by showing that there is a total failure of the consideration for which that undertaking was given; there may be such a failure as a result of a breach of the underlying contract.

(c) A person may deny liability to the person seeking to enforce the bill by showing that that person has no title to it.

(d) A person may deny liability by showing that he is not a party to the bill on the grounds that his signature on the bill was forged or placed there without his authority.

(e) A person may deny liability by showing that there is no valid bill, because the statutory requirements for a valid bill are not fulfilled.

(f) A person other than the acceptor may avoid liability by showing that the required proceedings were not taken on dishonour.

(g) A person may avoid liability by showing that the bill has been materially altered without his consent. If a bill is materially altered and the alteration is apparent, the bill is wholly avoided as against all persons who became party to the bill before the alteration, unless they consent to it. Where the alteration is not apparent, a holder in due course may enforce the bill against persons who became party to it prior to the alteration in accordance with its original terms.

An altered bill may be enforced as *altered* against any person who becomes party to it after the alteration.

The following are material alterations:

(i) alteration of the date or amount of the bill or of the time or place of payment (BoEA 1882, s. 64(2));

(ii) alteration of the name of the payee (*Slingsby* v *District Bank* [1932] 1 KB 544); and

(iii) any other alteration which affects the rights of the parties (*Koch* v *Dicks* [1933] 1 KB 307).

22.2.10 Discharge of a bill

The person primarily liable on a bill of exchange is the drawee/acceptor. However, if he fails to honour the bill, the holder may either:

(a) seek to enforce his undertaking on the bill by legal action; or

(b) enforce the bill against one of the other parties liable on it, providing the appropriate proceedings have been taken on dishonour.

If anyone other than the drawee/acceptor pays the bill, all subsequent parties are discharged from liability but the bill generally remains enforceable against prior parties.

An indorser who pays a bill may either:

(a) cancel all endorsements subsequent to his own and re-issue it for value; or

(b) enforce the bill against a previous party.

If the drawer pays the bill he may enforce it against the drawee/acceptor, unless it was an accommodation bill.

EXAMPLE

A draws a bill on B, payable to C. C transfers the bill to D by indorsing it and D transfers to E in the same way. If B fails to honour the bill on presentation, E should give notice of dishonour to D, C and A. He may then enforce it against any of them. If he enforces it against C, as indorser, D is discharged but C may either cancel D's indorsement and re-issue the bill, or enforce the bill against A or B.

The undertakings contained in the bill therefore remain enforceable until the bill is discharged.

A bill may be discharged in the following ways.

(a) By payment in due course by or on behalf of the drawee/acceptor. A payment is only 'in due course' if made:

(i)   on or after maturity;

(ii)   to the holder; and

(iii) in good faith without notice of any defect in the holder's title.

Payment to anyone other than the holder leaves the party making payment liable to pay the true owner, except that special statutory rules may protect a bank which pays a cheque other than to the true holder (see **22.3.2.4**). The payer may be able to recover the money by a restitutionary claim.

(b) By cancellation of the bill or of the liability of one or more parties (s. 63).

(c) By the holder renouncing his rights either on the bill as a whole or against one or more individual parties (s. 62).

(d) If the bill is negotiated back to the acceptor so that he becomes holder of it.

End Of Bills Of Exchange

22.3 Cheques

A cheque is defined by the Bills of Exchange Act 1882, s. 73 as 'a bill of exchange drawn on a banker payable on demand'. It follows therefore that a valid cheque must satisfy the requirements for a valid bill of exchange (see **22.2.4**).

In general the law applicable to bills of exchange applies equally to cheques; however, it is supplemented by certain provisions applicable only to cheques and contained, particularly, in the Cheques Acts 1957 and 1992.

Unlike other bills, a cheque is not accepted by the drawee, so that the bank on which it is drawn is under no obligation to the payee to honour the cheque. Instead, primary liability on a cheque falls on the drawer. This is slightly modified where a cheque is supported by a cheque guarantee card, in which case the bank does come under an obligation to the payee, but that obligation is based on the undertaking contained in the card rather than any undertaking in the cheque itself. However, the drawee bank is in all cases under an obligation to its customer to honour cheques drawn by him so long as there are sufficient funds credited to his account to meet the cheque.

22.3.1 The banker-customer relationship *⟶ 3rd topic*

Essentially, the relationship between banker and customer is one of debtor–creditor: when the customer deposits money with the bank the money becomes the bank's property, subject to an obligation on the bank to repay the sum deposited, with interest as agreed. The position is, of course, reversed if the customer's account is overdrawn so that he becomes a debtor of the bank. The bank's basic obligations are:

(a) to receive money from, and to collect bills of exchange on behalf of, its customer;

(b) to hold such moneys and the proceeds of bills so collected as a debtor of the customer;

(c) to repay the sum so held on demand, or against the customer's written order(s), to make payments during banking hours at the branch where the customer's account is held (*Joachimson v Swiss Bank Corp.* [1921] 3 KB 110).

The bank is therefore obliged to honour its customer's instructions to make payments. When it does so it pays its own money and reimburses itself by debiting the customer's account, thus reducing the amount of its debt to the customer.

22.3.1.1   The bank's mandate

The bank is obliged by the terms of its contract to honour its customer's instructions, or *mandate*, provided there are sufficient funds credited to the customer's account (including when the customer has been granted an overdraft) to allow the bank to reimburse itself. Failure to do so is a breach of the bank's contract with the customer, for which the bank may be liable in damages. Conversely the bank has no right to debit the customer's account for payments made without the customer's mandate.

The customer's mandate can be given in a number of ways, including by authorising standing order payments and direct debits or by signature of a slip used in conjunction with a bank payment card. In these cases the bank's authority to debit the customer's account depends on the customer's signature. Alternatively, where the customer uses an automated teller machine (ATM) or electronic funds transfer (EFT) system, he may author-ise a debit to his account by using a plastic card in conjunction with a personal identifi-cation number (PIN). However, for our purposes the most important form of bank mandate is that given by the customer's signature of a cheque.

22.3.1.2   Withdrawal of the mandate

The customer may generally withdraw the bank's mandate to make a payment at any time before payment is made. In the case of cheques this is done by countermanding or 'stop-ping' the cheque. Notice of countermand must be given to the branch on which the cheque is drawn (*Burnett* v *Westminster Bank Ltd* [1966] 1 QB 742) and is not effective until it reaches the teller or ledger clerk (*Curtice* v *London, City and Midland Bank Ltd* [1908] 1 KB 293). However, where the customer draws a cheque supported by a cheque card his freedom to withdraw his mandate may be restricted by the terms of the agreement under which the card is issued.

22.3.1.3   Use of cheque cards

Where the customer draws a cheque supported by a cheque guarantee card the bank is obliged to the payee to honour the cheque even if there are insufficient funds to the credit of the customer's account to cover the cheque, provided certain conditions are fulfilled. The conditions may be set out on the card or in a separate document; typically they require that:

(a) the cheque be signed in the presence of the payee;

(b) the card be produced to the payee when the cheque is signed;

(c) the signature on the cheque match the specimen signature on the cheque card;

(d) the payee write the number of the card on the reverse of the cheque (to allow the bank to confirm that the card was indeed presented); and

(e) the amount for which the cheque is drawn (together with any other cheque taken from the same cheque book in respect of the same transaction) should not exceed a stated amount, generally £50.

These conditions constitute the terms of an offer of a unilateral contract; if they are ful-filled the bank is contractually bound to honour the cheque. Where the terms are set out on the card the bank's offer is conveyed to the payee by the person in possession of the card acting as the bank's agent. In *First Sport* v *Barclays Bank plc* [1993] 3 All ER 789 it was held that even if the person presenting the card is not the authorised card holder he nevertheless has apparent authority to make the offer on behalf of the bank. The bank was therefore bound to honour a cheque when the conditions described above were satisfied, even though the person who presented the card and signed the cheque was not the true card holder. However, the standard conditions of the bank's offer have since been varied so that the first requires that the cheque be signed in the presence of the payee *by the person whose name appears on the card*. Thus if the person signing the cheque is not the true card holder the bank is not obliged to honour the cheque.

22.3.1.4   Duties of the parties

An essential function of the bank under the terms of its contract with the customer is the collection and payment of bills, including cheques. The bank owes its customer a duty of care in collecting and paying bills and cheques on his behalf. The customer owes the bank a reciprocal duty of care in drawing cheques and in operating his account, including a duty to notify the bank of any forgery or fraud on his account of which he becomes aware (*Greenwood* v *Martins Bank Ltd* [1933] AC 51) and a duty to take care in drawing cheques so as not to facilitate alteration or fraud (*London Joint Stock Bank Ltd* v *Macmillan and Arthur* [1918] AC 777). However, there is no duty on the customer, either in tort or in contract, to check bank statements or to seek to detect fraud on his account, unless such a duty is imposed by the express terms of the contract between him and the bank (*Tai Hing Cotton Mill Ltd* v *Liu Chong Hing Bank Ltd* [1986] AC 80).

22.3.2   Collection and payment of cheques

The payee of a cheque must collect payment from the bank on which it is drawn. This may be done in three ways:

(a) by presenting the cheque, in person, to the bank on which it is drawn at the branch where the drawer's account is held;

(b) by presenting the cheque through the clearing system; in this case the payee employs a bank to act as his agent to present the cheque and collect payment;

(c) by discounting the cheque for cash, in the same way as any other bill; in this case the payee is not concerned with collection of the cheque and the person to whom he transfers it will have to collect it or himself discount it.

22.3.2.1   The effect of crossings on cheques

A cheque may be marked on its face with a crossing. The way in which a cheque is presented and collected may be affected by any crossing on it.

(a) *General crossings*
A cheque may be generally crossed: two parallel lines are drawn across its face and the words '&Co' may be written between them. Such a cheque must be presented through a bank account; the payee may not present it in person for cash payment.

(b) *Special crossings*
A special crossing is like a general crossing, except that it names a particular bank. In that case the cheque must be presented by and paid through the named bank.

(c) *Not negotiable*
A cheque crossed 'not negotiable' can be *transferred* but cannot be *negotiated* so that if it is transferred the transferee cannot take free of any defects in the transferor's title (BoEA 1882, s. 81).

(d) *Account payee only*

A cheque crossed 'Account (or "a/c") payee only' can be collected only for the named payee and is therefore not transferable (BoEA 1882, s. 81A).

A crossing is a material part of a cheque (BoEA 1882, s. 78) so that alteration of the crossing will avoid the cheque if it is apparent. However, the holder of an uncrossed cheque may add a crossing, and the holder of a crossed cheque may alter the crossing so as to make it more, but not less, restrictive: e.g. by changing a general crossing to a special crossing; such altera-tions do not prejudice the drawer of the cheque and therefore do not invalidate it.

If a bank pays a crossed cheque other than in accordance with the crossing it runs the risk that it may not have paid the true owner. If that is the case, it remains liable to the true owner of the cheque for its value and has no right to debit its customer's account for the wrongful payment.

22.3.2.2 The clearing system

Most cheques are presented, collected and paid through the clearing system; where the cheque is crossed it cannot be presented for personal payment, and most cheques are printed crossed.

The payee pays the cheque into his bank account; his bank then presents the cheque to the drawer's bank for clearing through a central system in London. Cheques are not individually paid; a list of mutual debits and credits is drawn up summarising each bank's dealings with each of the other banks involved in clearing and the relevant balance is transferred between the two banks at the end of each day's trading.

The cheque is actually presented at the branch where the drawer's account is held. If it is dishonoured it will be returned to the payee's bank marked with a statement of the reason for the dishonour. In that case the payee's account with his own bank will be debited with the amount of the cheque and there will have to be an adjustment of the account between the two banks. The payee may then take up the matter with the drawer and may initiate proceedings for non-payment of the cheque.

The drawer's bank must take care in dishonouring cheques. First, it is a breach of contract for the bank to dishonour a cheque if there are funds to the credit of the drawer's account to satisfy the cheque. It will generally be assumed that a customer (whether a trader or not) suffers loss as a result of wrongful dishonour of a cheque by reason of damage to his reputation and damages will therefore be payable without specific proof of loss (see *Kpohraror* v *Woolwich Building Society* [1996] 4 All ER 119). Secondly, the statement of the reason for dishonour must be worded with care since if false, including by implication, it may be regarded as defamatory. It has been held that the words 'Refer to drawer' imply that the funds credited to the drawer's account are insufficient to cover the cheque and that this is defamatory if untrue (*Jayson* v *Midland Bank Ltd* [1968] 1 Lloyd's Rep 409).

Where a cheque is collected in the way described above, the payee's bank acts as his agent and therefore owes him a duty of care. Alternatively, if the bank credits the payee's account before the cheque is cleared and allows him to draw against the uncleared cheque, it may in effect purchase the cheque and present it for itself as holder for value.

22.3.2.3 Liabilities of collecting and paying banks

Banks which collect or pay cheques for customers, including through the clearing system, are potentially exposed to legal liability. A bank which pays a cheque without its customer's mandate is in breach of contract and may not debit its customer's account. Conversely it may incur liability if it wrongfully refuses to pay a cheque. In addition, a bank which collects or pays a cheque other than for the true owner may incur liability to the true owner. Either bank may be liable for conversion of the cheque; in addition the collecting bank may be liable for money had and received for the amount of the cheque. These liabilities are generally strict; however, both paying and collecting banks may be protected by a number of defences at common law and, more importantly, under statute.

22.3.2.4   Protection of the paying bank

The main risk for a paying bank is that it may pay without its customer's mandate so that it may not debit the customer's account (and may incur additional liability if its breach of contract causes the customer any additional damage).

(a) *Common law protection*

The bank may be protected against liability to its customer at common law in the following circumstances:

(i)   if it pays out on a forged or unauthorised signature but the customer is estopped from setting up the forgery or lack of authority, either as a result of a representation or as a result of a breach of his duty of care in management of his account (see *Greenwood* v *Martins Bank Ltd* [1933] AC 51);

(ii)   if it pays out an altered cheque it may debit the customer's account for the original amount of the cheque if the alteration was not apparent; and the customer may be estopped from complaining of the alteration if it was facilitated by his negligence in drawing the cheque (*London Joint Stock Bank Ltd* v *Macmillan and Arthur* [1918] AC 777).

In addition, if the bank's payment discharges a liability of its customer it may be able to debit the customer's account relying on principles of subrogation. Where the bank makes an unauthorised payment, as where it pays on a forged cheque or pays someone other than the true owner, it may be able to recover the payment from the payee as money paid under a mistake of fact. It cannot recover on this basis, however, if its payment is authorised—as for instance where the bank mistakenly pays a cheque when there are insufficient funds in the drawer's account to cover the cheque (*Lloyds TSB plc* v *Industrial Insurance Co. Ltd* [1999] 1 All ER (Comm) 8).

(b) *Statutory protection*

The most important sources of protection for a paying bank are contained in the Bills of Exchange Act 1882, ss. 60, 80 and the Cheques Act 1957, s. 1.

(i)   Where the bank pays someone who has no title to the cheque because his title depends on a forged or unauthorised indorsement and the bank pays the cheque in good faith and in the ordinary course of business, it is deemed to have paid the cheque in due course (BoEA 1882, s. 60). It is therefore entitled to debit its customer's account but may still be liable to the true owner of the cheque in conversion. Section 60 will generally apply where the cheque is paid over the counter.

(ii)   Where a bank pays a crossed cheque in accordance with the crossing and does so in good faith and without negligence, it is treated as if it had paid the true owner (BoEA 1882, s. 80). It is therefore entitled to debit its customer's account and is protected against liability to the true owner. This provision will apply to most payments made through the clearing system provided the bank can show that it acted in good faith and without negligence. In addition the section also protects the drawer: provided that the cheque has come into the hands of the true owner prior to payment, the drawer is placed in the same position as if payment had been made to the true owner.

EXAMPLE

D buys goods from P and draws a cheque on the BAC bank in payment. P loses the cheque and it is found by T, who pays it into his account at the XYZ bank, forging P's signature as indorser. The cheque is presented to the BAC bank which pays it. The effect of s. 80 is that BAC is protected from liability to P, provided that it acted in good faith and without negligence; BAC can debit D's account; moreover, D is discharged from liability on the cheque. The effect, then, is that P must bear the loss of the cheque.

(iii) Where a bank pays a cheque in good faith and in the ordinary course of business it incurs no liability by reason only of the absence of, or irregularity in, any indorsement and is deemed to have paid in due course (Cheques Act 1957, s. 1). The effect of this provision is to remove the need for cheques to be indorsed when paid in for collection. It only protects the bank where the missing indorsement is that of the person who pays it in or presents it for payment. It only applies where the cheque is paid through clearing rather than over the counter, since banking practice is to require indorsement in the latter case (in accordance with a circular issued by the Committee of Clearing Bank Managers in 1957), so that payment without indorsement is not in the course of business.

Section 1 applies to certain other instruments which are not, strictly, cheques, such as 'cheques' drawn payable to 'cash' (see 22.2.4.7).

22.3.2.5 Protection of the collecting bank

A bank which collects a cheque other than for the true owner may be liable to the true owner in conversion or for money had and received. However, it may be protected by the Cheques Act 1957, s. 4, which provides that where a banker in good faith and without negligence:

(a) receives payment of a cheque on behalf of a customer; or

(b) having credited the customer's account with the amount of the cheque, receives payment for itself

and the customer has no title, or only a defective title, to the cheque, the bank incurs no liability to the true owner by reason only of collecting the cheque.

Where the bank credits the customer's account and allows him to draw against the cheque before it is cleared, it effectively collects the cheque for itself and is potentially protected by s. 4. However, if it pays cash for the cheque at the counter, it buys the cheque and becomes a holder for value. Since it does not credit the customer's account it is not protected by s. 4 but may qualify as a holder in due course, in which case it is the true owner of the cheque.

Where the section applies the bank is protected against all liability including for conversion and in money had and received (*Capital and Counties Bank Ltd* v *Gordon* [1903] AC 240).

The bank is only protected if it collects the cheque for, or credits the account of, a customer, meaning a person who has an account with the bank. A person who opens an account for the purpose of paying in and collecting a cheque becomes a customer.

The bank is not protected unless it acts without negligence. The bank may be held negligent, and therefore be unprotected, if the circumstances are such that they would have put a reasonable banker on enquiry that the customer's title might be defective, as for instance if it collects for an agent a cheque drawn by him on his principal (*Lloyds Bank Ltd* v *Reckitt* [1933] AC 201); or for an employee a cheque drawn by him on his employer (*Lloyds Bank Ltd* v *E B Savory and Co.* [1933] AC 201); or for a shareholder in a company a cheque payable to the company (*A L Underwood Ltd* v *Bank of Liverpool and Martins* [1924] 1 KB 775). The bank may also be held negligent and denied the protection of s. 4 if its conduct prevents it having information which it would otherwise have had and which would have alerted it to the fact that the circumstances surrounding the collection of the cheque were suspicious. For instance, a bank which fails to take up references on a new customer, or to obtain details of his employer, may be negligent (*Lloyds Bank Ltd* v *Savory; Marfani & Co. Ltd* v *Midland Bank Ltd* [1968] 1 WLR 956).

22.4 Promissory notes

A promissory note is a promise to pay a sum of money. Bank notes are promissory notes; notes other than bank notes are no longer widely used other than in international transactions. They may be used as a form of security for a loan, the lender requiring the borrower to provide a promissory note for the amount of the loan. However, their use in this way is restricted by the Consumer Credit Act 1974 if the loan is a regulated credit agreement.

22.4.1 Definition of a promissory note

A promissory note is:

an unconditional promise made in writing by one person to another signed by the maker, engaging to pay on demand or at a fixed or determinable future time, a sum certain in money to, or to the order of, a specified person or to bearer (BoEA 1882, s. 83).

A valid note must comply with all aspects of this definition. A valid note may contain a pledge of property with a grant of authority to sell the property, and such a form may be used where the note is given by a debtor in order to give the creditor the dual security of both a promissory note and a pledge.

A note must be distinguished from an IOU which is a mere acknowledgement of a debt rather than a promise to pay.

The definition of a promissory note is similar to that of a bill of exchange and the law relating to bills and notes is largely similar. It follows that a note can be transferred and negotiated in the same way as a bill. The law relating to notes is contained in the Bills of Exchange Act 1882, Part III.

22.4.1.1 Notes distinguished from bills

The main difference between bills and notes is that a note is never accepted: it is a promise, rather than an order, to pay. The provisions of the Bills of Exchange Act 1882 concerned with presentment for acceptance and acceptance are therefore inapplicable to notes.

22.4.2 Liability on a note

Since, unlike a bill, a note is not accepted, liability to honour a note falls on the maker and any indorser.

22.4.2.1 Maker of the note

The maker of a note is primarily liable to honour it and his position is equated to that of the acceptor of a bill of exchange. He undertakes to pay the note in accordance with its terms and, if it comes into the hands of a holder in due course, is estopped from denying the existence of the payee and his capacity to indorse it. The maker's liability on the note is not complete until the note is delivered (BoEA 1882, s. 84).

22.4.2.2 Indorser of a note

The first indorser of a note incurs the same liabilities as the drawer of an accepted bill payable to drawer's order (see **22.2.7.4**). Subsequent indorsers are liable in the same way as indorsers of an order bill.

22.4.3 Presentation of the note

A bill payable on demand must be presented for payment within a reasonable time of indorsement; if not, the indorser is discharged from liability. However, there is no need for such a note to be presented to make the maker of the note liable on it, unless by its terms it must be presented at a particular place for payment.

22.5 Summary

After completing this chapter you should understand and be able to advise on:

- the concept of negotiability;
- the nature of a bill of exchange and the commercial uses of and the law relating to bills of exchange including their transfer and enforcement and liability on a bill;
- the nature of a cheque and the law relating to cheques and their role in the banking system;
- the nature of a promissory note and the use of and law relating to promissory notes.

Bankers' commercial credits

23.1 Introduction

The commercial community has developed special arrangements to finance international transactions. In this chapter we:

- consider the special problems of international transactions;
- examine the law and practice of one of the most important methods of financing international sales, the documentary credit; and finally
- briefly examine the operation of and law relating to another financial instrument often used in international commerce, the performance bond.

In international transactions the normal risks involved in a commercial transaction are magnified. Since the parties are in different countries, if one defaults the other will face legal and procedural difficulties in enforcing the contract against him. Moreover, goods are likely to be tied up for a considerable time in transit.

Where parties trade together on a regular basis the seller may be prepared to grant the buyer credit, and supply goods 'on open account'. In order to guard against the risk of the buyer's insolvency, the seller may retain property in the goods until payment. However, given the problems of enforcing a claim against a party in another country, the seller may be reluctant to part with control over the goods until he has received payment or some assurance of payment. A buyer may be similarly reluctant to pay until he has some assurance of performance by the seller. To meet these needs a number of special mechanisms may be used.

One option is for the seller to require payment by bill of exchange. If the bill is accepted the seller has some protection against the buyer's non-performance because of the autonomous nature of the payment undertaking in a bill. In order to meet the needs of both parties the bill may be presented to the buyer for acceptance with the shipping and other documents attached. The bill is then called a 'documentary bill'. If the buyer fails to accept the bill of exchange he may not retain the bill of lading, and no property passes to him if he does so (Sale of Goods Act 1979, s. 19(3)). The seller will often employ a bank as his agent to present the bill for acceptance and later payment under a 'documentary collection' arrangement.

A documentary bill therefore serves the interests of both parties: the presentation of the shipping documents with the bill of exchange gives the buyer an assurance of payment before he accepts the bill; the seller is protected by his retention of property until the bill is accepted. If the bill provides for deferred payment the buyer gains the benefit of a period of credit; the seller can discount the bill for immediate payment. A bill of exchange does not, however, give the seller a complete assurance of payment. If the buyer fails to honour the bill at maturity, the seller may have difficulty enforcing it in cross-border litigation. Moreover, for that reason a bill accepted by a buyer out of the jurisdiction may be less marketable, so that the seller will be unable to discount it for as much as he would obtain from a domestic buyer. In order to increase the bill's marketability the seller may therefore require the buyer to arrange for the bill to be accepted by a bank or other financial institution. As a further alternative, however, the seller may require the buyer to arrange for payment through a banker's commercial credit. Such an arrangement gives the seller the security of a promise of payment from a bank or other financial institution and, preferably, one within the jurisdiction. Similar arrangements, such as performance bonds, can be used to provide the buyer of goods with a similar assurance of the seller's performance.

23.2   Bankers' commercial credits

Bankers' commercial credits are used in connection with contracts for the international sale of goods (see **Chapter 21**). Essentially the buyer arranges with a bank that it will give the seller an undertaking that, provided certain conditions are fulfilled, it will make payment to the seller. The conditions to be fulfilled by the seller normally relate to the presentation by him of shipping documents relating to the goods to be sold.

23.2.1   The bank's undertaking

The bank's undertaking may take several forms:

    (a) to pay the seller, either immediately on presentation of the shipping documents, or at some fixed date thereafter, e.g. 90 days after presentation of shipping documents;

    (b) to accept bills of exchange drawn on it by the seller (an acceptance credit); or

    (c) to discount bills drawn by the seller on the buyer (a negotiation credit); the seller will normally indorse such bills 'without recourse' (see **22.2.7.4**).

23.2.1.1   The nature of the bank's undertaking

The bank's undertaking creates an obligation which is recognised by law and commercial practice as independent of the underlying sale contract. The seller therefore looks primarily to the bank for payment and, having agreed to accept a documentary credit in payment, cannot then look to the buyer unless the bank makes default. A banker's credit therefore gives the seller an almost absolute guarantee of payment, and allows him to perform his contract with certainty that he will receive payment. At the same time, since the bank's undertaking is to pay only in return for the seller's presenting documents showing that the goods have been shipped, the buyer can be confident that the seller will only be paid when he produces proof that he has performed his obligations under the contract of sale.

23.2.2   The law relating to bankers' credits

Bankers' commercial credits are not regulated by statute. The law relating to credits is therefore to be found in the common law, which in turn is largely based on commercial practice.

    Most credits are in fact governed by the Uniform Customs and Practice relating to Documentary Credits (UCP), drawn up by the International Chamber of Commerce. The UCP is revised from time to time: the current version is UCP 500 (1993). In order for the UCP to apply to a credit it must be incorporated, expressly or by implication. However, most credits do expressly incorporate the UCP.

In 1997, the ICC instituted a special dispute resolution service, 'DOCDEX', effectively a specialist arbitration service, which may be used to resolve disputes arising out of documentary credit transactions.

23.2.3 Types of credit transaction

The UCP defines a documentary credit as:

any arrangement, however named or described, whereby a bank (the issuing bank) acting at the request and in accordance with the instructions of a customer (the applicant for the credit)

(i) is to make payment to or to the order of a third party (the beneficiary) or is to pay or accept or negotiate bills of exchange (drafts) drawn by the beneficiary or

(ii) authorises another bank to effect such payment, or to pay, accept or negotiate such bills of exchange

against stipulated documents, provided that the terms and conditions of the credit are complied with (Art. 2).

There are therefore a range of different types of documentary credit arrangement.

23.2.3.1 Standby credits

These arrangements differ from true documentary credits in that whereas under a documentary credit the bank's obligation to pay is a primary one, the bank's obligation under a standby credit is to pay if its customer defaults in payment. Standby credits are therefore a form of guarantee and were developed in the United States in order to circumvent legal restrictions on the enforceability of guarantees in US law. They are, however, governed by the UCP and the rules applicable to documentary credits.

23.2.3.2 Revolving credits

Where two parties trade together on a continuing basis the buyer may, rather than opening a new credit for each transaction, arrange a revolving credit under which the bank undertakes to the seller to pay sums due from time to time, up to an agreed credit limit.

23.2.3.3 Transferable credits

Under a transferable credit the beneficiary (i.e. the seller) may require the bank to make the credit available wholly or in part to a third party. The seller may therefore use a transferable credit to make payment to his supplier.

23.2.3.4 Back to back credits

A back to back credit is also an arrangement used by a seller to pay his supplier. However, under this arrangement two credits are arranged, the first in favour of the seller and the second, 'back to back' with the first, by the seller in favour of his supplier. The first credit is used to finance the second.

23.2.3.5 Revocable and irrevocable credits

This is a fundamental distinction. If the credit is revocable the bank may revoke its undertaking to the seller at any time before presentation of the shipping documents, and is under no obligation to the seller to notify him of the revocation (*Cape Asbestos Ltd* v *Lloyds Bank Ltd* [1921] WN 274). It therefore offers the seller little real security since he may ship the goods only to find that the credit has been revoked and he has no right against the bank.

The bank's undertaking under an irrevocable credit cannot be revoked, even if the buyer requests revocation, unless there is clear evidence of fraud by the seller.

Where the seller has sufficient bargaining power he will therefore insist on the buyer opening an irrevocable credit.

23.2.3.6   Confirmed and unconfirmed credits

Where the bank has no branch in the seller's country, it will normally arrange for a bank in that country to act as its agent by notifying the seller that the credit is opened and the seller will then present the shipping documents to that bank. The bank which opens the credit is then known as the 'issuing bank', whilst the bank which notifies the seller of the opening of the credit is the 'correspondent bank'. Normally the correspondent undertakes no obligation to the seller but merely acts as intermediary between seller and issuing bank; it may even make payment to the seller but does so as agent for the issuing bank. This is a simple *unconfirmed credit*.

The seller will generally prefer to have an undertaking provided by an institution within his home jurisdiction. If the issuing bank has no branch in the seller's country, he may therefore require the buyer to arrange a *confirmed* credit, in which case the correspondent bank not only notifies the seller of the opening of the credit but also *confirms* the issuing bank's payment undertaking. The seller therefore has the benefit of payment undertakings from both the issuing and the confirming banks and has the added security provided by the fact that the latter is in his home jurisdiction. If the confirming bank does make payment it is entitled to be reimbursed by the issuing bank.

A correspondent bank will normally only confirm a credit which is irrevocable.

The confirming bank will have to be paid for adding its confirmation, so that a confirmed credit will cost the buyer more than an unconfirmed credit.

23.3   Stages in a documentary credit transaction

The typical stages in a documentary credit transaction are as follows.

(a) Seller and buyer enter into a sale contract which requires payment to be by documentary credit. The contract will specify the type of credit required.

(b) Buyer instructs his bank to open the required credit and gives the bank detailed instructions as to the documents to be presented by the seller to obtain payment. The buyer will have to pay the bank for the service so provided; the cost of opening the credit is therefore an additional cost of the transaction.

(c) If the bank has no branch in the seller's country it will instruct a bank there to act as its correspondent. Where the credit is confirmed the correspondent will be asked to confirm the issuing bank's undertaking. The issuing bank will give the correspondent instructions as to the documents to be presented by the seller to obtain payment.

(d) The seller is notified, normally by the correspondent bank, that the credit is opened.

(e) The seller ships the goods.

(f) The seller presents the documents stipulated by the terms of the credit and the sale contract to the correspondent bank. Typically he will be required to present a bill of lading showing the goods to have been shipped, a commercial invoice and a policy of insurance to cover the goods during transit. To give the buyer added confidence that the contract has been performed, further documents, such as a certificate of quality or of origin, may be required. Provided that the documents are in order the seller is entitled to be paid in accordance with the terms of the credit.

23.4 The contracts created by a documentary credit transaction

A documentary credit transaction involves a series of contracts, as follows:

    (a) the (underlying) sale contract between seller and buyer;

    (b) the contract between the buyer/customer and his bank;

    (c) a contract between the issuing bank and the correspondent bank which acts as its agent;

    (d) a contract between the issuing bank and the seller (the beneficiary) containing the bank's undertaking to pay on presentation of the stipulated documents; and

    (e) where the credit is confirmed, a further contract between the confirming bank and the seller containing that bank's undertaking to pay.

23.4.1 The contractual nature of the bank's undertakings

The key to the effectiveness of documentary credit arrangements, and their importance in commerce, lies in the fact that the undertakings of the issuing and confirming banks to the seller are regarded as contractually binding. It is not clear at what stage in the transaction the bank's undertakings become binding; it is generally accepted that the undertaking is binding and irrevocable at the latest when the seller acts in reliance on the credit by shipping the goods; however, there is some legal authority to support the view that it becomes binding at an earlier stage, as soon as the seller is notified that the credit is opened.

It is not clear what consideration the seller provides for the bank's undertakings to pay him. A number of different theories have been advanced; it may even be that the bank's undertakings are contracts enforceable without the seller providing consideration. The matter has never been considered by any English court and it is assumed that the commercial importance of documentary credits is such that, if the point were taken the courts would uphold the binding nature of the bank's undertaking.

23.4.2 The autonomy of the bank's undertakings

The contractual obligations created by the undertakings given by the banks to the seller are separate from the underlying sale contract between seller and buyer, and this separation is recognised by both commercial practice and by the courts (see UCP, Art. 3). The result is that, provided the seller has complied with the conditions of the credit, the bank cannot refuse to honour its payment undertaking even if it is alleged that the seller is in breach of the underlying sale contract. The court will not grant the buyer an injunction to prevent the seller drawing on the credit in such a case (*Hamzeh Malas Inc* v *British Imex Industries* [1958] 1 QB 542); nor will it grant the buyer an injunction against the bank to prevent it paying the seller (*Discount Records Ltd* v *Barclays Bank Ltd* [1975] 1 WLR 315). The only exceptional cases where payment can be withheld are (a) where there is clear evidence of fraud to which the seller is a party (*United City Merchants Ltd* v *Royal Bank of Canada* [1983] 1 AC 168) and (b) where the credit itself is illegal or void.

An injunction to restrain payment on grounds of fraud will rarely be granted. The court will require clear evidence of fraud, to which the seller is party and of which the bank is aware. Moreover, as the injunction will normally be sought at a pre-trial stage in proceedings, the court will only grant an injunction if satisfied that the balance of convenience favours the grant. This requirement will rarely be satisfied, since if the bank pays where it has knowledge of clear evidence of fraud it will be in breach of its contract with its customer, who will therefore have a remedy in damages against the bank (see *Czarnikow Rionda Sugar Trading Inc* v *Standard Bank London Ltd* [1999] 1 All ER Comm 890).

The reason for this approach is that, if payment could be withheld, the commercial value of credits as an assurance of payment, would be undermined. The effect is to reverse the balance of bargaining power between seller and buyer where the buyer alleges that the seller is in breach of the sale contract: the buyer cannot simply withhold payment. Instead the seller will be paid by the bank and the buyer will be forced to reimburse the bank leaving him to take proceedings against the seller for damages.

23.4.3   The doctrine of strict compliance

The corollary of the above rule is that the seller is only entitled to be paid when he presents the documents required by the terms of the credit. The documents presented by the seller must exactly correspond with the terms of the credit; if the documents do not exactly correspond the bank is entitled to reject the documents and refuse payment. This rule is strictly applied. For instance, where the terms of the credit required the seller to present a bill of lading relating to 'machine shelled groundnut kernels', the bank was entitled to reject a bill relating to 'coromandel groundnuts' even though there was evidence that it was well known in the trade that the two were the same (see *J H Rayner & Co. Ltd* v *Hambros Bank* [1943] 1 KB 37).

The rule of strict compliance is slightly modified where the credit is governed by the UCP which provides that the bank will not reject the bill of lading provided the quantity of goods shipped is within a tolerance of plus or minus 5 per cent of the contract quantity (Art. 39(b)).

The bank will be instructed by its customer, the buyer, as to the documents to be presented by the seller. If the bank does accept documents which do not exactly correspond with the terms of its instructions, it will be in breach of its duty of care to the customer; the customer may then refuse to take the documents from the bank or to pay for them, leaving the bank with the goods on its hands, and the bank may also be liable to the customer in damages.

In view of the rule of strict compliance the customer should be advised when arranging the credit to give the bank detailed instructions as to the documents to be presented. The seller should be warned of the importance of ensuring that the documents presented do correspond exactly to the terms of the credit.

23.4.4   Effect of non-payment

If the bank rejects the documents, the seller may re-present them or may contact the buyer and ask him to instruct the bank to accept them; however, having agreed to payment by documentary credit, he may not present them direct to the buyer for payment. However, the credit operates only as conditional payment so that if the bank fails to pay, the buyer's obligation to pay is revived and the seller can then claim payment direct from the buyer (*Alan* v *El Nasr* [1972] 2 QB 189).

23.4.5   Release of the goods

Having paid for the goods the bank will look to its customer, the buyer, to reimburse it. It may retain possession of the bill of lading as security for payment; however, it may often release the bill to the buyer in order that he can collect the goods and deal with them.

In order to preserve its security the bank will normally release the goods under the terms of a trust receipt, under which the buyer acknowledges that he receives the goods as trustee for the bank and that, if he resells them, he holds the proceeds of sale on the same basis.

23.5   Performance bonds

Performance bonds are used to secure performance of a wide range of contractual and other obligations. For instance, where a sale contract requires payment by documentary credit, the buyer may need a guarantee that the goods will be shipped and therefore require the seller to arrange a performance bond so that, in default of shipment in accordance with the contract, the sum fixed by the bond will become payable; or, where an advance payment is required under a contract, the payer may require the recipient to provide a bond to ensure repayment of the advance if the contract is not performed.

The person who arranges the bond is known as the 'account party'; the recipient of payment is the 'beneficiary'.

A wide range of arrangements is in use. The common features of them are that the bond is provided by a creditworthy institution, such as a bank, thus providing the beneficiary with a guarantee of performance and, in default, of payment of the amount payable under the bond. In many ways, therefore, such bonds perform the function of a guarantee; however, they have been treated by the courts as broadly analogous to documentary credits.

23.5.1   When is the bond payable?

The most important factor to be considered when agreeing to provide a bond is the nature of the conditions to be fulfilled before a call can be made under the bond. Where the sum is payable in the event of the account party being in default under his contract with the beneficiary, payment is only due if it is shown that the account party is in default; such a bond therefore provides little security for the beneficiary. In order to avoid this the bond may provide for the beneficiary to be paid on production of a certificate from a third party, such as a surveyor or valuer, certifying that the account party is in default. Such arrangements avoid the need for the bank to become involved in disputes relating to the contract between beneficiary and account party: providing the required certificate is produced, the bank must pay in accordance with the bond.

A further alternative is for the bond to provide for payment to the beneficiary on demand. The bank is then obliged to pay the agreed sum simply on a demand being made; it is not concerned with the question whether the demand is justified.

23.5.2   The autonomy of the undertaking in the bond

A demand bond is therefore particularly attractive from the points of view of the beneficiary and the bank providing the bond, but exposes the account party to the risk of an unjustified demand. This risk is exacerbated by the fact that, to date, the courts have tended to treat performance bonds as analogous to documentary credits and therefore treat them as autonomous of the underlying contract between beneficiary and account party.

The approach, and the risks for the account party, are illustrated by the decision in *Edward Owen Engineering Ltd* v *Barclays Bank International* [1978] 1 QB 179. Under a contract for the sale of glasshouses to a Libyan buyer, the buyer was required to arrange a documentary credit for the price and the seller was required to arrange a performance bond, payable on demand, to guarantee his performance. The buyer failed to arrange the credit and the seller refused to ship the goods; the buyer then made a demand under the bond and the Court of Appeal held that the seller could not obtain an injunction to prevent the bank paying. The bank had given an undertaking to pay on the buyer's demand and was obliged to fulfil that undertaking which was separate from the contract of sale.

The risk for the seller/account party in such a case is clear: the bank will make payment under the bond and will be entitled to be reimbursed by its customer, the account party. He, in turn, may be able to recover payment from the beneficiary but will be forced to take proceedings to do so and may face the difficulties of suing a defendant outside the jurisdiction. A party asked to provide a performance bond should therefore be advised of the risks involved in giving an 'on demand' bond.

Under a conditional bond the bank's payment obligation is still autonomous of the underlying contract, so provided that the condition in the bond is satisfied the benefici-ary is entitled to demand payment. The court will not restrain the bank from paying, or the beneficiary from drawing on the bond, unless there is clear and obvious evidence of fraud. In such a case, however, the court may restrain the beneficiary from receiving payment if there is evidence that the condition in the bond is not satisfied. So if a bond provides for payment on the beneficiary certifying that certain conditions are satisfied and the beneficiary seeks payment by falsely certifying that they are so satisfied, the court may restrain it from receiving payment and, where the paying bank is aware of the falsity of the statement, may restrain the bank from making payment. (See *Kvaerner John Brown Ltd v Midland Bank plc* [1998] Com LC 446.)

Even where a bond is payable only where the account party is in breach of contract, the beneficiary may be entitled to call on it without proof of loss. However, it seems that if the beneficiary recovers more than his actual loss he may be liable to refund the excess to the account party. In *Cargill International Sugar SA v Bangladesh Sugar and Food Industries Corp* [1996] 4 All ER 563, aff'd [1998] 2 All ER 406 a company submitted a tender to supply sugar and provided a performance bond for 10 per cent of the price. The supply contract stipulated that the bond was liable to be forfeited if the suppliers failed to fulfil any of the terms of the contract. The suppliers did commit a breach by tendering a cargo which arrived late and relying on that breach the buyers rejected the cargo and then made a call on the bond. The buyers' motive in rejecting the cargo was to escape from the contract, since the market price for sugar had fallen. They therefore suffered no loss as a result of the seller's breach. It was held that they were nevertheless entitled to call on the bond. However, it was further held that in the absence of clear words to the contrary it is norm-ally implicit in the nature of a bond that following the beneficiary's call there should be an accounting between the parties and that the beneficiary should refund to the account party any amount received by it in excess of its actual loss. The position might be different if, perhaps, the wording of the bond makes clear that the sum payable to the account party is payable by way of liquidated damages, but such wording is unlikely to be used.

23.6 Summary

Having completed this chapter you should:

- be aware of the main financing arrangements used in international commercial transactions;
- understand the legal status and commercial use of documentary letters of credit;

- understand and be able to advise on the key legal principles applicable to documentary credit operations—the autonomy principle and the rule of strict compliance; in particular you should be able to advise on the risks involved for seller and buyer in agreeing to payment by documentary credit;

- understand the commercial use of and legal principles applicable to performance bonds and similar arrangements;

- be able to advise on the legal and commercial risks inherent in agreeing to provide a performance bond.

Commercial credit and security

Part VI

Commercial credit and security

Commercial credit and security

24.1 Credit

Most businesses rely on credit facilities to operate. A business which does not have sufficient capital to finance its spending must obtain credit facilities, usually from fellow traders or financial institutions. Furthermore, as a business expands so too does its need for credit facilities.

In this short chapter:

- we consider the basic concepts of 'credit' and 'security';
- we identify and distinguish the different arrangements for the provision of credit to businesses, such as—
  - loan credit and sales credit;
  - fixed term and revolving credit;
- we consider the application of the Consumer Credit Act 1974 to businesses; and
- we outline the different types of security (real and personal) and quasi-security that can be used by businesses. Real security, personal security and quasi-security are considered, in greater detail, in the following three chapters.

24.1.1 Types of credit

Credit has been defined as 'the provision of a benefit (cash, land, goods, services and facilities) for which payment is to be made by the recipient in money at a later date' (Goode, *Commercial Law*, 2nd edn, Penguin, 1995, p. 637). Credit can therefore be provided by several different types of arrangement. Credit arrangements can be classified in two ways.

24.1.1.1 Loan and sales credit

Loan credit involves an advance of money; sales (or supplier) credit involves a deferment of a payment obligation under a supply contract.

A loan is a payment of money by a creditor to a debtor as a means of benefiting and enriching the debtor, upon the condition that the money paid, plus interest, shall be repaid by the debtor to the creditor at a specified rate over a specified period. Examples include bank loans and overdrafts.

A deferment of a payment obligation, on the other hand, occurs where the buyer of goods or services obtains the benefit of the goods or services without having to pay, immediately and in full, their price. Examples include credit sales, instalment sales and hire-purchase agreements.

The practical effect of these two arrangements is the same: the debtor/buyer receives a benefit without having to incur immediate expenditure and drain capital resources.

However, loan and sales credit have, historically, been treated differently by the law. The courts have tended to regard price deferment mechanisms as different from loan and security arrangements. However, the Consumer Credit Act 1974 (see **24.2**) applies to both types of arrangement.

A business which wishes to purchase goods or services on credit therefore has a choice of sources of credit. It may obtain the goods or services on credit terms from the supplier; alternatively it may obtain loan credit from a third party, such as a bank, and use that credit facility to finance the transaction.

Loan credit has the advantage of flexibility: the loan can be used for any purpose (although in some cases the debtor may be contractually obliged to use the loan for a particular specified purpose). Loan credit may appear to be more expensive, since the debtor will have to pay for the credit facility, for instance by payment of interest on the amount of the credit. However, the debtor will generally also have to pay for sales credit since the amount actually paid to the supplier will be increased:

(a) to compensate the supplier for the fact that he is deprived of the use of the price for the credit period; and

(b) to cover the risk of non-payment by the debtor.

In some cases the 'price' of sales credit may be disguised: for instance, where goods are supplied under a credit sale arrangement the price will generally be higher than would be charged to a cash customer as the price will not contain a separate, identifiable charge for credit.

24.1.1.2   Fixed term and revolving credit

Under a fixed term credit arrangement a fixed amount is drawn by the debtor and is repaid over a stated period. The arrangement comes to an end on completion of the repayments. Examples are a personal loan and a hire purchase arrangement.

Alternatively, credit can be provided through a revolving facility. Here the creditor is not given a fixed amount but an upper credit limit is set, as with overdraft or credit card facilities for example. The debtor can make one or more drawings of any amount provided that at any time the total amount outstanding does not exceed the fixed upper limit. He is not obliged to use the full facility. Each drawing reduces the amount of the credit facility and as the debtor repays amounts to the creditor the facility is replenished.

24.2   Consumer Credit Act 1974

This Act regulates the credit industry involved in the supply of credit to individuals. A licence is required to carry on a consumer credit business, a consumer hire business or ancillary credit businesses and the industry operates under the supervision of the Director General of Fair Trading.

The Consumer Credit Act (CCA) 1974 imposes controls on advertising and means of obtaining business and contains provisions regulating individual agreements. It covers such matters as:

(a) the formation and form of agreements;

(b) termination of agreements;

(c) default by the debtor;

(d) enforcement by the creditor.

The Act applies to all forms of credit, which is defined widely to include 'a cash loan and any other form of financial accommodation' (CCA 1974, s. 9). However, it applies only to 'regulated credit agreements', which are defined as agreements between an *individual debtor* and a creditor by which the creditor supplies the debtor with credit not exceeding £15,000 other than exempt agreements (CCA 1974, s. 189; s. 8). Some business credit agreements may therefore fall within the ambit of the Act, where the debtor is an individual. However, any agreement involving the supply of credit to a company is not regulated by the Act.

The Act's provisions are detailed and technical. Detailed coverage is outside the scope of this book but the commercial lawyer should be aware of it and its impact on any agreement where the debtor is an individual. (See further Goode, *Consumer Credit Law*, 2nd edn, Butterworths, 1989.)

24.3 Security

Before a creditor will be willing to advance money to a debtor, he will want to be satisfied that the debt will be repaid. If the potential debtor is a 'creditworthy' business, the creditor may be happy, on the basis of the strength of the business alone, that the debt will be repaid. However, it is not easy to assess creditworthiness, especially in times of recession. The creditor's fear is that if, for example, the debtor becomes insolvent before repaying the debt, the creditor may not be paid in full or even at all. The position of unsecured creditors has improved somewhat under the Enterprise Act 2002 which requires that a certain percentage of floating charge realisations should be set aside for the benefit of unsecured creditors (s. 252, 2002 Act; s. 176A, Insolvency Act 1986; the Enterprise Act 2002 (Commencement No. 4) Order 2003, SI 2003, No. 2093). But this measure will not ensure that the claims of all unsecured creditors are fully satisfied. Unsecured creditors will, at best, still receive only a proportion of the amount owing to them. A creditor can minimise this risk of insolvency by taking security.

24.3.1 Real and personal security

Security can be real (proprietary) or personal.

Real security gives the creditor real property rights over some or all of the debtor's assets. Examples include pledges, liens, mortgages and charges. Personal security involves a third party entering into a separate contract with the creditor and undertaking responsibility for the debt if the debtor defaults; for instance a guarantee.

Real security protects against the debtor's insolvency by providing the creditor with real rights over the debtor's assets, offering the creditor priority if the debtor becomes insolvent. Its effectiveness therefore depends on the value of the assets used as security. The effectiveness of personal security will depend on the creditworthiness of the guarantor. For this reason a personal security is often reinforced by requiring the guarantor to grant real security over his assets to secure the guarantee.

24.3.2 Security and quasi-security

A number of other arrangements are available to provide a creditor with security against the debtor's non-payment or insolvency. In particular a seller who supplies goods on credit terms can protect his interests by utilising the rules on passing of property.

Reservation of ownership under a conditional sale, hire purchase or similar arrangement allows the supplier to retake the goods if the debtor fails to pay and gives him priority over the debtor's other creditors if the debtor becomes insolvent. The practical effect of these arrangements is therefore to grant the supplier security. However, the courts have tended not to regard them as security devices, so they avoid the formality and registration requirements which apply to some security interests. Such devices can be referred to as 'quasi-security' devices. They are examined in more detail in **Chapter 27**.

24.3.2.1 Letters of comfort

Another means of reassuring a creditor that a debt will be repaid is by providing a letter of comfort. Letters of comfort are used as an alternative to a formal guarantee; they are therefore considered in **Chapter 26**.

25

Real security

25.1 Introduction

In this chapter, our focus is on real security. In it:

- we distinguish consensual from non-consensual security, and possessory from non-possessory security;
- we examine, in detail, the main security devices used by businesses, namely, the pledge, the lien, the mortgage and the equitable charge; and
- we consider the statuory control of non-possessory security, in particular, under the Bills of Sale legislation and the Companies Acts.

The provision of real security involves the creditor obtaining proprietary rights over property of the debtor.

Real security confers two basic rights on the secured creditor: the right of *pursuit* and the right of *preference*. This means that the secured creditor can:

(a) follow his asset, its products and proceeds into the hands of third parties other than those obtaining title under the *nemo dat* rules (see **Chapter 15**); and

(b) claim the asset or the proceeds of its sale to satisfy his claim in priority to the claims of other creditors (Goode, *Commercial Law*, 2nd edn, Penguin, 1995, p. 673).

Real security gives the debtor an incentive to pay the debt in order to recover his property. This may be particularly powerful if the goods are worth more (to the debtor) than the amount of the debt.

It may be classified as *consensual* or *non-consensual* and as *possessory* or *non-possessory*.

25.1.1 Consensual and non-consensual security

Security is consensual where it is created by the agreement of creditor and debtor. Examples include pledges, mortgages and some charges.

Security is non-consensual where it arises by operation of the law. Examples include liens and certain statutory charges.

25.1.2 Possessory and non-possessory security

Possessory security depends on the creditor having possession of goods. Examples include pledges and liens.

Under a non-possessory security the creditor's security interest is not dependent on possession. Examples include mortgages and equitable charges.

Non-possessory security may be preferable where the debtor needs the use of the goods which are to be offered as security, for instance plant and machinery, and is therefore not in a position to transfer possession of them. However, non-possessory securities tend to be subject to a higher degree of statutory control, especially in order to protect third parties. Where a debtor is left in possession of property which is in fact subject to a security interest, other potential creditors may believe him to be the unencumbered owner of that property and thus be misled as to his creditworthiness. In order to avoid this, non-possessory securities generally have to be registered (e.g. Bills of Sale Acts 1878–1882; Companies Act 1985: see **25.6**). Further statutory controls are imposed, especially on non-possessory securities, to protect the debtor (see **25.6.1**).

25.2 Pledge

A pledge is a type of real security which involves a debtor (the pledgor) delivering goods to a creditor (the pledgee) who has the right to retain possession of the goods as security until payment of a debt or until discharge of another obligation, upon an express or implied undertaking that the goods shall be restored to the pledgor as soon as the debt or other obligation is met. The debt may arise at the time the pledge is created, or may be pre-existing or, indeed, a future debt. A pledge is therefore a consensual, possessory security.

Pledges are commonly used in commerce; for example, where a buyer of goods under an international sale contract pledges a bill of lading to a bank as security for an advance of money to pay for them. In the consumer context the most common type of pledge is a 'pawn'. Pawns are regulated by the CCA 1974.

25.2.1 Possession

Since a pledge involves the transfer of possession to the pledgee it gives the pledgee a special property in the goods.

The pledgee's possession of the goods can be actual or constructive. However, if the creditor has only a contractual right to seize the goods to secure a debt, the contract will amount to a security bill of sale which will be void unless the relevant registration and formality requirements, under the bills of sale legislation, are satisfied (see **25.6.1**).

Actual possession of the goods brings with it the expense of storage and insurance, so the pledgee should make express provision in the pledge agreement that such costs are to be met by the pledgor. As a bailee of the goods, the pledgee is liable for loss of or damage to the goods caused by his negligence and the burden of proof is reversed so that the pledgee/bailee must prove that he was not negligent. A contract creating the pledge may include terms modifying or restricting this duty of care.

Today, it is far more usual for the pledgee to have constructive possession of the goods, for example, by holding the keys to the warehouse where the goods are stored or by having possession of a bill of lading (recognised as a document of title to the goods; see **20.2.3**) while the goods are at sea. Equally, an attornment (**11.2.1.4**) by the pledgor or his bailee would suffice.

25.2.1.1 Limitations of pledges

The main limitation of this type of security is that it is dependent on possession (actual or constructive) and so not applicable to intangible property which cannot be possessed in the physical sense. Other types of security fulfil this function (see **25.4**).

If the pledge agreement allows the pledgor to retain some control over the goods, the pledgee's security may be destroyed. A provision stating that the pledgor may repossess the goods whenever he likes would take precedence over the pledge. However, if the pledgee redelivers the goods to the pledgor for a limited purpose and on terms that the pledge is to continue, the pledge is not destroyed. For instance where a bill of lading is pledged with a bank as security for an advance of the price of goods, the bank may release the bill to the buyer for the purpose of collecting the goods.

25.2.1.2 Possession must be lawful

The pledgee's possession must be lawful. Where the goods are taken by force or the pledgor's consent to the pledge is obtained by fraud or misrepresentation, the pledgor is not bound.

25.2.1.3 Delivery to a third party

The pledgee's special property in the goods is a disposable interest which can be assigned or sub-pledged and delivery by the pledgee to a third party does not destroy the pledge or enable the pledgor to sue the pledgee or sub-pledgee in the tort of conversion. However, the pledgee cannot sub-pledge the goods for a sum greater than the original debt, as this would prejudice the pledgor's right to repossess the goods on payment of the debt.

If the pledgee purports to deal with the *general property* in the goods, for instance by pledging them, he commits a breach of contract *vis-à-vis* the pledgor and is liable in damages for any loss the pledgor suffers as a result. However, the pledge continues. The pledgor can sue the pledgee in conversion if he first pays the debt secured by the pledge.

The pledgor can deal with his general property in the goods while the pledge continues and may therefore sell the goods subject to the pledge. The buyer may then recover possession of the goods by redeeming the pledge.

25.2.2 Creation and formation

As a form of consensual security a pledge is created by the agreement of the parties. However, no formality is required for creation of a pledge. Registration is not required: the very fact of possession is sufficient evidence of the pledge and puts third parties on notice of the pledgee's interest.

There is no prescribed legal form for pledges unless the CCA 1974 applies. It is standard banking practice to require the pledgor to sign a document such as a 'letter of pledge'. A letter of pledge may often include terms by which:

(a) the pledgor agrees that the pledgee is to have a pledge over all goods or documents of title delivered by the pledgor or his agent into the possession of the pledgee or his agent;

(b) where the credit provided is a revolving facility, the pledgor agrees that the goods and documents are pledged as continuing security for the payment of all sums owed by the pledgor from time to time;

(c) the pledgor agrees that in the case of his default in repayment of any sum or sums on demand, the pledgee has the right to immediate actual possession of the goods and to sell the goods or any part of them, [X] days after the default;

(d) the pledgor agrees to keep the goods fully insured to their full value, with such persons as the pledgee may approve and provide proof of such insurance, the pledgor further agrees to notify the insurers of the pledgee's interest in the goods;

(e) the pledgor agrees to pay all the cost of storage of the goods;

(f) all risk of loss of or damage to the goods remains, at all times, with the pledgor whether the goods are in his possession, the pledgee's possession or the possession of a third party.

25.2.3   Powers of sale

If the debt is not paid by the date fixed by the pledge agreement the pledgee can sell the goods. If no date is stipulated the pledge must be redeemed within a reasonable time. If the pledge is governed by the CCA 1974 the pledgor must have at least six months to redeem the pledge.

A sale by the pledgee must be reasonable in that the goods must be sold at a reasonable price. The pledgee must account to the pledgor for any moneys received on the sale in excess of the debt. If the sale fails to meet the debt in full, the pledgee may pursue the pledgor personally for the amount outstanding.

25.2.4   Termination of the pledge

The pledgee's interest terminates where:

(a) the underlying debt is paid, releasing the security;

(b) the pledgee waives his rights by, for example, returning the goods to the possession of the pledgor; or

(c) the pledgee breaches an important term of the pledge agreement, for instance by intentional destruction of the goods. This will rarely occur: dealing with the goods does not destroy the pledge; use of the goods by the pledgee may not amount to a breach, at least where use does not adversely affect the goods, although use may be a breach if the goods are adversely affected (see *Cooke* v *Hadden* (1862) 3 F & F 229, where the pledge was destroyed when the pledgee of champagne started drinking it!).

Generally, pledges are not affected by lapse of time. Thus the pledgee's rights under the pledge remain even if the debt secured by the pledge is time barred. Equally, the pledgor can reclaim the goods on payment of the barred debt. However, lapse of time may amount to a waiver.

25.3   Lien

A lien is a relatively primitive form of real security. Essentially, it entitles a person (the lienee) who has done work for another (the lienor), to retain possession of the lienor's goods or documents until the charges for the work have been paid: the lienee is said to have a right of retention. It is a 'self-help remedy' (*Tappenden* v *Artus* [1964] 2 QB 185).

25.3.1   The lienee as bailee

While the goods are in the lienee's possession, he is a bailee of those goods; hence if the goods are lost or damaged as a result of his negligence he will be liable for that loss and the burden of proving that he was not negligent rests with him. To avoid this outcome, a lienee could expressly contract that:

all risk of loss of or damage to the goods remains with the owner of the goods while the goods are within the lienee's possession or control,

or

all risk of loss of or damage to the goods, in excess of [an agreed amount] remains with the owner of the goods while the goods are within the lienee's possession or control.

Exclusion or limitation of liability will be valid so long as it satisfies the test of reasonableness (UCTA 1977, s. 2(2)).

25.3.2 Types of lien

Liens can be based on the common law, contract, equity, statute and maritime law.

25.3.2.1 The common law lien

Common law has recognised that practitioners of certain trades or callings (especially those pursuing 'common callings') have a lien over their customers' property. This is a non-consensual form of security which arises by operation of the law.

Examples of common law liens include a ship's master's lien on cargo for freight or on luggage for passage, an innkeeper's (or hotelier's) lien over a guest's belongings and a repairer's lien over goods repaired for the cost of repairs.

(a) *Depends on possession*

Possession of the goods by the lienee is essential for both the creation and continued existence of a common law lien. Generally, the lienee must have an immediate right of possession so that if payment is tendered, at any time, the goods can be immediately returned to the lienor, their owner. Hence, a lien, unlike a pledge, cannot be transferred.

If the lienor retains some control over the goods, the lien may be overridden unless it is clear that the lienor's control is subject to the superior rights of the lienee. In *Forth* v *Simpson* (1843) 13 QB 680, a race horse trainer who claimed a lien over some horses failed because the owner had been given a right to take the horses away to race whenever he wished. This case can be compared with *Allen* v *Smith* (1862) 12 CBNS 638, where an innkeeper's lien was held to continue, despite the fact that a guest who had brought with him two horses and stayed several months at an inn without paying, regularly took the horses out of the stables for exercising and took them away for several days, because he had the intention of returning.

(b) *Exclusion of the lien*

Although the common law lien is non-consensual the terms of a contract may prevent a lien arising if it appears that the parties intend that the goods should not be retained until payment. The agreement excluding the lien may be express or implied. So, for example, where the owner of the goods is given credit and not expected to pay immediately, it may be argued that the intention of the parties overrides the operation of a common law lien. For instance in *Wilson* v *Lombard Ltd* [1963] 1 WLR 1294, a car mechanic was held to have no lien over a car because the cost of repair was to be charged to the customer's account.

25.3.2.2 Contractual lien

A right of lien may be reserved by contract and any provider of services may find it useful to include such a lien in its contracts as a means of reinforcing its common law rights. Such a term may be implied following a course of dealing or trade custom, but it is preferable that it be expressly provided for.

A contractual lien should include an express right to sell (see **25.3.4**).

25.3.2.3 Equitable lien

Possession is not necessary for an equitable lien. For instance the vendor of land has a lien to secure the purchase price, and the purchaser has a lien to secure repayment of the price if the transaction falls through. The seller of intangible property, including shares, debts and intellectual property, also has an equitable lien over the property to secure the price, but the unpaid seller of goods has no such lien.

Where a creditor is given a non-possessory equitable lien over *goods* not in his possession, this will amount to a security bill of sale which will be void if not formed and registered in accordance with the bills of sale legislation (see **25.6.1**).

25.3.2.4   Statutory lien

Certain statutes grant creditors liens or similar rights. The most important example of a statutory lien is in the Sale of Goods Act 1979, ss. 41–43, which provides that a seller of goods who has not been paid has the right to retain the goods even though property in the goods has passed to the buyer (see **16.4.2.1**).

25.3.2.5   Maritime lien

A maritime lien is a lien over a ship and its cargo for salvage, seamen's wages and damage caused by the ship.

25.3.3   General or particular

A lien may be general or particular.

A general lien allows the creditor to retain possession of any property of the debtor until any debt due from the debtor is paid. Solicitors, bankers, factors, insurance brokers and stock-brokers have all been recognised as having general liens as a matter of usage.

A particular lien allows the debtor to retain possession of goods or documents as security for payment of debts which relate to the property retained. For instance a warehouseman has a particular lien over goods for warehouse charges relating to those goods; a repairer can retain possession of the goods repaired until he is paid for the work done on them.

Although some general liens are recognised at common law, most common law and statutory liens tend to be particular, while general liens are usually the creation of contract.

Where parties are in a continuing trading relationship a general lien will usually be preferable. A general lien offers the lienee greater and more flexible security but also offers advantages to the lienor. If the lienee has only a particular lien he may be reluctant to release property until debts relating to that property are paid, thus restricting the lienor's trading ability as he will have to pay for each transaction as it is completed, in order to regain possession of the goods. If the lienee has a general lien, he will be more willing to release goods to the lienor without immediate payment, as long as he has possession of some of the lienor's other goods or will have possession of more of the lienor's goods at some future date.

A contract provision granting a general lien is perfectly valid even if the lienee would have only a particular lien at common law.

25.3.4   Power of sale

At common law, a lien does not confer a right of sale and such an act amounts to conversion. However, a number of statutes do give lienees powers of sale. These include the SoGA 1979 (see **16.4.2.1** and **16.4.2.3**) and the Torts (Interference with Goods) Act 1977.

25.3.4.1   Statutory power of sale

Under the Torts (Interference with Goods) Act 1977, s. 12, a bailee in possession of uncollected goods has a right to sell them where:

(a) the bailor is in breach of his obligation to take delivery or give directions as to delivery of the goods; or

(b) the bailee could require the bailor to take delivery but cannot trace him; or

(c) the bailee can reasonably be expected to be relieved of any duty to safeguard the goods by giving notice to the bailor but cannot trace him.

The right can only be exercised where the lienee has:

(i) given notice to the bailor of his intention to sell goods; or

(ii) taken reasonable steps to trace or communicate with the bailor but failed.

Section 13 provides for the bailee to sell goods with the authority of the court. Where there are doubts about the bailee's right to sell, or where the goods are of high value, the bailee may be advised to seek the authorisation of the court.

Where there is a dispute between bailee and bailor over any payment claimed by the bailee, for instance, where the owner of goods disputes liability for repair charges, the bailee can only sell with the authority of the court.

The 1977 Act prescribes the forms of notices imposing on the bailor an obligation to collect the goods and giving notice of intention to sell the goods.

25.3.4.2   Contractual rights of sale

The lienee may reserve a right of sale by contract and in view of the limited rights of sale under the general law this will generally be advisable.

25.3.4.3   Form of the sale

Where the lienee has a contractual right of sale, no particular method of sale is prescribed but the sale must be reasonable. If the goods are sold at an undervalue this may amount to an unreasonable sale. If the proceeds of the sale exceed the debt the lienee must account to the lienor for this surplus. If, however, the sale fails to satisfy the debt, the lienee may pursue a personal action against the lienor for the remaining balance.

Statute does prescribe formalities in certain areas: an unpaid seller must give reasonable notice, unless the goods are perishable (SoGA 1979, s. 48); and an innkeeper must sell at public auction after advertising the sale (Innkeepers Act 1878, s. 1); see further the Torts (Interference with Goods) Act 1977.

25.3.5   Termination of the interest

In general, a lienee's interest in the goods terminates in the following circumstances.

(a) On payment of the debt.

(b) Where the lienee loses possession of the goods. In *Pennington v Reliance Motor Work Ltd* [1923] 1 KB 127, car mechanics returned a repaired car before payment and without asserting a lien. When the car was later returned to their possession for other work, they sought to assert their lien for work previously done, but it was held that by returning the goods any potential lien had been destroyed.

(c) Where the lienee waives his right by returning the goods to the lienor or where, for instance, alternative security is provided.

(d) Where the lienee breaches a term on which he holds the goods, the lien will terminate and the immediate right of possession will revest in the lienor. There is such a breach if, for example:

(i) the lienor tenders payment of the debt and this is wrongly refused by the lienee; or

(ii) the immediate right to possession passes to a third party; this will restrict the lienee's ability to re-deliver the goods to the lienor on payment, and constitute a breach of his obligations under the lien; however, it has been held that the lienee is entitled to do what is reasonably incidental to his obligation under the lien, so that, in *Chesham Automobile Supply Ltd* v *Beresford Hotel (Birchington) Ltd* (1913) 29 TLR 584, a lienee, intending to exercise a right of sale, could send the goods to be repaired without losing his lien; or

(iii) perhaps even, the lienee asserts a lien for the wrong amount.

As with pledges, liens are not generally affected by lapse of time and limitations of actions do not affect a lienee's rights even if the debt is time barred. Equally, the lienor can reclaim the goods on payment when the debt is barred, but, again, such a lapse of time may amount to a waiver.

25.4 Mortgage

A mortgage is a non-possessory form of real security, which involves the transfer of ownership of an asset to a creditor (the mortgagee) by way of security upon condition that the asset will be transferred back to the debtor (mortgagor) when the sum secured is paid.

The mortgagor may retain possession of the mortgaged property, an advantage where the mortgaged property must be used by the mortgagor in its business.

The mortgagor has the right to recover ownership of the mortgaged property, known as the 'equity of redemption', on payment of the debt secured by the mortgage. A mortgage of personalty may be worded as an outright transfer subject to a proviso that the transfer is to be void on payment of the debt.

25.4.1 What can be mortgaged

Any property can be mortgaged, including real and personal, tangible and intangible, present and future property. This gives a mortgage an advantage over a pledge which cannot be granted over intangible or future property.

Mortgages of land are outside the scope of the book.

25.4.2 Legal or equitable

A mortgage can be either legal or equitable. A legal mortgage involves the transfer by way of security of legal ownership of the property. An equitable mortgage is created where:

(a) the mortgagor transfers the equitable ownership or confers an equitable interest in his property; or

(b) the mortgage is of equitable property; this includes a mortgage of future property to be acquired by the mortgagor, such as a mortgage of future book debts; or

(c) the parties enter into a contract to create a mortgage, including where they fail to comply with the necessary formalities for creation of a legal mortgage.

25.4.3 Formalities

Generally there is no prescribed form for a mortgage of personalty. The manner of transfer will depend on the type of property being transferred. No formality is required for the transfer of goods; property passes when the parties intend it to pass. However, it will generally be advisable for the mortgage to be in writing.

25.4.3.1   Intangible property

In the case of intangible property, transfer is usually by assignment in writing. In the case of a mortgage of a debt, notice should be given to the debtor to perfect the assignment to make the assignment a legal, as opposed to an equitable, assignment and to fix priority as against any other assignee of the debt in accordance with the rule in *Dearle* v *Hall* (1828) 3 Russ 1.

25.4.3.2   Impact of the Bills of Sale Acts 1878–1891

If the mortgagee does not take possession of the mortgaged property a written transfer by way of mortgage must correspond with the formal requirements of the Bills of Sale Acts (see **25.6.1**). Similarly a general assignment of future book debts must be registered in accordance with the Acts.

25.4.3.3   Equitable interests

A mortgage of an equitable interest in property must be in writing (Law of Property Act 1925, s. 53).

25.4.4   Enforcement

A mortgagee generally has four rights as a means of enforcing the mortgage:

(a) a right of foreclosure which terminates the mortgagor's right of redemption;

(b) a right to take possession of the mortgaged property; where the mortgage is a security bill of sale, the mortgagee has a special statutory right of seizure (see **25.6.1.5**);

(c) an implied power of sale;

(d) the right to apply to the court for an order for sale or the appointment of a receiver.

These rights are generally amplified and reinforced by express provisions in the security instrument.

25.4.4.1   The equity of redemption

The mortgagor's equity of redemption prevents the mortgagee claiming outright ownership and compels him to allow the mortgagor to redeem the mortgaged property, by tender of the amount due, plus interest, even after the agreed time for redemption is passed. The mortgagor's equity of redemption is extinguished by foreclosure and sale.

25.4.4.2   Foreclosure

If the debtor fails to redeem the mortgage within a reasonable time after the debt has become due, the mortgagor can apply for a court order for foreclosure.

The effect of foreclosure is to end the mortgagor's equity of redemption, leaving the mortgagee outright owner of the property. In the case of an equitable mortgage a further court order for the transfer to the mortgagor of the legal property is necessary. The debt secured by the mortgage is extinguished: the mortgagee is deemed to have taken the property in satisfaction of the debt.

Foreclosure may give the mortgagee a windfall where the value of the asset exceeds the debt, so the court tends to be reluctant to make a foreclosure order without giving the mortgagee the opportunity to redeem. In practice, the court makes an order *nisi* in the first instance, allowing the debtor to redeem within a specified period, after which the creditor can apply to have the order made absolute if the debtor has not paid.

Due to delays in this procedure, mortgagees usually prefer the remedies of possession and sale.

25.4.4.3 Power of sale

The mortgagee has a power of sale where:

(a) the mortgage is created by deed (Law of Property Act 1925, s. 101);

(b) it is expressly or impliedly included in the contract of mortgage;

(c) the mortgage is a security bill of sale under the Bills of Sale Acts.

(a) *Mortgage created by deed*
The Law of Property Act 1925, s. 101 gives the mortgagee a power of sale where the mortgage is created by deed. This provision applies to mortgages of any property other than goods (*Re Morritt* (1886) 18 QBD 222). Section 103 imposes restrictions on the statutory power of sale but these are usually excluded by the mortgage document.

(b) *Power reserved by the contract*
A well drafted mortgage will include an express power of sale. In the absence of an express power, a right of sale may be implied. There is extensive authority supporting the existence of a common law right to sell under a mortgage of intangible property (e.g. *Deverges* v *Sandman, Clark & Co.* [1902] 1 Ch 579). The position of a mortgagee of goods is unclear: there is authority that a legal mortgagee in possession of goods has a common law power of sale if the mortgagor defaults (*Re Morritt* (1886) 18 QBD 222) but this was queried in *Deverges* v *Sandman, Clark & Co.* [1902] 1 Ch 579 so that an express power should be reserved.

The position of an equitable mortgagee is unclear and an equitable mortgagee wishing to sell should seek the assistance of the court.

(c) *Where the mortgage is a security bill of sale under the bills of sale legislation*
In such cases the mortgagee has a power of sale subject to restrictions imposed by the legislation (see **25.6.1**).

25.4.4.4 Order for sale or appointment of a receiver

In any case, a mortgagee can apply to the court for an order for sale, or the appointment of a receiver (Law of Property Act 1925, ss. 109, 101).

As already noted, express powers of seizure, sale and for appointment of a receiver should be included in the security instrument creating the mortgage. The powers of the receiver should also be spelled out: if not the receiver has the powers given by statute (Law of Property Act 1925, s. 109; Insolvency Act 1986, sch. 1). For instance, debenture documents creating a mortgage over company property will usually empower the debenture holder to appoint a receiver who will act as the mortgagor company's agent, with authority to run the business, enter into contracts, realise assets and eventually dispose of the business if possible as a going concern.

25.4.4.5 Duty of care

Although a mortgagee exercising a power of sale sells for his own benefit rather than on behalf of the mortgagor, he is nevertheless under a duty of care to obtain a reasonable price.

This duty may be excluded by a carefully drafted term in the mortgage (*Bishop* v *Bonham* [1988] 1 WLR 742 at 752).

25.4.4.6 **Distribution of proceeds**

If sale of the mortgaged property realises more than is required to pay the debt, the mortgagee must account to the mortgagor for the surplus (Law of Property Act 1925, s. 105). The Court of Appeal has held that even a mortgagee, misled by fradulent misrepresentation into making a mortgage advance, who chooses to enforce his rights as a secured creditor by selling the mortgaged property, can only retain an amount to cover the debt: any surplus must be held on trust for the debtor (*Halifax Building Society* v *Thomas* [1996] Ch 217).

25.5 Equitable charge

An equitable charge involves the debtor (chargor) granting the creditor (chargee) the right to have designated property of the debtor appropriated to discharge the debt. It involves no transfer of possession or ownership of the property; the debt is satisfied by the proceeds of sale of the property which can be transacted voluntarily by the chargor or result from an application by the chargee for a court order.

As a mere encumbrance without any conveyance or assignment, a charge exists only in equity or under statute.

A charge can be created over any class of property, including goods, intangible property and property to be acquired by the debtor.

Although charges can be conferred by an individual, they are most often utilised by companies to secure loans.

25.5.1 Fixed or floating

Equitable charges can be fixed or floating.

A fixed (or specific) charge is one which attaches to the property as soon as the charge is created or the chargor acquires the rights over the property to be charged, whichever is the later. The chargor cannot dispose of the property free of the charge without the chargee's consent, unless the debt secured by the charge is paid.

Any person can create a fixed charge. Charges created by an individual are subject to the bills of sale legislation; those created by companies are subject to the companies legislation.

More flexible is the floating charge which is not dedicated to any particular asset(s) but floats over a designated class of assets, present or future, allowing the chargor to deal with those assets free from the charge as long as it remains floating. The security fund is therefore constantly changing; but if, for example, the chargor defaults on a repayment, or goes into liquidation, the charge *crystallises*, that is to say it attaches to those assets then owned by the chargor which correspond with the description specified in the charging instrument, limiting the chargor's right to deal with them. Details of the circumstances in which a floating charge will crystallise should be provided for in the charging instrument.

Because of restrictions imposed by the bills of sale legislation on charges by individuals over acquired property, only a limited company can create a floating charge.

From the creditor's perspective the main advantage of a floating charge was that it would normally allow the chargee to appoint an administrative receiver of the chargor company's property. As a result the chargee was entitled to be notified of any application for an administration order and could effectively block the making of such an order by appointing an administrative receiver. Moreover, where the floating charge covered the whole of the chargor's business as was often the case, any administration receives appointed would be enhanced to take over the management of the whole of the chargor's business. A creditor secured by fixed charges would often take a floating charge over the same property (a so-called 'light weight floating charge') in order to obtain the power to appoint an administrator. However, the appointment by a floating charge holder of an administrative receiver is now (subject to certain special exceptions) prohibited by s. 250 of the Enterprise Act 2002 (inserting a new s. 72A into the Insolvency Act 1986). As a result floating charges may in future be less attractive to creditors than in the past.

An institution lending to a company will usually take a fixed charge over certain assets of a company (for example, by way of a legal mortgage on its premises, plant and machinery) and then a floating charge over the remainder of its assets.

25.5.2 Debentures

A charge may be created by contract or trust, but a commercial charge is generally created by contract. A charge created by a contract is often referred to as a 'debenture'. The Companies Act 1985 defines debenture as including debenture stock, bonds and any other securities of a company whether constituting a charge on the assets of the company or not, but the term can more generally be used to refer to a type of instrument which creates a charge on the company's assets.

Lending institutions such as banks have their own printed form of debenture which will normally contain:

(a) an undertaking by the company to repay on demand all monies owing, including interest and charges;

(b) an undertaking by the company to create:
   (i)   a fixed charge on assets X, Y and Z; and
   (ii) a floating charge over the company's remaining assets, present and future;

(c) an undertaking by the company to create no mortgage or charge that would rank in priority to or *pari passu* with the floating charge created herein;

(d) provision that the monies secured by the debenture become payable on the happening of any of the following events:
   (i)   a written demand for payment by the bank;
   (ii) the commencement of winding-up proceedings in respect of the company; or
   (iii) the cessation of business by the company;

(e) power for the bank to appoint a receiver in certain circumstances, usually at any time after it has demanded payment of the monies secured and whether or not they have become due;

(f) an undertaking by the company to provide the bank quarterly, or on demand, with up to date financial records, including a trading account, profit and loss account and balance sheet representing the true position of the company and duly audited, to enable the bank to review the financial situation and health of the company;

(g) an undertaking by the company to insure all its assets to their full value with such persons as the bank may approve, and provide proof of such insurance.

25.6 Statutory control

Non-possessory securities, i.e. mortgages and equitable charges, are subject to a high degree of statutory control, which requires the registration of security interests as a means of providing third parties with notice of them. Where the debtor is an individual, the bills of sale legislation lays down various requirements as to form and registration. Where the debtor is a company, security interests in the form of a charge, including mortgages (Companies Act 1985, s. 396(4)), must be registered under the Companies Act 1985, ss. 395–397. Moreover, there exists a number of separate registers setting out different rules for specific types of property.

(a) Merchant Shipping Act 1894, s. 31 and Merchant Shipping Act 1988, sch. 3.

(b) Agricultural Credits Act 1928, ss. 8 and 14, and Agricultural Marketing Act 1958, s. 15.

(c) Trade Marks Act 1994, s. 25.

(d) Registered Designs Act 1949, s. 19.

(e) Industrial and Provident Societies Act 1967, s. 1.

(f) Patents Act 1977, s. 33.

(g) Civil Aviation Act 1982, s. 86 and Mortgaging of Aircraft Order 1972, SI 1972 No. 1268 (as amended).

For our purposes, the two most important systems of regulation are those in the bills of sale legislation and the Companies Act. We will also examine one of the more important specific registers, to see how it operates.

25.6.1   Bills of sale

Broadly speaking, a bill of sale is an instrument in writing whereby one party transfers property in goods to another party but remains in possession.

There are two types of bill of sale:

(a) an absolute bill; and

(b) a conditional bill, more usually called a 'security bill'.

A bill is absolute if given otherwise than as security for payment of money; a bill is a conditional, or a security bill if it is given to secure a money payment.

25.6.1.1   The legislation

The bills of sale legislation provides for a public registration system for bills of sale to protect third parties who are contemplating taking security in return for credit. The potential creditor has the opportunity to examine the register to see if other prior security interests exist, before advancing the credit. The legislation also seeks to protect the debtor from poor deals and oppressive enforcement measures, by requiring bills to be in a prescribed form and restricting enforcement procedures. The courts have been astute to prevent creditors evading the statutory controls; therefore where an individual or other non-corporate entity, such as a trading partnership, gives security over goods, the bills of sale legislation comes into play and the transaction must be considered in order to decide if it applies.

There are four Bills of Sale Acts in force:

(a) the Bills of Sale Act 1878 (which applies to absolute bills of sale);

(b) the Bills of Sale Act (1878) Amendment Act 1882 (which applies specifically to security bills of sale);

(c) the Bills of Sale Act 1890 (which amends the 1882 Act); and

(d) the Bills of Sale Act 1891 (which amends the 1890 Act).

The 1878 and 1882 Acts must be read together regarding bills of sale given by way of security for a money payment. A transaction comes within the scope of the Acts if five conditions are met:

(a) there must be a document: oral transactions are not affected by the legislation;

(b) the document must be a bill of sale as defined by the legislation;

(c) the document must relate to personal chattels as defined in the legislation;

(d) the document must confer on the transferee a right to seize or take possession of the goods; and

(e) this right to possession must derive from the document.

25.6.1.2   Exclusions

(a) The legislation does not apply when security is given by a company. The 1882 Act, s. 17 provides that a bill of sale does not include a debenture issued by a company and indeed no other form of company security comes within the remit of this legislation.

(b) The 1878 Act, s. 4 states that the term 'bill of sale' only applies to 'documents' relating to 'personal chattels' so that security over intangible property is excluded, although under the Insolvency Act 1986, s. 334, a general assignment of book debts by way of security is registrable as if it was a general bill of sale.

(c) Oral transactions are exempt.

(d) Further exclusions are found in the 1878 Act, s. 4: assignments for the benefit of creditors and marriage settlements which involve security, and transfers of goods in the ordinary course of business of any trade or calling.

25.6.1.3   Registration

The 1882 Act requires that all security transactions covered by the Acts must be registered within seven days (s. 8) and, if necessary, the registration is to be renewed every five years (s. 11). If the bill of sale is not duly registered, it is void and not enforceable. Bills are registered at the Filing and Record Department of the Central Office at the Royal Courts of Justice in London.

25.6.1.4   Formalities

The 1882 Act, s. 9 makes a security bill of sale void unless made in a deed in the form prescribed in the schedule to the Act. The bill must include:

(a) the names, addresses and descriptions of the parties;

(b) the consideration given by the creditor;

(c) the details of the repayment: amount, interest, time and manner;

(d) the details of insurance;

(e) the enforcement terms;

(f) a reasonably detailed inventory of the chattels affected (1882 Act, s. 4); and

(g) an attestation by one or more credible witnesses (1882 Act, s. 6).

This form must also be contained in a deed. Non-compliance not only means that the security interest cannot be enforced but also that the underlying loan is void.

25.6.1.5   Enforcement

The 1882 Act gives the creditor limited powers to seize and sell personal chattels secured by the bill of sale. The secured chattels may be seized by the creditor on five grounds (s. 7) if:

(a) the debtor is in default, or fails to comply with any obligations necessary to maintain the security;

(b) the debtor becomes bankrupt, or suffers the goods to be distrained for rent, rates, or taxes;

(c) the debtor fraudulently removes or allows the goods to be removed from the agreed premises;

(d) the debtor fails to comply with a written request for his last receipt of rents, rates or taxes; or

(e) execution has been levied against the debtor's goods.

If seized, the goods cannot be removed from the debtor's premises for five days and in that time the debtor can apply to the court for relief (s. 7).

25.6.1.6 Practical use of bills of sale

The extensive formality and registration requirements means that in practice, in spite of the draconian effect of failure to comply, the vast majority of bills of sale are not registered. Coupled with the statutory restrictions on enforcement procedures, the formal requirements of the legislation mean that mortgages and charges of goods by individuals are little used.

25.6.2 Companies Acts

The Companies Act 1985, ss. 395–397 require certain charges (including mortgages) created by a limited company to be registered with the Registrar of Companies.

Unlike the bills of sale legislation, the Companies Act protects only third parties, not the debtor company itself: companies are considered to be in a sufficiently strong bargaining position to protect themselves.

The Companies Act 1989, Part IV contains provisions intended to reform the registration provisions of the 1985 Act but they have not yet been implemented.

25.6.2.1 Registration

The Companies Act 1985, s. 396 sets out a list of classes of charges which must be registered. Particulars of a registrable charge, together with the instrument by which the charge was created or evidenced, must be registered at Companies House within 21 days of its creation. Failure to register a charge as required renders the charge void against a liquidator and any creditor of the company.

The duty to register the charge is imposed on the company but in practice, to ensure registration, the secured creditor usually does so. When registration is completed the Companies Registrar issues to the applicant a certificate of registration which is conclusive evidence of registration.

The register of charges is a public register, available for consultation by the public for a small fee. Any person contemplating advancing loan or credit facilities on the basis of security offered by a limited company, should inspect the register for prior registered charges. The company is also required to maintain its own register of charges. Non-compliance with these registration requirements means that the security is void *against the liquidator and any creditor* of the company so that against them the creditor is unsecured. It remains valid against all other persons, however, and so it continues to bind the company and any purchaser of the charged assets.

25.6.2.2 Priority

Registration of a charge is required to perfect the chargee's security. Where there are two or more charges over the same property, priority depends primarily on the date of creation of the charge.

(a) *Priority of competing fixed or floating charges*

As between two similar charges, priority depends on the date of creation so that, provided it is registered within the 21 day period, the first created charge has priority over the second, even if the latter is the first registered.

EXAMPLE

Charge 1: registered 10 June 2000, created 5 June 2000.
Charge 2: registered 21 June 2000, created 1 June 2000.
Here, Charge 2 has priority.

(b) *Floating charge versus fixed charge*

Where a fixed charge is created over property covered by a prior floating charge, the normal rule is varied so that the later fixed charge may have priority because it is regarded as having being completed under an implied licence from the holder of the floating charge.

In order to avoid this the chargee may include in the floating charge a 'negative pledge' clause providing as follows:

The company undertakes not to create any mortgages or charges on any of its assets which would rank in priority to or *pari passu* with the floating charge.

This clause will only be binding upon a subsequent chargee if he has notice of it; registration of the charge at Companies House is not itself notice that the charge contains a negative pledge clause. One way to avoid this outcome is to recite the clause in the documentation used when registering the charge.

25.6.3 Ship mortgages

Ship mortgages are commercially very important.

Ship ownership in the UK is governed principally by the Merchant Shipping Act 1894. The Act divides property in a ship into 64 notional shares, and imposes restrictions on who can own a ship or a share in a ship and on the form of dealings in ships or shares in them.

Every ship (over a certain tonnage) must be registered; registers of ownership are kept at most ports in the UK and some abroad. Upon registration, the registrar issues a 'certificate of registration' containing details of the ship. Shares are transferred following a form prescribed in the Act.

Ships, or shares in them, may be mortgaged. The deposit of the certificate of registration as security is illegal and void. A ship may be mortgaged following one of two forms set out in the First Schedule of the 1894 Act. The mortgage is complete when the relevant form is registered at the ship's port of registry and the required fee paid. However, lending institutions often go further by requiring execution of a memorandum which contains clauses similar to those found in bank mortgage forms providing, for instance, that:

(a) the mortgagor undertakes that the advances will be repaid upon demand;

(b) the security will be enforceable in the event of one month's default;

    (c) the mortgagor undertakes to keep the ship insured and in good repair so as to maintain her classification with Lloyd's.

Ships can be difficult to realise, especially in times of recession. The last provision seeks to ensure that the ship maintains its value.

If the mortgagor is also a limited company, the charge must also be registered under the Companies Act.

The Merchant Shipping Act 1894, s. 33 provides that mortgages of ships or shares therein take priority according to the date at which each mortgage is registered and not according to the date of the mortgage itself. A registered mortgage will always take priority over an unregistered mortgage. A creditor considering the advance of money secured by a mortgage must check the ship's register so as to determine if any prior mortgages have been registered. Mortgages are postponed to maritime liens so, to avoid the danger of a superseding maritime lien, lending institutions will often include in the memorandum an undertaking from the mortgagor that the risk of these liens arising will be covered by insurance and that the mortgagors will notify the insurers of the bank's interest in the ship.

The mortgage is discharged when the mortgage deed, with a receipt for the mortgage money endorsed thereon, duly signed and attested, is produced to the registrar (s. 32). The registrar then notes in the register that the mortgage has been discharged.

If the mortgagee finds that he must realise the ship, s. 35 empowers him to dispose of the ship or the share in respect of which he is interested.

25.7 Summary

At the end of this chapter, you should:

- be familiar with the different classifications of security as consensual or non-consensual and possessory or non-possessory;
- be familiar with the range of security options available to businesses and understand how the different types of security operate;
- be aware of the schemes of statutory control in relation to non-possessory security.

Personal security

26.1 Introduction

In this chapter our focus is on personal security. In it:

- we concentrate on the use of guarantees as a means of providing personal security. In doing so we:
    - classify guarantees as once-off or continuing, demand or conditional, and requested by debtor or creditor;
    - examine the rules on the formation of guarantees;
    - consider the legal relations between guarantor and creditor, and surety and debtor;
    - outline the rights against co-guarantors; and
    - analyse the position on discharge of a guarantee;
- we also briefly consider alternatives to the guarantee, such as indemnities, letters of credit, performance guarantees and letters of comfort.

Personal security is provided by means of contracts of suretyship, whereby one person, the surety, agrees to be answerable for the debt of another, the principal debtor. It therefore involves a tri-partite relationship between creditor, principal debtor and surety. It should be noted that the debtor is not a party to the contract of surety.

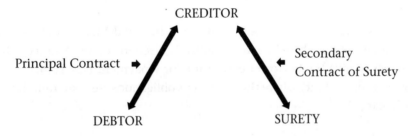

A contract of surety gives the creditor a personal right of action against the surety but no real rights over property. Its value thus depends entirely on the creditworthiness of the surety. However, the surety may be required to reinforce his personal undertaking by providing real security to secure his performance: for instance, he may be required to mortgage his house.

Contracts of suretyship take two forms: guarantees and indemnities.

26.1.1 Guarantees defined

A guarantee is an undertaking, given by a third party, to answer for another's default.

EXAMPLE

X will loan money to Y, subject to Z providing security by guaranteeing the loan. The guarantor, Z, will only become liable under the guarantee if the principal debtor, Y, defaults.

The guarantee is based on the debtor's default so, it is referred to as a secondary obligation; the primary obligation to pay lies with the principal debtor (Y).

26.1.2 Guarantees and indemnities distinguished

The secondary liability of a guarantee can be compared with the surety's primary liability under an indemnity.

Like a guarantee, an indemnity is a personal security undertaking given by a third party, but under an indemnity the surety's obligation is independent of the debtor/creditor relationship. It is therefore a primary liability, not dependent on the debtor's default.

An indemnity does not have to be in any specific form.

The difference between indemnities and guarantees can be illustrated by example.

EXAMPLE

If X says to Y: 'Supply goods to Z and if he does not pay, I will', X's undertaking is a contract of guarantee, as payment by X is conditional on Y's default. But if X says to Y: 'Supply goods to Z and I will see you paid', this is a contract of indemnity because X's liability to pay is not contingent on Y's default (*Birkmyr* v *Darnell* (1704) 1 Salk 27).

Guarantees and indemnities are often used to reinforce each other (see e.g. *Gulf Bank K.S.C.* v *Mitsubishi Heavy Industries Ltd (No. 2)* [1994] 2 Lloyd's Rep 145). A standard provision in a contract for guarantee might state:

Without prejudice to the guarantee herein given, the guarantor agrees to indemnify the Bank against any loss or damage which the Bank may suffer as a result of providing the debtor, named above, with credit facilities

or:

[The guarantor] undertakes, as a separate and independent obligation, that all sums due under the guarantee, shall be recoverable by the creditor from [the guarantor], as principal debtor and/or by way of indemnity.

A clause such as the latter is known as a 'principal debtor clause'. Its main purpose is to exclude the rules by which a guarantor is discharged, for instance, where the creditor agrees to give the borrower extra time for repayment (see **26.8.1**), or to preserve the guarantor's liability where the borrower's obligations are void from the outset or are later discharged.

26.2 Guarantees

A guarantee can be used to secure both fixed and revolving debts. For example, before agreeing to sell goods on credit terms, a seller, unsure of the potential buyer's creditworthiness, may require that a creditworthy third party guarantees payment of the price. Similarly, a bank contemplating providing loan or overdraft facilities, may require a creditworthy third party to guarantee repayment.

Common instances of the use of guarantees include a parent guaranteeing a child's loan; directors of a private limited company guaranteeing a loan to the company; and a parent company guaranteeing a loan to a subsidiary company. The export trade also relies heavily on a system of institutional guarantees, whereby the Government, through the Export Credits Guarantee Department, protects sellers of goods abroad against default by buyers and also guarantees bank loans for capital development. A similar system operates in most trading nations world-wide. A del credere agent who arranges an international sale contract guarantees payment by the buyer (see **4.3.3**).

26.2.1 Performance guarantees

Guarantees are used not only to secure the repayment of a loan or overdraft but also can be given to guarantee tender or performance of a contract. Such transactions are known as performance guarantees or bonds but they do not comply with the strict legal meaning of guarantees (see **26.10**).

26.3 Types of guarantee

Guarantees can be classified in several ways.

26.3.1 Once-off and continuing guarantees

A guarantee may secure a single, 'once-off', obligation, such as the price under a sale contract, or a loan of fixed sum credit. Alternatively it may secure a continuing obligation, such as rental instalments due under a lease or equipment hire contract, or sums due under a revolving credit facility such as an overdraft.

A 'once-off' guarantee secures the single transaction until the debtor's obligation has been discharged. A continuing guarantee imposes a continuing obligation on the surety; if it secures a revolving facility it continues so long as the facility remains available and the amount of the guarantor's liability will vary in accordance with the extent of the debtor's borrowing.

A creditor will usually require a guarantee of a revolving facility to include a provision that the guarantee will continue despite intermediate discharge of the debt; for example:

> The guarantor's liability under the guarantee will be of a continuous nature and apply to the balance outstanding from time to time and shall not be terminated by any intermediary payment or satisfaction of the debt owed by the debtor.

The effect is that the guarantor remains liable throughout the period of the credit facility and is not released merely because the debt is cleared from time to time.

26.3.2 Demand and conditional guarantees

Under a conditional guarantee the guarantor's obligation to pay is conditional on the happening of a specified event, such as the production of a written statement that the principal debtor is in default or a court judgement in favour of the creditor, so the clause might take the following form:

> The guarantor undertakes that, if the debtor defaults in the payment due to the creditor, he, the guarantor, will pay that sum to the creditor on the production of a written statement that the principal debtor is in default.

Under a demand guarantee the guarantor must pay on first demand by the creditor. An 'on demand' clause could be drafted along the following lines:

> The guarantor undertakes that, if the debtor defaults in the payment due to the creditor, he, the guarantor, will pay that sum to the creditor on demand.

Banks most often use demand guarantees so as to avoid disputes. Other financial institutions, such as insurance or surety companies, often agree to conditional guarantees.

Under a demand guarantee the surety's liability arises as soon as a demand is made. However, if the guarantee also contains what is termed a 'principal debtor' clause, the surety's liability is not even contingent on a demand being made (*MS Fashions* v *Bank of Credit & Commerce International SA* [1993] 3 All ER 769, cf. *Re Bank of Credit & Commerce International SA (No. 8)* [1994] 3 All ER 565).

26.3.3   Guarantees may be requested by debtor or creditor

Guarantees can also be classified according to whether they are requested by the debtor or creditor. Where the guarantee is requested by the creditor there is no contractual relationship between surety and debtor; this has important consequences for the guarantor's rights (see **26.6**).

In hire purchase agreements, where a finance company supplies goods on hire purchase to a debtor introduced by a dealer, from whom the finance company buys the goods, both these situations can arise: the finance house (the creditor) may require that a third party act as guarantor for the debtor, so that the debtor must ask a parent or friend to provide the guarantee; or the finance house may agree with the dealer that the dealer will guarantee payment by all debtors he introduces.

26.4   Formation of a guarantee

Guarantees must conform to the general requirements for formation of a contract. Those requirements are slightly modified in some respects.

26.4.1   Consideration

Unless made under seal the guarantee must be supported by consideration. Where the guarantee is of a future debt or transaction, the creditor provides consideration for the guarantor's promise by making the loan to the principal debtor, and the agreement should recite that the guarantee is given in consideration of the loan.

A guarantee of an existing debt may be expressed to be in consideration of the creditor's forbearance to sue the principal debtor; otherwise it must be made by deed, since the loan itself would be past consideration.

26.4.2   Written memorandum

A guarantee is not enforceable as a contract unless evidenced by a note or memorandum in writing and signed by the guarantor or other authorised person (Statute of Frauds 1677, s. 4). The relevant document(s) should record the existence of the guarantee and all the material terms (see e.g. *Carlton Communications plc & Granada Media plc* v *The Football League* [2002] EWHC 1650 (Comm)).

It can be argued that a defendant by his conduct is estopped from relying on section 4 (e.g. *Amalgamated Investment & Property Co Ltd (in liquidation)* v *Texas Commerce International Bank Ltd* [1982] QB 84) but such an argument will not succeed where the only inducement is the oral guarantee itself. In *Actionstrength Ltd* v *International Glass Engineering and Another* [2003] UKHL 17; [2003] 2 All ER 615, the claimant was a labour-only sub-contractor providing services to the main contractor, the first defendant, in connection with the building of a factory for the second defendant. The main contractor defaulted on a number of payments and ultimately the claimant withdrew its labour. It obtained default judgment against the main contractor for unpaid invoices but the main contractor became insolvent. The claimant issued proceedings against the second defendant on an alleged oral guarantee of the main contractor's liability. The claimant contended that in reliance on an oral promise from the defendant the claimant had not withdrawn its labour for one further month. The defendant argued that the claimant's action was precluded by the requirements of s. 4 of the Statute of Frauds 1677. The House of Lords found that while the claimant believed itself to be the beneficiary of an effective guarantee, the issue was whether the defendant had induced or encouraged the making of that belief. On the facts, there had been no representation by the defendant that it would honour the agreement despite the absence of writing; or that it was not a contract of guarantee; or that it would confirm the agreement in writing. Nor had the defendant made any payment direct to the claimant which could be relied on as affirming the oral guarantee or inducing the claimant to go on supplying labour. Lord Bingham stated that if the defendant were held to be estopped in this case, it would be hard to see why any oral guarantee, where credit was extended to a debtor on the strength of a guarantee, would not be similarly estopped. Such a result would render nugatory a provision (s. 4, SoF 1677) which despite its age, Parliament had chosen to retain.

26.4.3   Revocability of the guarantor's undertaking

A guarantee may be a unilateral or a bilateral contract.

If the creditor agrees that, in consideration of the surety's guarantee, it will provide credit to the debtor, the contract is bilateral. More often the creditor will not actually promise to advance credit. In that case the contract is unilateral: the surety's undertaking is that *if* the creditor advances credit, the surety will guarantee the debt. The creditor accepts that offer, and provides consideration for the surety's promise, by advancing the credit.

Where the contract is unilateral the surety can revoke its offer at any time before it is accepted. Once credit is advanced the surety is bound. In some cases, however, such as where the surety guarantees a revolving credit facility, the correct analysis may be that the surety's undertaking is a standing offer which the creditor accepts each time it makes a new advance to the debtor. In that case the surety can at any time revoke its offer and thus terminate its liability in respect of future advances; it remains liable in respect of advances made before revocation. The terms of the guarantee will normally require the surety to give notice before revoking the offer in this way.

Whether a continuing guarantee is revocable in this way depends on the construction of the contract. The undertaking is revocable where the consideration provided by the creditor is severable. Where the creditor's consideration is entire, for instance where the surety guarantees payment of rent if the creditor accepts the debtor as a tenant, the surety is irrevocably bound once its offer is accepted.

26.4.4   Duress and undue influence

If the surety's undertaking is obtained by duress, undue influence or misrepresentation by the creditor, the guarantee will be voidable (see *Lloyds Bank Ltd* v *Bundy* [1975] QB 326; *National Westminster Bank plc* v *Morgan* [1985] AC 686).

Unlike contracts of insurance, contracts of suretyship are not contracts of *utmost good faith*, i.e. the creditor is not under a duty to disclose all material facts to the guarantor. However, the law has recognised a limited duty on the creditor to disclose information to the guarantor. The principle appears to be that a creditor is under a duty to disclose to the surety, what in general terms can be described as unusual features unknown to the surety. In *Levett* v *Barclays*

Bank plc [1995] 2 All ER 615, at first instance, the court in applying this principle held that a creditor was under a duty to disclose to the surety, contractual arrangements made between the debtor and the creditor which make the terms of the principal contract something materially different in a potentially disadvantageous respect from those which the surety might naturally expect (see further *Geest plc* v *Fyffes plc* [1999] 1 All ER (Comm) 672).

26.4.4.1 Improper conduct by the debtor

The guarantee may also be invalidated by duress, undue influence or misrepresentation by the *debtor* if:

(a) the debtor was acting as the creditor's agent, for instance, in obtaining the surety's agreement to the transaction; or

(b) the creditor has actual or constructive notice of the debtor's improper conduct.

In *Barclays Bank* v *O'Brien* [1994] 1 AC 180, the House of Lords held that, where a wife gave a guarantee to secure her husband's debt, the guarantee was not to the wife's advantage and there was a substantial risk of the husband committing a wrong which would allow the wife to set the transaction aside, so that the creditor would have constructive notice of any improper conduct by the debtor unless the creditor took reasonable steps to ensure that the guarantee had been properly obtained. The same rule applies where surety and debtor are cohabitees and the creditor is aware of the personal relationship between them, or in any other relationship where the creditor is aware that the guarantor reposes trust and confidence in the principal debtor (see, for example, the Court of Appeal decision in *Credit Lyonnais* v *Burch* [1997] 1 All ER 144, where the relationship between surety and principal debtor was that of employee and employer).

In *Royal Bank of Scotland plc* v *Etridge and ors* [2001] UKHL 44; [2001] 4 All ER 449; [2001] 3 WLR 1021, their Lordships sought to indicate clear, simple and practically operable minimum requirements for the procedures followed when a bank is obtaining security. In particular, a bank would satisfy the minimum requirements to take steps to bring to the wife's attention the risks of standing as surety for her husband if it insisted that the wife attend a private meeting with a representative of the bank where she was:

(a) told of the extent of her liability as surety; and

(b) warned of the risk she was running; and

(c) urged to take separate legal advice.

To be safe, a bank could insist that she take separate legal advice from a solicitor on whose confirmation the bank could rely that she understood the nature and effect of the transaction. The House of Lords also set out the minimum content of the legal advice that a solicitor advising the wife should give.

Where the guarantee is not for the *sole* benefit of the debtor, as, for instance, where a wife guarantees a loan made to her and her husband jointly and secures the guarantee by giving a mortgage over her property, the creditor is not fixed with constructive notice of improper conduct by the debtor (*CIBC Mortgages plc* v *Pitt* [1994] 1 AC 200).

26.5 Relations between the guarantor and the creditor

Unless agreed otherwise, the guarantor's liability is coterminous with that of the principal debtor, so that the guarantor is not liable unless the debtor defaults, and, where the debtor pays the secured debt in full, the guarantee terminates.

If the debtor defaults, it is not necessary for the creditor to sue or even to make a claim against the principal debtor before calling on the guarantor unless the contract of guarantee expressly so provides; it is unlikely that a bank would agree to such a provision.

26.5.1   Nature of the guarantor's liability

The extent of the guarantor's liability depends on the construction of the contract but usually the guarantor's responsibility is not merely to pay a sum of money to the creditor if the principal debtor fails to do so, but to procure the debtor's performance.

In *Moschi* v *Lep Air Services Ltd* [1973] AC 331, freight forwarders agreed to relinquish their lien over the debtor's goods in return for the debtor's agreement to pay £40,000 in instalments. The appellants guaranteed performance of the debtor's obligation. The debtor defaulted and the creditors, treating this as a repudiation of the agreement, terminated the contract and claimed against the appellants. They argued that termination of the contract with the principal debtors released them from liability. The House of Lords held that the appellants' undertaking was not to pay the instalments on the debtor's default but to procure performance by the debtor of his obligations under the contract, so that the guarantors were liable for damages equal to the amount the debtor would have paid, plus interest.

26.5.2   Invalidity of the principal contract

The effect on the surety's liability of invalidity or unenforceability of the main contract depends on the construction of the surety contract and whether it is classified as a guarantee or an indemnity.

26.5.2.1   Guarantees

Since a guarantee is ancillary to the main contract, if the principal contract is void and unenforceable, so too is the contract of guarantee. This point is illustrated by the case of *Coutts & Co.* v *Browne-Lecky* [1947] KB 104, where a guarantee of a minor's overdraft at a bank could not be enforced due to the Infants Relief Act 1874 which provided that the infant was not liable to repay the loan.

26.5.2.2   Indemnities

If the surety is properly construed as an indemnity, the surety incurs primary liability so that he remains liable even though the principal contract is unenforceable against the principal debtor. To avoid any uncertainty over classification of the surety, an express provision should be included that the surety shall be liable even in circumstances where the principal debtor is not: see *Heald* v *O'Connor* [1971] 1 WLR 497.

26.5.2.3   Surety contract void

If the surety contract itself is void or voidable it is irrelevant that it is an indemnity rather than a guarantee. In *Associated Japanese Bank (International) Ltd* v *Crédit du Nord SA* [1988] 3 All ER 902, the defendants guaranteed payment of rentals due to the plaintiffs under a sale and lease-back arrangement of machinery and undertook that they would be liable as 'sole or principal debtor'. In fact the machinery which was the subject of the sale and lease-back contract did not exist. It was held that the guarantee contract itself was void *ab initio* for mistake so that the plaintiffs could recover nothing under the guarantee. In addition the court found that on the construction of the contract there was an express (or at least implied) condition precedent to the guarantee agreement that the machinery existed.

26.6 Relations between surety and debtor

The guarantor has two basic rights against the principal debtor:

(a) a right to indemnity; and

(b) a right of subrogation.

Where there is a contract between surety and debtor these may be supplemented by express, or implied, provisions of the contract.

26.6.1 The right to indemnity

If the guarantee is given at the request of the debtor, the guarantor has an implied contractual right to be indemnified by the debtor against all liabilities he incurs. This is an example of the general rule that if one party incurs expenditure or liabilities at another party's request or with his authority, then that party is entitled to be compensated or indemnified, since the request or authority implies a promise to compensate or indemnify the creditor (*Re a Debtor* [1937] 1 All ER 1 at 7–8, *per* Greene LJ).

The guarantee may include terms which restrict the guarantor's right of indemnity; for example:

The guarantor undertakes not to pursue a claim for indemnity in competition with the creditor in the bankruptcy of the principal debtor until the creditor has received payment in full.

The effect is that the guarantor cannot pursue his right of indemnity, and hence reduce the pool of assets available to satisfy the creditor's claim, until the creditor's claim has been satisfied.

Where a guarantor entitled to indemnity is sued on the guarantee he may claim indemnity from the debtor in third party proceedings.

26.6.2 A right of subrogation

Where the guarantor discharges the debt which he has guaranteed, he is entitled to step into the shoes of the creditor and, under the doctrine of subrogation, pursue any claims against the debtor which the creditor had, including by enforcing securities held by the creditor for the debt, whether made before or after the guarantee.

The doctrine of subrogation arises by operation of the law to prevent the debtor being unjustly enriched; it is available whether the guarantee was given at the request of the debtor or the creditor.

For the purposes of subrogation, although the payment of the debt extinguishes the debt, any other securities are kept alive for the benefit of the guarantor who is entitled to have them transferred to him together with any judgement obtained by the creditor. The guarantor ranks in the same priority as the creditor.

The guarantor can only claim a right to subrogation to securities or other rights of the creditor where he has paid the debt in full: a proportionate right of subrogation does not exist.

26.7   Rights against co-guarantors

Where two or more guarantors are liable for the same obligation to the same amount, the extent of the liability is shared equally between them, unless otherwise agreed. So, where one guarantor has paid the full guaranteed amount, he is entitled to claim reimbursement from his co-guarantor in an equitable action for contribution (the debtor and any other co-guarantors should be joined as co-defendants in the action to avoid multiplicity of actions).

The guarantees need not be created by the same instrument and indeed the fact that each guarantor was unaware of the other's existence does not affect the right to contribution.

Where the guarantees cover the same obligation but in different amounts, each guarantor must contribute in proportion to their respective liabilities.

26.8   Discharge of the guarantee

A guarantee is usually discharged where:

(a) the creditor does any act which alters the guarantor's rights, or

(b) the debtor is discharged from liability.

26.8.1   Where the guarantor's rights are altered

Unless otherwise agreed, any acts or omissions by the creditor which alter or extinguish the guarantor's rights (for example, by releasing a co-guarantor or varying another security from the debtor) operate to discharge the guarantee. The guarantor does not have to prove loss or damage. To avoid this outcome, the guarantee should include a provision such as:

The guarantor agrees and consents to any alteration, variation, amendment or extinction of his rights to indemnity and subrogation made by the creditor.

26.8.2   Discharge of the debtor

26.8.2.1   Under a guarantee

Since a guarantor's liability is coterminous with that of the debtor, the guarantor's liability is discharged if the debt is paid, or the debtor is discharged from liability, or the liability to pay is extinguished by operation of the law.

If, on construction of the guarantee, the guarantor is responsible for procuring the debtor's performance the guarantor is not released if the creditor terminates the principal contract in response to a serious breach of contract by the debtor (see **26.5.1**). The debtor's primary liability in debt is converted into a liability in damages and this secondary obligation is also guaranteed.

26.8.2.2   Under an indemnity

Since under an indemnity the surety's liability is independent of the debtor's, discharge of the debtor does not necessarily release the surety under a contract of indemnity.

26.9   Letters of credit

Letters of credit (see **Chapter 23**), or documentary credits, are utilised as a means of securing payment in international sales contracts. They are used, especially under an international contract, to give a seller of goods an assurance of payment: the buyer arranges for a bank to give the seller an undertaking to pay the price if certain conditions are fulfilled. They thus resemble a guarantee. However, the bank's undertaking under a letter of credit is generally a primary obligation, independent of the underlying contract and the seller looks to the bank rather than to the buyer for payment.

26.10   Performance guarantees

Performance guarantees (sometimes referred to as bank guarantees or performance bonds) are not guarantees in the strict common law sense, in that they are not secondary obligations which come into operation on the debtor's default, but are primary autonomous obligations. They are undertakings by a bank or similar institution to pay money, used in a similar way to letters of credit to provide an assurance of payment or performance of another obligation.

Like letters of credit, performance guarantees are independent of the underlying contract; see **23.5**.

26.11   Letters of comfort

A letter of comfort may be used as an alternative to a guarantee. The use of letters of comfort has become more common recently, as a means of reassuring potential creditors that their loan or credit facilities will be repaid, without actually guaranteeing repayment. It is usually given by a parent company to support an advance of credit facilities to its subsidiary by a lending institution.

26.11.1   Contents of the letter

A typical comfort letter usually provides:

(a) a statement of the awareness of the parent company of the advances made to the subsidiary;

(b) a promise that the parent company will not, without the lender's consent, relinquish or reduce control of the subsidiary before repayment; and

(c) words of comfort, stating how far the parent company is prepared to go in supporting its subsidiary, often beginning 'it is our intention', or 'it is our policy'.

26.11.2   Contractual effect of the letter of comfort

Whether the words of comfort in (c) above have contractual effect depends on the construction of the letter; however, it seems that generally they will be regarded as not intended to be binding. In *Kleinwort Benson Ltd* v *Malaysia Mining Corp. Ltd* [1989] 1 WLR 379 a creditor agreed a loan with a subsidiary company based on two letters of comfort provided by the parent company (who had been unwilling to guarantee the loan) along the following lines:

It is our policy to ensure that the business of the subsidiary is at all times in a position to meet its liabilities to you under the loan agreement.

The subsidiary company went into liquidation and the creditors sought repayment from the parent company. The Court of Appeal held that the letter of comfort was not intended to create a contractual promise as to future conduct. The court did not consider the possibility that the letters contained an *implied* future promise but took the view that letters of comfort are generally commercially regarded as intended to create a moral, but not a legally binding, obligation.

As a result of this case a letter of comfort represents a poor substitute for a binding personal security undertaking and creditors may be reluctant to advance credit on the basis of letters of comfort alone. However, where a parent company is unwilling to provide a guarantee, a letter of comfort may be the only 'security' available to the creditor.

26.12 Summary

Having read this chapter you should:

- be able to advise a client of the different forms of personal security devices available to him; and
- be familiar with all aspects of the formation of guarantees, the various rights and obligations under a guarantee, and the position on discharge of a guarantee.

Quasi-security

27.1 Introduction

In order to avoid the formality and registration requirements of legislation such as the bills of sale legislation and Companies Act, a creditor may seek security which falls outside the legislation, or disguise the arrangement as something else, such as a sale. For example, in order to raise finance on the security of goods the owner may agree to sell them to the proposed lender subject to an agreement that he may buy them back on repaying the price.

Such devices are referred to as 'quasi-security' because they perform a function similar to other security devices but strictly speaking are not classified as types of security. In this chapter:

- we consider the fine line between a sale and a security interest;
- we consider a number of different quasi-security arrangements, such as
  - retention of title arrangements;
  - the use of assets as security;
  - bills of exchange and
  - set-off agreements;
- lastly, we identify the factors that should be considered in deciding what type of security device to use.

27.2 Sale and security

A transfer of property intended to operate by way of security is not governed by the provisions of the Sale of Goods Act 1979 (s. 62(4)). If the agreement really creates a security interest, then, depending on the nature of the agreement, it may be unenforceable for lack of formality and/or non-registration. It may therefore be necessary to decide:

(a) whether a transaction is a genuine sale or a disguised security arrangement; and

(b) if it is a security arrangement, what kind of security it creates.

27.2.1 Classifying the transaction

In assessing the nature of the agreement, the court looks beyond the form of the agreement and enquires into the facts of the case and the intention of the parties, to determine whether the agreement was a sham or a genuine sale or other type of agreement.

Relevant facts which a court will take into account include the relationship between the parties, the normal pattern of business of the credit provider and the factual accuracy of statements in the contract document (*North Central Wagon Finance* v *Brailsford* [1962] 1 All ER 502).

27.2.2 Sale or security

There are three basic distinctions between a sale and a security arrangement, such as a mortgage or charge.

(a) Under a sale the vendor is not entitled to get the subject-matter back by returning the purchase price. In the case of a mortgage or charge, the mortgagor is entitled, until he has been foreclosed, to recover the subject-matter of the mortgage or charge on payment of the debt.

(b) If the buyer resells the subject-matter of the sale at a profit, that profit is his. A mortgagee who realises the subject-matter of the mortgage for a sum greater than is sufficient to repay himself, must account to the mortgagor for the surplus.

(c) A buyer who resells the goods at a loss must bear that loss. A mortgagee who realises the subject-matter for a sum insufficient to satisfy his debt is entitled to look to the mortgagor to make good the balance (*Re George Inglefield Ltd* [1933] Ch 1 at 27 *per* Romer LJ).

27.3 Quasi-security devices

Despite these guidelines the distinction between a true sale and a disguised security may be difficult to draw. In addition there exists a number of legitimate quasi-security devices which are available, especially to a sale as opposed to a loan creditor, as alternatives to true security.

27.3.1 Title retention arrangements

A supplier of goods on credit terms can secure himself against the buyer's inability to pay by supplying the goods under an arrangement by which he reserves ownership of the goods until their price is paid.

27.3.1.1 Hire purchase

Under a hire purchase agreement the owner/creditor retains property in the goods until all the instalments and the final option payment are paid by the hirer/debtor. If the hirer/debtor becomes insolvent before this time, the owner/creditor can reclaim his property before it is realised to meet the claims of other creditors.

27.3.1.2 Conditional sale

Similarly, under a conditional sale, property in the goods does not pass to the buyer until the condition is met: typically, until the price is paid in full. Hence the seller can demand redelivery if, before paying for the goods in full, the buyer becomes insolvent.

A sale subject to a reservation of title clause is a conditional sale, expressly sanctioned by the Sale of Goods Act 1979, s. 19(2). It is now standard practice for sellers to include a clause to the effect that the property in the goods will not pass from the seller to the buyer until the price is paid (see **16.4.3**). If the buyer/debtor becomes insolvent before the price has been paid, the seller/creditor can demand the redelivery of his goods. Again the goods cannot be realised to meet the claims of other creditors because they still belong to the seller. A number of attempts have been made to challenge the effectiveness of reservation of title clauses and to argue that they create registrable charges. It is now settled that a simple clause which reserves title in goods until their price is paid does not create a charge (*Clough Mill Ltd* v *Martin* [1985] 1 WLR 111). The seller may even reserve property in goods supplied as security for payment of other debts (*Armour* v *Thyssen Edelstahlwerke GmbH* [1990] 3 All ER 481). Attempts to claim rights over other property than the goods supplied may be construed as creating a charge (see **16.4.3.1(c)**).

27.3.1.3 Finance leases

Under a lease the owner of goods transfers possession of the goods to a hirer, for use by the hirer, in return for payment, while retaining ownership. Since ownership is retained, the lessor can repossess the goods if the lessee defaults, and is thus effectively granted some security against the lessee's insolvency.

Leases can be classified as operating leases and finance leases. An operating lease usually involves goods being hired out to a series of different lessees in return for payment of rental; it can be used for a variety of arrangments, e.g. anything from the hire of a car for a day, to a five-year lease of an aeroplane. The owner is often responsible for such things as maintenance and repair of the goods.

A finance lease, on the other hand, is viewed as a financial tool where the retention of ownership is nominal. Here the goods (usually equipment) are acquired by the owner/lessor and hired out for a period equivalent to the working life of the equipment, to one lessee, who is responsible for their maintenance. The rental is calculated so that the 'owner' will recoup the cost of the goods and a profit. In effect, therefore, the lessor provides financial assistance to the lessee to acquire the goods while the lease provides the lessor with security against the lessee's default. Commercially such an arrangement achieves much the same effect as a secured credit sale of the goods but it is not recognised at law as creating a security interest.

27.3.1.4 Sale with a right to re-purchase

This involves a transaction whereby X sells goods to Y, payment to be by instalments. X and Y also agree that if Y defaults on the instalments, X has the right to purchase back the goods, setting off the amount outstanding against the repurchase price. Although this resembles a mortgage arrangement, if genuine, it will be regarded as a sale.

27.3.2 Use of assets as quasi-security

There are a number of arrangements which may be used by a business which wishes to raise finance using its assets as security, but without entering into formal legal security arrangements.

27.3.2.1 Sale and lease-back

Instead of agreeing a mortgage, an owner may sell goods to a finance house, for the purpose of raising funds, and then take them back under a lease, hire purchase, or conditional sale agreement. He thus has use of the goods and use of their capital value. The effect is very similar to a mortgage of the goods to secure a loan: ownership of the goods is transferred; the original owner gets their cash price, the equivalent of the mortgage advance; the price, together with a payment to cover the finance house's charges, is repaid by instalments; the reservation of title under the hire purchase or other agreement is equivalent to security over the goods.

Under a variant on this arrangement the goods are leased back not to the original owner but to his nominee. Alternatively, the owner may sell the goods to a dealer who then sells them to a finance house which leases them back to the original owner on hire-purchase, i.e. a refinancing transaction.

A genuine sale and lease-back is a valid transaction and is not regarded as a disguised mortgage.

27.3.2.2   Discounting of receivables

Just as a company may use its tangible property to obtain financial accommodation in a quasi-security arrangement, it can use its intangible property in the same way. It may sell its receivables (future debts and other obligations owed by third parties) to a creditor in return for an immediate cash payment. Since the creditor is providing a cash advance against future receivables it will pay less than the full face value of the debts, which are thus said to be 'discounted'; it may also discount to cover the risk of non-payment. The borrower may be required to guarantee payment of the assigned debts.

EXAMPLE

A company, X Ltd, wishes to borrow money from Y Ltd, using its receivables as security. However, X Ltd has already given its bank a debenture to secure a loan, and that debenture restricts its power to make further secured borrowings. X may achieve its objective by selling its receivables at a discount to Y Ltd, guaranteeing payment by the debtors.

This has the same effect as a secured loan. X Ltd, gets money at a cost (the discount on the sale) while Y Ltd pays money but is guaranteed to get it back, in full, at a later date. X Ltd effectively avoids the restrictions placed on its borrowing in the debenture.

A genuine discounting arrangement does not create a charge, even though its effect is to provide security for a cash advance: see *Lloyds and Scottish Finance Ltd* v *Cyril Lord Carpet Sales Ltd* (1979) 129 NLJ 366.

This arrangement is less advantageous to an unincorporated business: a general assignment of future book debts by an individual is registrable as if it was a general bill of sale (Insolvency Act 1986, s. 344).

27.3.3   Bills of exchange

Because a bill of exchange creates a contractually binding obligation to pay money which is separate from any underlying contract in connection with which it is given, bills may be used as an alternative to, or to reinforce, other security. For instance, a creditor providing a loan to a debtor may require the debtor to accept bills of exchange for the instalments of the loan; if there is doubt about the debtor's ability to meet the repayments the creditor could require the debtor to have the bills accepted by some creditworthy third party, such as a bank: see **22.2.1**.

27.3.4   Set-off agreements

It is common in commercial contracts, where there is a payment obligation on one party, to find a provision which allows that party to set-off against the sum he is obliged to pay under the contract any amount owing to him by the other.

This contractual right of set-off can operate in a similar fashion to a security, but in law it does not create a security interest. It establishes no rights over the creditor's assets but is merely an entitlement to set-off one personal obligation against another. It therefore does not need to be registered.

27.4   Type of security

If it can be established that what is created is a security interest, it may still not be exactly obvious what type of security interest it is. Is it a pledge, mortgage, lien or charge? For instance, a pledge involves the transfer of possession, but transfer of possession may indicate the creation of an equitable charge or a mortgage or merely a bailment rather than a pledge. It is well established that these types of security are mutually exclusive, so that an arrangement cannot be both a mortgage and a pledge.

In assessing the nature of the transaction the court must examine the agreement of the parties. Lending institutions usually use standard form contracts when taking security; however, a court will look beyond the form of the contract and assess the substance of the contract.

27.5   Deciding what type of security

The different types of security and quasi-security have different characteristics and advantages. A commercial lawyer needs to be aware of these in order to advise a debtor on the type of security which will suit his needs, and a creditor on the most secure form of security for him. Between fellow traders of equal size, the balance of power is more or less equal and so the type of security a debtor gives a creditor is often a matter of negotiation. However, when dealing with relatively large traders and lending institutions, the balance of power is clearly with these larger institutions and usually they can demand the type of security which suits them.

Some basic points should be remembered.

(a) Registration requirements can be time consuming and administratively inconvenient. They can be avoided by using quasi-security devices but care must be taken to draft the terms of the agreement clearly and precisely.

(b) Real security offers the creditor more protection than personal security and a lending institution may often require a guarantor to secure his guarantee by offering some form of real security.

(c) Possessory security deprives the owner of the property of the use of the property used as security, although this may be avoided by giving the pledgee constructive possession. Pledges are most often used in international trade where a bill of lading is pledged to a lending institution as security for a loan.

(d) A letter of comfort may be used as an alternative to security. However, it appears that it offers little protection to the creditor and lending institutions often require some other form of security as well. They may be accepted by a lender if no other security can be agreed.

(e) Different forms of security may be combined. For instance, a bank lending money to a company may require the company to grant a charge over its assets and the directors of the company personally to guarantee the loan. The directors may be further required to grant mortgages or charges over their own property to secure their guarantees.

Part VII

Competition law

Sources of competition law

28.1 Introduction

Competition law regulates the way businesses compete and promotes open competition in the interests of economic efficiency and the protection of consumers. It regulates three main areas:

(a) agreements between businesses which restrict competition, such as cartels to fix prices;

(b) the exercise of market power by a business which enjoys either a monopoly or a large market share; and

(c) takeovers and mergers which reduce the number of competitors in a market and which may create a new business with considerable market power.

Political factors, such as employment policies and encouraging inter-state trade, can be as important as purely economic considerations.

In this short chapter we:

- identify the main sources of European and domestic competition law; and
- consider the relationship between these two sources of law.

28.2 European and domestic law

Both domestic and European law contain rules designed to promote competition.

28.2.1 European law

Articles 81 and 82 of the EC Treaty form the basis of European Community competition law, dealing with cartels and abuse of market power respectively. Regulation 139/2004 (the Merger Regulation) deals with mergers which have a Community dimension.

From 1 May 2004, Articles 81 and 82 have been directly applicable in Member States and hence the application and enforcement of Articles 81 and 82 is shared between the Commission and national competition authorities (NCAs) and courts. The Merger Regulation is administered by a subdivision of DG Competition, the Merger Task Force.

28.2.2 UK competition law

The main source of UK competition law is now the Competition Act 1998, which regulates cartels and anti-competitive agreements and abuse of market power. The Act is closely modelled on the provisions of Arts 81 and 82. It came into force on 1 March 2000 and replaces controls previously contained in the Restrictive Trade Practices Act 1976, Resale Prices Act 1976 and the Competition Act 1980. There are additional controls on mono-polies in the Enterprise Act 2002, which also contains a system of merger control.

28.2.3   Relationship between domestic and European law

Some conduct is prohibited by domestic law, some by European law, some by both. Solicitors must therefore be familiar with both systems. However, the task of advising on competition law has been greatly simplified by the coming into force of the Competition Act 1998, as its main substantive provisions are very similar to those of Arts 81 and 82 and it expressly provides that it is to be interpreted and applied consistently with relevant provisions of European competition law.

In general EC law applies wherever conduct has an effect on trade within the community between Member States. Where conduct has effect only within the UK, domestic law applies. In the past the European authorities have adopted a fairly broad interpretation of 'conduct which has effects on trade between Member States' effectively widening the area of application of EC law. Where conduct with such effect is permitted by domestic law but prohibited by EC law, EC law takes priority and the conduct is prohibited. There is no authoritative decision of the European Court of Justice covering the situation where conduct with effects on inter-state trade is prohibited by national law but permitted by EC law, but there are dicta to the effect that the conduct should be permitted in order that EC law can be applied consistently in all Member States (see *Walt Wilhelm* v *Bundeskartellamt* [1969] ECR 1). This issue is addressed in Article 3 of Regulation 1/2003 which came into force on 1 May 2004. Article 3(1) provides that NCAs and national courts must *always* apply Art. 81 to agreements (as defined by Art. 81) which 'may affect trade between Member States within the meaning of that provision'. Moreover, Art. 3(2) provides that the application of national competition law may not lead to the prohibition of agreements which may affect trade between Member States that do not restrict competition within the meaning of Art. 81(1) or that fulfil the conditions of Art. 81(3). These provisions have the effect of establishing the supremacy of European law over national law where the jurisdictional requirements of the former are satisfied.

Where conduct is prohibited by both domestic and EC law, both sets of authorities can, in theory, intervene and impose sanctions, although any domestic investigation should not impede that of the European Commission. EC law provides that where fines are imposed under both systems for the same conduct, the first fine must be taken into account when fixing the level of the second, so that the offender is not punished twice. Where, however, the fines are imposed in respect of even slightly different conduct, the second fine may be levied in full (*Wilhelm* v *Bundeskartellamt*; *Boehringer Mannheim* v *Commission* [1972] ECR 1281).

The Competition Act 1998 envisages that conduct with a European, as opposed to purely domestic, effect will normally be dealt with under EC law. It remains possible, however, that where conduct has effect both on trade within the UK and on inter-state trade, both domestic and EC authorities will have jurisdiction, and the Act expressly permits the UK authorities to investigate agreements permitted by EC law in certain circumstances. In relation to the situation where both systems are infringed, it expressly requires that, when penalties for infringement of that Act's provisions are imposed, any penalty or fine imposed by the European Commission, or by the competition authorities of any other Member State, must be taken into account (s. 38(9)).

European Community competition law

29.1 Introduction

No business person or legal practitioner can afford to be ignorant of EC competition law. This applies whether the lawyer is engaged in non-contentious work (such as drafting an agreement) or contentious work (such as taking or defending a legal action).

In this chapter:

- we begin by highlighting how competition law impacts on various aspects of legal practice;
- subsequently, we examine the three substantive rules of European competition law, that is:
  - the rules dealing with cartels, under Art. 81;
  - the rules on abuse of market power, under Art. 82;
  - the rules dealing with take-overs and mergers, under the Merger Regulation;
- we analyse the procedures put in place to enforce Arts 81 and 82, at European and national levels.

29.1.1 Drafting an agreement

Much of a practitioner's time can be spent drafting agreements such as standard terms of trading, distribution agreements, leases, employment contracts etc. From the client's point of view the purpose of such an agreement is to ensure that the rights and duties of the parties to the agreement are set out clearly and, should a disagreement arise, that these rights and duties are legally enforceable. However, if the agreement, or part thereof, is in breach of the EC competition rules, the agreement, or the relevant part, may be unenforceable. As a damage limitation exercise, it is important for every commercial agreement to include a severance clause (*e.g. any clause, or part hereof, which is or may be void or unenforceable shall be treated as severable from the remainder of this agreement and shall not affect any other provision of this contract*) to ensure that where a particular aspect of the agreement breaches competition law, the remainder is left intact and enforceable.

When drafting, for example, a patent licensing agreement which would have a significant effect on inter-state trade, it is vital for the legal practitioner to have the relevant block exemption at hand: this prohibits the inclusion of certain clauses (known as 'hardcore restrictions' or black list clauses). Essentially, block exemptions are drafting tools (see further **29.2.4.3**).

29.1.2 Commercial litigation

EC competition rules are enforceable in private proceedings in national courts and so can be used to challenge the alleged anti-competitive actions of another party, such as a supplier who refuses to supply a client, or a competitor (see further **29.5.2**). It is also useful to consider whether competition law can be used to defend an action. For instance, where someone is seeking to enforce a contract against a client, one can argue that the contract (e.g. a tie-in sale), or the part being sued upon, is unenforceable for breach of competition law.

Moreover, the ECJ has held that a party to a contract may sue the other party for damages for losses arising from the operation of the contract in so far as it infringes competition law (see *Courage* v *Crehan* [2001] ECR I-6297; *Crehan* v *Inntrepreneur* [2004] EWCA Civ 637).

29.1.3 Disclosure requirements

Under EC law the European Commission is given various fact-finding powers in order to investigate whether a breach of the competition rules has occurred. Officials from the European Commission might present themselves at a clients' business premises without warning and ask to be admitted, request various documentation, and seek interviews. Must the client comply; would it be advisable to try to hide certain evidence; can the client have legal representation during the visit; can business secrets be protected? In a situation like this, time is of the essence and one cannot afford not to be able to deal with these types of questions (see further **29.4**).

29.1.4 Fines, penalties and other sanctions

At Community level, the sanctions for breach of competition law include fines and penalties. A business person might ask whether the threat of a fine might not be out-weighed, for example, by the potential to earn monopoly profits for a period of time. A legal practitioner's response is that the fines and penalties can be hefty: up to 10 per cent of the fined undertaking's previous annual world-wide turnover. Other sanctions are also available. A party in breach of competition law may find himself the subject of an injunction and may be ordered to pay damages.

29.1.5 Negligence action

As a matter of pure self-interest, a legal practitioner should be aware of the possibility of a disappointed client taking a negligence action alleging that he was given poor or defective legal advice on a competition matter.

The main provisions of EC law dealing with competition law are Arts 81 and 82 of the EC Treaty which deal respectively with cartels and abuses of market power. There are also provisions to deal with mergers.

29.2 Article 81

Article 81 of the EC Treaty prohibits as incompatible with the common market:

all agreements between undertakings, decisions by associations of undertakings and concerted practices which may affect trade between Member States and which have as their object or effect the prevention, restriction or distortion of competition within the common market, and in particular those which:

(a) directly or indirectly fix purchase or selling prices or any other trading conditions;

(b) limit or control production, markets, technical development, or investment;

(c) share markets or sources of supply;

(d) apply dissimilar conditions to equivalent trading transactions with other trading parties, thereby placing them at a competitive disadvantage;

(e) make the conclusion of contracts subject to the acceptance by other parties of supplementary obligations which, by their nature or according to commercial usage, have no connection with the subject of such contracts.

Initially, only the Commission had the power to grant exemption from this general prohibition under Art. 81(3), but from 1 May 2004, under Regulation 1/2003, Art. 81(3) has been directly applicable by national courts and NCAs (Art. 1). In particular, subject to the final control of the ECJ, national courts have the power and obligation to rule on the application of Art. 81(3) to agreements in litigation where damages for breach of Art. 81 and/or the enforceability of an agreement are at issue. Any agreement prohibited by Art. 81 and not covered by an exemption under Art. 81(3) is automatically void (Art. 81(2)).

29.2.1 Article 81(1)

The prohibition in Art. 81(1) only applies if four conditions are fulfilled.

29.2.1.1 Undertakings

Article 81 applies to agreements between and decisions and concerted practices of 'undertakings'. The Commission has defined an undertaking as 'any entity carrying on a commercial activity' (*Re Polypropylene Cartel* [1988] 4 CMLR 347). Companies, partnerships, individuals and nationalised industries are therefore all 'undertakings'.

Agreements between different members of a corporate group are not covered by Art. 81(1), provided that the subsidiary companies do not have economic independence.

Article 81(1) expressly includes decisions of trade associations in the category of agreements between undertakings.

29.2.1.2 Agreements and concerted practices

Article 81 does not apply only to legally enforceable contracts but also to 'concerted practices' so that it can cover informal 'gentlemen's agreements'. In the *Sugar Cartel case* [1975] ECR 1916 the ECJ explained that Art. 81 prohibits 'a form of co-ordination between undertakings which, without having reached the stage where an agreement properly so-called has been concluded, knowingly substitutes for the risks of competition practical cooperation between them which leads to conditions of competition which do not correspond to the market'.

Economic theory suggests that, where there are only a few undertakings in any market (a so-called 'oligopoly') prices and market shares tend to remain stable, because any attempt by one undertaking to cut prices will lead to retaliation from the others: this is known as 'parallel behaviour'. ⟶ not prohibited

The Community authorities, recognising this theory, have held that 'parallel behaviour' does not infringe Art. 81 where the market is oligopolistic (*Zinc Producer Group* [1985] 2 CMLR 108; *Woodpulp* [1993] 4 CMLR 407). As the ECJ explained in *Woodpulp*, Art. 81(1)

requires undertakings to determine their policy independently; but it does not deprive them of the right intelligently to adapt their behaviour to the existing and anticipated conduct of their competitors. The fact that a number of undertakings appear to act in an identical fashion is proof of a concerted practice only if there is no other plausible explanation for their behaviour.

Opinions will always differ as to the reasons for parallel behaviour, and undertakings accused of collusion may find it time-consuming, difficult and expensive to show that they did not engage in a concerted practice.

It is no defence for an undertaking party to an agreement or concerted practice to say that it appeared to join the cartel with the intention of secretly cutting prices or otherwise not complying with the agreement (*Polypropylene* [1992] 4 CMLR 84, Court of First Instance). Once a representative of an undertaking is shown to have attended a cartel meeting, the undertaking will be guilty of membership of the cartel unless it can prove its innocence by showing that the representative discussed 'innocuous' issues or that the representative was too junior to set prices for his firm. Otherwise the undertaking must show that the other people at the meeting knew that it would not abide by cartel decisions (in which case it is most unlikely that it would have been allowed to be represented at the meeting). The Commission's policy is to encourage whistleblowing among members of a cartel, by offering a reduction in fines for whistleblowers (see **29.4.2.2**).

29.2.1.3 The object or effect of preventing, restricting or distorting competition

If the object of an agreement is the restriction of competition, it contravenes Art. 81 (*Société Technique Minière* v *Maschinenbau Ulm* [1966] ECR 235, ECJ). Thus any agreement to fix prices, limit production or divide markets will contravene Art. 81, even if the agreement would not in fact have achieved its object. There is no need to examine the subjective intentions of the parties: if the agreement would restrict competition if implemented, its object is to restrict competition even if the participants honestly believe otherwise (*Sugar Cartel* [1975] ECR 1663).

If the object of the agreement is not the restriction of competition, one must consider its effect. The Commission must consider not only the agreement itself, but any surrounding agreements and the generally prevailing market conditions: *Brasserie de Haecht SA* v *Wilkin-Janssen* [1967] ECR 407, ECJ. In that case the owner of a cafe in Belgium claimed that his agreement to purchase beer exclusively from the defendant contravened Art. 81(1) and was therefore void. Clearly a restriction on the conduct of one cafe-owner will not have an effect on inter-state trade; but the Court held that the prevalence of such agreements should be considered: if the entire market were dominated by them, they might all infringe Art. 81.

Article 81(1) lists five types of distortion or restriction of competition; however, it has also been applied to conduct far less obviously restrictive of competition.

(a) It has been held that Art. 81 is contravened if certain types of information are exchanged: any exchange of information as to prices, terms and conditions, customers, market shares, general business strategy and product differentiation contravenes Art. 81(1) (*Soda Ash Cartel* case [1991] 4 CMLR 502, Court of First Instance). If businesses have access to this sort of information, they may be inclined to match but not undercut competitors' prices. Therefore the only information which may be exchanged is information which is no longer current (normally when it is a few months old) or statistics on the industry in general which do not highlight the relative positions of individual undertakings.

(b) Article 81 is infringed if there is any kind of restriction on the right of a party to the agreement to export or import goods to or from other Member States. Community authorities have consistently used Art. 81 to further the political goals of a single market. In *Consten SA and Grundig-Verkaufs GmbH* v *Commission* [1966] ECR 299, Grundig, the German manufacturer of electrical goods, wished to penetrate the French market, and needed a distributor with good local knowledge to promote its products. Consten agreed to set up a distribution system, to promote the products, and to keep minimum stocks of the products themselves and of spare parts. In return, Grundig agreed not to sell to anyone else in France. The ECJ held that this was a restriction on competition, which could not be justified by showing that competition between manufacturers was increased by the restriction of competition between retailers. This approach has been followed ever since (e.g. *Gosme/Martell-DMP* 1991 OJ L189/23).

(c) More generally, Art. 81 has been held to apply to most restrictions in contracts between manufacturers and their distributors. Many distribution agreements will involve restrictions on the conduct of the manufacturer and the distributor (see **Chapter 8**). Such restrictions are usually in the public interest: they encourage competition between the products of competing manufacturers (inter-brand competition) at the expense of competition between retailers selling the same product (intra-brand competition). Such agreements will usually infringe Art. 81(1), but may be granted individual or group exemption (see **29.2.4.3**).

(d) Resale price maintenance is almost certain to contravene Art. 81, and it is most unlikely that exemption will be granted in respect of it.

29.2.1.4 Agency

In 1962 the Commission issued a Notice saying that, in certain circumstances, agreements between commercial agents and their principals do not infringe the Art. 81(1) prohibition. This Notice has been replaced by Chapter 2, Section II of the Commission Notice, Guidelines on Vertical Restraints, which accompanies the new Regulation on Vertical Restraints (1999 OJ L336/21). The Guidelines provide that an agency agreement will fall outside the Art. 81(1) prohibition if the agent does not bear any, or only insignificant, risks in relation to contracts negotiated and/or concluded on behalf of the principal and in relation to market specific investments on behalf of the principal.

Risk is assessed on a case-by-case basis and the Commission looks at the economic reality of the situation. The fact that a relationship may be regarded as one of agency in national law is irrelevant if the agent is taking too much financial risk. The Guidelines contain a non-exhaustive list of circumstances where the Art. 81(1) prohibition will generally not apply. For example, Art. 81(1) will probably not apply where the property in contract goods bought or sold does not vest in the agent, or the agent does not itself supply the contract services and where the agent:

(a) does not maintain at its own cost or risk stocks of contract goods;

(b) does not create and/or operate an after-sales service;

(c) does not take responsibility for customers' non-performance of the contract.

The Guidelines also list obligations on the agent's behalf which generally will be considered inherent to the agency relationship, such as limitations on the territory in which the agent may operate, and the prices and conditions under which the agent sells or purchases the goods or services.

29.2.2 Effect on inter-state trade

Article 81 applies only where the agreement (not necessarily the restriction) in question has an effect on inter-state trade. The ECJ and Commission have, unsurprisingly, taken a wide view of what is meant by an effect on inter-state trade: the Commission need only prove that there is a possibility of an impact on trade, which can be direct or indirect (*Consten and Grundig* v *Commission* [1966] ECR 299). Thus an agreement will affect inter-state trade whenever it causes a change in the volume of trade that is not *de minimis*, or has the potential to cause such a change. There will also be an effect on inter-state trade if there will be a significant change in the structure of the market, for example, if there is a possibility that new firms will enter the market or an existing supplier will leave it (*Commercial Solvents* [1974] ECR 223, a case on Art. 82).

Agreements with only a minimal impact on inter-state trade are not caught by Art. 81, but this *de minimis* doctrine is narrowly construed. Whether an agreement is too trivial to come within the terms of Art. 81 is a matter of fact in each case (*Volk* v *Vervaecke* [1969] CMLR 273), but the Commission has issued Notices of Guidance which, while not binding on it, indicate the approach which it will take. The latest Notice on agreements of minor importance ([2001] OJ C368/07; see also Chapter 1, Section 11, of the Commission Notice, Guidelines on Vertical Restraints [2000] OJ C291/1) provides that an agreement does not fall under the prohibition in Art. 81(1) if the aggregate market shares of the participating undertakings do not exceed:

(a) in the case of 'horizontal' agreements—i.e. agreements made between undertakings operating at the same level in the market—10 per cent of the relevant market;

(b) in the case of 'vertical' agreements—i.e. agreements between undertakings operating at different levels in the market, such as between manufacturers and retailers—15 per cent of the relevant market.

The Notice also indicates that agreements between small and medium-sized undertakings (as defined in the Annex to Commission Recommendation 96/280 EC, 1996 OJ L107/4) will not, as a general rule, be caught by Art. 81(1) even if the above thresholds are exceeded. On the other hand, the Notice also indicates that the Commission will no longer classify as of minor importance agreements containing hardcore restrictions, such as agreements between competitors which have as their object the fixing of prices, the limitation of sales, or the allocation of markets, even if the parties' market shares fall below the thresholds set out in the Notice.

The *de minimis* doctrine applies to agreements of minor importance, not to restrictions of minor importance.

29.2.3 Article 81(2)

An agreement which contravenes Art. 81(1) is automatically void unless exempted under Art. 81(3). It cannot be enforced by any of the parties, and, in addition, third parties who are adversely affected can bring civil proceedings (see **29.5.2**). The parties may also be liable to substantial fines (para **29.4.4.1**).

29.2.4 Exemption under Art. 81(3)

Under Art. 81(3), Art. 81(1) may be declared inapplicable to:

any agreement or category of agreements between undertakings;
any decision or category of decisions by associations of undertakings;
any concerted practice or category of concerted practices;

which contributes to improving the production or distribution of goods or to promoting technical or economic progress, while allowing consumers a fair share of the resulting benefit, and which does not:

(a) impose on the undertakings concerned restrictions which are not indispensable to the attainment of these objectives;

(b) afford such undertakings the possibility of eliminating competition in respect of a substantial part of the products in question.

This power may be exercised to grant exemption to an individual agreement; it has also been used to grant 'block' exemptions to certain categories of agreement.

Four conditions must be satisfied before an exemption can be given to an agreement which contravenes Art. 81(1). They are:

(a) that the agreement contributes to the production or distribution of goods or to promoting technical or economic progress;

(b) that the agreement allows consumers a fair share of the resulting benefit;

(c) that the agreement does not impose restrictions which are not indispensable to the attainment of conditions (a) and (b);

(d) that competition is not eliminated in a substantial part of the relevant product market.

29.2.4.1   Benefit to consumers

An exemption can be granted only if its restrictions provide some concrete benefit to consumers, but in recent years the Commission has taken a wider view of what amounts to a benefit. It has recognised that, in relation to certain products, a reduction in price is not always in the consumers' interests. For instance, in the *Yves St Laurent Perfumes* case (1992 OJ L12/24), a system of distributing luxury perfumes was granted exemption even though the system ensured that prices were kept higher than would otherwise have been the case. As the Commission explained, 'The customer is thus ensured that the luxury product will not become an everyday product as a result of a downgrading of its image'.

29.2.4.2   The restriction must be indispensable

The requirements that all restrictions must be 'indispensable', and that there must not be an elimination of competition in a substantial part of the product market, are used to just-ify a policy of refusing individual exemptions to agreements which attempt to partition the markets in Member States or which impose absolute bans on exports to other Member States.

29.2.4.3   Block exemptions

There are six 'block' or 'group' exemptions in which the Commission has set out the conditions under which particular types of agreement will qualify for exemption from Art. 81(1).

The block exemptions relate to:

(a) certain categories of vertical agreements and concerted practices (Reg. 2790/99 until 31 May 2010: see [1999] OJ L 336/21);

(b) motor vehicle distribution (Reg. 1400/02 until 31 May 2010: see [2002] OJ L 203/30);

(c) specialisation (Reg. 2658/2000 until 31 December 2010: see [2000] OJ L 304/3);

(d) research and development (Reg. 2659/2000 until 31 December 2010: see [2000] OJ L 304/7);

(e) certain categories of agreements, decisions and concerted practices in the insurance sector (Reg. 358/2003 until 31 March 2010: [2003] OJ L53/8;

(f) technology transfer agreements (Reg. 772/2004 until 30 April 2014: see [2004] OJ L123/11).

From a lawyer's perspective, block exemptions are a drafting tool. Earlier block exemptions were prescriptive as to the types of clauses which should and should not be included in an agreement. Since 1999 however, the newer block exemptions are less restrictive and more economics orientated. Some block exemptions contain provisions which parties should include in their agreement if they are to benefit from the exemption. For example, Art. 3 of Regulation 1400/02 on motor vehicle distribution contains provision which, although not mandatory *per se*, are usually included to avoid falling foul of Art. 81(1) and (2). The block exemptions also included provisions, known as the 'black list', which must not be included in an agreement. Examples include provisions dealing with export and import bans and resale price maintenance. Otherwise, the parties are free to agree terms.

For example, the Regulation on Vertical Agreements, with accompanying Guidelines (see Commission Notice—Guidelines on Vertical Restraints (2000 OJ C 291/1)), came into force on 1 January 2000 and applies with effect from 1 June 2000 (Art. 13). The Regulation replaces three previous block exemptions on exclusive distribution, exclusive purchasing and franchising agreements. It is notable for a number of reasons. First, the Regulation is capable of application to *all* vertical agreements, subject to its terms, and does not apply only to exclusive distribution, exclusive purchasing and franchising agreements. It does not apply, however, where there is a sector specific block exemption (Art. 2.5). Secondly, the Regulation applies to both goods and services agreements, and to goods supplied for resale and use. Thirdly, the block exemption does not apply to undertakings with a market share of more than 30 per cent, thereby creating a presumption of legality—a 'safe harbour'—for undertakings below this threshold. This reflects the more economics orientated approach of the Regulation.

In 2000, the Commission also issued a Notice—Guidelines on the applicability of Art. 81 to horizontal co-operation agreements (2000 OJ C 3/2). As well as distinguishing between agreements which *almost all, do not, and may,* fall under Art. 81(1), the Guidelines also consider the principles applicable to a number of specific categories of horizontal agreements, such as R&D, commercialisation and standardisation agreements.

29.2.4.4 Individual exemption

As noted above, from 1 May 2004, the Commission's monopoly over the granting of individual exemptions under Art. 81(3) has been eliminated pursuant to Regulation 1/2003. Accordingly, Art. 81(3) is now directly applicable by national courts and NCAs (Art. 1). In particular, subject to the final control of the ECJ, national courts and NCAs have the power and obligation to rule on the application of Art. 81(3). Importantly, however, national courts and NCAs are not empowered to grant individual exemptions to applicants under Regulation 1/2003. Instead, as with the Commission, individual NCAs will apply Art. 81(3) in the context of other proceedings, such as infringement proceedings. Similarly, national courts will apply Art. 81(3) in the context of ordinary civil proceedings, such as where damages for breach of Art. 81 and/or the enforceability of an agreement are at issue.

Furthermore, Regulation 1/2003 introduced a new element into the application of Art. 81(3). Article 2 shifts the burden of proof in respect of Art. 81(3) on to the person relying on the provision. Consequently, Art. 2 provides that in respect of Art. 81(1) the burden of proof lies upon the person alleging the infringement of that provision. However, once that burden has been met, the burden shifts to the party seeking to rely on Art. 81(3), who then has the burden of proving that the exemption provisions of Art. 81(3) apply.

From the parties' perspective, this devolution of the individual exemption power will mean an increased burden on undertakings to ensure that their agreements do not fall foul of Art. 81(1), or if they do, that they fall within the exemption criteria of Art. 81(3) or within the scope of a block exemption. Until such time as a competition authority or court becomes involved, undertakings will have to engage in self-assessment of the legal status of their agreements and such assessment will need to be based on sophisticated legal and economic analysis. Moreover, undertakings will need to keep a permanent eye on such matters, since whether the criteria of Art. 81(3) are met can vary from time to time depending on prevailing market conditions.

To assist undertakings in this task, the Commission has issued a series of Notices setting out principles developed by the ECJ and the Commission's interpretation of these principles, including *Guidelines on the effect on trade concept contained in Articles 81 and 82*, [2004] OJ C101/81; and *Guidelines on the application of Article 81(3)*, [2004] OJ C101/97. Moreover, the Commission has issued a *Notice on informal guidance relating to novel questions concerning Articles 81 and 82 that arise in individual cases*, whereby undertakings can seek informal guidance on a novel question in a written statement, known as 'guidance letters', from the Commission (see further [2004] OJ C101/78). Such guidance letters are not Commission decisions and hence are not legally binding though, as stated in the Notice, NCAs and courts may take such guidance letters into account as they see fit in the context of a case.

29.3　Article 82

Article 82 of the EC Treaty is designed to prevent the exploitation of market power. It reads as follows:

Any abuse by one or more undertakings of a dominant position within the common market or in a substantial part of it shall be prohibited as incompatible with the common market in so far as it may affect trade between Member States. Such abuse may, in particular, consist in:

(a) directly or indirectly imposing unfair purchase prices or unfair trading conditions;

(b) limiting production, markets or technical development to the prejudice of consumers;

(c) applying dissimilar conditions to equivalent transactions with other trading parties, thereby placing them at a competitive disadvantage;

(d) making the conclusion of contracts subject to acceptance by the other parties of supplementary obligations which, by their nature or according to commercial usage, have no connection with the subject of such contracts.

There are thus three crucial questions to be addressed when considering the application of Art. 82.

(a) What is 'dominance'?

(b) What is a 'substantial' part of the common market?

(c) What amounts to an 'abuse' of a dominant position?

29.3.1   The relevant market

An undertaking cannot simply be 'dominant'; it must be dominant in relation to a particular product and geographical market. The definition of the product market therefore becomes of crucial importance: if the market is defined narrowly, the undertaking in question will have a larger share than it would if the market were to be given a wide definition. For example, in one of the first major Art. 82 decisions, *Europemballage Corp. and Continental Can Co. Inc* v *Commission* [1973] ECR 215 (the *Continental Can* case), the Commission found that the undertaking in question was dominant because of its large share in the markets for cans for meat, cans for fish, and metal tops. The appellant successfully contended that the market should have been defined more widely, as the market for packaging for food generally. As its market share for packaging generally was not as high, it was not in a dominant position.

29.3.1.1   The definition of the market

A number of factors are relevant to defining the relevant market. The first is the interchangeability of demand and supply (or, to use economic language, 'cross-elasticity'). If consumers will buy product A instead of product B when the price of product B goes up, then A and B are part of the same market. Similarly, if manufacturer C puts up its prices and manufacturer D starts supplying similar products, there is interchangeability of supply, and any consideration of C's market power has to take into account the threat to it from D.

Other factors are relevant in identifying the relevant market.

EXAMPLE

In *United Brands* v *Commission* [1978] 1 CMLR 429 the ECJ held that price, physical characteristics and intended use must be taken into account so that, applying these criteria, the market for bananas was separate from that for fruit generally (for example, bananas are soft and seedless, relatively cheap, and particularly attractive to sick people, children and the elderly).

This definition is vague, and will be difficult to apply in practice. To address this concern the Commission, in 1997, adopted a *Notice on the definition of the relevant market for the purposes of Articles 85 and 86* (now Arts 81 and 82) (1997 OJ C372/5; [1998] 4 CMLR 117). The stated purpose of the Notice is to provide guidance on how the Commission applies the concept of the relevant product and geographical market. Much of the Notice is not new but acts as a useful summary of the Commission's approach. For example, there is express support for the use of hypothetical price rises to determine whether two products, or services, are in the same market. More generally, the Notice evidences the Commission's support for more advanced econometric and statistical approaches to defining markets.

29.3.2   Dominance

Having defined the relevant market, the next question is whether the undertaking is 'dominant'. A company is dominant where it is able to act independently of its suppliers and customers (for example, by dictating the prices at which it will buy and sell things), and where it is able to prevent effective competition (*Hoffman La Roche* v *Commission* [1979] ECR 461 ECJ). In later cases, undertakings have been found to be dominant where competition is seriously restricted, but is not altogether eliminated (e.g. *United Brands* v *Commission; AKZO Chemie BV* v *EC Commission* [1991] 1 ECR 3359).

29.3.2.1 Relevant factors

(a) The most important factor in determining dominance is the market share of the undertaking, together with the market shares of other members of the market. In *Hoffman La Roche* the ECJ said that a high market share (probably in excess of 65–70 per cent) will almost certainly be enough to prove dominance, unless the undertaking can show that special factors exist (for example, that there is a major producer ready to enter the market if customers no longer believe that they are getting a good deal). However, dominance can exist where the market share is as low as 40–45 per cent, provided that the other members of the market are too small and fragmented to present a serious threat (for example, United Brands was dominant with a market share of 40–45 per cent).

(b) The Commission can also take into account the power resulting from:

(i) intellectual property rights *(Tetra Pak v Commission* [1997] 4 CMLR 662);

(ii) superior distribution systems *(United Brands v Commission)*; and

(iii) overall size and strength *(Hoffman La Roche)*.

It can also take into account evidence of managers saying that they enjoy a dominant position *(Boosey and Hawkes* [1988] 4 CMLR 67): this is more dubious, because some executives may boast about enjoying market power without in fact doing so, and possibly without fully understanding what it means.

The conduct complained of as an abuse may also be evidence of dominance. In *Michelin* v *Commission* [1983] ECR 3461 the ECJ allowed the Commission to find that the practice of price discrimination between customers (the abuse) was itself evidence of dominance.

29.3.3 'A substantial part of the common market'

There is no simple definition of what amounts to a substantial part of the common market based on geographical or other criteria. An entire Member State will be regarded as a substantial part of the EC *(BRT v SABAM* [1974] ECR 313), as will a large part of a large Member State (e.g. southern Germany: *Suiker Unie* v *Commission* [1975] ECR 1663). In *RTE* v *Commission* [1991] 4 CMLR 586 it was held by the Court of First Instance that where dominance exists over the whole of one Member State and part of another, there is definitely dominance in a substantial part of the common market. Where the dominance covers only part of a Member State, it will be necessary to consider the share of the total EC market represented by the area in question, along with geographical considerations.

29.3.4 Abuse

Article 82 includes a non-exhaustive list of types of conduct which may be regarded as an 'abuse' for its purposes. Other conduct which may attract sanctions includes:

(a) predatory pricing, where the monopolist prices below cost to drive out competitors (with the intention of raising prices once it is alone in the market again) *(AKZO Chemie BV* v *EC Commission* [1991] 1 ECR 3359);

(b) the practice of giving 'loyalty' discounts when a purchaser obtains all or most of its requirements from the dominant firm *(Hoffman La Roche* v *Commission* [1979] ECR 461; *Michelin* v *Commission* [1983] ECR 3461);

(c) the use of intellectual property rights to restrict access to the market by competitors *(Tetra Pak Rausing* v *Commission* [1991] 4 CMLR 344);

(d) any attempt to impose export bans on trade between Member States in order to keep prices high (*United Brands* v *Commission* [1978] ECR 207);

(e) refusing to supply a customer with raw materials which will be used to make products to compete with the manufacturer in another market, or to discriminate between customers when allocating scarce goods (*Commercial Solvents* [1974] ECR 223; *BPB Industries plc* v *Commission* [1993] 5 CMLR 32).

The ECJ has developed the concept of 'objective justification' to determine whether particular conduct is abusive. For example, in deciding whether a system of rebates and discounts contravenes Art. 82, the Commission should look at whether they reflect matters such as economies of scale or reductions in cost arising from the reduced risk of not being able to sell all one's products, or whether they are unrelated to such factors but are designed to deter customers from finding new suppliers. Similarly, a refusal to supply may be objectively justified on the grounds that the purchaser does not know how to use the products properly, and so may cause accidents or otherwise damage the reputation of the manufacturer.

29.4 Enforcement of Articles 81 and 82

For the last forty or so years the principal enforcement measure has been Regulation 17/62. However, Regulation 17/62 proved ill-suited to the pursuit of a focused enforcement agenda and, following a consultation process, a decentralised and modernised system of enforcement was implemented under Regulation 1/2003 which replaced Regulation 17/62, as from 1 May 2004 (see [2003] OJ L1/1; see further Regulation 773/2004 relating to the conduct of proceedings by the Commission pursuant to Arts 81 and 82, [2004] OJ L123/18).

The principal stated aim of Regulation 1/2003 is to enable the Commission to concentrate 'its resources on curbing the most serious infringements' of Community law (Recital 3). The Regulation seeks to achieve this aim in two ways: first, it frees-up Commission resources by decentralising the enforcement of Art. 81 and secondly, it strengthens the Commission's enforcement powers.

As of 1 May 2004, Regulation 1/2003 places a legal obligation on the Commission, NCAs and national courts to apply and enforce Arts 81 and 82 (Arts 4, 5 and 6). As already noted, the Commission's monopoly over the grant of individual exemptions under Art. 81(3) and the system requiring prior notification of agreements as a pre-condition to individual exemption has been eliminated (Art. 1). With the participation of more actors in the implementation of Arts 81 and 82 comes the challenge of maintaining consistency. Controlling diversity is addressed in a number of key provisions of the Regulation. Article 3 deals with the relationship between Arts 81 and 82 and national competition laws and establishes the supremacy of community law over national law where the jurisdiction requirements of the former are satisfied. Article 3(1) provides that NCAs and national courts must always apply Art. 81 to agreements (as defined by Art. 81) which 'may affect trade between Member States within the meaning of that provision'. Moreover, Art. 3(2) provides that the application of national competition law may not lead to the prohibition of agreements which may affect trade between Member States that do not restrict competition within the meaning of Art. 81(1) or that fulfil the conditions of Art. 81(3). This supremacy of Community competition law over national competition law is likely to mean that in most smaller EU states Art. 81 will become the predominant restrictive business practice competition law to be applied. There is likely to be more room to apply national competition rules in states with larger economies and geographical areas. In contrast, as regards Art. 82, Member States retain the power to impose more restrictive national competition rules. Recital 8 makes it clear that stricter national rules may include provisions which prohibit or impose sanctions on abusive behaviour towards economically dependant undertakings. Recital 8 also takes national criminal antitrust statutes, such as the Enterprise Act 2002, out of the scope of Art. 3. Recital 9 also seeks to protect national law, particularly unfair trading legislation, from the effects of Art. 3. So long as the national measures have a different object to competition law and comply with the general principles of Community law, Art. 3 will not apply.

The Regulation also requires that the Commission, NCAs and the national courts cooperate in the application of competition rules (Arts 11–16). Importantly, in the relationship between the Commission and NCAs, the Commission is given a right of pre-emption in Art. 11(6) whereby the Commission can initiate proceedings, even if an NCA is already acting on the same case (although the Commission must first consult the NCA). Such initiation by the Commission has the effect of relieving the NCA of jurisdiction to act in the case. This power will be used as a disciplining force by the Commission of NCAs, if needed. Moreover, the Commission is given the power to intervene before national courts as *amicus curiae* (Art. 15(3)). Other 'information rules' in Arts 11–16 require the sharing of information between the Commission, NCAs and national courts as a means of achieving consistency. Lastly, Art. 16 also addresses this issue of consistency by requiring that when national courts or NCAs rule on agreements, decision or practices under Arts 81 and 82 they must avoid conflict with Commission decisions.

This decentralised system of enforcement involves parallel competence of the Commission, NCAs and national courts, and, in order to further limit inconsistent application of Arts 81 and 82, the Commission has issued a series of Notices, including:

- *Notice on cooperation within the Network of Competition Authorities*, [2004] OJ C101/43;
- *Notice on co-operation between the Commission and the courts of EU Member States*, [2004] OJ C101/54;
- *Notice on the handling of complaints by the Commission*, [2004] OJ C101/65;
- *Notice on informal guidance relating to novel questions concerning Articles 81 and 82 that arise in individual cases*, [2004] OJ C101/78;
- *Guidelines on the effect on trade concept contained in Articles 81 and 82*, [2004] OJ C101/81; and
- *Guidelines on the application of Article 81(3)*, [2004] OJ C101/97.

The decentralisation of enforcement is coupled with an increase of the Commission's investigative powers. The investigative process will be outlined below in terms of its commencement; investigative powers, interim measures; and infringement proceedings and decisions.

29.4.1 Commencing an investigation

Commission investigations originate from a variety of sources. The Commission may take up a case when its own monitoring of the financial press and trade journals reveals something suspicious. Other investigations derive from a complaint (see Notice on handling of complaints by the Commission, [2004] OJ C101/65). The Commission takes a wide view of the persons who have a sufficient interest to have *locus standi* to complain of infringement (including, for example, competitors, trade unions and consumers). Complaints must comply with Form C, available from the Commission (at http://europa.eu.int/dgcomp/ complaints_form). An important new source of investigations result from 'whistle-blowing' by cartel members. Through the use of Leniency Notices the Commission has offered incentives, in the form of a reduction in fines, to undertakings participating in cartels to 'blow-the-whistle' on the cartel. Under the Commission's latest Leniency Notice [2002] OJ C45/3 the first member of a cartel involved in a price-fixing or market allocation agreement to disclose the agreement, receives no fine from the Commission provided certain conditions are met, including that the member never put pressure on other members to take part.

29.4.2   Investigative powers

At first sight the Commission's investigative powers appear to be similar to those under Regulation 17/62; in particular the power to obtain information by decision and the power to carry out on-the-spot investigations. However, there are a number of significant extensions of the Commisssion's investigative powers under Regulation 1/2003.

First, the power to obtain information is contained in Art. 18, under which the Commission has a choice: it can proceed either by request and, if this is not acceded to, by decision (as under the old rules) or, it may proceed immediately to a decision requiring that information be provided. Article 19 grants the Commission entirely new powers to take voluntary statements from witnesses. This provision seems to add little to the Commission's investigative powers because the Commission cannot compel testimony and no fines can be imposed where incorrect or inaccurate answers are provided.

The Commission's powers of inspection ('dawn-raids') are outlined in Art. 20. Accordingly, the Commission can, in the course of its investigations:

- enter any premises, land or means of transport of an undertaking;
- examine and copy any books or records, irrespective of the medium on which they are stored;
- seal any premises, books or records; and
- ask any representative or member of staff of an undertaking for oral 'on-the-spot' explanations concerning both facts and documents within the scope of the inspection and record the answers.

As a counter-balance, Art. 20(8) provides that where national law requires judicial authorisation for an inspection (a search warrant), the national judicial authority shall ensure that the Commission decision is authentic and that the coercive measures envisaged are neither arbitrary nor excessive. Further, Recital 23 indicates that there are some limits on the questions that the Commission can ask representatives and members of staff of undertakings. In particular, undertakings cannot be forced to admit that they have committed an infringement, but they are obliged to answer factual questions and to provide documents, even if this information may be used to establish the existence of an infringement against them. Recital 23 reproduces the ruling from *Hoechst AG v Commission* (Case 227/88 [1989] ECR 2859) thereby ensuring a minimum protection against self-incrimination. For the first time, pursuant to Art. 21, the Commission can carryout inspections in employees' and executives' homes. Strict standards apply to the authorisation of such inspections and a national court order is required before such a search can be undertaken.

Lastly, the Commission can impose substantial fines for non-compliance with procedural rules relating to inspections—up to 1 per cent of the company's worldwide turnover and up to 5 per cent of the company's average daily turnover in the case of periodic penalties (Arts 23 and 24).

29.4.2.1 Cooperating with the Commission

A legal adviser may find that a client under investigation may be tempted to destroy evidence of suspicious conduct. The client should be advised that this is most unwise. Apart from the fact that solicitors are bound by professional ethics which would require them not to encourage such conduct, destroying evidence is likely to prove to be counter-productive.

(a) The client under investigation will not know what the Commission has discovered elsewhere, for example, from other undertakings in the cartel, competitors, or disgruntled employees.

(b) The client may also be unable to destroy all evidence of its conduct: for example, the minutes of a price-fixing meeting may disappear, but can the managers be sure that they have got rid of all the agendas, all the cryptic diary entries referring to the meeting and any memos mentioning it?

(c) When the Commission launches a 'dawn raid', it is likely to do so simultaneously at all the premises of the alleged participants in the breach. Can the client be sure that nothing will be found there?

The client who destroys evidence will be faced with increased fines. A client who cooperates, and who takes advantage of cooperation to justify or mitigate its behaviour stands a far greater chance of receiving lower penalties. In 2002, the Commission published a revised *Notice on the immunity from fines and reduction of fines in cartel cases* ([2002] OJ C45/3) which offers incentives, primarily a reduction in fines, to undertakings participating in cartels to 'blow the whistle' (see e.g., *British Sugar plc, Tate & Lyle plc, Napier Brown & Co. Ltd, James Budgett Sugars Ltd* [1999] OJ L076/01).

29.4.3 Interim measures

The pre-existing law (*Camera Care* v *Commission* [1980] ECR 119) has been largely codified under Art. 8 of Regulation 1/2003 which provides for the granting of interim measures. Art. 8(1) states:

In cases of urgency due to the risk of serious and irreparable damage to competition, the Commission, acting on its own initiative may by decision, on the basis of a *prima facie* finding of infringement, order interim measures.

Such a decision can apply for a specified period and may be renewed if necessary and appropriate (Art. 8(2)).

29.4.4 Infringement proceedings and decisions

Most minor contraventions of competition law are settled informally on the basis of the parties undertaking to comply in the future; only a minority of cases lead to formal infringement proceedings.

Before the Commission can take a decision, parties under investigation must be given a right to be heard (see Regulation 1/2003, Arts 27 and 28 and Regulation 773/2004 relating to the conduct of proceedings by the Commission, [2004] OJ L123/18). The Commission begins infringement proceedings by serving a notice of objections on the parties. Parties under investigation have a right of access to the Commission's file, but not to confidential information, and internal documents of and communications between the Commission and NCAs (Reg. 1/2003, Art. 27(2) and Reg. 773/2004, Arts 15–16). The parties may reply in writing within a deadline set by the Commission (often two months), and they may also request an oral hearing. Oral hearings are very different from English court proceedings: they rarely last for more than a day; they are inquisitorial; they are held in private; and the parties may be heard separately. A Hearing Officer will be appointed to try to ensure 'fair play' between the Commission and the undertakings, but he can be expected to take a more active role than that of a judge in an English court.

Similarly, under Regulation 1/2003, before the Commission can take a decision undertakings under investigation must be given a right to be heard and their rights of defence are protected (Arts 27 and 28). For example, an undertaking under investigation has a right of access to the Commission's file (excluding confidential information and Commission internal documents).

29.4.4.1 Decisions

Articles 7 to 10 of Regulation 1/2003 set out the main decision-making powers of the Commission. Most of these powers existed previously under Regulation 17 or case law from the ECJ. For example, Art. 7 provides that the Commission has the power to find an infringement and by decision to require that an undertaking bring the infringement to an end. Further, Art. 7 expressly grants the Commission the power to adopt behaviour and structural remedies. While the ECJ had previously determined that the Commission has this power (see e.g. *Continental Can* [1973] ECR 215 where an order was made requiring the undertaking to sell off a newly acquired company) the express conferment of such a power may encourage greater application of this type of remedy than hitherto.

In contrast, Arts 9 and 10 provide the Commission with new decision-making powers. Article 9 grants the Commission power to adopt a decision imposing commitments on undertakings. The provision envisages the Commission adopting a commitment decision in the course of infringement proceedings where an undertaking offers commitments that meet the concerns of the Commission. Such a decision will be adopted for a specified period and will provide that given the commitment of the undertaking there are no longer grounds for action by the Commission. Article 10 grants the Commission the power to adopt a decision of inapplicability, where the Community public interest so requires, that the provisions of Art. 81(1) do not apply or that the provisions of Art. 81(3) are satisfied. This type of decision is intended to be declaratory in nature and its purpose is to clarify the law in particular as regards new types of agreement or practice that have not been addressed by existing case law.

In addition, breach of Arts 81 and 82, interim measures and commitment decisions are punishable by fixed fines of up to 10 per cent of the turnover in the preceding business year of each of the undertakings participating in the infringement (Art. 23), and periodic penalties at up to 5 per cent of the average daily turnover of the undertaking concerned (Art. 24). The Commission will consider the length and gravity of the offences in fixing the level of fines. Further guidance on fining policy can be found in the Commission's *Guidelines on the method of setting fines* ([1998] OJ C9/3). Fines are enforced as civil judgments.

29.5 Affected third parties

A third party adversely affected by an infringement of competition law may complain to the Commission, thus initiating the investigation procedure, or bring a civil claim for damages.

29.5.1   Complaint or litigation?

A complaint to the Commission will normally be the best course of action. Complainants enjoy qualified privilege from the tort of defamation, and the Commission is under a duty to keep a complainant's identity secret if there is a risk of reprisals (*Adams* v *Commission* [1985] ECR 3539). Although the complainant is not entitled to costs, the costs of making a complaint are much lower than the equivalent costs of bringing an action in the domestic courts. The Commission's investigative powers are likely to lead to more evidence being uncovered than would be the case in discovery in civil proceedings, and the Commission can grant interim relief in appropriate cases.

29.5.2   Civil litigation in English Courts

Infringement of Arts 81 and 82 is actionable in English law as a breach of statutory duty (*Garden Cottage Foods Ltd* v *Milk Marketing Board* [1984] AC 130). However, in *Garden Cottage Foods* the House of Lords suggested that damages will normally be a sufficient remedy, so that interlocutory injunctions to prevent the conduct complained of will generally not be granted. Some applications for injunctions have succeeded where the applicant could show that a refusal would have led to the collapse of his business and the loss of his livelihood.

An action for damages is likely to be unattractive to all but the most single-minded litigant, because the difficulties are enormous (but see e.g. *Crehan* v *Inntrepreneur* [2004] EWCA Civ 637). In a case of infringement of Art. 81, the claimant will have to prove the existence of an agreement or concerted practice, and the mere existence of parallel behaviour will not in itself be enough. The claimant will then have to show that the infringement caused it to suffer a loss. Actions based on Art. 82 will be even more difficult, because the claimant will have to provide economic evidence to prove the existence of a dominant position, as well as proving abuse and causation.

29.5.3   Infringing agreements are void

The most significant aspect of EC competition law in civil litigation is likely to be Art. 81(2). It renders any agreement which infringes Art. 81(1) void and unenforceable. Consequently, in an action for breach of contract the defendant can plead breach of Art. 81(1) as a defence and avoid liability if it can show that the contract restricted competition and affected inter-state trade, and was not protected by Art. 81(3) or a block exemption.

29.6   European Community control of takeovers and mergers

Articles 81 and 82 of the EC Treaty are not particularly well suited to dealing with takeovers and mergers, although they were on occasion applied to them (e.g. *Europemballage Corp. and Continental Can Co. Inc* v *Commission* [1973] ECR 215, where it was held that a dominant company abuses its power when it takes over a rival).

The first Merger Control Regulation was introduced in 1989. From 1 May 2004, Regulation 139/2004 (the Merger Regulation, [2004] OJ L24/1) governs all mergers or 'concentrations' with a 'Community dimension' (see also Regulation 802/2004 implementing Regulation 139/2004, [2004] OJ L133/1). The new Merger Regulation has altered the substantive test for the assessment of mergers; streamlined the system for merger referrals between the Commission and Member States; and introduced more flexibility at a procedural level. Accompanying the new Merger Regulation is a Commission Notice providing guidelines on the appraisal of horizontal mergers, ([2004] OJ C31/5) and the Commission has also published Best Practice guidelines on the conduct of EC merger control proceedings.

29.6.1 Concentrations

The Merger Regulation requires all 'concentrations' of a particular size to be notified to the Commission before they are put into effect. A 'concentration' occurs when two or more undertakings (see the *Notice on the concept of undertakings* 1998 OJ C66/14) merge, or when one person who already controls one undertaking acquires direct or indirect control over another (Art. 3). A person has 'control' if, for example, he has sufficient voting rights to exercise 'decisive influence' over the undertaking in question (Art. 3(2)). Acquisition of a substantial minority shareholding can thus amount to a concentration. (See further the *Notice on the concept of concentrations*, 1998 OJ C66/5.)

29.6.1.1 Joint ventures

The creation of a joint venture performing on a lasting basis all the functions of an autonomous economic entity, constitutes a concentration (Art. 3(4); see further the *Notice on the concept of full function joint ventures*, 1998 OJ C66/1).

29.6.2 Community dimension

Under Art. 1, a concentration has a Community dimension if:

(a) the combined aggregate world-wide turnover of all the undertakings concerned exceeds Eur 5,000 million; and

(b) the aggregate EC turnover of each of at least two of the undertakings concerned exceeds Eur 250 million.

If, however, each of the undertakings concerned achieves more than two-thirds of its EC turnover in one Member State, the concentration will not have a Community dimension but will be left to the Member State where the bulk of the turnover occurs to deal with it.

Furthermore, a concentration which does not meet the above thresholds has a Community dimension where:

(a) the combined aggregate world-wide turnover of all the undertakings concerned is more than Eur 2,500 million;

(b) in each of at least three Member States, the combined aggregate turnover of all the undertakings is more than Eur 100 million;

(c) in each of at least three Member States included for the purpose of (b), the aggregate turnover of each of at least two of the undertakings concerned is more than Eur 25 million; and

(d) the aggregate Community-wide turnover of each of at least two of the undertakings concerned is more than Eur 100 million;

unless each of the undertakings concerned achieves more than two-thirds of its aggregate Community-wide turnover within one and the same Member State (Art. 1(3)).

Article 5 contains more detailed rules on the calculation of turnover (see also the *Notice on the calculation of turnover*, 1998 OJ C66/25).

29.6.3 Compatibility with the Common Market

Once a concentration has been notified, the Commission considers whether it would be compatible with the Common Market. A concentration will be incompatible with the Common Market when it would significantly impede effective competition, in the Common Market or in a substantial part of it, in particular as a result of the creation or strengthening of a dominant position (Art. 2(3)). In deciding whether a concentration is compatible with the Common Market, the Commission is to have regard to (Art. 2(1)):

(a) the need to maintain and develop effective competition;

(b) the market position of the undertakings concerned and their economic and financial power;

(c) alternatives available to suppliers and users;

(d) their access to supplies or markets;

(e) legal and other barriers to entry;

(f) trends of supply and demand;

(g) the interests of consumers; and

(h) the development of technical and economic progress where this is not achieved at the expense of the consumer.

The criteria on which decisions are to be made are exclusively economic. Other factors, such as employment, are not relevant.

29.6.4 Notification

The Commission must be notified of a concentration with a Community dimension prior to implementation and following:

(a) the conclusion of the agreement; or

(b) the announcement of the public bid; or

(c) the acquisition of the controlling interest whichever is the earliest (Art. 4(1)).

Fines of up to 10 per cent of the aggregate turnover of the undertaking concerned can be imposed for failure to notify a concentration (Art. 14(2)).

29.6.4.1 Procedure

Procedures are set out in the Implementing Regulation 802/2004, [2004] OJ L133/1.

Notification is made on Form CO (see Annex I of Reg. 802/2004) and is obtainable from the Commission or its UK offices. Where a merger is agreed between undertakings, there should be joint notification. Otherwise, the party acquiring the controlling interest should notify.

An immense amount of information must be provided. The form sets out the requirements. In brief, the notification must be accompanied by:

(a) copies of the documents bringing about the concentration (e.g. the agreement between the undertakings, or the offer document in a public bid);

(b) copies of the most recent annual reports and accounts of all the parties;

(c) copies of all analyses, reports, etc., used by any of the notifying parties to assess the impact of the concentration on the relevant markets.

The notifying parties must also provide information on:

(d) the nature of the concentration;

(e) the economic and financial structure of the concentration;

(f) the turnover of the parties to the concentration;

(g) details on ownership and control.

If any of this information is regarded as confidential, it should be marked as such; if the Commission agrees that it is to be regarded as a business secret, it will not be revealed to third parties. Twenty copies of the notification and fifteen copies of the supporting documents have to be sent. The Commission has a discretion to require less information. In practice, therefore, formal notification is usually preceded by a meeting with the relevant Commission officials to determine exactly what information they require.

Parties can be fined for providing false or misleading information; and the relevant time limits for the investigation do not run until all the correct information has been supplied.

In July 2000, the Commission adopted a Notice on a simplified procedure for treatment of certain concentrations that do not raise competition concerns under the Merger Regulation (2000 OJ C217/11, see also Form CO). Under this procedure, provided that the necessary conditions are met and there are no special circumstances, the Commission will adopt a short-form clearance decision within a month from the date of notification. The Notice identifies categories of concentration to which the simplified procedure will apply, including where two or more undertakings acquire joint control of a joint venture, provided that the joint venture has no, or negligible, actual or foreseen activities within the EEA, or where two or more undertakings merge, provided that none of the parties to the concentration are engaged in business activities in the same product or geographical market, or in a product market which is upstream or downstream of a product market in which any other party to the concentration is engaged.

In order to assess the applicability of the simplified procedure, the Commission welcomes pre-notification contact from parties.

29.6.5 The investigation

There are two stages to a Commission investigation.

29.6.5.1 First stage

The first lasts for 25 working days (Art. 10), during which the Commission consults third parties, analyses the information provided with the notification, and considers the impact of the concentration on the relevant markets. At the end of the first stage, the Commission decides whether or not there are serious doubts about the compatibility of the concentration with the Common Market. If there are no serious doubts, the concentration will be cleared (Art. 6(1)(b)).

29.6.5.2 Second stage

If the Commission has serious doubts about the compatibility of the concentration with the Common Market, the investigation enters the second stage (Art. 6(1)(c)). In practice, only about ten per cent of cases reach this stage. There will be further investigation and consultation, and other sections of the Commission whose responsibilities overlap with the markets affected by the concentration will be consulted. If the Commission is minded to reach a conclusion unfavourable to the parties, it will serve them with a notice of objections to which they can respond, if necessary at an oral hearing. Finally, the decision of the Commission will be considered by the Advisory Committee and, if controversial, by the full Commission.

29.6.6 The involvement of Member States

EC law takes precedence over national law so that if a merger has a community dimension, validity of the concentration is to be decided by the Commission alone. There are, however, three situations in which national competition authorities can become involved.

29.6.6.1 Dominance in a distinct local market

Article 9 of the Merger Regulation (the 'German clause') provides that the Commission may refer a Community dimension concentration to a Member State for adjudication where the Member State informs the Commission that the particular concentration threatens to affect significantly competition in a market within that Member State, which presents all the characteristics of a distinct market, or affects competition in a market within that Member State, which presents all the characteristics of a distinct market and which does not constitute a substantial part of the common market.

29.6.6.2 National powers to block approved concentrations

A Member State may take appropriate measures to protect legitimate interests other than those taken into account by the Merger Regulation, provided that they are compatible with the general principles and other provisions of Community law. Public security, plurality of the media and prudential rules are listed as 'legitimate interests'.

29.7 Summary

Having completed this chapter you should:

- be conscious of the practical implications of competition law;
- be familiar with the substantive rules of, and procedures for enforcement under, Arts 81 and 82 and the Merger Regulation.

UK competition law

30.1 Introduction

Domestic competition law operates alongside EC competition law to regulate and control anti-competitive behaviour which has effects only in the UK rather than on trade between Member States.

In this chapter we examine the main provisions of domestic competition law and their commercial effects including:

- controls on anti-competitive agreements;
- controls on abuse of a dominant position;
- the role of the Office of Fair Trading and other enforcement authorities;
- penalties and sanctions for breach of competition law;
- controls on mergers and cartels.

30.1.1 The statutory framework

The main sources of UK competition law are now the Competition Act 1998 and the Enterprise Act 2002. The 1998 Act controls cartels, anti-competitive agreements and abuse of market power. The 2002 Act controls mergers and other anti-competitive practices which may affect competition and distort the operation of markets. Primary responsibility for enforcing the law falls on the Office of Fair Trading (OFT), which has extensive powers of investigation under the 1998 Act, and on the Competition Commission (CC).

The OFT plays a central role. In addition to its enforcement responsibilities its statutory functions include the obtaining, compiling and keeping under review of information about matters relating to the carrying out of its functions for the purpose of ensuring that it has sufficient information to carry out its statutory functions (Enterprise Act 2002, s. 5), the provision of information to the public (s. 6) and the provision of information and advice to Ministers (s. 7).

The Enterprise Act 2002 also creates a new Competition Appeals Tribunal, supported by a Competition Service, which hears appeals under the 1998 Act against decisions made by the OFT and actions for damages under the 1998 Act and reviews decisions of the OFT, Secretary of State and Competition Commission in respect of mergers and market investigations under the 2002 Act.

30.1.2 The Competition Act 1998

The Competition Act 1998 came into force on 1 March 2000, replacing earlier controls on anti-competitive agreements and abuse of market power contained in the Restrictive Trade Practices Act 1976, Resale Prices Act 1976 and the Competition Act 1980. The twin objectives of the 1998 Act were to improve the effectiveness of UK competition law and bring it into line with EC law. To this end the Act introduced a 'prohibition-based approach' to competition law, introducing two new prohibitions on anti-competitive agreements and abuse of dominant position, closely based on the provisions of Arts 81 and 82 of the EC Treaty, and the Act seeks to ensure that, so far as possible, they are interpreted consistently with Arts 81 and 82 by:

(a) closely following the wording of Arts 81 and 82 in the wording of the new prohibitions; and

(b) expressly providing that when applying the substantive provisions of the Act the courts and regulatory authorities are to have regard to relevant provisions of EC law, including those of the Treaty, decisions of the ECJ and decisions or statements of the European Commission (s. 60).

One objective of the 1998 Act was to make it easier to advise businesses, since compliance with EC law will generally involve compliance with UK law and vice versa. However, recent reforms to EC competition law (see Chapter 29) have produced new differences between the two regimes and it is anticipated that reforms to the domestic legislation will be needed to realign the two systems. There are criminal and civil sanctions for breach of the prohibitions. Breach is punishable by a fine. In addition, any person injured by a breach may seek damages, so that competitors and consumers injured by anti-competitive behaviour will, in the future, be entitled to redress.

30.1.2.1   Enforcement

Primary responsibility for enforcing the new prohibitions falls on the OFT concurrently with the sector regulators for telecommunications, gas, electricity, water and rail. Regulations have been made to ensure cooperation between the OFT and other regulators with authority to enforce provisions of the Act (The Competition Act 1998 (Concurrency) Regulations 2004, SI 2004, No. 1077). Appeal from a decision of the OFT (or regulator) lies to a new Competition Appeal Tribunal.

In order to improve the effectiveness of the law the 1998 Act gives the OFT and regulators significantly enhanced powers of investigation, similar to those enjoyed by the European Commission.

30.1.2.2   Guidelines

In order to assist businesses and their advisers, the OFT (and regulators) are required to publish guidelines containing advice and information on the application and enforcement of the new Act. They will be revised from time to time to take account of changing circumstances and changes in the law resulting from decided cases and EC case law. The guidelines, which are available on the OFT website (www.oft.gov.uk), are a valuable source of guidance as to the application of the law, but it must be noted that they are not binding on the OFT.

30.2   Anti-competitive agreements: the Chapter I prohibition

The 1998 Act prohibits 'agreements between undertakings, decisions by associations of undertakings or concerted practices which–

(a) may affect trade within the United Kingdom, and

(b) have as their object or effect the prevention, restriction or distortion of competition within the United Kingdom' (s. 2).

This provision, known as 'the Chapter I prohibition', is closely based on Art. 81 of the EC Treaty and it is intended that its application should closely mirror that of Art. 81 (see **29.2**). Agreements and decisions covered by the prohibition are automatically void. In addition, contravention of the prohibition may expose a business to criminal penalties and to actions for damages. However, certain categories of agreement are excluded from the prohibition, whilst others may benefit from exemptions.

30.2.1   Scope and definition

The DGFT has published guidance on the application of the Chapter I prohibition (OFT 401, The Chapter I Prohibition). In general, it is intended that the prohibition should apply to 'horizontal' agreements etc.—that is agreements, etc., between businesses operating at the same level in the production and distribution chain. It is felt that, in general, 'vertical' agreements, other than price fixing agreements, do not raise competition concerns. 'Agreement', 'decision' and 'concerted practice' will be interpreted in the same manner as under Art. 81. Thus an agreement need not be a binding contract to be subject to the prohibition; nor is it a defence for a party to claim that they entered into an agreement as a result of pressure from other parties (see **29.2.1.2.**).

Section 2(2) of the Act sets out a non-exhaustive illustrative list of the types of agreement etc. which may be covered by the Chapter I prohibition. The list is identical to that contained in Art. 81 (see **29.2**).

An agreement, decision or practice is only subject to the Chapter I prohibition if it may affect trade in the UK and has as its object or effect the prevention, restriction or distortion of competition in the UK (or, in the case of an agreement which operates or is intended to operate in part of the UK, on trade in that part of the UK) (s. 2(7)). This provision is likely to be interpreted in the same way as Art. 81, save only that it requires effects (etc.) on trade or competition within the UK, rather than on inter-state trade (see **29.2.1.2, 29.2.1.3**). Thus agreements which may potentially affect trade, which affect trade in a positive way, or which have an indirect effect, are all subject to the prohibition.

There is no minimum size below which a market is too small to be covered by the prohibition on agreements etc. which may affect trade. However, the OFT (following the line of European competition law) takes the view that in relation to agreements etc. which have as their object or effect the prevention (etc.) of competition, the prohibition will not be breached unless the agreement (etc.) has an appreciable effect on competition, and for this purpose an effect is unlikely to be regarded as 'appreciable' where the combined market share of the parties to the agreement, decision or practice is less than 25 per cent (OFT 401, para. 2.19.). In addition, agreements in breach of the Chapter I prohibition between businesses whose combined turnover does not exceed £20 million are exempt from penalty (see Competition Act 1998 (Small Agreements and Conduct of Minor Significance) Regulations 2000, SI 2000, No. 262, below at **30.5.3**).

30.2.2   Exclusions

Section 3 of the Act contains a list of cases in which the application of the Chapter I prohibition is excluded. They include mergers, agreements etc. subject to scrutiny under other legislation, planning restrictions etc., and professional rules. There is power for the Secretary of State to vary the list by adding to it or by amending or removing any of the exclusions. An exclusion has already been made for 'vertical agreements' and land agreements (Competition Act 1998 (Land and Vertical Agreements Exclusion) Order 2000, SI 2000, No. 310).

A 'vertical agreement' is one between undertakings operating for the purposes of the agreement at different levels in the supply chain (such as manufacturers and distributors) and relating to the conditions under which the parties may purchase, sell or resell certain goods or services (Art. 2). In the past the prevailing thinking has been that, in general, 'vertical' agreements, other than price-fixing agreements, do not raise competition concerns. The exclusion therefore does not apply to any vertical agreement which, directly or indirectly, has the object or effect of restricting the buyer's ability to determine its sale price (Art. 4), although it is permissible for a supplier to fix a maximum resale price or to stipulate a recommended resale price. However, vertical agreements are subject to Art. 81 of the EC Treaty (subject to a block exemption: see **29.2.4.3**) and in March 2004 the Secretary of State for Trade and Industry announced that the UK government intends to revoke the blanket exclusion for vertical agreements in domestic law.

'Land agreements' are defined as agreements between undertakings which create, alter, transfer or terminate an interest in land, or agreements to enter into such agreements (Art. 2). The provisions relating to land agreements are complex, but broadly speaking they exclude from the Chapter I prohibition certain categories of restrictions and obligations accepted by parties to land agreements. Thus, for instance, certain covenants between landlord and tenant contained in a tenancy agreement and certain classes of covenant contained in a transfer restricting the user of land by transferor or transferee are excluded from the Chapter I prohibition.

30.2.3 Exemptions

An agreement, decision or practice may be exempted from the Chapter I prohibition. The Act provides for three classes of exemption—individual, block and parallel.

Individual and block exemptions

The OFT may grant an individual exemption to a particular agreement on the request of one of the parties to it (s. 4). In order to obtain individual exemption for an agreement, therefore, the agreement must be notified to the OFT. A detailed analysis of the relevant market and the effect on it of the agreement in question will normally be required before the decision whether or not to grant exemption can be made. Exemption may be granted for such period, and be made subject to such conditions and obligations, as the OFT thinks fit (s. 4(3)) and there is power for the OFT, acting on its own initiative or on a complaint by any person, to cancel an exemption or vary, add to or remove any conditions to which it was subject if, after granting it, it has reasonable grounds for believing that there has been a material change of circumstances since it was granted, or reasonable suspicion that the information on which its decision was based was incomplete, false or misleading in a material particular, or in the event of failure to comply with any obligation. Where the exemption is granted subject to a condition, breach of that condition automatically cancels the exemption (s. 5(3)). It is therefore important that where parties obtain an exemption they take care to comply with its terms.

Exemption may be granted to entire classes of agreement by block exemptions made by the Secretary of State on the recommendation of the OFT (ss. 6–7). It is not necessary for an agreement covered by a block exemption to be notified to the OFT.

An individual or block exemption can only be granted if the criteria in s. 9 are satisfied. Section 9 is in terms almost identical to those of Art. 81(3), save only that it is not limited to the production or distribution of goods, but can also apply to agreements which contribute to improving the production or distribution of services. As under Art. 81(3), therefore, there are four conditions which must be satisfied before exemption can be granted (see **29.2.4**). The burden of proving that the conditions are satisfied lies on the party seeking exemption.

Parallel exemptions

Section 10 provides for agreements to benefit from 'parallel exemptions'. This provision is intended to promote harmony between domestic and European law. An agreement is exempt under this provision if it is exempt from Art. 81 by virtue of an individual or block exemption under Art. 81. In addition, an agreement may benefit from parallel exemption if it falls into a class covered by a Community block exemption but is not covered by that block exemption solely because it does not affect inter-state trade (s. 10(2)). It is not necessary for an agreement covered by a block exemption to be notified to the OFT. There is power for the OFT to make rules permitting it to impose conditions on or even to vary or cancel a parallel exemption (s. 10(5)).

30.2.4   Notification for guidance or decision

Where a party to an agreement thinks that it may infringe the Chapter I prohibition they may notify the agreement to the OFT for guidance, or a decision, as to whether or not it does infringe or is, or may be, protected by an exemption. Notifying an agreement for guidance or a decision means that no penalty can be imposed for any infringement of the Chapter I prohibition by the agreement during the period from the date of notification to that when the application is determined (s. 13(4), s. 14(4)). The procedure for making such applications is set out in the Schedule to the Act and accompanying regulations (Competition Act 1998 (Director's Rules) Order 2000, SI 2000, No. 293). A fee, of £5,000 on an application for guidance and £13,000 on an application for a decision, is payable.

30.2.4.1   Guidance

Notification for guidance is, in effect, an application to the OFT for its opinion whether the agreement infringes the Chapter I prohibition and, if so, whether it is likely to be covered by a block or parallel exemption or whether it would be likely to grant it individual exemption. It does not lead to a binding decision so that, for instance, the OFT is not bound to grant exemption to an agreement even if it has given guidance to the effect that it would be likely to grant it exemption. However, if the OFT does give guidance to the effect that the agreement does not infringe the prohibition, that it is likely to be covered by a block or parallel exemption, or that it would be likely to grant an individual exemption, the parties to the agreement are given a broad measure of protection. After giving such guidance the OFT may take no further action with respect to the agreement unless:

(a) it has reasonable grounds for believing that there has been a material change of circumstances since it gave its guidance;

(b) it has a reasonable suspicion that the information on which it based its guidance was incomplete, false or misleading in a material particular;

(c) one of the parties applies to it for a decision in relation to the agreement; or

(d) a complaint is made by a person not party to the agreement (s. 15(2)).

Moreover, guidance that an agreement does not infringe or is likely to be exempt provides the parties to the agreement with immunity from any penalty under the Act (s. 15(3)). The OFT may however withdraw the immunity from penalty by written notice in any of the circumstances listed in (a)–(d) above (s. 15(4)), and where the grounds for withdrawal are that the OFT has a reasonable suspicion that incomplete, false or misleading information was provided to it by one of the parties to the agreement, such notice may be retrospective (s. 15(5)).

30.2.4.2   Notification for decision

Where application is made for a decision, the OFT may respond by deciding that the agreement does not infringe the prohibition, or that it is covered by the terms of an exclusion or exemption. An application for a decision may include a request for it to be granted individual exemption (s. 14(3)). Details of all applications for a decision, including their outcome, are kept in a register open to public inspection.

The OFT's decision that an agreement does not infringe the prohibition, or is protected by an exemption, provides the parties with a greater measure of protection than mere guidance, for after giving such a decision the OFT can take no further action in respect of the agreement unless it has reasonable

(a) grounds for believing that there has been a material change of circumstances since it gave its decision, or

(b) suspicion that the information on which it based its decision was incomplete, false or misleading in a material particular.

The OFT therefore cannot withdraw its decision merely on the grounds that a third party makes a complaint about an agreement. Such a complaint may, however, lead to its investigating the agreement and deciding either that there has been a change of circumstances, or that its original decision was based on false information.

As in the case of guidance, a decision that the agreement does not infringe the Chapter I prohibition provides the parties to the agreement with immunity from penalty under the Act (s. 16(3)). That immunity may be withdrawn on notice to the party who sought the decision in either of the circumstances listed in (a)–(b) above if the OFT considers it likely that the agreement will infringe the prohibition. The withdrawal of immunity may be retrospective where the OFT has a reasonable suspicion that incomplete, false or misleading information was provided to it by one of the parties to the agreement (s. 16(5)).

Where the parties to an agreement are concerned that it may infringe the Chapter I prohibition they may therefore in the first instance notify it to the OFT for guidance. If the response to that notification is favourable they must decide whether or not to notify it for a formal decision, or to seek an individual exemption. A formal decision, if granted, will offer the agreement a measure of protection against sanction even in the event of a third party complaint to the OFT. In so doing, however, it must be borne in mind that in the event of an application for a formal decision the OFT is not bound by its guidance, and the immunity from sanction under the Act is lost.

30.2.5   Notification to the European Commission

An agreement which infringes the Chapter I prohibition will normally also infringe Art. 81 if it affects, or may affect, inter-state trade. In the past it was possible for parties to an agreement to notify it to the European Commission to obtain an exemption from Art. 81. If granted such exemption would give the agreement a 'parallel exemption' under the 1998 Act (see **30.2.3**). However, the pre-notification system has been abolished with effect from 1 May 2004. It will therefore no longer be possible for an agreement to be exempted from the 1998 Act on this basis.

30.2.6 Transitional provisions

Prior to the coming into force of the 1998 Act, anti-competitive agreements were controlled by the RTPA 1976 and RPA 1976. Under the RTPA 1976, any agreement which imposed certain categories of restrictions on the conduct of the parties was required to be registered with the DGFT. Failure to register a registrable agreement made it void and unenforceable. On registration the DGFT was required to refer the agreement to the Restrictive Practices Court, where the agreement would be declared void unless the parties could show that its restrictions were justified in the public interest. In practice, however, most agreements were dealt with by a different procedure under s. 21(2) of the RTPA, which allowed the Secretary of State to release the DGFT from the duty to refer an agreement to the Court where its restrictions were considered to be of too little significance to justify investigation by the Court. The DGFT would therefore negotiate with the parties to remove objectionable restrictions before recommending that the Secretary of State give an appropriate direction.

The RPA 1976 sought to control the practice of resale price maintenance whereby manufacturers and suppliers impose on their customers conditions as to the prices at which their goods should be resold. Under the Act it was unlawful for a supplier to include in a contract with a dealer any term which purported to set a minimum resale price to be charged by the dealer, or to withhold supplies from a dealer, or to supply him only on terms less favourable than those offered to other dealers, on the grounds that he had sold, or was likely to sell, goods at a price below the stipulated resale price. It was also unlawful for two or more suppliers of goods to make or carry out any agreement or arrangement to withhold supplies from a dealer, or to supply them only on terms which were less favourable than those offered to other dealers.

All agreements previously covered by these regimes are now covered by the 1998 Act. However, because the new competition regime introduced by the 1998 Act is substantially different from this old regime, the Act provides for a transitional period during which the Chapter I prohibition will not apply to agreements made prior to its coming into force. The details of the transitional provisions are complicated. Broadly speaking their effect is as follows.

- Agreements other than price-fixing agreements made prior to the enactment of the 1998 Act and not caught by the RTPA are entitled to a one-year transitional period.

- Agreements covered by directions under s. 21(2) of the RTPA are exempt from the Chapter I prohibition for their duration (although this exemption may be lost if there is a material variation of the agreement).

- Agreements found not to be contrary to the public interest under the RTPA are entitled to a five-year transitional period.

- Agreements void under the RTPA or RPA are immediately subject to the Chapter I prohibition as from the commencement date.

There are special provisions for certain agreements relating to utilities, and power for the OFT to extend the transitional periods. Such extensions will only be granted where there is good reason. An extension is unlikely to be granted in respect of an agreement which is likely seriously to infringe the Chapter I prohibition. There is also power for the OFT to terminate the transitional period where an agreement would infringe the prohibition.

Agreements made during the period between the passing of the 1998 Act and its coming into force are subject to the Chapter I prohibition.

Agreements made after the commencement of the 1998 Act are fully subject to its provisions.

30.3   Abuse of a dominant position: the Chapter II prohibition

Section 18 of the 1998 Act provides that:

'any conduct on the part of one or more undertakings which amounts to the abuse of a dominant position in a market is prohibited if it may affect trade within the United Kingdom.'

This provision, known as 'the Chapter II prohibition' is an almost verbatim reproduction of Art. 82 of the EC Treaty (see **29.3**) save only that it prohibits abuses which have effects on trade within the UK, or in any part of it. It should be noted that, like Art. 82, the prohibition does not prohibit dominance but the *abuse* of a dominant position. There are no transitional arrangements applicable to the Chapter II prohibition which has immediate effect from 1 March 2000.

30.3.1   Scope and exclusions

There are exclusions from the Chapter II prohibition including for:—

(a) conduct which results in a merger covered by Pt 3 of the Enterprise Act 2002 or which is subject to the exclusive jurisdiction of the European Commission under the EC Merger Regulation;

(b) undertakings entrusted with the operation of 'services of a general economic interest' or a 'revenue producing monopoly';

(c) conduct engaged in to comply with a legal requirement;

(d) avoidance of conflict with international obligations;

(e) conduct relating to coal or steel products where the European Commission has exclusive jurisdiction pursuant to the European Coal and Steel Treaty; and,

(f) on the order of the Secretary of State, 'exceptional and compelling reasons of public policy'.

On the whole these exceptions cover cases where the conduct in question is subject to control under a separate regime, or is sanctioned by law.

There is no scope for conduct to be exempted from the Chapter II prohibition. However, infringement which consists of 'conduct of minor significance', where the annual turnover of the business involved does not exceed £50 million, is exempt from penalty (see **30.5.3**).

It is intended that the interpretation and application of the Chapter II prohibition should closely follow that of Art. 82, and the OFT has issued draft guidance (OFT 402: *The Chapter II Prohibition*, OFT 403, Market Definition) indicating that it intends to follow the jurisprudence of the ECJ and the practice of the European Commission in relation to such matters as market definition, dominance and abuse (see **29.3**). Thus market definition will take account of both the product market, including the possibility of product substitution, and the geographic market. Previous investigation of a market, by the OFT or the European Commission, may offer a precedent but will not be binding, for as the OFT notes, markets may change over time.

30.3.2   Dominance

As under Art. 82, the principle test of dominance is the ability of a business to act independently of competitive pressures. The definition laid down by the ECJ in the *United Brands* case will be applied (OFT 402 para. 3.10; see **29.3.2**). Thus, as under Art. 82 a number of factors may be relevant in assessing whether a business enjoys a dominant position. They include market share; customer power, which may balance the power of an otherwise dominant business; and barriers to the entry of new businesses into the market, which may include regulatory barriers such as licensing requirements, intellectual property rights, strategic advantages enjoyed by a business' being the first in a particular market, and any evidence of predatory behaviour designed to exclude or deter new market entrants. The OFT has indicated that a business with a market share of less than forty per cent is unlikely to be considered 'dominant', but dominance may be established with a smaller market share in appropriate circumstances, as for instance where the weakness of competitors provides evidence of dominance (see OFT 402, para. 3.13).

The scope of the prohibition is not limited to the case where a single business is dominant. Cases of joint dominance are also covered, although where two or more businesses are jointly dominant in a particular market and act in a concerted fashion to abuse that dominance there is likely also to be a breach of the Chapter I prohibition.

30.3.3   Abuse

Section 18(2) contains the following non-exhaustive list of the types of conduct which may amount to abuse of a dominant position:

(a) directly or indirectly imposing unfair purchase or selling prices or other unfair trading conditions;

(b) limiting production, markets or technical development to the prejudice of consumers;

(c) applying dissimilar conditions to equivalent transactions with other trading parties, thereby placing them at a competitive disadvantage;

(d) making the conclusion of contracts subject to acceptance by the other parties of supplementary obligations which, by their nature or according to commercial usage, have no connection with the subject of the contracts.

Again this repeats almost verbatim the language of Art. 82. The OFT has indicated that conduct for which there is an objective justification will not be regarded as an abuse, so that for instance a manufacturer's policy of restricting supplies to selected customers might be justifiable if shown to be based on safety considerations. However, it is for the business charged with abuse to justify its conduct and it will be necessary to show that the behaviour challenged is proportionate to the justification. Mere enforcement of intellectual property rights will not *per se* be regarded as an abuse.

The OFT suggests that abusive behaviour will normally fall into one of two categories: exploitation of customers or suppliers, or conduct which removes or limits actual or potential competition. The first category would include excessively high selling prices (or unfairly low purchasing prices by a dominant purchaser) and discriminatory pricing or contract terms. The second would include predatory behaviour, vertical restraints, such as resale price maintenance, selective distribution, refusal to supply and tie-in sales.

30.3.4   Applications for guidance and decisions

Although there is no scope for exemption from the Chapter II prohibition, the Act provides for a person whose conduct may be considered to infringe the prohibition to apply to the OFT for their conduct to be considered by the OFT for guidance or decision (s. 20). Applications for guidance or decision should be made in the form prescribed by regulations

(Competition Act 1998 (Director's Rules) Order 2000, SI 2000, No. 293). A fee, of £5,000 on an application for guidance and £13,000 on an application for a decision, is payable.

30.3.4.1   Applications for guidance

On an application for guidance the OFT may give the applicant guidance as to whether, in its opinion, the conduct in question is likely to infringe the prohibition. It is not obliged to give such guidance, but if it does give guidance that the conduct is not likely to infringe the prohibition it may not subsequently take action in respect of the conduct in question unless:

(a) it has reasonable grounds for believing that there has been a material change of circumstances since it gave its guidance;

(b) it has a reasonable suspicion that the information on which it based its guidance was incomplete, false or misleading in a material particular;

(c) a complaint about the conduct is made to it (s. 23(2)).

In addition, where such guidance has been given no penalty may be imposed for breach of the Chapter II prohibition (s. 23(3)). The OFT may however withdraw the immunity from penalty by written notice in any of the circumstances listed in (a)–(c) above (s. 23(4)), and where the grounds for withdrawal are that the OFT has a reasonable suspicion that information on which it based its guidance and which was supplied by one of the undertakings engaging in the conduct in question was incomplete, false or misleading, such withdrawal may be retrospective (s. 23(5)).

30.3.4.2   Application for decision

On an application for a decision, the OFT may make a decision whether or not the conduct in question does infringe the Chapter II prohibition and, if not, whether that is because it is covered by one of the exclusions (s. 22). Details of applications for a decision, including their outcome, are kept in a register open to public inspection. As is the case under the Chapter I prohibition, a decision that there is no infringement offers greater protection than mere guidance. Where the OFT makes a decision that there has been no infringement of the Chapter II prohibition it may not subsequently take action in respect of the conduct in question unless:

(a) it has reasonable grounds for believing that there has been a material change of circumstances since it gave its guidance;

(b) it has a reasonable suspicion that the information on which it based its guidance was incomplete, false or misleading in a material particular (s. 24(2)).

In addition such a decision confers on the conduct immunity from penalty under the Act (s. 24(3), save that the OFT may withdraw the immunity by written notice in either of the circumstances listed above (s. 24(4)), and where the grounds for withdrawal are that the OFT has a reasonable suspicion that information on which it based its guidance and which was supplied by one of the undertakings engaging in the conduct in question was incomplete, false or misleading, such notice may be retrospective (s. 24(5)).

It will be noted that, as under the Chapter I prohibition, a decision by the OFT offers greater protection against subsequent sanction or penalty than does guidance. However, the protection offered by either decision or guidance in respect of infringement of the Chapter II prohibition is narrower than that offered by a decision or guidance in respect of the Chapter I prohibition. In particular, an application for guidance or a decision in relation to the Chapter II prohibition provides no interim protection pending the OFT's response.

30.4   Powers of investigation

The OFT has extensive powers of investigation which may be utilised to determine if there has been a breach of the Chapter I or Chapter II prohibition. They include powers to require the production of documents and/or the supply of information and to enter premises with or without a court warrant. It is a criminal offence, punishable by fines and/or imprisonment to fail or refuse to comply with such a requirement or to obstruct or interfere with the exercise of these powers. Although the powers of investigation are given to the OFT, they are exercisable by any officer authorised to act on its behalf.

30.4.1   Grounds for an investigation

The OFT's powers of investigation are only available where it has reasonable grounds for suspecting that there has been a breach of the Chapter I or Chapter II prohibition (s. 25). In the draft guidance on the investigation provisions the OFT suggests that information which might provide such reasonable grounds for suspicion include copies of cartel agreements, statements from employees or ex-employees, substantiated complaints, and economic evidence of price movements. It also indicates that it would expect in many cases to obtain information informally, without invoking the formal powers of investigation. Of course, information gathered informally may provide the OFT with reasonable grounds for suspecting an infringement and thus provide the grounds for invoking the formal powers of investigation.

30.4.2   Power to require production of documents and/or provision of information

The OFT indicates that it expects the power to require the provision of information and/ or the production of documents to be the most commonly used of its powers of investigation. It may require the production of documents and/or information relevant to any matter relevant to its investigation, and from any person, including not only parties to the suspected infringement but third parties including competitors and customers of the suspected infringer. It may take copies of and require an explanation of any document produced. 'Document' for this purpose is defined as including 'information recorded in any form' so that it would include computer files (s. 59(1)).

In order to invoke the power against any person the OFT must serve written notice, specifying:

(a) the subject matter and purpose of the investigation

(b) the information and/or documents required

(c) the time, place, manner and form in which they are to be produced and

(d) the offences created by the Act in relation to non-compliance etc. with the notice (s. 26(2)).

30.4.3   Power to enter premises without warrant

The Act gives the OFT power to enter premises without warrant (s. 27). The power is not limited to premises of the parties under investigation but may also be exercised in relation to premises of third parties. However, it only be exercised in relation to a domestic house if it is used in connection with the business or if business documents are stored there (s. 59(1)).

The power of entry is normally only exercisable on the OFT giving at least two working days' notice, in writing, stating the subject matter and purpose of the investigation, including the type of infringement suspected, and the offences which may be committed by a person who fails to comply with the notice (s. 27(2)). There is also power to enter premises without prior written notice but this is only available where the OFT has reasonable suspicion that the premises are, or have been, occupied by a party to an agreement under investigation, or a business whose conduct it is investigating OR where the investigating officer has been unable to give written notice to the occupier of the premises despite taking reasonable steps to do so (s. 27(3)).

Where an officer exercises the power to enter premises without warrant he may require the production of any document he considers relevant to the investigation, which may then be copied, an explanation of any document and the production of any information held on computer and accessible from the premises.

A business being investigated will generally be able to contact its legal advisers during an on-site investigation. Regulations provide that where an investigating officer enters premises the occupier of premises may request that reasonable time be allowed for the occupier's legal adviser to arrive before the investigation continues. The investigating officer must grant such a request if he considers it reasonable in all the circumstances to do so and he is satisfied that any conditions he thinks appropriate to impose on the grant of such a delay will be satisfied (Competition Act 1998 (Director's Rules) Order 2000, SI 2000, No. 293, reg. 13). The officer might therefore make the grant of such a request conditional on, say, the sealing of files or the suspension of external communications. The OFT has indicated that where entry is sought on prior written notice, it will not normally delay the investigation to allow legal advice to be taken.

30.4.4   Power to enter premises with warrant

The Act gives the OFT a further power to apply to the court (the High Court in England and Wales, Court of Session in Scotland) for a warrant to enter and search premises (s. 28). This is a power of last resort, to be used when entry without warrant either is impossible or would be ineffective. A warrant may only be granted where the court is satisfied that there are reasonable grounds for suspecting that there are documents on the premises:

(a) which have not been produced in response to a request for their production; or

(b) which, if the OFT were to require their production, would be concealed, tampered with, destroyed or removed; or

(c) whose production the officer could have required if the premises had been entered without warrant

AND, in case (c), that the officer has been unable to obtain entry without a warrant (s. 28(1)). If a warrant is granted the investigating officer may use reasonable force to obtain entry to the premises. He may then search the premises, take copies of documents of the kind to which the warrant relates and even, where it appears necessary to preserve or prevent interference with the documents, remove the originals and keep them for up to three months, require any person to provide an explanation of any document of a kind to which the warrant relates, and require the production in readable form of any information held in computer accessible from the premises.

30.4.5   Protection for certain classes of information

The OFT's powers to require the production and explanation of documents and information are subject to certain limitations. It cannot require production or disclosure of any 'privileged communication' which, for this purpose, means a communication between a professional legal adviser and his client or a communication made in connection with or contemplation of, and for the purposes of, legal proceedings, which would be protected by legal professional privilege in High Court proceedings (s. 30(2)). The category of documents protected by privilege in relation to an investigation of infringement of domestic competition law is therefore wider than the category recognised by the ECJ for the purposes of investigations under Arts 81 and 82 and extends, for instance, to communications with an in-house lawyer (see **29.4.2.1**).

Secondly, since the Act requires the OFT to act in accordance with the relevant principles of Community law (s. 60), it has indicated that the privilege against self-incrimination recognised by the ECJ will apply to investigations of infringement of domestic competition law (OFT 404, paras 6.3–6.4). Thus no person can be required to answer a question which might involve an admission of an infringement by him (see **29.4.2.1**).

There are also restrictions on the disclosure of information obtained in the course of an investigation. Any such information which relates to the affairs of any individual or any business of an undertaking, cannot be disclosed during the lifetime of the individual or while the business is carried on, as appropriate, without the consent of both the person who provided it and the person to whom it relates (s. 55). Disclosure outside these circumstances is a criminal offence. Outside this restriction the OFT and Secretary of State are required when considering whether to disclose any information acquired during an investigation to have regard to the need to exclude, so far as possible, disclosure of information disclosure of which would be contrary to the public interest, commercial information whose disclosure might significantly harm the legitimate business interests of the person to whom it relates, and information relating to the private affairs of any person disclosure of which might significantly harm his interests (s. 56).

30.4.6 Offences in relation to investigations

A person who fails to co-operate with, or who obstructs or interferes with, an investigation by the OFT may commit a number of criminal offences. Thus it is an offence:

(a) to fail to comply with a requirement to produce a document or to supply information (s. 42);

(b) intentionally to obstruct an officer carrying out an investigation on premises with or without warrant (s. 42);

(c) intentionally or recklessly to destroy, falsify or conceal a document whose production has been required (s. 43);

(d) knowingly or recklessly to provide information which is false in a material particular (s. 44).

Where an offence is committed by a company with the consent or connivance, or as a result of the neglect of any officer of the company, then the officer is also guilty of an offence (s. 72).

The offences may be tried summarily or on indictment. All are punishable by fines. In addition the offences of obstructing an officer searching premises with a warrant, falsifying (etc.) a document and supplying false information are punishable on indictment by up to two years' imprisonment.

30.4.7 Conclusion of the investigation

Where the OFT has conducted an investigation it may make a decision that there has been an infringement of either the Chapter I or II prohibition. Before doing so it must give written notice to the persons likely to be affected by its decision, and offer them a chance to make representations (s. 31). The person to whom such notice is given may make written representations and may also request an appointment to supplement this with oral representations and/or to inspect the OFT's file. Any confidential information will be removed from the file before such inspection.

30.5   Penalties and sanctions

Where the OFT concludes that there has been an infringement it may issue directions to bring it to an end. In addition, it has power to give interim directions which take effect before and pending completion of an investigation, and to impose financial penalties for any infringement. An infringer may also face a civil law action for damages from a person adversely affected by an infringement. Although proceedings leading to the imposition of penalties by the OFT share some of the features of criminal proceedings, it has been held that the appropriate standard of proof is the civil standard, that is to say proof on the balance of probabilities. The OFT may therefore rely on inferences from proved facts in order to draw a conclusion that a business has been party to an anti-competitive agreement or has abused a dominant position (*NAPP Pharmaceutical Holdings Ltd* v *DGFT (No. 4)* [2002] Comp A R 13).

30.5.1   Directions

Where the OFT concludes that there has been an infringement of the Chapter I or II prohibition it may give such directions as it considers appropriate to bring the infringement to an end (ss. 32, 33). They may include directions to terminate or modify an agreement or to end or modify a course of conduct. Such directions may be addressed not only to the infringer but to such person or persons as the OFT considers appropriate. This might include, for instance, a parent company of an infringer. The directions must be given in writing, and will be published on a register kept by the OFT which will be available for inspection and on the Internet. Where the OFT gives a direction, it is required at the same time to inform the person to whom it is addressed of (a) the facts on which it bases the direction, and (b) its reasons for giving it (Competition Act 1998 (Director's Rules) Order 2000, SI 2000, No. 293, reg. 17).

If any person fails without reasonable excuse to comply with directions addressed to him, the OFT may seek a court order requiring him to comply. Failure to comply with such a court order is punishable as a contempt of court (s. 34).

30.5.2   Interim measures

Directions may be given on completion of an investigation. However, more immediate action may sometimes be necessary. The Act therefore empowers the OFT to make 'interim measures' (s. 35). This power is available where the OFT has a reasonable suspicion that the Chapter I or II prohibition has been infringed but has not yet completed its investigation, and considers it necessary to act as a matter of urgency to prevent serious, irreparable damage to a person or undertaking or to protect the public interest. The power might therefore be exercisable where, for instance, a business is suspected of abusing a dominant position and there is a danger that a smaller competitor will be driven out of business. The OFT notes that the power is more readily available than the corresponding power of the

European Commission which is only available where there is established a *prima facie* case of infringement of Arts 81 or 82 (see **29.4.3**).

The imposition of interim measures, like the initiation of an investigation, may therefore result from a complaint of infringement, for instance by a competitor harmed by the alleged infringement. A business which makes a complaint of infringement can also request the imposition of interim measures and specify the measures it wishes to be imposed.

If the OFT decides to impose interim measures it must give written notice to the person(s) to whom they are addressed specifying the nature of the measures and the grounds upon which they are made, and offering the addressee an opportunity to make representations before the measures take effect (s. 35(3)). It must give the person(s) to whom the measures will be addressed a reasonable opportunity to inspect documents in its file relating to the proposed measures, although it may withhold from inspection documents which contain information given in confidence, or which it considers to be confidential (Competition Act 1998 (Director's Rules) Order 2000, SI 2000, No. 293, reg. 18). If a direction is made the OFT must give the person to whom it is addressed a statement in writing of (a) the facts on which it bases the direction and (b) its reasons for giving it. If interim measures are imposed, they will be published on the register of directions maintained by the OFT.

30.5.3 Penalties

Although non-compliance with a direction is not *per se* an offence, the Act allows the OFT to impose financial penalties for any intentional or negligent infringement of the Chapter I or II prohibition (s. 36). Penalties may be up to ten per cent of the UK turnover (or combined turnover) of the undertaking or undertakings involved in the infringement. This is a wholly new power and a radical change from the position under the old domestic competition regime. The OFT has indicated that it will make use of the power to impose penalties as a deterrent to infringement and has observed that, in the USA, penalties of up to $300 m have been imposed.

Although penalties may only be imposed in the event of an intentional or negligent infringement, the OFT has indicated that the fact that the Competition Act system is 'new' will be not prevent the imposition of penalties. Nor will it be a defence that an undertaking party to an infringement acted under duress, although that fact may lead to a reduction of the penalty imposed.

There are, however, a number of exemptions. Most important, there is provision for 'small agreements' and 'conduct of minor significance' to be immune from penalty for infringement of the Chapter I and II prohibitions respectively (ss. 39 and 40). These terms are defined by reference to the (combined) turnover of the business(es) involved in the agreement or conduct in question, and the levels will be set by statutory instrument from time to time. Initially, 'small agreement' has been defined as an agreement between undertakings whose combined turnover during the calendar year preceding that in which the infringement occurs does not exceed £20 million, and 'conduct of minor significance' as conduct by an undertaking whose turnover in the year preceding that of the infringement does not exceed £50 million (Competition Act 1998 (Small Agreements and Conduct of Minor Significance) Regulations 2000, SI 2000, No. 262). The immunity will also protect businesses with turnover in excess of the stipulated thresholds if they act on the basis of a reasonable assumption that they are protected by the immunity (s. 36(4) and (5)). The OFT, however, has power to withdraw the immunity from penalty if it concludes after an investigation that there has been an infringement of either prohibition.

In addition, as already noted, a business may enjoy immunity from penalty where it has notified an agreement to the OFT for decision or guidance, or where the OFT has given a decision or guidance that an agreement or course of conduct does not infringe the relevant prohibition (see **30.2.4, 30.3.4**). Similarly, where an agreement is notified to the European Commission for an individual exemption under Art. 81 it will be immune from penalty for infringing the Chapter I prohibition from the time of notification until the date of the Commission's decision. If the Commission grants an exemption, the agreement will benefit from a parallel exemption from the Chapter I prohibition, subject to the OFT's power to investigate such an agreement and, if it thinks appropriate, cancel the parallel exemption (see **30.2.3**). (The pre-notification system will end from 1 May 2004: see **29.2.4.4**.)

The Act requires the OFT to publish guidance as to the level of penalties to be imposed under the Act (s. 38). In the published guidance (*OFT 423: Director General of Fair Trading's Guidance as to the Appropriate Amount of a Penalty, 28 April 2000*) the OFT has indicated that the following steps will be followed in calculating the level of penalty in any particular case.

1. The appropriate level of penalty for the infringement will be determined in the first instance as a percentage of the undertaking's turnover, up to a maximum of 10 per cent. (Turnover for these purposes will be determined in accordance with the Competition Act 1998 (Determination of Turnover for Penalties) Regulations 2000, SI 2000, No. 309). The appropriate percentage will be determined primarily by reference to the seriousness of the infringement.

2. The penalty so determined may then be increased to to take account of the duration of the infringement.

3. The level of penalty may then be adjusted to ensure that the penalty operates as a sufficient deterrent against infringement of the Act and to ensure that the undertakings party to the infringement do not profit from it. As the OFT observes, this adjustment may result in a substantial increase in the level of penalty as initially determined.

4. The level of penalty may then be further adjusted to take account of any aggravating or mitigating factors: for instance, an undertaking which took a leading role in an infringement might receive an increased penalty, one which participated reluctantly, under duress, a reduced one. The fact that a business has a compliance program may be relevant to the level of penalty as a mitigating factor.

5. Finally the 10 per cent cap will be applied so that the overall level of penalty will never exceed 10 per cent of turnover.

The OFT will follow the Commission's policy on whistleblowers, so that a business which reveals the existence or activities of a cartel may be subject to reduced penalties (see **29.4.2.2**). Finally, in fixing the level of penalty the OFT will take account of any penalty imposed by the Commission or the competition authorities of other EU Member States to avoid a business being penalised twice for the same conduct.

Penalties imposed for infringement are recoverable by the OFT as civil debts. It must serve notice on the business concerned indicating the level of penalty and the period for payment (three months will normally be allowed). If the penalty is not paid voluntarily the OFT may bring civil proceedings to recover it as a civil debt (s. 37).

30.5.4 Appeals

Decisions of the OFT are subject to appeal to the Competition Appeal Tribunal. Where the OFT decides that there has been an infringement of either prohibition, to grant or cancel an exemption or to impose a penalty for an infringement, any person whose conduct is the subject of the decision may appeal to the Tribunal (s. 46). Where a party appeals against a decision in this way it may also apply to the Appeal Tribunal to suspend any directions made against it by the OFT.

In addition any third party, or representative of third parties, whom the Competition Appeal Tribunal considers to have sufficient interest in the relevant decision may appeal to the Tribunal against a decision of the OFT (or sectoral regulator) other than as to the imposition of a penalty (s. 47).

The Tribunal has wide powers on an appeal to confirm or set aside the decision, remit the matter to the OFT, impose, revoke or vary the amount of any penalty imposed, grant or cancel an individual exemption, or make any other decision which the OFT could have made.

30.5.5 Civil liability

In addition to penalties imposed by the Act, a business which infringes either prohibition may be held liable in civil damages to any person injured by the infringement. The Act does not in terms create such civil liability, but it was clearly stated by the Government when introducing the Competition Bill that it would be possible for any person injured by an infringement to sue for damages. A person injured by infringement of Art. 81 or 82 may bring a civil claim (see **29.5.2**), and the courts applying the Act are expressly required to have regard to the provisions of Community law and to the practice of the ECJ in relation to the civil liability for harm caused by infringement (s. 60(6)(b)).

Such a claim may be brought before the ordinary civil courts. Alternatively, by virtue of s. 47A inserted by the Enterprise Act 2002, a person who has suffered loss as a result of infringement of the Chapter I or Chapter II prohibition or the prohibition in Art. 81 or 82 of the EC Treaty may bring a claim for damages before the Competition Appeal Tribunal.

Such an infringement will often adversely affect the interests of consumers but individual consumers may lack the resources to bring a compensation claim. However, s. 47B allows bodies specified by Order by the Secretary of State to bring claims for compensation on behalf of consumers before the Competition Appeal Tribunal.

A third party bringing such proceedings will be entitled to rely on any findings of fact made by the OFT in any investigation or in response to an application for a decision for the Chapter I or II prohibition. The Act provides that if following such an investigation or decision no appeal is made within the time allowed, or if the Commission confirms the OFT's decision, any findings of fact made by the OFT in the course of the investigation or as a result of the application for a decision become binding in any subsequent proceedings for breach of the Chapter I or II prohibitions brought by a third party, unless the OFT exercises its powers under the Act to reconsider a decision on the limited grounds permitted (s. 58).

30.6 Control of cartels under the Enterprise Act 2002

Although cartel arrangements infringe the Chapter I prohibition in the 1998 Act, Part 6 of the Enterprise Act contains powerful additional provisions applicable to 'hard core' cartels. Part 6 creates a new 'cartel offence' by which it is an offence for any person dishonestly to agree with another to make or implement or cause to be made or implemented arrangements which fix prices for, limit supply of or divide markets for goods or services in the UK (s. 188).

30.6.1   The cartel offence

The precise definitions of the types of arrangement caught by the new provisions are complex. However, they include arrangements which

(a) directly or indirectly fix the price for *or*

(b) limit or prevent the supply of *or*

(c) limit or prevent the production of

a product or service by two parties in the UK at the same level of the supply chain. It is not necessary that the arrangements restrict both parties in the same way or that they apply to the same class or type of products or services, so that an arrangement which (say) fixes the price to be charged by A for the supply of widgets whilst limiting the manufacture by B of bodgets would be within the scope of the definition.

In addition the provisions apply to arrangements which would

(d) divide between two or more parties at the same level of the supply chain the supply of a product or service in the UK *or*

(e) divide between two or more parties customers for the supply of a product or service in the UK *or*

(f) be bid rigging arrangements.

A prosecution for a cartel offence may only be brought by the Director of the Serious Fraud Office or with the consent of the OFT (s. 190(2)). However, the offence is punishable summarily by a fine and/or imprisonment for a term not exceeding six months and on indictment by a fine and/or imprisonment for a term not exceeding five years (s. 190(1)). No prosecution can be brought unless the agreement is made or implemented, wholly or in part, in the UK (s. 190(3)). However, provision is made for the offence to be made extraditable (s. 191).

30.6.2   Investigation of cartels

Investigation of cartel arrangements is the task of the OFT which is empowered to conduct an investigation if there are reasonable grounds for suspecting that a cartel offence has been committed (s. 192). The OFT is given wide powers of investigation, similar to those available in investigations under the Competition Act. Thus it may, by notice in writing indicating the subject matter and purpose of the investigation and the potential criminal liabilities for non-compliance, require the person under investigation or any other person it has reason to believe has relevant information, to answer questions or provide information on any matter relevant to the investigation (s. 193(1)) or to produce specified documents or documents of a specified description which appear to relate to any matter relevant to the investigation (s. 193(2)), and may take copies or require an explanation of any documents so produced (s. 193(3)).

In addition the OFT may apply to the court for a warrant to enter and search premises (s. 194). A warrant can be issued if the court is satisfied by the OFT that there are reasonable grounds for believing that there are on the premises documents which the OFT could require to be produced for the purposes of the investigation and that a person has failed to comply with a notice to produce them, or that it is not practicable to serve a notice for their production, or that service of such a notice might prejudice the investigation (eg: because the documents would be destroyed). A warrant issued under this section may authorise the OFT to enter the premises, using force if necessary, search them, take possession of any relevant documents or take other steps for their preservation, and require any person to provide an explanation of any relevant document, indicate where it may be found or produce electronically-stored information in a form in which it can be taken away and is visible and legible.

The chairman of the OFT may also grant authorisation for intrusive surveillance of any person under the Regulation of Investigatory Powers Act 2000 if necessary for the purposes of preventing or detecting a cartel offence (s. 199).

Failure to co-operate with or obstruction of an OFT investigation into a cartel offence is itself a criminal offence which may attract serious penalties. Thus

(a) it is a summary offence, punishable by fine and/or up to six months imprisonment to fail to comply with a requirement to answer questions or supply information or to produce or explain documents, either in response to an OFT notice or following issue of an entry warrant;

(b) it is an offence, punishable by fine and or imprisonment, on indictment for up to two years, knowingly or recklessly to make a false or misleading statement in response to an OFT notice to provide information etc, or following entry pursuant to a warrant;

(c) it is an offence, punishable by fine and or imprisonment, on indictment for up to five years, knowing that an OFT investigation into a cartel offence is being or is likely to be carried out, to falsify, conceal, destroy or dispose of, or to cause or permit the falsification, concealment, destruction or disposal of any documents knowing or suspecting them to be relevant to the investigation;

(d) it is an offence, punishable by fine and or imprisonment, on indictment for up to two years, intentionally to obstruct any person exercising powers of entry etc pursuant to an entry warrant.

30.6.2.1   Privileged information

The duty to co-operate with the OFT is subject to some limitations. No person can be required to produce information or documents which would be protected in High Court proceedings by legal professional privilege, save that a lawyer may be required to provide the name and address of his client (s. 196). Similarly no person may be required to to disclose any information or document in relation to which he owes a duty of confidence as a result of carrying on a banking business, unless the OFT specifically authorises the requirement to disclose (s. 196(2)).

A person who is required to supply information to the OFT is also protected by the privilege against self incrimination. A statement made in response to a requirement to provide information either in response to an OFT notice or following issue of an entry warrant cannot be used in evidence against the maker except (a) on a prosecution for knowingly or recklessly making a false or misleading statement to the OFT (see above, **30.6.2**) or (b) on a prosecution for another offence if in evidence he makes a statement inconsistent with it (s. 197). A similar restriction applies to the use of statements made in response to a requirement imposed by virtue of ss. 26–28 of the Competition Act in the course of an OFT investigation of a breach of the Chapter I or Chapter II prohibition (Competition Act 1998, s. 30A).

30.6.2.2   Immunity from prosecution

As we have noted, cartel arrangements may be extremely difficult to prove. To encourage whistle blowing and co-operation with the OFT, there is therefore power for the OFT to grant immunity from prosecution. Section 190(4) provides that if the OFT for the purposes of a cartel investigation or prosecution gives any person written notice that he will not be prosecuted for cartel offences specified in the notice, no prosecution may brought against him for such offences except as specified in the notice.

30.7 Market investigations under the Enterprise Act 2002

Part 4 of the Enterprise Act 2002 creates a new system of market investigations designed to allow the Competition Commission, acting on a reference from the OFT, to investigate markets in cases where there has been no breach of any specific competition law provision such as the Chapter I or II prohibition. These provisions replace the system of monopoly control formerly contained in Part IV of the Fair Trading Act 1973. A key feature of the new regime is that, as compared with the old FTA regime, it contains a much reduced role for the Secretary of State who can generally intervene only in cases where there are public interest considerations.

The OFT and Commission are required to prepare and publish advice and information for persons affected by Part 4 explaining its provisions and indicating how they expect those provisions to operate (s. 171).

30.7.1 Market investigation references

Market investigations are carried out by the Competition Commission on reference either from the OFT or the Secretary of State.

Where the OFT has reasonable grounds for suspecting that the

(a) structure of any market for goods or services in the UK,

(b) conduct of any person or persons who supplies or acquires goods or services, or

(c) conduct in relation to the market of customers of a person who supplies or acquires goods or services

restricts or distorts competition in connection with the supply or acquisition of any goods or services in the UK, it may make a market investigation reference to the Competition Commission (s. 131).

As an alternative to making a reference the OFT may seek and accept such undertakings as it considers appropriate for the purposes of remedying, mitigating or preventing any adverse effect on competition or any detrimental effect on consumers resulting therefrom (s. 154). Where the OFT proposes to accept an undertaking in lieu of making an investigation it must first publish details of the proposed undertaking (s. 155). If the OFT accepts such an undertaking it cannot make a reference in respect of the market to which the undertaking relates for a period of 12 months, unless either the undertaking is broken or the person giving any undertaking supplied the OFT with information which was false or misleading in a material respect (s. 156).

Before deciding to make a reference to the Commission or accept undertakings in lieu, the OFT must consult with any person on whose interests it thinks its decision will have a substantial impact, taking into account the timetable for making its decision and any need to keep information confidential (s. 169).

Generally a reference to the Commission will be made by the OFT but there is power for the Secretary of State to make a reference where he has reasonable grounds for believing that any feature of a market as described above restricts or distorts competition in connection with the supply or acquisition of any goods or services in the UK and either

(a) he is not satisfied with the OFT's decision not to make a reference; or

(b) he has brought to the attention of the OFT information he considers relevant to the question whether the OFT should make a reference but he is not satisfied that the OFT will decide within a reasonable time whether or not to make a reference (s. 132).

Before making a reference the Secretary of State is under a similar duty to the OFT to consult with any person on whose interests he thinks his decision will have a substantial impact (s. 169).

30.7.2   Commission investigations

If a market investigation reference is made to it the Commission must decide whether any feature or combination of features of the relevant market prevents, restricts or distorts competition in connection with the supply or acquisition of goods or services in the UK (s. 134(1)). If it does there is an 'adverse effect on competition' and the Commission must also decide whether, and if so, what, action it should take, or recommend others to take, for the purpose of remedying, mitigating or preventing the adverse effects on competition or any detrimental effect thereof on consumers (s. 134(4)–(5)). Such detrimental effect may take the form of higher prices, lower quality or less choice of goods or services in any market or less innovation in relation to goods or services. In deciding whether to take action the Commission may take in to account any consumer benefits in the form of lower prices, reduced quality, increased choice or increased innovation, which result from the relevant feature of the market concerned, which are unlikely to have accrued without that feature and which may be affected by its proposed actions (s. 134(7)–(8)). Before making any decision on these issues the Commission must consult with any person on whose interests it thinks its decision will have a substantial impact, taking into account the timetable for making its decision and any need to keep information confidential (s. 169).

The Commission must then, within a period of two years from the date of the market investigation reference prepare and publish its report containing its decisions on these questions, the reasons for its decisions and such supporting information as it considers appropriate for facilitating a proper understanding of the questions and its decisions (s. 136).

If the Commission concludes that there is any adverse effect on competition it is under a duty to take such action by obtaining undertakings or making orders as it considers reasonable and practicable to remedy, mitigate or prevent the adverse effect on competition and any detrimental effects on consumers resulting therefrom (s. 138). Again in deciding what action to take the Commission may take into account any benefits accruing to consumers from the relevant features of the market.

Where on publication of the Commission's report the market investigation is not finally concluded the Commission obtain interim undertakings (s. 157) or make interim orders (s. 158) to protect the *status quo* by preventing pre-emptive action which would impede the making of final orders by the Commission.

30.7.3   Intervention by the Secretary of State

There is power for the Secretary of State to intervene in the process where he believes that there are public interest considerations relevant to a case, by serving notice on either the Commission or OFT.

30.7.3.1 Intervention notice to the Competition Commission

Where a reference has been made to the Competition Commission and the Secretary of State believes that there is one or more public interest consideration relevant to the case the Secretary of State may give the Commission an intervention notice specifying the relevant public interest consideration. Such notice must be given not later than four months after the date of the reference to the Commission and before the reference is finally determined. On receipt of such a notice the Commission must determine in the normal way whether there is any adverse effect on competition and, if so, what, if any, action should be taken by the Secretary of State, itself or any other person to remedy mitigate or prevent that adverse effect (s. 141). If, however, the Commission concludes that there is an adverse effect on competition and that it should take remedial action, the Commission is required not to publish its report but in the first instance to present it to the Secretary of State (s. 143(3)). The Secretary of State must then decide whether any public interest considerations as specified in his intervention notice are relevant to the action proposed by the Commission and publish his decision within 90 days of receipt of the Commission's report. The Secretary of State's discretion is limited to the effect of the identified public interest consideration: he may not challenge the decision of the Commission that there is an adverse effect on competition (s. 147(4)).

If the Secretary of State concludes that an eligible public interest consideration is relevant he may then decide what remedial action should be taken to remedy, mitigate or prevent the adverse effects on competition or any detrimental effect thereof on consumers. taking account of the relevant public interest consideration (s. 147).

If the Secretary of State decides that there is no eligible public interest consideration or he fails to publish his decision within the 90 day period as required the matter reverts to the Commission which may publish its report and proceed as if there had been no public interest intervention notice (s. 148; see above, **30.6.2**).

In effect in such a case therefore the Act requires the Secretary of State to be given the opportunity to determine whether any public interest consideration is relevant and, if so, what remedial action should be taken.

30.7.3.2 Intervention notice to the OFT

The Secretary of State may serve an intervention notice on the OFT where it is considering accepting an undertaking under s. 154 in lieu of making a reference to the Competition Commission (s. 149). Again the notice must specify the relevant public interest consideration. Its effect is to give the Secretary of State the right to veto, on public interest grounds, acceptance of the proposed undertaking. So long as the notice remains in force the OFT may not accept the proposed undertaking without the consent of the Secretary of State (s. 150(1)). The Secretary of State must withhold his consent if he believes that the proposed undertaking will operate against the public interest because the public interest concerns specified in his intervention notice outweigh the considerations which lead the OFT to propose accepting the undertaking (s. 150(2)–(3)). Again the Secretary of State's discretion is limited to consideration of the public interest: he cannot challenge the OFT's view of what undertakings would be appropriate to remedy, mitigate or prevent the adverse effects on competition or detrimental effects on consumers (s. 150(4)).

30.7.4 Enforcement

The OFT is required to keep under review compliance with any enforcement undertakings or orders and to advise the Competition Commission and Secretary of State as the case may be on the variation, release or enforcement of existing orders or undertakings or the making of new ones (s. 162). To that end it is required to maintain a register of enforcement undertakings and orders which is open to the public (s. 166).

Breach of any enforcement order or undertaking may be restrained by the OFT, Competition Commission or Secretary of State (as appropriate) seeking an injunction (s. 167(6)). However, an enforcement order or undertaking also takes effect as a duty owed to any person who may be affected by breach of it and breach of an undertaking or order is therefore actionable by any such person who suffers loss or damage as a result as a breach of statutory duty (s. 167(3)–(4)).

30.7.5 Investigations

The OFT has extensive powers for the purposes of deciding whether to make a reference or accept undertakings in lieu, to serve notice on any person requiring him to attend and give evidence and/or produce documents in his custody or control and to copy documents (s. 174). It is an offence, punishable by a fine or on indictment by up to two years' imprisonment and/or a fine, intentionally and without reasonable excuse to fail to comply with such a notice (s. 175).

The Commission has similar powers to require persons to attend before it, give evidence and produce documents for the purposes of any reference. It may also take evidence on oath and has the power to impose penalties on any person who without reasonable excuse fails to comply with the requirements of any such notice or who intentionally obstructs or delays another person seeking to make copies of any document produced for the purposes of the investigation (s. 176). Such penalties may be of such amount as the Commission considers appropriate up to an amount to be specified by the Secretary of State (s. 111; see **30.7.6**). A person aggrieved by a penalty imposed on him by the Commission may appeal to the Competition Appeal Tribunal (s. 114).

In addition it is an offence punishable by fine or imprisonment intentionally to alter, suppress or destroy a document required to be produced for the purposes of the reference (s. 110(5)), although the same act cannot be the subject of both a criminal prosecution and a penalty imposed by the Commission.

30.7.5.1 Provision of false or misleading information

It is an offence for any person to provide to the OFT, Commission or Minister in connection with their functions in respect of market investigations any information which is false or misleading in a material respect knowing that, or being reckless whether, it is false or misleading in a material respect (s. 180).

30.7.5.2 Offences by bodies corporate

As under the Competition Act (see **30.4.6**) where an offence is committed by a company with the consent or connivance of or is attributable to the neglect of any officer of the company, an offence is committed by that individual as well as the company (s. 180).

30.7.6 Appeals

Any person aggrieved by a decision of the OFT, Secretary of State or Competition Commission—including a failure to take a decision permitted or required by the Act—may appeal to the Competition Appeal Trinbunal (s. 179).

30.8 Merger control under the Enterprise Act 2002

Part 3 of the Enterprise Act 2002 contains new powers to control mergers replacing the powers formerly contained in Part V of the Fair Trading Act 1973. The major difference between the old and new regimes is that the Secretary of State plays a much reduced role under the new regime. Under the old FTA regime merger situations were subject to investigation by the Competition Commission on reference from the Secretary of State and, although the Secretary of State generally acted on advice from the Director General of Fair Trading he had a discretion whether or not to refer. Under the new regime the decision to refer a merger to the Commission is normally taken by the OFT, the Secretary of State having power to intervene in cases only where the merger raises public interest as opposed to merely competition or consumer benefit considerations.

The OFT and Commission are required to prepare and publish advice and information for persons affected by Part 3 explaining its provisions and indicating how they expect those provisions to operate (s. 106).

30.8.1 OFT jurisdiction to refer a merger

Generally the OFT has a duty to refer a merger to the Competition Commission if it believes that

(a) a relevant merger situation has been created and

(b) the creation of that situation has resulted in, or may be expected to result in, a substantial lessening of competition within any market in the UK for goods or services (s. 22(1)).

A 'relevant merger situation' is created if two or more enterprises cease to be distinct and either (i) the value of the UK turnover of the enterprise taken over exceeds £70m or (ii) as a result of the merger at least one quarter of the goods or services of a particular description are supplied by a single person (s. 23). Enterprises cease to be distinct for this purpose if they are (directly or indirectly) brought under common ownership or control (s. 26). 'Enterprise' is defined widely to include 'the activities or part of the activities of a business' (s. 129). A merger situation may therefore arise as a result of a share transfer or a transfer of the undertaking of an incorporated or an unincorporated business.

The OFT, however, has a discretion not to refer a merger if it considers either that the relevant goods or services market concerned is not sufficiently important to justify the making of a reference or that the merger creates consumer benefits which outweigh the lessening of competition and any adverse effects thereof (s. 23(2)). The benefit may consist of lower prices, higher quality, greater choice of or increased innovation in relation to goods or services in any market in the UK, and the OFT must be satisfied that the benefit has accrued as a result of the merger and was unlikely to result without the reduction of competition resulting from the merger (s. 30).

In certain prescribed circumstances the OFT may not refer a merger situation. Those circumstances include where the merger relates to newspaper ownership (for which there is a special regime under the FTA 1973: see **30.8.8**) and where the merger is being dealt with by the European Commission at the request of the UK government under the European Merger Regulation (s. 22(3)) (see **29.6.6.3**).

The OFT is empowered to require any person carrying on the enterprises involved in the merger to provide it with information to determine whether or not to make a reference to the Competition Commission (s. 31). It is an offence to supply false or misleading information (s. 117).

In the interests of commercial certainty the OFT is required when deciding whether to make a reference to have regard to the need to make a decision as soon as is reasonably practicable (s. 103).

30.8.1.1 Anticipated mergers

The OFT has a similar duty, subject to similar qualifications and restrictions, to refer an anticipated merger if it believes that there are or may be arrangements in progress or even contemplation which, if carried out, will result in a relevant merger situation resulting in a a substantial lessening of competition within any market in the UK for goods or services, provided that the OFT has a discretion not to refer an anticipated merger if it believes that the arrangements are not sufficiently far advanced or sufficiently likely to proceed to justify a reference (s. 33). (See *Office of Fair Trading* v *IBA Health Ltd* [2004] EWCA Civ 142.)

30.8.1.2 Cases referred by European Commission

As noted in Chapter 29, the new EC Merger Regulation (EC No. 139/2004) allows the European Commission to refer a concentration with a Community dimension to a Member State for consideration (see **29.6.6.1**) Where a completed or anticipated merger is referred in this way the OFT has a duty to consider whether to make a reference to the Competition Commission (s. 34A). The OFT may decide not to make such a reference but to deal with the matter by seeking or accepting undertakings from the parties under s. 73 (see **30.8.1.3**).

30.8.1.3 Enforcement action pending a reference

Where the OFT is considering making a reference under s. 22 in respect of a completed merger it has power to accept undertakings (s. 71) or make orders (s. 72) for the purpose of preventing any pre-emptive action which might prejudice the reference concerned or impede the taking of any enforcement action which might be justified by the final decision on the reference.

Where the OFT considers that it has a duty under to make a reference in respect of a completed (s. 22) or anticipated (s. 33) merger it may proceed instead by accepting undertakings from such of the parties and in such terms as it considers appropriate for the purposes of remedying, mitigating or preventing the lessening of competition resulting from the merger or the adverse effects thereof (s. 73). It is reasonable to suppose that in many cases the OFT will proceed by negotiating appropriate undertakings rather than making a reference. Where such an undertaking is accepted no reference can be made in respect of the merger to which the undertaking relates so long as the undertaking is in force, unless it transpires that material facts relating to the merger were not notified to the OFT or made public before the undertaking was accepted (s. 74). However, if the OFT considers that such an undertaking has been, or will be, broken, or that information supplied to it in respect of the undertaking by the person giving the undertaking was false or misleading in any material respect, it may make such orders as it thinks necessary for the purposes of remedying, mitigating or preventing the lessening of competition resulting from the merger or the adverse effects thereof (s. 75). The making of such an order terminates the undertaking it replaces (s. 73(6)), and therefore terminates the prohibition on the making of a reference.

30.8.2 Competition Commission Investigation and Report

If a merger is referred to the Commission no person carrying on the business to which the reference relates, no subsidiary or associated of such a person, may, without the

Commission's consent, complete any outstanding matters, make any further arrangements or transfer ownership of any business to which the reference relates, whilst the reference is pending (s. 77). In the case of an anticipated merger no such person may directly or indirectly acquire an interest in shares in any company by or under the control of which the relevant business is carried on (s. 78). Breach of this prohibition can be restrained by injunction at the suit of the OFT and/or Competition Commission and is actionable as a breach of statutory duty by any person affected by the breach who suffers loss or damage thereby (s. 95). Pending determination of a reference the Commission may accept undertakings or make orders to prevent pre-emptive action (ss. 80–81).

Once a reference is made the Commission must, within 24 weeks beginning with the date of the reference, prepare and publish a report (ss. 38–9). The report must consider

(a) whether a relevant merger situation has arisen; and

(b) if so whether it has resulted or may be expected to result in a substantial lessening of competition within any market in the UK for goods or services.

If both questions are answered in the affirmative the Commission must decide what, if any action should be taken by it or any other person, either by making appropriate orders or by obtaining undertakings, to remedy, mitigate or prevent the lessening of competition or the adverse effects resulting from it (s. 35). The report must contain reasons for the Commission's decisions and such additional information as the Commission considers necessary to facilitate a proper understanding of the issues and the reasons for its decisions.

If the Commission concludes that there is a merger with an anti-competitive outcome, it must take such action as may be practicable and reasonable by way of seeking final undertakings or making final orders to remedy, mitigate or prevent the lessening of competition or any adverse effects resulting therefrom (s. 41).

30.8.3 Intervention by the Secretary of State

Although in most cases it is for the OFT to initiate a merger reference the Secretary of State retains a residual power to intervene in cases where an actual or proposed merger raises public interest or similar considerations.

30.8.3.1 Intervention on grounds of public interest considerations

The Secretary of State may initiate a merger investigation by issuing an 'intervention notice' to the OFT if

(a) he has reasonable grounds for suspecting that a relevant merger situation has been created or that arrangements are in progress or contemplation which if carried through will result in a relevant merger situation; AND

(b) no reference in respect of that merger situation has been made by the OFT; AND

(c) he believes that a public interest consideration is relevant to consideration of the merger (s. 42).

The Secretary of State has an apparently wide discretion to determine what is a 'public interest consideration' for this purpose. The only public interest consideration specified in the Act is national security (s. 58) but for the purposes of a public interest intervention notice a public interest consideration may be any other consideration which 'in the opinion of the Secretary of State ought to be specified' (s. 42(3)). However, the public interest consideration relied on must be specified by the Secretary of State in his intervention notice, which must also identify the relevant merger situation (s. 43).

Where an intervention notice is issued the OFT must investigate the situation and report to the Secretary of State within the time specified in the notice (s. 44). The report should include advice from the OFT on the considerations relevant to the question whether the merger should be referred to the Competition Commission and a summary of any representations made to the OFT about the public interest consideration specified in the notice which may be relevant to the decision to refer the merger.

On receipt of the OFT's report the Secretary of State may refer the merger to the Competition Commission if he believes that

(a) a relevant merger situation has been or will be created and

(b) one or more public interest considerations is relevant to consideration of the merger and

(c) that taking account only of the public interest consideration and, if he believes that the merger will result in a lessening of competition within any market in the UK for goods or services, the lessening of competition

the merger operates or will operate against the public interest. Public interest considerations may operate either against or in favour of a merger. Thus where the merger results in a lessening of competition public interest considerations may nevertheless mean that it does not operate against the public interest. Conversely even if the merger does not result in a lessening of competition, public interest considerations may mean that it does operate against the public interest.

On receipt of any reference from the Secretary of State the Commission must within 24 weeks from the date of the reference produce a report determining whether there is a relevant merger situation, if so whether it results, or is likely to result, in a substantial lessening of competition and whether, taking account of any lessening of competition and the public interest consideration specified in the reference the creation of the merger situation operates against the public interest (s. 50). If the Commission concludes that the merger does or will operate against the public interest it must continue to decide whether any, and if so, what action should be taken by the Secretary of State or any other person to remedy, mitigate or prevent the adverse effects of the merger (s. 47(7)).

On receipt of the Commission's report the Secretary of State must decide within 30 days whether to make an adverse public interest finding (s. 54). If he does so he may make orders or seek undertakings covering a range of matters specified in Sch 8 of the Act, including (for instance) prohibiting the making or performance of an agreement, the withholding from any person of any goods or service, the discrimination against any person in relation to the prices charged for any goods or services; prohibiting or restricting the acquisition of the whole or part of the assets or undertaking of any business; requiring the division of any business.

30.8.3.2   Intervention in special public interest cases

The Secretary of State may also initiate a merger investigation by serving on the OFT a 'special intervention notice' (s. 59). This power is available in 'special merger' situations, to deal with mergers affecting government defence contractors which are not covered by the normal investigatory regime because of the size of the businesses involved. A 'special merger situation' is created where two or more enterprises cease to be distinct enterprises but the merger does not constitute a 'relevant merger situation' solely because neither the £70 million turnover nor quarter market share requirement (see above **30.8.1**) is satisfied (s. 59(3)).

The Secretary of State may serve a special intervention notice where

(a) he has reasonable grounds for suspecting that a special merger situation has been created or that arrangements are in progress or contemplation which if carried through will result in a special merger situation; AND

(b) immediately prior to the merger at least one of the enterprises concerned was carried on in the UK or by or under the control of a body corporate registered in the UK; AND

(c) a person carrying on one of the enterprises was a 'relevant government contractor' (s. 59(4)(b)) who has been notified by the Secretary of State of confidential information etc relating to defence; AND

(d) he believes that a public interest consideration specified in s. 58 is relevant to consideration of the merger.

Where a special intervention notice is served the procedure is broadly similar to that where an intervention notice is served. The OFT must investigate the situation and report to the Secretary of State within the time specified in the notice (s. 61). The report should include the OFT's decision whether it believes that a special merger situation has been or will be created, advice from the OFT on the considerations relevant to the question whether the merger should be referred to the Competition Commission and a summary of any representations made to the OFT about the public interest consideration specified in the notice which may be relevant to the decision to refer the merger.

On receipt of the OFT's report the Secretary of State may refer the merger to the Competition Commission if he believes that

(a) a special merger situation has been or will be created and

(b) one or more public interest considerations is relevant to consideration of the merger and

(c) that taking account only of the public interest consideration the merger operates or will operate against the public interest.

The Commission must within 24 weeks from the date of any reference from the Secretary of State produce a report determining whether there is a special merger situation and, if so, whether it operates or may be expected to operate, against the public interest (s. 62). If the Commission concludes that the merger does or will operate against the public interest it must continue to decide whether any, and if so, what action should be taken by the Secretary of State or any other person to remedy, mitigate or prevent the adverse effects of the merger (s. 62(4)).

On receipt of the Commission's report the Secretary of State must make and publish his decision. He is bound by the Commission's finding on the question whether a special merger situation has been or is about to be created but must decide in light of the Commission's report whether, taking account of the public interest consideration specified in the case, the creation of the special merger situation operates or may be expected to operate against the public interest. If he does so decide he may make such orders or seek such undertakings as he considers reasonable and practicable to remedy, mitigate or prevent the adverse public interest effects of the merger (s. 66).

30.8.3.3   Mergers with a European dimension

In accordance with the principle of supremacy of Community law, where a merger has a European dimension it is normally dealt with by the European Commission under the European Merger Control Regulation (137/2004: see **29.6.6**). However, under the

Regulation Member States retain power to take action to protect 'legitimate interests' threatened by a merger or proposed merger. The Secretary of State therefore retains power to intervene in a merger or proposed merger by serving a 'European intervention notice' where a merger or proposed merger with a European dimension threatens legitimate interests (ss. 67–8). The notice must specify the relevant merger situation concerned and the public interest considerations considered to be relevant to its consideration. Once such a notice is given the Secretary of State may make orders providing for action to be taken to remedy, mitigate or prevent the adverse effects of the merger on the relevant public interest (s. 68).

30.8.4 Prior notification of mergers

To avoid the uncertainty of a reference and investigation of a merger there is a system of pre-notification which allows parties to give the OFT advance notice of a planned merger (s. 96). The notice must be in the form prescribed from time to time by notice in the London Gazette and state that the relevant merger proposals have been made public. A fee is payable.

Where such a merger notice is given the OFT has 20 days beginning with the day after its receipt to consider it (s. 97). During that period the OFT must take such action as it considers appropriate to bring the existence of the proposal and the notice to the attention of those who would be affected by the proposed arrangements (s. 99). It may by notice require the provider of the notice to provide additional information and may for certain purposes give notice extending the period for consideration of the merger notice.

If the period for consideration of the merger notice expires without its being rejected or a reference being made, no reference can subsequently be made in relation to the arrangements to which the notice relates (s. 96(3)), except in certain specified circumstances, including where any information supplied by the person giving the notice is false or misleading in any material respect (s. 100(1)(g)).

30.8.5 Enforcement

The OFT is required to keep under review compliance with any enforcement undertakings or orders (s. 92) and to advise the Competition and Secretary of State as the case may be on the variation, release or enforcement of existing orders or undertakings or the making of new ones. To that end it is required to maintain a register of enforcement undertakings and orders which is open to the public (s. 91).

Breach of any enforcement order or undertaking may be restrained by the OFT, Competition Commission or Secretary of State (as appropriate) seeking an injunction. However, an enforcement order or undertaking also takes effect as a duty owed to any person who may be affected by breach of it and breach of an undertaking or order is therefore actionable by any such person who suffers loss or damage as a result as a breach of statutory duty (s. 94).

30.8.6 Investigations

The Competition Commission has wide powers for the purposes of the investigation of any merger referred to it to serve notice on any person requiring him to attend and give evidence and/or produce documents in his custody or control, to copy documents and to take evidence on oath (s. 109). The Commission has power to impose penalties on any person who without reasonable excuse fails to comply with the requirements of any such notice or who intentionally obstructs or delays another person seeking to make copies of documents of any document produced for the purposes of the investigation. Such penalties may be of such amount as the Commission considers appropriate up to an amount to be specified by the Secretary of State (s. 111). It is clear that penalties for non-compliance with or obstruction of a Commission investigation may be substantial: the Act provides that the maximum amount specified by the Secretary of State may not exceed a fixed amount of £30,000 or a daily rate of £15,000.

30.8.6.1   Destruction etc of documents

In addition it is an offence punishable by fine or imprisonment intentionally to alter, suppress or destroy a document required to be produced for the purposes of the investigation (s. 110(5)), although the same act cannot be the subject of both a criminal prosecution and a penalty imposed by the Commission.

30.8.6.2   Provision of false or misleading information

It is an offence for any person to provide to the OFT, Commission or Secretary of State in connection with their functions in respect of mergers any information which is false or misleading in a material respect knowing that, or being reckless whether it is false or misleading in a material respect (s. 117).

30.8.6.3   Offences by bodies corporate

As under the Competition Act (see **30.4.6**) where an offence is committed by a company with the consent or connivance of or is attributable to the neglect of any officer of the company, an offence is committed by that individual as well as the company (s. 125).

30.8.7   Appeals

Any person aggrieved by a decision of the OFT, Secretary of State or Competition Commission in connection with a reference or possible reference of a merger situation—including a failure to take a decision permitted or required by the Act—may appeal to the Competition Appeal Trinbunal (s. 120).

30.8.8   Special schemes

Newspaper mergers are not covered by the scheme in Part 3 of the Enterprise Act. They are covered by a separate scheme of control, more strict than that applicable to ordinary mergers, in ss. 57–62 of the FTA 1973.

Mergers of water and sewerage enterprises are also subject to a special, separate scheme of control, again involving reference by the OFT to the Competition Commission, under ss. 32–35 of the Water Act 1991.

30. 9   Summary

Having completed this chapter you should:

- understand and be able to advise on the main provisions of domestic competition law;
- understand the relationship between domestic and EC competition law;

- understand the rules relating to anti-competitive agreements and be aware of the procedures for seeking guidance or a decision on a potentially anti-competitive agreement;

- understand the rules relating to abuse of a dominant position under domestic competition law;

- be able to advise on the investigatory and enforcement procedures available in the event of an infringement of domestic competition law;

- understand the rules governing control of cartels under domestic competition law;

- understand the rules governing control of mergers under domestic competition law and be able to advise on the appropriate steps to be taken by parties to a proposed merger.

Part VIII

Intellectual property

The nature and importance of intellectual property

31.1 Introduction

Intellectual property law has an impact on almost every area of commercial legal practice and its importance is growing. All commercial practitioners must therefore have at least an outline knowledge of intellectual property law and of its importance.

In this and the following chapters we examine the commercial importance of intellectual property law and the principal intellectual property rights recognised by law. In particular in this chapter we examine in overview:

- the commercial importance of intellectual property;
- the different types of intellectual property law;
- the relationship between intellectual property law and other legal rules, including contract, competition law and human rights law;
- the principal remedies for infringement of intellectual property rights.

31.1.1 What is intellectual property?

Intellectual property consists of a series of legal rights. Such property is therefore intangible: it exists only because it is recognised by law. It is nevertheless a valuable commercial commodity which, if properly exploited, can generate great profits for its owner. Like any other item of property, it can be exploited in a variety of ways, for instance by outright disposition such as an assignment in return for a cash payment, or by the owner permitting others to exploit his property, either exclusively or jointly with him, for instance, by granting a licence or licences to one or more other persons to exploit the property or by granting security over it.

31.2 The commercial importance of intellectual property

Intellectual property rights underpin much modern commercial activity. When a business manufactures and markets a product, it may need advice on a complex network of interlocking intellectual property rights. It may patent the product and market it under a trade name which it may protect by a trade mark or by the law of passing off; its own corporate name may also be protected by a trade mark; instructions for the use of the product may be protected by copyright; its marketing plans may be regarded as confidential.

A business therefore needs to know:

(a) what intellectual property rights it has;

(b) what it must do in order to protect those rights;

(c) how they may best be exploited;

(d) what action it may take against anyone who infringes those rights;

(e) how it may avoid infringing the rights of others.

31.3 The different types of intellectual property right

Intellectual property law takes in a range of rights, including the following:

(a) patents, which protect inventions;

(b) copyrights, which protect such works as written and artistic works, musical compositions, films, recordings and computer programs;

(c) moral rights, which are rights granted to authors and artists of copyright works concerned primarily with protection of the artist's reputation, rather than with his economic interests;

(d) design rights, which protect designs for products; registered design rights protect designs with 'eye-appeal'; unregistered design rights give protection similar to copyright to purely functional designs;

(e) performers' rights, which enable performers to prevent their performances being recorded without their permission;

(f) trade marks, which protect a business's reputation and goodwill by allowing it to register a mark as distinctive of its goods/services and prevent others using that or a similar mark; they therefore guard against (unfair) competition;

(g) passing-off, which is a tort which performs a similar role to the law of trade marks, protecting businesses against unfair competition by allowing A to prevent B passing off its goods as A's;

(h) confidentiality, which allows a person who entrusts information to another in confidence to restrain the unauthorised use or disclosure of that information by that person. It may protect both commercial and industrial information, such as secret formulae and marketing plans, and personal information.

In addition there are special systems of protection for plant varieties and semiconductor topographies.

31.3.1 Classifications of intellectual property

These rights can be categorised in a number of ways.

31.3.1.1 Statutory and common law rights

Copyrights, patents, design rights, moral rights, performers' rights and trade marks are all statutory rights; passing off and confidentiality depend solely on the common law.

31.3.1.2 Registrable and non-registrable rights

Patents, trade marks and registered design rights are all registrable under statutory schemes; protection is lost if the relevant right is not registered. The other rights do not depend on registration.

31.3.1.3 What is the interest protected?

Most of the rights listed above relate to acts of invention or creativity; however, trade marks and passing off protect trading reputation and the law of confidence fulfils a hybrid role since it is capable of protecting inventions and know-how as well as commercial/trading information such as customer lists, prices etc.

31.3.1.4 Exclusive and non-exclusive rights

The owner of intellectual property generally has a monopoly right to exploit the property. In some cases this is an absolute monopoly: e.g. a patent holder has an exclusive right to exploit the patented invention. In other cases the right is only a qualified monopoly: e.g. a copyright holder can prevent anyone copying his work but has no right to prevent any other person producing the same or a similar work without copying.

31.4 Relationships with other legal rules

When considering questions of intellectual property law it is important to bear in mind that other legal rules may be relevant. For instance, although trading reputation is primarily protected by the law of trade marks and passing off, the law of defamation and malicious falsehood may also be relevant. Contract and competition law have a particularly important impact on intellectual property law.

31.4.1 Contract

Contract may be relevant in a number of ways.

(a) A contract may protect information which would otherwise be unprotected, for instance, by imposing an obligation of confidence. It may often be necessary to disclose information in order to exploit it: for instance, a games inventor with an idea for a new game may wish to discuss it with a toy manufacturer with a view to their exploiting his idea. Although the law might impose an obligation of confidentiality on the manufacturer to prevent it 'stealing' the idea, the inventor would be well advised to require the manufacturer to enter into an agreement to treat the information as confidential before disclosing it. Similarly where an employee has access to confidential information the contract of employment will generally impose an obligation on the employee to keep the information confidential. However, the effectiveness of contract as a means of protecting intellectual property is limited by the doctrine of privity.

(b) Contract may permit acts which would otherwise be an infringement of intellectual property rights: for instance, the owner of a patent may license another person to exploit it. Again privity is important: the contract may permit the other contracting party to do acts which would otherwise be an infringement of intellectual property rights but the owner of the rights can assert them, despite the contract, against any other potential infringer.

A contract may perform both these roles: for instance, a patent licence may require the patent holder to disclose to the licensee technical information which would otherwise be confidential. The agreement would therefore permit exploitation of the patent and at the same time impose an obligation to keep such know-how confidential.

Contracts are particularly important when the owner of intellectual property wishes to exploit it. The drafting of such agreements will be a particularly important part of the work of a specialist intellectual property lawyer.

31.4.2 Competition law

Since intellectual property law grants monopoly rights there is obviously a tension between it and competition law. The intellectual property lawyer must therefore have an understanding of the relationship between intellectual property law and competition law. This is particularly important when drafting licensing and other agreements.

Two sets of rules restrict the anti-competitive effects of intellectual property law:

(a) those within intellectual property law itself; and

(b) those imposed by competition law.

31.4.2.1 Internal restrictions on monopoly

Intellectual property law limits the monopoly rights of the intellectual property owner in order to balance his rights with those of competitors and the general public. For instance:

(a) the monopoly granted by intellectual property may be limited in time, as in the case of patents and copyright and related rights;

(b) the monopoly granted to the owner may be qualified: e.g. copyright only protects the owner against copying and not against the competitor who independently produces a similar work;

(c) the law may permit third parties to obtain licences to exploit intellectual property without the consent of the intellectual property owner: e.g. the Comptroller of Patents may grant a compulsory licence permitting a person to exploit a patent which is unused or underused, regardless of the wishes of the patent holder (see **33.3.2.2**).

31.4.2.2 Restrictions under EC competition law

Articles 81, 82 and 28–30 of the Treaty of Rome are all relevant to intellectual property.

(a) *Art. 81*

Many agreements relating to the exploitation of intellectual property would, *prima facie*, fall within the ambit of Art. 81 which prohibits agreements whose object or effect is to prevent, restrict or distort competition within the Common Market (see **29.2**). However, patent licences, know-how licences and research and development agreements are all covered by block exemptions (Reg. 240/96 on technology transfer agreements in the case of patent and know-how licences; Reg. 2659/2000 in the case of research and development agreements). Such agreements will therefore not fall foul of Art. 81 provided that they are drafted in accordance with the terms of the relevant block exemption. All include a 'black list' of prohibited terms which must not be included in the licence if it is to be protected by the exemption: in addition the technology transfer exemption includes a further 'white list' of terms which must be included in the licence.

(b) *Art. 82*

Intellectual property rights may enable a business to acquire a dominant position in a particular product market. Abuse of such position may contravene Art. 82 (see **29.3**). However, the mere ownership or assertion of the relevant intellectual property rights is not *per se* an abuse. Thus, for instance, it is not an abuse for an i.p. right holder to refuse to licence others to exploit his rights, or to refuse to do so on reasonable terms: see *CICRA* v *Renault* [1988] ECR 6039; *Volvo* v *Veng* [1988] ECR 6211; *Philips Electronics N.V.* v *Ingram Ltd* [1999] FSR 112.

(c) *Arts 28–30*

Articles 28–30 prohibit national measures which impose quantitative restrictions on imports from other Member States, or have equivalent effect. Since intellectual property laws are primarily national rather than Community laws they may potentially fall foul of this prohibition. However, restrictions are permitted for, *inter alia*, the protection of industrial and commercial property unless they constitute a means of 'arbitrary discrimination or a disguised restriction on trade' (Art. 30) and national property rights are expressly preserved by Art. 222. The European Court of Justice has interpreted these provisions as permitting the *existence* of intellectual property rights but not their unfettered *exercise*, which is governed by the rules relating to free movement of goods. The Court has also developed a doctrine of exhaustion of rights: when goods are first placed on the market in any Member State by or with the consent of the owner of the relevant intellectual property, his rights are 'exhausted' so that he cannot use them to control trade in the goods within the Community. This prevents intellectual property owners using their intellectual property rights to divide up the Common Market.

EXAMPLE

Phil's Fashions Ltd registers its trade mark, 'Fine Threads' for use on suits, and then licenses Herge, in Belgium, to use the mark. Nigel buys suits from Herge in Belgium and imports them into the UK; Phil's cannot use its trade mark to prevent Nigel importing the suits: its rights are exhausted when the suits are placed on the market by Herge with Phil's' consent.

31.4.2.3 Restrictions under UK competition law

UK competition law is now governed by a regime closely modelled on that of EC competition law under the Competition Act 1998 (see generally **Chapter 30**). Thus agreements for the exploitation of intellectual property may offend the Chapter I prohibition on agreements which affect trade in the UK and which have as their object or effect the prevention, restriction or distortion of competition in the UK, while exploitation of intellectual property may expose the property owner to a charge of abuse of a dominant position, contrary to the Chapter II prohibition. As already noted. these prohibitions are based on and closely mirror the terms of Arts 81 and 82 of the Treaty of Rome and an agreement which is exempt from Art. 81 under an individual or block exemption will automatically be exempt from the Chapter I prohibition. It follows that patent and know-how licences and research and development agreements drafted in accordance with the terms of the appropriate EC block exemption will automatically gain exemption from both systems.

31.4.3 Impact of the Human Rights Act 1998

One of the rights protected by the European Convention on Human Rights and thus by the Human Rights Act 1998 is the right to freedom of expression. Section 12 of the Act requires a court considering whether to grant any relief which might affect the right to freedom of expression to have regard to the importance of the right. Intellectual property rights, and especially copyright and confidentiality, may operate as a restriction on the right of freedom of expression, and an action for infringement of an intellectual property right may therefore require the court to consider the impact of the remedy sought on the right of freedom of expression. However, the Convention recognises that the exercise of the right of freedom of expression is subject to such conditions and restrictions as are prescribed by law 'and are necessary in a democratic society . . . for the protection of the . . . rights of others' and also provides (Art. 1 of the First Protocol) that 'every natural or legal person is entitled to the peaceful enjoyment of his possessions'. Infringement of intellectual property rights such as copyright constitutes interference with 'the peaceful enjoyment of possessions'. Thus an action for infringement of an intellectual property right may require the court to consider whether the action will interfere with the Convention right to freedom of expression and to balance that right with the right to protection of property (see *Ashdown* v *Telegraph Group Ltd* [2001] EWCA Civ 1142; [2001] 4 All ER 666).

As noted above, most intellectual property rights are qualified so that acts which would otherwise constitute infringement are permitted in certain circumstances. In general such qualifications seek to strike the necessary balance between the opposing interests of the right holder and other members of society and thus reflect the balance required to be struck under the 1998 Act. However, there may be occasions when the right to freedom of expression is inadequately protected by the specific qualifications contained in intellectual property legislation so that it will be necessary for the court to consider the facts of each case to determine whether the right of freedom of expression is adequately protected by the relevant provisions, and, if necessary, to interpret the relevant law so as to accommodate and protect the right.

31.5 Remedies for infringement

There is a range of remedies available to the owner of intellectual property rights against a person who infringes those rights, including damages, accounts of profits and injunctions.

Injunctions may be particularly important and the practitioner advising on intellectual property matters should be aware of the orders which may be made and the bases on which they will be made.

31.5.1 Interim injunctions

Often the intellectual property owner will first seek an interim injunction during proceedings without prior notice to the other party. Since such injunctions are made when the court has heard only one party's case, they are granted for only a limited period until a further hearing with both parties before the court when the court will often have to grant a further interim injunction to cover the position until a full trial. Such injunctions will generally be granted in accordance with the principles outlined in *American Cyanamid Co.* v *Ethicon Ltd* [1975] AC 396: provided that the claimant can show a serious issue to be tried, the court will grant an injunction if the balance of convenience favours the grant of an injunction. The balance of convenience will often favour the grant of an injunction, since the claimant's interests are likely to suffer serious damage if the defendant's (alleged) infringement is not restrained. The position may however be different where the right of freedom of expression is engaged. Section 12 of the Human Rights Act 1998 applies where a court is considering whether to grant any relief which might affect the Convention right of freedom of expression. It provides that the court should not grant such relief so as to restrain publication before trial unless the court is satisfied that the applicant for relief is likely to establish at trial that publication should be prevented (s. 12(3)). Moreover it requires the court to have 'particular regard' to the Convention right of freedom of expression. An interim injunction will therefore not be granted in such cases merely on the basis of a serious issue to be tried and the balance of convenience. The court must consider the likely outcome of the case at full trial and not grant an interim injunction prior to trial unless satisfied that, having regard to all the relevant factors including the defendant's right of freedom of expression, the applicant is likely to succeed. However, this does not require the applicant to prove on the balance of probabilities that his claim will succeed at trial. The court must be satisfied in light of all the facts that the applicant has a 'real prospect of success, convincingly established' (*Cream Holdings Ltd* v *Bannerjee* [2003] EWCA Civ 103; [2003] 2 All ER 318). This is likely to be especially important in copyright and breach of confidence actions.

31.5.2 Search orders and freezing injunctions

In many cases the claimant will also seek further interim orders without notice. In particular, he may seek a search order in order to seize infringing material and gather further evidence of the defendant's infringement, and where it is feared that the defendant may dissipate funds prior to trial so as to frustrate an eventual order for damages or account of profits, he may also seek a freezing injunction, freezing some or all of the defendant's assets (see **37.4.1** and **37.4.2**).

31.5.3 Final injunctions

If the intellectual property owner succeeds at trial he will normally seek damages or an account of profits to compensate him for the defendant's past infringements of his rights. He will normally also want to restrain the defendant from repeating the infringement and will therefore seek a final injunction to that effect. The form of an injunction is always in the discretion of the judge and should seek to balance the interests of the parties (including now the defendant's right of freedom of expression under the European Convention on Human Rights). It is, however, essential that a person restrained by an injunction should know what acts it restrains, especially as breach of an injunction is punishable as a contempt of court. In the case of patent infringement it may be appropriate to grant an injunction which simply enjoins the defendant from infringing the complainant's patent. In the case of other intellectual property rights, such as breach of confidence or passing off, a more detailed injunction may be required specifying in detail what the defendant is enjoined from doing: see *Coflexip SA* v *Stolt Comex Seaway MS Ltd* [2001] 1 All ER 952. In a case where the defendant's infringement was not deliberate and no future infringement is threatened the court may refuse altogether to grant injunctive relief.

31.6 International aspects

If intellectual property is to be fully exploited in global markets it must be capable of protection internationally. Measures have therefore been designed to harmonise intellectual property laws both throughout the EC and also on a truly international basis. In some cases these measures seek to harmonise the substantive laws of states; in others merely to secure a degree of international cooperation and mutual recognition of intellectual property rights. Many of these international conventions are administered by the World Intellectual Property Organisation (WIPO), a United Nations organisation. The growth of international trade has led to further international developments and, in particular, the General Agreement on Tariffs and Trade (GATT) at its Uruguay Round in 1994 established the World Trade Organisation (WTO). All member states of the WTO are required to give mutual protection to intellectual property rights in accordance with the WTO Agreement on Trade Related Aspects of Intellectual Property (known as 'TRIPS').

31.7 Summary

Having completed this chapter you should:

- be aware of the significance of intellectual property and of the main categories of intellectual property rights;
- be aware of the relationship between intellectual property law and other areas of law, including contract and competition law; in particular you should understand:
  - the role of contract in protecting and exploiting intellectual property through licences, etc.;
  - the potentially anti-competitive effects of intellectual property law and the restrictions imposed by competition law on the exercise of intellectual property rights;
- the principal remedies available for infringement of intellectual property rights and, in particular, the role played in the protection of intellectual property rights by special procedures such as interim injunctions, search orders and freezing injunctions.

Copyright

32.1 Introduction

This chapter deals with copyright and the associated rights which protect designs and performances. In it we examine:

- what works are protected by copyright;
- the nature of the rights of the copyright owner;
- what constitutes infringement of copyright, the remedies available for infringement and the possible defences to an infringement claim;
- the so-called 'moral rights' of the author of a copyright work;
- the protection available for designs through copyright and registered and unregistered design right;
- performers' rights.

32.1.1 The legal framework

Copyright protects a wide range of works against unauthorised exploitation in various forms, including but not limited to making copies. Several other intellectual property rights are closely connected with copyright, including registered and unregistered design rights, moral rights and performers' rights (see **32.8** to **32.10**). The law is now contained in the Copyright, Designs and Patents Act 1988, as amended (CDPA 1988 — all references to this chapter are to the CDPA unless otherwise indicated).

There are two international conventions designed to achieve a degree of harmonisation of copyright law: the Berne Convention, originally opened in 1886, and the Universal Copyright Convention of 1952. Most, but not all, states are signatories to at least one of these conventions; some states are party to both. Both prescribe minimum levels of protection which Member States must give to copyright owners and provide for mutual recognition of copyrights. The UK is party to both conventions. The countries to which the UK gives reciprocal recognition under the Convention are specified by statutory instrument (SI 1999/1751). In recent years the EC has adopted a number of Directives to harmonise the laws of Member States on various aspects of copyright and related rights. They have been implemented in the UK by regulations amending the 1988 Act. In May 2001 the Council and Parliament of the EU completed a new Directive on harmonisation of certain aspects of copyright and related rights in the information society (Directive 2001/29/EC). The Directive makes some amendments to the EU copyright regime in order to take account of new forms of expression, publication and transmission of works made possible by the use of new digital technology, and implements two WIPO Treaties, on copyright and on performances and phonograms, of 1996. It seeks to ensure that authors and performers receive a high level of protection and requires Member States, *inter alia*, to ensure that there is adequate legal protection against the circumvention of technological methods, such as scrambling and encryption, designed to protect works against unauthorised copying or dissemination. The Directive is implemented in the UK by the Copyright and Related Rights Regulation 2003 (SI 2003, No. 2498) which came into effect on 31 October 2003.

32.2   What is protected?

Copyright is defined as:

a property right which subsists . . . in the following descriptions of work:

    (a) original literary, dramatic, musical or artistic works,

    (b) sound recordings, films, broadcasts (as defined), and

    (c) the typographical arrangement of published editions (CDPA 1988, s. 1).

32.2.1   Original literary, dramatic, musical or artistic works

Works may be protected under this heading regardless of artistic quality or merit; for example, examination questions and lists of TV programmes and football fixtures have all been held to be protected as 'literary works', and the design drawings for a motor car exhaust system were protected as an 'artistic work'.

Literary work means 'any work other than a dramatic or musical work, which is written, spoken or sung' and the Act expressly states that tables, compilations and computer programs are 'literary works' (s. 3(1)). Thus the instructions for use of a product or a set of standard terms of trading would be protected by copyright.

32.2.1.1   Work

'Work' is not defined. To be regarded as a 'work' something must have a degree of substance: single words, such as titles, are rarely regarded as 'works' (*Exxon Corp.* v *Exxon Insurance Consultants International Ltd* [1981] 3 All ER 341).

32.2.1.2   Originality

The requirement that the work must be 'original' is more important. It excludes works which have been simply copied (*Interlego AG* v *Tyco Industries Ltd* [1989] 1 AC 217): for a work to be protected there must be an element of creativity or effort involved in its production.

32.2.1.3   Idea/expression

Copyright law protects expressions, not ideas. Thus, e.g. an idea for a format of a new television programme is not protected by copyright. This 'idea/expression dichotomy', as it is called, may be difficult to apply. It is particularly important in relation to computer software, where it has proved particularly difficult to apply.

32.2.1.4   The work must be recorded

A work is only protected under this heading if it is recorded, in writing or otherwise (s. 3(2)), but there is no need for the recording to be done by, or even with the permission of, the creator of the work. Thus, for instance, if a lecture is tape-recorded by students, the lecturer can claim copyright in the lecture.

32.2.2 Sound recordings, films or broadcasts

All of these works attract a separate copyright even if they are based on a prior literary or other work. Thus where a lecture is recorded there are two copyrights: one in the lecture itself and another in the recording (although the recording might itself be a breach of copyright *vis-à-vis* the lecturer).

32.2.3 Published editions

The typographical arrangement of a published edition of a book or other literary work attracts a separate copyright from that of the work. The published edition is not necessarily the same as the work in which copyright exists. For instance in the case of a newspaper or magazine each article will be a separate 'work' protected by its own copyright, but the relevant published edition will be the newspaper or magazine as a whole: see *Newspaper Licensing Agency Ltd* v *Marks & Spencer plc* [2001] 3 All ER 977.

32.2.4 Databases

A database may qualify for copyright protection as a compilation, and therefore a literary work. However, a database is only entitled to copyright protection if (a) it is original and (b) by reason of the selection or arrangement of its contents it constitutes the author's own intellectual creation (s. 3A).

Regardless of whether it qualifies for copyright protection a database may also be protected by the separate database right provided for in the Copyright and Rights in Databases Regulations 1997, SI 1997 3032, which implement an EC Directive, No. 96/9/EC. Under these regulations a database is protected for a period of 15 years against unauthorised extraction or re-utilisation of a substantial part of its contents.

32.2.5 Qualification for copyright protection

A work which falls into one of the above categories is protected by UK copyright law provided one of the following conditions is fulfilled (ss. 153–162).

(a) The author is a 'qualifying person' as defined (s. 154). This includes:
   (i)   British citizens, subjects and citizens of British dependent territories;
   (ii) persons domiciled or resident in the UK;
   (iii) companies incorporated in the UK;
   (iv) persons domiciled or resident in countries of other Berne Convention or Universal Copyright Convention states as specified by Order in Council (SI 1999, No. 1751).

(b) The work was first published in the UK or in a state party to either the Berne or Universal Copyright Convention, or was published elsewhere but was 'simultaneously' published in the UK or in a Convention state. A work is 'simultaneously published' for this purpose if it is published in one of the relevant states within 30 days of its first publication elsewhere (s. 155). A person who publishes a work in a non-convention state should therefore arrange for it to be published within 30 days in a Convention state to ensure protection in the UK and other Convention states.

32.2.6 Multiple copyrights

There may be several copyrights in what appears to be one 'work'. For instance where a book is published there are separate copyrights in the literary work contained in the book and in the typographical arrangement. In the case of an anthology or collection each piece included may be a separate work entitled to its own copyright, whilst there may be additional separate copyrights in the collection as a whole and in the typographical arrangement of the collection. In the case of a CD music album there may be a literary copyright in the lyrics, musical copyright in the music and a separate copyright in the sound recording; there will be a further artistic copyright in the inlay card artwork.

32.2.7 Publication right

A person who publishes a previously unpublished work after expiry of copyright in the work is entitled to a 'publication right' which gives him rights broadly equivalent to the economic rights (but not the moral rights) granted to a copyright holder for a period of 25 years from the date of publication, provided that (a) first publication occurs in a Member State of the European Economic Area and (b) the publisher is a national of a Member State of the EEA. (Copyright and Related Rights Regulations 1996, SI 1996, No. 2967, Reg. 16).

32.3 Who has the rights?

The copyright in a work is generally owned by the person who creates the work. However, this rule is modified in some cases.

(a) Copyright in literary, dramatic, musical and artistic works is generally owned by the author, composer or artist.

(b) Copyright in a sound recording is owned by the producer. Copyright in a film is owned jointly by the producer of the film and its principal director (s. 10A as amended by the Copyright and Related Rights Regulations 1996). 'Producer' is defined as 'the person who made the arrangements for' the recording or film (s. 178).

(c) Copyright in broadcasts is owned by the broadcaster.

(d) Copyright in typographical arrangements of published editions is owned by the publisher.

32.3.1 Employees' works

Where a copyright work is produced by an employee in the course of his employment, the first owner of the copyright is the employer, unless otherwise agreed (s. 11).

Such agreement may be express or implied. Thus if an employer allows employees to treat works produced in the course of employment as their own property that may be construed as evidence of an implied term that copyright shall vest in the employees (see *Noah* v *Shuba* [1991] FSR 15).

Determining whether a work is produced 'in the course of employment' will require consideration of the facts of each case. The fact that a work is produced using the employer's or employee's resources or during the employer's or employee's time will not be conclusive. The key question in most cases is likely to be whether production of the work formed part of the employee's contractual duties in the sense that (s)he could be contractually required to produce it (see *Stephenson Jordan and Harrison* v *MacDonald and Evans* [1952] 69 RPC 14: lectures written by employed accountant not produced in the course of employment). On the other hand in the absence of a detailed contractual specification of the employee's duties evidence that the work was produced in the employer's time or using the employer's resources may provide inferential evidence that the work was produced in the course of employment.

32.3.2 Commissioned works

Where a work is commissioned, copyright vests in the author of the work in the usual way. Thus if an independent contractor is retained to produce a work, such as a report or a computer program, he will own the copyright in the work. In order to avoid this the person commissioning the work may require the contractor to agree to assign to him the copyright in the work.

32.3.3 Disposition of copyright

Copyright is transmissible as personal property (s. 90). The owner may license others to exploit his copyright or may assign the copyright.

32.3.3.1 Assignments

An assignment may be of the whole or of only part of the copyright. Thus the copyright owner can license different persons to do different things with the work, or may make several partial assignments of it. For instance, an author of a book may make separate assignments to publishers to publish soft and hardback editions, license a newspaper to publish extracts from the book and a film producer to make a film based on it. Assignments may also be limited in time.

Any assignment of copyright must be in writing and signed by the copyright owner.

The prospective owner of copyright may make an assignment of future copyright; in that case, provided that the assignment is in writing, the copyright vests in the assignee when the work comes into existence (s. 90).

32.3.3.2 Licences

A copyright owner can grant others exclusive, or non-exclusive, licences to do things which would otherwise be an infringement of copyright. An exclusive licence must be in writing and signed by the licensor (s. 92).

A licence may be granted in respect of a prospective copyright (s. 91).

32.4 Duration of copyright

The duration of copyright varies according to the nature of the work.

32.4.1 Literary, dramatic and artistic works

Copyright expires 70 years after the end of the year in which the author or, in the case of works of joint authorship, the last author, of the work dies (s. 12 as amended by the Duration of Copyright and Rights in Performances Regulations 1995). Prior to 1995 the copyright period was 50 years; it was increased in order to give effect to an EC

Directive. As a result of the extension some works which were out of copyright, following the expiry of the relevant 50-year period prior to 1995, have been restored to copyright protection from 1995. The 1995 Regulations contain transitional rules to deal with this point.

Where a copyright work is published for the first time after expiry of copyright the publisher may be entitled to a 'publication right' which gives much the same protection as copyright for a period of 25 years from the date of publication (see **32.2.7**). Effectively, therefore, the period of copyright protection may be extended, in favour of the publisher, if a copyright work is not exploited during the primary copyright period.

Copyright in computer generated works expires 50 years after the end of the year in which the work was produced.

32.4.2   Sound recordings and films

Copyright in a sound recording expires at the end of the period of 50 years from the end of the calendar year in which the recording is made or, if the recording is published during that period, 50 years from the end of the calendar year in which it was published. If the recording is not published but is released to the public during the period of 50 years from the end of the year of recording, the copyright period expires 50 years from the end of the year of release (s. 13A).

Copyright in a cinematographic or audiovisual work created after 1 July 1994 expires 70 years after the death of the last principal director, the author of the screen play, the author of the dialogue and the composer of the music created for the work. Again, the period was extended and other changes were made in 1995 in order to implement the EC Directive on copyright duration. For works created prior to 1 July 1994 the relevant period is 50 years.

32.4.3   Broadcasts

Copyright expires 50 years after the end of the year in which the broadcast is made (s. 14).

32.4.4   Published editions

Copyright expires 25 years after the end of the year in which the edition was first published.

32.5   The rights of the copyright owner

The copyright owner is given the following exclusive rights (s. 16).

(a) To make copies of the copyright work.

(b) To issue copies of the work to the public.

(c) To rent or lend the work to the public.

(d) To perform, show or play the work in public.

(e) To communicate the work to the public.

(f) To make an adaptation of the work or to do any of the above acts to an adaptation of the work.

Copyright is therefore infringed if any such acts are done by any other person without permission of the copyright owner.

32.5.1 Infringement

The Act recognises two categories of infringing acts: primary and secondary infringements.

32.5.1.1 Primary infringement

Primary infringement involves doing, without permission of the copyright owner, any of the acts which are the sole right of the copyright owner. The following are therefore prim-ary infringements.

(a) Copying a work (s. 17). A literary, dramatic, musical or artistic work is copied if it is reproduced in any material form. There is clearly an infringement if an entire work is copied; however, copying part of a work may also amount to infringement if the part copied is substantial in quantity or quality. Copying of an artistic work includes copying a two-dimensional work in three dimensions or a three-dimensional work in two dimensions.

(b) Issuing copies of any work to the public (s. 18).

(c) Renting or lending copies of the work to the public (s. 18A).

(d) Performing in public any literary, dramatic or musical work (s. 19)

(e) Playing or showing in public any sound recording, film, broadcast or cable transmission (s. 19).

(f) Communicating to the public any work other than a typographical arrangement (s. 20).

(g) Making an adaptation of a literary, dramatic or musical work, or doing any of the acts in (a)–(e) above in relation to such an adaptation (s. 21).

Liability for primary infringement is strict.

A person who authorises any act of primary infringement is also liable for primary infringement. However, a person who merely facilitates infringement does not thereby authorise infringement (*Amstrad Consumer Electronics plc* v *CBS Songs Ltd* [1988] 2 All ER 484).

32.5.1.2 Secondary infringement

Secondary infringement includes a number of acts which involve dealing in infringing copies of copyright works and doing acts which facilitate breaches of copyright, such as making an article designed to make infringing copies (ss. 22–26). In general liability for secondary infringement requires the defendant to be aware of the infringement.

32.6 Defences

A number of defences are available to a breach of copyright claim.

32.6.1 No copyright

The defendant may challenge the claimant's copyright.

32.6.2 No breach

Where the alleged breach is by copying a copyright work it is a defence for the defendant to show that he produced his work independently, without copying the claimant's work.

However, if there are close similarities between the two works and it is shown that the defendant was aware of the claimant's work, the court is likely to infer that the defendant's work was copied in the absence of rebutting evidence from the defendant. Expert evidence may be called to testify as to the degree of similarity and the likelihood of the defendant having produced his work independently.

It is no defence that the defendant copied the claimant's work subconsciously. Thus where copying of a popular work, such as a piece of popular music, is alleged the court may infer copying if there is a close similarity between the defendant's work and that of the claimant.

In cases of secondary infringement where some degree of 'guilty' knowledge or belief is generally required it is a defence to show that the defendant lacked the relevant knowledge or belief.

32.6.3 Permitted acts

Permitted copying is not an infringement. Copying may be permitted by a licence granted by the copyright holder or by some person acting on his behalf, such as a collective licensing agency; in addition a number of acts which would otherwise involve breach of copyright are permitted by the CDPA 1988. It is therefore a defence to show that an alleged copying falls into a category of 'permitted acts'.

The permitted acts are set out in Part III of the CDPA and take up 48 sections of the Act. The more important are set out below.

32.6.3.1 Temporary copies

The making of a temporary copy of a literary work (other than a computer program or database), a dramatic, musical or artistic work, in a typographical arrangement or in a sound recording or a film is permitted provided that the copy is 'transient or incidental' and is an integral and essential part of a technological process the sole purpose of which is the transmission of the work in a network between third parties via an intermediary or a lawful use of the work, and which has no independent economic significance (s. 28A). So, for instance, if a copyright work is transmitted via e-mail or over the Internet, the service provider does not infringe copyright merely by making a temporary copy of the work in the course of transmitting it.

32.6.3.2 Fair dealing

Copying is permitted provided that it amounts to a 'fair dealing' with the copyright work for one of four permitted purposes:

(a) research for a non-commercial purpose (s. 29(1));

(b) private study (s. 29(1C));

(c) criticism or review (provided that the work has been made available to the public) (s. 30);

(d) reporting current events (s. 30(2)).

There is no statutory definition of 'fair dealing'; what is 'fair' is a matter of fact and degree in each individual case. The court will consider, amongst other factors, the amount and importance of the copied material, the manner in which it was obtained and the commercial purpose and effect of the copying. Thus where copied material is intended to compete commercially with the original work it is unlikely that the defence of fair dealing will be made out.

Where work is copied for the purposes of research, criticism or review or reporting current events there must be 'sufficient acknowledgement' of the copyright work, unless such acknowledgement would be impossible for reasons of practicality or otherwise.

32.6.3.3 Time shifting (s. 70)

Making in domestic premises a recording of a broadcast for private or domestic purposes and solely for the purpose of enabling it to be watched or listened to at a more convenient time does not infringe copyright in the broadcast/programme or in any work included in it.

32.6.3.4 Incidental inclusion (s. 31)

Copyright in a work is not infringed by its incidental inclusion in an artistic work, film, sound recording, broadcast or cable programme. Inclusion of music, lyrics and recordings of musical works will not be regarded as 'incidental' if it is deliberate.

32.6.3.5 Free public showings of broadcasts/cable programmes (s. 72)

The showing or playing of a broadcast to a public audience does not infringe copyright in the broadcast provided that the audience have not paid for admission to the premises where the broadcast is shown/played. However, such showing etc. may infringe copyright in any literary, dramatic or musical work included in the broadcast.

Persons resident in premises are treated as not having paid for admission and so hotels can show broadcasts etc. to residents.

32.6.3.6 Education and libraries

A number of acts are permitted if done for the purposes of education (ss. 32–36) or by an educational establishment (s. 36A) or by librarians for the purposes of the provision of library services (ss. 37–44).

32.6.3.7 Public administration (ss. 45–50)

A number of acts are permitted if done for the purposes of public administration, including for the purposes of parliamentary or judicial proceedings (s. 45). Copyright is not infringed by producing a report of such proceedings, but copying a published report of proceedings may infringe copyright in the report.

32.6.4 Common law defences

The common law will not recognise copyright in a work if it is immoral (*Glyn v Weston Feature Film Co.* [1916] 1 Ch 261). Copying which would otherwise amount to a breach of copyright may be permitted where the copying is in the public interest, and this defence is expressly recognised by s. 171(3). This might cover cases where publication of copied material reveals criminal acts or corruption but also applies more widely. It might, for instance, permit copying so as to give effect to the right of freedom of expression protected by the Human Rights Act 1998.

32.7 Remedies

The law offers a copyright holder a range of remedies against an infringer. In addition breach of copyright may be a criminal offence.

32.7.1   Civil remedies

Civil remedies for breach of copyright include actions for damages and accounts of profits and certain rights to seize infringing copies.

32.7.1.1   Damages

Breach of copyright is a civil wrong for which the copyright owner may claim damages. The aim of an award of damages is to put the copyright holder in the same position as if the breach had not been committed and damages are quantified accordingly. However, the basic rule is modified in two situations.

(a) If it is shown that at the time of the infringement the defendant did not know and had no reason to believe that the material was copyright, no damages may be awarded (s. 97(1)).

(b) The court may award additional damages having regard to the circumstances of the case, and, in particular, to the flagrancy of the breach and any benefit accruing to the defendant as a result of the breach (s. 97(2)).

32.7.1.2   Account of profits

As an alternative to an action for damages the claimant may seek an account of profits. This remedy will be preferable where the claimant cannot show that the defendant's actions have caused him financial loss, where the amount of the loss is difficult to quantify or where the defendant has profited from his breach.

32.7.1.3   Injunction

The copyright owner may seek an injunction to restrain the defendant from committing breaches of copyright. Often he will seek an injunction along with a claim for an account or for damages.

Where an information society service is being used to infringe copyright in a work the copyright owner may seek an injunction against the service provider provided that the service provider has actual notice of the infringing use of the service (s. 97A). Thus for instance if a service is being used to distribute infringing copies of a sound recording or film the copyright owner may be entitled to an injunction requiring the service provider to terminate the infringing use. In order to ensure that the service provider has actual knowledge of the infringing use the copyright owner should first serve him notice giving full details of the alleged infringement.

32.7.1.4   Delivery up of infringing copies

Where a person has in his possession an infringing copy of a work or an article specifically designed or adapted for making copies of a particular work, such as plates for printing copies of a picture, the copyright owner may apply to the court for an order that the copy/article be delivered up to him (s. 99) for him to retain or destroy (s. 114). The court will not make such an order if other remedies (including damages) would be adequate to protect the plaintiff's interest.

32.7.2   Criminal remedies

Certain breaches of copyright are also criminal offences. However, the defendant is generally only criminally liable if he knows, or has reason to believe, that a breach is involved (s. 107).

The court may make an order for delivery up to the copyright owner of infringing copies in criminal proceedings (s. 108).

32.7.3 Seizure

In addition to the right to seek delivery up of infringing copies the copyright owner is given a limited right to seize infringing copies which are offered for immediate sale or hire (s. 100). However, he must first give notice to the police and may not seize anything in the possession of a person at a permanent or regular place of business. This right is therefore only useful against street vendors and the like.

The copyright owner may also request the Commissioners of Customs and Excise to treat infringing copies of his work as prohibited goods, and thus prevent the import of infringing copies (s. 111).

32.8 Design rights

The design of a product may be an important feature affecting customer choice of that product and therefore giving a business a 'marketing edge'. A business will wish to protect its designs and prevent competitors copying them.

The law of trade marks or passing off may protect certain product designs; for instance, where a company had established a reputation for supplying lemon juice in plastic containers shaped like lemons, it could use the law of passing off to prevent a rival manufacturer selling juice in similar containers (*Reckitt & Colman Products Ltd v Borden Inc* [1990] 1 All ER 873). Such cases will be rare, but protection for designs per se may be available under three regimes:

(a) registered design right under the Registered Designs Act 1949;

(b) copyright; and

(c) unregistered design right under the CDPA 1988.

The relationship between these three rights is complex. Broadly speaking, copyright protects only artistic works which are not commercially exploited; registered design right protects industrial designs with 'eye appeal'; and unregistered design right protects purely functional industrial designs.

32.8.1 Registered design right

The Registered Designs Act 1949 gives designs similar protection to that available for patents, for a maximum period of 25 years. Registration is available for a design, provided that it is novel and has 'individual character'. Design is defined as

the appearance of the whole or a part of a product resulting from the features of, in particular, the lines, contours, colours, shape, texture or materials of the product or its ornamentation (s. 1(2))

Product is widely defined as

any industrial or handicraft item other than a computer program; and, in particular, includes packaging, get-up, graphic symbols, typographic type-faces and parts intended to be assembled into a complex product. (s. 1(3)).

No design right can exist in features of appearance of a product which are solely dictated by the product's technical function (s. 1C(1)) nor in 'must fit' or 'must match' features of a product which must necessarily be exactly reproduced in shape and size to enable the product to be connected (etc.) to another product so that either product may perform its function (s. 1C(2)). In addition no design right can exist in a design which is contrary to public policy or to accepted principles of morality (s. 1D). Registration is not permitted for a design which involves the use of various emblems or devices including the flags or emblems of the UK, the Royal family, other nations or certain international organisations (Sch. A1).

In order to obtain protection the design must be registered at the Designs Registry, a branch of the Patent Office. The application form used to seek registration can be downloaded from the Patent Office website at www.patent.gov.uk. Registration gives the registered proprietor monopoly rights to exploit the design, similar to the rights of a patent proprietor, for an initial period of five years. The period may be extended, on payment of further fees, for up to four further periods of five years (s. 8).

32.8.1.1   Ownership of designs

The proprietor of a design is normally its author. However, where an employee creates a design in the course of his employment, the design is the property of his employer and where an independent contractor is commissioned to produce a design, the design belongs to the person who commissioned it.

Registered designs can be assigned, mortgaged and licensed. Dealings with designs must be registered in the same way as dealings with patents (s. 19).

Licences of right and Crown licences are available in respect of registered designs in the same way as patents.

32.8.1.2   Infringement

The registered proprietor of a design has the exclusive right to use the design and 'any design which does not produce on the informed user a different overall impression.' (s. 7(1)) including by

(a) making, offering, putting on the market, importing, exporting or using a product in which the design is incorporated or to which it is applied; or

(b) stocking such a product for those purposes.

Subject to certain exceptions, the proprietor's rights are infringed by any person who does any of these acts without his permission. The proprietor's rights are also infringed by doing a number of other, ancillary acts, such as making anything which enables an article to which the design is applied to be made.

Remedies for infringement are similar to those for patent infringement. Orders for delivery up and destruction can be made; no damages can be awarded against a defendant who was unaware that the design was registered (s. 9). Articles in respect of which a design is registered should therefore be marked with that fact to put potential infringers on notice.

There is provision for persons aggrieved by threats of infringement proceedings to bring an action to establish that they are groundless and restrain them (s. 26). In addition it is a criminal offence falsely to represent that a design has been registered (s. 35).

32.8.2   Copyright

Design drawings and models are protected by copyright but that copyright is not infringed by making a finished article corresponding to the design unless the finished article itself is entitled to copyright (CDPA 1988, s. 51(1)). Thus the copyright in the design drawings for an exhaust system is no longer infringed by making an exhaust system corresponding to the design. On the other hand, if a sculptor prepares drawings for a sculpture and a rival makes a sculpture based on the drawing, the copyright in the drawing is infringed.

In addition, where a finished article is protected by copyright, copyright protection is reduced if the article is 'industrially exploited' by making copies by an 'industrial process' and marketing them within the United Kingdom. In that case, at the end of 25 years from the end of the year in which the article was first marketed, copies of it can be made without infringing copyright (s. 52). An article is deemed to have been 'industrially exploited' for this purpose if 50 or more have been made (Copyright (Industrial Processes and Excluded Articles) (No. 2) Order 1989 (SI 1989, No. 1070)).

32.8.3   Unregistered design right

Purely functional designs lacking the 'eye appeal' necessary to make them registrable under the 1949 Act are protected by 'unregistered design right' under Part III of the CDPA 1988. The right may protect 'any aspect of the shape or configuration (whether internal or external) of the whole or part of an article' (s. 213) provided that the design is 'original'. A design is not original if it is 'commonplace in the design field in question at the time of its creation'.

No design rights exist in:

(a) methods or principles of construction; or

(b) features of shape or configuration which are intended to enable the article to fit or match with other articles.

Thus design right cannot be used by a product manufacturer to prevent competitors making spare parts for his product.

32.8.3.1   Ownership of design rights

Design rights are normally owned by the designer who creates the design. However, designs created by an employee in the course of employment belong to his employer and designs created by a person commissioned to produce a design belong to the person who commissioned the design (s. 215). What is 'in the course of employment' is determined in much the same way as for the purposes of copyright (see **32.3.1** above), by reference primarily to the employee's contractual duties.

32.8.3.2   Duration

Design rights last for a maximum period of 15 years from the end of the year the design was first recorded in a design document or a product was first made to the design. However, if products manufactured in accordance with the design are marketed within five years of that date, the period of protection ends 10 years from the end of the year of first marketing (s. 216).

32.8.3.3   Infringement

The owner of the design has the exclusive rights to:

(a) make products to the design and

(b) make design documents recording the design to enable such products to be made.

A person who does either of these acts without his permission infringes his rights. His rights are also infringed by anyone who, without permission:

(a) imports or has in his possession for commercial purposes; or

(b) sells or lets for hire or offers or exposes for sale or hire in the course of business

an article which he knows, or has reason to believe, is an 'infringing article', i.e. an article made to the design in infringement of the design right (ss. 227–8).

Remedies similar to those for breach of copyright are available for infringement of design right (ss. 229–231).

32.8.3.4 Dealings in design rights

Design rights can be transferred in the same way as copyright.

Licences of right are available in the last five years of design right protection (s. 237). The terms of such licences are fixed by the Comptroller of Patents in the absence of agreement by the parties. There is also provision for the Crown, for certain limited purposes, to exploit designs and do acts which would otherwise infringe design right (s. 240).

32.9 Moral rights

The Berne Convention (Art. 6 bis) requires that:

independently of the author's economic rights, and even after transfer of the said rights, the author shall have the right to claim authorship of the work and to object to any distortion, mutilation or other modification of, or other derogatory action in relation to, the said work which would be prejudicial to his honour or reputation.

These rights are normally referred to as the rights of 'paternity' and 'integrity'. As a signatory to the Convention, the UK is required to protect these rights. They may be protected by the common law of contract, passing off and defamation but the CDPA 1988 (Chapter IV) now contains specific statutory protection for these rights, together with the right to object to a false attribution of authorship and rights of privacy in respect of certain photographs.

Although the author's moral rights are linked to copyright, they exist independently of the economic copyright and are retained by the author even after assignment of the copyright. They may therefore bind, and be asserted against, the owner of the copyright.

32.9.1 The right of paternity

The author of a literary, dramatic, musical or artistic work in which copyright subsists, and the director of a copyright film, has the right to be identified as the author (etc.) each time the work is published, performed, broadcast, issued to the public or, in the case of an artistic work, displayed in public (s. 77). However, the author can only complain of infringement of his right of paternity if it has first been asserted. The right may be asserted by including a statement to that effect in an assignment of the copyright, or by separate notice in writing (s. 78). An assertion in an assignment is binding on the assignee and anyone claiming title through him, regardless of notice, but a separate notice of assertion is only binding on persons who have notice of it. Authors who wish to enforce the right should therefore assert it and include a notice of assertion on copies of the work issued to the public.

There are a number of exceptions to the right (s. 79); for instance, where copyright in the work originally vests in the author's employer, the right is not infringed by anything done by or with the consent of the copyright owner; nor by anything which would be regarded as 'fair dealing' for the purposes of criticism or review and would therefore not infringe copyright.

32.9.2   The right of integrity

The author of a copyright literary, dramatic, musical or artistic work and the director of a copyright film has the right not to have his work subjected to 'derogatory treatment' (s. 80). Treatment is derogatory if it amounts to 'distortion or mutilation of the work or is otherwise prejudicial to the honour or reputation of the author or director'. This leaves considerable scope for dispute as to what is 'derogatory treatment'. Again, the right is subject to a number of exceptions (s. 81).

32.9.3   Duration

The rights of paternity and integrity last for the same period as copyright in the relevant work. They are personal to the author and therefore cannot be assigned (s. 94); however, they are transmissible on death (s. 95).

The author may waive any or all of his moral rights, either generally or in relation to a specific act or acts. Publishers and others taking assignments of copyright may wish to require authors to waive their moral rights. Care must be taken, however, in drafting a contract containing such a waiver: it may be possible to challenge its validity if it can be shown that the author's agreement was obtained by undue influence or that the contract was in restraint of trade.

Even in the absence of an express waiver, an author may be held to have waived, or be estopped from asserting, his moral rights under the general law of waiver or estoppel.

32.9.4   Other rights

Every person has the right not to have a work falsely attributed to him (s. 84). The right subsists until 20 years after the person's death so that it can be asserted by a person's personal representatives (s. 86).

A person who commissions photographs or the making of a film 'for private and domestic purposes' has the right, subject to certain exceptions, not to have the work issued to or shown in public (s. 85). This is important since copyright in a commissioned photograph or film will generally vest in the photographer; the moral right of privacy therefore prevents the commercial exploitation of private commissioned photographs.

32.9.5   Remedies

Breach of the author's moral rights is actionable as a breach of statutory duty, so that damages may be available. In addition the court may grant an injunction preventing any derogatory treatment unless it is accompanied by a disclaimer dissociating the author from the treatment (s. 103).

32.10 Performers' rights

Since copyright protects *expressions* which are fixed in some medium, performances such as a singer's rendition of a song or an actor's performance in a role are not protected by copyright. However, performers are given certain rights to restrain unauthorised recording, broadcasting and making available to the public of their performances under CDPA 1988, Part II (ss. 180–212).

The law was amended in 1996 by the Copyright and Related Rights Regulations 1996 (SI 1996, No. 2967), introduced to implement an EC Directive, and again in 2003 by the Copyright and Related Rights Regulations 2003 (SI 2003, No. 2498) implementing EC Directive 2001/29/EC. As a result the law is now particularly complicated. What follows is a brief summary of the relevant law.

A performer's rights are infringed by anyone who without their consent:

(a) makes a recording direct from a performance, other than for private or domestic use (s. 182);

(b) broadcasts a performance (s. 182);

(c) makes a recording of a performance from a broadcast, other than for private or domestic use (s. 182);

(d) makes a copy of a recording of a performance (s. 182A);

(e) issues to the public copies of a recording of a performance (s. 182B);

(f) rents or lends to the public copies of a recording of a performance (s. 182C);

(g) makes available to the public a recording of a performance by an electronic transmission in such a way that members of the public can access the recording individually at a time and place of their own choosing (s. 182CA), so that (e.g.) the performer's rights are infringed if a recording of a performance is posted on a web site;

(h) shows or plays in public, or broadcasts a recording of a performance, knowing or having reason to believe that it was made without the performer's consent (s. 183);

(i) imports, other than for private use, or commercially deals with an unauthorised recording of a performance (s. 184).

In addition a performer is entitled to 'equitable remuneration' if a commercially published recording of a performance is played in public or included in a broadcast. The amount of such remuneration is to be fixed by the Copyright Tribunal if not agreed (s. 182D).

The rights in paragraphs (d)–(g) above are classified as 'performers' property rights' and may be transferred by written assignment signed by the transferor, or by testamentary disposition (s. 191A). The rights in paragraphs (a)–(c) and (h)–(i) and the right to equitable remuneration under s. 182D may be transmitted by testamentary disposition but cannot be assigned, save that the right to equitable remuneration can be assigned to a performers' rights collecting society.

Infringement of a performer's property rights is actionable in the same way as interference with any other property, and the performer may seek damages, accounts, injunctions and declarations as appropriate, but no damages will be awarded for infringement of those rights unless at the time of the infringement the defendant either knew, or had reason to believe, that the performer had not consented to the act in question.

Infringement of a performer's *non-property* rights is actionable by the performer as a breach of statutory duty for which damages may be awarded, and similar rights of action are given to any person with whom the performer has an exclusive recording contract. Thus if a concert by the rock group Wasted Years is recorded without their consent by a 'bootlegger', both Wasted Years and their record company can take action against the bootlegger.

There is power for the court to order delivery up of recordings etc. made in breach of performers' rights. There is also criminal liability for certain breaches of performers' rights, including making an unauthorised recording and selling or offering (etc.) for sale such a recording (s. 198).

The court has power to order forfeiture and destruction of recordings which infringe rights in performances, and such an order may be made whenever such recordings come into the possession of a person in connection with the investigation of an offence, whether there is a prosecution or not.

32.11 Summary

Having completed this chapter you should:

- understand the nature of copyright;
- know in broad terms what types of work are protected by copyright and in whom ownership of copyright vests;
- be able to advise on what constitutes infringement of copyright, the remedies available for infringement and the possible defences to an infringement claim;
- understand the nature of the author's 'moral rights', their relationship to copyright and the remedies for their infringement;
- understand the essentials of the systems of protection for designs through copyright, registered and unregistered design right;
- understand the nature of the protection given to performers' rights and their infringement.

Patents

33.1 Introduction

In this chapter we examine the legal protection afforded to inventions through the patent system. In particular we examine:

- the nature of the domestic and international patent systems;
- what is patentable;
- the procedure for obtaining a patent;
- the nature of the rights of a patent holder, remedies for their infringement and the possible defences to an infringement claim.

Patent law protects inventions. The patent system is now governed by the Patents Act 1977 as slightly amended by the Copyright, Designs and Patents Act 1988. A number of international treaties seek to promote a measure of harmonisation and mutuality in international patent law, including the Paris Convention of 1883, the Patent Co-operation Treaty of 1970 and the European Patent Convention of 1973 which established the European Patent Office. These conventions and treaties enable an inventor to obtain protection for his invention in other states of the EC and elsewhere in the world.

33.2 Obtaining a patent

A patent can be obtained for any patentable invention provided the proper statutory procedure is followed.

33.2.1 What is patentable?

A patent can be awarded for an invention unless it is excluded from patentability by the statute.

33.2.1.1 Invention

'Invention' is not defined by the Patents Act 1977. However, the following are not inventions (s. 1(2)):

(a) a discovery, such as the discovery of a natural substance;

(b) a scientific theory;

(c) a mathematical method;

(d) a literary, dramatic, musical or artistic work or any other aesthetic creation whatsoever;

(e) a scheme, rule or method for performing any mental act, playing a game or doing business;

(f) a computer program;

(g) the presentation of information.

These things are only excluded from the category of 'inventions' 'to the extent that a patent or application for a patent relates to that thing *as such*'. Thus although a discovery is not patentable, a person who discovers a naturally occurring substance and a practical use for it may patent the use. It will often be difficult to apply this distinction. Similarly, although a patent will not be granted for a computer program as such, the European Patent Office has held that under the European Patent Convention a patent can be granted for a computer system comprising hardware and software together, and a patent can be granted for a technical effect produced by a computer program—such as making computer hardware operate in a particular way. (See *IBM's European Patent* [1999] RPC 861.) This issue has not yet been considered by the UK courts but since the 1977 Act is modelled on the European Patent Convention it may be expected that the position will be the same under the Act.

Subject to this list of exclusions, an invention may be a thing, such as a new type of mousetrap, a process, such as a new method of manufacture, or even a new use for an existing item, such as a drug.

33.2.1.2 Patentable inventions

An invention is only patentable if it is new, involves an inventive step and is industrially applicable.

(a) *New*

An invention is 'new' if it did not form part of the 'state of the art' known to the public at the date of application for the patent (the priority date) (s. 2(1)). The 'state of the art' includes all information made available to the public by written or oral description, by use or otherwise. Thus a patent cannot be granted for a process if it has already been described in a technical or academic journal; similarly a windsurfing board was not patentable when it was revealed that a crude version of the board had been used in public prior to the application for the patent. A person who thinks he has made an invention must therefore carry out a careful search of the 'prior art' before applying for a patent in order to decide if the invention is patentable. This may be an expensive and time-consuming process.

(b) *The invention must involve an 'inventive step'*

This means that the invention, as well as being novel, must not be 'obvious to a person skilled in the [relevant] art' (s. 3). Thus if a person familiar with the state of the art in the relevant area, but lacking the ability to make inventions, could have produced the 'invention' in question simply by using his knowledge of the prior art, the 'invention' is not patentable. This too is a difficult test to apply and the courts have proposed a number of tests to decide if an 'invention' is obvious; for instance, if an invention satisfies a 'long felt want', that is evidence that it was not obvious; however, the fact that an invention has been commercially successful is not necessarily proof that it was not obvious. The requirement of 'inventive step' generally excludes from patentability devices which simply combine two or more existing items.

(c) *The invention must be capable of industrial application (s. 4(1))*

The invention must be capable of being made or used in any industry other than agriculture.

33.2.1.3 Inventions excluded from patentability

The following may not be patented:

(a) an invention the commercial exploitation of which would be contrary to public policy or morality; however, exploitation will not be regarded as contrary to public policy or morality only because it is prohibited by any law in force in the UK or any part of it (s. 1(3) and 1(4) as amended by the Patents Regulations 2000, SI 2000, No. 2037);

(b) any variety of animal or plant or any essentially biological process for the production of animals or plants not being a microbiological process or the product of such a process; thus genetically engineered micro-organisms can be patented. Plants cannot be patented but a person who breeds a new plant variety may obtain protection for his discovery under the Plant Varieties Act 1997. Most new plant varieties, potatoes, trees and vines are protected for up to 30 years;

(c) a method of treatment of the human or animal body by surgery or therapy or a method of diagnosis practised on the human or animal body (s. 4A inserted by Patents Act 2004). However, this does not apply to 'a substance or composition for use in any such method' so that a patent can be granted for a particular new use of a drug.

33.2.1.4 Biotechnological inventions

Biotechnology is now an important industry. The Patents Act was amended by the Patents Regulations 2000 (SI 2000, No. 2037) which inserts a new Schedule A2 into the Act to make provision for the patenting of biotechnological inventions and implement the EC Directive on the legal protection of biotechnological inventions (Directive 98/44/EC). The regulations are detailed and complex. Many aspects of their meaning are unclear and/or disputed. However, their main effect is that it is now expressly provided that an invention is not to be considered unpatentable *solely* on the ground that it concerns a product consisting of or containing biological material or a process by which biological material is produced, processed or used. Biological material which is 'isolated from its natural envir-onment or produced by means of a technical process' may also be the subject of an invention, and therefore be patentable, even though it occurs in nature (Sch. A2, para. 1).

Certain things are excluded from patentability, including the human body, processes for cloning human beings, processes for modifying the germ line genetic identity of human beings, uses of human embryos for industrial or commercial purposes and 'any variety of animal or plant or any essentially biological process for the production of animals or plants, not being a micro-biological or other technical process or the product of such processes.' (Sch. A2, para. 3).

33.2.2 Procedure

Patents are granted by the Patent Office. The application procedure is technical, complex and potentially expensive. Some guidance is contained in The Stationery Office publications (see *Introducing Patents: A Guide for Inventors*, The Stationery Office 1988); however, an inventor will generally require specialist advice from a patent agent or someone with similar experience of the patent procedure (see **33.2.2.5**).

Broadly speaking the application procedure is as follows.

(a) The inventor files the application for the grant of a patent. The application form can be downloaded from the Patent Office website (www.patent.gov.uk) and can be completed on computer, but must be returned to the Patent Office in printed (paper) form.

(b) The application is considered by the Patent Office.

(c) A patent is either granted or refused; if refused it is possible for the applicant to amend his application.

Each stage must be completed within prescribed time limits.

Fees are payable to the Patent Office at each stage; in addition the applicant may have to pay professional fees to patent agents. An inventor must therefore consider very carefully whether his invention is worth patenting, taking into account, *inter alia*, the likely commercial exploitability of the invention and whether it could be protected without a patent by keeping it confidential. In addition, the inventor may have to decide whether to apply simply for a UK patent, or to seek wider protection for his invention through one of the international patent systems.

33.2.2.1   The application

The application must be in the form prescribed by the Patents Rules 1992 and must contain:

(a) the name of the applicant;

(b) a request for the grant of a patent;

(c) a specification: this is a detailed, technical description of the invention, often including plans and drawings; it should contain sufficient information to enable a person skilled in the art to understand the invention and carry it out by performing the process or making the item described;

(d) the claim for the patent: a detailed description of what the invention does; and

(e) an abstract: a summary description of the patent to be used by the Patent Office in preliminary consideration of the application (s. 14(2)).

The applicant must also pay the proper fee.

33.2.2.2   The priority date

The 'priority date' fixes the date at which the prior art is to be considered for the purpose of assessing the novelty of the invention; it is generally the date of filing the application. In addition, infringement proceedings may be taken in respect of acts done after the priority date. The inventor will therefore wish to apply for a patent as soon as possible in order to gain early priority and to ensure that no competitors pre-empt his application. However, the patent specification and claim must be prepared with care. If the specification is inaccurate any resulting patent may be invalid; if the claim does not cover all uses of the invention competitors may use the invention for such uses without liability for infringement. Conversely, an overly broad claim may be invalid on the grounds that the claim, which defines the scope of the protection granted by the patent sought, is not supported by the patent specification. In order to gain early priority the inventor may therefore simply file a description of the invention with an indication of his intention to apply for a patent. Provided he then files a detailed specification, claim and abstract within 12 months, his application will proceed but priority will be given from the date of the initial filing (s. 15).

A patent may be amended after grant (s. 27) but amendment is at the discretion of the Comptroller of Patents. Amendment is likely to be refused if, for instance, the patentee deliberately made an over-wide claim in the original application. Moreover an amendment will not be permitted if it results in the specification disclosing additional matter not in the original specification or seeks to extend the scope of the patent's protection (s. 76). So a patent cannot be amended so as to cure the insufficiency of the initial specification.

33.2.2.3 Consideration by the Patent Office

After filing, the patent application is considered by one of the Patent Office's patent examiners to ensure that it complies with the formal requirements for a valid application. There is then a search of relevant technical materials to consider whether the application complies with the requirements of novelty and inventive step. There may be dialogue between the examiner and the applicant, during which the applicant may provide further information in support of the application.

On completion of the search the examiner issues a search report. The applicant must then decide whether to proceed with, or withdraw the application. Within 18 months of service of the search report the patent application is published. If the applicant wishes to proceed with the application he must request formal examination of the application for novelty and inventive step within six months of service of the search report; a further fee is then payable. If no such request is made the application will lapse.

33.2.2.4 Grant of a patent

On completion of consideration of the application the Patent Office may either grant or refuse the application. If the application is refused, the applicant may file further information to rectify his application within four and a half years of the original priority date. If the application is granted the applicant becomes 'proprietor' of the patent (Patents Act 1977, s. 72(2)).

33.2.2.5 The role of patent agents

An inventor may need professional assistance to prepare the patent specification and claim. The CDPA 1988 allows any individual or body corporate to carry out the functions of a patent agent (CDPA 1988, s. 274) but restricts the use of the titles 'patent agent' and 'patent attorney' (s. 276). Only a patent agent registered by the Chartered Institute of Patent Agents can use the title 'patent agent'; in addition a solicitor may use the title 'patent attorney' (s. 278). Special rules apply to partnerships and companies (s. 276).

Communications between an inventor and his patent agent in relation to any matter relating to the protection of an invention, design or technical information are privileged from disclosure in legal proceedings in the same way as communications between a client and his solicitor.

33.2.3 Ownership

The person entitled to apply for a patent in respect of an invention is normally the inventor, defined as 'the actual deviser of the invention' (s. 7(3)). There may be joint inventors so that where an invention is produced by (say) a research team, the team may apply for a patent as joint inventors.

33.2.3.1 Employees' inventions

Inventions made by an employee will belong to the inventor's employer if they are made:

(a) in the course of:
   (i)   the employee's normal duties; or
   (ii) duties specifically assigned to him

   if, in either case, an invention might reasonably be expected to result from the employee carrying out those duties (s. 39(1)(a)); thus e.g. an invention made by a research scientist during the course of his research will belong to his employer;

(b) in the course of the employee carrying out his duties where the employee had a special obligation to further the interests of his employer's undertaking (s. 39(1)(b)).

Inventions made by employees outside these situations belong to the employee.

Where an employee's invention belongs to his employer in accordance with s. 39 and a patent is granted in respect of it, the employee is entitled to share in the profits from the invention or patent by being awarded compensation to be paid by the employer if the invention or patent is of outstanding benefit to the employer and it is just that the employee should therefore be awarded compensation (s. 40). In such circumstances the employee may apply to the court or to the Comptroller of Patents for compensation and may be awarded such sum as will secure for him/her a 'fair share' of the benefit of the patent or invention (s. 41).

Any term in an employee's contract of employment which diminishes his rights under these provisions is unenforceable. Thus, for instance, a term which seeks to vest an employee's inventions in his employer outside the scope of s. 39, or one which seeks to deprive him of his right to compensation under s. 40 would be unenforceable.

33.3 Effect of grant

The grant of a patent gives the proprietor a monopoly right to exploit the invention. The patent is presumed valid unless successfully challenged. A challenge to the validity of a patent may be made by the defendant in infringement proceedings. There are also provisions which allow a patent to be revoked.

33.3.1 Duration

The maximum period of patent monopoloy is 20 years. Patents are initially granted for a period of four years. Thereafter they may be renewed annually, on payment of a fee. At the end of the initial four year period the proprietor must therefore decide whether or not to renew the patent, taking into account the commercial success of the invention in the initial period.

If the patent is not renewed it will lapse. However, there is provision for the proprietor to restore a lapsed patent (s. 28).

33.3.2 Owner's rights

The proprietor of a patent can deal with it as property, by outright disposal, by mortgaging it or by licensing others to use it. Any disposition or mortgage of a patent is void unless in writing signed by both parties. Licences may be exclusive or non-exclusive. Patent and know-how licences are granted block exemption from the provisions of Art. 81 of the Treaty of Rome, and must be drafted with attention to the terms of the exemption (Reg. No. 772/2004—technology transfer agreements) to ensure that they contain none of the prohibited 'black list' terms.

All dealings with a patent must be registered at the Patent Office. Failure to register a disposition may prevent the disponee obtaining certain remedies in the event of infringement.

In certain circumstances the proprietor's freedom to deal with his patent is restricted. The Act contains provisions for the grant of licences of right and of compulsory licences. In addition it permits the Crown, in certain circumstances, to exploit a patent without the consent of the proprietor.

33.3.2.1   Licences of right

A proprietor who is unable to exploit his patent may ask the Comptroller of Patents to endorse the Register with a notice that licences to exploit the patent are available 'as of right' (s. 46). The fees for renewal of a patent so endorsed are halved. Any person who wishes to take a licence of such a patent may approach the proprietor with a view to negotiating a licence; if the parties cannot agree the terms of the licence, they can be fixed by the Comptroller.

33.3.2.2   Compulsory licences

Any person can apply for a compulsory licence to exploit a patent at any time after three years have elapsed from the grant (s. 48). A compulsory licence will only be granted if the applicant can show the Comptroller that the patent has been unused or underused, or that failure to grant licences has damaged British exports or industry.

33.3.2.3   Crown use of patents

There is provision for the Crown to make use of a patent, or to authorise its use by another person, in certain limited circumstances in the national interest (s. 55). Where the Crown does make use of a patent under these provisions it must pay compensation to the proprietor or to any exclusive licensee.

33.3.3   Infringement

A patent is infringed by any person who, without the express or implied authority of the proprietor:

(a) makes, disposes of, offers to dispose of, imports, uses or keeps, whether for disposal or otherwise, a patented product or a product made from a patented process;

(b) uses, or offers for use in the UK, a patented process, knowing, or in circumstances where it would be obvious to a reasonable person, that its use would be unauthorised and an infringement of the patent;

(c) supplies or offers to supply any means, relating to an essential element of the patented invention, for putting the invention into effect knowing, or where it would be obvious to a reasonable man, that the means are suitable for and intended for putting the invention into effect; thus, for instance, a person who supplies a patented product in kit form commits an infringement.

It should be noted that a UK patent is infringed only by acts done in the UK. A person who has only a UK patent therefore cannot prevent a person manufacturing a competing product in another country, although he can prevent its import into the UK if it would infringe his patent here. It should also be noted that for the purposes of the third category of infringement listed above ('supplying any means for putting the invention into effect') it is not necessary that the infringing invention be located in the UK provided that the means for putting it into effect in the UK are supplied in the UK. In *Menashe Business Mercantile Ltd* v *William Hill Organisation Ltd* [2003] 1 All ER 279 a patent had been granted in respect of a computerised gaming system using a host computer and remote terminals. The defendants devised a similar gaming system which they made available to their customers in the UK by supplying them with a CD ROM which enabled the customer's computer to operate as a remote terminal. The defendants' host computer infringed the patent but was located in Antigua. The Court of Appeal nevertheless held that when the defendants' UK customers accessed the remote host they put it into effect in the UK. The defendants had therefore infringed the patent by supplying in the UK the means for putting the remote host into effect in the UK.

In the age of the Internet this decision represents an important extension of the patent holder's protection. In general however the UK patent holder's protection remains limited to the UK. A person who wishes to gain wider protection must therefore obtain patents in other states or take advantage of the international patent registration schemes.

33.3.3.1   Infringement proceedings

Infringement proceedings may be taken by the proprietor of the patent or by an exclusive licensee, provided he joins the proprietor as a party to the proceedings. Proceedings may be taken in the High Court or in a county court designated as a Patents County Court and in March 1996 new rules of court introduced a system of arbitration in Patents County Courts. Alternatively, with the consent of the parties, infringement disputes can be adjudicated by the Comptroller of Patents.

No infringement proceedings can be taken until publication of the patent specification; however, after publication, proceedings can be taken in respect of acts done prior to publication but after the priority date.

33.3.3.2   Interpretation

A claim of infringement will often turn on the proper interpretation of the patent. The court will adopt a purposive rather than a literal approach, interpreting the patent in the way it would be understood by a reasonable person skilled in the relevant art so as to give the patent holder the full extent of the monopoly which such a person would think he was claiming (*Catnic Components* v *Hill & Smith* [1982] RPC 237; *Kirin Amgen Inc* v *Hoechst Marion Roussel Inc* [2004] UKHL 46). A similar approach is taken under the European Patent Convention.

33.3.3.3   Defences

A number of defences are available to an alleged infringer. The main ones are as follows.

(a) *No infringement*

A decision whether a product infringes the patent in another product depends upon consideration of the specification and claim filed for the patented product. Where the allegedly infringing product differs slightly from the patented product the court may have to consider whether the differences are material.

(b) *Private and non-commercial use*

It is a defence to an infringement claim to show that the allegedly infringing act was done privately and for non-commercial purposes (s. 60(5)(a)).

(c) *Experimental purposes*

It is a defence to show that the alleged infringement was done for experimental purposes relating to the invention (s. 60(5)(b)). This might permit reverse engineering, where an invention is disassembled in order to discover how it works.

(d) *Use of seeds and/or reproductive material*

There is no infringement where a farmer grows a crop from patented seed of certain specified plants which was sold to him for agricultural use by, or with the permission of, the patent holder, and saves part of the crop for the purpose of further sowing (s. 60(5)(g)). Similarly, there is no infringement where a farmer uses an animal or animal reproductive material for an agricultural purpose following the commercial supply to him of breeding stock or other animal reproductive material (s. 60(5)(h)). In each case the exemption is conditional on the farmer paying 'equitable remuneration' to the patent holder. Thus although biological material, including genetically modified crops and animals, are now patentable, a farmer who grows crops from modified seed covered by a patent, or breeds animals from modified stock covered by a patent, does not necessarily thereby infringe the patent.

(e) *Continuance of activities done before the priority date*

It is a defence to show that the alleged breach was merely a continuation of activities the defendant carried on before the priority date of the claimant's patent (s. 64).

(f) *Licensed activities*

There is no infringement in respect of acts done with the claimant's licence. A customer who buys a product may have an implied licence to do acts necessary to repair it, including making replacement parts, if it breaks down.

(g) *Exhaustion of rights*

Where the proprietor has consented to goods made in accordance with his patent being placed on the market within the EC, the concept of exhaustion of rights may prevent him complaining of the import of products, which would otherwise infringe his patent, into the UK (see **31.5.2.3**).

(h) *No valid patent*

An alleged infringer may defend the infringement claim by challenging the validity of the patent itself: for instance by asserting that the claimant's 'invention' was part of the prior art, or was obvious and lacked the necessary inventive step, or on the grounds that the patent claim contains insufficient disclosure to enable a person skilled in the art to perform the invention (s. 74). A patent proprietor contemplating infringement proceedings should consider this possibility, since a successful challenge to the patent will lead to revocation of the patent, meaning that he not only loses the case in question but is also deprived of his patent and therefore of protection against all others.

33.3.3.4   Threats of infringement proceedings

The threat of infringement proceedings may be used to damage the business of a competitor. For instance, if A is proprietor of a patent and B makes and sells a competing product, B's customers are guilty of infringement if B's product infringes A's patent. A may therefore threaten them with infringement proceedings and such a threat may be sufficient to deter them from buying B's product and damage B's business, *even if in fact B's product does not infringe A's patent*. The Act therefore permits a person in B's position to seek a declaration that a threat of infringement proceedings is groundless, an injunction to prevent the repetition of such threats and damages for any losses caused by such threats (s. 70). Any person aggrieved by a threat of infringement can bring proceedings. However, no such proceedings may be brought where the threat relates to infringement by making or importing a product for resale, or to using a process (s. 70(4)).

It is not a threat simply to point out the existence of a patent; a proprietor who believes that someone is, or is about to infringe, his patent may therefore be advised simply to draw the attention of those concerned to the existence of his patent, rather than threatening proceedings. A threat of proceedings made during the course of genuine 'without prejudice' negotiations in an attempt to settle an existing dispute is not actionable. However, merely adding the words 'without prejudice' to a threat of proceedings will not make the threat non-actionable if it is made outside the context of genuine settlement negotiations (see *Unilever plc* v *The Procter & Gamble Company* [2000] FSR 344; *Kooltrade Ltd* v *XTS Ltd* [2001] FSR 13).

It is a further defence to a claim in respect of a groundless threat of proceedings for the person who made the threat to show that before (s)he made the threat (s)he used best endeavours to identify the person who made or imported the allegedly infringing product or used or offered for use the allegedly infringing process. To rely on the defence the person making the threats must notify the person threatened before or when making the threats that (s)he has so used best endeavours and identify the endeavours used (s. 70(6)). This procedure may therefore provide a defence where a patent is infringed but the patent holder is unable to identify the infringer.

A person who is unsure whether his proposed actions will infringe a patent may apply to the proprietor for an acknowledgement that the proposed acts will not infringe his patent. If no such acknowledgement is given he may apply to the court for a declaration that his acts will not amount to an infringement.

33.3.3.5 Remedies

If an infringement action succeeds the following remedies may be awarded.

(a) An injunction to restrain further infringement. A final injunction will normally be granted in a 'broad' form, to restrain any infringement of the patent. In an appropriate case the injunction may extend beyond the expiry of the patent in order to prevent the defendant gaining an unfair 'springboard' advantage from his infringement (see *Dyson Appliances Ltd* v *Hoover Ltd (No. 2)* [2001] RPC 544).

(b) A declaration of the validity of the patent.

(c) Damages to compensate the proprietor for any losses suffered as a result of the infringement. They may be assessed on the basis of the royalty which would have been payable by the infringer had the infringing acts been done under licence.

(d) An account of profits: for instance where damages are difficult to assess.

(e) An order that infringing articles be delivered up to the claimant and destroyed.

Neither damages nor accounts can be awarded if either:

(a) the defendant shows that at the time of the infringement he neither knew nor had reasonable grounds to suppose that the patent existed (s. 62(1)); where a proprietor believes that his patent is being infringed he should therefore bring its existence to the notice of the infringer; such notification will not amount to a threat of proceedings but will provide the infringer with notice and allow the proprietor to claim damages if the claim succeeds;

(b) the claimant has not registered his interest in the patent (s. 68).

Remedies are also restricted where a licence of right is available in respect of a patent. In that case no injunction may be granted if the defendant undertakes to obtain a licence, and damages in respect of past infringements are limited to double the amount which would have been payable under a licence had he already obtained one.

33.3.3.6 Patent Office opinions

A claim for infringement of a patent is therefore potentially hazardous. A patent owner who threatens infringement proceedings may incur liability for a groundless threat; if (s)he brings proceedings (s)he runs the risk that the validity of the patent may be challenged. In addition, infringement proceedings are likely to be expensive. In any case, infringement proceedings are generally expensive, requiring specialist representation and expert evidence. As an alternative there is provision for a patent owner or any other person to seek an opinion from the Patent Office as to the validity of a patent or whether a particular act would constitute infringement (s. 74A). An opinion will then be prepared by a patent examiner from the Patent Office. An opinion might therefore be sought by the patent owner before commencing proceedings, by an alleged infringer threatened with proceedings, or by a person contemplating (e.g) manufacturing a product which it fears may infringe an existing patent. Such an opinion may provide valuable guidance to the parties, but it should be noted that such an opinion is not binding for any purpose.

33.4 International dimension

Registration of a UK patent gives the proprietor a monopoly to exploit his invention in the UK but does not allow him to restrain activities outside the UK. If he wishes to obtain international protection he could, of course, register his patent separately in each State in which he wishes to exploit his invention. Alternatively he may take advantage of several international cooperation and harmonisation measures to simplify the process of getting international protection.

33.4.1 European patents

The European Patent Treaty established a European patent system and a European Patent Office. The criteria for patentability of an invention are similar in all States which are party to the Convention. A person who wishes to exploit an invention in several Convention States may, as an alternative to making separate patent applications in each State, make a single application for a European patent to the European Patent Office, specifying the States in which he wants protection. This has the advantage of giving wider protection more simply than if separate applications are made, and will generally be cheaper than making separate applications. However, the risk for the applicant is that if the application is rejected then his patent will automatically fail in each Convention Member State.

33.4.2 European community patents

The Community Patent Convention which came into force in 1993 allows an applicant to apply for a Community patent. Such a patent is valid in all Member States of the Community. If the applicant wishes to obtain protection in all EC Member States a Community patent will generally be cheaper than an application under the European Patent Treaty. However, since some non-EC Member States are party to the European Patent Treaty Convention the applicant may prefer to apply under the earlier system if he wishes to obtain protection beyond the EC.

33.4.3 Patent Cooperation Treaty

Even wider protection can be obtained by applying for a patent under the Patent Cooperation Treaty specifying the states in which a patent is sought. An application under the Treaty may be made to the London Patent Office.

33.5 Summary

Having completed this chapter you should understand and be able to advise on:

- the nature of a patent;
- what is patentable;
- the procedure for obtaining a patent;
- the availability of international protection for patents;
- what constitutes infringement of a patent, the remedies for infringement and the possible defences to an infringement claim.

Confidentiality

34.1 Introduction

In this short chapter we briefly examine the commercial uses of the law of confidence including:

- how an obligation of confidence may arise, including through the use of confidentiality agreements and with particular reference to the duty of confidence owed by an employee;
- remedies for breach of confidence;
- defences to a breach of confidence claim.

When information is imparted by one person to another in confidence, the law may impose on the recipient an obligation to respect that confidence and may therefore restrain the use or disclosure of that information without the consent of the confider.

Protection of confidential information is governed by the common law and the boundaries of the law are unclear. The law is flexible and protects trade secrets, such as secret formulae, and commercial information, such as customer details or marketing plans (e.g. *Thos Marshall (Exports) Ltd* v *Guinle* [1976] FSR 345). It may also protect personal (e.g. *Stephens* v *Avery* [1988] 1 Ch 457) and government information (*A-G* v *The Observer Ltd* [1989] AC 109).

34.1.1 Commercial and legal significance

In protecting business and commercial information, confidentiality operates as an adjunct to the statutory intellectual property regimes and, especially, patents and copyright. Thus a business may use confidentiality to protect details of a secret invention or process, as an alternative to patenting it. Often confidence may be used alongside patent protection, for instance, to protect details of manufacturing processes used in the exploitation of a patentable invention. Where the business is satisfied that it can keep details of a process or invention secret, confidentiality may provide greater protection than would be obtained by patenting the invention, since the information will be protected so long as it remains confidential whereas patent protection is limited in time. However, confidentiality will not provide adequate protection if the invention can be reverse engineered, for in that case details of the invention will fall into the public domain, and cease to be confidential, as soon as it is marketed.

Confidentiality may also be used to protect ideas which would not be protected by copyright: for instance, the idea for a television programme format (*Fraser* v *Thames Television Ltd* [1969] 2 All ER 101).

34.1.2   Basis of the obligation

Where the parties are in a contractual relationship, as are, say, employer and employee, an obligation of confidence may take effect as an express or implied term in the contract (*Faccenda Chicken Ltd* v *Fowler* [1986] 1 All ER 617). However, it is clear that an obligation of confidence may be imposed even where the confider and confidee are not in a contractual relationship and the protection of confidential information is generally said to rest on 'broad equitable principles' (see *Seager* v *Copydex* [1967] 2 All ER 415; *Duchess of Argyll* v *Duke of Argyll* [1967] Ch 303).

34.2   What information is protected?

In order for information to be protected as confidential two conditions must be fulfilled.

(a) The information must have the 'necessary quality of confidence'; it must not be information which is in the public domain (*Saltman Engineering Co. Ltd* v *Campbell Engineering Co. Ltd* [1963] 3 All ER 413). Thus, for instance, information about customers, such as their addresses and the most convenient routes to their premises, which could be discovered from public sources, could not be regarded as confidential (*Faccenda Chicken Ltd* v *Fowler* [1986] 1 All ER 617).

(b) It must have been imparted in circumstances importing an obligation of confidence, as, for instance, where the confider emphasises that the information is to be kept confidential. Note that if the information does not fulfil the first requirement a person cannot make it confidential merely by claiming that it is confidential.

34.2.1   Confidential relationships

In certain relationships a duty of confidentiality is imposed automatically by law, so that some or all information received during the course of the relationship must be regarded as confidential. These include the relationships between solicitor and client, banker and customer and employee and employer.

34.2.2   Third parties

The obligation of confidence binds the person to whom information is confided. It is not clear if third parties to whom confidential information is passed, or those who come by confidential information without it being confided, are bound by such an obligation. It seems that a third party recipient who knows that information is passed to him in breach of a duty of confidence may be held liable to respect the confidence. However, the position remains unclear. It could be relevant to e.g. acts of industrial espionage.

Where an obligation of confidence arises under a contract, a third party who induces the confidee to break the duty may commit the tort of inducing a breach of contract. This is particularly important in cases where employees who have access to confidential information are 'poached' by rival employers.

34.2.3   Confidentiality agreements

In order to avoid the uncertainties of the law, where a business needs to disclose confidential information, for instance, an idea for a computer program or a secret process, in order to obtain finance to exploit it, it will normally seek to impose a duty of confidence by an express agreement that, in consideration of the disclosure of the information, the recipient agrees to respect its confidence and neither to make use of it nor disclose it to any other person without the express consent of the discloser.

34.3 Breach of duty

The duty of confidentiality is broken if the confidee, without the consent of the confider, uses the information for his own benefit or discloses it to any other person. It seems that it is irrelevant that the use or disclosure was entirely innocent, as where the confidee uses information having forgotten that it was imparted to him in confidence (*Seager* v *Copydex Ltd* [1967] 2 All ER 415).

34.4 Defences

The only defences to a claim of breach of confidence are:

(a) to deny that the information was confidential; or

(b) to claim that disclosure was justified.

Disclosure may be justified where it is in the public interest, e.g. to disclose wrongdoing or iniquity. For instance, disclosure of inaccuracies in police breath test equipment used to test motorists suspected of drink-driving could be justified on this basis (*Lion Laboratories Ltd* v *Evans* [1984] 2 All ER 417). The public interest may justify disclosure to law enforcement or other authorities (*Francome* v *Mirror Group Newspapers Ltd* [1984] 1 WLR 192) or, possibly, to the media where the information relates to wrongdoing by the authorities, but it will not justify commercial exploitation of the information.

In an action for breach of confidence it may also be necessary now to consider the right of freedom of expression protected by the European Convention on Human Rights and the Human Rights Act 1998. The right may be particularly important in considering whether disclosure of information is justified in the public interest. However, the Convention also recognises the right to respect for private and family life (Art. 8) and protection of property (Art. 1 of the First Protocol). Moreover, exercise of the right of freedom of expression is expressly stated by the Convention to be subject to such 'formalities, conditions, restrictions or penalties as are prescribed by law and are necessary in a democratic society . . . for the protection of the . . . rights of others, [or] for preventing the disclosure of information received in confidence' (Art. 10(2)). The Convention right of freedom of expression therefore does not override obligations of confidence but requires a court to undertake a balancing exercise between the competing rights of the parties.

34.5 Remedies

The court may award an injunction to restrain a breach of confidence—e.g. by restraining publication or use or requiring delivery up of lists or documents, and damages or an account of profits in respect of past breaches.

Where a breach of confidence puts trade secrets or commercial information into the public domain, other businesses may be free to make use of them. However, an injunction may be granted to prevent the person who broke confidence exploiting the information. The injunction will be limited in time in accordance with the 'springboard principle', which means that the defendant is restrained from using the information so as to gain a head start over other businesses (see *Terrapin* v *Builders Supply Co. (Hayes) Ltd* [1967] RPC 375; *Roger Bullivant* v *Ellis* [1987] FSR 172).

Damages may be assessed in the same way as for conversion. They will generally reflect the market value of the information which may be either:

(a) the fee a consultant would have charged for supplying it; or

(b) the price a willing buyer would have paid the claimant for the information (*Seager* v *Copydex Ltd (No. 2)* [1969] RPC 250).

Alternatively, the claimant may seek an account of profits made by use of the information (*Peter Pan Manufacturing Corp.* v *Corsets Silhouette* [1963] RPC 45).

34.6 Employees

Employees often have access to confidential or other sensitive information and employers may wish to prevent them exploiting that information, either for their own benefit or for a new employer, on termination of their employment.

34.6.1 During employment

All employees are subject to an implied duty of fidelity during employment. This prevents them doing anything for their own purposes which conflicts with the interests of their employer, including, for instance, copying lists of customers etc.

34.6.2 After employment

After employment there is a more restricted implied duty to respect confidentiality in information such as secret processes and trade secrets (*Faccenda Chicken Ltd* v *Fowler* [1986] 1 All ER 617). This may not prevent the employee using information such as details of customers etc. and information which becomes part of his general skill and expertise. In deciding what information is covered by this implied duty a court will consider:

(a) the nature of the information;

(b) the nature of the employment: did the employee regularly handle confidential information?

(c) whether the employer stressed that the information was confidential;

(d) whether the genuinely confidential information can be isolated from other, non-confidential information.

34.6.3 Express contract terms

In order to avoid relying on the implied duty, the contract of employment will often impose express restrictions on an employee:

(a) preventing him using confidential information during or (for a limited time) after employment; and

(b) preventing him competing with the employer, either on his own behalf or for another employer, after termination of the employment.

Such restrictions may be easier to enforce than the implied duty of confidentiality. However, they are subject to restrictions on their effectiveness. An express term cannot protect information which would not be protected by the implied duty and a restraint on the employee's post employment activities will be invalid and unenforceable if it is in restraint of trade.

34.7 Summary

Having completed this chapter you should have an outline knowledge of the law of confidence and its role in protecting commercial information, trade secrets and the like and be able to advise on:

- what constitutes a breach of confidence;
- the remedies available for such a breach;
- possible defences to a breach of confidence claim.

Trade marks and passing off

35.1 Introduction

Image and reputation are important to businesses; brand names are especially valuable as an element of goodwill. They may attract custom and also be a marketable commodity in their own right. Brand names and trade reputation are protected by the law of trade marks and passing off.

In this chapter we examine the legal protection afforded to registered marks through the trade mark system and for unregistered marks through the law of passing off, including:

- what is registrable as a trade mark;
- the rights of a trade mark owner;
- what constitutes infringement of a registered trade mark, the remedies for infringement and possible defences to an infringement claim;
- the system for international trade mark protection through the Community trade mark system;
- dealings in trade marks;
- the nature of the protection afforded to trade and similar marks through the tort of passing off, including the essential elements of the tort, remedies for passing off and defences to a passing off claim.

35.1.1 Trade marks and passing off

Passing off is a tort; in order to bring an action for passing off a trader must show that he has an established reputation and that he has been damaged by the defendant's activities. Registration of a trade mark allows the trader to prevent others using that mark without showing that he has established a reputation or that he has suffered damage; a trade mark can therefore be used for a wholly new product or by a new business. It also grants nationwide and even international protection. However, the trader must comply with the formalities for registration and pay a fee, both for initial registration and subsequent renewals. In addition, passing off may apply in some situations in which a trade mark cannot be registered. In many cases, however, the same act may amount to infringement of a trade mark and passing off; in that case there is nothing to prevent the owner of the mark suing for infringement of the mark and for passing off together or in the alternative.

35.2 Trade marks

The system of registration of trade marks was introduced in 1875. The law is now governed by the Trade Marks Act 1994 (TMA 1994) which replaced the Trade Marks Act 1938. The Act is intended, in part, to implement an EC Directive to harmonise trade mark law throughout the EC adopted in 1988 ([1989] OJ L40/1) and should be interpreted in accordance with the Directive.

In 1996 a Community Trade Mark Office was established pursuant to a Community Regulation of 1993 (Regulation 40/94 20.12.93) as a further step towards harmonisation of intellectual property law within the European Community. The Regulation permits nationals of EU Member States and others to seek registration in the Community Trade Mark Office of a single mark for the whole of the Community. There is wider international cooperation under the Madrid Agreement Concerning International Registration of Marks (1891) which allows a mark registered in one contracting State to be registered in other contracting States by applying to the International Registry of the International Bureau of the World Intellectual Property Organisation (WIPO). The UK ratified the Convention in 1995 and gave effect to it by the Trade Marks (International Registration) Order 1996 (SI 1996, No. 714).

35.2.1   What is registrable?

A trade mark is registrable unless it is excluded from registration. A trade mark is a badge of origin or source. Its function is to distinguish goods having one business source from goods having a different business source (per Lord Nicholls in *Scandecor Developments AB* v *Scandecor Marketing AV* [2001] UKHL 21). The mark must therefore be distinctive, in the sense that it must be such that it can provide end-users with a commercial guarantee that the goods to which it is applied originate from a particular source. Accordingly a trade mark is defined as 'any sign capable of being represented graphically which is capable of distinguishing goods or services of one undertaking from those of other undertakings' (TMA 1994, s. 1(1)). The TMA 1994 provides that it may consist of 'words (including personal names), designs, letters, numerals or the shape of goods or their packaging'. Smells, sounds and colours are all potentially capable of being registered provided that they are capable of distinguishing the goods or services of one undertaking from those of another and they are capable of graphic representation. In *Sieckman* v *Deutsches Patent und Markenamt* [2003] EYMR 466 the ECJ laid down seven criteria which must be satisfied for registration of an olfactory mark. Similar criteria are used for sound and colour marks (see *Shield Mark BV* v *Joost Kist* [2003] (unreported) (sounds); *Libertel Groep* v *Benelux Merkenbureau* [2003] (unreported) (colours)). The graphic representation must be clear, precise, self-contained, easily accessible, intelligible, durable and objective. In *Sieckman* it was held that a smell was not represented by a chemical formula, which represented not the smell but the chemical substance producing it, nor by a written description of the smell nor by the deposit of an odour sample. On the other hand in *Vennootschap Onder Firma Senta Aromatic Marketing's Application* [1999] ETMR 429 the registration of the verbal description 'the smell of fresh cut grass' was permitted as a trade mark.

35.2.1.1   The trade marks register

Marks are registered in one of 42 classes—34 for trade marks (used in connection with goods) and 8 for service marks. The classification is not entirely logical and a business may have to register in more than one class for goods which might be thought to be similar.

Although marks can be registered in respect of services it was held under the 1938 Act that a mark could not be registered in respect of the service of retailing goods (*Re Dee Corp plc* [1990] RPC 159) and it was thought that the position had not been changed by the 1994

Act. However, in 2001 the Trade Marks Registry announced a Change of Practice on Retail Services ([2001] RPC 33) in which it indicated that it will henceforth allow registration of service marks for retail services, including those of supermarkets, specialist retailers and catalogue and internet sales. The service in such a case is the bringing together of goods of different kinds or of different manufacturers in such a way as to enable customers conveniently to view and purchase them. In order to qualify for registration the description of the services must include a description of the nature of the particular retail service and the relevant market sector, so that (for instance) an attempt to register a mark for 'retail services' or 'mail order' will not be acceptable. A retailer may, of course, register a mark in respect of a brand of goods sold.

35.2.2 Exclusions from registrability

Certain marks are expressly made unregistrable even though they satisfy the definition of 'trade marks'. They include the following.

(a) Trade marks devoid of any distinctive character (TMA 1994, s. 3(1)(b)).

(b) Trade marks which consist exclusively of signs or indications which may serve, in trade, to designate characteristics of the goods or services including their kind, quality, quantity, intended purpose, value, geographical origin or time of production (TMA 1994, s. 3(1)(c)). Such marks are only unregistrable if they consist exclusively of descriptive words. A mark composed of descriptive words may therefore be registrable if there is some other factor, such as the manner in which the words are represented, which makes it distinctive. Thus the ECJ has held that the mark 'Baby-Dry' was registrable as a trade mark for babies' nappies because, although the words 'baby' and 'dry' were common and indicated the function of the goods, the combination as a whole was syntactically unusual and therefore distinctive (see *Procter & Gamble Co* v *Office for Harmonisation in the Internal Market (Trade Marks and Designs)* Case C-383/99 [2002] Ch 82).

(c) Trade marks which consist exclusively of signs or indications which have become customary in the current language or bona fide and established practices of the trade (TMA 1994, s. 3(1)(d)).

In these cases the mark is, effectively, not inherently distinctive. However, marks in these categories are not incapable of distinguishing goods or services of one undertaking from those of another and a mark in these categories is therefore registrable if it is shown that the mark has become distinctive before the application for registration.

35.2.2.1 Shapes of goods or packaging

The shape of goods, or their packaging, may be registered as a trade mark provided that it is distinctive. It is not necessary that there be some 'capricious addition or embellishment' to make the shape distinctive. However, the shape of goods or packaging is not registrable where that shape is purely functional, as where it results from the nature of the goods themselves, or the shape is necessary to achieve a particular technical result or gives substantial value to the goods (TMA 1994 s. 3(2)), and it makes no difference that the same technical result can be obtained by goods of a different shape. In this case, registration is not permitted in order to prevent one manufacturer obtaining a permanent monopoly over a particular design or shape. Therefore a mark of this type cannot be registered even if the shape of the goods has become distinctive. In *Philips Electronics NV* v *Remington Consumer Products Ltd,* Case C-299/99 [2002] All ER (EC) 634, P had registered as a trade mark a drawing of a three headed shaver, with the heads arranged in a triangular pattern. When R began to market a similar shaver, P claimed that it infringed that trade mark. The ECJ, on a reference from the Court of Appeal, held that the mark was not registrable, as the drawing showed an aspect of the shaver which was necessary to achieve a technical result. It made no difference that the same technical effect could be achieved by other means.

35.2.2.2 Marks contrary to policy or law

A mark is not registrable if it is contrary to public policy or accepted principles of morality, likely to deceive the public or if its use is prohibited by UK or EC law (TMA 1994, s. 3(3) and (4)).

35.2.2.3 National and other emblems

Marks consisting of certain national and international emblems, such as the Royal arms or national flag, are not registrable (TMA 1994, s. 4).

35.2.2.4 Marks similar to earlier registered marks

A mark is not registrable if it is identical or similar to an earlier registered UK or EC trade mark (TMA 1994, s. 5).

(a) A mark may not be registered if it is identical to an earlier mark registered for identical goods or services.

(b) A mark may not be registered if either:

  (i) it is identical to a mark registered for similar goods or services; or

  (ii) it is similar to a mark registered for identical goods or services and, as a result, there is a likelihood of confusion on the part of the public.

(c) In addition a mark which is identical or similar to an earlier mark may not be registered even though it is not for similar or identical goods or services if the earlier mark has a reputation in the UK and the use of the mark would take unfair advantage of, or be detrimental to, the distinctive character of the earlier mark (TMA 1944, s. 5(3)).

Registration may be refused by the Registrar on the grounds of similarity with an existing mark, or the issue may be raised in opposition proceedings (see **35.2.3**). However, if the issue is raised in opposition proceedings, registration will not be refused on these grounds if the prior mark was registered more than five years before publication of the new application unless either (a) within that five year period the earlier mark was put to genuine use as a trade mark in the UK for the goods or services for which it is registered or (b) there are 'proper reasons' for the failure to put it to use (s. 6A).

35.2.3 Application for registration

Application for registration of a UK trade mark is made to the Trade Marks Registry, a division of the Patent Office, in accordance with s. 32 of the TMA 1994 and the Trade Marks Rules 2000. The application form can be downloaded from the Patent Office Website (www.patent.gov.uk) and can be completed by computer, but it must (at present) be returned to the Patent Office in physical form (there is provision for the Registrar to permit filing of documents by electronic means: Trade Mark Rules 2000, r. 69). Application must be made for registration in one or more of the 34 classes for goods and 8 classes for services. The applicant may have to register in more than one class in order to protect all its uses of the mark, but one application can be made for registration in more than one class.

On receipt of the application the registrar considers whether the application satisfies the requirements for registration in order to decide whether or not to accept it. If he decides to accept it he must publish it in the Trade Mark Journal; any person who wishes to oppose the registration may then do so within three months of the publication (s. 38(2); see TMR 2000, r. 13).

If the application succeeds the mark is initially registered for ten years. On expiry it is renewable for periods of ten years on payment of a renewal fee. There is no limit to the number of renewals which can be sought.

35.2.4 Infringement

The registered proprietor of a trade mark has exclusive rights in the mark which are infringed by any person who, in the course of trade, without the proprietor's consent:

(a) uses an identical mark for goods or services which are identical to those for which it is registered;

(b) either

    (i)   uses a mark identical to the registered mark for goods or services which are similar to those in respect of which it is registered; or

    (ii) uses a mark similar to the registered mark for goods or services identical to those in respect of which it is registered

    so that there is a likelihood of confusion on the part of the public;

(c) uses a mark identical to a registered mark which has an established reputation in the UK for goods or services which are not similar to those in respect of which the mark is registered but in such a way as to take unfair advantage of or to be detrimental to the distinctive character or reputation of the mark (TMA 1994, s. 10).

35.2.4.1 Infringement proceedings

Injunctions, damages and accounts of profits may all be awarded in an action for trade mark infringement (TMA 1994, s. 4). The claimant will normally seek an injunction to prevent the defendant continuing to use the mark, together with either damages for any losses caused by the defendant's use of the mark or, where the claimant cannot prove that infringement caused him loss, an account of the profits made by the defendant.

The court may order marks to be removed from goods or, if the mark cannot be removed or erased, order the destruction of the goods (TMA 1994, s. 15).

35.2.4.2 Defences

A number of defences are available to a claim for trade mark infringement.

(a) A's registered trade mark is not infringed by B's use of his own registered mark (TMA 1994, s. 11(1)).

(b) A registered mark is not infringed by a person who, acting in accordance with the 'honest practices in industrial or commercial matters':

    (i)   uses his own name or address (it is not clear if this defence is available to a legal, as opposed to a natural, person, and in *Scandecor Developments AB* v *Scandecor Marketing AV* [2001] UKHL 21 the House of Lords referred the question to the ECJ);

    (ii) uses indications of the kind, quality, intended purpose, geographical origin, time of production etc. of goods or services;

    (iii) uses the mark where it is necessary to indicate the intended purpose of goods or services—for instance as spare parts for the goods in respect of which the mark is registered (s. 1(2)); or

(iv) uses the mark to identify goods or services as those of the registered proprietor or licensee (s. 10(6)); however, such use will be an infringement if it is 'not in accordance with the honest practices in industrial or commercial matters' and without due cause takes unfair advantage of or is detrimental to the distinctive character or repute of the mark. There thus might be an infringement on this basis where, in an advertisement for his own goods, A compares them with B's goods, using B's trade mark, in such a way as to disparage B's goods.

It should be noted that in all of these cases the test is whether the defendant acted in accordance with 'honest practices in industrial or commercial matters' and not whether the defendant acted honestly. The test is therefore objective, not subjective (*European Ltd* v *Economist Newspapers Ltd* [1996] FSR 431; *Cable & Wireless plc* v *British Telecommunications plc* [1998] FSR 383).

In addition the proprietor of a mark cannot complain that his rights are infringed when the mark is used on goods which have been placed on the market within the European Economic Area with his consent. In that case his rights are exhausted when the goods are placed on the market (TMA 1994, s. 12). However, the proprietor may complain of infringement where he has 'legitimate reasons . . . to oppose further dealings in the goods'—for instance where the goods have been altered after being first marketed.

A defendant in infringement proceedings may challenge the validity of the registration of the mark—for instance, on grounds that it should not have been registered (TMA 1984, s.47). If such a challenge succeeds the trade mark will be declared invalid and removed from the register.

35.2.4.3   Threats of proceedings

Threats of infringement proceedings may be used to damage the business of a competitor, for instance the proprietor of a mark might threaten proceedings against retailers selling the goods of a competitor alleging that the goods infringe his mark. The TMA 1994 therefore allows any person aggrieved by a threat of proceedings to bring court proceedings for a declaration that the threats are unjustified and/or an injunction to restrain further threats and/or damages except where the alleged infringement consists of:

(a) the application of the mark to goods or services;

(b) the importation of goods to which the mark has been applied; or

(c) the supply of services under the mark (TMA 1994, s. 21).

Where such an application is made the defendant responsible for the threats must show that the acts complained of in his threat of proceedings would constitute an infringement of his mark. As in the case of other threats of infringement proceeedings a threat made in the context of genuine 'without prejudice' negotiations will not be actionable.

35.2.5   Criminal liability

Trade marks are valuable commercial commodities. They also serve as a badge of origin for consumers and other purchasers. The sale of counterfeit goods which infringe a registered mark therefore damages the trade mark owner by trading on, and possibly damaging, his reputation, and also the consumer who buys the goods believing them to be genuine. Counterfeiting is a particularly serious problem in relation to goods such as computer software, CD's and tapes, videos, perfumes and fashion and designer clothing. Counterfeiting and dealing in counterfeit goods is therefore made subject to criminal penalties. A person commits an offence, if without the trade mark owner's consent and with a view to gain for himself or another or with intent to cause loss to another, he:

(a) applies to goods or their packaging a sign identical to, or likely to be confused with, a registered mark;

(b) deals with such goods by way of sale, hire or distribution; or

(c) has such goods in his possession for sale, hire or distribution (TMA, s. 92).

Further offences are committed by any person who applies a sign identical to, or likely to be confused with, a registered mark to material intended to be used *inter alia* for labelling, packaging or advertising goods, or has such material in his possession, or who makes or possesses an article specially designed or adapted for making copies of a sign identical to, or likely to be confused with, a registered mark. The section is intended to deal with the problem of counterfeit goods so that in each case an offence is committed only if the goods to which the mark is applied are goods in respect of which the mark is registered or the mark has a reputation in the UK of which the use would take advantage *or* to which the use would be detrimental.

EXAMPLE

Phil's Fashions of Fulchester has registered the trade mark 'Felipe'. The men's clothing shop Knott's Landing buys from Natty Nigel's counterfeit clothing bearing labels marked 'Felipe' and offers it for sale. An offence is committed by both Knott's Landing and Natty Nigel's. An offence is also committed by the person who supplied the counterfeit clothing to Natty Nigel's, by the person who applied the 'Felipe' mark to the clothing and possibly by the person who produced the labels or the machine used to manufacture the labels.

A defendant charged with an offence under s. 92 has a defence if he shows that he believed on reasonable grounds that the manner of the use of the mark would not be an infringement of the registered mark. However, this is a very limited defence. It has been held that it is no defence for the defendant to show that he did not intend to infringe the mark, or that he believed that no trade mark was registered (*Torbay DC* v *Singh* [1999] 2 Cr App R 451).

Responsibility for enforcing TMA, s. 92 is in the hands of local authority Trading Standards Officers. The offence may be tried either summarily or on indictment. If tried on indictment it is punishable with an unlimited fine and/or up to ten years' imprisonment (TMA, s. 92(6)). Moreover, where an offence is committed by a partner in a firm, every other partner may also be prosecuted individually, unless he can show that he was ignorant of the offence or tried to prevent its commission. Where an offence is committed by a body corporate an offence is committed by every director, secretary or other officer with whose consent or connivance the offence was committed (TMA, s. 101). In addition, a court may order the seizure and destruction of counterfeit goods, including where there is no prosecution (TMA, s. 97).

35.2.6   Removal from the register

The registration of a mark may be revoked on a number of grounds, including that it has not been used within the period of five years following its registration, that without proper reason it has not been used for a continuous period of five years or that as a result of the acts or inactivity of the proprietor it has become a common name for goods or services in respect of which it is registered (TMA 1984, s. 46). Any person may apply to the registrar or to the court for a registered mark to be revoked. A business which wishes to register a mark may find that a similar mark is already registered for similar goods; however, if the mark is not used, he may apply under these provisions to have the existing registration revoked.

Proprietors of registered marks should be aware of these provisions: a registered mark is a valuable piece of commercial property; if it is revoked it cannot be relied on against any competitor. The proprietor should be particularly astute to protect his mark against unauthorised use which may lead to its becoming a generic word for a type of goods or services.

35.2.7   Dealings in trade marks

The registered proprietor of a mark can deal with the mark as property. Dealings with trade marks, including by way of assignment, or the granting of a licence or charge, must be registered in accordance with the Act (TMA 1994, s.25).

35.2.7.1   Assignment

A mark can be assigned (TMA 1994, s. 24), either for all or some of the goods in respect of which it is registered, either absolutely or by way of security. An assignment must be in writing, signed by the assignor. A charge may also be granted over a registered mark in the same way as over other personal property.

On a sale of a business the buyer will normally wish to take an assignment of the seller's trade marks and if a business is transferred by a sale of assets the buyer's legal adviser should take instructions on the question of transfer of any trade marks.

35.2.7.2   Licences

The proprietor may license others to use his trade mark, and this is commonly done, so that goods sold under a familiar trade mark may be manufactured 'under licence'. A licensee may call on his licensor to bring proceedings against any person infringing the mark so as to affect the licensee's interests.

An exclusive licence prevents any person, including the licensor, using the mark in the manner authorised by the licence (TMA 1994, s. 29). An exclusive licence may give the licensee the right to bring proceedings in respect of infringement of the mark (TMA 1994, s. 31).

A licence must be in writing, signed by or on behalf of the licensor. It will be binding on the licensor's successors in title unless it otherwise provides.

Under the 1938 Act it was held that a mark could not be registered where the applicant's sole intention was to license the use of the mark by others, rather than to use it himself (*American Greeting Corpn's Application* [1984] FSR 199) so that trade mark law could not be used to protect character merchandising. However, under the 1994 Act there seems to be nothing to prevent a mark being registered in such a case. One of the grounds on which a registered mark may be revoked is that as a result of the use made of the mark by the proprietor, or with his consent, it is liable to mislead the public. In *Scandecor Developments AB* v *Scandecor Marketing AV* [2001] UKHL 21 it was argued that where a mark owner granted a licensee a bare exclusive licence to use its mark, the mark, became liable to mislead and should be revoked. Such a licence would permit the licensee to apply the mark to goods which did not originate from the owner of the mark, without the mark owner exercising any control over the quality of goods to which it was applied. The House of Lords inclined to the view however that in modern circumstances such use was unlikely to mislead the public, so that there is nothing objectionable in the grant of such licences. However, it declined to express a concluded view and referred the question to the ECJ.

35.2.8 Community trade marks

The protection given by registration of a national trade mark is geographically restricted to the territory for which the mark is registered. Within the European Union this territorial aspect of national trade mark protection was felt to be inconsistent with the objectives of the European Single Market. Although the 1989 EC Trade Mark Directive is intended to bring a large degree of harmonisation to the trade mark laws of Member States, some anomalies remain. Thus, for instance, a business seeking trade mark protection in more than one Member State must still seek registration in each state, or make use of the Madrid Agreement procedure to obtain recognition of a domestically registered mark (see **35.2**) and it is still possible for a business to register different marks for the same goods in different states or for different businesses to own similar marks registered in different Member States.

In order to try and overcome such problems it was decided to establish a Community Trade Mark system and in 1993 such a system was set up by the Community Trade Mark Regulation (Reg. 40/94, 20.12.93). The Regulation established a Community Trade Mark Office (CTMO) in Alicante (officially known as the Office for Harmonisation in the Internal Market (Trade Marks and Designs)) to which trade mark owners can apply to obtain registration of a community trade mark (CTM), which automatically gives protection for the mark in all Member States of the EU.

The substantive law governing what marks may be registered and the rights of the holder of a registered CTM is broadly similar to that contained in the EU Trade Marks Directive and therefore broadly similar to domestic law, discussed above. Thus decisions on the interpretation of the Regulation will also be authoritative as to the proper interpretation of the Directive, and vice versa. The procedure for application for a CTM is laid down in the Regulation and rules made under it. An application for a CTM can be made by a national of an EU Member State, a national of any state party to the Paris Convention for the Protection of Intellectual Property, a person domiciled in an EU Member or Paris Convention State or a national of any country which gives reciprocal protection to the trade marks of nationals of EU Member States (Art. 5). Application can be made either to the CTMO or through the domestic Trade Mark Registry of any EU Member State (Art. 25). An application for a CTM can be made in any of the official languages of the EU (Art. 115), but the same mark must be registered for the whole of the territory of the EU. Thus, for instance, if a business wants to register an invented word as a CTM it must use the same word in all states of the EU. This may cause difficulties if (say) the invented word has an unpleasant or unacceptable meaning in the language of one of the Member States: if a mark would be unregistrable—for instance because it is such as to deceive the public as to the nature, quality or origin of the goods—in any state of the EU it may not be registered as a CTM (Art. 7). Similarly, a mark which is merely descriptive, say of the function of the goods, in any one of the languages used in the Community, is unregistrable as a Community Trade Mark (see *Procter & Gamble Co* v *Office for Harmonisation in the Internal Market (Trade Marks and Designs)* Case C-383/99 [2002] Ch 82.)

The grounds on which registration may be refused are broadly similar to those applicable under ss. 3–5 of the TMA 1994 (see **35.2.2**) but registration of a CTM will not necessarily be refused on grounds of the mark's similarity to an existing mark. Instead where an application is made for registration of a mark identical or similar to an existing mark, the owner of the prior mark will be notified of the application and given the opportunity to oppose its registration (Art. 8).

If registration is granted, the mark is registered in the first instance for ten years, although the registration may be renewed for further periods of ten years on payment of a fee (Art. 46). The mark must be put into genuine use as a trade mark within the EU within five years of registration, failing which the registration may be revoked (Art. 15). It seems that it may not be enough for a mark registered as a CTM to be put into use in only one Member State (although there is provision for a registration of a mark as a CTM to be converted into a domestic registration).

The CTMO is required to publish a Bulletin giving details of marks registered and an Official Journal containing official guidance on its procedures and decisions (Art. 85). As yet, however, there is little evidence of its practices.

Registration of a CTM gives the owner of the mark protection throughout the EU. However, enforcement of the owner's rights is a matter for domestic law so that any litigation to enforce a CTM must be taken before the domestic courts of the country where the defendant is domiciled or established (Arts 90–101), and each Member State is required to designate courts to hear cases relating to CTMs. In England and Wales the High Court has been designated as 'Community Trade Mark Court'. If the defendant has no domicile or establishment in the EU the domestic courts of the Member State where the claimant is domiciled or established have jurisdiction. If neither party has a domicile or establishment within the EU the Spanish trade mark courts have jurisdiction.

A CTM is an item of property and may be exploited as such, including by transfer (Art. 17), licensing (Art. 22) and use as security (Art. 19). The Regulation contains provisions dealing with some aspects of the exploitation of a CTM; thus, for instance, an assignment of a CTM is not effective unless in writing, signed by the parties, and registered at the CTMO. However, except insofar as covered by the express provisions of the Regulation, the dealings in a CTM are governed by the law of the Member State where the proprietor of the mark is domiciled or established (Art. 16).

A business which wishes to register a trade mark for use in more than one Member State of the EU therefore now has a choice. It may apply in for registration of a CTM, either in Alicante or via its own national Registry. In that case it must register the same mark for the whole of the EU and must therefore ensure that the mark is acceptable in all Member States of the Union. Alternatively it may register a mark in its national registry and then seek registration under the Madrid Agreement procedure in other Member States where it wishes to use the mark; or it can make separate applications in each State where it wishes to use the mark, in which case it will be possible to amend the mark for national conditions and, if desired, register a different mark in each State (for instance, to take account of differences in language). The various advantages and disadvantages of each course of action may have to be weighed carefully and the business may well need specialist advice from a trade mark agent on how best to proceed.

35.3 Passing off

The common law protects trade reputation via the tort of passing off. The tort is flexible and its scope has developed over the years, taking account of developments in the market place. It has been said that 'an underlying principle is the maintenance of what is currently regarded as fair trading' (Laddie J in *Irvine* v *Talksport Ltd* [2002] EWHC 367 (Ch); [2002] 2 All ER 414).

35.3.1 Nature of the tort

The tort is committed when the defendant supplies goods or services and presents them as the claimant's goods or services, for instance, by using a name similar to the claimant's brand name or imitating the packaging or 'get-up' of the claimant's goods (see e.g. *Reckitt*

& *Colman Products Ltd* v *Borden Inc* [1990] 1 All ER 873). A person who supplies counterfeit goods thus commits the tort. In such a case the defendant effectively trades on the claimant's goodwill and may divert business away from the claimant. However, the tort may also be committed in several other ways.

(a) The defendant claims to be the manufacturer/supplier of goods or services actually manufactured/supplied by the claimant. In that case the defendant claims the claimant's reputation.

(b) The defendant advertises his goods in such a way as to damage the claimant (see, e.g. *McDonalds Hamburgers Ltd* v *Burgerking (UK) Ltd* [1986] FSR 45).

(c) The defendant supplies or offers goods or services in such a way as to make it appear that his offer is sanctioned by or connected with the claimant. In *Associated Newspapers Holdings Ltd* v *Insert Media* [1991] 3 All ER 535, the defendants arranged for advertising leaflets to be inserted in newspapers published by the plaintiffs, but without the plaintiffs' permission. It was held that this was passing off: the defendant's actions made it appear that their advertising was approved by the plaintiffs. This form of passing off may also provide protection for character merchandising (see *Mirage Studios* v *Counterfeit Clothing Ltd* [1991] FSR 145; attempts to protect character merchandising through passing off had been unsuccessful in earlier cases).

35.3.2   Definitions of passing off

There are several judicial definitions of passing off. According to Lord Diplock in *Erven Warnink BV* v *Townend & Sons (Hull) Ltd* [1979] AC 731 (the *Advocaat case*) the tort is committed where:

(a) a misrepresentation (which may be express or implicit)

(b) is made by the defendant in the course of a trade or business carried on by him

(c) to prospective customers or ultimate consumers of his goods or services

(d) which misrepresentation is calculated to injure the goodwill of the claimant ('calculated to' here means 'foreseeably likely to') and

(e) does in fact cause damage to the claimant or, where the claimant seeks a *quia timet* injunction to restrain a passing off, is likely to cause such damage if the injunction is refused.

More simply, Lord Oliver in *Reckitt & Colman Products Ltd* v *Borden Inc* [1990] 1 All ER 873 said that in order to succeed the claimant must show:

(a) that he has established a reputation or goodwill in respect of his goods or services, by association with their get-up, which is recognised as distinctive;

(b) that the defendant has made a misrepresentation to the public leading them to believe that his goods are those of the claimant; and

(c) that as a result the claimant has suffered, or is likely to suffer, damage.

35.3.2.1   Requirements for a passing off claim

Reading these definitions together, and considering other cases, it is possible to identify the following requirements for the claimant to succeed in a passing off action.

(a) Both claimant and defendant must be in trade or business: it is not passing off for the defendant to represent that his goods are (say) endorsed by a private individual.

(b) The claimant must have an established goodwill or reputation. Passing off thus provides less protection than registration of a trade mark.

(c) That goodwill must be damaged by the defendant. The damage may take several forms, including:

(i)   D stealing P's market;

(ii)   D damaging P's reputation by supplying an inferior product or service;

(iii) D undercutting the exclusivity of P's reputation;

(iv)   D depriving P of the opportunity to expand his business;

(v)   D falsely claims that his product or service is endorsed by P.

The circumstances in which a court will intervene by injunction to restrain passing off were reconsidered by the Court of Appeal in *British Telecommunications plc* v *One in a Million Ltd* [1998] 4 All ER 476. The Court concluded that an injunction will be granted in three types of case:

(a) where actual passing off is established or threatened;

(b) where the defendant is a joint tortfeasor with another in passing off, actual or threatened;

(c) where the defendant has equipped himself or intends to equip another with an instrument of fraud in which case the court will intervene on a *quia timet* basis.

In *One in a Million Ltd* the defendants had registered Internet domain names identical or similar to those of several well known commercial organisations (e.g. 'sainsbury's.com', 'marksandspencer.com', 'bt.org'.) The Court of Appeal held that the registration of such names amounted to a representation to the public that the person registered was connected with the name and thus to passing off. In addition it held that the registration of a domain name would amount to the creation of 'an instrument of fraud' which could be restrained by injunction either if the name, by reason of its similarity to that of an existing business, would inherently lead to passing off *or* even if the name would not inherently lead to passing off, if it was produced to enable passing off to be committed, was adapted to be used for passing off or was likely to be used fraudulently.

35.3.2.2 Geographical limitations

The scope of the claimant's claim may be limited by the scope of his goodwill. Where the claimant has a reputation in a particular area, or in a particular field of activity, he may be unable to sue if the defendant uses a similar business name etc. in a different area, either because the defendant's actions cause no confusion and therefore do not amount to a misrepresentation, or because the claimant's goodwill is not damaged by the defendant's activities.

EXAMPLE

If Phil's Fashions Ltd is a small but exclusive outlet, based in Sheffield, it cannot use passing off to prevent another trader opening a shop called 'Phil's Phashions' in Weston-super-Mare.

However, if Phil's Fashions Ltd is known nationally, for instance, because the 'Phil's Fashions' label is sold through other shops, or because its goods are available by mail order, or even because they are well known because of their exclusivity, even if its only retail outlet is in Sheffield, it may be able to bring a passing off action against the shop in Weston.

A claimant who has only a localised reputation may nevertheless succeed in an action against a business trading in another area if the defendant's activities prevent the claimant expanding into that area.

35.3.2.3 Common field of activity

Some cases suggest that the claimant will only succeed where he and the defendant have a 'common field of activity', so that where the claimant's reputation relates to a particular product he may not be able to prevent a defendant marketing a totally different product under a similar name (see, e.g. *McCulloch* v *May* (1948) 65 RPC 68; *Granada Group Ltd* v *Ford Motor Co. Ltd* [1973] RPC 79; *Nationwide Building Society* v *Nationwide Estate Agents Ltd* [1987] FSR 579). However, recent cases have doubted the need for a common field of activity, so that a celebrity sportsman succeeded in a claim for passing off against a radio station which falsely represented that its service was endorsed by the sportsman (*Irvine* v *Talksport Ltd* [2002] EWHC 367 (Ch); [2002] 2 All ER 414; [2003] EWCA Civ 423; [2003] 2 All ER 881). It is clear that, if the claimant's reputation is sufficiently well known, he may be able to bring a passing off action to restrain the marketing of even a wholly dissimilar product under a similar name (*Lego Systems* v *Lego Lemelstrich* [1983] FSR 155).

35.3.2.4 Temporal connection

The claimant must have a current reputation and goodwill at the time of the defendant's actions. Therefore if he has abandoned a brand name he cannot use passing off to prevent another trader using it.

35.3.2.5 Confusion of the public

The claimant must generally show that the defendant's actions/misrepresentations have caused confusion in the minds of the public. The claimant must adduce evidence of such confusion, and evidence of public surveys may be admissible for this purpose. In the absence of evidence of such confusion, however, the claim will fail (see, e.g.: *Arsenal Football Club plc* v *Reed* [2001] RPC 922).

35.3.3 Defences

A defendant will normally contest a passing off case by denying one or more of the elements of the tort: for instance, by claiming that the claimant has no goodwill, or that his activities have caused no damage to the claimant's goodwill.

He may also defend the claim on the grounds that the claimant has acquiesced in his activities, or that he is merely making bona fide use of his own name or the name of his business.

35.3.4 Remedies

The normal remedies in a passing off action are an award of damages and/or an injunction to restrain the defendant's activities. The court may also make an order for delivery up and destruction of offending articles in pursuance of its inherent jurisdiction.

35.4 Malicious falsehood

In some cases the claimant may be able to use the tort of malicious falsehood to restrain certain forms of unfair competition. The elements of the tort are that:

(a) the defendant made a false statement

(b) maliciously and

(c) that statement has caused the claimant economic loss.

Thus the tort may be committed if e.g. the defendant advertises his goods and makes disparaging comments about the claimant's goods. However, malicious falsehood will generally be less attractive to the claimant than passing off because of the need for the claimant to prove malice.

35.5 Summary

Having completed this chapter you should:

- understand the essentials of the trade mark system and the law of passing off, and the relationship between the two;
- know and be able to advise on what is registrable as a trade mark and the necessary steps to be taken to obtain registration;
- in particular be able to advise on the relative merits of seeking a national or Community trade mark;
- know and be able to advise on what constitutes infringement of a trade mark, the remedies for infringement and the possible defences to an infringement claim;
- be able to advise on the commercial exploitation of trade marks through licensing and assignment;
- know and be able to advise on what constitutes passing off, including what must be established to bring a claim, the defences available to a passing off claim and the remedies available on a successful claim.

Part IX

Commercial dispute resolution

Commercial arbitration

36.1 Introduction

No matter how well planned a transaction or comprehensively drafted a contract, disputes arise. Parties, in negotiating commercial transactions, should therefore be mindful of this and include in their contracts dispute resolution mechanisms. Whether such mechanisms are invoked will depend on the nature of the dispute: some breaches of contract may be too important or too costly to be left unchallenged; however, if the breach is minor the innocent party might be best advised not to get involved in costly and time-consuming proceedings.

The main forms of commercial dispute resolution are:

(a) negotiation;

(b) arbitration;

(c) litigation; and

(d) alternative dispute resolution mechanisms, such as, conciliation, mediation and mini-trials.

Negotiation should always be the first step in resolving a dispute. As a form of self-help, the details of the transaction in dispute remain private and the individual parties to the transaction remain in control of the process. However, where a negotiated settlement cannot be reached, recourse to other mechanisms may be necessary. Each method listed has its own distinct features and advantages. A commercial lawyer should be aware of these in order to advise a client in choosing the mechanism most suitable to his circumstances and needs. In this Part, we will concentrate on the use of arbitration proceedings and litigation to resolve commercial disputes, though it should be remembered that a negotiated settlement is still an option even after other dispute resolution mechanisms are set in motion (see **36.3.4.4**).

In this chapter:

- by way of introduction we
    - define arbitration;
    - outline its advantages; and
    - consider the different classifications of arbitration.
- we concentrate on arbitrations under the Arbitration Act 1996 and examine
    - the arbitration agreement;
    - the role of arbitrators and the arbitral tribunal;
    - arbitral proceedings;
    - the award and its enforcement;

- court intervention at the various stages of the process.
- with regard to international arbitration we consider
  - the impact of UNCITRAL;
  - the role of the ICC;
  - the enforcement of arbitration awards internationally under the New York Convention.

36.2   What is arbitration?

Arbitration is a process whereby parties voluntarily refer their disputes to an impartial third person, an arbitrator, selected by them, for a decision based on evidence and arguments to be presented before him. The parties agree in advance that the arbitrator's determination, the award, will be final and binding upon them. This definition highlights some of the salient features that distinguish arbitration from other means of dispute resolution:

(a) it is a consensual process which offers finality;

(b) it is a private process, hearings are in private and awards are usually not published; and,

(c) it offers parties the opportunity to select their own 'judge' or arbitrator(s), often on the basis of some expert skill or knowledge but, like a High Court judge, the arbitrator must be impartial and independent, and the procedures followed by both can be very similar.

36.2.1   What are its advantages?

Arbitration has, for many years, been the main form of dispute resolution in certain fields of business activity such as construction, commodity sales and shipping. Arbitration is said to avoid many of the drawbacks of litigation and to offer the following advantages:

(a) speed;

(b) costs savings;

(c) freedom to choose the arbitrator, who may have technical qualifications or trade experience;

(d) power to control the time and place of the proceedings;

(e) absence of publicity;

(f) flexible procedures; and

(g) finality of the award.

However, this is not always the case: arbitrations can be time-consuming and costly (for instance, with ICC arbitrations (see **36.4.3**) there is an administration fee and the arbitrator's fees and expenses to be paid, and because these are calculated with reference to the amount in dispute, the total bill can be substantial). There are opportunities to appeal an arbitrator's award before a court of law, negativing the finality of the award, and, in many circumstances, the arbitration tribunal, having limited powers, may have to rely on the assistance of the court (see **36.3** generally).

36.2.2   Types of arbitration

Arbitration can be either domestic or international; and institutional or ad hoc.

36.2.2.1   Domestic

An arbitration may be termed domestic where all the relevant factors in the dispute, i.e. subject matter, domicile of the parties, place of arbitration, applicable law, etc., converge in a single place.

36.2.2.2   International

The more diverse these connecting factors, the more likely that the arbitration will be international (see **36.4**).

36.2.2.3   Ad hoc

Ad hoc arbitration is conducted under rules of procedure that are adopted for the specific dispute. These rules can be:

(a) drawn from an international organisation, such as UNCITRAL'S Arbitration Rules 1976; or,

(b) drafted by the parties, the arbitration tribunal, or both, thus meeting the exact needs of the dispute.

In effect, an infrastructure for the arbitration process must be designed. Business persons who are wary of institutional arbitration because of its formality, or apparent lack of neut-rality will often prefer ad hoc arbitration for these reasons. Ad hoc arbitration depends entirely on the parties' goodwill and is time-consuming in terms of establishing the infrastructure which already exists in institutional arbitration.

36.2.2.4   Institutional

Institutional arbitration, on the other hand, is administered by one of the many specialised arbitration institutions under their own arbitration rules. In the UK there is the London Court of International Arbitration (LCIA), in Paris, the International Chamber of Commerce (ICC), while in the USA there is the American Arbitration Association (AAA), to name but a few. This method has the advantage that there is a pre-drafted set of rules under which the arbitration will be conducted and each institution provides experienced and trained staff to administer the arbitration. However, institutional arbitrations can be expensive and the rules, for example as to time limits, can be inflexible. The matters dealt with by such rules tend to include:

(a) request for arbitration;

(b) response by respondents;

(c) the arbitral tribunal;

(d) communications between the parties and the tribunal;

(e) conduct of the proceedings;

(f) submission of written statements and documents;

(g) place of arbitration;

(h) language of arbitration;

(i) party representatives;

(j) hearings;

(k) witnesses;

(l) experts appointed by the tribunal;

(m) additional powers of the tribunal;

(n) jurisdiction of the tribunal;

(o) deposits and security;

(p) the award;

(q) correction of the award and additional costs;

(r) costs;

(s) exclusion of liability; and

(t) general rules.

Source: Index to the London Court of Arbitration Rules.

36.3 English arbitration

The Arbitration Act 1996, is described in its preamble as an Act to restate and improve the law relating to arbitration. Prior to its coming into force on 31 January 1997, arbitration in English law was governed by the Arbitration Acts 1950, 1975 and 1979. The 1996 Act repeals Part I of the 1950 Act, formerly the principal Act governing arbitration (Part II dealing with the Geneva Convention—the forerunner to the New York Convention—remains in force), and the whole of the 1975 and 1979 Acts, which, respectively, gave effect to the New York Convention on the enforcement of certain arbitration awards and restricted the availability of judicial review of arbitration awards in certain circumstances (see Arbitration Act 1996, s. 107 and schs 3 and 4) and the Consumer Arbitration Agreements Act 1988. The new Act is intended to improve English arbitration law: it follows the structure and frequently the wording of the UNCITRAL Model Law. It was passed after lengthy consultation and in response to fears that existing law was not meeting the needs of the business community and that, as a result, London and other arbitration centres in the UK would lose business to other jurisdictions where party autonomy was more respected and court interference was kept to a minimum. It restates many of the provisions from earlier legislation, and places some established common law rules on a statutory basis. However, it also makes a number of significant changes to the prior law.

The 1996 Act attempts, among other things, to reinforce party autonomy; to facilitate institutional arbitration; and to minimise court intervention. These aims are reflected in s. 1 which sets out three general principles:

- the object of arbitration is to obtain a fair resolution to disputes without delay or expense;

- parties should be free to agree how their dispute should be resolved; and

- the court should not intervene, except as provided for in the legislation.

The 1996 Act is in four parts: Part I, our main concern, covers the law of arbitration pursuant to an arbitration agreement; Part II covers various other matters including modifications of Part I in relation to domestic arbitration agreements; Part III deals with the recognition and enforcement of certain foreign arbitration awards (basically a re-enactment of the 1975 Act); and Part IV contains the general provisions including provisions on repeals and commencement.

The 1996 Act (apart from ss. 85–87 which modify Part I in relation to domestic arbitration agreements) was brought into effect from 31 January 1997 (see Arbitration Act 1996 (Commencement No. 1) Order 1996, SI 1996, No. 3146; see also the Civil Procedure Rules 1998, Part 62 and the Practice Direction on Arbitrations (which replace Order 73) (see **37.2**).

It is worth bearing in mind, however, that where the 1996 Act merely restates the earlier legal position, pre-1996 Act case law will remain authoritative. *References in **36.3** are to the 1996 Act unless stated otherwise.*

36.3.1   The arbitration agreement

The foundation stone of modern commercial arbitration is an agreement between the parties to submit any dispute between them to arbitration. Part I of the 1996 Act contains the rules of arbitration pursuant to an arbitration agreement and applies to arbitral proceedings commenced on or after the date of commencement of the Act, regardless of when the arbitration agreement was made (s. 84). The provisions of Part I apply where the seat of the arbitration is in England and Wales or Northern Ireland (s. 2). The 'seat of the arbitration' is defined in s. 3 as the juridical seat (not necessarily the geographical area where the hearings take place) designated by the parties, or their delegate, including the tribunal, or, in the absence of any designation, having regard to the parties' agreement and all the relevant circumstances.

Section 4 provides that certain sections of Part I (listed in sch. 1) are of mandatory effect, so that the parties cannot contract out of them. Other provisions are non-mandatory allowing the parties to make their own arrangement by agreement (including by choosing a set of institutional rules) but providing fall-back or default rules where there is no such arrangement.

36.3.1.1   Submission or arbitration clause

The phrase 'arbitration agreement' can comprise:

(a) a submission (*compromis*)—an agreement to submit an existing dispute to arbitration; or

(b) an arbitration clause (*clause compromissoire*)—an agreement to submit future disputes to arbitration.

A submission is usually a very detailed document concerning the constitution of the arbitration tribunal, the procedure to be followed etc., whereas an arbitration clause often consists of a brief phrase:

All disputes arising in connection with this contract shall be finally settled by reference to arbitration in London: English law shall apply.

The Arbitration Act 1996 applies to both types of agreements: s. 6(1) provides that an arbitration agreement means an agreement to submit to arbitration present or future disputes (whether they are contractual or not).

36.3.1.2   Form

While a valid oral arbitration agreement may exist at common law, Part I of the 1996 Act only applies where the agreement is in writing (s. 5(1), this was also the case under the prior law). 'In writing' is given a broad definition and includes an agreement recorded by any means (s. 5(6)). This would include the use of fax, video, e-mail or voice mail to record the agreement, or indeed any future means of recording yet to be developed. Section 5(2) provides that there is an agreement in writing where:

(a) the agreement is made in writing whether or not it is signed by the parties;

(b) the agreement is made by exchange of communication in writing; or

(c) the agreement is evidenced in writing.

Furthermore, where the parties agree otherwise than in writing to arbitration terms which are in writing, there is a written agreement (s. 5(3)). An example of this is given in the DTI's Notes on Clauses where an oral salvage agreement is made by the master of a ship in distress incorporating Lloyd's Salvage Rules which contain an arbitration clause. Reference in an agreement to a written form of arbitration clause also constitutes an arbitration agreement so long as the reference is such as to make the clause part of the agreement, i.e, the reference is express and clear to ensure incorporation (s. 6(2); see further *Twigg Hansa Insurance* v *Equitas* [1998] 2 Lloyd's Rep 439).

An arbitration agreement in a contract with a consumer, meaning a natural or legal person (s. 90), is subject to the Unfair Terms in Consumer Contracts Regulations 1999 and is conclusively presumed to be unfair, where it relates to a claim which does not exceed £5,000 (s. 91 and the Unfair Arbitration Agreements (Specified Amount) Order 1999 (SI 1999, No. 2167)). It will therefore not be binding on the consumer (see **3.4.4.2**).

36.3.1.3   Scope of the arbitration clause

The arbitration agreement determines what disputes can be submitted to arbitration and the scope of the arbitrator's jurisdiction: the arbitrator must not exceed the power the parties have conferred upon him. Two questions need to be addressed in this regard:

(a) can the arbitrator decide the extent of his own jurisdiction?; and

(b) if the arbitration clause is contained in the contract, can the arbitrator decide whether that contract is void *ab initio*, due, for example, to mistake or illegality?

Can the arbitrator decide the extent of his own jurisdiction?

Prior to the 1996 Act, the extent to which an arbitrator could pronounce on his own jurisdiction in English law was unclear (*Dalmia Dairy Industries Ltd* v *National Bank of Pakistan* [1978] 2 Lloyd's Rep 223; *Christopher Brown Ltd* v *Genossenschaft Oesterreichischer Waldbesitzer Holzwirtschaftsbetriebe* [1954] 1 QB 8) but s. 30 of the 1996 Act now provides that unless otherwise agreed by the parties, the arbitral tribunal may rule on questions relating to its own substantive jurisdiction as to:

(a) whether there is a valid arbitration agreement;

(b) whether the arbitral tribunal is properly constituted; and

(c) what matters have been submitted to arbitration in accordance with the agreement.

Sections 31 and 73, both mandatory provisions, when combined require parties with objections to the substantive jurisdiction of the tribunal to make them known as early as possible in the proceedings. For instance, s. 31(1) specifies that an objection to the tribunal's lack of substantive jurisdiction *at the outset of proceedings* must be raised by a party not later than the time he takes the first steps in the proceedings to contest the merits of any matter in relation to which he challenges the tribunal's jurisdiction, although the appointment, or participation in the appointment, of an arbitrator does not preclude raising an objection. Similarly, s. 31(2) requires that any objection *during the course of the arbitral proceedings* to the tribunal exceeding its jurisdiction must be made as soon as possible after the matter alleged to be beyond its jurisdiction is raised. Section 31(3) softens the effect of these requirements somewhat by stating that the tribunal may admit an objection later than specified above. The effect of not raising the objection in time is set out in s. 73, which provides, *inter alia*, that a party who takes part or continues to take part in arbitral proceedings without making an objection to the substantive jurisdiction of the tribunal within the time specified in s. 31(1) or (2) may not raise that objection later before the tribunal or a court, unless he shows that at the time when he took part or continued to take part in the proceedings he did not know or could not with reasonable diligence have discovered the grounds for the objection. In effect, he will, by his conduct, be treated as having waived his right to object.

Section 32, also of mandatory effect, provides for an application to the court by a party to the proceedings to determine any preliminary question about substantive jurisdiction (this right to object can be lost under s. 73). A court will not consider an application under this section unless it is made:

(a) with the written agreement of all the parties, or

(b) with the permission of the tribunal and the court is satisfied that:

  (i)   the determination of the question is likely to produce substantial savings in costs,

  (ii) the application was made without delay, and

  (iii) there is good reason why the matter should be decided by the court.

Leave to appeal will only be given where the court is satisfied that the question involves a point of law which is of general importance or is one which, for some other special reason, should be considered by the Court of Appeal.

Can an arbitrator rule on the validity and existence of the contract?

In relation to the question whether the arbitrator can pronounce on the existence or validity of the contract, historically a distinction was drawn between the *initial* and the *continued* existence of the contract. Where the issue was one of the *continued* existence of the contract—i.e., where the contract did originally exist but for some reason, for example, repudiation or frustration, the contract had come to an end—the approach of the courts was to treat the arbitration clause as separate from the rest of the contract, allowing the arbitrator to make a decision about the continued existence of the contract. However, the traditional view was that an arbitrator could not make a binding award about the *initial* existence of the contract: if there was no contract to begin with, an arbitration clause in this non-existent contract could not empower the arbitrator to decide on the initial validity of the contract. More recent case law however, suggests that a suitably worded clause can be severed from the rest of the contract thereby allowing the arbitrator to deal even with issues of initial validity (see *Harbour Assurance Co. (UK) Ltd* v *Kansa General International Insurance Co. Ltd* [1993] QB 701).

Section 7 of the Arbitration Act 1996 removes the previous common law distinction between initial and continued existence of the contract and simply provides that, unless otherwise agreed by the parties, an arbitration agreement which forms part of another agreement (whether written or not) shall not be regarded as invalid, non-existent or ineffective because the other agreement is invalid, or did not come into existence or has become ineffective. Effectively, therefore, the legislation treats the arbitration agreement as distinct and separate from the remainder of the agreement, and capable of being severed from the remainder of the agreement. In practice, whether the arbitration clause can be severed from the main contract, to determine the initial or continued existence of the contract, is essentially a matter of construction dependent on the parties' intention and wording of the clause. A formulation often used and which has been recognised by the courts as being broad enough to cover a wide range of possibilities is that: 'all disputes or differences arising out of or in connection with the contract shall be submitted to arbitration' (see for examples *Woolf* v *Collis Removal Services* [1948] 1 KB 11; *Ashville Investments Ltd* v *Elmer Contractors Ltd* [1989] QB 488; *Ethiopian Oilseeds and Pulses Export Corporation* v *Rio del Mar Foods Inc.* [1990] 1 Lloyd's Rep 86).

36.3.1.4   Domestic or non-domestic

An arbitration agreement can be either domestic or non-domestic. This distinction, which existed under the earlier legislation, was provided for in the 1996 Act, but the rel-evant provisions have not been brought into force. Hence, domestic and non-domestic arbitrations are now treated alike in English law. A dual regime would not comply with EC law because it would treat nationals of other EC Member States less favourably than UK nationals.

36.3.1.5   Getting the arbitration started—staying legal proceedings

Where, despite the existence of an arbitration clause, both parties agree to pursue their claims through the courts, the clause is overidden by this new agreement and rendered redundant: it cannot be enforced. Where, however, one party, in opposition to the arbitration agreement, commences litigation, the courts have the power, at the request of the other party, to stay the litigation in order to give effect to the arbitration agreement (ss. 9–11: mandatory provisions). Section 9(1) provides that a party to an arbitration agreement against whom legal proceedings are brought (by way of claim or counterclaim) in respect of a matter which under the arbitration agreement should be referred to arbitration may (upon notice to the other parties to the proceedings) apply to the court in which the proceedings have been brought to stay the proceedings so far as they concern that matter. Section 9(4) states that the court *shall*, i.e., must, grant the stay unless satisfied that the arbitration agreement is null and void, inoperative, or incapable of being performed (for consideration of the meaning of these terms see *The Rena K* [1979] QB 377; *Metal Scrap Trade Corporation Ltd* v *Kate Shipping Co. Ltd* [1988] 1 WLR 115; *Government of Sierra Leone* v *Marmaro Shipping Co. Ltd* [1989] 2 Lloyd's Rep 130; *Finnish Marine Insurance Co. Ltd* v *Protective National Insurance Co.* [1990] 1 QB 1078; and *Channel Tunnel Group Ltd* v *Balfour Beatty Construction Ltd* [1993] AC 334). In effect, these provisions make it very difficult to avoid the arbitration agreement though there are procedural requirements: s. 9(3) provides that an application may not be made by a person before taking the appropriate procedural steps (if any) to acknowledge the legal proceeding against him or after he has taken any steps in those proceedings to answer the substantive claim (*Patel* v *Patel* [2000] QB 551). The old law on what constitutes a step in the proceedings remains good law under the 1996 Act. So, for example, where a party makes clear that its primary application is for a stay, it may also make alternative applications such as an application for summary judgment, without losing the right to a stay (*Capital Trust Investments* v *Radio Design TJ AB* [2002] EWCA Civ 125; [2002] 1 All ER (Comm) 514).

36.3.1.6   Getting the arbitration started—*Scott* v *Avery* clauses

The inclusion of a *Scott* v *Avery* clause is a useful addition to an arbitration agreement as it seeks to ensure that the matter in dispute is referred to arbitration. A typical clause might read as follows: 'The making of an arbitration award shall be a condition precedent to the commencement of any legal proceedings'. Basically, it makes arbitration a condition precedent to litigation, and is legally enforceable because it does not seek to oust the jurisdiction of the courts but merely to ensure that arbitration occurs (*Scott* v *Avery* (1856)

5 HL Cas 881; see further *Heyman v Darwins Ltd* [1942] AC 356 at p. 377). However, it has its limitations: for example, s. 9(5) provides that where the court refuses to stay the legal proceedings, any provision that an award is a condition precedent to the bringing of legal proceedings is of no effect.

36.3.1.7 Getting the arbitration started—*Atlantic Shipping* clauses

Another standard clause often found in arbitration agreements is the *Atlantic Shipping* clause (see *Atlantic Shipping and Trading Co.* v *Louis Dreyfus & Co.* [1922] 2 AC 250). Such a clause sets out strict time limits for the arbitration, e.g.:

> Arbitration proceedings must be commenced within six months of the dispute arising; failure to commence proceedings within this time limit will result in the claim being barred and the claimant's rights under the arbitration agreement extinguished.

This offers the parties some certainty about whether the arbitral proceeding will commence. However, the court has jurisdiction to extend such time limits under s. 12 (a mandatory provision, akin to s. 27 of the 1950 Act). Case law under the Arbitration Act 1950, s. 27, indicated that time limits were being less stringently applied (see *Libra Shipping and Trading Corporation Ltd* v *Northern Sales Ltd* [1981] 1 Lloyd's Rep 273; *Graham H Davies (UK) Ltd* v *Marc Rich & Co. Ltd* [1985] 2 Lloyd's Rep 423; *Comdel Commodities Ltd* v *Siporex Trade SA (No. 2)* [1991] 1 AC 148), but the new grounds set out in s. 12 of the 1996 Act suggest a stricter approach. Section 12(2) provides that any party to the agreement may apply for a court order to extend the time limits but only after a claim has arisen and after exhausting any available arbitral process for obtaining an extension. Section 12(3) states that the court shall make an order only if satisfied:

(a) that the circumstances are such as were outside the reasonable contemplation of the parties when they agreed the provision, and that it would be just to extend the time, or

(b) that the conduct of one party makes it unjust to hold the other party to the strict terms of the provision.

Leave is required for an appeal from a decision of the court under s. 12 (s. 12(6)).

36.3.2 Arbitrators and the arbitration tribunal

The arbitration tribunal may comprise a sole arbitrator or a panel of arbitrators which may include a chairman and/or an umpire.

The chairman's function may be prescribed by the parties but if not, his role is similar to that of the other member(s) of the tribunal in that decisions, orders and awards are made by all or a majority of the arbitrators, including the chairman (s. 20(3)). However, where there is neither unanimity nor a majority, the decision of the chairman prevails (s. 20(4)).

An umpire, in contrast, normally acts as a second tribunal. If an umpire is appointed the parties are again free to agree what his functions are: for example, whether he should attend proceedings and when the umpire should take over from the tribunal. If no provision is made in this regard, s. 21 provides that the umpire shall attend proceedings and be supplied with the same documentation as the other arbitrators. All decisions, orders and awards shall be made by the other arbitrators unless and until they cannot agree on a matter, in which case they shall give notice in writing to the parties and the umpire, and the umpire shall replace them as sole arbitrator with all necessary powers (s. 21(4)). This has the effect of encouraging the arbitrators to reach agreements especially regarding more minor matters.

Finally, where the parties agree that there shall be two or more arbitrators with no chairman or umpire, unless the parties agree otherwise, decisions, orders and awards shall be made by all or a majority of the arbitrators (s. 22).

36.3.2.1   Appointment

The general rule is that parties are free to decide the number of arbitrators they wish to appoint and whether to appoint a chair and make provision for an umpire (s. 15(1)). However, the presumption is for a sole arbitrator (s. 15(3)). It should be borne in mind that the greater the number of arbitrators the greater the arbitrators' fees and expenses! Where the parties have agreed on an even number of arbitrators, s. 15(2) spe-cifies that an additional arbitrator shall be appointed as chairman, unless otherwise agreed by the parties.

Where both parties are to appoint an arbitrator and one party refuses or fails to do so within the time specified, the other party, having appointed his arbitrator, may give notice in writing to the defaulting party that he proposes to appoint his arbitrator as sole arbitrator (s. 17). The defaulting party has seven days from the notice within which to make the required appointment and notify the other party, otherwise the sole arbitrator may proceed and his award is binding on the parties as if he had been appointed by agreement (s. 17(2)). There is provision to apply to the court to set the appointment aside (s. 17(3)).

36.3.2.2   Appointment procedures

Section 16 provides that the parties are free to agree on the procedures for the appointment of the tribunal, but where no such provision is made, it contains a number of default rules to facilitate getting the arbitration started:

(a) where there is a sole arbitrator, the parties shall appoint the arbitrator not later than 28 days after service of a request in writing by either party to do so;

(b) where there is a two-person tribunal, the parties have 14 days in which to appoint their respective arbitrators following a request;

(c) where there is a three-person tribunal, the parties have 14 days to appoint one arbitrator each and the two appointed arbitrators must then appoint a third arbitrator as chairman of the tribunal;

(d) where there is a two-person tribunal and an umpire, the parties have 14 days to make their respective appointments, and then the two arbitrators may appoint an umpire but must do so before, or shortly after, any substantive hearing begins.

The above time limits may be extended by the court under s. 79. Section 78 contains detailed rules on the reckoning of time periods for the purposes of Part I.

Where there is a failure in the appointment procedure and the parties have not made provision for it, any party to the agreement may (upon notice to the other party) apply to the court under s. 18, whereupon the court may:

(a) give directions as to the making of any necessary appointment;

(b) direct that the tribunal shall be constituted by such appointments already made;

(c) revoke any appointments made;

(d) make any necessary appointments itself.

36.3.2.3   Revocation of authority or removal by court

An arbitrator's authority derives from the agreement of the parties, and the parties are therefore free to revoke this authority. Where the parties have not provided for the revocation of an arbitrator's authority, s. 23 sets out the default rules including that:

(a) revocation must be the act of the parties acting jointly or of a person or institution vested with the necessary power by the parties; and

(b) revocation must be in writing unless the parties also agree to terminate the arbitration agreement.

As well as the power a court has under s. 18 to revoke an appointment, s. 24 (a mandatory provision) gives the court further power to remove an arbitrator, upon application by a party to the agreement, on any of the following grounds:

(a) that circumstances exist which give rise to justifiable doubts about his impartiality;

(b) that he does not possess the qualification required by the arbitration agreement;

(c) that he is physically or mentally incapable of conducting the proceedings or there are justifiable doubts about his capacity to do so;

(d) that he has refused or failed:

    (i) properly to conduct the proceedings, or

    (ii) to use all reasonable dispatch in conducting the proceedings or making the award, and that substantial injustice has been or will be caused to the applicant.

This power will only be exercised if all other avenues have been exhausted (s. 24(2)).

In *European Grain and Shipping Ltd* v *Johnston* [1983] QB 520, for example, the signing of a blank award form by an arbitrator, because he was to be in Australia when the award was to be made, amounted to misconduct (this term is no longer used in the 1996 Act, though there appears to be no change in the law) by himself and by the other arbitrators who endorsed his action: all the arbitrators were under a duty to participate in the decision-making process and to reach a joint decision.

36.3.2.4 Filling a vacancy

Unless the parties have agreed otherwise, the provisions of s. 16 (appointment of arbitrator) and s. 18 (failure of appointment procedures) apply in relation to filling a vacancy as in relation to an original appointment (s. 27).

Where the parties make express provision for filling a vacancy they should at least consider:

(a) whether the vacancy has to be filled and if so how;

(b) to what extent previous proceedings stand; and

(c) what effect the arbitrator's ceasing to hold office has on appointments made by him.

36.3.2.5 Fees

Section 28 (of mandatory effect) expressly provides what was previously implied by s. 19 of the Arbitration Act 1950 that the parties are jointly and severally liable to pay the arbitrators such *reasonable* fees and expenses as are appropriate. Application to the court for adjustment of the fees or expenses is possible.

36.3.2.5 Immunity

Section 29 (a mandatory provision) deals with the immunity of the arbitrator, an issue not addressed in previous legislation and on which the common law was unclear. The rule is that an arbitrator (and his employee or agent) is not liable for anything done or omitted in the discharge of his functions unless the act or omission is shown to have been in bad faith. The burden is on the complainant to prove bad faith. This provision is similar to the rules which apply to regulators (see, for example, the Financial Services Act 1986, s. 187; see further *Melton Medes Ltd* v *Securities and Investments Board* [1995] Ch 137). Similar immunity is given to arbitral institutions, for instance, with regard to an appointing function, under s. 74 (also of mandatory effect).

36.3.3   The arbitral proceedings

In practice, arbitral proceedings can vary from the very informal at one extreme (this often occurs where the parties have an established trading relationship and a degree of trust exists between them) to court-like proceedings at the other (this might arise where large sums of money are at stake or where the trading relationship has broken down and there is little likelihood of it being resurrected). Parties will need to be advised which type of proceedings would best meet their needs.

Prior to the 1996 Act there were no specific procedural rules prescribed in the general law, save the duty to observe the rules of natural justice. The legislation did require an arbitrator to act impartially (Arbitration Act 1950, s. 24; on procedures see further the Arbitration Act 1950, ss. 12, 13 and 15, and the Arbitration Act 1975, s. 5). Sections 33–41 of the 1996 Act now deal with the arbitral proceedings in some detail. In general, the parties are free to agree on the procedures, so, for example, if the parties have designed their own ad hoc arbitration or adopted an institutional arbitration, the relevant rules of procedure will apply. Otherwise, there are a number of default rules. However, there are two important mandatory provisions which parties cannot contract out of. First, s. 33 provides that the tribunal has a general duty:

(a) to act fairly and impartially between the parties, giving each a reasonable opportunity to state his case; and

(b) to adopt procedures suitable for the circumstances of the case, avoiding unnecessary delay or expense.

Secondly, s. 40 places a general duty on the parties to do all things necessary for the proper and expeditious conduct of the proceedings including:

(a) to comply without delay with any determination of the tribunal about procedures and evidence, or any other order or direction; and

(b) where appropriate, to take without delay any necessary steps to obtain a decision of the court on a preliminary question of jurisdiction or law (ss. 32 and 45).

36.3.3.1   Procedural and evidential matters

Subject to the right of the parties to agree any matter, it is for the tribunal to decide all procedural and evidential matters including (s. 34):

(a) when and where the proceedings are to be held and in what language;

(b) whether written statements of claim and defence are to be used;

(c) whether to apply the strict rules of evidence;

(d) whether there should be oral or written evidence etc.

In this regard the tribunal can adopt a variety of approaches: inquisitorial or accusatorial; formal or informal.

36.3.3.2   Consolidation of proceedings

The consolidation of proceedings was not addressed in the earlier legislation. Now s. 35 provides that the parties, or the tribunal with the agreement of the parties (though not the tribunal in its own right), may consolidate the arbitral proceedings with other arbitral proceedings, or concurrent hearings can be held. This provision should be welcomed in construction disputes where similar issues often arise between building owners and contractors and between contractors and sub-contractors. The same applies to maritime disputes between ship-owners and charterers and charterers and sub-charterers. Where proceedings cannot be consolidated there may be problems of conflicting decisions and of allocating liability for costs.

36.3.3.3   Representation

A party may be represented in arbitral proceedings by a lawyer or other person (s. 36). Previously, a party to an arbitration agreement did not always have the right to be represented by another person. Section 36 is not mandatory though.

36.3.3.4   Experts

Section 37 is new and provides that, unless agreed otherwise by the parties, the tribunal can appoint experts or legal advisers or assessors to report to it and the parties. The parties must be given an opportunity to comment on such reports. It is a mandatory provision that the fees and expenses of such experts are expenses of the arbitration and hence payable by the parties.

36.3.3.5   Powers of the tribunal

Unless otherwise agreed by the parties, the arbitral tribunal has the following general powers (s. 38):

(a) to order a claimant to provide security for costs (previously parties could give arbitrators the power to order security, but in the absence of such agreement only a court could order security for costs);

(b) to give directions in relation to property subject to the arbitration, for example, for inspection, copying, preservation, taking samples etc.;

(c) to direct that a party or witness be examined on oath or affirmation, and to administer the oath or affirmation.

Also, the parties may confer power on the tribunal to make provisional orders, for example, an order for the payment of money, the disposition of property or an interim payment on account of the costs of the arbitration (s. 39).

Section 41 provides a series of rules to deal with the situation where a party to the proceedings fails to do something necessary for the proper and expeditious conduct of the proceedings. For example, and unless otherwise agreed by the parties, the tribunal may make an award dismissing the claim where the tribunal is satisfied that there has been an inordinate and inexcusable delay on the part of the claimant and that the delay:

(a) gives rise, or is likely to give rise, to a substantial risk that it is not possible to have a fair resolution of the issues, or

(b) has caused or is likely to cause, serious prejudice to the respondent (s. 41(3): derived from the Arbitration Act 1950, s. 13A inserted by the Courts and Legal Services Act 1990, s. 102).

Also, if without sufficient cause a party fails to attend an oral hearing or provide written evidence where notice was given, the tribunal may continue the proceedings in his absence and make any award on the basis of the evidence before it (s. 41(4)).

Again, if without sufficient cause a party fails to comply with any order or direction of the tribunal, the tribunal may make a peremptory order to that effect and prescribe a time limit for compliance (s. 41(5)). Where a party fails to comply with a peremptory order the tribunal may:

(a) direct that the party in default may not rely on the allegation or material the subject of the order;

(b) draw such adverse inferences from non-compliance as the circumstances justify;

(c) proceed to an award based on materials properly provided;

(d) make such order as it thinks fit for costs in consequence of the non-compliance (s. 41(7)).

36.3.3.6   Powers of the court

The court is given various powers to support the arbitral process: many of these are derived from s. 12 of the 1950 Act. For instance, a party, with the permission of the tribunal or the parties, can use the same court procedures as are available in litigation to secure the attendance of a witness to give oral testimony or produce documentation (s. 43, a mandatory provision). This applies only where the witness is in the UK and the proceedings are being conducted in England, Wales or Northern Ireland.

Unless otherwise agreed by the parties, the court has the same powers to make orders, such as freezing injunctions, dealing with matters ancillary to arbitration as in litigation including orders concerning:

(a) the taking of evidence of witnesses;

(b) the preservation of evidence (e.g., search orders);

(c) property, its inspection, copying, preservation, etc;

(d) the sale of goods the subject of the proceedings;

(e) the granting of an interim injunction or the appointment of a receiver (s. 44).

Furthermore, s. 42 provides that an application may be made by a party or the tribunal to the court requiring compliance with a peremptory order of the tribunal.

Finally, s. 45 provides that, unless otherwise agreed by the parties, a court may on application of a party determine any preliminary question of law arising in the course of proceedings which the court is satisfied substantially affects the rights of one or more of the parties (this derives from the Arbitration Act 1979, ss. 2 and 3). An arbitration agreement can exclude this jurisdiction before the proceedings commence. An application under this section shall not be considered unless:

(a) it is made with the agreement of all the parties, or

(b) it is made with the permission of the tribunal (previously the permission of 'an arbitrator' was sufficient) and the court is satisfied:

(i)   that the determination of the question is likely to produce a substantial saving in costs, and

(ii) that the application was made without delay (s.45(2)).

An agreement to dispense with a reasoned award is interpreted as excluding the court's jurisdiction under s. 45.

Leave to appeal will only be given where the court is satisfied that the question is one of general importance or is one which, for some other special reason, should be considered by the Court of Appeal.

36.3.4   The award

Sections 46–58 deal with the award. Section 46 is new—it covers the issue of the applicable law. It states that the arbitral tribunal shall decide the dispute:

(a) in accordance with the law chosen by the parties (thus if the arbitration agreement states that 'English law shall apply', English substantive law governs the dispute), or

(b) if the parties so agree, in accordance with such other considerations as are agreed by them and determined by the tribunal.

The UNCITRAL Model Law provides that the arbitral tribunal can decide the case *ex aequo et bono* or as *amiable compositeur*, rather than in accordance with strict law, if so authorised by the parties (Art. 28). The effectiveness at common law of such 'equity clauses', empowering the arbitrator to decide the issues based on what is fair and equitable and not necessarily in strict accordance with the law was unclear in English law. In *Eagle Star Insurance Co. Ltd* v *Yuval Insurance Co. Ltd* [1978] 1 Lloyd's Rep 357, the Court of Appeal unanimously agreed that a clause which required an arbitrator to decide on equitable grounds rather than strict legal interpretation was valid and of full effect: it did not oust the jurisdiction of the court. However, in *Home and Overseas Insurance Co. Ltd* v *Mentor Insurance Co. (UK) Ltd* [1990] 1 WLR 153, it was stated, again in the Court of Appeal, that a clause allowing an arbitrator to settle a dispute, according to what seemed fair and reasonable, as opposed to according to settled principles of law, would be legally invalid and unenforceable. This clearly diminishes the extent to which the arbitrator can rely on his skill and expertise to decide a case and undermines the effectiveness of the arbitral process. Section 46(1)(b) allows the parties to authorise the tribunal to decide the dispute in accordance with such other considerations as are agreed by them or determined by the tribunal. This of course allows decisions based on equity or any other criteria, limited only by public policy. It should be noted that by agreeing that a dispute shall be resolved in this manner, the parties are in effect excluding any right of appeal to a court, in that there is no 'question of law' to appeal (see **36.3.6.3**).

Section 47 makes it clear that the tribunal can make more than one award: this was implied in the previous legislation (Arbitration Act 1950, s. 13(1)).

Section 48 is new and provides that, unless agreed otherwise by the parties, the tribunal has the following powers:

(a) to make a declaration about any matter to be determined in proceedings;

(b) to order a payment of money in any sum;

(c) as in the case of a court, to order a party to refrain from doing anything;

(d) as in the case of a court, to order specific performance of a contract;

(e) as in the case of a court, to order the rectification, setting aside or cancellation of a deed or other document;

(f) to award simple or compound interest (s. 49: the latter is new);

(g) to extend the time for making an award (s. 50).

36.3.4.1   Form of award

The parties are free to agree the form of the award. Where no provision is made the following default rules apply (s.52).

(a) The award shall be in writing and signed by all the arbitrators.

(b) The award shall be reasoned unless this has been dispensed with by the parties (see *Al Hadha Trading* v *Tradigrain SA* [2002] 2 Lloyd's Rep 512).

(c) The award shall state the seat of the arbitration and the date when the award is made.

(d) Unless otherwise agreed by the parties, where the seat of the arbitration is England, Wales or Northern Ireland, any award in proceedings shall be treated as made there, regardless of where the award is signed, dispatched or delivered to any of the parties (s. 53, reversing the effect of the decision in *Hiscox* v *Outhwaite* [1992] 1 AC 562, where it was held that an arbitration award was made in the place where it was signed).

36.3.4.2   Arbitrator's lien

Section 56, a mandatory provision, gives statutory recognition to the arbitrator's lien over the award, i.e., his right to retain possession of the award until his fees and expenses are paid in full. An application to the court to challenge the arbitrator's action can be made under s. 56(2).

36.3.4.3 Costs

Sections 59–65 deal with the matter of costs. Section 59 provides a new definition of the costs of arbitration which includes:

(a) the arbitrator's fees and expenses;

(b) the fees and expenses of any arbitral institution; and

(c) the legal or other costs of the parties.

Section 61 provides that the tribunal may make any award as to costs subject to any agreement of the parties, the general rules being that costs should follow the event. Section 60, a mandatory provision, states that an agreement which has the effect that a party is to pay the whole or part of the costs in any event is only valid if entered into after the dispute in question has arisen.

36.3.4.4 Settlement

Section 51 provides a set of default rules regarding settlement of the dispute. If during the arbitral proceedings the parties settle the dispute, the tribunal shall terminate the substantive proceedings, and if so requested by the parties and not objected to by the tribunal, the tribunal shall record the settlement in the form of an agreed award (sometimes called a 'consent award'), having the same status as any award of the tribunal.

36.3.5 Enforcing the award

Section 58, derived from s. 16 of the 1950 Act, states that the award is final and binding on the parties. In many cases, the parties will carry out the award faithfully, but sometimes it is necessary to enlist the force of the law. Section 66, a mandatory provision, provides that an award may, by leave of the court, be enforced in the same manner as a judgment or order of the court to the same effect.

For the enforcement of foreign awards see **36.4.4**.

36.3.6 Court intervention

As noted already, English arbitration, as an extrajudicial means of dispute resolution, is limited in the sense that recourse to judicial assistance may be needed. While it is essentially a private process between parties, the courts do intervene to enforce, support and supervise the arbitral process. We have already seen how the court gives effect to the arbitration agreement by staying litigation, by aiding in the constitution of the arbitration tribunal where necessary, and by determining preliminary points of law. Furthermore, the court has complementary powers to assist the arbitration process and to enforce the award where necessary. Once an award has been made there are a number of grounds on which it can be challenged before a court, although it may be possible to exclude this appellate jurisdiction.

36.3.6.1 Challenging the award: substantive jurisdiction

Section 67, a mandatory provision, provides that a party may apply to the court challenging an award on the basis that the tribunal lacked substantive jurisdiction. Before bringing the application the applicant must have exhausted all other processes and the application must be brought within 28 days of the date of the award (s. 70(2) and (3)—for the date of the award see s. 54). This right can be lost under s. 73 if the party wishing to object took part in the proceedings without objecting to the alleged lack of jurisdiction.

Following an application, the court may:

(a) confirm the award;

(b) vary the award; or

(c) set aside the award in whole or in part.

Leave is needed for any appeal from a decision under this section.

36.3.6.2   Challenging the award: procedural grounds

Section 68, another mandatory provision, provides that a party may apply to the court to challenge an award on the basis that there was a serious irregularity affecting the tribunal. An application under s. 68 involves a two-stage investigation: first, whether there has been an irregularity; and secondly, whether the irregularity has caused or will cause substantial injustice. Again, before bringing the application the applicant must have exhausted all other processes and the application must be brought within 28 days of the date of the award (s. 70(2) and (3)—for the date of the award see s. 54). Again this right may be lost if the objector took part in the proceedings without objecting to the irregularity (s. 73). Case law suggests that intervention on grounds of serious irregularity will be exceptional (e.g. *The Pamphilos* [2002] EWHC 2292 (Comm); [2002] 2 Lloyd's Rep 681).

Section 68(2) defines 'serious irregularity' as one which has 'caused or will cause substantial injustice to the applicant' including:

(a) failure of the tribunal to comply with s. 33 (general duty of tribunal);

(b) failure of tribunal to conduct proceedings as agreed by the parties;

(c) uncertainty or ambiguity as to the effect of the award;

(d) failure to comply with the requirement as to the form of the award, etc.

If there has been a serious irregularity affecting the proceedings, the tribunal or the award, the court may:

(a) remit the award to the tribunal to reconsider in whole or in part;

(b) set the award aside in whole or in part;

(c) declare the award to be of no effect, in whole or in part.

Leave is needed for any appeal from a decision under this section.

36.3.6.3   Challenging the award: appeal on a point of law

Unless otherwise agreed by the parties, a party can appeal to the court on a question of English law (not fact) arising out of the award (s. 69 and s. 82(1), derived from the Arbitration Act 1979, s. 1 and the *Nema* Guidelines: see *The Nema* [1982] AC 724). This jurisdiction can be excluded in the arbitration agreement before proceedings commence. An agreement to dispense with a reasoned award shall be treated as an agreement to exclude the court's jurisdiction under this section. An appeal cannot be brought without either:

(a) the agreement of the parties, or

(b) the leave of the court.

All other processes must be exhausted and the appeal must be brought within 28 days of the award (s. 70(2) and (3)).

Leave will only be given if the court is satisfied:

(a) that the determination of the question will substantially affect the rights of one or more of the parties;

(b) that the question was one the tribunal was asked to determine;

(c) that on the basis of the findings of fact in the award:

    (i)   the decision of the tribunal on the question is obviously wrong, or

    (ii) the question is of general public importance and the decision of the tribunal is at least open to serious doubt; and

(d) that despite the agreement of the parties to resolve the dispute by arbitration, it is just and proper in all the circumstances for the court to determine the question.

Leave is needed for any appeal from a decision under this section. It has been noted that while the statutory criteria are clearly strongly influenced by the *Nema* Guidelines, they do not follow them entirely. In *The Northern Pioneer* [2002] EWCA Civ 1878; [2003] 1 All ER (Comm) 204, it was stated that the new statutory criteria 'open the door a little more widely' than previously.

On appeal, the court may:

(a) confirm the award;

(b) vary the award;

(c) remit the award to the tribunal, in whole or in in part, for reconsideration in light of the court's determination; or

(d) set aside the award in whole or in part.

36.4   International arbitration

There may be aspects of a national arbitration system which parties to a dispute consider undesirable—in particular the possibility of judicial interference—and so they may turn to international arbitration to resolve their dispute.

Various bodies have devised international procedures for commercial arbitration: the London Court of International Arbitration, the American Arbitration Association and the Court of Arbitration of the International Chamber of Commerce have already been mentioned. Also, many large trading centres have developed their own international arbitration facilities in an attempt to enlarge their slice of the dispute resolution cake. Examples include: Japan's Commercial Arbitration Association; and the Netherlands Arbitration Institute.

Where the parties adopt one of these systems the arbitration is governed by the rules of the particular association or institute, and the mandatory rules of the forum where the actual arbitration takes place. We will briefly examine some of these systems later.

36.4.1   Is the arbitration international?

Traditionally, two means of determining whether an arbitration is international or not have dominated, i.e. the nature of the dispute and the nationality of the parties. The former approach is favoured by the International Chamber of Commerce (ICC). Article 1.1 of its Rules of Arbitration states that the function of the Court of Arbitration is to provide for the settlement by arbitration of 'business disputes of an international character' in accordance with these Rules. The latter approach is adopted in the UK Arbitration Act 1996.

A combination of the two approaches can be found in the UNCITRAL Model Law Article 1.3 which provides:

An arbitration is international if:

(a) the parties to the arbitration agreement have, at the time of the conclusion of that agreement, their place of business in different States; or

(b) one of the following places is situated outside the State in which the parties have their place of business:

    (i)   the place of arbitration if determined in, or pursuant to the arbitration agreement;

    (ii) any place where a substantial part of the obligations of the commercial relationship is to be performed or the place with which the subject-matter of the dispute is most closely connected; or

(c) the parties have expressly agreed that the subject-matter of the arbitration agreement relates to more than one country.

36.4.2 UNCITRAL

UNCITRAL is the United Nations Commission on International Trade Law. Its functions are to prepare and promote conventions and model laws; encourage wider acceptance of trade terms, customs and practices; disseminate information; and collaborate with other institutions responsible for the harmonisation of international trade law such as the ICC, UNIDROIT (the International Institute for Unification of Private Law) and UNCTAD (the UN Commission for Trade and Development). As part of this process, it has drafted a set of ad hoc arbitration rules and a model law.

36.4.2.1 Arbitration rules

These rules were devised in 1976 and are used in countries throughout the world with different legal, social and economic systems, in ad hoc arbitrations. They offer parties neutrality which national arbitration systems may not. The rules do not have the force of law but must be expressly adopted by the parties.

The following model arbitration clause is recommended in the rules.

Any dispute, controversy or claim arising out of or relating to this contract, or the breach, termination, or invalidity thereof, shall be settled by arbitration in accordance with the UNCITRAL Arbitration Rules as at present in force.

Note—Parties may wish to consider adding:

(a) The appointing authority shall be ... (name of institution or person).

(b) The number of arbitrators shall be ... (one or three).

(c) The place of arbitration shall be ... (town or country).

(d) The language(s) used in the arbitral proceedings shall be ...

Notable features of the rules include that:

(a) the arbitration clause must be in writing (Art. 1);

(b) any notice, including a notification of communication or proposal, is deemed to be received when it is physically delivered to the addressee or his habitual residence (Art. 2);

(c) the notice of arbitration must contain certain details (Art. 3.3);

(d) no arbitration can fail for lack of appointment or if an arbitrator cannot act: ultimately, either party can request the Secretary-General of the Permanent Court of Arbitration at the Hague to designate an appointing authority (Art. 6);

(e) the arbitration tribunal has jurisdiction to rule on objections that it has no jurisdiction and to determine the existence or the validity of a contract of which the arbitration clause forms part (Art. 21(1) and (2));

(f) the arbitration clause is severable from the contract and exists independently of it: a finding that the contract is null and void does not necessarily mean that the arbitration clause is invalid;

(g) periods of time fixed by the arbitration tribunal should not exceed forty-five days, though extensions are possible (Art. 23); and

(h) the award must be in writing, dated, signed, reasoned, not published without the consent of the parties and is final (Art. 32).

36.4.2.2   Model Law

The Model Law is an off-the-peg set of arbitration rules which can be used as the basis for a national set of arbitration rules. Several countries have arbitration laws based on the UNCITRAL Model Law. They include Australia, Bulgaria, Canada, Cyprus, Hong Kong, New Zealand, Nigeria, the states of California, Connecticut, Oregon and Texas in the USA, and Scotland.

36.4.3   Court of Arbitration of the International Chamber of Commerce

The ICC Court of Arbitration has been described as 'the most truly international of all arbitral systems' (*Bank Mallet* v *GAA Development and Construction Co.* [1988] 2 Lloyd's Rep 44 at 48 *per* Steyn J).

36.4.3.1   Who arbitrates?

The Court of Arbitration does not itself settle disputes but if the parties have not agreed on the arbitrator(s), the Court will choose a National Committee of the ICC which, from a list of competent and suitable persons, will propose the arbitrators. The arbitration is initiated by a request for arbitration to the Secretariat of the Court. The arbitration is then conducted under the ICC Rules which 'provide a code that is intended to be self-sufficient in the sense that it is capable of covering all aspects of arbitrations conducted under the rules, without the need for any recourse to any municipal system of law or any application to the courts of the forum' (*per* Kerr LJ in *Bank Mallet* v *Helliniki Techniki SA* [1984] QB 291 at 304).

36.4.3.2   The clause

The Arbitration Rules recommend a standard arbitration clause in seven languages. The English version states:

All disputes arising out of or in connection with the present contract shall be finally settled under the Rules of Arbitration of the International Chamber of Commerce by one or more arbitrators appointed in accordance with the said Rules.

Parties are reminded that it may be desirable for them to stipulate in the arbitration clause itself the law governing the contract, the number of arbitrators and the place and language of the arbitration. The parties' free choice of the law governing the contract and of the place and language of the arbitration is not limited by the ICC Rules of Arbitration.

Attention is called to the fact that the laws of certain countries require that parties to contracts expressly accept arbitration clauses, sometimes in a precise and particular manner.

36.4.3.3   Features of ICC arbitrations

Article 6.4 of the rules empower the arbitrator to determine questions as to his own jurisdiction and he has jurisdiction even if the contract containing the arbitration clause is 'inexistent, or null and void'. There are three further distinctive characteristics of ICC arbitrations.

(a) Article 18 provides that the arbitrator is required to draw up terms of reference before proceeding with the case, in order to clarify the issues subject to the arbitration.

(b) Before the arbitrator signs the award, under Art. 27 it must be submitted in draft form to the Court of Arbitration for scrutiny, as a means of ensuring enforcement in the relevant jurisdiction: the Court may lay down modifications to the award.

(c) The cost of the arbitration is covered by a deposit which the parties usually pay in equal shares to the Court in advance (Art. 30).

36.4.3.4   The award

An award is deemed to be made at the place of the arbitration proceedings and at the date when it is signed by the arbitrator (Art. 25). Article 28 states that the award shall be binding on the parties and it has been held that the adoption of ICC Rules could operate as an advance exclusion agreement under the Arbitration Act 1979 (*Marine Contractors Inc.* v *Shell Petroleum Development Co. of Nigeria Ltd* [1984] 2 Lloyd's Rep 77). The same would probably be the case under ss. 45 and 69 of the 1996 Act.

36.4.4   Enforcement—the New York Convention

A party to an arbitration award made in jurisdiction X may need to enforce it in jurisdiction Y. The main vehicle for such enforcement is the New York Convention on the Recognition and Enforcement of Foreign Arbitral Awards (1958) originally adopted in England in the Arbitration Act 1975 and now governed by Part III of the Arbitration Act 1996.

The New York Convention has been ratified by about 134 States.

36.4.4.1   Application

The Convention applies to foreign awards, that is, awards made in the territory of a State other than the State where the recognition and enforcement of the award is sought (Art. I). Article III states that each Contracting State is to enforce arbitral awards in accordance with the rules set out in the Convention, so there exists a general presumption for eligibility for enforcement.

36.4.4.2   Enforcement procedures

To obtain enforcement, the party must supply a duly authenticated original award or duly certified copy thereof, and the original agreement or duly certified copy thereof (Art. VI). Enforcement can only be refused, under Art. V, at the request of the party against whom enforcement is sought, if that person can prove, for instance, that:

(a) a party to the arbitration agreement is under some incapacity;

(b) the arbitration agreement is not valid under the law to which the parties subjected it . . . ;

(c) a party was not given proper notice of the proceedings . . .;

(d) the award deals with matters not within the arbitration agreement . . .;

(e) the arbitral tribunal was improperly constituted . . .; or

(f) the award is not yet binding on the parties or has been set aside by a competent authority . . .

Enforcement can also be refused if the competent authority where enforcement is being sought finds that the subject-matter is not capable of settlement by arbitration, or is contrary to public policy under the law of that country (Art. V.2). See *Dardana Ltd* v *Yukos Oil Co.* [2002] EWCA Civ 543; [2002] Lloyd's Rep 326, for a useful explanation of the scheme giving effect to the New York Convention under the 1996 Act.

36.5 Summary

Having read this chapter you should:

- be aware of and able to advise on the advantages and disadvantages of arbitration as an alternative to litigation;

- be aware of the different types of arbitration and be able to advise a client which type best suits his needs;

- be familiar with the legal framework which supports arbitration, in the form of the Arbitration Act 1996, in particular, in terms of commencing arbitration, the arbitral process, the arbitration award and the judicial support available to support the whole process;

- be aware of the particular features of international arbitration, including enforcement of awards under the New York Convention;

- be aware of the main points to consider when drafting an arbitration agreement or arbitration clause in a commercial context.

Commercial litigation

37.1 Introduction

There are many disadvantages to litigation. It can be time-consuming (especially where permission to appeal is granted), costly, and lack privacy. However, litigation does offer a final solution to a dispute, supported by the force of law and may be the only means to resolve a dispute.

When commencing litigation, a claimant needs to consider a number of questions.

(a) Can the claimant afford the litigation, in terms of money and time? Although usually the successful party is awarded costs, he may have to finance the litigation as it proceeds and recover his costs after judgment; moreover, any costs awarded will be taxed and will rarely fully reimburse the successful party's outlay; and, of course, there is always the risk of losing in litigation.

(b) Will litigation damage the goodwill and trading interests of the business?

(c) Is there sufficient evidence to substantiate the allegations?

(d) Will the defendant be able to meet any judgment against him?

Where a dispute relates to an international transaction there may be further problems of conflict of laws. The English courts may not have jurisdiction over the matter. Even if they do, English law may not apply, leading to the further expense of obtaining expert evidence on and proving foreign law. Even after judgment is obtained there may be difficulties in executing it.

Conflict of laws issues, for instance, the jurisdiction of the English courts over international litigation and the recognition and enforcement of judgments abroad, are outside the scope of this book. (For detailed discussion see Dicey and Morris, *Conflict of Laws*, (London: Sweet & Maxwell, 13th edn, 2000).)

In this chapter:

- we look briefly at the Civil Procedure Rules as they relate to commercial litigation;
- we consider the conduct of litigation in the Commercial Court, and, in particular
  - we examine the main forms of interim relief that have been developed to aid commercial litigation, that is, freezing injunctions and search orders;
  - we highlight certain devices that can be used to encourage settlement, such as summary judgement, interim payments, and, without prejudice payments;
- finally, we consider alternative dispute resolution (ADR) and the enforceability of ADR agreements.

37.2 The Civil Procedure Rules

With effect from 26 April 1999, a new procedural code, the Civil Procedure Rules (CPR), regulates the conduct of cases before all courts in England and Wales (see The Civil Procedure Act 1997; The Civil Procedure Rules 1998 (SI 1998, No. 3132), and the Civil Procedure (Amendment) Rules 1999 (SI 1999, No. 1008(L8)). The rules can be accessed via the internet and downloaded at www.dca.gov.uk/civil/procrules_fin/. The CPR replace the County Court Rules and the Rules of the Supreme Court. The CPR make no change to the jurisdiction of any of the courts, nor do they affect the conduct of arbitration (though arbitrators may adopt aspects of the CPR to suit any individual arbitration). Furthermore, the CPR and the relevant Practice Directions relate only to procedure and not substantive law.

The CPR are designed to simplify litigation. The 'overriding objective' (see Part 1, CPR) to be applied by courts at all stages of a case, is to ensure the just resolution of the case in a way that is proportionate to the sums at stake, the importance and complexity of the case and the financial position of each party. In pursuing this objective, the court has a duty actively to manage each case (see Part 3, CPR). This involves:

(a) encouraging the parties to co-operate with each other;

(b) identifying issues at an earlier stage;

(c) disposing summarily of issues where possible;

(d) encouraging settlement of whole or part of the claim;

(e) fixing timetables and controlling the progress of the case (see Rule 1.4, CPR).

This concept of case management by the court is reinforced by a structured regime whereby failure by a party or his solicitor to comply with any procedural timetable laid down by the court will result in the imposition of a costs sanction which will be payable within a fixed timetable. The overall objective of the new rules is to make civil litigation faster, simpler and therefore cheaper.

Under the CPR, familiar terms have been replaced. Plaintiff becomes *claimant*; writ becomes *claim form*; pleading becomes *statement of case; ex parte* becomes *without notice; Mareva* injunctions become *freezing orders*; Anton Piller Orders become *search orders*; and *permission* and not leave is needed when the approval of the court is required.

The pleading process has been simplified. As part of this, the former discovery procedure has been replaced by a process of *disclosure* (see Part 31, CPR). *Statements of Truth* need to be signed to verify certain documents, such as the statement of case and witness statements (Rule 22, CPR). Solicitors will have to consider the issue of authority to determine whether it is appropriate for the solicitor in charge of the case, or the client, to sign the statement of the case, for instance. The court has greater power to control the way in which evidence is given at trial (Parts 32–35, CPR). Other significant changes include the fact that both the claimant and the defendant can apply for summary judgment. Previously this procedure was only available to the claimant. The power to give summary judgment has been widened. Summary judgment can now be given if either the claimant or the defendant has no real prospect of succeeding on a claim or issue, or if generally the court considers that the claim or issue should be dealt with prior to full trial (Rule 24, CPR). The availability of summary judgment may be particularly important in commercial litigation where speedy resolution of disputes is generally considered to be of the essence. Contracts are often drafted so as to maximise the chances of a party being able to obtain summary judgment, by use of devices such as 'no set off', exclusion, and similar clauses (see **1.2.1** and generally **Chapter 18**). As a further incentive to encourage the early settlement of claims, there is now an entitlement for both the claimant and the defendant to make offers (under the Part 36 procedure) effectively to protect their positions as to costs. This procedure was previously only available to the defendant by a payment into court. Finally, the CPR alter the way in which costs are assessed and awarded (see Parts 43–48, CPR).

37.3   The Commercial Court

A large number of commercial disputes fall under the jurisdiction of the county court since the raising of jurisdictional limits, from £5,000 to £50,000, under the Courts and Legal Services Act 1990. Otherwise, commercial litigation is usually brought before the High Court, in the Queen's Bench Division (equitable claims come within the Chancery Division which has specialised courts to deal with company and patents law). A specialised court, the Commercial Court, which originated in 1895 by the creation of the 'commercial list', deals with commercial litigation. It was given statutory recognition in the Administration of Justice Act 1970 as a constituent of the Queen's Bench Division.

37.3.1   Rationale of the Commercial Court

Its rationale is to provide a court where there is greater familiarity with commercial disputes and to provide a procedure that would enable these disputes to be resolved quickly, effectively and without undue formality. The Commercial Court is staffed by judges with particular expertise in commercial law (they can also act as arbitrators: see the Arbitration Act 1996 s. 93 and sch. 2) and the Commercial Court's procedures are characterised by speed and simplicity.

37.3.2   The CPR, Part 58 and the Commercial Court Guide

The rules governing the Commercial Court are to be found in Part 58 of the CPR which deals with Specialist Proceedings, and the related Practice Direction. Together, these rules replace Order 72 of the Rules of the Supreme Court. There is also a Commercial Court Guide which is revised periodically (latest revision, 6th edn, 2002, see www.courtservice.gov.uk).

(a) *What is a commercial claim?*
The Practice Direction on the Commercial Court defines a 'commercial claim' as including any case arising out of trade and commerce in general, including any case relating to—

(i)   a business document or contract;

(ii)   the export or import of goods;

(iii) the carriage of goods by land, sea, air or pipeline;

(iv) the exploitation of oil and gas reserves;

(v)   insurance and re-insurance;

(vi) banking and financial services;

(vii) the operation of markets and exchanges;

(viii) business agency; and

(ix) arbitration.

(b) The Commercial Court Guide

The CPR apply to cases in the Commercial List subject to the provisions of the Guide. The Guide adapts some of the Rules and puts them within the specific context of a 'commercial claim'. Accordingly, the Guide contains further procedural requirements not found in the CPR. However, the Guide is not a substitute for the CPR.

The Guide deals with matters in relation to commercial claims, such as:

- commencement, transfer and removal
- particulars of claim, defence and reply
- case management in the Commercial Court
- disclosure in cases in the Commercial Court
- applications
- alternative dispute resolution
- evidence for trial
- trial
- after trial
- multi-party disputes
- litigants in person
- arbitrations

37.4 Interim relief

Part 25 of the CPR contains a list of interim remedies which may be granted to aid the litigation process. However, it should be noted that the list is not exhaustive (Rule 25.1(3), CPR). Expressly included are reliefs such as: interim injunctions and declarations; non-party disclosure; and interim payments. Two particular forms of interim relief, 'freezing injunctions' and 'search orders' deserve further analysis.

37.4.1 Freezing injunctions

A 'freezing injunction' is more commonly known as a *Mareva* injunction (from the case *Mareva Compania Naviera S.A.* v *International Bulkcarriers S.A.* [1975] 2 Lloyd's Rep 509, though the first case in which such an injunction was given was *Nippon Yusen Naviera* v *Karageorgis* [1975] 2 Lloyd's Rep 509). At its simplest, the freezing injunction is a court order freezing some or all of the respondent's assets, or ordering him not to deal with, dispose of, or remove them, from the court's jurisdiction. Its purpose is to prevent injustice to the claimant by ensuring that the respondent cannot remove or dissipate his assets to frustrate any judgment made against him. However, it does not give the claimant any security rights over the assets (see *Capital Cameras Ltd* v *Harold Line Ltd* [1991] 3 All ER 389) and preferential and secured creditors maintain their position of priority, for example, in the case of insolvency.

37.4.1.1 Legislative authority

Section 37(3) of the Supreme Court Act 1981 provides:

The power of the High Court . . . to grant interlocutory [now interim] relief restraining a party to any proceedings from removing from the jurisdiction of the High Court, or otherwise dealing with, assets located within that jurisdiction shall be exercisable in cases where that party is, as well as in cases where he is not, domiciled, resident or present within that jurisdiction.

37.4.1.2   Pre-conditions for granting the injunction

Before granting the injunction, usually the court will need to be satisfied that:

(i)   the applicant has a good arguable case;

(ii)   the claim is one over which the court has jurisdiction (*The Siskina* [1979] AC 210); and,

(iii)   that there is a real risk that the respondent will try to dissipate the assets or remove the assets out of the court's jurisdiction.

This places a heavy duty on the applicant's lawyers to present sufficient evidence to support the application.

Like all injunctions, the freezing (or *Mareva*) injunction is a discretionary order granted on the balance of convenience. So as not to give the respondent advance warning, the injunction is usually granted without notice. In such circumstances, the applicant is required to make a full and fair disclosure of all relevant facts (*The Assios* [1979] 1 Lloyd's Rep 331). The injunction may be granted at any stage: before, during or after a claim.

A freezing injunction can also be granted supporting proceedings pending, contemplated or concluded in a court of a Member State of the EU (Civil Jurisdiction and Judgments Act 1982, s. 25).

37.4.1.3   Assets that can be frozen

Assets which can be frozen include personal property, bank accounts and land and are not limited to assets within jurisdiction. For examples of freezing injunctions which froze assets worldwide, see *Babanaft International Co. Ltd* v *Bassatne* [1990] Ch 13; *Republic of Haiti* v *Duvalier* [1990] 1 QB 202; *Derby & Co. Ltd* v *Weldon* [1990] Ch 48; and *Derby & Co. Ltd* v *Weldon (Nos. 3 & 4)* [1990] 2 Ch 65.

Freezing injunctions have a profoundly restrictive effect on a respondent's business and so are not usually granted against banks (*Polly Peck International plc* v *Nadir (No. 2)* [1992] 4 All ER 769).

37.4.1.4   Undertakings by the applicant

Before granting the injunction, the court usually requires the applicant to give various undertakings to the court, which are incorporated in the order:

(a) an undertaking to pay damages, that the respondent sustains, which the court considers the applicant should pay;

(b) if made without notice, an undertaking to inform the respondent of the injunction and to serve all papers as soon as practicable;

(c) if made without notice, a return date for a further hearing at which either party can be present;

(d) an undertaking to inform third parties, for example banks, of the injunction and their right to apply to the court for directions and variation; and

(e) an undertaking to indemnify any third party regarding expenses in complying with the order.

See further the Practice Direction on Interim Injunctions which supplements Part 25, CPR.

37.4.1.5   The order

The order should only cover the amount needed to satisfy the applicant's claim: a maximum amount to be frozen is set in most orders. Provision for the respondent's living expenses, legitimate trading expenses and the right to deal with any remaining sum is usually made.

The order may be granted 'until trial or further order' or it may be granted for a limited period of time in which case the applicant will have to apply for its continuance.

The order, though directed at the respondent, also binds third parties with knowledge of it. A third party who assists in dealing with the frozen assets is in contempt of court. This is why it is important to notify third parties, such as banks, of its existence.

Supporting orders include disclosure orders against the respondent or third parties to disclose information of the whereabouts of the respondent's assets and orders which require the respondent to surrender his passport and not leave the jurisdiction.

It is good practice to draft an injunction so that it includes a proviso which permits acts, (which would otherwise breach the injunction) to be done with the written consent of the applicant's solicitors, thereby enabling the parties to vary the injunction without further recourse to the courts. If the injunction is breached the offending party is in contempt of court and subject to a fine and/or imprisonment.

Standard form orders and guidance notes are annexed to the Practice Direction on Interim Injunctions which supplements Part 25, CPR.

37.4.2   Search orders

Search orders (previously known as *Anton Piller* orders) are another form of interim, injunctive relief designed to facilitate the litigation process. They are usually granted without notice and were developed to respond to the ever increasing problem of piracy in the sound and video industry (*Anton Piller K.G.* v *Manufacturing Processes Ltd* [1976] Ch 55). Typically, a search order is used where a manufacturer claims that a business rival is infringing his intellectual property rights. It is an order requiring one party (the respondent) to allow another party (the applicant and/or his representative) to enter the respondent's premises and inspect and remove documents or assets. Its purpose is to preserve evidence which could otherwise be removed or destroyed.

37.4.2.1   Legislative authority

Search orders are now granted under s. 7 of the Civil Procedure Act 1997.

37.4.2.2   Pre-conditions for granting the order

The element of surprise is vital to this procedure so application is made without notice on affidavit in the Chancery Division. Again, the applicant is required to make a full and fair disclosure of all relevant facts. Before granting the order, the court must be satisfied that:

(a) there is a strong basic case on the merits;

(b) the respondent's activities pose serious potential or actual harm to the applicant's interests; and

(c) there is clear evidence that the respondent possesses the items and that there is a real danger that they will be removed or destroyed before an application can be made (*Anton Piller K.G.* v *Manufacturing Processes Ltd* [1976] Ch 55, per Ormrod LJ).

Once more, the relief is discretionary and cannot be obtained as of right.

37.4.2.3 Undertakings by the applicant

Again, the applicant is usually required to give various undertakings, which are usually incorporated in the order, before the court will grant this interim relief. The applicant is required to give:

(a) an undertaking as to damages;

(b) an undertaking to have the order (with supporting affidavits) served by a supervising solicitor;

(c) an undertaking to issue process (where the order is sought before commencement of the proceedings).

Furthermore, the applicant's solicitor will usually undertake, among other things:

(d) to explain the order to the respondent in everyday language;

(e) to inform the respondent of his right to seek legal advice before allowing the execution of the order;

(f) to make a list of all items removed and provide a copy to the respondent;

(g) to keep safe all documents and items seized;

(h) not to use the items seized for any purpose other than the action without the permission of the court; and

(i) after copying the documents, to return such items to the respondent's solicitors.

See further the Practice Direction on Interim Injunctions which supplements Part 25, CPR.

37.4.2.4 The order

The order does not permit the applicant to enter premises, like a civil search warrant, but is a court order requiring the respondent to permit the applicant to enter premises for the purpose of inspecting and removing documents or items. If the respondent fails to comply he is in contempt of court. The order will generally include other restrictions as to the respondent's future conduct (see Part 25, CPR and the relevant Practice Direction on Interim Injunctions). There are usually restrictions on the number of persons who can enter and at what time of day (see *Universal Thermosensors Ltd* v *Hibben* [1992] 3 All ER 257).

The order should only be used where it is essential due to its Draconian nature and the conditions for the granting of an order must be strictly complied with. It has been recognised that the order may be oppressive; see *Universal Thermosensors Ltd* v *Hibben* [1992] 3 All ER 257. In the *Chappell Case* [1989 Eur Court H.R. Series A No. 152–A] the European Court of Human Right upheld the use of search orders provided they were accompanied by adequate and effective safeguards against abuse such as: requiring the applicant's solicitor or an officer of the court to execute the order and allowing the respondent time to contact his solicitor and take the appropriate steps to challenge the execution of the order. A standard form order and guidance notes are annexed to the Practice Direction on Interim Injunctions which supplements Part 25, CPR.

37.4.2.5 Significance of the order

A search order can have a huge impact on a respondent's business—it may have to close down. A respondent who does not comply with the order will be in contempt of court and may be fined and/or imprisoned (see *Bhimji* v *Chatwani* [1991] 1 WLR 989).

37.4.2.6   Respondent's remedies

The respondent may apply to have an order set aside or varied, for instance on the grounds that it should not have been granted, or that it is too wide. The order will normally fix a date for a hearing for continuation of the negative injunctions included in it and the respondent can make an application at that hearing. Where the applicant has failed to make a full and frank disclosure, or has not proceeded with dispatch, the order may be discharged. However, a respondent's most effective remedy will often be damages.

37.5   Other means of resolving disputes

In the process of litigation, certain procedural devices can be used to encourage settlement.

37.5.1   Summary Judgment

Summary Judgment is now available to both the claimant and the defendant under Rule 24, CPR. Summary judgment can be given if either the claimant or the defendant has no real prospect of succeeding on a claim or issue, or if the court considers that the claim or issue should be dealt with prior to the full trial.

37.5.2   Interim payments

Under Part 25, CPR the defendant may be required to make an interim payment on account of damages if the court considers that if the claim went to trial, the claimant would obtain judgment for a substantial amount of money (other than costs) against the defendant (Rule 25.7). This can be used to encourage early settlement.

37.5.3   Without prejudice payments

The use of 'without prejudice' offers, by the claimant or the defendant can also encourage settlement (see Part 36, CPR).

37.6   Alternative dispute resolution

Under the CPR, it has been recognised that parties have a duty to consider seriously the possibility of alternative dispute resolution (ADR) mechanisms as part of their duty to further the 'overriding objective' of the CPR (Rule 1.3) and the court also has a duty to further the 'overriding objective' by 'active case management' and this includes encouraging parties to use ADR mechanisms (Rule 1.4, see further *Dunnett* v *Railtrack plc* [2002] EWCA Civ 303; [2002] 2 All ER 850). In particular, Rule 26.4 allows the court to stay proceedings, where the parties request it or of its own initiative, to facilitate ADR (see **37.6.3**). Two ADR mechanisms are outlined below.

37.6.1   Conciliation/mediation

Conciliation and mediation aim to achieve an amicable settlement of the dispute through the use of an independent and impartial third party. A conciliator will seek to find common ground between the parties and encourage them to find a settlement, whereas a mediator may play a more active role in trying to bring the parties together. These methods are best suited to parties that have a close, continuing, and relatively friendly trading relationship. The Clerk of the Commercial Court keeps a list of individuals and bodies offering alternative dispute resolution services. There is no statutory regulation of conciliation or mediation equivalent to the Arbitration Act and hence there are no default rules to govern the relevant procedure. It is therefore important that parties that parties identify a set of procedural rules either expressly or by adopting a exist set of rules. UNCITRAL has drafted a set of Conciliation Rules which can be adopted by parties seeking to use this method of dispute resolution. The ICC has also produced a set of Rules of Conciliation.

37.6.2 Mini-trials

This is a form of small scale, in-house litigation. It usually involves a presentation of the issues in dispute by each party's lawyers before a panel of senior executives, one from each side, who are unconnected with the dispute. Often there is a neutral chairman, such as a retired judge. Following the presentations, which are time-limited, the panel retires to negotiate a settlement. The success of this alternative to actual litigation is dependent on a willingness to settle and a realisation that either party may win. Where the parties reach a settlement, it is advisable that this is incorporated in a written agreement and can be enforced as a contract if necessary. This procedure has been successfully used in the USA to resolve some major commercial disputes.

37.6.3 Enforceability of ADR agreements

While the CPR require courts to encourage parties to use ADR, courts do not have any statutory power to stay proceedings commenced in breach of an agreement to refer disputes to ADR similar to the power under the Arbitration Act to stay proceedings in support of an arbitration clause. The court has an inherent jurisdiction to stay proceedings however. In *Channel Tunnel Group Ltd* v *Balfour Beatty Construction Ltd* [1993] AC 334; [1993] 1 All ER 664 the parties had agreed that disputes would be referred, in the first instance, to a panel of experts, and following that to arbitration. The House of Lords held that the court had an inherent jurisdiction to order a stay in order to support the parties' chosen method of dispute resolution. But the non-enforceability of agreements to negotiate may deter against the grant of a stay. In *Halifax Financial Services Ltd* v *Intuitive Systems Ltd* [1999] 1 All ER (Comm) 303, the parties entered into a contract which included a structured dispute resolution procedure. Accordingly, the parties were first required to meet in 'good faith' to negotiate a settlement. If unsuccessful, either party could call for 'structured negotiations' with a neutral advisor. If unsuccessful again, either party could refer the dispute to court unless both agreed to arbitration. When one party commenced court proceedings the judge refused to grant a stay to allow the structured dispute resolution procedure to be invoked because there was nothing in the agreement to make the procedure a condition precedent to litigation. Further, the procedure, if invoked, would not lead to a legally binding result. This case was distinguished in *Cable & Wireless plc* v *IBM United Kingdom Ltd* [2002] EWHC 2059 (Comm); [2002] 2 All ER (Comm) 1041 where the parties first agreed to attempt in good faith to resolve any dispute through negotiation. If unsuccessful, the parties agreed to attempt in good faith to resolve the dispute through an ADR procedure as recommended to the parties by the Centre for Dispute Resolution. In referring to the duty to promote ADR (*Dunnett* v *Railtrack plc* [2002] EWCA Civ 303, [2002] 2 All ER 850), the court held that because the agreement prescribed the means by which the attempt at ADR should be made, that is through the Centre for Dispute Resolution, the agreement included a sufficiently defined mutual obligation upon both parties to go through the process of initiating a mediation, selecting a mediator and at least presenting that mediator with its case. Colman J went on to state *obiter* that contractual references to ADR which do not include provision for an identifiable procedure would not necessarily fail to be enforceable by reason of uncertainty. An important issue would be whether the obligation to mediate was expressed in unqualified and mandatory terms or whether the duty was qualified, such as, 'shall take such serious steps as they may be advised'.

37.7 Summary

At the end of this chapter you should:

- be aware of the main thrust of the Civil Procedure Rules as they relate to commercial litigation and the role of the Commercial Court, in commercial litigation;
- be familiar with the reliefs and devices which have been developed to assist commercial litigation;
- be conscious that other methods of dispute resolution exist, such as arbitration or mediation, some of which are legally enforceable, and of their advantages and disadvantages.

Further reading

Part I

Anderson, *Drafting & Negotiating Commercial Contracts*, Butterworths, 1997

Berg, *Drafting Commercial Agreements*, Butterworths, 1991

Benjamin's Sale of Goods, 6th edn, Sweet & Maxwell, 2002, chapters 18–21

Bradgate, *Drafting Standard Terms of Trading*, 2nd edn, FT Law & Tax, 1995

Cheshire, Fifoot and Furmston, *The Law of Contract*, 14th edn, Butterworths, 2001

Chitty on Contracts, 28th edn, Sweet & Maxwell, 1999

Christou, *Boilerplate: Practical Clauses*, 3rd edn, Sweet & Maxwell, 2002

Christou, *Drafting Commercial Agreements*, 2nd edn, Sweet & Maxwell, 1998

Furmston (ed), *The Law of Contract*, 2nd edn, Butterworths, 2003

Lawson, *Exclusion Clauses and Unfair Contract Terms*, 6th edn, Sweet & Maxwell, 2000

Lewison, *The Interpretation of Contracts*, 3rd edn, Sweet & Maxwell, 2003

Treitel, *The Law of Contract*, 11th edn, Sweet & Maxwell, 2003

Yates and Hawkins, *Standard Business Contracts: Exclusions and Related Devices*, Sweet & Maxwell, 1986

Part II

Bowstead and Reynolds on Agency, 17th edn, Sweet & Maxwell, 2001

Bradgate, *Commercial Law*, 3rd edn, Butterworths, 2000, chapters 3–6

Christou, *Drafting Commercial Agreements*, 2nd edn, Sweet & Maxwell 2002, chapters 6–8

Christou, *International Agency Distribution and Licensing Agreements*, 2nd edn, Sweet & Maxwell, 2003

Fridman's Law of Agency, 7th edn, Butterworths, 1996

Markesinis and Munday, *Outline of the Law of Agency*, 4th edn, Butterworths, 1998

Randolph and Davey, *Guide to the Commercial Agents Regulation*, 2nd edn, Hart, 2001

Schmitthoff's Agency and Distribution Agreements, Sweet & Maxwell, 1992

Schmitthoff's Export Trade, 10th edn, Sweet & Maxwell, 2000, chapters 15, 16

Part III

Atiyah, *The Sale of Goods*, 10th edn, Pitman, 2000

Benjamin's Sale of Goods, 6th edn, Sweet & Maxwell, 2002

Bradgate, *Drafting Standard Terms of Trading*, 2nd edn, FT Law & Tax, 1995

Bradgate, *Commercial Law*, Butterworths, 3rd edn, 2000, chapters 7–19

Bradgate and Twigg-Flesner: *Blackstone's Guide to Consumer Sales and Associated Guarantees*, OUP, 2003

Christou, *Drafting Commercial Agreements*, 2nd edn, Sweet & Maxwell, 2002, chapters 1–5

Goode, *Commercial Law*, 3rd edn, Penguin, 2004, chapters 6–16

Goode, *Payment Obligations in Commercial and Financial Transactions*, Sweet & Maxwell, 1983

Goode, *Proprietary Rights and Insolvency in Sales Transactions*, 2nd edn, Sweet & Maxwell, 1989

McCormack, *Reservation of Title Clauses*, 2nd edn, Sweet & Maxwell, 1995

Part IV

Benjamin's Sale of Goods, 6th edn, Sweet & Maxwell, 2002, chapters 18–21

Bradgate, *Commercial Law*, 3rd edn, Butterworths, 2000, chapters 31–33

Bridge, *The International Sale of Goods, Law and Practice*, OUP, 1999

Goode, *Commercial Law*, 3rd edn, Penguin, 2004, chapters 32–37

Hardy Ivamy, *Marine Insurance*, Butterworths, 1985

Schmitthoff's Export Trade, 10th edn, Sweet & Maxwell, 2000, chapters 1, 2, 3, 27 and 28

Templeman, *Marine Insurance*, Pitman, 1986

Part V

Benjamin's Sale of Goods, 6th edn, Sweet & Maxwell, 2002, chapters 22–23

Bradgate, *Commercial Law*, 3rd edn, Butterworths, 2000, chapters 27–30 and 34

Byles on Bills of Exchange, 27th edn, Sweet & Maxwell, 2001

Chitty on Contracts, 28th edn, Sweet & Maxwell, 1999

Goode, *Commercial Law*, 3rd edn, Penguin, 2004, chapters 17–21

Richardson's Guide to Negotiable Instruments, 8th edn, Butterworths, 1992

Part VI

Bell, *Modern Law of Personal Property in England and Ireland*, Butterworths, 1989, chapters 6, 8

Bradgate, *Commercial Law*, 3rd edn, Butterworths, 2000, chapters 20–23

Chitty on Contracts, 28th edn, Sweet & Maxwell, 1999, Part II, chapters 6 and 12

Christou, *Drafting Commercial Agreements*, 2nd edn, Sweet & Maxwell 2002, chapter 16

Davies, *Textbook on Commercial Law*, Blackstone Press, 1992, chapters 12–17

Goode, *Commercial Law*, 3rd edn, Penguin, 2004, chapters 22–30

Goode, *Legal Problems of Credit and Security*, 2nd edn, Sweet & Maxwell, 1988

Wood, *Comparative Law of Security and Guarantees*, Sweet & Maxwell, 1995

Part VII

van Bael & Bellis, *Competition Law of the European Community*, Kluwer, 2004

Downes and Ellison, *The Legal Control of Mergers in the EC*, Blackstone Press, 1991

Freeman & Whish, *A Guide to the Competition Act 1998*, Butterworths, 1998

Goyder, *EC Competition Law*, 2nd edn, Clarendon Press, 1993

Harding, *European Community Investigations and Saunders*, Leicester University Press, 1993

Singleton, *Blackstone's Guide to the Competition Act 1998*, Blackstone Press, 1998

Whish, *Competition Law*, 4th edn, Butterworths, 2000

Part VIII

Annand & Norman, *Blackstone's Guide to the Trade Marks Act 1994*, Blackstone Press, 1994

Bainbridge, *Intellectual Property*, 4th edn, Pitman, 1999

Copinger and Skone James on Copyright, 13th edn, Sweet & Maxwell, 1991

Cornish, *Intellectual Property*, 5th edn, Sweet & Maxwell, 2003

Dworkin and Taylor, *Blackstone's Guide to the Copyright Designs and Patents Act 1988*, Blackstone Press, 1988

Holyoak & Torremans, *Intellectual Property Law*, 3rd edn, Butterworths, 2001

Kerly's Law of Trade Marks and Trade Names, 12th edn, Sweet & Maxwell, 1986

Pearson and Miller, *Commercial Exploitation of Intellectual Property*, Blackstone Press, 1990

Phillips and Firth, *An Introduction to the Law of Intellectual Property*, 4th edn, Butterworths, 1999

Reid, *A Practical Guide to Patent Law*, 2nd edn, Sweet & Maxwell, 1992

Part IX

Bernstein et al, *Handbook of Arbitration Practice*, London: Sweet & Maxwell, 3rd edn, 1998

Christou, *Drafting Commercial Agreements*, 2nd edn, Sweet & Maxwell, 2002, chapter 17

Colman et al, *The Practice and Procedure of the Commercial Court*, London: LLP, 5th edn, 2000

Gee, *Mareva Injunctions and Anton Piller Relief*, 4th edn, 1998

Goode, *Commercial Law*, 2nd edn, Penguin, 1995, chapters 38–39

Mustill and Boyd, *Commercial Arbitration—2000 Companion Volume*, Butterworths, 2000

Mustill and Boyd, *The Law and Practice of Commercial Arbitration in England*, 2nd edn, Butterworths, 1989

Ough, *The Mareva Injunction and Anton Piller Order, Practice and Precedents*, 2nd edn, Butterworths, 1993

Redfern and Hunter, *The Law and Practice of International Commercial Arbitration*, 3rd edn, Sweet & Maxwell, 1999

Russel on Arbitration, Sweet & Maxwell, 22nd edn, 2002

Rutherford and Sims, *Arbitration Act 1996: A Practical Guide*, FT Law & Tax, 1996

York, *Practical ADR Handbook*, Sweet & Maxwell, 2nd edn, 1999

INDEX